Designing for Zero Waste

'In a world where more and more people are consuming more and generating more waste this book is vital reading. In a society where most of us are consciously and sub-consciously detached from the reality of our own supporting ecosystems this book is vital reading. In an economy where precious resources are produced so cheaply that we can throw so much of them away this book is vital reading. In an environment being stripped of its resources, being polluted and made toxic on an industrial scale this book provides a real chance to re-connect and re-think our relationship with the supply and waste streams we take for granted in our unsustainable lifestyles. That re-connection is essential and this book shows us ways to make it happen. Please read it.'
Professor Susan Roaf, *Heriot-Watt University, Edinburgh, UK*

'Designing for Zero Waste is a timely resource and guide covering basic principles to city and regional governance. The flows of the waste created in our daily lives and building processes are largely ignored, misunderstood, or misinterpreted. This book should inspire a better understanding of material efficiency, avoidance of waste, and re-thinking material flows at a variety of scales and professions.'
Professor Alison Kwok, *University of Oregon, Eugene, USA*

Materials and resources are being depleted at an accelerating speed, and rising consumption trends across the globe have placed material efficiency, waste reduction and recycling at the centre of many government policy agendas, giving them an unprecedented urgency. The complex nature of the problem requires an increasing degree of interdisciplinarity. Resource recovery and the optimization of material flow can only be achieved with behaviour change to reduce the creation of material waste and wasteful consumption. *Designing for Zero Waste* aims to develop a more robust understanding of the links between lifestyle, consumption, technologies and urban development.

Professor Steffen Lehmann, PhD, is the Director of the Zero Waste SA Research Centre for Sustainable Design and Behaviour at the University of South Australia. Steffen is a widely published author and scholar and is Founding Director of the s_Lab Space Laboratory for Architectural Research and Design (Sydney–Berlin), as well as editor of the US-based *Journal of Green Building* and an advisor to Australian and German governments, city councils and industry. See www.slab.com.au.

Dr Robert Crocker is a Senior Lecturer in the School of Art, Architecture and Design at the University of South Australia, and teaches both the history and theory of design and the School's Master of Sustainable Design. With an Oxford doctorate in modern history (1987), Robert has published one monograph and two edited books. He is currently working on the role and idea of the national past in shaping Anglo-American domestic design and consumer culture in the 1920s and 1930s, and is developing another project on the role of technology in shaping consumer behaviour and attitudes towards waste. Find Robert's homepage at www.unisa.edu.au.

Earthscan Book Series on Sustainable Design
Editor of Series: Professor Steffen Lehmann (Steffen.Lehmann@unisa.edu.au)

All books in this series are authored and/or edited by leading academics and practitioners in the field of sustainable design.

Although there has been an immense amount of theory- and technology-focused writing published on the topic of sustainable design, many of these books have failed to introduce readers to the wider challenge of what the rethinking of design, production, operation and recycling of all products, buildings and cities really means.

Sustainability is not a passing fashion, and people are constantly searching for more information, ideas and products in this area. This new book series will aim to develop a more coherent theoretical framework for how different theories of sustainable design might engage with the practice of architects, designers, urban planners and related professions. The knowledge gained from this book series will equip the readers with the tools for realizing the full potential of the good intentions of sustainable design.

The aim is that these books will provide a novel alignment of interdisciplinary perspectives on the problems of global consumerism, sustainable design and strategies to avoid resource waste, on the scales of products, buildings, districts and cities.

The books will become essential reading for architects, industrial designers, urban designers and researchers/students in these disciplines. Potential readers for the books will also include industry and government agencies. Global relevance and the potential for use as textbooks will be essential.

The book series has been developed in coordination with UN-Habitat and will become a highly useful addition to the literature on sustainable design, urban development and city culture, focusing on the key topics encountered by students and scholars of urban studies, pointing towards related bibliographic material.

If you have an idea for the series then please contact the series editor.

Series Editor of the Sustainable Design Book Series
Professor Steffen Lehmann, PhD, is an internationally highly respected architect, urbanist and scholar, the Professor of Sustainable Design, Director of the ZWSA Research Centre for Sustainable Design and Behaviour (sd+b), at the University of South Australia. Steffen Lehmann has also been the UNESCO Chair in Sustainable Urban Development for Asia and the Pacific since 2008, the first such chair created with a particular view towards the rapid urbanization process in Asian cities. Since 1992, he has practised as a registered and licensed architect and urban designer in Berlin, where he established his own practice, the Space Laboratory for Architectural Research and Design (s_Lab).

Designing for Zero Waste

Consumption, technologies and the built environment

Edited by
Steffen Lehmann and
Robert Crocker

publishing for a sustainable future
LONDON AND NEW YORK

First published 2012
by Earthscan
2 Park Square, Milton Park, Abingdon, Oxon OX14 4RN

Simultaneously published in the USA and Canada
by Earthscan
711 Third Avenue, New York, NY 10017

Earthscan is an imprint of the Taylor & Francis Group, an informa business

British Library Cataloguing in Publication Data
A catalogue record for this book is available from the British Library

Library of Congress Cataloging in Publication Data
Designing for zero waste: consumption, technologies and the built environment / [edited by] Steffen Lehmann and Robert Crocker.
    p. cm.
    Includes bibliographical references and index.
    1. Waste minimization. 2. Urban ecology (Sociology) I. Lehmann, Steffen, 1963– II. Crocker, Robert, 1952–
    TD793.9.D47 2012
    628.4—dc23   2011025638

ISBN: 978-1-84971-434-1 (hbk)
ISBN: 978-1-84971-435-8 (pbk)
ISBN: 978-0-203-14605-7 (ebk)

Typeset in Times New Roman and Gill Sans
by Florence Production Ltd, Stoodleigh, Devon

Printed and bound in Great Britain by
CPI Antony Rowe, Chippenham, Wiltshire

Contents

Figures

Tables

Contributors

Editors

Robert Crocker is a Senior Lecturer in the School of Art, Architecture and Design at the University of South Australia, and teaches both the history and theory of design and the School's Master of Sustainable Design. With an Oxford doctorate in modern history (1987), Robert has published one monograph and two edited books (in The International Archives in the History of Ideas series). He is currently working on the role and idea of the national past in shaping Anglo-American domestic design and consumer culture in the 1920s and 1930s, and is developing another project on the role of technology in shaping consumer behaviour and attitudes towards waste. For a brief publication list, see Robert's homepage: www.unisa.edu.au.

Steffen Lehmann is the Professor of Sustainable Design and Director of the Zero Waste SA Research Centre for Sustainable Design and Behaviour (sd+b), at the University of South Australia. Prior to this, he held the Chair of Architectural Design in the Architecture School at the University of Newcastle (NSW). He has held a personal Chair in Australia since December 2002. He is the General Editor of the US-based *Journal of Green Building* and a member of the editorial boards of five academic journals. Steffen has held the UNESCO Professorship in Sustainable Urban Development for Asia and the Pacific since 2008. In 2009–10 he was the DAAD Professor at TU-Munich and a Visiting Professor at NUS in Singapore. He was also a Visiting Professor at the TU-Berlin and at Tongji University in Shanghai (2005). He received his doctorate in architecture from the TU-Berlin, an AA Diploma degree from the Architectural Association School in London, and a Masters degree from the University of Applied Sciences in Mainz. Between 1990 and 1993, he worked as an architect with James Stirling in London and with Arata Isozaki in Tokyo. In 1993, Steffen established his own ideas-driven, research-based practice in Berlin: the Space Laboratory for Architectural Research and Design (s_Lab), to pursue a more ethically correct practice. In 2010, he wrote *The Principles of Green Urbanism* and, in 2009, he edited *Back to the City*. For more information, see: www.slab.com.au.

Contributors

Simon Beecham is Head of the School of Natural and Built Environments at the University of South Australia. He is also the former Director of the SA Water Centre for Water Management and Reuse (CWMR). Simon is a Fellow of Engineers Australia and is also a Board Director for Water Quality Research Australia Ltd (WQRA). Simon's research interests include water-sensitive urban design (WSUD), siphonic roof water harvesting and the effects of climate change on integrated urban water management (IUWM). Simon is also the author of the Syfon software program, which has been used to design the roof water harvesting system for Sydney's Stadium Australia and the MCG, as well as the siphonic roof-drainage systems at the Norman Foster-designed Chek Lap Kok airport in Hong Kong and the new International Terminal Buildings at Adelaide, Sydney and Kuala Lumpur airports.

Sue Bigwood was raised on Kangaroo Island, South Australia. She discovered an innate passion for wildlife among a rural culture and strong community spirit. She graduated from Murdoch Veterinary School in 1989, and has spent her veterinary career largely at Zoos SA, in wildlife medicine and *in situ* conservation work. With developing interests in biodiversity, biosecurity, landcare and human health, her role at Zoos SA is now one of networking and coordinating the multidisciplinary, cross-agency core of wildlife health stakeholders. The benefits will be increased capabilities in the wildlife health sector through improved education, research and leadership. Her spare time is full of family and growing fine red wine, back on Kangaroo Island.

Victor Buchli is a Reader in Material Culture within the Material Culture Group at University College London and works on architecture, domesticity, the archaeology of the recent past, critical understandings of materiality and new technologies and the anthropology of sustainability and design. He has conducted fieldwork in Russia, Britain, Kazakhstan and Turkey and is currently researching new materials and rapid manufacturing, or 3D printing. He is a member of the interdisciplinary Templeton Scholars Group and is managing editor of the *Journal of Material Culture and Home Cultures*.

Nicholas Chileshe is a Senior Lecturer in Construction and Project Management in the School of Natural and Built Environments at the University of South Australia, where he is also the Research Education and Portfolio Leader. Dr Chileshe obtained his PhD in Construction Management from Sheffield Hallam University. Prior to his appointment in July 2009, he worked in the United Kingdom for ten years at Sheffield Hallam University. Nicholas is a Fellow of the Chartered Institute of Building (FCIOB), Fellow of the Australian Institute of Building (FAIB), Fellow of the Association of Building Engineers (FEBng) and Fellow of the Higher Education Academy (FHEA), Member of the Chartered Institute of Management (MICM) and Member of the Australian Institute of Project Management (MAIPM). His current research interests are in total quality management, sustainability, construction management, risk management, project management and project success.

Sandra Davison is a psychologist and a lecturer in Psychology at the University of South Australia and the South Australian Institute of Business Technology in Adelaide. She holds a Masters degree in Clinical Psychology and is currently a PhD research scholar on the mixed-methods project 'Zeroing in on food waste: Measuring, understanding and reducing food waste'. Sandra is interested in the social and psychological drivers of behaviour change. Clinically, much of Sandra's past work has been in health and rehabilitation areas, where she has assisted people to adapt and change health and lifestyle behaviours. With a deep concern for future world sustainability, and as a member of a research team at the University of South Australia, Sandra is now focusing on the psychological aspects of community pro-environmental behaviour.

Drew Dawson is internationally recognized for his contributions to the scientific community and to industry in the areas of sleep and fatigue research, organizational psychology and human factors, industrial-relations negotiations, and the human implications of hours of work. He has worked extensively with the aviation, manufacturing, retail, entertainment, transportation and mining sectors in Australia and is an expert on fatigue in the workplace. He has instigated fatigue-management programmes, developed shiftwork and fatigue policy, undertaken pre-employment assessments and facilitated shiftwork education sessions. Drew also regularly presents at national and international conferences and has provided expert-witness testimony in many fatigue-related court cases.

Jane Dickson is a PhD candidate in the Material Culture department at University College London. She is researching the governance of sustainability through housing in London. She has previously undertaken research in America into contemporary crafting, anti-consumerist and local history movements and in the UK into grass-roots environmental movements.

Angelique Edmonds is an architect interested in public architecture, fostering agency, participation and engagement, and has a particular interest in social sustainability in design, fostering socially inclusive design, engaging cross-cultural and broad participation from diverse groups and design approaches that foster resilience. She completed a PhD in interdisciplinary Cross-Cultural Research at the Australian National University in 2007, which focused upon the agency of Aboriginal people in South East Arnhem Land in Australia in determining the order of their lives, as evidenced through their responses to the living practices, planning and built forms of imposed sedentary life. Prior to that, she completed a Master of Philosophy in the History and Philosophy of Architecture at Cambridge University and completed her Architecture degrees at Kingston University in London and UNSW in Sydney. She is currently a Lecturer at the University of South Australia, in the School of Art, Architecture and Design and teaches at undergraduate and Masters levels.

Jane Edwards is an adjunct Research Fellow at the Centre for Work and Life at the University of South Australia and has a background in the sociology of health, as well as public health. She has developed an interest in the notion of community in contemporary society and has investigated this in various settings. Jane is particularly committed to work–life balance and spends long periods walking on the beach and in the bush to demonstrate this commitment.

Wendy Foster is the Manager of Conservation Programs for Conservation Ark (Zoos SA). She has studied and researched across a range of disciplines, including environmental biology, psychology, reproductive biology and medical research. She is currently a member of several species-recovery teams, is involved in a range of national and international conservation projects and oversees the research activities of Conservation Ark (Zoos SA) across Adelaide Zoo, Monarto Zoo and Warrawong Wildlife Sanctuary, as well as in the field. One of her key interests is looking at the ways people in different disciplines can bring together their skill sets and perspectives to provide increased conservation benefit.

Jaco Huisman is Scientific Advisor to the United Nations University Institute for Sustainability and Peace (UNU–ISP), a position he has held since 2006, focusing on electronics recycling in a global context. He leads UNU's Electronics Recycling Group and co-coordinates the TaskForce Capacity Building and Knowledge Management of the UNU-based StEP Initiative (Solving the e-waste Problem; see: www.step-initiative.org). In this role, he is responsible for a large project to further quantify the amounts and problems of e-waste worldwide in cooperation with research institutes and universities in Europe, China, the US and the Middle East. He is also leading various international research projects related to e-waste, including the UNU study supporting the European Commission's 2008 Review of the EU WEEE Directive. Jaco obtained a Masters degree in Chemical Engineering at Eindhoven University of Technology in 1999 and a PhD in 2003 from Delft University of Technology. Since 2004, he has run his own consultancy company, OsevenfortytwO (see: www.osevenfortytwo.com), and, as a consultant, he has given advice to a large number of producers, governments and recyclers in Europe, the US and China to improve eco-efficient operations, waste policies, system organization and product design. Since 2003, he has been an Associate Professor at Delft University of Technology, the Netherlands.

Sadasivam Karuppannan is a lecturer in Urban and Regional Planning at the University of South Australia. He is a planner with experience in urban planning, in particular, housing, the provision of affordable housing, geographical information systems and land-use planning. His research interests include evaluation of housing demand, urban-growth modelling, land-use planning, development and the application of spatial information systems (including geographical information systems) in urban planning, including land-use modelling. In 2008, he and his colleagues at the University of South Australia won an Australia Research Council Linkage grant on an integrated model for the assessment of urban sustainability. He has published on sustainability, urban planning, urban development, housing and ageing.

Carla Litchfield is a scientist involved in research and community work with organizations that promote animal psychological and physical well-being (in captivity and natural environments), responsible tourism and conservation. She has a PhD in Psychology (Animal Behaviour) from the University of Adelaide. She is a lecturer at the University of South Australia, and, as an adjunct researcher on the science team of Conservation Ark (Zoos SA), is developing the area of conservation psychology, addressing human behaviour change to conserve wildlife and natural environments, and ways to minimize human–animal conflict. In 1994, Carla spent a year observing a community of wild chimpanzees in Uganda – the start of an ongoing commitment to the African great apes. The Australian Science Communicators awarded her the 'Unsung Hero of Australian Science' in 2000. Carla is the Vice President of Zoos SA and President of the Australasian Primate Society. She is also on the board of the United Nations' Great Ape Survival Project (GRASP, Australasia). She has written four science and conservation books for children about animals (gorillas, chimpanzees, pandas and tigers), to inspire a love for nature, science and conservation, and with practical suggestions about sustainable human behaviour.

Kurt Lushington graduated from the Flinders University of South Australia in 1998 with a PhD in Psychology and a Masters degree in Clinical Psychology. Associate

Professor Lushington has been an academic with the University of South Australia since 1996 and is currently the Head of the Discipline of Psychology and the Associate Head of the School of Psychology, Social Work and Social Policy. In addition to his clinical and research work in sleep medicine, he has a keen interest in all issues to do with sustainability and especially the role of e-books and e-book reading devices and the paperless office. He has published numerous peer-reviewed journal articles in psychology, eight book chapters (including several specialist chapters on sleep written for senior high school students studying psychology) and three review/research papers on e-book technologies.

Sue Nichols is an education researcher at the University of South Australia whose investigations of children's learning in social and cultural contexts often take her into family and community, as well as educational, settings. She is the first author of *Resourcing Early Learning: New players, new networks* (Routledge, forthcoming) as well as numerous book chapters and articles in journals including *Contemporary Issues in Early Childhood*, *Early Years* and *Early Childhood Development and Care*.

Michelle Philp is an environmental engineer and scientist working with the Barbara Hardy Institute and the Australian Climate Change Adaptation Research Network for Settlements and Infrastructure (ACCARNSI) at the University of South Australia. Her professional experience includes modelling urban water and transport systems, sustainable surface water planning, assessment and design and researching climate-change mitigation and adaptation strategies in the urban environment.

Barbara Pocock is Director of the Centre for Work + Life at the University of South Australia in Adelaide. Barbara has been researching work, employment and industrial relations for over twenty-five years. She has worked in many jobs – advising politicians, on farms, in unions, for governments and as a mother. Her main areas of research have been work, employment relations, unions, inequality and vocational education. She was initially trained as an economist. She is widely published. Her books include: *Living low paid: The Dark Side of Prosperous Australia* (with Helen Masterman-Smith) (2008); *The Labour Market Ate my Babies: Work, Children and a Sustainable Future* (2006); *The Work/Life Collision* (2003); *Strife: Sex and Politics in Labour Unions* (1997); and *Demanding Skill: Women and Technical Education in Australia* (1988).

Stephen Pullen is a building scientist with twenty years' experience in the study of the sustainability of construction materials, buildings and the urban environment. He teaches building science, performance of buildings, energy efficiency, building surveying and sustainability in assets and facilities, and is also a PhD supervisor in this area. His research interests include life-cycle energy analysis and the embodied energy of buildings and he has published numerous papers in these areas. He commenced research into embodied energy in 1993 and participated in the Australia Research Council (ARC)-supported project, Design of Environmentally Responsible Housing for Australia, at the University of Adelaide, South Australia. In 2003–4, he was a Chief Investigator in the ARC Linkage project at the University of New South Wales on Water and Energy profiles for Sydney: Towards Sustainability. As part of his PhD studies, he developed a model of the urban environment that spatially represents embodied energy consumption. He is currently a Chief Investigator in the

ARC Linkage project on an Integrated Model for the Assessment of Urban Sustainability and has just completed a research project on affordable and sustainable housing for South Australia.

Anne Sharp is a Senior Research Fellow at the Ehrenberg-Bass Institute for Marketing Science at the University of South Australia. She heads the sustainable marketing research of the Institute and has a particular interest in evaluating government interventions encouraging behaviour change for improved environmental outcomes. She has worked collaboratively with a wide range of industry partners, including city councils, ambulance services, regulatory bodies, educational groups and, of particular interest, environmental groups. Anne's research work has the common theme of helping to establish empirical generalizations in marketing. Anne has published numerous refereed papers, with her work appearing in top international journals such as the *European Journal of Marketing* and the *International Journal of Research in Marketing*. Dr Sharp is a member of the Australian Market and Social Research Society and teaches market research.

Alpana Sivam is a lecturer in Urban and Regional Planning at the University of South Australia. She is an architect and planner with a PhD in Housing Policy. Earlier, she worked with Housing SA and Planning SA in Adelaide, South Australia. She has extensive experience in both the public and private sectors, having held a variety of senior and executive positions in India, Australia and Singapore. She has eighteen years of professional and research experience in urban and regional planning, statutory and strategic planning, delivery of urban infrastructure, housing policies and issues in developing countries, urban design and environmental planning. She has published on housing, housing delivery models, ageing, housing the ageing population, urban development and urban design.

Natalie Skinner is a Research Fellow at the Centre for Work + Life at the University of South Australia. She is interested in health and well-being in the workplace, with a particular emphasis on psychological health (e.g. stress, burnout and job satisfaction), job quality (work intensity, flexibility and work hours) and work–life interaction. Her interest in well-being extends to the impact of paid work on individuals' capacity to be 'good environmental citizens'.

Albert L. N. ('Ab') Stevels was born in Eindhoven, The Netherlands, in 1944. He studied Chemical Engineering at the Technical University of Eindhoven and holds a PhD in Physics and Chemistry. In 1969, he started to work for Royal Philips Electronics in various capacities, in research on materials, production technology of glass, electro-optics and as a project manager for joint ventures in Asia. In 1993, he became a senior advisor at the Environmental Competence Center of Philips Consumer Electronics. In 1995, he was appointed as a part-time Professor in Environmental Design at Delft University of Technology and a Visiting Professor in the Mechanical Engineering Department of Stanford University. He was also teaching at TU Berlin and at Georgia Institute of Technology, Atlanta. In 2003, he was a Visiting Professor at the Industrial Ecology Program at NTNU in Trondheim, Norway, and in 2005 at Tsinghua University in Beijing. Ab has done trailblazing work in turning eco-design into day-to-day business and has researched in detail the setting up of take-back and recycling systems for electronics. He has developed tools and management procedures for these purposes that have proven their strength through their practical success. Ab is the author of numerous journal articles and conference contributions. His training courses on applied eco-design have been held at various universities and at various Philips departments and divisions around the globe.

Michael A. P. Taylor is the Director of the Barbara Hardy Institute and Professor of Transport Planning at the University of South Australia in Adelaide. The institute is the university's flagship for research on sustainable human settlements, covering the five core areas of transport and land-use, energy, water, agriculture, and the natural and built environments. He is internationally acknowledged as an expert on traffic flow theory, travel demand modelling, environmental impacts of road traffic, sustainable transport and intelligent transport systems. His current research is in four areas: future urban transport systems, fuel and emissions modelling for road traffic, transit-oriented development and transport-network vulnerability. Mike has published extensively in all of these areas. He has forty years of professional experience, as a traffic engineer, a research scientist and in academia. He gained his PhD at Monash University in Melbourne. He is a Chartered Professional Engineer and a Fellow of the Institution of Engineers, Australia, the UK Chartered Institute of Transport and Logistics and the US Institute of Transportation Engineers.

Kirrilly Thompson is a cultural anthropologist working in the Centre for Sleep Research at the University of South Australia. She has conducted qualitative and ethnographic research across a diverse range of topics, spanning mounted bullfighting, equestrian safety, crowding in the rail industry and, currently, food waste. Her theoretical interests coalesce around risk, performance, boundaries and the sociocultural role of the non-human. Kirrilly is a research associate on the Australia Research Council linkage project, Zeroing in on Food Waste: Measuring, understanding and reducing food waste, being undertaken in South Australia.

Alexander (Sandy) Walker is an industrial designer who has worked extensively in R&D and management roles in the UK, the US and Canada, as well as in China, Thailand, Singapore and Korea, with manufacturing and consulting organizations. In 2001, he began the design, development and commercialization process of the 'Orbcourt' range of low environmental impact, multi-sport flooring products. Orbcourt was awarded a Commendation in the 2002 Design Institute of Australia Design Awards. He has a Bachelor of Science in Industrial Design, from Napier University, Edinburgh, and an MBA, from the University of South Australia. Sandy currently coordinates the final year of the Industrial Design programme and teaches in the Masters of Sustainable Design and Bachelor of Technology (Kaplan, Singapore) at the University of South Australia. His design and management qualifications have led to membership of the Chartered Society of Designers, associate membership of the Institute of Industrial Managers and Fellowship of the Design Institute of Australia. His interest in and passion for sports equipment design and biomechanics have been the inspiration for PhD studies at RMIT's School of Aerospace, Mechanical and Manufacturing Engineering.

Feng Wang has been undertaking PhD research into modelling and the eco-efficiency assessment of e-waste recycling systems at Delft University of Technology since 2009. Wang works in the UNU–ISP CYCLE as a Research Associate on e-waste recycling technologies, take-back systems, regional management and policies. He is involved in the project Best of 2 Worlds, seeking technical solutions to combine deep-level manual dismantling and professional end-processing technologies in mainland China. He has extensive investigation experience and knowledge of formal and informal e-waste recycling systems, trading structures and associated legislative developments in China.

Stephen Ward is an architect and educator with a long interest in issues of environmental and cultural sustainability, design practice and education, and conservation in the built environment. He has contributed to and organized exhibitions in art and architecture, and has published academic papers and professional articles on sustainable architecture and architectural education. As an advocate for a closer relationship between education and practice, Stephen has provided leadership on national working groups and committees. As a project director for ArchiVision, a seminar series for educators and practitioners, he has facilitated a joint forum to speculate on, and plan for, the future of architecture. Stephen is Programme Director of the Bachelor of Architectural Studies and Master of Architecture programmes at the School of Art, Architecture and Design at the University of South Australia. Prior to his focus on architectural education, Stephen was the architect for a range of award-winning public and private projects, specializing in the design of institutional and civic facilities and the adaptive reuse and conservation of heritage buildings.

Philippa (Pip) Williams is a Research Fellow at the Centre for Work and Life at the University of South Australia. She has a multidisciplinary background in psychology, sociology and public health. Her particular research interests focus on community, social support, work–life integration and the social and developmental needs of adolescents. In her private and professional life she is particularly interested in the rights of children and adolescents to be active citizens, to inherit a healthy planet and to have the skills to improve the well-being of themselves, their families and their environments.

Lou Wilson is a Senior Lecturer at the University of South Australia, where he teaches courses in social planning and research methods in the School of Natural and Built Environments. Lou is a Chief Investigator on two large projects funded by the Australian Research Council to investigate sustainable urban futures and green building design. He also has research interests in social policy, social inclusion and social justice. He is an active member of the Australian Sociological Association and publishes regularly on sustainability and social issues.

George Zillante is Associate Professor and Head of Construction and Project Management at the University of South Australia. He has qualifications in Architecture, Urban and Regional Planning, Building Surveying, Business Administration and Construction and has worked (and continues to work) at the professional level in those fields. Over the years, George has done a lot of work in the field of building legislation, and this has resulted in his appointment to many government committees, including, inter alia, Chair of the South Australian Building Advisory Committee, member of the South Australian Development Policy Advisory Committee and member of several Australian Building Codes Board committees, as well as his representing the Australian Construction Industry on the International Association for the Professional

Management of Construction. His interest in building legislation led George to establish the Centre for Building and Planning Studies at the University of South Australia in 1993, and this has resulted in several research projects dealing with the impact of legislation on development and, more recently, on bushfires and government policy responses to the impact of bushfires and organizational change. George is also a member of several professional bodies (including RICS, AIBS and ACCE) and serves on a number of their education and accreditation committees.

Jian Zuo has a PhD from the University of South Australia and a Masters degree in Engineering from Wuhan University, in the People's Republic of China. Currently, he is a lecturer and researcher in the School of Natural and Built Environments. His main research interests relate to achieving a low-carbon built environment by means of innovation and behavioural changes.

Acknowledgements

This book is the result of a collaborative effort far greater than the sum of its two lead authors and editors. The editors are grateful to all of the authors and reviewers who made this publication possible. The interdisciplinarity and diversity of the research papers contributed has made this a special book, and we hope it will be widely used and applied. As always, when you produce a book, there are many people who deserve to be personally acknowledged.

First, we would like to thank the team at Zero Waste SA and its chief executive, Vaughan Levitzke, who enthusiastically supported the idea of this publication from the very beginning. This book has slowly emerged from this initial idea, and the research work on which it is based continues.

We wish to thank all our colleagues at the University of South Australia for their valuable support during the development of this publication. We hope you find the book a worthy reflection of your excellent contributions and your generous support in reviewing draft chapters. We are very fortunate to have colleagues who are committed to creating an intellectually engaging atmosphere and have been so supportive in providing constructive feedback. We especially appreciate the thoughtful reflections of Professor Pal Ahluwalia, Professor Andrew Parfitt and Professor Mads Gaardboe, who helped us to develop the structure and sharpen the ideas included in the book's four parts.

The research in this book could have never been undertaken without the tireless support of many more people – too many to name them all here – in university centres, government departments and industry partner organizations, who have generously shared and supplied their information and insight.

Our particular thanks go to the publishing team at Earthscan and Routledge (an imprint of Taylor & Francis, the Informa Group) in the UK, who were very helpful in the book's production. We especially wish to thank Michael Jones, Jonathan Wilson Sinclair, Nicki Dennis, Alice Aldous, Anna Rice and Claire Lamont for their patience and support. Our grateful thanks also to: the inspirational Professor Emeritus Peter Brandon for the enthusiastic essay he contributed as the preface and for his ongoing friendship; Cida de Aragon, who created the great design for the front cover; Pamela Hart, for her efficient and cheerful administrative support; Gilbert Roe, for his nice photo of us and the interesting chat; Katharine Thornton, whose editing and proof-reading made this a better book; and PhD student Atiq Zaman, for compiling a list of journals and relevant web pages.

We are also grateful to Joan Clos, Paul Taylor and Bernhard Barth of UN-Habitat for their support and endorsement of this book series.

Finally, we would like to thank our families for their patience and support during the intensive period of creating this book. We could not have done it without you.

We hope this publication will become a useful resource for academic teaching, further scholarly research and policy formulation in the process of transforming the way we design, produce and recycle products, buildings and cities.

Steffen Lehmann and Robert Crocker
May 2011

Professor Steffen Lehmann and Dr Robert Crocker

Foreword
Designing for zero waste

Vaughan Levitzke

This book is for policymakers, designers, engineers, architects, sociologists, psychologists, recycling and waste practitioners, economists, resource developers, students, lecturers – and everyone who cares about how we use, reuse and value our resources in a resource-constrained world. For the first time we have a book that views the 'zero waste' concept from the perspective of four key interrelated areas – sustainability and behavioural change, consumption and technologies, the sustainable design of our built environment, and, finally, governance and material flows. Zero waste is a concept that ultimately envisages a thriving society that exists within nature's resource constraints and its ability to assimilate waste.

This book brings together global leading-edge research about the achievement of zero waste and a more sustainable society. This is a truly collaborative and multidisciplinary approach – the type of approach we should use if we are to reduce our ecological footprint, combat global warming and make the best use of the resources we need to sustain our societies. The authors are passionate experts in their respective fields. They have been brought together to contribute through the persuasive and motivating powers of Professor Steffen Lehmann at the University of South Australia's Zero Waste SA Centre for Sustainable Design and Behaviour.

The concept underpinning this book is based on the idea that design and human behaviour are interlinked. Bad design results in waste throughout the life cycle of a product, from raw-materials extraction to its use and final recycling and disposal. Starting with an examination of behaviour and the psychology of our consumption and the choices we make, the book continues with articles exploring the newest waste issues facing us – electronic waste, energy consumption and life-cycle analysis. Next, the way we design our urban and household infrastructure, including green infrastructure, is discussed, and, finally, how we can bring these concepts together in our cities, where there are some extraordinary growth pressures and challenges.

The term 'zero waste' is believed to have first been used by chemist Paul Palmer when he created his company, Zero Waste Disposals, in California in the 1970s. Three decades later, Robin Murray's book, *Zero waste*, was published by the Greenpeace Trust. The term is now being increasingly used throughout the community. It is shorthand for the better management of resources in an increasing number of corporations and governments around the world. Zero waste is a way of thinking and doing that will become even more commonplace and important as we attempt to deal with the big environmental, social and economic issues facing all of us. The concept of zero waste challenges the assumption that waste is inevitable or unavoidable. Zero waste shifts the focus from 'end-of-pipe' solutions and disposal practices, to promote the cyclical use of materials in the economy.

When Zero Waste SA was formed in 2003 as a government statutory authority in the state of South Australia, many commentators and waste-industry professionals thought that zero waste was impossible, and that the term was nonsensical because 'humans will always produce waste'. Many of those deriders are still around today. However, there is an increasing global engagement around the concept of zero waste, with many large corporations adopting the principle as an aspirational goal.

Although our community effort has largely, until now, been about recycling, the reduction of waste and extending the life of goods remain the Holy Grail of the waste industry. Much of the waste we create need not be created in the first instance. While it provides benefits by extending the life of materials in our economy, recycling is of lesser value than not producing waste in the first place.

This leads us to question how we can expect to be able to do this in such a consumer-driven, economic growth-focused society. For many years we have understood that design and behaviour are linked. The 'throwaway society' is a product of these forces at work. Many products are not designed for reuse, use rare materials in their construction and have a short lifespan before the next model comes on to the market; electronic gadgets are probably the best example of this carelessness.

In 1999, the world's population reached 6 billion. Just twelve years later, during 2011, the world's population is expected to reach 7 billion, and it continues to grow. Most of these people will, for the first time in history, be living in urban environments, and it is expected that the city-based proportion of the world's population will rapidly increase. The prospects of new employment opportunities and improved lifestyles will continue to encourage rural people to move to cities. These issues are not just the province of the world's megacities, as the trend is for all principal cities to grow for the foreseeable future. Urban populations are growing much faster than rural populations.

Resource scarcity, increased resource demand, growing pollution, the use of more complex materials in manufacturing and the distances goods and materials are transported in our modern economy will, in all likelihood, exert significant upward price pressures on products and materials into the future, making it even more difficult for poor communities to be released from their poverty.

Greater urbanization places increased demands on urban infrastructure and services, to the extent that governments find it difficult to cope with these demands. How do we live more sustainable lifestyles in an urban context where we must import our food, clothing, shelter and other basic materials? How do we build an urban form that is sensitive to people's needs, without further negative impact on the natural environment or human health?

The responses to this growth have been varied, depending upon local demands and circumstances. The lessons learned by one city are not necessarily transferred to others. Given these challenges and pressures, we can ill afford to replicate the mistakes of others, as this is inevitably both expensive and time consuming. In an interconnected world, these issues should be more easily overcome. We can use social media for political revolution; can we use the same media for sharing information and concepts in a more creative way, to bring about these other changes?

Increasing volumes of waste and the increasing complexity of our waste streams have also caused concerns about public health and the environment to grow. Increasing waste volumes closely correlate with increased affluence, and the cycle of technological advancement quickly outstrips social and legislative reform. These challenges confront all of us, as we live in an increasingly resource-constrained world.

Zero waste requires new designs for the environment: designs that influence our behaviour to reduce our generation of greenhouse gases, reduce our consumption of materials and reduce our ecological footprint. Designs may include those that allow for disassembly for reuse; better insulation properties for buildings; lighter construction and fabrication materials; and the use of materials that can be easily recycled. Given that the built environment is created by major capital investment and is expected to last at least 30, 50 and preferably 100 years or more, it is fundamentally important to identify materials, techniques and systems that will last the distance and that can be reused or recycled when the structure is no longer needed or when it needs to be upgraded.

To achieve this we need data. Data about life-cycle assessment of products and materials are sorely lacking, as are data that reflect the amount and types of waste being collected and disposed of every day. Without this information, how can we expect to identify the better products and services and reduce our waste?

Maximizing the value of our resources focuses our attention on local infrastructure, economic interventions and incentives for change. It also aims to maximize the social and economic benefits from the resources we consume. Avoiding and reducing waste require a more thoughtful approach to the way we use resources and the choices we make as governments, businesses and individuals. Committing to zero waste is about making long-term choices based on behavioural change and principled engagement.

It is my hope that reading this book will change the way you approach your work, your home life, choices you make and the way you perceive, use and reuse resources.

Vaughan Levitzke is the Chief Executive of Zero Waste SA (ZWSA), a position he has held since the South Australian government agency's establishment in 2003 within the Environment and Conservation portfolio. The objective of Zero Waste SA is to promote waste-management practices that, as far as possible, eliminate waste or its consignment to landfill, advance the development of resource recovery and recycling and are based on an integrated strategy for the state. South Australia is staying at the forefront of waste recycling and resource management in Australia and attracting international interest. Having helped reduce waste to landfill in South Australia by 16.1 per cent in six years, Zero Waste SA continues to stimulate investment in infrastructure, foster partnerships and collaboration and drive industry resource efficiency.

Vaughan has been the ministerial representative on the board of Keep South Australia Beautiful for twelve years. He is currently on the advisory boards of two University of South Australia research centres and is a member of the management committee of the Zero Waste Centre for Sustainable Design and Behaviour. He is a former member of the national projects group established under Australia's national packaging covenant. He is an *ex officio* member of Zero Waste SA and is a member of the Environmental Protection Authority board's waste reform subcommittee. Prior to ZWSA, Vaughan spent ten years with the South Australian Environment Protection Authority. His role focused on regulation in the waste sector (recycling, tyres, composting), litter policy development and the expansion of container deposit legislation. He was also responsible for managing eco-efficiency and industry sustainability programmes and grant schemes.

Preface

Zero waste: towards a vision of a new model for humankind

Peter Brandon

This book is both timely and visionary. Human consumption is increasing ever more rapidly, and this book addresses how we might reverse the trend, particularly in the developed world. The aspiration to consume, however, is just as high among people in the developing world, and so this book is equally applicable to those countries and their populations. As consumption, and the resultant waste, requires an understanding of human behaviour, the technologies adopted and the way in which humans choose to live, it is an extremely broad canvas. It is to the credit of the editors that the assembled authors have explored so many important issues and thus improved our understanding of the topic. Good practice comes from good theory. This book provides an introduction to the underlying theory and knowledge on which the practices required to move towards the concept and vision of zero waste will be based. The way in which humans choose to accommodate their activities in buildings and cities is central to the issues raised. The United Nations' Environment Programme's Sustainable Buildings and Construction Initiative (2007) estimated that the built environment uses 20 per cent of the land, 20 per cent of the water, 30 per cent of the raw materials and 40 per cent of the energy in global resource usage. From this activity, it generates 20 per cent of global waste effluents, 30 per cent of solid waste and 40 per cent of human global carbon dioxide emissions. By 2040, it is estimated that two-thirds of the world's population will be living in cities, with a consequent rise in the production of waste. This is not a trivial matter – it is at the very root of human existence and even survival.

Life context

Perhaps the greatest question we can ask ourselves is 'Why are we here?'. Is there a meaning to life, or are we just the result of chance processes? Don't worry; this essay is not attempting to answer these intriguing questions. There is, however, an observation that we can make and that does not seem especially contentious. If we look at life in general, and the human race in particular, all species want to survive. It appears that we are hardwired to procreate and to sustain our existence for as long as circumstances allow. When the context is benign, then all species will thrive and produce more offspring. This was brought home to me by the trailer for a new natural history documentary narrated by the veteran broadcaster David Attenborough. He started his narration by explaining that, during his working life (some six decades), the population of the world had trebled. This is extraordinary exponential growth, which has lead to some of the greatest challenges we face today.

In the spectrum of universal time, the last sixty years form a very short span indeed, and we can see that those decades have provided favourable circumstances for humans to flourish. The human ability to flourish, however, has not meant that other species have also found the environment conducive to expansion. In fact, the rise of human beings and their technologies has often resulted in the devastation of other species' habitats and, consequentially, the demise of many, at a speed that this world has not experienced before, except in times of natural disaster. Much of this is related to humans' consumption and the subsequent waste and pollution created. The loss of other species has already had an impact on the ability of human beings to provide our food and shelter.

Survival

In his 2003 book, *Our final century*, Martin Rees, a recent Astronomer Royal, posed the question as to whether the human race can survive for another 100 years. It is not so long ago that such a question would have been considered ridiculous, because the world was considered to be a stable entity, and the interdependence within nature was not considered to be a major problem.

Rees identifies disease, war, famine and, above all, technology as the major reasons for concern. Virtually all technologies have an upside and a downside. They provide a solution to one problem but at the same time create a problem elsewhere. In the hands of those perceived to be 'good', the technology can be a force for improvement, but, in the hands of those who are thought to be 'bad', the technology can create a monster that we find difficult to control. Nuclear fission, the internal combustion engine, genetic engineering, the Internet, global alliances or antibiotics can all be seen as either good or bad, depending on the lens through which we view them. If human beings are in charge of them, and human circumstances are such that they find a use to suit their own ends, then it is likely that both the good and the bad aspects of any technology will be found in our societies. Sometimes, human motivation is openly malevolent (as in war), but in most cases a new technology is adopted with the best of intentions, only to result in a by-product of its use having a detrimental effect on something else.

To take one example, the Aswan Dam in Egypt was built for two main reasons. First, to provide a substantial proportion of Egypt's electricity by damming the River Nile and providing hydroelectric power. Second, to avoid the frequent flooding of the Nile and the inconvenience that event caused to communities along its length. The Aswan Dam did indeed provide electricity and it did reduce the river's propensity to flood. Unfortunately, the lack of flood waters simultaneously prevented the rich silt associated with the floods from being spread across the land, and thus the land became less fertile. To counteract this, it was necessary to produce artificial fertilizer (requiring energy-demanding processes and transport), which eventually seeped into the river and polluted it. Consequently, the natural systems became unbalanced, and new problems arose. It has yet to be seen what trade-off was sensible in a complex ecosystem such as this, but the example does reveal the need to consider environmental problems in a holistic manner.

Consumption, waste and values

The urgent issue of human consumption is one of this book's major themes. How do we avoid increased consumption, which leads to more waste being generated and more pollution affecting the planet? Human population growth, and the increase in consumption that follows it, is the root cause. It is the countries that industrialized first and that gained wealth accordingly which have created the problems being observed today. The aspirations of others to do likewise are beginning to cause similar concerns. The most populated nations of earth, namely China and India, have the potential to consume and waste more than any others. They, like those in the developed world, have been seduced by the desire to accumulate wealth, and the technology they are using to do so has been adopted from countries that now face major environmental problems.

To address such large questions, which engage nearly every aspect of human life and include our relationship to the planet on which we live, it is time to revisit some of the values upon which we have built our culture and which influence our behaviour. This requires a fundamental rethink, and some would say a 'new world view', to establish what we are trying to achieve and what we need to do to change our behaviour. Albert Einstein observed that we tend to look for solutions using the tools that caused the problem in the first place. We need new thinking and we need to adopt everything at our disposal that might lead to a reduction in the harm created by our own existence and behaviour.

The solutions could be in the technologies we employ, the behaviour we adopt, the policies we implement and/or the investments we make in research in order to improve our understanding. A good practical starting point is often thought to be to set targets that we can use to focus our efforts. However, the adoption of targets can often lead to a reductionist view of the world and also to sub–optimization of the kind that leads to the dilemma suggested by the Aswan Dam example. To avoid this, we need to espouse a philosophy that allows us to look at our cosmos as a whole. We also need to describe our values and make them transparent, to identify interrelationships and to provide direction for our thoughts. We need a common framework within which we can think, communicate and act, so that we can share experience and build knowledge. This, of course, is not an easy thing to achieve, but, if we could provide such a framework, share a common vocabulary and have a shared understanding of the values on which we can build, then just maybe we might be able to make a major advance in uniting our efforts for mutual advantage.

A common holistic framework

Such a common and holistic framework could be based on the writings of the Dutch philosopher Herman Dooyeweerd (Brandon and Lombardi, 2010). He argued for a 'cosmonic idea of reality'. Dooyeweerd's arguments are complex and in some cases difficult to penetrate, but in outline consist of a hierarchy of fifteen modalities (irreducible areas of the functioning of a system or entity) that are nested within each other (thus creating a platform for interdependence) and that express the strength of the dependence by the distance of the relationship of one modality from another. The hierarchy encompassed not only physical measurements and relationships, such as counting and scientific measurement, but also the human aspects that influence performance. The latter are central to the introduction of any policy or strategy for sustainable development. At the pinnacle of the hierarchy is the modality related to commitment and vision, without which no policy for change could be implemented. The vision would be based on the second modality, that of ethics, which is related to the perceived morality of the decision (and based on agreed values). This would be followed by the judicial or regulatory framework that a society had chosen to express the parameters within which the values would be implemented. Following this would be the aesthetic considerations, the economic framework, the social framework and the manner of communication, all separate modalities but related to the others. Creativity, analysis and formal knowledge, plus the perceptions of people and their required health, biodiversity and ecology, followed before consideration of the physical aspects that can be measured using conventional methods. These last modalities relate to the physical environment, mass and energy, followed by transportation, space, shape and extension and finally numerical accounting.

This list can only give a flavour of Dooyeweerd's thought and, at its simplest, offers a checklist for consideration of sustainability matters. It is, however, much richer and can be experienced at a number of different levels, which enable it to be intuitively accepted by all those engaged in making decisions about sustainable development. For understanding the movement and vision towards zero waste, it provides a framework that is much more comprehensive than traditional assessment and implementation measures and it prompts new thinking. All the matters raised in this book could be found within such a framework, and the likelihood of items being overlooked or not considered is reduced. Such a framework provides a useful basis for dialogue and debate, but much still needs to be done to make it an effective tool for evaluation.

The point is that the challenge of zero waste is not just one of measurement and reduction, but a much more fundamental understanding of the vision and its implementation within a holistic framework. This is bound to include the values and commitment to zero waste found within our culture.

Complexity and rich knowledge

Searching relevant websites, including those that list government initiatives on waste in developing countries, reveals an extraordinary number of activities attempting to make the issue of reducing waste part of the culture of many industries (particularly construction) and communities. These activities are creating a pool of rich knowledge that deserves collation, recording and analysis to provide information for current and future generations.

This book plays its part in revealing the diversity of these activities. It deals with behaviour change and the consumption culture, and also with the technologies that may help to reduce waste. In so doing, it does not claim that using technology is the only way to achieve zero waste. It also addresses the part designers can play in achieving the goal of zero waste, and the fact that every citizen, not just those formally employed to deal with it, shares responsibility for the management of waste. Finally, it engages with the politics of waste at individual, regional and urban levels to find the commitment that enables zero-waste policies to be developed and adopted.

Part of the problem is the complexity of a subject that has so many facets and that demands so many different skills and so much knowledge across so many conventional boundaries. Zero waste is not always prescribed by national or other physical boundaries. It is not dealt with by one profession's repository of knowledge. It should engage both user and provider in an understanding of mutual benefit. It requires governments to be ahead of public opinion and not to respond reactively. It involves highly specialized research and yet also requires those who can bring these specializations together in a holistic way (and these 'bridge builders' are hard to find). It requires an understanding of values and a communication system that allows for democratic processes. In fact, it needs a full and thorough understanding of human behaviour that is not yet available in any readily accessible form.

It is this complexity that makes it difficult for zero waste to become part of the thinking of every person and every institution involved in decision-making. However, its successful solution depends on a holistic view that all humankind can endorse, at least in principle. The past three decades have seen great progress in making the world sensitive to these issues, and it is to the credit of many governments that they are taking it seriously.

For designers, there is a need to have a simple creed that spells out their belief in sustainability and that includes waste management. In the 1960s, a simple saying was being promoted that, if followed, would have had far reaching consequences for the way designers think and behave towards the environment. The maxim was called the 'three Ls concept' and the Ls stood for long life, loose fit and low energy (Gordon, 1974). Even now, such a simple check in thinking as a design develops would have a profound impact on the eventual physical product. Long life would ensure better materials and more recycling, and would probably involve less waste. Loose fit would ensure flexibility in, and more resilience to, the building over time. Low energy would encompass the desire for zero carbon and a reduction in many of the pollutants we see today. All three would help to reduce waste. Of course, much more knowledge is required as to how to implement such a concept, but it would set the scene for a cultural change that should engage every designer. Many designers have already embraced this change, but many more could do so. What is encouraging is that the markets are at last seeing the need for the three Ls (McGraw Hill Construction, 2008), and this is likely to have greater impact than any other impetus to move towards zero waste.

Whether you are a designer, researcher, policymaker, businessperson or a concerned global citizen, please enjoy, digest and implement the knowledge within this book! Good luck!

Professor Emeritus Peter Brandon is the Director of the Salford Think Lab, researching sustainable development in construction management, with a focus on knowledge-based systems for sustainable development. Peter is the former Pro-Vice Chancellor for Research of the University of Salford in Manchester and has published more than twenty books. His latest book, co-authored with Dr Patrizia Lombardi, *Evaluation of the built environment for sustainability* (2010), offers a new structure for sustainable development based on the 'Philosophy of the Cosmos' by Herman Dooyeweerd, encouraging a holistic and integrated systems approach.

References

Brandon, P. and Lombardi P. (2010) *Evaluating Sustainable Development in the Built Environment* (2nd edn), Wiley-Blackwell, Oxford

Gordon, A. (1974) 'The economics of the 3 L's concept', *Chartered Surveyor B and QS Quarterly*, Winter

McGraw Hill Construction (2008) *Global Green Building Trends – Market Growth and Perspectives from Around the World*, McGraw Hill Construction

Rees, M. (2003) *Our Final Century: Will the Human Race Survive the Twenty-first Century?*, Arrow Books, London

United Nations Environment Programme (UNEP) Sustainable Buildings and Construction Initiative (SBCI) (2007) *Buildings and Climate Change: Status, Challenges and Opportunities*, UNEP, Nairobi, Kenya

Introduction

People, policies and persuasion: the future of waste reduction and resource recovery in households and urban settings

Steffen Lehmann and Robert Crocker

Designing for Zero Waste is a timely, topical and necessary book. Materials and resources are being depleted at an accelerating speed, and rising consumption trends across the globe have placed material efficiency, waste reduction and recycling at the centre of many government policy agendas, giving them an unprecedented urgency. Although there is a considerable body of scholarly literature addressing consumption and waste reduction from different disciplinary perspectives, the complex nature of the problem demands interdisciplinary exploration. Resource recovery and the optimization of material flow can only be achieved alongside and through behaviour change to reduce both the creation of material waste and wasteful consumption.

Rethinking the way we deal with material flows and changing behaviour in regard to waste streams, we believe, can deliver significant improvements, curbing the threat of environmental degradation and global warming. We have borrowed from the planet for a long time, exceeding the planet's carrying capacity, and if our societies and the global economy are not transformed we risk descent into unhealthy urban conditions and further depletion of virgin materials. Our current model of economic and urban growth is driving this unhealthy system, and, as a consequence, we have now passed the limits of our planet's capacity to support us. Over the last twenty years, for example, the amount of waste Australians produced has more than doubled, and it is likely that this amount will double again between 2011 and 2020, because the amount of waste generated in Australia grows by 6 to 7 per cent per person, per year. In addition to this, 40 per cent of all food in Australia is not eaten; it is thrown out instead of being composted as organic kitchen waste to return nutrients as fertilizer to the soil, or recycled in a biogas plant to generate energy. Discarded television sets and outdated computers (known as e-waste) are another hazardous time bomb. For instance, around 32 million new television and computer products were sold in Australia in 2008, with an estimated 16.8 million units reaching end of life in the same year. However, only 10 per cent were recycled, well below the average rate of recycling for all waste in Australia of 52 per cent (2009 data, National Waste Report, 2010). Too much e-waste still ends up in our soil and rivers, polluting our drinking water.

Overall, things do not look good. In fact, endless consumption and growth are impossible. Everybody understands that, if you cut down more trees than you plant, at some point you run out of trees. In 1996, the German philosopher and urban planner Karl Ganser came up with the idea of 'change and prosperity without growth', something still unimaginable for most politicians and economists (Hannemann, 2000, p99). Passing the limits must have consequences, as we see in increasing global warming, changing weather patterns and a change in the way the whole system of 'Spaceship Earth' (Buckminster-Fuller, 1973) behaves. Topics such as food security (possible solution: urban farming?), water scarcity (solution: storm-water harvesting?), rising energy costs (solution: decentralized energy production on roofs and facades?), depletion of virgin materials (solution: closing the loop of material cycles?) and increasing traffic congestion (solution: increased investment in public transport?) have emerged as major concerns, and researchers at universities worldwide are now looking into better ways for us to live together in more liveable and sustainable cities in the future.

It is clear that things are going to change, and we must make every effort to future-proof the built environment by designing and building more resilience into urban systems. By doing so, we will increasingly learn from nature's complex ecosystems and natural ordering principles, in redefining our industrial ecology to change the way we produce, manufacture, package, transport and reuse products. We are embarking on nothing less than a silent green revolution, which has already started to transform our society, economy, energy and transport systems, waste-management systems and the way we design, build, operate, renew and reuse/recycle cities and buildings. New strategies for the reorganization of the urban landscape are emerging. It makes sense that the next step is to rethink industrial and urban systems and production methods. In 2009, sustainability activist Paul Gilding stated that we 'have entered a period of global ecological crisis and economic stagnation that will lead to an economic and social transformation of significance in the history of humanity'. According to Gilding, this crisis is inevitable, because the fundamental causes are not public opinion or politics, but the established momentum of changes in the ecosystem. As a result, he suggests our current model of economic growth is finished, and a new one must be forged based on the principles of sustainability and with human relationships at its core. Gilding has an optimistic vision of our shared future: he believes that 'we will break our addiction to growth, accept that more stuff is not making our lives better and focus instead on what does' (Gilding, 2009, np).

At the same time, new research agendas are emerging as open platforms for collaboration and interdisciplinary exploration. Demonstration projects accompanied by relevant research are essential in this change process, as these have the potential to deliver more and better solutions to curb global warming. Universities are at the forefront of a meaningful, relevant search for such solutions. Advances in knowledge, together with an awareness of the complexity of today's world, have led scholars to pursue multifaceted problems that cannot be resolved from the vantage point of a single academic discipline. Therefore, universities are increasingly engaged with industry, governments, community groups and other institutions worldwide to support multidisciplinary and integrated approaches to research in urban-systems thinking. Now is the time to scale up our scholarship in low-carbon urban solutions to match the size of the challenges we are facing and to support the development of appropriate policies. Collaboration across sectors is critical, because, in addition to influencing policy and legislation, collaborative research into low-carbon and zero-waste futures will help to develop a responsive plan for the transformation of existing cities as an important part of the solution. It is therefore critical that our efforts support long-term planning and research in line with agreed national priorities, for holistic, whole-of-life-cycle approaches. This book is the result of such interdisciplinary and cross-sector investigations.

We have arranged the following chapters in four parts. Part I is titled 'Zero waste, *Structure* sustainability and behaviour change: principles', and Part II is titled 'Zero waste, *of this* enabling technologies and consumption: policies'. *book*

An important aspect of the discussion of zero waste is the analysis of consumerism, behaviour change, particularly at the household and building scale. Parts I and II of the book deal with these issues. These chapters explore the complexity of consumption and lifestyle, people's motivations and attitudes, shifts of values and behaviours – and the dynamics of social change. Such an analysis requires the involvement of a series of disciplines, including sociologists, psychologists and researchers in cultural studies. It is obvious that sustainable consumption is still a controversial concept politically, economically, socially and culturally. Part I outlines the principles of behaviour change. It opens with Robert Crocker's assessment of the connections between consumerism, zero waste and mobility behaviour. In Chapter 2, Natalie Skinner, Barbara Pocock, Pip Williams and Jane Edwards describe the difficulties of changing behaviour while balancing work, home and community. Sue Nichols looks at the relationship between early-childhood education and sustainable consumption in Chapter 3. Sandra Davison, Kirrilly Thompson, Drew Dawson and Anne Sharp examine the psychology of consumption in regard to food waste in Chapter 4. Angelique Edmonds explores collaborative consumption and local resilience in Chapter 5. Part II introduces a debate on enabling technologies that will help us to live more sustainably: Robert Crocker explores the new mobile communications paradigm in Chapter 6, followed by Ab Stevels, Jaco Huisman and Feng Wang's discussion of the issue of e-waste in Chapter 7. Alexander Walker contributes an important chapter on life-cycle thinking and analysis from the viewpoint of the designer in Chapter 8, and Jane Dickson and Victor Buchli discuss the ontology of the house (or household) in Chapter 9. In Chapter 10, Carla Litchfield, Kurt Lushington, Sue Bigwood and Wendy Foster present a different view by looking at wildlife habitat and its relationship to sustainable living.

Sustainability theorist Tim Jackson noted that 'Consumption drives our economies and defines our lives; making it sustainable is an enormous and essential challenge', and he observes that 'the problem of changing consumer behaviour and making our lives more sustainable continues to challenge opinion-formers and policy-makers alike' (2006, pp132–6). Household behaviour in everyday life is increasingly seen as the essential starting point for change. There is a complex interplay between policy initiatives and individual behaviour (for instance, the difficulty of mobilizing shifts in attitudes, lifestyle values and consumption patterns). Our behaviour in our own homes – our recycling habits, consumer choices and transport preferences – has a huge impact on the environment locally and globally. This is clearly visible in household behaviour in regard to waste and recycling, food consumption and food waste, and transportation patterns and mobility choices. Among the researchers who have explored these links is Patrik Söderholm, who explains that, 'We need to gain a better understanding of how environmental policy enters the private, domestic sphere, and how it influences house-hold behaviour, to generate behaviour change at the household level and the move towards sustainable societies' (2010, p28). Designers Tom Fisher and Janet Shipton offer the view that 'the home is a system in which objects are processed' (2009, p127).

Part III of this book is titled 'Zero waste in sustainable architecture and design at the household and building scale', and Part IV is titled 'Zero waste in cities, urban

Structure of book

governance and material flows'. The chapters in these parts explore the complex problem of sustainable materials and their embodied energy, the enabling of low-carbon technologies and the principles of sustainable design. The chapters in Part III explore this multifaceted topic at the micro level of individual households and buildings, and those in Part IV examine zero waste at the macro scale of integration: the city.

The urbanized environment of the city is increasingly the place where solutions for waste reduction must and will be found. In this effort, every city will have to find its ideal set of particular solutions, or 'localized responses', to resolve questions of material flows and the management of waste streams (Lehmann, 2010, pp261ff.). However, local responses to globalizing forces depend partly on the nature of the interlinkages in governance from international structures, through multilateral organizations to nation-states, regions and localities, as these are mediated through social–local identity. This complex includes the transformation of production processes, green infrastructures and systems, as well as concepts of resource efficiency (especially material efficiency), decoupling concepts (decoupling the raise of consumption from the use of materials), clean technologies, and design for sustainability, industrial ecology and life-cycle analysis. Industrial production as a whole has to be transformed. In their book *Natural capitalism: the next industrial revolution*, Paul Hawken et al (2000) clearly set out the path that we must take to ensure the future prosperity of our civilization and our planet. A decade ago, *Natural capitalism* rocked the world of business and manufacturing with its authors' innovative approach – an approach that fused ecological integrity with business acumen via the radical concept of natural capitalism.

Part III of this book analyses the opportunities for zero waste in building and the construction sector. In Chapter 11, Steffen Lehmann explores sustainable building design and material efficiency, and Stephen Ward describes the many advantages of adaptive reuse of entire building structures in Chapter 12. In Chapter 13, Alapana Sivam and Sadasivam Karuppannan look at the densities and design of residential development, and Nicholas Chileshe, Jian Zuo, Stephen Pullen and George Zillante evaluate the potential for zero waste in construction management in Chapter 14. In Part IV, zero-waste concepts are related to urban planning and governance. Steffen Lehmann explores material flows and the metabolism of the city in Chapter 15, and Michael Taylor and Michelle Philp look at sustainable transport systems in regard to behaviour change in Chapter 16. In Chapter 17, Lou Wilson uses the city of Adelaide as a case study in urban planning for the sustainable consumption of urban resources. Simon Beecham presents concepts of multifunctional urban land uses and water-sensitive urban design in Chapter 18.

To identify holistic approaches of the kind discussed in these chapters requires the involvement of scholars in a range of disciplines, including economics, design and materials, working together to enable the systemic environmental restructuring of consumption and provision in energy, water and waste systems. In the context of this change process, designers – architects, urban planners, industrial, interior or product designers – axiomatically play a major part. In short, to advance the subject of design one has to engage in the activity of designing. In his book *Sustainable by design*, Stuart Walker (2006) offers a design-centred approach and a new understanding of the complexity and potential of sustainable design, extolling the contribution of design to the creation of a more meaningful material culture. As Peter Stasinopoulos and his colleagues point out, it is possible to apply a 'whole system design' approach alongside a more integrated approach to engineering. They argue that 'Whole System Design is increasingly being seen as one of the most cost-effective ways to both increase the productivity and reduce the negative environmental impacts of an engineered system' (Stasinopoulos et al, 2008, pp2–10). Consequently, the focus on design is critical, as the output from the design stage of the project locks in most of the economic and environmental performance of the designed system throughout its life cycle, which can span from a few years to many decades. Indeed, it is now widely acknowledged that all designers – particularly engineers, architects and industrial designers – need to be able to understand and implement a whole system design approach, because, as Stasinopoulos and his colleagues explain:

> Advances in energy, materials and water productivity can be achieved through applying an integrated approach to sustainable engineering, to enhance the established systems engineering framework, from passenger vehicles and computer systems, to the temperature control of buildings and domestic water systems.
>
> (2008, p10)

Designing with an eye to resource or energy efficiency, however, is not a straightforward solution. In *The myth of resource efficiency*, John Polimeni et al (2009) describe what is known as the 'Jevons paradox', which was first identified in 1865 by Australian engineer William Stanley Jevons in relation to the use of coal. The paradox Jevons observed is that an increase in the efficiency of using a resource frequently leads to an increased use of that resource rather than to the desired reduction. This effect is also called the 'rebound effect', where previous gains in efficiency are absorbed and lost. The paradox has subsequently been proved to apply not just to fossil fuels, but also to other resource-use scenarios, including material and water usage. Polimeni and his co-authors point out that, for example, doubling the efficiency of food production per hectare over the last fifty years (owing to the green agricultural revolution) did not solve the problem of hunger. Instead, this increase in efficiency increased production and, paradoxically, worsened hunger because of the resulting increase in population. This has substantial implications for today's world. Many scientists and policymakers argue that future technological innovations will reduce consumption of resources; the Jevons paradox, however, explains why we have to examine such an assumption carefully, as it may be a false hope.

But how do you engage with those who cannot or do not want to imagine a different future? What are the main drivers towards sustainable consumption? What are the determinants of consumer behaviour? Behaviour change has frequently been listed as the number one hurdle to a more energy- and material-efficient, low-carbon future. If we could only plan better cities and design better buildings and products that needed less energy, water, materials and other resources, thus generating less waste, and facilitating positive behaviour change simply through their design; for instance, enabling people to be less dependent on air conditioning and car driving, by offering attractive new housing typologies in the city centre based on passive design principles. The most successful research projects related to sustainability and behaviour change are probably those in which the community is involved and those that enable participants to identify with the outcomes of their activities. However, changing the behaviour of a community or building occupant is not easy; it usually starts with greater awareness (e.g. through visualization of carbon emissions or energy use based on smart metering systems) and involves incentives. Education to raise awareness is essential. Equally important is that the rules and benefits of waste separation, resource recovery and recycling are well explained. This suggests that the real problem is not technology, but social acceptance and behaviour change.

Understanding reuse is increasingly important, but designing for reuse in the domestic (household) context is still under-researched and little understood. We can reuse and recycle products, packaging and even buildings (through adaptive reuse). The common slogan is: every reused item is another item not purchased. A good example of the problem is the proposed legislation to reduce packaging and introduce extended producer responsibilities recently introduced by the Australian government. Packaging is seen as ephemeral; its purpose is to be 'wasted' once the product it contains has been removed. Alternatively, Fisher and Shipton have explained that 'the reuse of packaging has a significant effect on the quantity of material that enters the waste stream and the energy and consequently carbon that is expended in its production' (2009, p127). Most of the factors influencing the potential for reuse relate to the specifics of the design, including the types of material used, the flexibility and adaptability of a building's plan and section or the symbolism of the product's branding. Other factors are more social: for instance, the effects of reuse on the perception of different consumer orientations. Fisher and Shipton point out that 'understanding consumers' behaviour is significant for moving towards sustainability through design' (2009, p127ff.). Although research into consumption patterns and behaviour change is still in its infancy, no doubt it will continue to grow in importance.

Short-term and long-term strategies capable of implementation in the developed and developing world are required to bring about the desired change towards zero waste. How can it be achieved? In their report *State of the world 2010: transforming cultures from consumerism to sustainability*, the Worldwatch Institute (2010) lists many of the environmental and social problems we face today as symptoms of a deeper systemic failing, a dominant cultural paradigm that encourages living in ways that are often directly counter to the realities of a finite planet with finite resources. Consumerism has already spread to cultures around the world, and 'hyper-consumerism' has led to consumption levels that are vastly unsustainable. If this pattern spreads further, to rapidly developing and rapidly urbanizing societies in China and India, there will be little possibility of solving climate change or any of the other environmental problems that are poised to disrupt human civilization. The Worldwatch Institute's programme director, Eric Assadourian, notes soberly 'It will take a sustained, long-term effort to redirect the traditions, social movements and institutions that shape consumer cultures towards becoming cultures of sustainability' (Worldwatch Institute, 2010, p20ff.). If we can bring about a cultural shift to make living sustainably as 'natural' as today's consumer lifestyle, we will not only address urgent environmental crises, we will also contribute solutions to other problems, such as extreme income inequity, obesity and social isolation, that are not usually seen as environmental issues. To this end, *Designing for Zero Waste* aims to develop a more robust understanding of the links between lifestyle, consumption, technologies and urban development. It's not too late to change.

References

Buckminster Fuller, R. (1973) *Earth, Inc.,* Anchor Books, Random House, New York

Fisher, T. and Shipton, J. (2009) *Designing for Re-Use: The Life of Consumer Packaging*, Earthscan, London

Gilding, P. (2009) 'Economic growth version 1.0 is finished: the great disruption has begun', Institute of Sustainable Solutions Future Focus lecture given at the University of Sydney, Sydney, Australia, 29 April, http://sydney.edu.au/sydney_ideas/lectures/2009/great_disruption.shtml, accessed 25 April 2011

Hannemann, C. (2000) 'Zukunftschance Schrumpfung – Stadtentwicklung in Ostdeutschland – eine Skizze', in F. Hager and W. Schenkel (eds) *Schrumpfungen. Chancen für ein anderes Wachstum: ein Diskurs der Natur- und Sozialwissenschaften*, Springer-Verlag, Berlin, Germany

Hawken, P., Lovins, A. and Lovins, H. (2000, republished 2010) *Natural Capitalism: The Next Industrial Revolution*, Little, Brown and Company, California

Jackson, T. (ed) (2006) *The Earthscan Reader on Sustainable Consumption*, Earthscan Reader Series, Earthscan, London

Lehmann, S. (2010) *The Principles of Green Urbanism: Transforming the City for Sustainability*, Earthscan, London

Environment Protection and Heritage Council and Department of Environment, Water, Heritage and the Arts (2010) *National Waste Report 2010*, Australian government, Canberra, ACT, www.environment.gov.au/wastepolicy/publications/national-waste-report.htm, accessed 25 April 2011

Polimeni, J., Mayumi, K., Giampietro, M. and Alcott, B. (2009) *The Myth of Resource Efficiency: The Jevons Paradox*, Earthscan, London

Söderholm, P. (2010) *Environmental Policy and Household Behaviour: Sustainability and Everyday Life*, Earthscan, London

Stasinopoulos, P., Smith, M., Hargroves, K. and Desha, C. (2008) *Whole System Design: An Integrated Approach to Sustainable Engineering*, Earthscan, London

Walker, S. (2006) *Sustainable by Design: Explorations in Theory and Practice*, Earthscan, London

Worldwatch Institute (2010) *State of the World 2010: Transforming Cultures From Consumerism to Sustainability* (27th edn), W. W. Norton, Washington, DC/Earthscan, London

Part I

Zero waste, sustainability and behaviour change

Principles

Chapter 1

'Somebody else's problem'

Consumer culture, waste and behaviour
change – the case of walking

Robert Crocker

Summary

Most efforts at improving the sustainability of our products, systems and environments are currently focused on their role in consumption and use. This 'consumption'
focus, broadly defined here to include the consumption and use of raw materials and
services, necessarily distances us from the natural environment or 'commons' from which
various desired materials are extracted and into which – once processed and used – these
are later discarded as 'waste'. It also tends to silence our pre-existing relationship to,
and dependence on, each other and our local environments, as these too are reduced to
producing some economic value conceived of in relation to consumption. What remains
outside this 'consumption frame' becomes 'somebody else's problem', but increasingly
our environmental crisis is forcing us to question the effects of this narrow focus.

Using the sporadic but ongoing example of government attempts to get more people
out of their cars and walking, this chapter argues that progress towards greater sustainability in this and many other instances can only occur when a 'socialization' of
behaviour change can occur, that is when the social normalization of a desired behaviour
becomes habitual, and any barriers, either structural or behavioural, to this desired change
are minimized or removed. In the case of walking, this requires a substantial revision
of the traditional methods and concerns of the traffic engineer, and a return to the local
scale of 'walkable' environments and short journeys envisaged by the urban designer.
Recalling ten years' personal involvement in pedestrian safety advocacy, this chapter
reflects upon the experiences of local communities confronted with the dominant
system's barriers to walkable local environments and considers the successful 'socialized' strategies that have been developed to get people out of their cars and into these
environments as walkers.

Introduction: consumption, 'distance' and responsibility

In Douglas Adams's sci-fi novel, *Life, the universe and everything* (1982), space
engineers, faced with the expensive challenge of making a spaceship invisible for
defensive purposes, decide to go for a new, cheaper option, a technology wryly named
'somebody else's problem'. This makes the spaceship in question not really invisible,
but 'almost' so, through the device of the observer's inattention. Instead of seeing a ship
clearly or not seeing it at all, Adams's ship can only be seen with great difficulty out
of the corner of one's eye (Adams, 1982, pp28–9). Like many of the background systems

we take for granted, such as the supply of water, electricity and gas to our homes and the weekly rubbish collection, along with the roadways that enable our car-based commute to and from work, we seem to be able to focus only on the 'consumption phase' in the life cycle of any particular domain. Everything else outside the parameters of what we now take for granted becomes 'somebody else's problem', something perhaps 'they' should do something about, sooner or later.

Indeed, most of our more serious environmental problems now seem to be 'somebody else's problem'. A conceptual distancing or 'distantiation' is apparent in our aware-ness of, not only the origins and ordinary functioning of the things and services we use on a daily basis, but also what happens to them when they fail to function or when we no longer need them. The 'stuff' we use and enjoy appears in our lives almost magically, often having been transported thousands of kilometres in trucks, trains and planes, from processing, manufacturing and distribution locations hidden from us behind barcodes, brochures, branded labels and the 'fine print' on packages or delivery notes (Princen, 2002b). While even as children we can identify the logos and brands of well-known products, and retell the simple myths they recount, the real origins, life cycle, technical function in use and 'end-of-life' destination of these same products and services have been skilfully airbrushed out of the picture. This is not a product of corporate conspiracy but the result of long-term historical processes that have transformed our relationship to the world of goods: from being a much smaller population of face-to-face 'customers', of small shop, workshop and farm-based providers, over about 150 years we have become a 'side-to-side' army of consumers, dependent on vast, often global, mass-production and mass-distribution systems, whose complexity and lengthy supply chains render them opaque to us (Strasser, 2003). This means that, even if we wanted as individuals to do something about many of the downsides of our vastly distanced global production and distribution system, there is usually insufficient information available to us to act with any certainty or clarity of purpose (Princen, 2002a; 2002b; 2005).

For example, in New York or London, the delicious fresh tuna on our plate in a restaurant may have come from the other side of the world, pulled out of the sea perhaps only three days ago, and flown thousands of kilometres to us on ice to retain its fresh-ness (de Botton, 2009, pp53ff.). The modern miracle of the logistics responsible for bringing the tuna to our plate remains concealed, but its extraordinary costs, in fuel, emissions and energy, not to mention its impact on the tuna's population and the distant habitat in which it lived, are unknowable to us and remain silenced by this conceptual distance (Paché, 2007). Worse, there is no visible global oversight of the shared natural environment or 'commons' from which this tuna has been extracted, just as there are no effective global limits to our profligate use of other increasingly limited natural resources (Conca, 2008). As we eat our tuna, we can have no certainty that the fish was farmed or caught responsibly, and it remains a possibility that it was taken by 'illegal' fishermen and then somehow 'legalized' on paper during its journey to the restaurant (Bestor, 2003). Extraction and distribution, whether of tuna, oil, timber or diamonds, occur on a 'first come, first served' basis, with the richest, most technologically sophisticated or most powerful getting in first, staking a 'claim' and taking a 'share' that may create serious problems for the rest of us in the future (Princen, 2003; 2005). It is perhaps no wonder that there has been a substantial decline in public trust closely coinciding with this self-evident triumph of globalization (Putnam, 2000; Hardin, 2006).

Waste products, like the resources and by-products from which our food, clothing and other 'stuff' are made, are largely hidden from us, and we have developed efficient disposal systems and corresponding metaphors to ensure that what is discarded is taken away and disposed of, 'out of sight, and so out of mind' (Clapp, 2002; Princen, 2010). The environmental costs of over-extraction, over-consumption and excessive pollution and waste, like the real costs of our road toll, for example, are never made transparent to us, but can only be made visible with considerable effort, against a prevailing culture of 'use and enjoy, dispose and forget'. Part of the problem is economic 'externalization', where costs are shifted so that environmental 'debts' can pile up and be passed on, back to the population living on the 'frontier' from whence the 'resource' was first extracted, or where the items in question were manufactured (Princen, 2002b; Smart, 2010, pp110ff.). Just as transport departments around the world do not have to pay for the costs of road accidents, such as emergency medical staff, ambulances, surgery, insurance, or deal with the many personal tragedies, grief and suffering caused by most serious accidents, so miners, manufacturers and other producers, shippers and retailers, and the many consumers at the end of our lengthy and complex supply chains, usually do not have to pay for the environmental costs embedded in the 'stuff' they are using, or the waste it will eventually become (Frascara, 1996).

The problem is not only one of distantiation and the inevitable concealment from view that comes with lengthy supply chains, but also the way that our present economic system focuses attention and attributes value only at the 'owned' consumption or 'in-use' phase of any life cycle, and then only on the specific owner and the 'job' in question. This leads to a crisis of oversight and responsibility: we are accustomed to efficiently managing and focusing upon only what is 'owned' by some identifiable person, corporation or nation in its use phase. However, we seem unable to deal with what is there before this 'resource' is 'claimed' and then 'owned' at the beginning of this cycle, or what happens to the consumed material at its end, when it is turned again into what is 'unowned' or unwanted. For no one wants to 'own' garbage, unless it has some special material value, and when this is not identified it returns again to the commons, to what technically has not yet been given value or 'owned' (Strasser, 2000; Linebaugh, 2010). As Princen points out, much of this depends on widely accepted and unquestioned metaphors taken directly from economics and misapplied in the 'real world' of human and environmental relationships (Princen, 2010).

Witness the 'great Pacific garbage patch' made up of plastics and other industrial products floating in the northern Pacific gyre, which has become a hazard to shipping and wildlife and is now so large it can be seen from space (Moore, 2003; Coulter, 2009–10; Wikipedia, 2011). It lies beyond the responsibility of any government, ship owner or industrial producer and remains, mysteriously, without a determining or responsible cause, very much 'somebody else's problem'. But, as Moore and others have pointed out, while this continent-sized patch of floating garbage might damage many distant fish and birds directly, its toxins affect us too, entering the food chain and becoming a part of what we eat, perhaps thousands of miles distant, its tell-tale toxins now being identifiable in many commercially caught and consumed fish (Moore, 2003).

Distantiation and externalization have also become serious problems when it comes to more 'normal' waste and pollution issues, because, while what might be associated with the interests of a government or a corporation can be represented and dealt with fairly efficiently, what lies in the interests of everyone beyond this consumption or use phase seems to elude most systems of governance and consumption-focused economic thinking, just as it eludes our ability to focus on them in our daily lives. Like many 'undiscovered' resources and much waste, what lies in our metaphorically distanced biosphere or commons becomes obscure and tenuous, a global 'frontier' (Princen, 2002b; Linebaugh, 2010). Typically, this then becomes open to a free-for-all competition between corporate actors whose interests might include mining or exploiting an identified 'resource' within an area of the commons. These often operate under 'flags of convenience' or some similar 'legal' fiction to limit responsibility for the environmental damage caused by their exploration or extraction, as was the case in the recent disaster in the Gulf of Mexico (Princen, 2005; Courselle, 2010). As Maniates, Princen and others have argued, it is vital that we come to grips collectively with the lack of social and environmental responsibility embedded in the now global political, economic and legal infrastructures that foster and support this 'frontier mentality', rather than simply treating it as an abstract theoretical problem, involving only the 'pricing' of untapped natural resources, as though they can be magically reconstituted by some future technological wizardry (Maniates, 2002; Princen, 2002b; Conca, 2008).

The central metaphor for this distantiation and externalization I want to return to later in this chapter is that of walking in relation to the automobile: through the perceptual window provided by consumption we have been led to assume there is more economic and social value in driving than in walking, that, without the 'flexibility' and 'freedom' the car provides, many economic benefits will be lost or closed to us. We also assume that driving (or being driven) is socially as well as technologically more 'advanced' and therefore more important, and more worthy of investment than 'just' walking, something suggested by the metaphorical meaning often applied to the word 'pedestrian'. At present, the social and environmental costs of driving or being driven are nearly all externalized to the larger community and natural environment, to the commons from which the oil used to power cars is extracted, to the polluted air, water and environment created by our car dependence, and the 'sprawl' this dependence locks in place.

In aiming for zero waste, the car is an extremely problematic object of consumption: however 'advanced' we might be able to make it in the future, reducing its emissions to zero, and cleverly engineering its shell and guidance system until it is 'perfectly safe' (for those others, presumably, in their cars), it is still one of the world's most economically expensive and environmentally and socially destructive products, with one of its most significant and least considered costs being its direct restriction of walking. For, when we can drive we usually do, and this discourages us from walking (thus creating the grounds for many health problems in those driving or being driven, including obesity, diabetes and other, stress-related disorders), especially when we live or work in urban environments where other cars dominate, travel distances are great, public transport is limited and walking is a socially stigmatized, dangerous and unpleasant option (Hass-Klau, 1990; Freund and Martin, 1993; Litman, 2011).

The everyday domain of personal transport and the car's hold on it provides a particularly useful lens through which to examine the problem of behaviour change, partly because it has been so thoroughly documented and discussed in a very large literature involving many different disciplines (Paterson, 2000; Davison and Yelland, 2004), but also because it directly impacts on the problem of our waste stream: cars and other road-based vehicles are large objects producing tonnes of environmental waste, including around 20 per cent of the world's greenhouse-gas emissions, with much of it extremely toxic and contributing directly to climate change (for a summary of 2007 global figures, see CAIT, 2011). Cars are also deadly weapons, killing each year, in both America and Australia, proportionally as many people as were killed during our ten-year involvement in the Vietnam War, and maiming a similar proportion too (Sharma, 2008; Australian Government, 2009). Recent figures suggest that the annual road toll worldwide is approaching 1.5 million people, with around 50 million people maimed, a population the size of a significant country. The World Health Organization (WHO) estimates that the cost of this destruction (which does not include animals and birds killed on the road) totals a staggering US$52 billion per year (Australian Government, 2009; WHO, 2009, 2011).

As with the negative consequences of other 'unsustainable' systems and their infrastructures that we have developed and normalized over long periods of time, the car does not bear the costs of its destructive consequences, as these are routinely and invisibly externalized (Freund and Martin, 2009). It is sold to us through the promise of the freedom and flexible mobility it can provide, but, as its use begins to dominate our urban spaces, alternative means of transport, unless vigorously defended, tend to wither and die. Whereas the fact that it employs so many people, providing jobs, essential services and transport, and much work for large sections of the economy is well known, the true costs of the pollution of the atmosphere, land and waterways that our present transport system causes, its use of up to 50 per cent of land in many cities, and the death and destruction it causes, are rarely accounted for or even mentioned in public, because it seems so 'essential' to our lives (Davison and Yelland, 2004). Again, this cost is substantially externalized back to the community through government, with car manufacturers, retailers and others involved in the industry paying the same taxes other, much less destructive industries must pay, and often enjoying generous subsidies from governments afraid of the consequences any downturn in the industry might have on the national economy (Paterson, 2000).

Driving, however much we can improve it technically, is invariably a resource- and energy-intensive activity, and, as the above suggests, socially and environmentally destructive, with many negative side effects, including social isolation, obesity and other conditions that follow such sedentary activity. These well-known economic, social and environmental costs can be contrasted with the invariably low infrastructure costs and otherwise positive social balance-sheet for walking: improved health and fitness, improved oversight of local paths that are walked, so that quite often petty crime diminishes, and increased economic activity associated with pedestrian movements in commercial areas (Litman, 2011). Why then is walking so routinely dismissed as 'ordinary', 'pedestrian' and unworthy of attention or funding as a 'transport' mode, even as a 'link' between other (public) transport modes? Why do we insist on spending so much money on the automobile and its infrastructure, and on heavily subsidizing the manufacturers of this most deadly of everyday weapons? Questions such as these need to be asked, not just of our car dependency, but of many other domains of everyday life, where long-term sociotechnical development, government funding and established commercial interest, and often massive investment, combine to encourage and 'lock in' similarly destructive sociotechnical routines and behaviours. Improving them, and making them qualitatively 'greener', may not result in the desired solution of lower emissions, as, with the rapid development occurring in India and China, massive sales in new cars are making the gradualist solutions popular in the industry ineffective in both the short and long terms. We have to stop pretending that we can continue depending on the automobile as we did in the 1950s: the game plan has changed irrevocably. 'Sustainable transport' has to be reimagined as much more than simply 'smarter', greener cars.

Sustainability and consumer desire

Behind our car dependence, as well as our present preference for many other unsustainable practices, sits the 'elephant in the room', the engine of our economies and of the profitability that justified the kinds of risk BP recently took in the Gulf with such catastrophic results. This is consumer desire. Given the money and the opportunity, most of us seem to want 'more', and many of us also seem oblivious to the fact that the objects or systems we desire may cause some form of environmental damage in the process of their extraction, making, distribution, use or disposal. This, after all, is 'somebody else's problem', and it seems it cannot be seen clearly from where we stand before the shop's windows, saturated as we are with 'infotainment' and advertising that routinely misinforms us about the social and environmental consequences of our purchasing habits (Smart, 2010, pp60ff.).

But the question remains, what is it precisely that we want, and why? Although scholars have identified four typical motives towards consumption, in practice these can be seen to act together as they entangle us in unsustainable behaviours. We do not necessarily choose these behaviours consciously, but often find ourselves inheriting practices or ways of living from systems or product domains that have developed in each domain of our lives over time, and many of these have given birth to monumental self-replicating infrastructures, such as that which currently supports the automobile (Shove, 2003a; Quitzau and Ropke, 2008).

To understand our motives to consumption, a good starting point, which is often rather neglected in the vast literature on consumption, is our desire to improve ourselves and to extend or enhance our knowledge through expanding our experience of the world, of others and ourselves. Educational services, media, music and many other 'invisible' forms of consumption are tied up in this impulse, and it is a fundamental force in the great 'churn' of material flows and other 'grosser', more noticeable forms of consumption (Lees-Maffei, 2001; Miller, 2010). For, when we explore the world or try to understand something, we also consume: we buy newspapers and books, we go to university and do courses and degrees, we produce and read information on websites, through computers and other devices, and use up many services associated with expanding our knowledge or understanding each other and the world (McCracken, 2008). This impulse to consume through understanding, often resulting in some form of self-transformation, affects everyone, including those who cannot read well and have little education and no aspiration to get a degree or improve their prospects through training. Evidence of this can be seen in the daily horoscope in the newspaper, or in the huge array of 'lifestyle' magazines: we all want a 'better' future and a more enriching experience of ourselves, of others and of the world around us, and our consumer culture promises to deliver this 'better' future of 'more', where this year's novelty will soon be eclipsed by next. Travel, now the biggest consumer industry in the world, is to a great extent a reflection of this impulse among others (Urry, 2007), as is much IT business, with Apple having largely identified its brand and marketing campaigns with a promise to enable its customers to know more and understand 'better' (Apple, 2011).

(2) Second, consumption is often driven by a desire for more precise control over our environment and over the things we like doing; this is particularly evident when buying gadgets, appliances, machines and other things that seem to improve the functional aspects of our lives, perhaps saving time or doing something that cannot be done otherwise (Shove, 2003b; Ingram et al, 2007). Often, greater convenience, comfort or cleanliness are alibis we use to ourselves to justify this second 'technological' or 'functional' impulse towards consumption (Ingram et al, 2007). We become frustrated with some functional limitation or failure in one or more of our appliances, and so we go out and buy another to replace it, frequently when the appliance in question still works. We may want to replace something that does not work very well, or has certain functional limitations, with something that we think does. For many of us, this functional impulse is often perceptual rather than 'real': we think we 'need' that new iPhone, not because we cannot manage with our two-year-old BlackBerry, but because we imagine greater competency and functionality that we might be able to enjoy with the iPhone, and we will happily invent alibis to ensure that this happens. This 'functional' motive might be the result of real frustrations with what we now have: for example, wanting an apartment with more than one bedroom, or wanting to replace a mobile phone that will no longer work properly. Although these are 'real' problems, they come to our notice because we can imagine a future alternative: again, we imagine a future that is in some way preferable to, and in this case more efficient than, that which we enjoy in the present. This is the 'functional' incentive that retailers of electronic gadgets work very hard on in their advertising: 'thinner, faster, lighter, and with two cameras!' they will say (Apple, 2011). As this suggests, just as we desire what is apparently more efficient in our quest for a more sustainable future, more efficiency in itself can lead to more consumption, as Jevons noted many years ago (Verbeek and Slob, 2006; Herring and Roy, 2007).

(3) Third, we are attracted to many things, places and experiences on aesthetic or emotive grounds: we like the look or feel of something, and this leads us to buy it. This might be a computer game, a holiday in Bali, a new movie with our favourite actors in it, a Spanish cooking course or a beautiful pair of new shoes, or anything else that takes our fancy (McCracken, 1988, 2008; Miller, 2008). This motive has been of particular interest to a large number of scholars, probably because it seems to be so closely tied in to our sense of identity and our place in the world (Campbell, 2004). In his exploration of individuals in their homes, *The comfort of things* (2008), Daniel Miller, for example, describes the way each of us tends to layer our homes with things over time, in very specific, individually enhancing and fulfilling ways. He repeatedly identifies objects that his interviewees keep and display which for them represent valued experiences, special relationships, places we love or some passion such as music. As Miller and others have shown, we need to consume things like these in order to express ourselves, and to experience who we think we are or who we want to become, and also to position ourselves in relation to others we know and love. Gifts, awards or items of clothing that appear to be a special marker of an event or relationship that is important to us fall into this category, perhaps more than any other. As this suggests, perceived value and how one

thing more than another might seem to enhance the self play a critical role in consumption, as much consumption starts with a strong belief in our inadequacies; and, of course, our alleged 'incompleteness' is continually manipulated by advertisers and marketers and the fashion system through which they operate (Belk, 1988; Kasser, 2002).

 Finally, we also buy or 'update' things because we feel that it is socially necessary, that, for example, if we do not replace those curtains or that old sofa, we will be embarrassed when friends or relatives come to visit. This final motive is partly the result of our sense of what is a reasonable standard of 'decency', what is acceptable and normal, a standard that continually expands and rises with media encouragement (Dwyer, 2009a). So, if we work in sales or in a marketing organization where looking good is very important, we might think we need a new suit every year or so and a new car every two or three years, because otherwise the people we work with might think we are 'falling behind' or 'not keeping up'. To some extent, we all share this preoccupation, although perhaps not to the same extent as a real-estate salesman or someone whose job involves 'looking good'. This is not really the 'conspicuous' consumption it is often made out to be, but a 'positional' or 'comparative' motive for consumption (Dwyer, 2009a; Schor, 2007), the result of a largely unthinking tendency to measure what we do, how we dress, what we own, where we live or what we experience against what we see or experience around us as 'normal'. Sociologist Pierre Bourdieu's much-cited idea of 'cultural capital' is essentially a concept deriving from this 'positional' role that consumption has always played (Bourdieu, 1984; Schor, 2007).

None of these four motives usually occurs in isolation from the others, but rather they tend to coalesce around a particular desire or interest we might have in time. So we will chose an iPhone over a BlackBerry, not because it will do so much more (although we might use this as an excuse), but because it looks 'cooler' (the aesthetic impulse), has more useful 'apps' (self-improvement), and our friend Bill has one (the positional impulse). We will take our holiday in Bali rather than in Europe or closer to home because it is always fascinating to us (self-improvement), very beautiful and charming (aesthetic), cheaper and more convenient for us (functional), and our friends love the place where we will be staying (positional). Needless to say, all four motives are to a great extent enhanced and shaped by the media and retail, whose main function is to sell more products, and this means playing on these motives with great psychological precision and creative flair. So, for example, most of us know about the 'Gruen Transfer', that moment of 'scripted disorientation' that occurs when we enter most large stores or malls, which is intended to encourage us to 'consider' and buy more than we perhaps intended to (Crawford, 1992; Hardwick, 2003).

Over time, these four motives to consume, combined with the effect of constant media 'advice' and advertising, slowly ramp up, extend, expand or 'improve' what we think of as 'normal' (Lees-Maffei, 2001; Quitzau and Ropke, 2009): the standard of 'decency' we cling to slowly expands in quantity, if not always in quality, largely because of 'improvements', 'add-ons', innovations and technical enhancements and, consequently, relatively lower costs. For example, only two generations ago, a home for most people in Australia meant a fairly modest, two-bedroom, double-brick house, with perhaps one inside bathroom and kitchen, both innovations that were prized for being 'the very latest' in the 1940s and 1950s (as opposed to the outdoor toilet and 'lean-to' kitchen). Now, for many Australians and Americans, a 'normal' home is either a two- or three-bedroom, inner-city 'luxury' apartment or a suburban 'McMansion' that is nearly twice as big as its 1950s ancestor, with at least three or four bedrooms, a luxurious open-plan kitchen and up to two living areas, and two or more bathrooms, plus a double garage (Allon, 2008; Dwyer, 2009b). This kind of slow 'space inflation' is usually only noticed retrospectively, as the rising standards of what is 'normal' are attractive and seductive: everyone loves to get 'more' for what seems to be only slightly more money, even when this price itself has slowly and imperceptibly increased over time. The fact that the block of land on which the home is built is now much smaller, and internal walls are mostly now plasterboard, and there are many other ways builders cut their costs, is not noticed in the retail housing market, where what is valued is 'more' spaces such as bedrooms, bathrooms and living areas, and an increase in total square metres.

This ratchet-like forward motion, where every novelty or former luxury is progressively democratized through technical improvement and relatively lower prices, is a major issue for behaviour change: we are led to think we 'need' what everyone else regards as 'normal', even when this 'need' turns out to have major negative environmental consequences (Hamilton, 2002; Shove, 2003a). Once set in motion, it is very difficult to reverse this ratchet-like expansionary trend, as the media sell much of their product through the enticement of additional technological 'improvements', extended functions or 'special' credit-based deals or plans that appear to give us more, or even a 'bargain', but effectively lock us in to what is 'more' than perhaps we really need or even considered at the time, especially if it claims to save more energy or 'the environment' (Verbeek and Slob, 2006). This expansionary trend is particularly strong in technological markets such as that for mobile phones and laptops, where the 'normal' is being upgraded very rapidly. For example, the recently released iPad 2 makes last year's iPad 1 seem 'slower, fatter, and with a smaller screen', and thus less desirable (Smart, 2010; Crocker, Chapter 6 below). As cars become more computerized, a similar, even if still slower, expansion can be discerned, driven by marketing, minor improvements, technological 'breakthroughs', fashion styling and, increasingly, 'green-wash'. A newer, more up-to-date car with lower emissions targets our environmental anxieties, but completely misleads us, as often the improvements are extremely marginal in impact, and the environmental load of manufacturing and distributing the new car we are buying is swept out of the picture, again becoming 'somebody else's problem'.

Changing behaviour in this retail and media-saturated world can be very difficult, as what is 'normal' changes rather like the background landscape we might notice out of the window in a train: suddenly, the fields have given way to a forest or a mountain, and we were unaware that this was happening. So, for example, the introduction and normalization of the supply of milk and other juice drinks in plastic bottles or plasticated cardboard containers in the early 1970s in Australia and Britain happened relatively quickly, in response to a major business 'rationalization' in the sector, and without many people realizing what was really happening. These new plastic containers were purchased from the supermarket or corner store and were 'free': and so those who used to have their milk delivered by a milkman in reusable bottles now had the 'convenience' of having their milk in 'unbreakable' but throwaway containers that were supposed to be more hygienic. In Britain and Australia, the larger international food corporations had in fact bought out the smaller cooperative dairies delivering milk the older and more sustainable way, and, in a matter of years, for many people it became only possible to buy milk in the supermarket and in disposable plastic or cardboard containers. From being presented with a 'choice' to buy milk in more 'convenient', 'hygienic' and unbreakable containers in the supermarket, consumers were now forced to buy milk in this way, as the more sustainable alternative (buying milk in reusable bottles) in most places had been withdrawn from the market as 'uneconomic' (Vaughan et al, 2007; and see also Princen, 2005).

A similar 'ratchet-like' path-dependency created by the present logic of the mass market can be seen in the story of the spread of plastic shopping bags from the late 1970s onwards, which has led to the expectation that even small numbers of fruit and vegetables should be separately bagged or wrapped before purchase, with many outlets in our larger cities now selling individually wrapped apples, bananas or even two or three carrots (Djeru, 2006; Clapp and Swanston, 2009). Bought in this way, each smaller plastic bag joins other goods pre-packed in plastic inside a larger plastic shopping bag, and all this invariably ends in the waste stream. Although some bags might be recycled, many are not. So, instead of carrying home with our shopping perhaps a bit of newspaper and a reusable hessian bag, as we might have done in the 1950s, many shoppers now return home with between thirty and fifty separate plastic bags, all of which will need to be disposed of in some way. This, together with the packaging of drinks in plastic bottles, has led to an avalanche of plastic food and drink containers in various states of integrity clogging waterways and waste streams and increasing the levels of the chemicals these contain in the food chain (Mulder, 1998; Zero Waste SA, 2011). Referring to this phenomenon, my local vet jokingly calls himself a 'plastic surgeon', as a large proportion of his time is taken up with extracting pieces of this now universal material from domestic pets and rescued wild animals.

The economic and sociotechnical system that provides us with the 'convenience' of food bought and stored in plastic bags is usually experienced through a narrow 'consumption window' of use and enjoyment that leaves its environmental consequences to 'others' to deal with. In a similar manner, the convenience, flexibility and value we all find in car-ownership and driving lock us in to patterns of use and enjoyment whose environmental consequences we are unable or unwilling to see or understand: we all 'need' our cars, especially in our much larger cities, and this need becomes self-replicating, as transport alternatives become 'uneconomic' or inconvenient. The environmental costs in both systems, as well as those of their extensive infrastructures, have been up to now routinely 'externalized'.

The 'wicked problem' of global demand

As India and China modernize, and increasing numbers of people aspire to the consumption-centred lifestyles we have become accustomed to, more scholarly attention has been given to western-style consumption and the environmentally destructive behaviours it entails (Smart, 2010; Urry, 2010). The unfolding crisis, together with any solution's minimum requirement that, collectively, we will have to change the way we mine, make, distribute, use and dispose of much of what we currently possess, has all the hallmarks of a classic dilemma or 'wicked problem' (Bernstein et al, 2007). This consists, first, of the fact that current levels of prosperity and unprecedented material well-being (in the wealthier half of the world) are founded upon mining diminishing resources and then manufacturing, transporting, buying and rapidly 'using up' the products these resources contribute to at an unprecedented rate, with quite a lot of them wasted or even thrown away before they are even used (Hamilton, 2002; Zero Waste

SA, 2011). But, if the 'over-consumption' on which this prosperity depends were to be abruptly stopped by some miraculously binding agreement, a massive global economic, social and political dislocation might occur, curtailing the possibility of the kind of international cooperation and policy change that seems to be required to reduce energy and resource use and adjust our way of life to more sustainable levels. If, on the other hand, nothing is done, and we continue to produce and consume at current accelerating rates, it is very likely that we will soon face serious dislocations of supply and shortages of critical fuels and resources, and bring about more rapidly the catastrophe we are now all trying to avoid (Princen, 2005; Bernstein et al, 2007).

There are, at present, three interrelated kinds of response to the 'wicked problem' just outlined that have been widely taken up and endorsed, but none on its own is entirely satisfactory, and to a great extent they rely on each other to gain social and economic traction. The first approach responds to the widespread belief that this crisis can be ameliorated by more effective international cooperation and governance and more targeted legislation to limit the destructive results of over-consumption, nationally and internationally, and to encourage and reward the spread of 'sustainable development' and 'sustainable consumption' (Jackson, 2006; Conca, 2008). Through this approach, we are being encouraged to change the way we do business, the way we move goods, people and information, and the way we work and live, substituting more sustainable, less wasteful and less toxic approaches to making, using and doing things, whether in a local council area, a city or a nation. This also implies a much greater degree of articulated agreement on limits of, for example, allowed pollution or the exploitation of limited resources (Mazmanian and Kraft, 2009). Often set in terms of greater efficiency and agreed 'targets', this approach has so far failed to deliver many of the hopes that have been placed on it, with many international negotiations stalling, seriously compromised or failing (Princen, 2005; Conca, 2008).

Closely related to this, a second related approach is a push to redesign our material goods and services, so that our cities and transport and communication systems, as well as the material composition of the appliances and gadgets we use, will become less resource intensive, more energy efficient and able to be reused or recycled more easily (Lehmann, 2010). This promises to substantially reduce material flows while maintaining, to a great extent, our present state of prosperity. Both these interrelated approaches, from a political and economic standpoint and from a material flow and design standpoint, try to redesign or reset the framework in which we all live, and in this way to materially create limits or barriers to what have become evidently unsustainable practices (Hawken et al, 1999; Dorf, 2001). Unfortunately, both approaches suffer from the fact that many of these changes can only be the result of lengthy efforts at policy development, planning and considerable investment, often across different domains within each nation, across national boundaries and sometimes with groups who may be unwilling to recognize the problem for what it is, or to change their more individually profitable way of doing things, or even to negotiate at all (Mazmanian and Kraft, 2009).

Third, as part of an apparently easier 'lower hanging fruit' strategy, many governments and policymakers have attempted to individualize the unfolding crisis and insist on the user's responsibility, and promote the idea that, with better education and oversight, it should be possible to persuade everyone to live and do business within a more environmentally and socially responsible set of parameters. This impulse to 'behaviour change' sits comfortably with the democratic individualist and neo-liberalist beliefs that many governments hold so dear. Most of us are familiar with this model: we are asked to do something such as stop smoking, save water, get a health check or avoid drinking while driving. At first sight, this individualization does not appear to require the kind of massive investment of money, resources, negotiation and policy development that is required in the first and second approaches described above. However, individualization on its own rarely works without a socialization of the desired behaviour and without some clear incentives to change: what 'you' can do for the world or for climate change (McKenzie-Mohr and Smith, 1999; Maniates, 2002; Seyfang, 2008).

The problem with individualization is that we can achieve very little on our own as individuals, except perhaps choosing to consume 'greener' products; and it is this individualized market response that is also the engine of consumer culture. Most of the examples of more substantial success cited in support of 'individualizing' programmes are in fact not quite truthful, as the programmes or initiative described are more often the result of 'socialized' efforts at behaviour change (Seyfang, 2008). In these, the normalization of a more sustainable practice or behaviour comes about, not just through moral appeals to individuals to 'do the right thing', but through collective action, inspired perhaps by 'carrots and sticks' that can push or 'nudge' individuals to change their behaviour (McKenzie-Mohr and Smith, 1999; Verbeek, 2006). In the case of household recycling in South Australia, for instance, many local councils now provide householders with half-size household rubbish bins (a 'stick', as these are deliberately too small for most household needs without recourse to recycling) and much larger, full-size yellow-lidded recycling bins for cans, bottles and paper products, and similarly large 'green' bins for garden rubbish ('the carrot') (see Zero Waste SA, 2011). Although, on the surface, this scheme seems to be based on appealing to individuals directly, it is in fact reshaping a communal response to waste management by making the normal 'standard of decency' one of separating and recycling our rubbish (Dwyer, 2009a). The apparent individualization of this scheme is part of a social marketing strategy, but in truth we do not 'individually' have to make up our mind to recycle goods, but simply to choose to comply with what is effectively a new regime of provision that 'nudges' our behaviour towards more responsible waste disposal (see also Edmonds below, Chapter 5).

Individualization, socialization and behaviour change

Without a clear linkage to policy and legislative development and integrative strategies that attempt to redesign and remake our urban environments, systems and products, and the 'socialization' that can cement individual behaviour into more desirable lines, an overemphasis on individualization can become a morally problematic and ineffective strategy (McKenzie-Mohr and Smith, 1999; Maniates, 2002). The ignorance of most people about what they are buying, using and throwing away is often deeply engrained by media influence and convention; occasional educational and information campaigns to 'reduce, reuse and recycle', unaccompanied by a comprehensive integrated approach to changing behaviour, may encourage only a few dedicated individuals to 'do the right thing'. So, for instance, against the desires of most of the soft-drink manufacturers and retailers, South Australia alone of the Australian states has had a deposit scheme to encourage bottle and can recycling for about thirty years (Sun, 2010). This means that many poor people in Adelaide (South Australia's capital city) go around and pick bottles and drink cans out of rubbish bins to recycle them because of the ten cents paid by the scheme for each item surrendered. As a result, South Australia has consistently achieved a much higher rate for the take-back and recycling of these items than any other state in Australia (Zero Waste SA, 2011). This strategy is a socialized one and disliked by the soft-drink manufacturers, who naturally prefer to shift responsibility and costs downstream to the individual, as in the 'voluntary' schemes operating in the other Australian states. What is apparent is that even modest financial incentives, such as a promise of ten cents to be paid on surrender of a bottle or can, will lock in long-term changes in behaviour and involve many charity groups and others also. Individualization on its own, such as the overtly 'moral' appeals to recycle cans and bottles, widely used in the other Australian states, fails to achieve very much at all, and the other states, concerned about the failure of their own ineffective individualized schemes, are now seriously examining the 'South Australian' scheme.

Unfortunately, individualization closely reflects the psychology involved in our normative consuming behaviour, and therefore the promoted behaviour rarely manages effectively to compete with the established, unsustainable behaviour (McKenzie-Mohr and Smith, 1999; and see below, Davidson et al, Chapter 4). Contemporary consumer culture is based on a narrow, usually brief, 'flat' type of 'relationship' created by the transaction: a 'one-shot' symmetrical form of exchange where, unless it is legally defined otherwise, all responsibility seems to end after the transaction is completed or fulfilled. To make this transaction happen more quickly (and cheaply), we have become accustomed to shopping 'side by side', and not 'face to face' as was once the case (Strasser, 2003). This 'fast' consumption is very convenient for the seller, but not good for social capital (Putnam, 2000; McCracken, 2008). Like our exchange of money for a particular good or service, individualizing approaches to behaviour change tend to model 'good' or sustainable behaviour as a more 'responsible' transaction, and this encourages the delusion that we can change the world, either through moralizing the individual concerned, or through yet another series of 'greener' transactions, as though our problems can be fixed by just a different kind of fashion-driven consumption, a valued 'choice' made as a sort of moral protest against the consumerist mainstream (Seyfang, 2008). So we might be encouraged to believe that we can reduce our carbon footprint by selling our SUV and purchasing a small hybrid car (despite the additional 'eco-load' involved in the manufacture and sale of any new product, however 'green' it might be), and we might sell a big, power-hungry house and move to an 'eco-efficient' one specially built for us, or we might expensively retrofit our house with solar panels, water-tanks and energy-efficient lighting. All this may help, and make us feel better about ourselves, but in the bigger picture may have only a tiny effect on the overall consumption volumes we collectively share with our community, nation or globalized world (Maniates, 2002).

Opposed to this, the socialization of more sustainable behaviour is often to be found based on schemes that have the potential to develop longer-term, 'face-to-face' asymmetrical relationships between individuals over time, through sharing an activity or behaviour that is mutually enjoyable, beneficial or fulfilling in some way (often an important but neglected 'carrot'), such as swapping fruit and vegetables from the garden, community gardening or voluntary activities such as reading at your child's primary school. Somewhat akin to sociologist Thorstein Veblen's expected 'standard of decency' (Dwyer, 2009a), sustainable-behaviour programmes often mimic the building of asymmetrical relationships, over a period of time, that are naturally found in the 'close-grain' activities, ones that Putnam describes in his work on the development of social capital (Putnam, 2000, pp93ff.; Seyfang, 2008). This kind of 'social-capital-building' activity often involves some mutual interest or social obligation, whether it is a hybrid one developed 'online', or whether it is a real one with your local garden cooperative or voluntary walking group. Although this kind of 'sustainable' behaviour might be individually enacted (riding a bike, going for a walk, growing your own vegetables and fruit, or going to buy honey from a neighbour), it is often most effectively supported if this behaviour can be woven into the fabric of existing local relationships or groups, especially with people who share the same activity or interest. This kind of asymmetrical relationship transcends the social 'flatness' of the standard consumer transaction, which is both limited in duration and involves a 'one-shot' obligation ending at the till. Unlike the now 'normal', mass-choreographed and mass-marketed 'flat' consumer transaction, much sustainable consumption involves a richer, 'face-to-face' and localized element (Seyfang, 2008; and see below, Edmonds, Chapter 5).

Innovation, normalization and unsustainable behaviour

As many historical and sociological studies have made clear, 'unsustainable' habits develop over time in response to sociotechnical regimes or breakthrough innovations that create an unsustainable, 'ratchet-like' path-dependency (Shove, 2003b; Strasser, 2003; Shove et al, 2007). As an innovation becomes 'normalized', we adopt it, not necessarily because we choose to, but because, once an innovation attains a position of cultural dominance, it becomes much harder to find or choose an alternative: as the big box warehouses and malls were built, the small family-run stores went out of business; as the motorways were built, it became more dangerous to travel anywhere except in a car. Few of us can now shop entirely without a car, and without using plastic bags or buying 'throwaway' plastic drinks containers, as few alternatives are readily available, even if we are able, as a moral protest, to carry our groceries home in a string or hessian bag. Our daily routines change slowly, but sometimes more quickly in response to what seem breakthrough technological innovations at the time, and it is rare for us to be able to question the environmental consequences of these changes until long after they have been established, as the advantages of each much-touted 'advance' can seem dramatically to outweigh any of its disadvantages. Mass-marketers are adept at presenting only what is more convenient or beneficial to us in the products and services they are promoting: their task cannot involve drawing attention to any of their negative environmental or health consequences.

To return to our example, over a twenty-year period in the USA and Europe, the car moved from being a luxury toy for the very wealthy, without any obvious benefit to the 'average man', to being an increasingly affordable means of 'convenient' transport for the middle classes (starting in the 1920s and 1930s in the USA), and subsequently, after the Second World War, becoming a vehicle for mass transportation in most modern cities and priced within the reach of almost everyone (Paterson, 2000; Claydon, 2004; Freund and Martin, 2009). The car, in a story told many times, has since reconfigured and vastly extended our cities and towns and transformed our expectations around mobility and land-use, a configuration sociologists Peter Freund and George Martin term 'hyperautomobility' (2009). While giving us the freedom of 'convenience', it has also become a means of coercion, locking us into path-dependent behavioural routines that are destructive in environmental, and often also in social and physical, terms (Sheller and Urry, 2000; Urry, 2004). We expect now to be able to jump into our cars, kept 'ready at hand' in our garages, and drive to work, without having to pay for the environmental damage our vehicles effect. The car is in many ways emblematic of the individualization involved in consumer culture: as drivers and passengers, we travel 'side by side', oblivious of the small local landscapes through which we pass, and able to avoid all face-to-face relationships with those who might be present between the A and B of our journey (Augé, 1995). In our cars, we become convinced of our own independence and freedom, and we are encouraged to overlook the larger environmental costs of our technological individualism (Freund and Martin, 2009).

Our dependence on the car in many ways is typical of the kind of dilemma or 'wicked problem' represented by the challenge of behaviour change. Unless governments are prepared to intervene, plan for, and spend considerable sums on, alternative, more sustainable transport systems on our behalf, our car-based transport systems will lead inexorably towards growing emissions and climate change. The problem is that the car has not only come to dominate urban life, shaping our routines and the way we live, but has greatly shaped the modern city itself, even breaking up our experience of city life into disparate 'islands' of activities, such as 'dormitory' suburbs, industrial or business parks, shopping malls and leisure and other precincts. All the land between these precincts where our activities might take place fades into 'non-places', hurriedly passed on our way from A to B (Augé, 1995; Paterson, 2000). These roadways carve up the urban environment and make much of it unnavigable, except for those in cars. And because the car can take us long distances very quickly, it also alters how we experience and manage our time, so that we get used to the idea of scheduling our day around a series of car journeys.

The car is also a symbol of the individual consumer's social, aesthetic and functional aspirations, and emblematic of the narrow 'consumer window' through which we now tend to see the world (Freund and Martin, 2009). Everything else in the car's supply chain, its negative impacts and the pollution and waste it creates as we use and enjoy it, is rendered largely invisible and becomes 'somebody else's problem'. Because of its great speed and the distances it can travel, it has also shaped our sense of time, to the extent that 'useful' time is contrasted to 'waiting time' as we sit behind the wheel waiting to get to our destination. This 'fast–slow' perception of time means that any attempt to encourage people to take more 'incidental' exercise, to walk the dog or pick up shopping during a short walk, for example, not only has to reconfigure what have become established routines and remove what are often dangerous physical barriers to such exercise, but also has to change the idea that everything has to be done so quickly, within a tight set of deadlines created by and around the constraints and flexibility of 'car-time'. This need to 'allow' us to enjoy such 'slow time' is an extraordinary challenge to those interested in furthering behaviour change, when so many have become addicted to the 'fast' time imposed by the automobile (Freund and Martin, 2000).

Cars and pedestrians: a personal recollection

As many suburban residents are apt to complain, those who live alongside major roadways or on the wrong side of them become hostages to the needs of those just 'passing through', and subject to the excessive noise, pollution and the real physical dangers represented by heavy traffic (Hass-Klau, 1990; Davison and Yelland, 2004). As a parent or grandparent with young children, you are forced periodically to get them across a major road to enjoy a park on the other side, or to get them to a kindergarten or school. In a car-dominated world, children, the elderly and the disabled become completely dependent on able-bodied carers, preferably with cars, as it is too dangerous for them to attempt to cross any major roads on their own (Hillman et al, 1990; Tolley, 2003). This naturally restricts them to live within their homes and is now widely understood to be one cause of childhood obesity and also of the restricted lives many elderly and disabled people endure.

Near where I lived for many years, I can remember one particularly dangerous corner on a major road that intersected with another 'feeder' road leading to the local primary school. Most of the parents with children at this school who lived on the wrong side of the major road would drive their children the 100 metres or so to the school, simply to avoid the dangers of crossing this particular intersection on foot with their young children. The schoolteachers also felt this problem keenly, as they would either have to try and stop the traffic to take their little charges on expeditions across the road in the other direction, to the local beach, or else persuade the police to stop the traffic for them. Many times I witnessed this little piece of local theatre, with the rather nervous-looking teachers trying to stop traffic with wands while the children crossed the road.

For over twenty years, the school principal and many parents had repeatedly petitioned the local council and the state government to install a pedestrian crossing, not only so that the parents and children could walk to school, but also so that all those living on the school side of the major road could walk to the park and beach on the far side of the same road. Even though, over the same twenty-year period, two pedestrians had been killed attempting to cross at or near this point, it seemed nothing could be done: putting in a pedestrian crossing was simply 'too expensive' and could not be justified by the relatively small numbers of pedestrians attempting to cross the road, against about 10,000 vehicles a day. Ironically, during this period, many programmes were offered at the school promoting road safety, but most of these moralized the children about attending to their own safety rather than making use of their knowledge of the local environment and its safety problems. These well-intentioned programmes, from 'Safe Routes to School' to a 'Virtual Bus', an attempt to get children to walk together to school in an invisible bus 'driven' by a trained parent (Tolley, 2003), all failed to have any impact on the infrastructure of the nearby main road or to remove the real barriers to walking it represented. Changing this infrastructure, apart from putting in a few well-intentioned pedestrian islands, was apparently off limits, as the engineers managing the system could see no compelling reason to justify spending approximately US$120,000 for a handful of schoolchildren. The fact that, if a child had been killed, the cost to the state would have been US$2 million or more was not a problem for them, but for the health bureaucracy, out of whose coffers at least some of this money would come.

At least four traffic management consultant reports paid for by the local council recommended pedestrian lights at this corner, and many of us local residents over time witnessed 'near misses' at the crossing, either between emerging cars and the traffic or between cars and the elderly, who often walked to the local doctors' clinic or chemist situated on the other side of the road. Although, very recently, a crossing has been installed at this point, ironically this was a product of the gentrification of the nearby beachside area, with the local council having just spent very large sums on 'up-grading' the area; the provision of the once hotly disputed pedestrian crossing was added as a 'bonus' to what was a much more expensive remodelling of nearby infrastructure.

I first came across this case, along with many similar ones, through my involvement with a local pedestrian-safety advocacy group. For about ten years (1995–2004), I was the secretary of this group (WalkSafe SA) and heard many similar and sometimes much worse and more tragic stories, from all over Adelaide where I live. The majority were cases involving the shortcomings of local pedestrian infrastructure and often a complete lack of sensible pedestrian safety regulation, and an official, usually economically justified, refusal to act on behalf of local pedestrians or residents, many of whom were unable to make themselves heard or deal effectively with the system where, it was always clear, keeping the traffic moving was the main priority. Local and state governments effectively silenced these usually local pedestrian voices, as being able to walk around their own neighbourhoods was not really seen as a 'real' transport issue nor, ultimately, even a 'right'. I also heard many tragic stories involving the death or injury of children, elderly and disabled people, fathers and sons, mothers and daughters, friends and strangers, all victims of our otherwise superbly calibrated and 'efficient' car-based transport system.

When our little group would present ourselves to local authorities, I remember we were readily supported by most health professionals and also, sadly, the local priests or counsellors, who were often called upon to deal with the darker side of our road system and the death, serious injury and grief it frequently involves, and of course most teachers and parents who, like us, were often quite baffled about why it seemed so difficult to 'get anything done'. Interestingly, politicians rarely came to our support, as there has always been little political mileage to be made out of what is so 'pedestrian' and 'every-day' as pedestrian safety, and the press were similarly disinterested. Unless we could beat up a good story about a particularly awful tragedy, or some local conflict with the council that might result, there was 'nothing' in it for them. But what stands out in my memory of this period was the strange incomprehension of most traffic engineers, who genuinely found it very difficult to understand the local, footpath-based perspective of most pedestrians. From their global vehicular-network perspective, pedestrians were an anomaly, interrupting an efficient and impressively functional transport system by attempting to cross roads, and often seemingly for no particular rational or economic purpose.

While this is very much a local story based in Adelaide, South Australia, the routine externalization of the social and environmental costs of our car-based transport systems is in many ways emblematic of how unsustainable behaviour can become normalized and 'locked in' over time by the forces of policy, governance and commercial interest. As I have tried to argue in this chapter, it is very difficult for individuals to oppose such 'normalization' or 'lock-in', whether it is the prioritization of vehicular traffic over pedestrians, or of supermarket and packaged foods over local, fresh produce. In this kind of historical, developed, sociotechnical and economic 'lock-in', 'efficiency' and economic utility are often used as weapons to justify the marginalization of the more sustainable activity in question and those who might want to promote it. This is not to say that traffic engineers were deliberately marginalizing or victimizing pedestrians, but simply that their training did not provide them with the kind of information that allowed them to understand the importance of pedestrian movement. In the experience of our little group, they seemed to picture pedestrians as mysterious and ill-disciplined anomalies, who often wilfully got in the way of the traffic the engineers aimed to control and efficiently direct.

What was most striking was the way that, in the regime of the traffic engineer we encountered, pedestrians seemed to be denied visibility until large groups of them had been observed and counted, such as adjacent to a supermarket, a school or a hospital, or in a city centre. Taking refuge in their procedural 'warrant' (routinely used at this time), which required sixty pedestrians to cross within a 30m length of roadway on an average hour on an average day, they could then 'justify' refusing to act on behalf of those local people who often needed help to negotiate very dangerous, fast-moving traffic. Despite this official procedure, we discovered that they practised their humanity by suspending the warrant if two or more pedestrians had been killed or seriously injured at one particular section of roadway. It seemed to us as observers that the procedure they followed was anything but scientific, or even rational, and resembled expecting a car to cross a creek on a goat track to 'prove' the need for a road or bridge. Pedestrians were expected, by these long-standing rules, to routinely expose themselves to danger when attempting to cross a major road, and only if there were sufficient numbers of them could a pedestrian crossing be considered and, if there was funding, authorized.

This rational methodological support of what was then the majority practice seems to me again somewhat emblematic of the similar situations found in many other domains, where unsustainable systems and infrastructures have developed over time. This is simply because the massive historical investment involved in developing and maintaining these systems tends to disguise and reshape our appreciation or understanding of the social and environmental costs involved, and the resulting political and economic status quo seems to outweigh the more sustainable systems or practices one might want to support or encourage in their place. Cars, after all, despite their heavy environmental and social costs, are efficient, long-distance vehicles, and their immediate utility and social benefits are many. However, the present system and its infrastructure inevitably hampered our attempts to encourage pedestrian movement, as, without relative basic safety for those attempting to cross major roads, any pedestrian movement becomes problematic, or only available to the able-bodied or swift of foot.

In recalling my own experience as a pedestrian activist, I am very aware that, over the ten years of my involvement, the incomprehension and hostility of the traffic engineers I had encountered during the late 1990s began to melt away by 2000, when a preoccupation with sustainable transport became the norm in many transport bureaucracies. This meant that, by the time my group disbanded in 2005, I found myself on a number of advisory committees charged by the state government to shape a new, more 'sustainable' transport agenda, for which the views of cyclists, pedestrians and public-transport advocates were elicited as those of legitimate 'stakeholders', even if not much meaningful funding was being redirected to improve the kinds of problem I and others had brought to their attention. To provide a more 'walkable' city environment is to encourage behaviour change on an important local scale, which can, not only reduce carbon emissions, but also improve the health of many individuals, and government was beginning to respond to this message, even if the established system of prioritizing road building and maintenance funding made practical progress on the ground very difficult. At this time, all public-health indicators suggested that regular walking is among the best exercise options available, especially to those unable to access regular sports, gyms or other arenas. Yet many urban environments still make walking for many people, especially the young or more vulnerable, inconvenient or dangerous (Hillman et al, 1990). Getting people to walk regularly, even to the shops or a park, or to take their children to school on foot can have significant long-term health benefits, but obstacles to local walking can have a profoundly negative effect on getting people out and about (Litman, 2011).

Most attempts I witnessed to promote walking as 'the best thing I can do' only gained traction when there were supporting groups of people involved: for example, walking clubs, charity walks or 'walk to work days', or groups of friends committed to walk and talk together three or four times a week, all tended to be more successful than simple promotion. Once these group activities became visible, they effectively legitimized walking as an activity for others to join in (McKenzie-Mohr and Smith, 1999; Dwyer, 2009a). This can take many forms, including programmes that encourage the use of other modes of transport, such as catching the bus rather than driving to work (see Travel Smart, 2011; and Taylor and Philp, Chapter 16 below). This seems, in retrospect, to be an important insight: once pedestrians became visible, others would be attracted to the same or similar activities and arrangements, even if at first they might have hesitated to get involved. But what was really vital was traffic calming, or some reduction in the danger pedestrians faced engaging in the desired activity (Tolley, 2003).

Along the beach near where I live, I witnessed an extraordinary growth in walking for health over a twenty-year period. When I first came to live there in 1990, the majority of walkers were local dog owners, and so few were they that we all knew each other and would stop to chat as our dogs ran around us on the beach early most mornings. Now, there are at least ten times more walkers on the beach each morning, and much better infrastructure and pathways for walkers and cyclists have also been built along the beachfront, accommodating this much larger number of 'incidental' walkers. This has been facilitated by the fact that there are no major roads in the vicinity, no heavy traffic to deal with to gain access to the beach, and the nearest main road has had its speed limit lowered to ensure a greater degree of pedestrian safety. This increase in walking has been a boon for local cafes, which have also doubled in number over the same period, with many now opening at 7 a.m. to cater for this early-morning trade. Back in the 1990s, I remember well that it was impossible to get a coffee before 10 a.m. anywhere along the beachfront. The economic advantages of encouraging pedestrian activity are well known, but rarely taken sufficiently seriously (Litman, 2011).

What is most noticeable in this case is that, once walking has been rendered 'normal' or even 'respectable' as an activity, it seems to attract more adherents. Unsustainable alternatives may not be abandoned, but their hold on the participants becomes a little looser. But, for this socialization to occur, any physical barriers to walking need to be removed (McKenzie-Mohr and Smith, 1999), and, in our experience, a reduction in vehicle speed limits is the first and most important of all 'pedestrian infrastructures' (Tolley, 2003). In several attempts to survey pedestrians in many different areas, our little organization found again and again the presence of fast, heavy and, by definition, dangerous traffic was the strongest disincentive to walking, as was the absence of suitable pedestrian safety infrastructure, especially when volumes of traffic were over about 10,000 vehicles a day. Perhaps only slightly less important disincentives were the absence of reasonable lighting at night and, further down the list, the absence of sufficiently wide and level footpaths or clean, nearby, accessible public toilets. But what was most appreciated was the presence of others, whether sitting in nearby cafes or out walking their dogs.

Unfortunately, like cyclists, pedestrians are notoriously 'vulnerable' road users and not easily integrated into traffic planning as it tends to be organized today, often in vast hierarchies of engineers, with the 'important jobs' all going to those who manage large road systems and heavy traffic volumes. Unlike cyclists, pedestrians are extremely local users of the bigger road system, and they are 'road crossers' rather than, strictly speaking, 'road users', their paths rarely following the asphalt roadways built for cars, unless they absolutely have to. Choosing a direct route from A to B, they will also not expose themselves willingly to unnecessary delays, dangers or discomforts, and this can be a source of frustration to engineers expecting them to stand passively for three minutes or more at a set of traffic lights. But, above all, from my experience, pedestrian infrastructure needs to include pleasant, visibly interesting, walkable streets, with 'calmed' traffic and beautification, with occasional seating for the elderly and, in Australia especially, rows of shade trees (Soderstrom, 2010).

Conclusion

If walking (or walking in combination with other modes of transport, such as cycling, rail or bus) is seen as exemplary of the kind of policy, infrastructure and design changes required by 'behaviour change', we can afford to be moderately optimistic. Recent experiences from many cities and towns around the world reveal that the secret to the 'walkable city' is relatively simple, but it does require considerable incremental policy and planning interventions, progressive cost-related restrictions placed upon driving, traffic calming or reductions in speed limits, and much more thoughtful urban design, including well-funded policy and infrastructure changes to facilitate the choice of walking and the use of public transport (Soderstrom, 2010). These changes are most effectively built around programmes that engage directly with the everyday experience and the activities of groups of people. Our preferences can be 'nudged' collectively, often at modest cost, towards behaviours that encourage more sustainable practices such as walking. But this socialized behaviour change cannot be firmly established without 'follow-up' to important social initiatives or redesign of relevant infrastructures or supporting systems. This means that we cannot really expect more people to decide to walk to work or ride a bike, or even catch a bus, if the infrastructure is not there, or if the choice to do so is simply too difficult, dangerous, expensive or inconvenient to access, or if there is no enabling system in place to ensure that the more sustainable transport options are not only possible but attractive (McKenzie-Mohr and Smith, 1999).

Groups of people, supporting each other by their proximity and presence, must be led into a new practice in a particular setting, over a particular time, and learn its benefits through direct experience, preferably informed by knowledge and understanding that effectively counter the commercially derived misinformation that comes with many 'unsustainable' activities in our consumer culture. Like going to the cafe to drink coffee and meet a friend, 'incidental' walking (such as walking the dog on the beach) is an activity that, like other forms of more positive social behaviour, can be readily emulated once it is regarded as normal, easy, sociable and a 'standard' (Dwyer, 2009a). The consumption window that currently frames car use can only be broadened through a combination of knowledge and experience in a social setting. Sustainable behaviour has to be practised and normalized socially, so that its benefits can be realized and understood; and unsustainable systems and infrastructures need to be modified to ensure that the more sustainable behaviour envisaged can take place.

References

Adams, D. (1982) *Life, the Universe and Everything*, Pan Books, London

Allon, F. (2008) *Renovation Nation: Our Obsession With Home*, University of New South Wales Press, Sydney, Australia

Apple (2011) Apple iPad advertisement, www.apple.com/ipad/#if-you-asked, accessed 20 March 2011

Augé, M. (1995) *Non-places: Introduction to an Anthropology of Super-modernity*, Verso, London

Australian Government (2009) *Road Deaths Australia Statistical Summary 2008, Road Safety Report number 4*, Department of Infrastructure, Transport, Regional and Local Government, Canberra, www.infrastructure.gov.au/roads/safety/publications/2009/pdf/rsr_04.pdf, accessed 20 March 2011

Belk, R. (1988) 'Possessions and the extended self', *Journal of Consumer Research*, vol 15, no 2, pp139–68

Bernstein, S., Cashore, B., Levin, K. and Auld, G. (2007) 'Playing it forward: path dependency, progressive incrementalism, and the "super wicked" problem of global climate change', paper presented to the International Studies Association 48th Annual Convention, Chicago, IL, February 28, www.allacademic.com/one/prol/prol01/index.php?click_key=1, accessed 3 March 2011

Bestor, T. (2003) 'Markets and places: Tokyo and the global tuna trade', in S. M. Low and D. Lawrence-Zuniga (eds) *The Anthropology of Space and Place: Locating Culture*, Blackwell, Malden, MA

Bourdieu, P. (1984) *Distinction: A Social Critique of the Judgment of Taste*, R. Nice (trans) Harvard University Press, Cambridge, MA

CAIT (2011) 'GHG emissions by sector in 2007', World Resources Institute, http://cait.wri.org/cait.php?page=sectors, accessed 20 May 2011

Campbell, C. (2004) 'I shop therefore I know I am: the metaphysical basis of modern consumerism', in B. Ekstrom and H. Brembeck (eds) *Elusive Consumption*, Oxford, Berg, chapter 2, pp27–44

Clapp, J. (2002) 'The distancing of waste: overconsumption in a global economy', in T. Princen, M. Maniates and K. Conca (eds) *Confronting Consumption*, MIT Press, Cambridge, MA

Clapp, J. and Swanston, L. (2009) 'Doing away with plastic shopping bags: patterns of norm emergence and policy implementation', *Environmental Politics*, vol 18, no 3, pp315–32

Claydon, T. et al (eds) (1998) *The Motor Car and Popular Culture in the Twentieth Century*, Ashgate, London

Conca, K. (2008) 'Rethinking authority, territory, and knowledge: transnational socio-ecological controversies and global environmental governance', in J. Park, K. Conca and M. Finger (eds) *The Crisis of Global Environmental Governance: Towards a New Political Economy of Sustainability*, Routledge, London

Coulter, J. (2009–10) 'A sea change to change the sea: stopping the spread of the great Pacific garbage patch by small scale environmental legislation', *William and Mary Law Review*, vol 51, no 5, pp1959–96

Courselle, D. (2010) 'We [used to] make a good gumbo: the BP Deepwater Horizon Disaster and the heightened threats to the unique cultural communities of the Louisiana Gulf coast,' *Tulane Environmental Law Journal*, vol 24, no 1, pp19–39

Crawford, M. (1992) 'The world in a shopping mall', in M. Sorkin (ed) *Variations on a Theme Park: The New American City and the End of Public Space*, Hill and Wang, New York

Davison, G. and Yelland, S. (2004) *Car Wars*, Allen and Unwin, Sydney, Australia

De Botton, P. (2009) *The Pleasures and Sorrows of Work*, Pantheon, London

Djeru, J. (2006) 'The urban political economy of the waste bag problem in Nairobi, Kenya', *Geoforum*, vol 37, pp1046–58

Dorf, R. C. (2001) *Technology, Humans and Society: Towards a Sustainable World*, Academic Press, San Diego, CA

Dwyer, R. (2009a) 'Making a habit of it: Positional consumption, conventional action and the standard of living', *Journal of Consumer Culture*, vol 9, pp328–47

Dwyer, R. (2009b) 'The McMansionization of America? Income stratification and the standard of living in housing, 1960–2000', *Research in Social Stratification and Mobility*, vol 27, pp285–300

Frascara, J. (1996) 'Communication for change: strategies and difficulties', *Design Issues*, vol 12, no 3, pp44–59

Freund, P. and Martin, G. (1993) *The Ecology of the Automobile*, Black Rose, Toronto, Canada

Freund, P. and Martin, G. (2009) 'The social and material culture of hyperautomobility: "Hyperauto"', *Bulletin of Science, Technology and Society*, vol 29, no 6, pp476–82

Hamilton, C. (2002) 'Overconsumption in Australia', report by the Australia Institute, www.tai.org.au/documents/dp_fulltext/DP49.pdf, accessed 20 March 2011

Hardin, R. (2006) *Trust*, Polity Press, Cambridge

Hardwick, M. J. (2003) *Mall Maker: Victor Gruen, Architect of an American Dream*, University of Pennsylvania, Philadelphia, PA

Hass-Klau, C. (1990) *The Pedestrian and the City*, Belhaven Press, London

Hawken, P., Lovins, A. B. and Lovins, L. H. (1999) *Natural Capitalism: The Next Industrial Revolution*, Earthscan, London

Herring, H. and Roy, R. (2007) 'Technological innovation, energy efficient design and the rebound effect', Technovation, vol 27, pp194–203

Hillman, M., Adams, J. and Whitelegg, J. (1990) *One False Move: A Study of Children's Independent Mobility*, PSI, London

Ingram, J., Shove, E., and Watson, M. (2007) 'Products and practices: selected concepts from science and technology studies and from social theories of consumption and practice', *Design Issues*, vol 23, no 2, pp3–16

Jackson, T. (2006) 'Challenges for sustainable consumption policy', in T. Jackson (ed) *The Earthscan Reader in Sustainable Consumption*, Earthscan, London

Kasser, T. (2002) *The High Price of Materialism*, MIT Press, Cambridge, MA

Lees-Maffei, G. (2001) 'From service to self-service: advice literature as design discourse, 1920–1970', *Journal of Design History*, vol 14, no 3, pp187–206

Lehmann, S. (2010) *The Principles of Green Urbanism: Transforming the City for Sustainability*, Earthscan, London

Linebaugh, P. (2010) 'Enclosures from the bottom up', *Radical History Review*, vol 108, pp11–27

Litman, T. (2011) 'Economic value of walkability', Victoria Transport Policy Institute, Canada, www.vtpi.org/walkability.pdf, accessed 20 March 2011

McCracken, G. (1988) *Culture and Consumption: New Approaches to the Symbolic Character of Consumer Goods and Activities*, Indiana University Press, Bloomington, IN

McCracken, G. (2008) *Transformations: Identity Construction in Contemporary Culture*, Indiana University Press, Bloomington, IN

McKenzie-Mohr, D. and Smith, W. (1999) *Fostering Sustainable Behavior: An Introduction to Community-Based Social Marketing*, New Society Publishers, Gabriola Island, BC, Canada

Maniates, M. (2002) 'Individualization: plant a tree, buy a bike, save the world?', in T. Princen, M. Maniates and K. Conca (eds) *Confronting Consumption*, MIT Press, Cambridge, MA

Mazmanian, D. A. and Kraft, M. E. (eds) (2009) *Towards Sustainable Communities*, MIT Press, Cambridge, MA

Miller, D. (2008) *The Comfort of Things*, Polity Press, Cambridge

Miller, D. (2010) *Stuff*, Polity Press, Cambridge

Moore, C. (2003) 'Across the Pacific Ocean, plastics, plastics everywhere', *Natural History*, vol 112, no 9, November, www.mindfully.org/Plastic/Ocean/Moore-Trashed-PacificNov03.htm, accessed 10 March 2011

Mulder, K. (1998) 'Sustainable consumption and the production of plastics?', *Technological Forecasting and Social Change*, vol 58, pp105–24

Paché, G. (2007) 'Slowness logistics? Towards a new time orientation', *Time and Society*, vol 16, pp311–32

Paterson, M. (2000) 'Car culture and global environmental politics', *Review of International Studies*, vol 26, no 2, pp253–70

Princen, T. (2002a) 'Consumption and its externalities: where economy meets ecology', in T. Princen, M. Maniates and K. Conca (eds) *Confronting Consumption*, MIT Press, Cambridge, MA

Princen, T. (2002b) 'Distancing: consumption and the severing of feedback', in T. Princen, M. Maniates and K. Conca (eds) *Confronting Consumption*, MIT Press, Cambridge, MA

Princen, T. (2003) 'Principles of sustainability: from cooperation and efficiency to sufficiency', *Global Environmental Politics*, vol 3, no 1, pp33–50

Princen, T. (2005) *The Logic of Sufficiency*, MIT Press, Cambridge, MA

Princen, T. (2010) 'Speaking of sustainability: The potential of a metaphor', *Sustainability: Science, Practice and Policy*, vol 6, no 2, pp60–65

Putnam, R. D. (2000) *Bowling Alone: The Collapse and Revival of American Community*, Simon and Schuster, New York

Quitzau, M.-B. and Ropke, I. (2008) 'The Construction of normal expectations: consumption drivers for the Danish bathroom boom', *Journal of Industrial Ecology*, vol 12, no 2, pp186–206

Quitzau, M.-B. and Ropke, I. (2009) 'Bathroom transformation: from hygiene to well-being?', *Home Cultures*, vol. 6, no 3, pp219–42

Schor, J. B. (2007) 'In defence of consumer critique: revisiting the consumption debates of the twentieth century', *Annals of the American Academy of Political and Social Science*, vol 611: The Politics of Consumption/the Consumption of Politics, pp16–30

Seyfang, G. (2008) *The New Economics of Sustainable Consumption: Seeds of Change*, Palgrave Macmillan, London

Sharma, B. R. (2008) 'Road traffic injuries: a major global public health crisis', *Public Health*, vol 122, no 12, pp1399–406

Shove, E. (2003a) *Comfort, Cleanliness and Convenience: The Social Organization of Normality*, Berg, Oxford

Shove, E. (2003b) 'Users, technologies and expectations of comfort, cleanliness and convenience', *Innovation: the European Journal of the Social Sciences*, vol 16, no 2, pp193–206

Shove, E., Watson, M., Hand, M. and Ingham, J. (2007) *The Design of Everyday Life*, Berg, New York

Sheller, M. and Urry, J. (2000) 'The city and the car', *International Journal of Urban and Regional Research*, vol 24, no 2, pp737–57

Smart, B. (2010) *Consumer Society: Critical Issues and Environmental Consequences*, SAGE, London

Strasser, S. (2000) *Waste and Want: A Social History of Trash*, Henry Holt, New York

Strasser, S. (2003) 'The alien past: consumer culture in historical perspective', *Journal of Consumer Policy*, vol 26, pp375–93

Soderstrom, M. (2010) *The Walkable City: from Haussmann's Boulevards to Jane Jacobs' Streets and beyond*, Vehicule Books, Montreal, Canada

Sun, M. (2010) 'Push for 10c recycling refund scheme', *Adelaide Now*, July 2, 2010, www.adelaidenow.com.au/news/national/push-for-10c-can-recycling-refund-scheme/story-e6frea8c-1225887263662, accessed 20 March 2011

Tolley, R. S. (ed) (2003) *Sustainable Transport: Planning for Walking and Cycling in Urban Environments*, Woodhead, London, UK

Travel Smart SA (2011) 'Travel Smart SA', www.transport.sa.gov.au/environment/travelsmartsa/index.asp, accessed 20 March 2011

Urry, J. (2004) 'The "system" of automobility', *Theory, Culture and Society*, vol 21, pp25–39

Urry, J. (2007) *Mobilities*, Polity Press, Cambridge

Urry, J. (2010) 'Consuming the planet to excess', *Theory, Culture and Society*, vol 27, pp197–212

Vaughan, P., Cook, M. and Trawick, P. (2007) 'A sociology of reuse: deconstructing the milk bottle', *Sociologica Ruralis*, vol 47, no 2, pp120–34

Verbeek, P.-P. (2006) 'Materializing morality: design ethics and technological mediation', *Science, Technology and Human Values*, vol 31, no 3, pp361–80

Verbeek, P.-P. and Slob, A. (eds) (2006) *User Behaviour and Technology Development: Shaping Sustainable Relations Between Consumers and Technologies*, Springer, London

World Health Organization (WHO) (2009) *Global Status Report on Road Safety: Time for Action*, WHO, Geneva, whqlibdoc.who.int/publications/2009/9789241563840_eng.pdf, accessed 20 March 2011

World Health Organization (WHO) (2011) 'United Nations road safety collaboration' (news), www.who.int/roadsafety/decade_of_action/en/index.html, accessed 19 May 2011

Wikipedia (2011) 'The great Pacific garbage patch', Wikipedia, en.wikipedia.org/wiki/Great_Pacific_Garbage_Patch, accessed 10 March 2011

Zero Waste SA (2011) 'Resource centre', www.zerowaste.sa.gov.au/resource-centre, accessed 10 March 2011

Chapter 2

Twenty-first-century life

How our work, home and community lives affect our capacity to live sustainably

Natalie Skinner, Pip Williams, Barbara Pocock and Jane Edwards

Summary

We are living in a world of rapid change, and this includes changes in the way that we work and live. Yet in discussion and debate about the urgent need for individuals, families and communities to adopt more sustainable lifestyles, the modern and changing systems in which we work, study, parent and live are often ignored. In this chapter, we apply a social systems theory to describe how the domains of work, home and community, separately and together, affect scope and opportunity for reducing water, waste, energy, transport and carbon emissions, at home and at work. The Intergovernmental Panel on Climate Change (IPCC) (2007, p59) observed that changes to individual and household consumption, transport, housing and lifestyle are an important part of the broader effort to address climate change. These changes will only be achieved when we break through the myth of the autonomous individual with the freedom to make sustainable choices armed with the right information and attitude. Instead, we must understand, and engage with, the complex nexus of employment, social, financial, temporal and spatial factors that interact to create daily life and, hence, the barriers or levers for change that create the capacity to live more sustainably.

Introduction

How we work, play, parent, socialize, age, communicate and travel is in many ways radically different from even a decade ago. When we think about change, it is technological innovation that often receives the most attention, with its clear and immediate impact on our lives. Many young people could not imagine life without being connected 24/7 to friends via online social networks. Smartphones are seen as essential work tools for many. A substantial part of the global response to climate change involves innovations that reduce carbon emissions from existing technology and create new ways of generating energy via solar, wind and other sustainable sources.

Technological change can be exciting. It can be easy to overlook that, in most countries, there have also been deep and fundamental changes to the ways that we work and live that have been slowly gaining momentum over the past few decades. It is these social changes – to our workplaces, our households and our communities – that we argue have received too little, if any, attention in research, policy and public debate on how we can reduce our energy consumption and waste in order to live more sustainably.

We are particularly interested in paid work, as that is where substantial change is occurring. Paid work has major implications for how we live. The influence of twenty-first-century patterns of work extends beyond the individual worker: they also affect children, family, friends, neighbours and the larger community. In this chapter, we argue that these changes also have a major impact on our individual and collective willingness and capacity to adopt and maintain more sustainable lifestyles. Paid work is the central pivot around which much of our routines, habits, time schedules and 'windows of opportunity' for change depend (see Stø et al, 2008, for a discussion of the concept of 'windows of opportunity'). It has a substantial impact on how easy or hard it is to change individual and household behaviours, and the benefits or drawbacks of change.

We are emphasizing the role of paid work as it is increasingly a major part of twenty-first-century life for women, men, older and young people. In industrialized countries, the rate of participation in paid work is increasing. More women are entering the workforce, and dual-earner households with children are increasingly common (Hofacker, 2008; Stadelmann-Steffen, 2008). For young people, working and studying is becoming the norm (Patton and Smith, 2009; Staff and Schulenberg, 2010). Hence, the prominence of paid work in households is rising – more household members are working, and the household is contributing more hours to paid work than ever before. Dual-earner households usually double the commute of the traditional, sole-breadwinner household, with major implications for congested roads and carbon footprints. Busy households with complex combinations of work, education, care, travel, domestic and social activities contribute to the ubiquity of time pressure as a part of modern life (Hochschild, 1997; Pocock, 2003; Zuzanek, 2004).

In this chapter, we take firm aim at what is often an implicit assumption that, if people's awareness and attitudes can be changed, then behaviour change in the desired direction will naturally follow. This individualistic perspective ignores the broader contexts of household, workplace and personal commitments and relationships (Stø et al, 2008). Finances, time and logistics influence and often constrain choices and behaviours. Peace and good relations in the household may take priority over an individual's desire to change household practices around diet, waste or energy use (Grønhøj, 2006). The two case studies presented in this chapter demonstrate this argument. The first case study looks at the common circumstance of young people bound within their parents' work and household routines, which constrain opportunities to translate their environmental concerns into action. In our second case study, we observe that, even within a custom-designed eco-village with motivated and knowledgeable residents, comfort and convenience are often the key drivers of energy consumption.

We are deliberately focusing on behaviours, rather than attitudes and intentions. The gap between attitudes or intentions and behaviours is well established and the focus of much psychological research. A meta-analysis of international research indicates that intentions account for a modest 27 per cent of change in self-reported environmental behaviours (Bamberg and Möser, 2007). In some circumstances, pro-environmental attitudes coexist with unsustainable behaviours. Labelled the 'green attitudes, brown behaviour' paradox, this pattern reflects the tendency for higher levels of income and education to be associated with both greater concern and activism for the environment (Edwards and Pocock, 2011) and a higher ecological footprint related to higher levels of greenhouse-gas emissions, larger houses and greater consumption of material goods (Anker-Nilssen, 2003; Stø et al, 2008; Fielding et al, 2010). Financial capacity often trumps environmental concern, as one of our interview participants from the eco-village case study (see below) explains: 'we just had the money, [so] we paid the bills'.

In this chapter, we describe a social systems approach to understanding the demands, constraints, resources and supports that affect the capacity of individuals, families and households to adopt and sustain behaviour change to reduce their waste, material consumption and energy use. The IPCC (2007, p59) has made it very clear that individuals, families and communities need to change their lifestyles and behaviours as part of the global response to climate change, and this includes changes in patterns of consumption, transport, housing and lifestyle. This cannot be achieved by attitudes and intentions alone. Interventions to change behaviour, whether by legislation, community programmes and initiatives, urban planning or housing design, must engage with the complex social systems in which people are intertwined, to create the most effective 'windows of opportunity', supports and levers for behaviour change.

A social systems approach to behaviour change

In our research, we employ Bronfenbrenner's (1979) and Voydanoff's (2007) ecological systems theory to frame the linkages between work, family and community and understand how these domains interact to influence behaviour (Pocock et al, in press). Bronfenbrenner's original model was constructed to explain children's development. It identifies four ecological domains, each nested within the next, which together make up the 'ecology' within which children develop. Voydanoff (2007) adapted this theory to analyse the relationships between work, family and community domains for adults. She adds to this model by using the notion of the demands and resources that are created in each sphere. For example, in the sphere of the workplace, access to paid leave is a resource, whereas long hours are a demand. In the household domain, sick children are a demand, and extended family support is a resource. In the broader community, good neighbours can be a resource, whereas poor local schools can create demands.

This social systems approach, overlaid with consideration of the demands and resources in each domain, has some important strengths. It takes us away from individualistic notions of freedom of choice and absolute autonomy. It locates the three interlocking domains of work, home and community in a larger 'macrosystem' of social norms and institutions. It encourages study of the 'microsystem' in each domain, as well as the 'mesosystem' of interaction between the three core domains of work, home and community, and implies that each domain creates demands and resources that support or impede particular behaviours and choices (see Figure 2.1).

This system of interconnected domains affects social, educational, economic and well-being outcomes for individuals, families, communities and workplaces. In our research, we have used it to analyse how Australians fit together their work, home and community lives, the supports and constraints that affect their behaviours and lifestyles and the outcomes for individuals, families and communities (Williams et al, 2009). The findings from this research indicate four universal factors that intersect these domains and consistently affect outcomes:

1   time: number, predictability, control and scheduling of hours spent in each domain, fit of these hours with personal and household preferences, cross-domain spillover of the experience of time (e.g. intensive paid work impeding quality of family time),

timing of activity in each sphere (e.g. working at night, caring at night), cross-domain fit of time schedules (e.g. school, work hours);

2   space: spatial separation between domains, how long it takes to commute these distances, whether domains are virtually connected;

3   life stage: how work, family and community needs and experiences vary by life stage, including for infants, children, teenagers, adults in pre-family formation, adults forming families, parents, pre-retirees, retirees and the aged;

4   power: relative power between socio-economic groups, men and women, workers of varying levels of education and skill, employers and employees, ethnic groups and age groups. This includes the nature and availability of 'voice' in suburban, social and political arrangements.

The interrelationship between time, space, life stage and power constructs the activities and well-being of those who live in suburban 'ecosystems', their economic productivity, social reproduction and the ease with which they can engage in sustainable behaviour. Figure 2.1 sets out a model that brings all of these elements together. In this model, the domain of paid work needs to be unpacked to make sense of how work intersects with the other domains of households and community. In sum, it is interaction between the contexts of everyday life – work, home and community – and the broader factors of life stage, space, time and power, that constructs both the willingness and the capacity to live sustainably. In the case study below, we show how these complex social systems interact to constrain or enhance young people's capacity to engage in pro-environmental behaviours. It is important to pay attention to young people, as they are being socialized into our future as workers, consumers, policymakers and 'agents of change'.

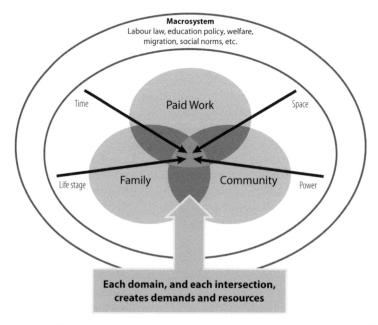

Figure 2.1 Social systems model of factors influencing engagement in sustainable behaviours.
Photo courtesy of the authors

Case study: a social systems approach to understanding the enablers and constraints affecting young people's sustainable behaviour

Adolescents are the consumers, scientists and policymakers of the future. How they are enabled to engage in the environmental issues of today affects their attitudes and behaviour in the short and longer term. It also affects their ability to be agents of change in their families, workplaces and communities (United Nations, 2002; Bentley et al, 2004; Ballantyne et al, 2006). The United Nations (2009) recognizes young people as key to a societal shift in attitudes and behaviours toward the environment and seeks to 'promote a global movement through which children and young people worldwide will actively participate in environmental activities and use the power of their numbers to influence politicians, leaders and society to make environmental changes' (p2). However, there are significant constraints and barriers to engagement that limit young people's participation and erode their potential as agents of change, putting an environmentally sustainable future at risk (Bentley et al, 2004).

How young people think and behave in relation to the environment is the result of a complex interaction between individuals' emotional and intellectual engagement in environmental issues and the way their daily lives are organized in relation to home, school, community and work (their own and their parents'). As Schultz and Stieß (2008) observe, environment-related behaviours such as consumption, waste and energy use are determined in large part by the structure and routines of daily life, with individuals, 'taking their own preferences as well as the wishes of other family or household members into account' (p289).

Surprisingly, there is little research examining how the rituals and habits of home, school, community and work interact to affect young people's engagement with environmental sustainability. Environmental education can raise awareness and facilitate pro-environmental attitudes (Loughland et al, 2002; Ballantyne et al, 2006), but there is little evidence that education alone leads to behaviour change (Gralton et al, 2004). We know that physically connecting with the environment can motivate young people to behave sustainably (Blanchet-Cohen, 2008), and also that positive adult role models, particularly parental attitudes and behaviour, can enhance sustainable behaviours in young people (Chawla, 1999). What has been overlooked in most research is how the contexts of daily life, especially parental work, influence young people's sustainable behaviours.

Here, we describe a qualitative study that applied a social systems model (Figure 2.1) to examine how different contexts of daily life interact to enable or constrain sustainable behaviour in adolescents. Participants were recruited from both metropolitan and semi-rural areas in order to explore the role of residential location on adolescents' opportunities to engage in issues of environmental sustainability. Participants included sixteen boys and girls from one metropolitan state secondary school and sixteen boys and girls from one semi-rural state secondary school in South Australia. Participants were aged from thirteen to sixteen years old, boys and girls were equally represented, and they came from a range of socio-economic and cultural backgrounds. Focus-group discussions addressed the demands and resources available within and between home, school, community and parental work, and how these demands and resources affected young people's knowledge, attitudes and behaviour in relation to the environment.

Key findings

One of the major findings, consistent with previous research, was that awareness of environmental issues does not necessarily translate into concern or a sense of responsibility (Gralton et al, 2004; Deniss, 2005; Carlsson and Jensen, 2006). Parental work and the characteristics of home, school and community interacted to create spatial and temporal demands and resources that either empowered and enabled young people to behave sustainably, or significantly undermined their capacity to do so. These characteristics can be understood in regard to time, space, power and life stage.

Time and space

What young people do with their time, where they live in relation to daily activities and how these activities are scheduled in relation to other people in their household all affect their capacity to behave sustainably. For many young people, time to think about the environment was curtailed by the busyness of their daily lives, by the requirements of school and the schedules of their parents:

> I've never thought of [the environment] as a big issue, my parents are focussed on schoolwork. I get up, go to school, do homework, go to bed. I haven't got time to think about the environment – I'm stuck in my parents' world.
>
> (Girl, fourteen years old, urban)

Parents' pro-environmental attitudes and behaviours can also have a positive influence on young peoples' knowledge and attitudes towards the environment, but this positive influence was often undermined by working time and commuting:

> We don't go camping as much as we used to 'cos dad works so much more . . . I miss it.
>
> (Boy, fourteen years old, urban)

When parents' work required long hours or a long commute, they were also more likely to model unsustainable consumption and waste behaviours, such as increased food waste and consumption of take-away food:

> If mum gets home about 8 o'clock and dad's home at 9 there's not enough time. We'll just get a takeaway.
>
> (Boy, fifteen years old, semi-rural)

Community characteristics also created demands and limited resources in relation to time and space. It takes time to get from one activity to another. Sustainable mobility among young people depends on easy access to daily activities such as education, recreation, entertainments and social interaction. When local access was not possible, young people would use public transport if it was scheduled to meet their activity needs; otherwise, they had no choice but to rely on less sustainable forms of private transport:

> It's pretty easy for me. The bus comes every 5 minutes. It's really convenient so I use it all the time.
>
> (Girl, fourteen years old, urban)

On like weekends and stuff I have to get taken down [to town] because my bus only comes on school days.

(Girl, fifteen years old, semi-rural)

Time to think and act sustainably was also determined by the characteristics of school. Participants at both the metropolitan and semi-rural schools indicated a lack of opportunities to learn about environmental sustainability: 'Just one or two lessons in science'. They were also critical about how this precious time was used: 'It's not very fun'.

When we consider the amount of time young people spend at school, it is useful to think about how well this time integrates environmental sustainability with other activities. The following discussion among a group of Year 8 students highlights the disconnect between the messages received through environmental education and the school experience. It also demonstrates that young people themselves are a resource that schools could make better use of when developing sustainable systems.

Boy 1: I went and got a doughnut, right, and there was packaging on the outside but she put it in another plastic bag . . . there's no point. I am going to eat it straight away.

Girl 1: When you take it out it's just a fresh piece of paper then it just goes in the bin, because there is no recycling in the hall.

Facilitator: What else could the canteen do though to help you reduce your waste?

Boy 2: Just not have a canteen.

Girl 2: Ask them, 'do you want a bag?'

Boy 1: And then charge 10 cents if you want one.

(thirteen–fourteen years old, semi-rural)

Power and life stage

Young people have very little control over the temporal and spatial configuration of their daily activities. They are not consulted about the design of the internal and external spaces they inhabit, and their daily activities come a poor second to the needs of voting/working adults in the planning of community amenities and the provision of public transport. Many participants felt they had some responsibility to behave in a way that protected the environment, but their belief in their capacity was diminished because of a perceived lack of power to make a difference:

I care about it sometimes, but I can't do anything about it.

(Girl, fourteen years old, urban)

This attitude could be countered when adults at home, school or in the community encouraged young people to speak up, empowering them to act.

I've sent letters to the editor about the weir at the Murray . . . Dad's not really into it, but he encouraged me to do it.

(Boy, fourteen years old, urban)

Unfortunately, these young people identified many lost opportunities for empowerment. Although some indicated they had an influence on their parents' behaviour – 'I'm like, "Dad, why have you got the TV on?" and I turn it off' – none considered they had any power to influence school systems or local council.

> You could write a letter to the council and they'll say, 'We'll think about it'.

Conclusion

This case study demonstrates how young people's attitudes and behaviours are developed within, and supported or constrained by, the relationships between home, school, community and (parents') work. Time, space and power interact to create barriers or supports to sustainable behaviours. As a result of these complex connections, sustainable behaviours were particularly difficult for some young people, such as those: who were not already connected to natural environments; whose parents work long hours or model unsustainable behaviours; whose homes are isolated from good amenity and mobility resources; and who lack a voice in their home, school or community. These young people struggled to internalize and act on their pro-environmental attitudes, born of their increasing knowledge of humans' role in climate change and environmental degradation.

Living sustainably – a twenty-first-century challenge

As the previous case study demonstrates, the systems and structures that shape adults' patterns of working and living significantly affect adolescents' capacity to change patterns of waste, consumption and energy consumption. We now turn to a more in-depth examination of the dynamics of working and living in the twenty-first century.

Rising levels of household consumption and energy use have been noted across a range of countries, and calls to reduce consumption are becoming more common (Hamilton and Denniss, 2005; Jackson and Papathanasopoulou, 2008; Stø et al, 2008). Shove (2010) observes that contemporary thinking around these issues is dominated by a focus on 'attitudes' (A), 'behaviour' (B) and 'choice' (C). Such 'ABC' frameworks do not sufficiently acknowledge that behaviours are social and cultural practices, not merely individual choices predicated on attitudes, knowledge and values. Put simply, policies and programmes for individual or household behaviour change must take account of the routine practices of household life and the sociocultural, institutional and systemic contexts in which they are enacted (Schultz and Stieß, 2008; Shove, 2010).

The configuration of domestic and working life makes a powerful contribution to relatively high levels of consumption. Jensen (2008) observes that many individuals and households are caught in a somewhat contradictory position. They are simultaneously asked to practise environmentally responsible behaviour, while the structure of social life in effect demands relatively high levels of consumption of things that promote comfort and convenience. Many aspects of consumption, rather than being discretionary, are often conditioned by the requirements of ordinary household routine (Shove, 2003). Greater use of private cars is the result less of a desire for individual car journeys than of a need to get to distant workplaces, or shopping centres, as conveniently as possible (Jackson and Papathanasopoulou, 2008). The increasing use of clothes dryers and microwaves is another example of 'locked-in' consumption, due to the demands made on women, in particular, by the labour market and the domestic division of labour.

It is worthwhile paying attention to gender. As we observed earlier, women's employment participation is increasing in most industrialized countries. It is a common observation across diverse countries, including Australia, the United States and Europe, that working women are especially likely be time poor, regardless of whether they work full time or part time (van der Lippe et al, 2006; Bianchi, 2009; Pocock et al, 2010). Much of this time pressure and time poverty is due to unequal distributions of care and domestic work (Hook, 2006; Budlender, 2010). This gender inequity also extends to the work of maintaining an 'eco-friendly' household, where routines, behaviours and purchasing decisions are developed to reduce consumption, waste and energy use (Grønhøj and Ölander, 2007; Judkins and Presser, 2008). Transport patterns are also highly gendered. Women's commutes often include diverse purposes such as shopping, social/recreational activities and passenger services (i.e. taking children to school or other activities), whereas men's commutes mainly relate to work and education (Noland and Thomas, 2007; Primerano et al, 2008). Asking households to change their routines, purchasing decisions, waste management practices and commuting is, for most households, asking women to do more, or to figure out how to do things differently (which in itself involves an investment of time) (Carlsson-Kanyama and Lindén, 2007).

Much more needs to be done to improve gender equity in the work and private spheres to make behaviour change realistic, sustainable and achievable for most households. Working conditions and arrangements are some of the most important structural barriers that can be addressed, and there are examples of countries that have already undertaken major reforms in this area, such as Sweden and Norway. Hook's (2006) analysis of twenty countries found that men's unpaid work in the household, including childcare, increases as women's working hours increase, but also with the length of available parental leave and men's eligibility for parental leave. To increase the capacity of individuals and households to live more sustainably, gender equity in the workplace and in the home must be addressed. Busy, time-poor, stressed individuals are not in a position to be good eco-citizens.

Our second case study (described below) demonstrates these complex influences of gender, work and care on consumption behaviour, and highlights the difficulty of living sustainably within a modern lifestyle, even with optimal urban planning and housing design.

Comfort, convenience and cost – drivers of energy consumption in an eco-village

Lochiel Park is a master-planned community located 8 km from the capital city of Adelaide, in South Australia. Designed as an 'eco-village', Lochiel Park seeks to demonstrate that urban, medium-density housing developments can have sustainable living as their core principle. At the time of the study (2010), Lochiel Park was in the early stages of growth (fewer than thirty households), with the final community to include 106 dwellings. All houses in Lochiel Park are serviced by solar photovoltaic cells, recycled-water systems and gas-boosted solar hot-water systems and have a minimum

7.5-star thermal performance rating. Houses are equipped with 'ecovision' monitors to provide information externally (to researchers and the land development company) on household water and energy consumption, and feedback to the householders. Not all monitors were functioning in participating households at the time of the study.

Here, we discuss key findings from in-depth interviews with sixteen individuals (six couples, four individuals) who were resident or soon-to-be resident in Lochiel Park. These residents were financially comfortable and were well informed and highly motivated to practise pro-environmental behaviours. Yet, despite optimal financial resources, knowledge and attitudes, a very clear message emerged from this study – comfort, convenience and cost were the biggest influences on behaviour.

Comfort

Comfort was a uniform expectation for residents – the phrase was ubiquitous in discussions of household temperature. As one couple explained, 'being warm in the winter and being cool in the summer, they are important to us'. Despite the higher thermal performance rating of their houses, residents still used artificial heating and cooling, especially for upstairs rooms in hot weather. Summer heat was a common concern. Residents tried to use air conditioning efficiently and parsimoniously, but there were common tipping points that promoted air-conditioner use, including relief from extended heatwaves, heat-related tiredness that made everyday routines more difficult, comfortable temperatures for sleeping, children's needs and health concerns for those with medical conditions. There is also a bigger picture here around changing norms regarding comfort. The meaning of comfort in relation to indoor air temperature has changed dramatically in the last century, and new norms and expectations about comfort now define people's expectations of their indoor environment (Chappells and Shove, 2004). As one Lochiel Park couple explains, they persevere as much as they can through Australia's heatwaves, which can be a week of temperatures of 35°C and above. However, they have their limits: 'when we get these extreme periods of weather *we have the right* to have a choice to be comfortable' (emphasis added).

Convenience

In Lochiel Park, it was very clear that behaviours related to energy consumption are embedded in everyday household routines. Energy consumption that promotes convenience was commonly practised, even if it contradicted pro-environmental attitudes or incurred financial costs. Inconvenience was also one of the main barriers to pro-environmental behaviours. This was especially the case for participants with children, who are juggling a number of demands, with limited time every day. As one parent explains:

> One of the things about working and having to get kids off to school . . . your time is more limited . . . It's often more convenient to take the car or turn a heater on . . . As much as I would like always to do the environmentally [friendly] thing, it doesn't happen.

Another couple, also with a deep commitment to sustainability, testify to the way that behaviours have to mesh with individual and household routines, or they will not be practised:

> We basically do everything that we can think of that is reasonable and coming back to this convenience factor I suppose. We don't sit the bucket under the shower to catch the water ... I haven't got time to fiddle around ... there are a few things like that and you think, well it's just too much like hard work.

Paid work plays an important role in restricting the 'time to fiddle around'. For example, for one retired couple in Lochiel Park the contrast between their pre- and post-retirement lives was stark. They observed that busy working lives tend to narrow the focus to maintaining daily functions and routines, effectively pushing environmental concerns to the periphery. Their remarks also illustrate the benefits for pro-environmental behaviour of having time to think about the implication of their actions and to change accordingly:

> We were busy working people ... I don't think we thought about it [the environment] ... we were probably working 50 hours per week [each] ... You do things, you've got housework, got washing and whatever to do on the weekend ... and all of that just occupies your mind. Yeah, well I think we were indicative back then of most people – the environment is not the top of your tick list.

Cost

Even though the study participants were financially secure, and some were quite affluent, financial constraints were a common barrier to larger-scale home installations or modifications such as insulation and solar energy systems. Residents were strongly motivated to live sustainably and so, on occasion, they would practise behaviour that was not economically self-serving. For larger-scale financial investments, residents emphasized the importance of subsidies towards energy efficiency.

Conclusion

To the outside observer, Lochiel Park residents have an array of resources to enable sustainable living – pro-environment values, practical knowledge, well-designed housing and urban landscape, a supportive community and financial security. Their daily reality is quite different. The demands, pressures and requirements of living, working and parenting in a modern household mean that comfort, convenience and cost become the major determinants of energy and water consumption. There are deep cultural and social forces at play here, about what is defined as comfortable, normal and appropriate for cleanliness and comfort (Shove, 2003). There are also larger-scale structural factors, such as the way paid work is scheduled and experienced, that create busy, time-stressed households where lives are intricately organized and time-tabled, and what is quick and easy often wins over slower and more effortful eco-friendly behaviours.

Work–life configurations that support or impede sustainable behaviours

The challenges of managing work and other life commitments, such as parenting, feature prominently in the Lochiel Park case study. As paid work is becoming an increasingly prominent feature of modern life, a deeper examination of the impact of paid work on the capacity to reduce waste, consumption and energy use is warranted. Here, we consider three interrelated aspects of paid work that impact on the capacity to live more sustainably – commuting, work hours and flexible work schedules.

Work commutes and carbon footprint

For most people, participation in paid work requires commuting. Globally, transport is responsible for 23 per cent of energy-related greenhouse-gas emissions, and 44.5 per cent of these emissions are from light-duty vehicles (including cars for personal use). Transport emissions are increasing at a faster rate than any other sector (Kahn Ribeiro et al, 2007).

Telecommuting (working from home) is one obvious and effective strategy to reduce travel-related carbon emissions (Jensen-Butler et al, 2008). Excluding the self-employed, only 13.9 per cent of workers in Australia work at least some hours at home (Australian Bureau of Statistics, 2008).

Telecommuting is more common in Europe: around 20 per cent of workers work at least one-quarter of their work time at home (Parent-Thirion et al, 2007). There is clearly more room to improve access and uptake of telecommuting, although it must be recognized and acknowledged that this arrangement does not suit many types of job. Case studies that we have conducted of telecommuting in Australian organizations illustrate cost, time and environmental savings that arise from telecommuting, with benefits for employers, employees, households and the economy.

Much more can be done, of course, to better design many cities and suburbs to reduce the reliance on cars as the primary form of transportation, and Australian cities, along with those in other English-speaking countries, significantly lag behind our European counterparts (Mees, 2010). Governments and developers need to take on this challenge and make significant and innovative investments in better urban planning and transport systems. For example, well-designed and well-planned public transport, such as light rail, can support denser urban development (Handy, 2005). It is very clear from our interviews with Australians living and working in typical Australian suburbs that much more can be done to increase the opportunity and capacity for more sustainable and low-impact commuting between work, home, school and other activities (Williams et al, 2009).

Long on hours and short on sustainability

Modern life is often busy and time pressured, and hours of paid work at the individual and household level play a major role (Pocock, 2003; van der Lippe et al, 2006). Among most high-income nations such as the US, Canada, Australia and Western European countries, per capita ecological impacts increase as average work hours lengthen, via the effect on increasing GDP (i.e. the ubiquitous work–spend cycle) (Hayden and

Shandra, 2009). Work hours have a substantial impact on energy consumption. One study found that, if US workers were able to adopt European-style working arrangements (more holidays, shorter hours), the US would consume 20 per cent less energy (Rosnick and Weisbrot, 2006). A range of factors are likely to account for this observation, although there is evidence that it is the increase in income that is mainly responsible for greater consumption of energy and material resources (Pullinger, 2009; Nässén and Larsson, 2010). The relationship between higher income and higher levels of consumption of material goods and energy (cooling, heating, car use, house size) is well established (Schor, 2005; Abrahamse and Steg, 2009; Pullinger, 2009). It has also been observed that the strong link between increased prosperity and increased consumption significantly outweighs the contribution of technological advances to reducing environmental impact (Jackson, 2009). The more we work, the more we spend – on travel, car purchases, appliances and larger houses.

The relationship between work hours and ecological impact is not wholly a function of increased GDP. In their analysis, Hayden and Shandra (2009) observed that GDP growth did not account for all of the hours–GDP association, and they suggest that time scarcity and its effect on promoting various unsustainable lifestyle practices is also an important consideration. There is growing support for this time-scarcity hypothesis and its connection to the central role of paid work. Schor (2010) has put forward strong arguments that the dominance of paid work in the lives of individuals and households places significant constraints on the capacity and opportunity for pro-environmental behaviours. For example, in a study of family communication patterns around consumption of organic food, water and energy, waste and transport, Grønhøj (2006) observed that discussion centred primarily on issues of 'time, taste, convenience, health and economy', rather than environmental concern. Time pressures, particularly related to work expectations and family responsibilities, are a major factor that encourages car use in general, and a household model of a car for every adult in particular (Andrey et al, 2004). Paid work hours, their length, scheduling and intensity have a substantial impact on time availability, what is most convenient and, of course, what fits in with the household budget.

The argument for reducing work hours often includes the well-established principle that, beyond a certain level of material comfort, increasing wealth does not result in gains in happiness or well-being. Many authors have argued that reducing work hours can increase the quality of life, by increasing time for family, community, leisure and other enjoyable and meaningful life pursuits (Diener and Oishi, 2003; Schor, 2010). We must be careful here to acknowledge that reduced working hours are not a viable or realistic option for everybody, as they require decent rates of pay to support a reasonable quality of life. As Siegel (2007) observes, 'A simple living movement cannot spread widely as long as almost all the good jobs do not give you the option of working less and consuming less'.

There have been numerous calls in the research and policy literature for better-quality part-time jobs that provide security, stability of work hours and scheduling, and a sufficient income to support a decent quality of life (Lyonette et al, 2010). This type of industrial-relations and employment reform is needed, not only to increase the quality of life and capacity of the poorest and most vulnerable members of society, but also to create realistic and attractive alternatives for all workers to combine paid work with more sustainable lifestyles.

Flexibility for sustainability

Flexi-time (time-in-lieu) and variable start and finish times can also have a significant impact on commuting requirements by reducing car use or making alternative forms of transport that may have a time cost (bus, train, bike) more viable. More flexible schedules can also create 'windows of opportunity' for pro-environmental behaviours with a time cost or effort requirement, such as reducing appliance use (e.g. hanging clothes outside rather than using a spin dryer) and growing food in a home garden. Flexible work arrangements do not necessarily mean reduced hours and, hence, reduced income. For example, the US state of Utah implemented a compressed working week of four 10-hour days for its employees. This resulted in substantial reductions in energy consumption, such as a reduction of 4546 metric tons of carbon due to 3 million fewer miles travelled by the state vehicle fleet. This new arrangement also suited workers – 82 per cent wanted to keep the new four-day schedule (Facer and Wadsworth, 2010).

Conclusion

In this chapter, we have argued that the fundamental changes to paid work that have occurred over the past decades have rippled out across every aspect of modern life to create households that are often busy, tightly scheduled and time pressured. More women are in the paid workforce, and dual-earner households are increasingly common. There is also evidence, from a range of countries, that the gender divide in unpaid work extends to the business of organizing and managing an eco-friendly household, which can mean increasing women's domestic workload.

As a society, we need to think more radically and with greater courage and innovation about how we structure our paid work so as best to support the health and well-being of individuals, families, communities and the natural environment. There is much that can be done legislatively, culturally and socially to develop what the International Labour Organization calls 'decent working time' as the norm, where individuals and households have the time and energy to make more sustainable choices, including reducing their energy consumption and waste. Shorter working hours, telecommuting and employee-centred flexibility are some of the key elements of a system of paid work that supports, rather than impedes, more sustainable behaviours.

In light of the complex and changing circumstances of everyday life, researchers and policymakers must integrate the perspectives of social scientists, engineers, architects, geographers, scientists and public policymakers in the challenge of behaviour change. Improving design and technology is crucial. But the impact of these innovations on material consumption, waste and energy use will be limited if we do not take into account the complex, and often busy, lives that are becoming the norm. These innovations must take account of the lived reality of citizens, and especially how this varies by gender and socio-economic status. Both of these factors condition the nature and consequences of people's response to environmental challenges: not all citizens are equally positioned or affected by particular programmes, initiatives or innovations.

Understanding and addressing climate change requires a systems approach, engaging with complex and interdependent processes of nature and civilization. So, too, with human behaviour, as it is also embedded within complex and interacting systems of work, home, education, community and family life that have the capacity to both constrain and enable behaviour change for environmental sustainability.

References

Abrahamse, W. and Steg, L. (2009) 'How do socio-demographic and psychological factors relate to households' direct and indirect energy use and savings?', *Journal of Economic Psychology*, vol 30, no 5, pp711–20

Andrey, J. C., Burns, K. R. and Doherty, S. T. (2004) 'Toward sustainable transportation: exploring transportation decision making in teleworking households in a mid-sized Canadian city', *Canadian Journal of Urban Research*, vol 13, no 2, pp257–77

Anker-Nilssen, P. (2003) 'Household energy use and the environment: a conflicting issue', *Applied Energy*, vol 76, no 1–3, pp189–96

Australian Bureau of Statistics (2008) *Locations of work, Cat. No. 6275.0*, ABS, Canberra, Australia

Ballantyne, R., Connell, S. and Fien, J. (2006) 'Students as catalysts of environmental change: a framework for researching intergenerational influence through environmental education', *Environmental Education Research*, vol 12, no 3–4, pp413–27

Bamberg, S. and Möser, G. (2007) 'Twenty years after Hines, Hungerford, and Tomera: a new meta-analysis of psycho-social determinants of pro-environmental behaviour', *Journal of Environmental Psychology*, vol 27, no 1, pp14–25

Bentley, M., Fien, J. and Neil, C. (2004) *Sustainable Consumption: Young Australians as Agents of Change*, Department of Family and Community Services on behalf of National Youth Affairs Research Scheme (NYARS), Canberra, Australia

Bianchi, S. M. (2009) 'What gives when mothers are employed? Parental time allocation in dual-earner and single-earner two-parent families', in D. R. Crane and E. J. Hill (eds) *Handbook of Families and Work: Interdisciplinary Perspectives*, University Press of America, New York

Blanchet-Cohen, N. (2008) 'Taking a stance: child agency across the dimensions of early adolescents' environmental involvement', *Environmental Education Research*, vol 14, no 3, pp257–72

Bronfenbrenner, U. (1979) *The Ecology of Human Development*, Harvard University Press, Cambridge, MA

Budlender, D. (2010) 'What do time use studies tell us about unpaid care work? Evidence from seven countries', in D. Budlender (ed) *Time Use Studies and Unpaid Care Work*, Routledge, New York

Carlsson, M. and Jensen, B. (2006) 'Encouraging environmental citizenship: the roles and challenges for schools', in A. Dobson and D. Bell (eds) *Environmental Citizenship*, MIT Press, Cambridge, MA

Carlsson-Kanyama, A. and Lindén, A.-L. (2007) 'Energy efficiency in residences – challenges for women and men in the North', *Energy Policy*, vol 35, no 4, pp2163–72

Chappells, H. and Shove, E. (2004) 'Comfort: a review of philosophies and paradigms', Centre for Science Studies, Lancaster University, Lancaster, UK

Chawla, L. (1999) 'Life paths into effective environmental action', *Journal of Environmental Education*, vol 31, no 1, pp15–26

Deniss, R. (2005) 'The attitudes of young people to the environment', The Australia Institute, Canberra, Australia

Diener, E. and Oishi, S. (2003) 'Money and happiness: income and subjective well-being across nations', in E. Diener and E. M. Suh (eds) *Culture and Subjective Well-being*, MIT Press, Boston, MA

Edwards, J. and Pocock, B. (2011) *Comfort, Cost and Convenience: The Calculus of Sustainable Living at Lochiel Park*, Centre for Work + Life, University of South Australia, Adelaide, Australia

Facer, R. L. and Wadsworth, L. L. (2010) 'Four-day work weeks: current research and practice', *Connecticut Law Review*, vol 42, no 4, pp1031–46

Fielding, K. S., Thompson, A., Louis, W. R. and Warren, C. (2010) *Environmental Sustainability: Understanding Attitudes and Behaviour of Australian Households*, AHURI final report no 152, Australian Housing and Urban Research Institute (AHURI) Melbourne, Australia

Gralton, A., Sinclair, M. and Purnell, K. (2004) 'Changes in attitudes, beliefs and behaviour: a critical review of research into the impacts of environmental education initiatives', *Australian Journal of Environmental Education*, vol 20, no 2, pp41–52

Grønhøj, A. (2006) 'Communication about consumption: a family process perspective on "green" consumer practices', *Journal of Consumer Behaviour*, vol 5, no 6, pp491–503

Grønhøj, A. and Ölander, F. (2007) 'A gender perspective on environmentally related family consumption', *Journal of Consumer Behaviour*, vol 6, no 4, pp218–35

Hamilton, C. and Denniss, R. (2005) *Affluenza: When Too Much is Never Enough*, Allen and Unwin, Crows Nest, New South Wales, Australia

Handy, S. (2005) 'Smart growth and the transportation–land use connection: what does the research tell us?', *International Regional Science Review*, vol 28, no 2, pp146–67

Hayden, A. and Shandra, J. M. (2009) 'Hours of work and the ecological footprint of nations: an exploratory analysis', *Local Environment*, vol 14, no 6, pp575–600

Hochschild, A. (1997) *The Time Bind: When Work Becomes Home and Home Becomes Work*, Metropolitan Books, New York

Hofacker, D. (2008) 'Women's employment in times of globalization: a comparative overview', in H.-P. Blossfeld and H. Hofmeister (eds) *Globalization, Uncertainty and Women's Careers: An International Comparison*, Edward Elgar, Massachusetts, MA

Hook, J. L. (2006) 'Care in context: men's unpaid work in 20 Countries, 1965–2003', *American Sociological Review*, vol 71, no 4, pp639–60

Intergovernmental Panel on Climate Change (IPCC) (2007) *Climate Change 2007: Synthesis Report*, IPCC, Geneva, Switzerland

Jackson, T. (2009) *Prosperity Without Growth: Economics for a Finite Planet*, Earthscan, London

Jackson, T. and Papathanasopoulou, E. (2008) 'Luxury or "lock-in"? An exploration of unsustainable consumption in the UK: 1968 to 2000', *Ecological Economics*, vol 68, no 1–2, pp80–95

Jensen-Butler, C., Sloth, B., Larsen, M. M., Madsen, B., Nielsen, O. A., Glogger, A. F., Zangler, T.W and Karg, G. (2008) 'The impact of telecommuting on households' travel behaviour, expenditures and emissions', in M. M. Fischer, G. J. D. Hewings, P. Nijkamp and F. Snickars (eds) *Road Pricing, the Economy and the Environment*, Springer, Berlin/Heidelberg, Germany

Jensen, J. (2008) 'Measuring consumption in households: interpretations and strategies', *Ecological Economics*, vol 68, no 1–2, pp353–61

Judkins, B. and Presser, L. (2008) 'Division of eco-friendly household labor and the marital relationship', *Journal of Social and Personal Relationships*, vol 25, no 6, pp923–41

Kahn Ribeiro, S., Kobayashi, S., Beuthe, M., Gasca, J., Greene, D., Lee, D. S., Muromachi, Y., Newton, P. J., Plotkin, S., Sperling, D., Wit, R. and Zhou, P. J. (2007) 'Transport and its infrastructure', in B. Metz, O. R. Davidson, P. R. Bosch, R. Dave and L. A. Meyer (eds) *Climate Change 2007: Mitigation. Contribution of Working Group III to the Fourth Assessment Report of the Intergovernmental Panel on Climate Change*, Cambridge University Press, Cambridge

Loughland, T., Reid, A. and Petocz, P. (2002) 'Young people's conceptions of environment: a phenomenographic analysis', *Environmental Education Research*, vol 8, no 2, pp187–97

Lyonette, C., Baldauf, B. and Behle, H. (2010) *'Quality' Part-time Work: A Review of the Evidence*, Institute for Employment Research, University of Warwick, Warwick

Mees, P. (2010) *Transport for Surburbia: Beyond the Automobile Age*, Earthscan, London

Nässén, J. and Larsson, J. (2010) 'Would shorter work time reduce greenhouse gas emissions? An analysis of time use and consumption in Swedish households', unpublished working paper, Chalmers University of Technology and the University of Gothenburg, Gothenburg, Sweden

Noland, R. B. and Thomas, J. V. (2007) 'Multivariate analysis of trip-chaining behavior', *Environment and Planning B: Planning and Design*, vol 34, no 6, pp953–70

Parent-Thirion, A., Fernández-Macias, E., Hurley, J. and Vermeylen, G. (2007) *Fourth European Working Conditions Survey*, Eurofound, Dublin, Ireland

Patton, W. and Smith , E. (2009) 'School students and part-time work: workplace problems and challenges', *Youth Studies Australia*, vol 28, no 3, pp21–31

Pocock, B. (2003) *The Work/Life Collision: What Work is Doing to Australians and What to Do About It*, Federation Press, Sydney, Australia

Pocock, B., Skinner, N. and Pisaniello, S. (2010) *How Much Should We Work? Working Hours, Holidays and Working Life: The Participation Challenge. The Australian Work and Life Index 2010*, Centre for Work + Life, University of South Australia, Adelaide, Australia

Pocock, B., Williams, P. and Skinner, N. (in press) 'Conceptualising work, family and community: what's missing and how the field of employment relations can help', *British Journal of Industrial Relations*

Primerano, F., Taylor, M., Pitaksringkarn, L. and Tisato, P. (2008) 'Defining and understanding trip chaining behaviour', *Transportation*, vol 35, no 1, pp55–72

Pullinger, M. (2009) 'Work life balance policy as sustainable consumption policy: the environmental impacts of working time reduction in UK households with children', paper presented at the 8th International Conference of the European Society for Ecological Economics, Ljubljana, Slovenia, 29 June–2 July

Rosnick, D. and Weisbrot, M. (2006) 'Are shorter work hours good for the environment? – a comparison of U.S. and European energy consumption', Center for Economic and Policy Research, Washington, DC

Schor, J. (2010) 'Sustainable work schedules for all', in L. Starke and L. Mastny (eds) *2010 State of the World. Transforming Cultures. From Consumerism to Sustainability*, W.W. Norton and Company, New York

Schor, J. B. (2005) 'Sustainable consumption and worktime reduction', *Journal of Industrial Ecology*, vol 9, no 1/2, pp37–50

Schultz, I. and Stieß, I. (2008) 'Linking sustainable consumption to everyday life: a social-ecological approach to consumption research', in A. Tukker, M. Charter, C. Vezzoli, E. Stø and M. Munch Andersen (eds) *System Innovation for Sustainability 1*, Greenleaf Publishing, Sheffield, pp288–300

Shove, E. (2003) 'Users, technologies and expectations of comfort, cleanliness and convenience', *Innovation*, vol 16, no 2, pp193–206

Shove, E. (2010) 'Beyond the ABC: climate change policy and theories of social change', *Environment and Planning A*, vol 42, pp1273–85

Siegel, C. (2007) *Work Time and Global Warming: A Preservation Institute White Paper*, The Preservation Institute, Berkeley, CA

Stadelmann-Steffen, I. (2008) 'Women, labour, and public policy: female labour market integration in OECD countries. A comparative perspective', *Journal of Social Policy*, vol 37, no 3, pp383–408

Staff, J. and Schulenberg, J. E. (2010) 'Millennials and the world of work: experiences in paid work during adolescence ', *Journal of Business and Psychology*, vol 25, no 2, pp247–55

Stø, E., Throne-Holst, H., Strandbakken, P. and Vittersø, G. (2008) 'Review: a multi-dimensional approach to the study of consumption in modern societies and the potential for radical sustainable changes', in A. Tukker, M. Charter, C. Vezzoli, E. Stø and M. Munch Andersen (eds), *System Innovation for Sustainability 1*, Greenleaf Publishing, Sheffield

United Nations (2002) *Plan of Implementation of the World Summit on Sustainable Development*, United Nations, Geneva, Switzerland

United Nations Environmental Program (2009) 'Final review of the long term strategy on the engagement and involvement of young people in environmental issues', paper presented at the 25th session of the governing council/global ministerial environment forum, Nairobi, Kenya, 16–20 February

van der Lippe, T., Jager, A. and Kops, Y. (2006) 'Combination pressure: the paid work–family balance of men and women in European countries', *Acta Sociologica*, vol 49, no 3, pp303–19

Voydanoff, P. (2007) *Work, Family, and Community: Exploring Interconnections*, Psychology Press, New York

Williams, P., Pocock, B. and Bridge, K. (2009) *Linked Up Lives: Putting Together Work, Home and Community in Ten Australian Suburbs. Overview Report*, Centre for Work + Life, University of South Australia, Adelaide, Australia

Zuzanek, J. (2004) 'Work, leisure, time-pressure and stress', in J. T. Haworth and A. J. Veal (eds), *Work and Leisure*, Routledge, Hove, UK

Chapter 3

Young children and sustainable consumption

An early childhood education agenda

Sue Nichols

Summary

This chapter argues that sustainable consumption is an important and appropriate subject for young children's learning. Challenges are identified, including the disciplinary boundaries of early childhood education (ECE), the desires of practitioners to protect children from consumer society, a lack of curriculum specification, and definitions of sustainable consumption that fail to acknowledge the interwoven nature of children's needs and wants. An action research project involving preschool children is described. This project found that children value the continuity of significant objects and gain understandings of practices of conservation, reuse and redesign through families' activities related to possessions. These are all concepts related to sustainability and highlight the potential of building on children's values and experiences to promote learning about sustainable futures.

Introduction

Sustainability is a future-oriented concept. It has been defined as forms of progress 'that meet the needs of the present without compromising the ability of future generations to meet their own needs' (Bruntland, 1987). This chapter concerns those 'future generations' who are today's young children. Young children are often thought of as citizens of the future. When it comes to sustainability, the future that we are working towards is indeed the future in which today's young children will be the people in charge. In her assessment of the connections between schools, their curricula and citizenship, education scholar Marie Brennan identified a contradiction that applies equally to ECE when she observed that:

> If citizenship is about sustaining public life . . . then schools have to be seen as places of public life themselves . . . Yet schools are expected to treat their members as only 'in preparation' for later public life.
>
> (1996, p29)

In this chapter, I will argue that we need to think of young children as citizens of the present and engage with them, and their carers, to develop in them the dispositions that will orient them to work towards a sustainable future.

The theme of this chapter is sustainable consumption and childhood, a theme that arouses many responses, from moral indignation to resignation to hope. It has been said that treating children as citizens necessitates acknowledging 'how they see their "place" in the world and how they produce the world to come' (Katz, 1994, p109). Being socialized into practices of consumption and sustainability are ways in which children are invited to take up places in the world. Finding a way to bring these two activities and their associated values together is currently a critical challenge of parenting and education.

Children and youth are a significant consumer group. The Commission on the Development of the World Conference on Religion and Peace has stated that 'a child born in North America or England will consume, waste and pollute more in a lifetime than as many as 50 children in a developing country' (McGregor, 2002, p2). This makes the report that, in 2003, combined youth spending power in affluent nations was in excess of US$750 billion unsurprising (Department of Education Science and Technology (DEST), 2004).

The Australian government report, *Sustainable Consumption*, focuses specifically on youth, reflecting a view that influencing the current generation's consumption attitudes and habits is essential to achieving sustainability (DEST, 2004). This report defines sustainable consumption as 'privileging quality of life over material standards of living; minimising resource use waste and pollution; taking a life cycle perspective in consumer decision making and acting with concern for future generations' (DEST, 2004). The inclusion of the 'life cycle perspective' is particularly salient and suggests the need to find strategies suitable to the particular stage that individuals have reached in their lives. However, younger children are not mentioned, and so the interests of citizens at this particular stage of life in relation to consumption and sustainability remain to be addressed.

Another element of sustainable consumption included in the definition above, which I have separated out for comment, is described as 'satisfying basic human needs not the desire for wants and luxuries' (DEST, 2004, p2). The issue of how to define 'needs' as compared with 'wants' and how this may impact on those whose perceived 'needs' are redefined as 'wants' is by no means as simple as it is often made to sound. This is particularly the case when we consider the role consumption may play in children's identity formation, a matter that until recently has received very little attention. Historian of childhood, Daniel Cook, reviewing a number of key sociological studies of consumption (including Bourdieu's (1984) *Distinction*), notes the absence of any serious treatment of the child: 'The "child" does not appear as a social actor who enters the world, engages in meaning-making activities and who has and expresses desire for things' (Cook, 2008, p227). This is a serious omission if, as I argue, the desires of children are central to the question of how to approach the issue of sustainable consumption. Desire is, for Cook, an important dimension of consumption, which he defines as 'knowing of and the desiring of goods; the viewing and touching of things as much as ownership' (2008, p227) This emphasis on the sensory aspect of consumption is particularly relevant to children, as this is one of the major ways in which they experience and apprehend their worlds.

Cook states that consumption 'gains its meaning from the social relationships through which it occurs' (2008, p227). For young children, important social relationships are formed within the family and then with peers, usually at entry into preschool or school.

Although consumption studies often focus on individual choices, it is beginning to be appreciated that families function as dynamic, interdependent systems, with shared identities. Arguing for a re-theorization of consumption that takes this into account, marketing academics Amber Epp and Linda Price have written that family identity is 'mutually constructed . . . [and] contingent upon shared interactions', including those involved in consumption routines such as meal times (2008, p52). Epp and Price refer to the symbolic power of consumption practices – such as forms of gift giving – that are 'shared as resources for constructing and managing relational identities' (2008, p53).

The discussion that follows is an exploration of how to begin a meaningful engagement with young children and their carers on the issue of sustainable consumption. It reports on a project that investigated early childhood (EC) educators' views and then moved to an action research phase to explore preschool children's understandings and values related to consumption. The opportunity to become involved with developing an approach to working with young children and carers on the issue of sustainable consumption came about as a result of the initiative of the Zero Waste Research Centre at the University of South Australia. This research centre supports scholarship related to its four priorities: measuring consumption and ecological footprint; resource efficiency and life-cycle measurement; behavioural change; and decision-making. The last two of these priorities are clearly in concert with the aims of educators. In response to an invitation from the Zero Waste Research Centre, a group of education academics formed a collaborative project team with their colleagues from the University of South Australia's Schools of Marketing and Communication, which aims to develop strategies for engaging with young children, EC practitioners and parents on issues of sustainable consumption.

As this is very much an emerging area of research and practice, the aim is to begin a dialogue on the subject and to encourage those who work in the field of sustainability to take into account the perspectives of young children and their carers. An additional goal is to support EC practitioners and parents in coming to grips with the issue of consumption when considering how to foster children's learning about sustainability.

Early childhood education: perspectives on sustainability and children's consumption

In this section of the chapter, I look at how the field of ECE views the issue of sustainable consumption as a subject for young children's learning. Three sources are used to develop this analysis. First, the results of a literature review are presented; second, the curriculum within a state jurisdiction is examined; and, finally, the views of ECE practitioners are presented. Taken together, these perspectives show that, although there is considerable potential and support for engaging young children in learning about sustainability, there are challenges due to academic disciplines' boundaries, curriculum limitations and the professional values of some ECE workers.

Disjuncture between ECE and environmental education scholarship

An initial task of the project was to survey the relevant literature from the fields of ECE and environmental education. This task revealed a profound disconnect between the two fields, similar to that which Cook found when he looked for the child in sociological studies of consumption. A content analysis was undertaken of the full text of three ECE journals and three environmental education journals, inclusive of all issues since these journals began publication. In the EC field, the contents of the journals *Early Years*, *Contemporary Issues in Early Childhood* and the *Australian Journal of Early Childhood* were searched using the keywords 'environment', 'environmental', 'sustainable', 'sustainability', 'garden', 'waste' and 'recycling'. Only five relevant articles were found in the total contents of these three journals. All of those articles discussed children's learning and play in the outdoor environment, for example, advocating that there should be a natural environment for children to play in as part of their participation in ECE institutions.

In the environmental area, the following journals were searched: *Environmental Education Research*, *Australian Journal of Environmental Education* and *Organisation and Environment*, the last of these because the EC sector can be understood on an organizational level. Keywords used in this search were 'preschool', 'kindergarten', 'children' and 'early childhood'. Three relevant articles were found in the combined contents of all three journals. Davis (2005) describes a kindergarten's integration of sustainability objectives across all its programmes; Strife and Downey (2009) advocate for children's access to the natural environment; and Senier and her colleagues (2007) report on the elimination of toxic chemicals from school environments.

The disjuncture between ECE and environmental education in the scholarly literature is also evident in policy areas. In 2009, the South Australian minister for early childhood development was also, coincidentally, the minister for the environment. Opening that year's de Lissa Oration for Children's Week, the minister stated that these two portfolios had rarely been in contact. His point was supported by that year's de Lissa orator, Tanya Young, who had spent 2008 bringing EC centres in the Australian state of Victoria under the umbrella of the national 'Sustainable Schools' network, the first time that such centres had been invited to participate. In her lecture, Young observed that, in the ECE sector, there is a high value placed on protecting children, which translates to keeping them out of the public sphere. She argued that, to advance sustainability as an educational goal, childcare centres and kindergartens needed to be much more connected to public life, which could just be the 'local public', the activities of people in their communities (Young, 2009).

Curriculum context: potential for learning

The prior-to-school period has been an area of considerable educational development in the last decade, with structured learning pathways becoming evident in many national curricula. (This is no doubt partly owing to the substantial increase in out-of-home care for preschool-aged children, as more mothers of young children participate in paid work.) In the author's home state of South Australia, for example, the South Australian Curriculum Standards and Accountability (SACSA) framework's 'early years' band, which applies to children aged nought to eight years old, includes five essential learning areas:

1   Futures: 'Who I want to be and how I want the world to be for me and others';
2   Identity: 'Who I am';

3 Interdependence: 'Where and how I fit with others';
4 Thinking: 'How I understand the world'; and
5 Communication: 'How I express myself and interact with others'.

It is evident that this curriculum offers ample support to engage children in learning about sustainability, given its emphasis on futures thinking and interdependence. Indeed, this way of structuring learning connects the development of self-identity closely with an understanding of the relationship between self and others. This is made explicit in the curriculum guidelines, which state that children are to be encouraged to develop 'complex ideas of who they are, what they are like, what they feel' and to recognize that 'what they can do is interdependent with others and their environment' (DECS, 2001, p20).

The curriculum's Key Ideas (KIs) show how this idea is developed via specific learning foci. For example, one of the KIs in the 'Understanding our world' learning area for children aged three to five years old is: 'Children develop a sense of responsibility for natural and social environments and an understanding that their world is shared' (DECS, 2001, p66). This statement is further elaborated with several sub-points regarding what children should be doing to develop this aspect, including:

- observing changes in their environment and reflecting and acting on these observations;
- exploring the impact of manufactured materials, technologies and resources on the environment; and
- contributing towards the preservation of environments and the conservation of resources with a sense of influence and optimism (DECS, 2001, p66).

The current curriculum thus provides both scope and a degree of guidance for South Australia's ECE practitioners to engage young children in learning about sustainability. However, even though the environment is obviously part of the 'natural and social', it would be easy to interpret the curriculum as simply encouraging children's engagement with nature. The role of children as consumers is not made explicit; instead, they are positioned as young scientists and proto-conservationists, 'observing changes' and 'exploring'. It would, therefore, be reasonable if this curriculum, when put into practice, did not provide opportunities to develop children's understanding of consumption as an aspect of sustainability.

Interviews with early childhood educators

In order to gain a better sense of the views of those who work with young children, the project team conducted an interview study after obtaining the necessary approval from both the university's and the relevant government department's ethics committees. A total of sixteen practitioners from three sites – two childcare centres that offered a full preschool programme and one kindergarten – accepted the invitation to be interviewed. The interviewees included the directors of each centre. All three centres operate under the auspices of the South Australian Department of Education and Children's Services, and together they covered a wide range of the population. One was located in an affluent area, serving the children of highly educated parents (site 1), another was strongly multicultural (site 2), and the third was located in a neighbourhood of moderately high socio-economic disadvantage (site 3).

Interviews were conducted on site, in staffrooms. The interview time averaged 30 minutes, which was a generous amount of time shared by these exceptionally busy workers. Questions covered two major topics: attitudes to sustainability and consumer culture as subjects for young children's learning. Transcripts were analysed thematically. Despite the differences in their centres' client base, there were strong commonalities found in the ECE workers' answers.

EC educators see sustainability as a suitable topic for young children's learning and development, as well as important for the ethical management of centres as workplaces. When practitioners spoke about sustainability, they often connected the two concerns. At the same time as instituting waste reduction and ecologically friendly initiatives at an organizational level, they engaged children in learning the routines and language that went with being environmentally responsible, as seen in the two examples below.

> We talk about things at group time, about saving our water and in the yard looking after our flowers and our plants. We've got the taps that turn off by themselves, but we talk about that as well. I think that the stepping stone is just using that language before they understand about where the recycling bin goes or where the paper goes or that sort of thing.
>
> (site 1, respondent 1)

> There's nice conversations you can have at lunchtime . . . 'What's left in your bowl, where does that go?'. So talk about, it can go to the chickens, it can go to the special bin that we have here . . . We talk about where that goes and how they break it down and that gives them some sort of background as to what happens to their food when they're finished as opposed to just 'That's your job, that's your routine.'
>
> (site 1, respondent 2)

Most EC educators saw their centre as a non-commercial zone and took active steps to filter out signs of consumer culture. Views ranged from extreme disapproval, particularly of certain kinds of product (e.g. fast food, syndicated characters), to concern that children who lacked particular possessions could feel disadvantaged. Strategies employed to minimize the influence of consumer culture in ECE sites included not purchasing materials featuring syndicated characters, prohibiting children from bringing in personal possessions and discouraging talk about such possessions, as the next three extracts from the interview transcripts show:

> You've got to have everything neutral . . . We don't tend to have any Disney products or any of that sort of stuff, we don't have any books that are in that commercial, really promoted type stuff. Children might bring them from home but we don't tend to have that here in the centre because that's not what we're focused on.
>
> (site 1, respondent 3)

> We encourage children not to bring toys into childcare. And we also don't have toys that have like big stickers that say like *Fairies* [children's tv show], or High Five [children's performers]. Y'know, we play their music, but that's about it.
>
> (site 2, respondent 1)

We try and discourage them I think as much as we can to not talk about all their new fandangled things but it's not any written policy anywhere.

(site 3, respondent 1)

Potentially, the ECE curriculum, as seen in the SACSA framework analysed above, could support educators engaging children in exploring their experiences with consumer culture as an aspect of learning in the areas of futures, identity or thinking. A belief that entering the ECE site means leaving consumer culture at the door, however, makes it difficult for educators to integrate children's learning about sustainability and inter-dependence with their experience of consumption in their everyday lives.

Action research project: 'We love old things'

In this section of the chapter, I describe how the research team responded to the findings of the first phase (above) by designing an intervention using a performing-arts approach. This design followed a pilot study in which we attempted various methods of assisting ECE practitioners to engage children in activities related to the theme of sustainable consumption. The most successful of these activities involved a drama performance. It was decided to run this activity as a research project to collect and analyse data related to children's learning, and ethics approval was again gained from the university and the state government department.

The action research project was designed around an interactive experience called 'We love old things' (WLOT) and was intended to facilitate dialogue with children to explore their understanding and values. The idea of 'loving old things' relates to the theme of sustainable consumption, in that it implicitly challenges the notion that the only things of value are new. The approach engaged children's interest in the concrete nature of experience by using material objects to prompt interaction. It captured their cognitive engagement by using narratives to make connections, for instance, between an object's history and its present value, or between the action of conserving an object and its continued use.

WLOT involved children aged three to four years old at each of the three centres being visited on two occasions by actors playing the parts of 'Molly' and 'May', characters who express a great enthusiasm for 'old things'. On the first occasion, the actors brought a selection of objects to show to and talk about with the children. The objects were selected by the author to represent a wide range of materials and to prompt a range of storylines, with the aim of exploring different meanings related to valuing and conserving existing material culture. The actors were given a brief from which to improvise their roles. This included notes on each of the objects, for example:

- Handmade toy donkey:
  - This is my special donkey – it doesn't look like any other toy.
  - It's handmade – not from a shop.
  - It got a bit torn, but do you think I wanted to throw it away?
  - No, I wanted to keep it, so my grandma mended it.
  - It's still as good as ever.

- Vintage games console:
  - Back in the 80s, this is what people played computer games on.
  - You can still play cool games on this.
  - I'm glad my dad kept this old games console.
  - It still works just fine!
- Piece of petrified wood:
  - This looks like an ordinary stone . . . but it's special.
  - I found it at the beach.
  - My mum says it's maybe thousands of years old.
  - Do you know it used to be part of a tree?
  - It will last for another thousand years!

The performance included children being taught a simple 'rap' song with hand actions:

> Old things rap:
> We love old things, we think they're cool.
> [clap, clap, clap]
> Old things rule!

About a week after the initial performance, 'Molly' and 'May' returned. This time, the children were invited to bring along their own 'old things' from home and to describe what they most valued about them. Parents and caregivers were asked for their consent and sent information about how they could participate:

> You can talk with your child about all the things the child and family have which are old. Ask and talk about the value of these things to the child and others in the family – why they are interesting, useful, special or have a story to tell. This will help broaden your child's mind about all the reasons we have to keep, use and preserve objects even when they are old. You might ask and talk about the ways we have to preserve objects and extend their lives, e.g. repairing, mending, cleaning, handing them down when they are outgrown.
>
> (Excerpt from information for parents)

Data collection and analysis

Both sessions at the centres were recorded using digital video, digital audio and digital still photography. The talk component of interactions was transcribed. Additionally, as some children chose to create drawings of their 'old things' (particularly when these were too large or valuable to bring in), these drawings were photographed.

The main focus of analysis was the interactions between individual children and the 'Molly' or 'May' character. As young children's verbal abilities are still developing, attention to non-verbal communication is important in interpreting their meaning-making. Thus, analysis involved attending to spoken language, gesture, gaze and behaviours with the object. The five questions guiding this analysis were:

1   What object(s) has the child selected to bring in, draw or talk about?
2   How does the child communicate the value of the object?

3   What makes this object important to the child?
4   What is the child's understanding of the concept of 'old' as applied to material things?
5   What is the child's understanding of a possible future for the object?

Children's values and understandings related to 'old things'

In many cultures, babies are given soft toys (such as teddy bears) at birth, and often the child is encouraged to become attached to one of these objects and use it for company, especially at bedtime. Accordingly, it was not surprising to see that many of the children who chose to speak about their special 'old things' nominated a teddy or a similar cuddly toy. For some children, their cot blankets, which might be maintained as a comfort object into childhood, were their chosen 'old thing'. These objects are literally the children's oldest personal possessions, and maintaining possession is an important early experience of investing an object with special significance, as the following transcript of a conversation between a child and one of the actors illustrates:

Molly: Hello! Do you want to tell me about one of your special old things?
Melody: My blanky.
Molly: Your blanky?
Melody: I sleep with it at night.
Molly: And how long have you had your blanky?
Melody: [Holds up six fingers]
Molly: Is your blanky older than you?
Melody: [Nods]
Molly: Who had your blanky before you?
Melody: Um, no-one. I had it when I was a baby.

In several cases, the selected object had been given to the child by a previous owner, such as a parent; see Figure 3.1 for a necklace given by a mother to her daughter. In these cases, the object represented a link to the parent and also to that person's past as a child. A young boy, for example, brought in a set of four metal Matchbox-style toy cars:

Sam: Those are my old old daddy's cars. My daddy's cars.
Molly: Did you say this car belonged to your daddy?
Sam: And the other cars belong to my daddy too.
Molly: Right. So how long has your daddy had these cars?
Sam: He had it when he was a little boy. He was little and I have them.

The preservation and handing-down of childhood objects brings to life, for the child, the reality that the person s/he knows as an adult has been a child. These objects can create a sense of shared experience between older and younger family members, working in the same way as telling stories about 'when I was a little girl/boy'.

The meaning of 'old' is relative. For children, one meaning is in relation to the concept of growth from 'little' to 'big'. Seeing younger siblings come into the world and take possession of items now too small for the child gives her/him a concrete sense of getting older and/or bigger. Emma, for example, began talking about her teddy but soon moved

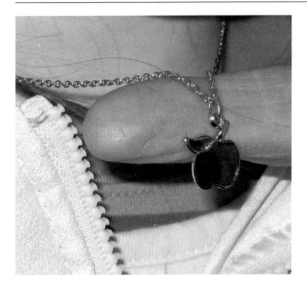

Figure 3.1 A necklace handed down from mother to daughter.
Photo courtesy of the author

to another important topic: 'I like him [teddy] and I've got a cot too. I had a big bed when I was a big girl. But Jordy [brother] he's got a little bed'.

In a relatively short life to date, the persistence of an object for several months may allocate it to the category of 'old' for a young child, as the following exchange shows:

Lachlan: Um I have an old scoop and when it was my birthday I got 'em.
Molly: Right. So are you saying that it's old because you've had it for a while?
Lachlan: Yeah I've had it for fifty-nine days.

When it comes to the future of comfort objects, it seems their status as symbols of childhood may make it hard for children to imagine continuing to value them once childhood is over. Even though his own father had kept the cars, Sam said he would 'chuck them out' when he was a grown up. Celine was similarly unsure about the future prospects of her teddy:

Molly: And what are you going to do with your teddy when you're a big girl?
Celine: My mum's gonna chuck it out.
Molly: How will you feel about that, is that fine?
Celine: Hmm.
Molly: And are you going to have different things then?
Celine: I might have a Ipod and a DX.
Molly: Well that's something to look forward to! Are there any old things that you want to keep forever and ever?
Celine: Uuum my teddy?

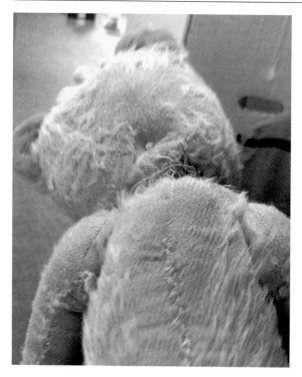

Figure 3.2 Mending on a grandfather's teddy bear.
Photo courtesy of the author

There was evidence in both the appearance of the objects and in the children's talk about them that efforts had been made to conserve these significant possessions. Stella, for instance, said that her teddy had been 'falling apart so mum sewed it back up'. Hamilton brought in a threadbare teddy (see Figure 3.2) which had belonged to his grandfather and was mended in several places.

While many of the examples showed children as gift recipients, others gave insight into children as active consumers. Ethan was less enthusiastic about the subject of 'old things' and keener to talk about his buying power:

Ethan: I didn't bought my things. But I've got a motorbike, a toy motorbike. And that's old.
Molly: Where did you get it?
Ethan: . . .
Molly: Where did it come from?
Ethan: I don't know.
Molly: And why do you like your motorbike?
Ethan: I've got fifty bucks! And I've got some paper money now.
Molly: And what are you going to do with that?
Ethan: Buy lollies.

Even as consumers, however, children are not necessarily always acquiring new possessions. Lachlan, for example, talked about shopping at garage sales. His conversation with Molly is also interesting for his strategies for improving the value of a broken toy:

Lachlan: When I went to a garage sale with my nanna and John and Sam and me, I found a Hot Wheels track that goes and it has four cars and it lost a little white piece.
Molly: Uhuh?
Lachlan: And um I realized when I watched *Toy Story* [children's film] you just have to push the car then they go up [demonstrating] and um the blue thing goes at the end so the cars go zhummm!
Molly: Woooh! So when you watched *Toy Story* you suddenly realized how you could play with that thing.
Lachlan: Yeah. But it lost a piece.
Molly: It did. But could you still play with it a bit?
Lachlan: Yeah. You just have to push it with that [demonstrating]. You just have to do that.

Popular culture is often blamed for enticing children into habits of continual consumption, particularly through the branding of multiple kinds of item with images of well-known characters (see, for example, Beder, 2009). Yet, in the above example, Lachlan explains that a popular movie series, *Toy Story*, was a source of valuable information on how to play with broken toys. Watching *Toy Story* had helped Lachlan discover how to make a broken electric car work by using the power of his hands and his imagination.

Conclusion

This exploration, ranging over areas of academic literature, the early childhood curriculum, ECE practitioners' perspectives and children's responses, has revealed some challenges for, and promising directions in, furthering the agenda of sustainable consumption in childhood. One of these challenges relates to the tension between protecting young children from the consumer marketplace and engaging with children's lives – which include their experiences of desiring, acquiring and managing possessions. It has been argued that educational sites are 'no longer a haven' from the commercial world (Beder, 2009, p3) and that marketers are shaping children from birth into a lifetime of thoughtless addiction to novelty (Lynn, 2004). This kind of nostalgic pessimism is of little use to those who wish to promote active and pragmatic engagement with children and families in order to create a sustainable future.

For many, the most promising direction lies in the 'greening' of early childhood education, as it does with schools more generally. ECE is already embracing some aspects of environmental learning for young children, particularly where these connect with the long history of the discipline's understanding of children as 'natural' beings (recall that the German word *Kindergarten* translates literally to 'children's garden'). Given the dearth of early years'-focused articles in environmental education journals, there is an obvious need for the mainstream environmental education movement to recognize young children and their educators as equally important as those in primary and secondary schools. Recent initiatives, such as the inclusion of childcare centres and preschools in the 'Sustainable Schools' network in Victoria, Australia, are a move in this direction. In many countries, the introduction of curriculum frameworks for the early years has helped environmental learning find a place in ECE curricula.

All of this is positive, but it does not necessarily address the issue of consumption and may even counter such a move, if the 'natural child' is seen as incompatible with the 'material child'. From our interview study, it appears that a certain fear of the influence of consumer culture may be inhibiting ECE practitioners from seeing consumption as a suitable subject for young children's learning. Perhaps, though, these fears give too much credence to the perception that the marketplace is the main influence on children's and families' values. It is worth acknowledging that many of the critiques of marketing to children (such as Lynn, 2004; Beder, 2009) rely on marketers' own claims about their power, claims that should be treated with caution, given that marketers are in the business of selling their ability to influence children.

The project 'We love old things' was a deliberate intervention into this debate in that it invited children and their families to express values other than those that fuel the consumption of the new and the short lived. It was undertaken in the awareness that what we learned from children would not be the whole story. However, it did enable children to share with us the value they place in the continuity of their significant objects. We gained some insights into the efforts children and their carers make to conserve special possessions. Some of the children's stories revealed that they are able to create new lives for old things. Continuity, conservation, redesign – all of these are important elements of sustainability, and they are particularly relevant when considering the place of material culture in sustainability.

The children's voices heard in this project also remind us of something fundamental but easily forgotten by adults – children are growing. As they experience themselves getting bigger and older, they also necessarily discard what they have outgrown and acquire possessions more appropriate to their current needs. Growing up is also a process of aspiring to be bigger, older and more capable. This makes needs and wants much more interwoven and harder to distinguish for children than some sustainability advocates may wish. The implication for those trying to develop a learning agenda related to sustainable consumption is that it should be open to, and build on, children's experiences and values. Children's aspirations to grow and their need to belong make them attractive targets for marketers; by the same token, they hold promise for sustainable futures.

References

Beder, S. (2009) *This Little Kiddy Went to Market: The Corporate Capture of Childhood*, Plutopress, London

Bourdieu, P. (1984) *Distinction: A Social Critique of the Judgement of Taste*, Harvard University Press, Cambridge, MA

Brennan, M. (1996) 'Sustaining new forms of school life? A response to Stuart Macintyre's "Diversity, citizenship and the curriculum"', in K. Kennedy (ed) *New Challenges in Civics and Citizenship Education*, Australian Curriculum Studies Association, Canberra, Australia

Bruntland, G. (1987) *Our Common Future: The World Commission on Environment and Development*, chapter 2: 'Towards Sustainable Development', section 1, from www.un-documents.net/ocf-02.htm#I, accessed on 20 March 2011

Cook, D. (2008) 'The missing child in consumption theory', *Journal of Consumer Culture*, vol 8, no 2, pp219–43

Davis, J. (2005) 'Educating for sustainability in the early years: creating cultural change in a child care setting', *Australian Journal of Environmental Education*, vol 21, pp47–55

Department of Education and Children's Services (DECS) (2001) *South Australian Curriculum Standards and Accountability Framework, Early Years Band*, Government of South Australia, Adelaide, Australia

Department of Education Science and Technology (DEST) (2004) *Sustainable Consumption*, Australian Government, Canberra, Australia

Epp, A. and Price, L. (2008) 'Family identity: a framework of identity interplay in consumption practices', *Journal of Consumer Research*, vol 35, pp50–70

Katz, C. (1994) 'Textures of global change: eroding ecologies of childhood in New York and Sudan', *Childhood*, vol 2, no 1, pp103–10

Lynn, S. (2004) *Consuming Kids: Protecting Our Children From the Onslaught of Marketing and Advertising*, Anchor Books, New York

McGregor, S. (2002) 'Consumer citizenship: a pathway to sustainable development?', keynote paper presented at the International Conference on Developing Consumer Citizenship, Hamar, Norway, April, www.consultmcgregor.com/documents/keynotes/norway_keynote.pdf

Senier, L., Mayer, B., Brown, P. and Morello-Frosh, R. (2007) 'School custodians and green cleaners', *Organization and Environment*, vol 20, no 3, pp304–24

Strife, S. and Downey, L. (2009) 'Childhood development and access to nature: a new direction for environmental inequality research', *Organisation and Environment*, vol, 22, no 1, pp99–122

Young, T. (2009) '"The crack where the light gets in": an examination of sustainable education in early childhood education', lecture given for the de Lissa Oration for Children's Week, Adelaide, Australia, 21 October

Chapter 4

Reducing wasteful household behaviours

Contributions from psychology and implications for intervention design

Sandra Davison, Kirrilly Thompson, Anne Sharp and Drew Dawson

Summary

In the quest for environmental sustainability, there is a pressing need for improved pro-environmental behaviour at the individual and community level. Achieving any type of behaviour change is rarely easy, however, with habitual behaviours and attitudinal resistance creating significant barriers (Zimbardo and Leippe, 1991). Several psychological models, theories and concepts have been put forward to better understand the behaviour change process and to support policymakers. One notable model is the Transtheoretical Model (TTM) of Change (Prochaska and DiClemente, 1983).

The TTM addresses readiness for change and personal barriers to change. It proposes a taxonomy of five change stages that people move through: 'pre-contemplation', 'contemplation', 'planning', 'action' and 'maintenance'. Each stage is measureable, and each stage is characterized by certain behavioural and psychological processes. Although the TTM has been cited as 'arguably the dominant model of health behaviour change' (Armitage, 2009, p195), rarely has it been extended to a pro-environmental behaviour change context.

This chapter outlines the concepts of the TTM and its current position within research, examining its usefulness as a tool to assess readiness for change and as a guide for the improved development of large-scale community interventions or public education programmes. The chapter explores how TTM concepts may offer a simple framework and method for understanding and changing attitudes and behaviours around sustainability, illustrating the discussion in the context of domestic food waste: a wasteful behaviour with significant environmental impact.

Issues around sustainability and behaviour change

Climate change is widely attributed to human behaviour in general (Geller, 1989), and wasteful human behaviour in particular. These behaviours have been addressed by environmentalism and waste management, respectively, from the realism of both research and management (Dwyer, 2009). Governments, for example, have introduced a range of initiatives to encourage increased pro-environmental behaviours (Lyon and Maxwell, 2004).

One of the greatest environmental challenges faced by governments is how effectively to persuade people to develop more environmentally friendly lifestyles and engage in pro-environmental behaviours such as saving and recycling water, conserving energy and reducing the waste of other significant resources, such as food. As the greatest impact in addressing environmental problems usually requires large-scale and long-term changes in people's behaviours, intervention at a public policy level is increasingly needed (Geller, 1989).

The overt marketing of social objectives is often met with consumer resentment and resistance as part of normal human responses to change (Geller, 1989; Carrigan et al, 2004). In these cases, behaviour-change strategies can be viewed by consumers as 'manipulative' or Orwellian (Kotler and Zaltman, 1971). A widespread forced change in behaviour, such as is typical with broad, government-level policy interventions, can cultivate perceptions of domination and cause resentment (Stern et al, 1995; Cherrier, 2006; Wall, 2007), particularly when the behaviour in question is habitual (Carrigan et al, 2004), such as the daily purchase, preparation, consumption and disposal of food. Where there is a risk of voter backlash (Wall, 2005), it is vital for policymakers to understand the impact of policies and the best path to implementation.

Strongly worded calls for action towards sustainability have little effect (Reich and Robertson, 1979), and government initiatives can have trouble graining traction (Davies and Macdonald, 1998). Research has quantitatively identified a weak or at best unclear relationship between attitudes and behaviour (Wicker, 1969; Andreasen, 1994; Davies and Macdonald, 1998; Wright and Klÿn, 1998), especially in the field of environmental attitudes (Scott and Willits, 1994; Wright and Klÿn, 1998), with typical correlations of less than 0.1. Thus, working on attitude change or behavior change alone is unlikely to be effective. Certainly, there may be many members of the general public who are neither listening to, nor accepting, current messages encouraging them to behave more sustainably.

In Australia, statistics suggest that there is a large percentage of the population who could reduce their consumption or waste of fuel, water and food (Australian Bureau of Statistics (ABS), 2006, 2008, 2010). For example, when travelling to work or places of study, 75 per cent of Australians prefer to use private transport as opposed to public transport. Although Australia is the driest inhabited continent on earth, 46 per cent of Australians do not use any grey water in their house or garden, and only 21 per cent of Australian households have a tank to harvest rainwater. Each household in Australian discards 17.7kg of waste each week, and Australians have been shown to waste over €3.6 billion worth of food annually (Baker et al, 2009).

Domestic food waste

Domestic food waste is a behaviour that is psychologically, socially and culturally entrenched and that has significant environmental impact, but that has shown to be resistant to behaviour-change initiatives. As noted by Lupton (1996, p1),

> food and eating habits are banal practices of everyday life; we all . . . must eat to survive. This apparent banality, however, is deceptive. Food and eating habits and preferences are not simply matters of 'fuelling' ourselves, alleviating hunger pangs, or taking enjoyment in gustatory sensations. Food and eating are central to our subjectivity, or sense of self.

Given the centrality of food to human existence and identity, it is no surprise that food purchase, storage, preparation, sharing, consumption and disposal are all habitual behaviours that are resistant to change. Behaviours and attitudes that result in food wastage are implicated in all of these stages of the domestic food chain.

While food riots are occurring in some countries, developed countries exhibit staggering levels of household food waste. Various studies estimate food losses and wastage of up to 50 per cent between production and consumption (Jones, 2005; Lundqvist et al, 2008). In Australia, food thrown away by households each year is equivalent to AU$616 (€460.68) per household, or AU$239 (€178.74) per person (Baker et al, 2009). In addition to being a waste of individuals' income, this waste has substantial economic, environmental and social impacts.

Food waste results in the depletion of natural resources, the emission of greenhouse gases and pressure on landfills, and a strain on food systems and security. The majority of this waste could be minimized or avoided if households adopted better food-management practices (Schneider, 2008; Ventour, 2008). This potential is being recognized internationally in the media (*The Age*, 2008; *The Economist*, 2009; Stuart, 2009; *The Sunday Telegraph*, 2009) and by government, industry and community groups, evidenced by their growing levels of activity around household food waste (IGD, 2007; Food Wise, 2009; United States Environmental Protection Agency, 2009; Neverwaste, 2010).

Increasing environmental behaviour

Important issues arise when endeavouring to increase environmental behaviours, including those related to a reduction of domestic food waste. Behaviour is a very complicated process to understand, with many underlying influences such as attitudes, values and beliefs, cognitions, motivation, prior learning, and social and cultural influences (Zimbardo and Leippe, 1991; Watson and Tharp, 2007). Research has highlighted many barriers to behaviour change. These include, but are certainly not limited to, competing personal needs and wants, time, financial costs, perceived discomfort or inconvenience, low motivation, personal values, status, behavioural opportunities, social norms, moral norms, intentions, choice or perceived choice, old, established attitudes, behaviours and habits (Zimbardo and Leippe, 1991; Bamberg and Möser, 2007; Pelletier et al, 2008; Arbuthnott, 2009; Kazdin, 2009). Beyond these predominantly intangible or conceptual barriers are physical barriers, such as the planning of domestic houses, the layout of rooms and the affordances of furniture and technologies (Sobal and Wansink, 2007).

As Zimbardo and Leippe (1991) noted, environmental problems are not always clearly visible, and, even when they are, many people do not see a connection between their own behaviours and environmental problems and possible solutions. Even if a connection is made, a behaviour change may not follow, for a variety of competing factors. A vast amount of human behaviour is also maintained by reinforcement. Well-established behaviours, such as food consumption and food waste, have usually been practised and reinforced across lifetimes and generations, to an extent that they have become entrenched habits or automatic responses (Watson and Tharp, 2007).

The habitual nature of much consumer behaviour, combined with resistance to change, presents significant challenges to successful and lasting behaviour change. In seeking to change something as complex as environmental behaviour, several important questions arise. How do we ready people for change? How do we know when people are ready to change? How do people develop pro-environmental behaviours? How can they be encouraged to relinquish entrenched behaviours?

In order to consider change, people need information they can accept, new skills they believe they can develop and, most important of all, they need the motivation to change. Self-knowledge is also an important precursor to self-change (Watson and Tharp, 2007). Before thinking about changing a behaviour, people need to reflect on their current behaviours, what they are doing and could be doing. Likewise, if large-scale community education programmes are developed, those charged with their creation first need to know as much as possible about their target audience. In response to barriers to personal behaviour change, policymakers need to understand how best to provide information to assist change and what calls to action are appropriate at given times. Information has to be accepted and acted upon to be effective (Zimbardo and Leippe, 1991), yet consumers are skilled at screening out much of the communication efforts to which they are exposed. So another set of questions arise. How and when should information be transmitted to people in the community? How do people discriminate in an information-saturated environment? How best can a 'cut-through' be achieved?

One model that has had great success in changing behaviours is the TTM. This model has been used extensively in public-health and social marketing to address harmful health behaviours, such as smoking and excessive use of alcohol. However, the model has not yet been applied to harmful environmental behaviours such as food waste.

In the following section, we describe the TTM. Owing to its popularity in public-health campaigns, most of our examples are drawn from health literature. This review is followed by an application of the TTM to food waste behaviours.

The transtheoretical model

The TTM is a psychological model of behaviour that identifies behaviour-change stages and behaviour-change processes. The TTM has been shown to be an effective model in assessing individual readiness for change and a useful guide for envisioning a developmental trajectory associated with behaviour change (Tierney and McCabe, 2005; Spencer et al, 2006). The delivery of different messages to people at different times during decision-making processes is not a new idea in social marketing. However, the TTM may extend this method of delivery. The TTM offers a useful framework for when and how to deliver messages, and the model attaches a strong psychological and cognitive component to the internal processes that are believed to be related to change. In addition, the TTM is not complicated to apply, and the simple and logical stages of change it identifies provide an understanding of the overall change process for both laypeople and professionals.

Although there do not appear to be any published studies that assess the TTM's application to community environmental behaviours, the model, either in part or in its entirety, has been applied in many other behavioural contexts, to a wide range of people. These include: sex offenders (Tierney and McCabe, 2005); quality improvement in the workplace (Levesque et al, 2001); adolescent offenders (Hemphill and Howell, 2000); cancer screening (Spencer et al, 2005); depression (Lewis et al, 2009); blood donors (Burditt et al, 2009); eating low-fat food (Armitage et al, 2004); gambling (Petry, 2005); substance abuse (DiClemente et al, 2004); and physical activity (Nigg et al, 2005).

The TTM is an integrative model of change that developed from an analysis of different theories of psychotherapy, including behavioural, cognitive, experiential, humanistic and psychoanalytic therapies (Prochaska et al, 1994), hence the name 'transtheoretical', as the concepts of the model span several theories. The TTM was originally devised in the context of health behaviour change for cigarette smoking (Prochaska and DiClemente, 1983). The model has been shown to be effective in assessing smokers' readiness for change and also as a guide for the provision of information to assist with quitting (Prochaska and Norcross, 2001; Velicer et al, 2007). Cigarette smoking is a highly addictive behaviour that is perceived by the smoker as having rewarding consequences in the short term (relaxation, pleasant feelings, an activity that can be shared socially). These typically outweigh the long-term consequences (such as poor health and reduced quality of life). The TTM may be equally useful for environmental behaviours such as those related to consumption and waste, as these behaviours provide similar trade-offs. For example, enjoying long, hot showers, buying large amounts of food for convenience (even if some is ultimately wasted) or driving to work alone in a motor vehicle as opposed to using public transport. All these behaviours provide some immediate personal benefits, with little thought for long-term environmental consequences, or even long-term personal consequences.

TTM constructs

The TTM is a multidimensional model and includes four separate but related dimensions or 'constructs'. These constructs are: the stages of change, the processes of change, 'decisional balance' and 'self-efficacy'. The constructs are believed to interact with one another as a person is considering, or attempting, a change in behaviour. For this reason, it is important to address all four constructs when developing behaviour-change programmes based on the TTM (Spencer et al, 2005).

Stages of change

Within the first construct, there are five stages of change that people are presumed to move through (in full or part) as they change a behaviour. The first stage is 'pre-contemplation', where a person is unlikely to identify any need for change or recognize that current behaviours need to change. The second stage is 'contemplation', where a person has given some serious thought to the idea of making a specific change, although they have not yet made a change. Next is a 'preparation' stage, which is predominantly a planning stage. Following preparation, a person will move into the 'action' stage. Once at the action stage, a person is acting in the desired manner. That is, they have either ceased an undesirable behaviour and/or acquired a new behaviour. The final stage is a 'maintenance' stage, which is defined by time, with the criterion of behaving in the desired manner for at least six months.

Although the stages are theorized qualitatively, they have been subject to extensive quantitative evaluation. The most common method for measuring the stages appears to be by use of a staging algorithm (Armitage et al, 2004; Spencer et al, 2006). As a categorical measure, the stages-of-change algorithm is usually a set of four or five simple questions or statements about a current behaviour. Responses are matched to a specific

Table 4.1 A suggested stages-of-change algorithm to measure a current food-waste behaviour

Notes:

(i) 'Food waste' refers to any food scraps (including bones), any unwanted leftover food, and/or any food that is unable to be consumed owing to its condition or because it is no longer wanted

(ii) Disposing of household food waste in an 'environmentally friendly manner' would refer to one or more of the following behaviours:

- placing food waste in a garden compost bin or compost heap;
- feeding food waste to worms in your worm farm;
- feeding food waste to an animal (dog, chickens, other);
- passing food waste to another person for use in one or more of the above manners.

Item 1	Do you currently dispose of all your household food waste in an environmentally friendly manner?	YES/NO
Item 2	Do you intend to dispose of all your household food waste in an environmentally friendly manner within the next 6 months?	YES/NO
Item 3	Do you intend to dispose of all your household food waste in an environmentally friendly manner within the next 30 days?	YES/NO
Item 4	Have you been regularly disposing of all your household food waste in an environmentally friendly manner for the past six months?	YES/NO

Scoring

If item 1 = no and item 2 = no: pre-contemplation stage
If item 1 = no and item 2 = yes: contemplation stage
If item 1 = no and item 3 = yes: preparation stage
If item 1 = yes and item 4 = no: action stage
If item 1 = yes and item 4 = yes: maintenance stage

stage. Participants either tick the one statement most like them, or, in some studies, participants provide yes/no responses. In an adaptation of previous tables (for example that used by Nigg et al, 2005), Table 4.1 presents an example of an algorithm that may provide information about a population's current disposal of food waste and its near-future intentions for disposal.

Staging algorithms can be arbitrary. Indeed, one criticism of the TTM has been the lack of a consistent instrument for measurement and the requirement to tailor it to the context in which behaviour change is sought. For example, Grant and Franklin (2007) adapted an algorithm to suit student study habits, with the pre-contemplation stage of their algorithm being 'I haven't given it any thought, and at present I do not intend to deliberately try to improve the way that I go about my studies' (Grant and Franklin, 2007, p103). In contrast to criticisms about inconsistent methods of measurement, the ability to tailor algorithms can also be seen as one of the model's strengths. Staging algorithms could be tailored to suit a variety of consumer behaviours with environmental impacts, such as those related to the use of food, water and power.

Other more elaborate questionnaires to measure the stages of change have also been developed. Examples include the University of Rhode Island Change Assessment Scale (URICA; McConnaughy et al, 1983) and the Stages of Change Readiness and Treatment Eagerness Scale (SOCRATES; Miller and Tonigan, 1996). Both of these are multiple-item questionnaires (with multiple scales) that measure behaviour, attitudes and motivation and were designed as more subtle measures of the stages, for use with mental health patients and substance abusers, especially those who may be entering treatment (DiClemente et al, 2004).

Decisional balance and self-efficacy

'Decisional balance', a second TTM construct, is the weighing up of the pros and cons related to performing a specific problem behaviour (Prochaska et al, 1994). However, decisional balance may also relate to the pros and cons of changing a problem behaviour. As individuals advance through the stages of change, decisional balance is likewise expected to change. Prochaska et al (1994) were able to show a cross-over from higher cons to higher pros as people moved through the stages of change in several health behaviour-related case studies. Similarly, after reviewing thirty-eight studies related to energy conservation, Abrahamse et al (2005) included in their recommendations the importance of problem diagnosis. Examination of factors that may help or hinder sustainable behaviour patterns (in other words, identifying barriers and enablers) would assist in identifying areas to be targeted by programme developers.

A third TTM construct is the use of the psychological concept of 'self-efficacy' (Bandura, 1982), which can be described as a person's belief in their own ability to perform or achieve a particular task. Higher self-efficacy is related to a greater likelihood that the specific behaviour will be successfully performed. Self-efficacy would most likely increase as stage progression occurs and has been noted as a significant predictor of waste management behaviour (Barr, 2007).

Decisional balance and self-efficacy are usually measured with simple Likert-type scales (with responses to a selection of relevant items ranging from strongly disagree to strongly agree). The number of actual items varies according to the behaviour and the type of study. For example, when assessing smokers, Schorr et al (2008) administered two five-item scales for decisional balance, and self-efficacy was assessed with a nine-item scale. Similar scales could be easily adapted for pro-environmental behaviours.

Processes of change

The final TTM construct, 'processes of change', relates to ten specific cognitive and behavioural processes, or strategies, that people may use or experience as they progress through the different stages of change. According to Norcross et al (2011, p144), 'The Stages of Change represent when people change; the Processes of Change entail how people change.' The processes have been used to explain how movement occurs through the stages in a variety of health behaviours, including smoking cessation (Prochaska et al, 1988), diabetes management (Gambling and Long, 2006) and mammography screening (Pruitt et al, 2010). Based on the processes of change (Tierney and McCabe, 2005; Prochaska and Norcross, 2010), Table 4.2 lists the ten processes of change and includes examples of corresponding areas that could be addressed in community education programmes, in order to encourage these processes and thus encourage people to change or to maintain change in environmental behaviours.

It is important to match the right process with the right stage, and at the right time, as a person will be more receptive to certain information or certain strategies at different stages (Perz et al, 1996; Prochaska and Norcross, 2010). For example, the first five

Table 4.2 Processes of change

Process	Areas that might be addressed
1 Consciousness raising	Provide information that can be accepted. Increase awareness of causes and consequences. Encourage positive ideas about succeeding.
2 Dramatic relief	Acknowledge emotions involved in changing.
3 Environmental re-evaluation	Note the benefits for an environment and for others if a change is made.
4 Self-re-evaluation	Help to hold on to and actualize some core values but to let go of others. Highlight intrinsic benefits. Decrease guilt.
5 Self-liberation	Foster the belief that change is possible. Encourage autonomy and commitment to change.
6 Social liberation	Note ability to influence the environment, to behave in socially acceptable ways.
7 Counter conditioning	Suggest alternative behaviours to replace an unwanted behaviour, or alternative ways of thinking about a problem or unwanted behaviour.
8 Helping relationships	Encourage social support and sharing of ideas.
9 Stimulus control	Emphasize triggers that maintain an unwanted behaviour, or hinder a new behaviour. Introduce new triggers to help change to a new behaviour.
10 Reinforcement management	Identify what may be supporting the unwanted behaviour. Introduce new rewards for a new behaviour. Highlight positive consequences of making a change.

processes of change are experiential or cognitive-affective processes thought to occur mostly in the early stages of change. This is when cognitive processes are most likely to be taking place, so this would be an ideal time to present information and ideas to encourage thought about environmental issues. The remaining five processes are more behavioural and may be more relevant to the action stage. At this stage of change, strategies should concentrate on information and opportunities to act in more environmentally friendly ways.

Hutchison et al (2009) noted some reported differences in the timing of behavioural and experiential processes between cigarette-smoking behaviour and physical-activity behaviour. Rosen (2000) reviewed forty-seven studies that all assessed the change processes and likewise noted some timing differences between some behaviours. However, for cigarette smoking, as predicted by the TTM, Rosen (2000) was also able to provide strong evidence for the use of experiential processes during early stages and behavioural processes mostly in the action stage. For example, in that review, over 84 per cent of all studies relating to health problems indicated the use of committing to change (a self-liberation process) and substituting new behaviours for old behaviours (a counter-conditioning process) in the action stage. This ability to match processes of change with stages of change (as relevant to a specific behaviour being targeted for change) demonstrates the flexibility of the TTM, especially as past research has shown that different psychological and contextual variables are associated with different environmental behaviours (Poortinga et al, 2004; Barr, 2007).

Targeting, tailoring or matching strategies

According to Noar et al (2007), most health-education materials could be described as 'targeted' communication, where messages are developed for specific segments of a population, whereas 'tailored' messages are individualized for each person. Stage 'matching' usually refers to interventions adapted to the psychological characteristics of people at different stages (Dijkstra et al, 2006), and it would be expected that TTM stage-matched interventions would address those factors associated with the processes of change at a particular stage of change. The best method of testing the true value of matching interventions to stages would be to include both matched and mismatched conditions, but few studies have done so. However, research by Dijkstra et al (2006) has provided some support for the matching of interventions by including both matched and mismatched conditions. Results indicated matched interventions were significantly more effective than mismatched interventions in promoting forward stage progression from pre-contemplation and contemplation stages.

Strategies for change, based on TTM assessments, have been customized or tailored for individual people, with past studies often including more than 1000 and sometimes more than 5000 participants (Prochaska and Norcross, 2001; Nigg et al, 2005). Compared with non-tailored information, tailored information can be more effective in attracting attention and in promoting greater comprehension and retention (Kreuter and Holt, 2001). Smoking cessation is one area where TTM studies have used tailored information to encourage behaviour change.

Information tailored on TTM constructs has been presented via stage-matched manuals, proactive phone calls and individual computer feedback generated from mail or telephone questions known as 'expert systems' (Prochaska and Norcross, 2001). The expert system involves the development of up to 20,000 computer-generated pieces of information. A participant receives information based on his/her responses to an initial questionnaire, with information advising him/her of his/her stage of change and the appropriate processes of change. In TTM studies, this individualized approach usually consists of a letter that begins by outlining the person's stage of change and then provides appropriate information for that stage. Prochaska and colleagues (Prochaska et al, 2001; Prochaska and Norcross, 2001) were able to show that the use of the expert system achieved significantly higher smoking abstinence rates than a control assessment group. Adding additional interventions (counselling and additional instruction materials) to the expert system did not increase effectiveness, and the extra instruction materials actually produced a significantly lower rate of abstinence eighteen months later.

One population-based study of 1277 overweight or obese participants demonstrated that fully tailored, TTM-based, multiple interventions were effective one year post-intervention, as measured by a progression to action and maintenance stages (Johnson et al, 2008). Tailored feedback (based on all TTM constructs) was provided initially and then at three, six and nine months and was related to improved healthy eating, increased exercise, managing emotional distress and weight loss. This appears to be one of the few studies where multiple behaviours were addressed in the same study.

Noar et al (2007) presented a meta-analytic review of fifty-six studies related to tailored print health messages intended to persuade people to change a health behaviour. Among concepts that produced larger effect sizes were stages of change and processes of change, as well as self-efficacy. The authors concluded that tailored messages were more effective than non-tailored messages, and that existing evidence suggests this type of message may be cost effective. Participation rates up to 80 per cent in past studies (Prochaska and Norcross 2001) suggest that tailoring information based on TTM constructs may also be effective in recruiting larger numbers of people in the general community.

Although the stages of change and the processes of change have been applied successfully to individuals, often in large numbers, there is scant evidence of TTM-based community interventions presented simultaneously to a whole community. Yet it may be that a series of information-type interventions that are matched to each stage, and the TTM constructs associated with that stage, could be presented over time, to suit a large group of people, although those people would be in different stages of change. For example, it may be possible for mass-media environmental education campaigns to be delivered to the general public. Such community campaigns may be able to address many, if not all, of the areas that are currently addressed in individual tailored letters and matched strategies that have frequently been used in successful TTM studies.

Limitations of the TTM

Although shown to be an effective model that can promote behaviour change in a variety of situations, the TTM has not escaped criticism. Conceptually, many criticisms of the TTM have been largely semantic. Suggestions have been made that the TTM stages of change may only be simple points along a continuum, rather than truly independent stages requiring capitalization (Belding et al, 1996; Hemphill and Howell, 2000; Napper et al, 2008; Dishman et al, 2009). As Herzog (2010) has stated, there is little empirical support for a discrete set of stages. However, these criticisms are based on an assumption that the model reflects 'real' stages of change, rather than conceding that it identifies probable stages for the specific purpose of providing an analytic model. Regardless of whether the TTM is envisaged as discrete stages, a continuum, or something else, its usefulness in understanding the readiness of a population to change has been established. Most importantly, the TTM indicates where behaviour change efforts should be targeted for increased success, and the form of the messages that should be employed.

Other criticisms of the TTM relate to practicalities of its application and evaluation. Armitage (2009) has noted that the stages-of-change construct is frequently used in isolation from the other dimensions of the TTM. Hutchison and colleagues' (2009) review of twenty-four TTM-based interventions related to physical activity behaviour change found that all twenty-four studies referred to the stages of change. Only seven of the studies developed interventions based on all four dimensions of the TTM. Six of those studies did produce effective results (mostly short term), in terms of significant stage progression or significantly increased activity-related variables when TTM-based interventions were compared with controls. At the same time, 71 per cent of studies that were based only on the stages of change also produced significant short-term results. Hutchison and his fellow reviewers (2009) concluded that there are numerous inconsistencies in the application of reported TTM interventions, and thus at present it is impossible accurately to assess the usefulness of the TTM.

As previously noted, there are no standardized methods for administering TTM questionnaires or algorithms. Consequently, comparisons of studies and evaluations of the model can be difficult. In a meta-analysis related to cancer, Spencer and colleagues (2005) noted several different methods of measuring stages of change in relation to mammography studies. One measure was specifically designed for mammography; a measure used in one study had been designed for tobacco use; and some measures were ones that had not been published previously.

An applied example: household food waste reduction and the TTM

After reviewing the literature on behaviour change and the TTM and its application in the area of health, there does appear to be significant potential for applying the TTM to the area of environmental behaviour. Although further empirical research is required to evaluate this potential, and to identify how the stages and processes may fit specific pro-environmental behaviours, we provide a hypothetical application of the TTM. In light of its environmental impact, the topic of food waste offers a complex case study for considering the TTM's application to pro-environmental behaviours.

The TTM and food waste

Initial surveys could identify the key barriers to reducing food waste that policy intervention might address. Decisional balance scales could identify the perceived pros and cons relevant to the reduction of household food waste. The cons may include the perceived inconvenience of, for example, the effort required to write a shopping list, check food stocks and/or create recipes to reuse leftover food. The perceived pros may include the financial gain from wasting less food, the positive feelings associated with more efficient use of food in the home and the added benefit of having to cook less often because leftovers are used more frequently. Self-efficacy scales could measure individual perceptions of ability to undertake the new behaviours required to reduce household waste: for example, the ability to compost food or to store food more efficiently.

Completing surveys based on TTM constructs may also encourage members of the general public to acknowledge their current beliefs, intentions and behaviours relating to specific food practices in the home. It is likely that some people may not yet have given any thought to how environmental issues connect to their own food-management behaviour. Some may not even realize the environmental implications of food waste.

The inclusion of a stages-of-change algorithm in large-scale surveys would provide a baseline regarding a population's aggregate stage of readiness for reducing food waste. Using the TTM stages-of-change construct could guide the development of novel community education programmes based on stage-matched information and strategies for change. A staggered series of messages and mass-media presentations could be delivered over time. Each presentation could focus on a separate stage of change, with the content and delivery relating to relevant processes of change. The first presentation would consist of message content that was appropriate for the first stage of change, for all pre-contemplators in the community. This could be followed, at a later time, by a second presentation, where the content was relevant for those members of the community who may be in the next stage of change (those contemplating a change in behaviour), and so on. Thus, the presentation of information would develop over time, targeting and attracting the attention of new groups of people in the community, as the content of specific presentations addressed that group's particular stage of change.

Matching programme content with TTM stages and also the processes of change would allow appropriate environmental information and strategies to capture people in every stage of change, from those who are not contemplating any change to their usual behaviour to those who are already practising some pro-environmental behaviour. With thought and planning, large community programmes directed at educating the general public about food waste could present a considerable number of useful strategies and messages. Some brief examples of how decisional balance, self-efficacy and the rationale of the processes of change could be presented in stage-matched messages to help reduce food waste follow.

Pre-contemplation stage and food waste

For those not contemplating any change, the general public's knowledge about environmental issues and awareness about personal behaviours could be increased (Doppelt, 2008). A useful focus for large-scale community messages could be making a connection between throwing away food and the effects of that behaviour on the environment, by explaining the harmful amounts of gas that rotting food produces and the wasted fertilizers, water and petrol or other fuels involved in the food supply chain. These types of strategy address the 'consciousness-raising' process of change.

Figure 4.1 'Pre-contemplation' stage: typical domestic food waste headed to municipal waste.
Photo courtesy of Kerry Thompson, Adelaide, SA, 2011

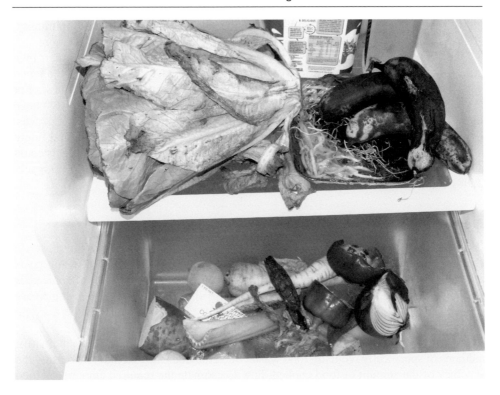

Figure 4.2 'Pre-contemplation' stage: refrigerators are the source of much food waste.
Photo courtesy of Sandra Davison, Adelaide, SA, 2011

At this initial stage, people may also be encouraged to consider behaviours they have changed in the past and also any pro-environmental behaviours they may already perform (e.g. they may recycle, even in a small way). Considering these past positive situations may help raise self-efficacy, a personal belief in the ability to make positive changes to behaviours associated with the purchase, use and disposal of food. Highlighting past desirable behaviour has been shown to encourage people to see themselves as more environmentally friendly (Cornelissen et al, 2008). That is, people can realign their self-perceived identity with the identity desired of the change strategy and consequently become more likely to act in a pro-environmental manner in other areas.

Contemplation stage and food waste

At this second stage of change, people have reached a stage of considering some change in the future. However, they are not yet ready for change, requiring in essence 'a little push'. To address this stage, a community message might ask people to consider the personal and environmental benefits of not wasting food. A list of benefits could be presented for consideration, and these might include monetary savings, interesting new menus to avoid food waste, new activities such as worm farms, composting and gardening, home-grown food and the sharing of produce within the community. Addressing these areas would help to encourage the process of self re-evaluation.

The contemplation stage is an appropriate time to ask people to identify their own core beliefs and values and critically reflect on the extent to which they are aligned with their current behaviour. Ambivalence, or mental conflict about acting one way or another, may begin to build up once people start to connect their own personal beliefs, their current behaviour and any associated negative environmental consequences. Explaining how global warming and certain behaviours may affect current and future generations and how reducing food waste can contribute to avoiding those effects could also create internal conflict and be a powerful motivator for change at this time (Doppelt, 2008).

Preparation stage and food waste

If people can be motivated to reach the preparation stage, they are moving closer to change. This could be the right time to encourage people to think about setting goals and making a commitment to change. Building in choices, or perception of choices, is also important. Making choices can enhance a sense of personal control and can increase self-efficacy, while choice, or a perception of choice, has been shown to be a strong component of an effective commitment (Cialdini, 1993).

Messages might now offer choices by presenting various acceptable, alternative methods of specifically reducing food waste. Such methods may include: increasing the accuracy of the amount of food cooked; how to estimate the required amounts of food to purchase; or learning new ways to combine leftovers for a meal. Examples of possible goal statements or commitments would be, 'next week I will purchase a compost bin' or 'next week I will make a start by only purchasing sufficient food for three days' meals' or 'commencing next shopping day I will adhere to purchasing only those food items that are on a prepared shopping list'.

Highlighting the positive consequences of achieving new goals would also be important to increase motivation and to help address the change process of 'reinforcement management'. The change process of 'stimulus control' could also be addressed by the provision of additional rewards or incentives to encourage positive behaviours. Incentives may be in the form of monetary rebates (reductions or refunds for the cost of compost bins and worm farms) or perhaps the free provision of small kitchen bins for the daily collection of any unavoidable kitchen food scraps (for later transfer to garden compost or worm farms).

Action stage

Ongoing strategies would still be required to encourage behaviours such as planning meals, adhering to a shopping list, reducing the accumulation of unused stored foods, preparing new recipes for leftovers and composting kitchen scraps. Public campaigns could help highlight these behaviours by the use of visual media messages that depict family 'models' acting in a desired manner. For example, messages could depict a family cooking a second meal with leftover food, or physically transferring small amounts of food waste to a compost bin, as a routine daily behaviour, and then show the benefits of compost use in their flourishing vegetable garden. Social learning theory (Bandura,

Figure 4.3 'Action' stage: a convenient means of storing food waste prior to environmentally friendly disposal.

Photo courtesy of Sandra Davison, Adelaide, SA, 2011

1977) states that people can learn new behaviours by observing and then imitating the behaviours of others.

Reminders about the positive consequences of behaving in ways that reduce food waste would also help strengthen and reinforce those new behaviours (and thus further address the process of 'reinforcement management'). Positives that could again be highlighted could include reduced shopping times through adhering to shopping lists, better, tastier planned and prepared meals, monetary savings, more organization and space in cupboards and fridges, fresh, home-grown vegetables, contributions to future sustainability and a sense of personal achievement, satisfaction and pride.

Maintenance stage

Information presented for an action stage could also fit for the maintenance stage. Incentives and ongoing reminders about the positive consequences of reducing food waste could help encourage the maintenance of new behaviours and may help prevent people reverting to former wasteful behaviours.

Personal effort is not only needed to change, it is also needed to maintain change, and sometimes that effort can wane. Therefore, addressing any relapse to wasteful food behaviours would be a crucial task during this final stage. Slipping back to old behaviours is not uncommon during any change process (Watson and Tharp, 2007), but a lapse to old behaviours does not mean failure and does not indicate that a person is incapable of change. Towards the end of any community campaign, it would be helpful to address the possibility of slipping back into old behaviours and the importance of not giving up, but instead starting over again, by recommencing the new behaviours.

Figure 4.4 'Action' and 'maintenance' stages: compost bins can blend in well with the gardens that composted food helps to grow.

Photo courtesy of Sandra Davison, Adelaide, SA, 2011

People may resume previously established behaviours owing to short-term rewards such as convenience and the comfort they experience when returning to an old habit (Watson and Tharp, 2007). For example, if simply placing any excess food straight into a generic garbage bin was an original behaviour, then returning to this habit would probably seem a quick, easy and convenient way to dispose of food. For a time, the effects of that behaviour on landfill and the environment could be easily ignored. Hence, restating the positive consequences of reducing food waste, reminding people about increased benefits for significant others, strengthening self-efficacy and the repetition of previous encouraging strategies could all be included when addressing the final stage of maintenance.

Evaluation of a TTM-based community food-waste campaign

There are numerous methods (charts, tables, symbols, diaries) that could be introduced during and after a change programme, in order to help people plot their stages of change

Figure 4.5 'Action' and 'maintenance' stages: a worm farm. Thousands of worms dispose of food, turning waste food into both liquid and solid garden fertilizer.

Photo courtesy of Sandra Davison, Adelaide, SA, 2011

and their progress with food-waste reduction over time. Large groups of people in the community could be invited to complete ongoing measures at various time intervals. Self-reporting would be a means of self-monitoring, which can help people maintain awareness of their current behaviours around food-waste reduction. Self-observation and self-reporting can also help maintain motivation (Watson and Tharp, 2007).

During campaigns to reduce food waste, TTM constructs would also be useful means of providing feedback to programme developers. The simple stages-of-change algorithm could be repeated at intervals in time, either as a subjective yes/no measure or combined with an objective measure (for example, the actual amount of food wasted weekly, and/or the monetary cost of food purchased weekly). Information from reassessments or additional phone or mail surveys could be a method of evaluating the effect that information and other strategies about food-waste reduction may be having on a community. The advantage of having five individual stages of change allows for easy assessment of stage progression, and also stage regression. The value of this feedback is that strategies for reducing food waste could then be addressed and adapted as necessary, either during a campaign, or when creating future campaigns.

Throughout, the marketing challenge remains the diminished salience of the messages at the time when a targeted behaviour is likely to be performed. Often, the message is no longer salient when the opportunity for the desired behaviour arises. Messages from mass media are encountered at times far removed from the moment when there is an opportunity to respond to the call to action with a change to the desirable behaviour. A key challenge, then, is for policymakers to try and have message exposure as close to the point of action as possible. This will maximize the likelihood that the messages will be salient at the time for action. An example of achieving this call-to-action close to the point of behaviour relevant to food waste is having correct storage information for fruit and vegetables printed on the plastic separation bags that are provided on a roll at supermarkets. If, for example, the bag has instructions that a particular fruit should be stored in the fridge to maximize its life, then there is a greater chance that this information will be seen and acted upon as the groceries are unpacked.

Conclusions and future steps

There is an urgent need to increase the adoption of pro-environmental behaviours in the community. This can only be achieved by large-scale behaviour change, but behaviour is complicated, and its habitual nature means it is difficult to change. Effective methods of community education and behaviour change are needed to increase the general public's awareness of environmental problems, and to help large numbers of people become more motivated and contribute more to solving those problems. Although the TTM is well established as a behaviour model for change in relation to public-health issues, it has not been well evaluated in relation to environmental behaviours where it could be effective. The TTM stands out as one psychological model of change that could provide a reliable framework for the delivery of messages to encourage increased pro-environmental behaviours.

The TTM appears to have the potential to guide large community education programmes that target pro-environmental behaviours and thus offers a way forward for policymakers and other change agents. For this reason, the TTM could be applied to the reduction of food waste – a key issue facing policymakers. As an example of a complex socio-psychological and cultural behaviour, our hypothetical application of the TTM to food waste suggests that the TTM could be easily adapted in relation to any environmental behaviour. Further research is required to substantiate this claim empirically. Although the TTM originated in psychology, further research by multi-disciplinary research teams would be useful. Human behaviour is inherently social and cultural and can be understood from the perspectives of economics, politics and gender, as well as those offered by design and architecture. Experts in these domains should be collaboratively engaged to deal with the problem of environmental behaviour change.

References

Abrahamse, W., Steg, L., Vlek, C. and Rothengatter, T. (2005) 'A review of intervention studies aimed at household energy conservation', *Journal of Environmental Psychology*, vol 25, no 3, pp273–91
Andreasen, A. R. (1994) 'Social marketing: its definition and domain', *Journal of Public Policy and Marketing*, vol 13, no 1, pp108–14

Arbuthnott, K. D. (2009) 'Education for sustainable development beyond attitude change', *International Journal of Sustainability in Higher Education*, vol 10, no 2, pp152–63

Armitage, C. J. (2009) 'Is there utility in the transtheoretical model?', *British Journal of Health Psychology*, vol 14, pp195–210

Armitage, C. J., Sheeran, P., Conner, M. and Arden, M. A. (2004) 'Stages of change or changes of stage? Predicting transitions in transtheoretial model stages in relation to healthy food choice', *Journal of Consulting and Clinical Psychology*, vol 72, no 3, pp491–9

Australian Bureau of Statistics (2006) *Environmental Issues: People's Views and Practices*, no 4602.0, Australian Bureau of Statistics, Canberra, Australia

Australian Bureau of Statistics (2008) *Australian Social Trends*, no 4613.0, Australian Bureau of Statistics, Canberra, Australia

Australian Bureau of Statistics (2010) *Australia's Environment: Issues and Trends*, no 4613.0, Australian Bureau of Statistics, Canberra, Australia

Baker, D., Fear, J. and Denniss, R. (2009) *What a Waste: An Analysis of Household Expenditure on Food*, The Australia Institute, Canberra, Australia

Bamberg, S. and Möser, G. (2007) 'Twenty years after Hines, Hungerford, and Tomera: a new meta-analysis of psychosocial determinants of pro-environmental behaviour', *Journal of Environmental Psychology*, vol 27, no 1, pp14–25

Bandura, A. (1977) *Social Learning Theory*, Prentice Hall, Englewood Cliffs, NJ

Bandura, A. (1982) 'Self-efficacy mechanism in human agency', *American Psychologist*, vol 37, pp122–47

Barr, S. (2007) 'Factors influencing environmental attitudes and behaviours: a UK case study of household waste management', *Environment and Behaviour*, vol 39, no 4, pp435–73

Belding, M. A., Iguchi, M. Y. and Lamb, R. J. (1996) 'Stages of change in methadone maintenance: assessing the convergent validity of two measures', *Psychology of Addictive Behaviours*, vol 10, no 3, pp157–66

Burditt, C., Robbins, M., Paiva, A., Velicer, W., Koblin, B. and Kessler, D. (2009) 'Motivation for blood donation among African Americans: developing measures for stage of change, decisional balance, and self-efficacy constructs', *Journal of Behavioural Medicine*, vol 32, no 5, pp429–42

Carrigan, M., Szmigin, I. and Wright, J. (2004) 'Shopping for a better world? An interpretive study of the potential for ethical consumption within the older market', *Journal of Consumer Marketing*, vol 21, no 6, pp401–17

Cherrier, H. (2006) 'Consumer identity and moral obligations in non-plastic bag consumption: a dialectical perspective', *International Journal of Consumer Studies*, vol 30, no 5, pp515–23

Cialdini, R. B. (1993) *Influence: Science and Practice* (3rd edn) Harper Collins College Publishers, New York

Cornelissen, G., Pandalaere, M., Warlop, L. and Dewitte, S. (2008) 'Positive cueing: promoting sustainable consumer behaviour by cueing common environmental behaviours as environmental', *International Journal of Research in Marketing*, vol 25, no 5, pp46–55

Davies, J. and Macdonald, G. (eds) (1998) *Quality, Evidence and Effectiveness in Health Promotion: Striving for Certainties*, Routledge, London

DiClemente, C. C., Schlundt, B. S. and Gemmell, L. (2004) 'Readiness and stages of change in addiction treatment', *The American Journal on Addiction*, vol 13, pp103–19

Dijkstra, A., Conijn, B. and De Vries, H. (2006) 'A match–mismatch test of a stage model of behaviour change in tobacco smoking', *Addiction*, vol 101, pp1035–43

Dishman, R. K., Thom, N. J., Rooks, C. R., Molt, R. W., Horwath, C. and Nigg, C. R. (2009) 'Failure of post-action stages of the transtheoretical model to predict change in regular physical activity: a multiethnic cohort study', *Annals of Behavioural Medicine*, vol 37, pp280–93

Doppelt, B. (2008) *The Power of Sustainable Thinking*, Earthscan, London

Dwyer, R. (2009) 'Keen to be green organizations: a focused rules approach to accountability', *Management Decision*, vol 47, pp120–6

Food Wise (2009) 'About FoodWise', http://foodwise.com.au/about-foodwise.aspx, accessed 5 February 2010

Gambling, T. and Long, A. F. (2006) 'Exploring patient perceptions of movement through the stages of change model within a diabetes tele-care intervention', *Journal of Health Psychology*, vol 11, no 1, pp117–28

Geller, E. S. (1989) 'Applied analysis and social marketing: an integration for environmental preservation', *Journal of Social Issues*, vol 45, no 1, pp17–36

Grant, A. M. and Franklin, J. (2007) 'The transtheoretical model and study skills', *Behaviour Change*, vol 24, no 2, pp99–113

Hemphill, J. F. and Howell, A. J. (2000) 'Adolescent offenders and stages of change', *Psychological Assessment*, vol 12, no 4, pp371–81

Herzog, T. A. (2010) 'A welcomed and overdue debate', *Health Psychology*, vol 29, no 1, pp102–3

Hutchison, A. J., Breckon, J. D. and Johnston, L. H. (2009) 'Physical activity behavior change interventions based on the transtheoretical model: a systematic review', *Health Education & Behavior*, vol 36, no 5, pp829–45

IGD (2007) *Beyond Packaging: Food Waste in the Home*, IGD, Watford, www.igd.com/index.asp?id=1&fid=2&sid=2&cid=280, accessed 14 April 2011

Johnson, S. S., Palva, A. L., Cummins, C. O., Johnson, J. L., Dyment, S. J., Wright, J. A., Prochaska, J. O., Prochaska, J. M. and Sherman, K. (2008) 'Transtheoretical model-based multiple behaviour intervention for weight management: effectiveness on a population basis', *Preventative Medicine*, vol 46, no 3, pp238–46

Jones, T. (2005) *Using Contemporary Archaeology and Applied Anthropology to Understand Food Loss in the American Food System*, Tucson, AZ

Kazdin, A. E. (2009) 'Psychological science's contributions to a sustainable environment: extending our reach to a grand challenge of society', *American Psychologist*, vol 64, no 5, pp339–56

Kotler, P. and Zaltman, G. (1971) 'Social marketing: an approach to planned social change', *Journal of Marketing*, vol 35, pp3–12

Kreuter, M. W. and Holt, C. L. (2001) 'How do people process health information? Applications in an age of individualized communication', *Current Directions in Psychological Science*, vol 10, no 6, pp206–9

Levesque, D. A., Prochaska, J. M., Prochaska, J. O., Dewart, S. R., Hamby, L. S. and Weeks, W. B. (2001) 'Organizational stages and processes of change for continuous quality improvement in health care', *Consulting Psychology Journal: Practice and Research*, vol 53, no 3, pp139–53

Lewis, C. C., Simons, A. D., Silva, S. G., Rohde, P., Small, D. M., Murakami, J. L., High, R. R. and March, J. S. (2009) 'The role of readiness to change in response to treatment of adolescent depression', *Journal of Consulting Psychology*, vol 77, no 3, pp422–8

Lundqvist, J., de Fraiture, C. and Molden, D. (2008) 'Saving water: from field to fork – curbing losses and wastage in the food chain', Stockholm International Water Institute, www.eldis.org/assets/Docs/39358.html, accessed 14 April 2011

Lupton, D. (1996) *Food, the Body and the Self*, SAGE, London

Lyon, T. and Maxwell, J. (2004) *Corporate Environmentalism and Public Policy*, Cambridge University Press, Cambridge

McConnaughy, E. A., Prochaska, J. O. and Velicer, W. F. (1983) 'Stages of Change in psychotherapy: measurement and sample profiles', *Psychotherapy: Theory, Research and Practice*, vol 20, pp368–75

Miller, W. R. and Tonigan, J. S. (1996) 'Assessing drinkers' motivation for change: the Stages of Change Readiness and Treatment Eagerness Scale (SOCRATES)', *Psychology of Addictive Behaviors*, vol 10, pp81–9

Napper, L. E., Wood, M. M., Jaffe, A., Fisher, D. G., Reynolds, G. L. and Klahn, J. A. (2008) 'Convergent and discriminant validity of three measures of stage of change', *Psychology of Addictive Behaviors*, vol 22, no 3, pp362–71

Neverwaste (2010) 'Preventing household food waste – the first project of its kind in Australia', www.neverwaste.vic.gov.au/news/food-saving-tools-to-avoid-food-waste-in-your-own-home/, accessed 5 February 2010

Nigg, C., Hellsten, L., Norman, G., Braun, L., Breger, R., Burbank, P. and Coday, M. (2005) 'Physical activity staging distribution: establishing a heuristic using multiple studies', *Annals of Behavioral Medicine*, 29, vol, pp35–45

Noar, S. M., Benac, C. N. and Harris, M. S. (2007) 'Does tailoring matter? Meta-analytic review of tailored print health behavior change interventions', *Psychological Bulletin*, vol 133, no 4, pp673–93

Norcross, J. C., Krebs, P. M. and Prochaska, J. O. (2011) 'Stages of change', *Journal of Clinical Psychology: In Session*, vol 67, no 2, pp143–54

Pelletier, L. G., Lavergne, K. J. and Sharp, E. C. (2008) 'Environmental psychology and sustainability: comments on topics important for our future', *Canadian Psychology*, vol 49, no 4, pp304–8

Perz, C. A., DiClemente, C. C. and Carbonari, J. P. (1996) 'Doing the right thing at the right time? The interaction of stages and processes of change in successful smoking cessation', *Health Psychology*, vol 15, no 6, pp462–8

Petry, N. M. (2005) 'Stages of change in treatment-seeking pathological gamblers', *Journal of Consulting and Clinical Psychology*, vol 73, no 2, pp312–22

Poortinga, W., Steg, L. and Vlek, C. (2004) 'Values, environmental concern, and environmental behaviour: a study into household energy use', *Environment and Behaviour*, vol 36, no 1, pp70–93

Prochaska, J. O. and DiClemente, C. C. (1983) 'Stages and processes of self-change of smoking: toward an integrative model of change', *Journal of Consulting and Clinical Psychology*, vol 51, pp390–5

Prochaska, J. O., Fava, J. L., Rossi, J. S. and Tsoh, J. Y. (2001) 'Evaluating a population-based recruitment approach and a stage-based expert system intervention for smoking cessation', *Addictive Behaviours*, vol 26, no 4, pp583–602

Prochaska, J. O. and Norcross, J. C. (2001) 'Stages of Change', *Psychotherapy: Theory, Research and Practice*, vol 38, no 4, pp443–8

Prochaska, J. O. and Norcross, J. C. (2010) *Systems of Psychotherapy: A Transtheoretical Analysis* (7th edn), Brooks/Cole, Cengage Learning, Belmont, CA

Prochaska, J. O., Velicer, W. F., DiClemente, C. C. and Fava, J. (1988) 'Measuring processes of change: applications to the cessation of smoking', *Journal of Consulting and Clinical Psychology*, vol 56, no 4, pp520–8

Prochaska, J. O., Velicer, W. F., Rossi, J. S., Goldstein, M. G., Marcus, B. H., Rakowski, W., Fiore, C., Harlow, L. L., Redding, C. A., Rosenbloom, D. and Rossi, S. R. (1994) 'Stages of change and decisional balance for 12 problem behaviors', *Health Psychology*, vol 13, no 1, pp39–46

Pruitt, S., McQueen, A., Tiro, J., Rakowski, W., Diclemente, C. and Vernon, S. (2010) 'Construct validity of a mammography processes of change scale and invariance by stage of change', *Journal of Health Psychology*, vol 15, no 1, pp64–74

Reich, J. W. and Robertson, J. L. (1979) 'Reactance and norm appeal in anti-littering messages', *Journal of Applied Social Psychology*, vol 9, pp91–101

Rosen, C. S. (2000) 'Is there sequencing of change processes by stage consistent across health problems? A meta-analysis', *Health Psychology*, vol 19, no 6, pp593–604

Schneider, F. (2008) 'Wasting food – an insistent behaviour', in *Waste – the Social Context: Urban Issues & Solutions*, Edmonton, Canada

Schorr, G., Ulbricht, S., Schmidt, C. O., Baumeister, S. E., Ruge, J., Schumann, A., Rumpf, H., John, U. and Meyer, C. (2008) 'Does precontemplation represent a homogeneous stage category? A latent class analysis on German smokers', *Journal of Consulting and Clinical Psychology*, vol 76, no 5, pp840–51

Scott, D. and Willits, T. (1994) 'Environmental attitudes and behavior: a Pennsylvania survey', *Environment and Behaviour*, vol 26, no 2, pp239–60

Sobal, J. and Wansink, B. (2007) 'Kitchenscapes, tablescapes, platescapes, and foodscapes: influences of microscale build environments on food intake', *Environment and Behaviour*, vol 39, no 1, pp124–42

Spencer, L., Adams, T. B., Malone, S., Roy, L. and Yost, E. (2006) 'Applying the transtheoretical model to exercise: a systematic and comprehensive review of the literature', *Health Promotion Practice*, vol 7, no 4, pp428–43

Spencer, L., Pagell, F. and Adams, T. (2005) 'Applying the transtheoretical model to cancer screening behaviour', *American Journal of Health Behavior*, vol 29, no 1, pp36–56

Stern, P. C., Dietz, T. and Guagnano, G. A. (1995) 'The new ecological paradigm in social-psychological context', *Environment and Behavior*, vol 27, no 6, pp723–43

Stuart, T. (2009) *Waste: Uncovering the Global Food Scandal*, Penguin, Harmondsworth

The Age (2008) 'Our tips are full of good food. Why the waste?', *The Age*, 3 February, www.theage.com.au/articles/2008/02/02/1201801098851.html, accessed 5 February 2010

The Economist (2009) 'A hill of beans: America's food-waste problem is getting worse', www.economist.com/node/14960159?story_id=14960159, accessed 5 February 2010

The Sunday Telegraph (2009) 'Shoppers waste millions on food', *The Sunday Telegraph*, 31 May

Tierney, D. W. and McCabe, M. P. (2005) 'The utility of the trans-theoretical model of behavior change in the treatment of sex offenders', *Sexual Abuse: A Journal of Research and Treatment*, vol 17, no 2, pp153–70

United States Environmental Protection Agency (2009) 'Food waste management tools and resources', www.epa.gov/osw/conserve/materials/organics/food/fd-res.htm, accessed 5 February 2010

Velicer, W. F., Redding, C. A., Sun, X. and Prochaska, J. O. (2007) 'Demographic variables, smoking variables, and outcome across five studies', *Health Psychology*, vol 26, no 3, pp278–87

Ventour, L. (2008) 'The food we waste', in *Food Waste Report*, Banbury

Wall, A. (2005) 'Government demarketing: different approaches and mixed messages', *European Journal of Marketing*, vol 39, pp421–7

Wall, A. P. (2007) 'Government "demarketing" as viewed by its target audience', *Marketing Intelligence and Planning*, vol 25, pp123–35

Watson, D. L. and Tharp, R. G. (2007) *Self-directed Behaviour* (9th edn), Thomson Wadworth, Belmont, CA

Wicker, A. W. (1969) 'Attitudes versus actions: the relationship of verbal and overt behavioural responses to attitude objects', *Journal of Social Issues*, vol 25, pp41–78

Wright, M. and Klÿn, B. (1998) 'Environmental attitude – behaviour correlations in 21 countries', *Journal of Empirical Generalisations in Marketing Science*, vol 3, pp42–60

Zimbardo, P. G. and Leippe, M. R. (1991) *The Psychology of Attitude Change and Social Influence*, McGraw-Hill Inc, New York

Chapter 5

Collaborative consumption and the remaking of local resilience

Reflecting upon enabling solutions

Angelique Edmonds

Summary

Current patterns of consumption are, quite clearly, unjust and unsustainable; the extent and nature of the transformation required are hotly debated, reflecting as they do competing, deep-rooted beliefs about society and nature (Seyfang, 2009). One of the greatest difficulties in effecting change is that, rather than creatively expressing their identity, consumers' choices are limited, and they are 'effectively trapped within particular consumption patterns and lifestyle practices by the overarching social structures of market, business, working patterns, urban planning and development' (Ropke, 1999, in Seyfang, 2009, p17; Sanne, 2002). As sustainability theorist Gill Seyfang notes, this has implications for locating agency and allocating responsibility: 'in the social practices approach, the responsibility of the individual towards environmental change is analysed in direct relation with social structure' (Spaargaren, 2003, p690, in Seyfang, 2009, p18). In expanding on this, Seyfang (2009, p18) presents an illustrative example:

> A person might choose one brand of washing machine over another because of its greater energy efficiency, but what they cannot easily choose is to purchase collectively and share common laundry facilities among a group of local residents, or to redefine social conventions to reduce the socially acceptable frequency of clothes washing.

This chapter speaks to the gap highlighted by Seyfang's example and is framed by these concerns regarding agency.

Context: individual agency and collective action

As sustainability theorist Gill Seyfang (2009, p18) notes, 'the shift to new systems of provision is neither easy nor straightforward, given that it involves, first contradicting and then challenging existing social institutions and socio-technological regimes'. In seeking to make the necessary changes to their consumption patterns, ecologically motivated citizens,

> see that their individual consumption choices are environmentally important, but that their control over those choices is constrained, shaped and framed by institutions and political forces that can be remade only through collective citizen action, as opposed to consumer behaviour.
>
> (Maniates, 2002, p65)

It is in response to this awareness that many report feeling overwhelmed by the task of addressing issues of sustainability, noting that the scale of the task requires coordination of their individual agency into collective action, and yet many of the customary gatherings that facilitate collective action have been eroded by modern lifestyles (Putnam, 2000). Seyfang also notes that, by focusing on analysis of sociotechnical regimes rather than individual decision-making, one can see that,

> in consciously exercising our individual incremental choices, we have sleepwalked into some larger choices and foreclosed others without even realizing it. The market can be an 'invisible elbow' shoving us into an unwanted corner rather than Adam Smith's benign 'invisible hand'.
>
> (Levett et al, 2003, p47, in Seyfang, 2009, p19)

In response to such constraints, the prospect of collaborative consumption offers refreshing ways to rethink consumption patterns and reverse the increasing atomization of society by drawing individuals back into customs of collective action. It avoids the perils of 'sleepwalking' described above, as it prompts active participation in fundamentally rethinking the way we connect with one another to use products. This catalyses an additional opportunity for rethinking the way a product is used. This occurs through organized sharing, bartering, lending, trading, renting, gifting and swapping through online and real-world communities – to get the same fulfillment and benefits of ownership with reduced personal burden and cost and lower environmental impact.

In addition to collaborative consumption, other collective-action initiatives reimagine the structures of distribution: for example, local food redistribution systems that bypass supermarket chains, or the establishing of community currencies that aim to value and reward unpaid work in society, incentivizing mutual aid rather than competition. Each of these initiatives is seen by its proponents as an embodiment of a different set of values, offering a more sustainable infrastructure within which to conduct lives of self-sufficiency rather than continually increasing consumption. Seyfang discusses these as instances of 'new economics'; design theorist Ezio Manzini discusses such initiatives as enabling solutions; whatever their nomenclature, they are creative acts to rethink the infrastructure of service systems, to redistribute markets, work and care within lifestyles of collaboration, which can in turn foster local resilience. Before proceeding to a number of examples of these initiatives from various countries, I will outline in further detail the evidence that demonstrates the increasing atomization of society referred to earlier. My interest in examining these practices of collective action and collaborative consumption in this chapter is as potential remedy to this decline, offering a means to foster more sustainable living practices.

Atomization of society: trends and their likely causes

Epidemiologists Richard Wilkinson and Kate Pickett begin their book, *Spirit level*, with a sobering observation:

> It is a remarkable paradox that, at the pinnacle of human material and technical achievement, we find ourselves anxiety-ridden, prone to depression, worried about how others see us, unsure of our friendships, driven to consume and with little or

no community life. Lacking the relaxed social contact and emotional satisfaction we all need, we seek comfort in over eating, obsessive shopping and spending, or become prey to excessive alcohol, psychoactive medicines and illegal drugs.

(Wilkinson and Pickett, 2009, p3)

After analysing surveys measuring social trust over the last century in America, political scientist Robert D. Putnam reports that:

Social trust rose from the mid 1940s to the mid 1960s, peaking in 1964 just as many other measures of social capital did. Middle-aged Americans in the 1960s were probably living in a more trusting society than the one in which they had grown up. In the mid 1960s however, this beneficent trend was reversed, initiating a long-term decline in social trust. If generalised reciprocity and honesty are important social lubricants, Americans today are experiencing more friction in our daily lives than our parents and grandparents did a generation ago.

(Putnam, 2000, p140)

These authors present alarming realities for the quality of our relationships, satisfaction and well-being with respect to sustaining the bonds that underpin collective action. Putnam notes that 'thick trust', confidence in personal friends, is as strong as ever. However, 'thin' trust, which he defines as 'the tenuous bond between you and your nodding acquaintance from the coffee shop, that crucial emollient for large complex societies like ours – is becoming rarer' (Putnam, 2000, p142). Elsewhere, Putnam describes this as 'bridging capital', something that develops when one forms a bond with someone unlike oneself. Such bonds and opportunities to extend the 'thin' trust are critical in the diversity of contemporary cities because, as he explains,

Thin, single stranded interactions are gradually replacing dense, multistranded, well-exercised bonds. More of our social connectedness is one-shot, special purpose, and self oriented. Place-based social capital is being supplanted by function-based social capital. We are withdrawing from those networks of reciprocity that once constituted our communities.

(Putnam, 2000, p184)

It is unlikely that we will succeed in organizing ourselves collectively in the face of sustainability pressures unless we can overcome and reverse this withdrawal. Wilkinson and Pickett believe that,

the contrast between the material success and social failure of many rich countries is an important signpost. It suggests that, if we are to gain further improvements in the real quality of life, we need to shift attention from material standards and economic growth to ways of improving the psychological and social well-being of whole societies.

(Wilkinson and Pickett, 2009, p4)

The concept of 'social capital' extends by analogy the notions of physical and human capital (i.e. tools and training that enhance individual productivity). According to

Putnam (2000, p19), the 'core idea of social capital theory is that social networks have value; social contacts can affect the productivity of individuals and groups'. If social capital has declined rapidly since the mid 1960s, then the increasing atomization that results from this means a decline in the social networks and norms of reciprocity and trustworthiness that arise from them. This also contributes to less civic participation, which makes collective action on social and environmental sustainability more difficult to establish, coordinate and carry out.

Putnam describes at length the suspected reasons for the decline in social trust and social capital, yet maintains that causal relations are difficult to determine. There are, however, strong correlations between four particular factors: (1) the pressures of time and money, and two-career families; (2) suburbanization, commuting and sprawl; (3) the effect of electronic entertainment and especially television; and (4) generational change, as the long civic generation is replaced by their less-involved children and grandchildren (Putnam, 2000, p283). Political scientists Howard and Gilbert (2008) have extended this analysis in nineteen European countries through their examination of the 'European Social Survey' (and have reported upon their findings from both eastern and western Europe). In addition, they also analysed the US Citizenship, Involvement, Democracy (CID) survey and found, 'for individuals in the Unites States and Europe involvement in voluntary associations is a relatively strong predictor of political action, life satisfaction and interpersonal trust' (Howard and Gilbert, 2008, p27). By reverse implication, a decline in participation in voluntary organizations correlates to a decline in social trust.

Wilkinson and Pickett suggest that, as a result of the decline of communities of the past and as a result of increasing geographic mobility, each of us as individuals has spread the locus of familiarity further, but with astonishingly reduced depth of familiarity, and that this has implications. They explain that,

> People's sense of identity used to be embedded in the community to which they belonged, in people's real knowledge of one another, but now it is cast adrift in the anonymity of mass society. Familiar faces have been replaced by a constant flux of strangers. As a result, who we are, identity itself, is endlessly open to question.
>
> (Wilkinson and Pickett, 2009, p42)

They go on to argue that the impact of that uncertainty regarding the stability of identity is one of the greatest drivers of consumption, because inequality increases evaluation anxieties, which people attempt to overcome through increased consumerism. They conclude that the 'weakening of community life and the growth of consumerism are related' (Wilkinson and Pickett, 2009, p126). They also suggest that, where this results in greater inequality in a society, such an outcome is also accompanied by poorer health and well-being measures (Wilkinson and Pickett, 2009). Thus, the decline in social capital is not a small inconvenience that modern lifestyles can continue to ignore, if we also seek to live sustainably and have equality and well-being.

Howard and Gilbert (2008), Putnam (2000) and Wilkinson and Pickett (2009) contribute to an impressive and growing body of research that suggests that civic connections help make us healthy, wealthy and wise. 'Living without social capital is not easy', Putnam (2000, p287) explains, 'whether one is a villager in southern Italy or a poor person in the American inner city or a well heeled entrepreneur in a high tech industrial district'. Social capital has many features that help people translate aspirations into realities and is vital for the 'collaborative' part of interest in this chapter discussing 'collaborative consumption'. Social capital allows citizens to resolve collective problems more easily. Putnam (2000, p288) argues that, '"collective action problems" are best solved by an institutional mechanism with the power to ensure compliance with the collectively desirable behaviour. Social norms and the networks that enforce them provide such a mechanism'.

What Putnam refers to as 'institutional mechanisms' seem similar to that which Seyfang (2009) describes as 'socio-technological regimes'. In addition, social capital 'greases the wheels' that allow communities to advance smoothly. Where people are trusting and trustworthy, and where they are subject to repeated interactions with fellow citizens, everyday business and social transactions are less costly. Social capital also improves our lot by widening our awareness of the many ways in which our fates are linked. According to Putnam (2000, p289), 'people who have active and trusting connections to others develop or maintain character traits that are good for the rest of society'. Having established the impact of the loss of community life and increasing atomization of society, and the vital need to restore social capital and foster trust, I will now describe the conceptual and value distinctions of framing in which collaborative consumption initiatives distinguish themselves from the mainstream market system.

Collaborative consumption as distinct from the mainstream market system

In his book *The value of nothing*, activist and academic Raj Patel (2009, p22) explains that 'What characterizes today's markets is exchange driven not by needs but by profit'. If we accept this assertion, could it be possible that – in order to overcome the current and future environmental consequences of resource depletion resulting from over consumption – we could recreate a market that is driven by needs? In addressing our first and foremost need, a transformation of the accepted system of exchange is required, to ensure it is one that can be sustained. Seyfang (2009) argues that new economics may be an approach that could do just that.

New economics is an environmental, philosophical and political movement founded on a belief that economics cannot be divorced from its foundations in environmental and social contexts, and that sustainability requires a realigning of development priorities away from the primary goal of economic growth towards well-being instead (Jackson, 2004). The term 'new economics' was first adopted in 1984 following a gathering of alternative thinkers, in a parallel conference to that year's G7 summit, that was known as 'The Other Economic Summit' (TOES). As Boyle explains:

> Old economics loses everything it fails to measure. Women are lost if economics simply tracks what happens to households as a whole. Nature is lost, because its services are not valued. People working in the informal economy – up to a third of people in poor countries – are lost. The contribution of traditional knowledge and cultural diversity are lost. New schools of economic study, study what old economics misses out: how organizations work (institutional economics), the contribution of

nature (ecological economics) and human behaviour (socio-economics). The approach relies on a broader understanding of wealth, a richer conception of work, new uses of money and on integrating ethics back into economic life.

(Boyle, 1993, p5, in Seyfang, 2009, p48)

System-wide changes in infrastructure provision are the objective of new economics, with progress measured by new indicators of sustainable well-being acknowledging that consumption is not necessarily related to well-being. New economics addresses 'ecological citizens' who act ethically in public and private to reconfigure the patterns of their lives to reduce environmental and social impacts on others (Dobson, 2003, in Seyfang, 2009, p23). Seyfang (2004, p21) explains the impact of ecological citizens' action: 'Through the participation of ecological citizens within communities of place, practice and interest and through collective action, socio-technical infrastructures of provision are reshaped, creating new systems and non market alternatives where necessary'.

What is interesting here for the possibilities of collaborative consumption is that such reframing of economic theory challenges mainstream economic assumptions of how humans satisfy their needs. Chilean economist Manfred Max-Neef's work allows an approach that posits a range of alternative methods of meeting needs that do not rely on private ownership of material goods, and 'a possibility that the culturally and historically specific consumerist economy is neither an inherent outcome of human-needs satisfaction, nor an inevitable one' (Max Neef, 1992, p203, in Seyfang, 2004, p50). This also reflects practices I observed in Ngukurr, an Aboriginal community in south-east Arnhem Land in the Northern Territory (NT) of Australia, during contract consultancy work I undertook for the NT government, which subsequently became the focus of my PhD (Edmonds, 2007). Aboriginal Australians' satisfaction of their needs relies upon the maintenance of webs of relatedness, rather than requiring exclusive ownership of items to satisfy needs.

Investment in relatedness over ownership

A prominent older lady in the Ngukurr community, who was very vocal, political and also much respected, discussed this issue with me at length. She commented, 'you whitefellas invest your future in houses, we invest ourselves in people, in knowing each other [because you are] secure in country when you know people'. This comment draws attention to the difference orientation can have on one's security. This woman expressed the view that whitefellas (a local term used to describe non-indigenous people) require tangible items of property to own in order to feel secure. The much-discussed Australian dream to own one's own house testifies to this. Yet such security is limited to the particular place where the ownership is exercised, or only in as far as that asset may be borrowed against to facilitate other desires (e.g. to travel). By comparison, an investment in relatedness, knowing your role and place within a broader identity structure of reciprocal kin obligations, offers an intangible security, yet one that can be exercised anywhere.

This lady went on to illustrate her statement by pointing out that she can travel anywhere and be looked after by other Aboriginal people in another country, because her country in the Roper River region has links all around, and Aboriginal people in neighbouring country, both near and far, would be able to trace a link or kin relatedness to each other within an extended network of kin. Thus, she felt secure in the knowledge that, in knowing other people via the system of kin relatedness, and being known by them, one would be safe in foreign territory. This is due to the system of reciprocal obligation to kin, which ensures that once kin relations have been established, hosts will be hospitable and ensure you are looked after. In conclusion, she explained that, 'whitefellas spend their effort making security with houses in just one little spot, whereas us mob got security wherever we go, because we got each other'. What she describes is doubtless an ideal scenario that has suffered considerably since colonization and the degradation of linkages and networks, in addition to the introduction of cash economies. However, as an orientation for understanding one's place in the world, and one's orientation to freedom, it suggests that ensuring relationships are sustained takes precedence over the accumulation of resources for private or exclusive use.

Freedom in this sense is not confined to one's perceived agency to leave the community. Thus, it is not a freedom from the constraints of the context that is sought. Rather, this custom of maintaining relatedness and investment in social capital is motivated by an obligation to ensure continuity in the conditions as they are, rather than an escape from them (Edmonds, 2007). Social capital can be understood as a resource for collective action: that is, access to social connections that help individuals to make decisions and to get things done (Hunter, 2004, p3). Relatedness of people and thus of country remains the baseline of order in some Aboriginal communities. Drawing on his observations of the Aboriginal community in Cape York, Queensland anthropologist David Martin (1995, p12) explains that, 'the resources and time invested into many enterprises [in Cape York] were not primarily used to develop a capital base for reinvestment, expansion and material productivity, but in the accumulation of social capital'. Maintaining this order based on the structure of relatedness and investment in social capital ensures the conditions for life are sustained in the present and into the future.

Indigenous Australians' approaches to understanding ownership embody and extend this emphasis, because, within understandings of collective ownership, Aboriginal people distinguish that certain individuals have the authority to speak for the use of an item. To give some context to this point, let me first note two meanings associated with the term 'property'. In his 'Survey of property theory and tenure types', anthropologist Bruce Rigsby quoted Hallowell's explanation that the term 'property' 'has two common senses; it signifies both the object that is owned, as well as the rights that are exercised over it' (Rigsby, 1998, p23, quoting Hallowell, 1955, p239). Consensus about, and observation of, these meanings, however, is contingent upon membership within an institution of behaviour that recognizes the distinction of 'property' indicating 'owner-ship' and resultant 'rights'. Thus, for Aboriginal people in the Roper region, authority to speak for the use of an item, or to be consulted regarding its use, stands as a measure of ownership, as expressed by the term 'property', and yet this authority is not understood as a property right subject to exclusivity in the manner of Western property rights, which underpin modern consumerism. As a result of the difference in Aboriginal Australians' institution of behaviour surrounding these matters, maintaining relationships among extended kin is often required to maintain access to the items over which they have authority. This provides the incentive to ensure that maintenance of relationships is prioritized over ownership of 'things' (Edmonds, 2007, p302).

In returning to Max Neef's work and considering indigenous Australians' alternative methods of meeting one's needs in a way that does not rely on private ownership of material goods, this chapter explores whether it is possible that urban resilience could be strengthened by the network of relatedness one experiences within it, rather than be measured by the accumulation of things. Furthermore, if this is possible, we need to understand what conditions are necessary to mobilize or support the development of such networks of relatedness and cooperation and whether collaborative consumption can make a contribution. As Patel explains, the fundamental impediment to overcoming inequality lies within our systems of ownership and distribution:

> The reason people go hungry today has nothing at all to do with a gap between the amount of food in the world and the number of people who are hungry. There's more than enough food on earth today to feed the world one and a half times over. The reason people go hungry is because of the way we distribute food through the market as private property, and the people who starve are simply too poor to be able to afford it.
>
> (Patel, 2009, p94)

Just as the indigenous-Australian understanding of property relies upon membership of an institution of behaviour that recognizes the distinction between 'property' indicating 'ownership' and resultant 'rights', in our modern society, for food to be treated as private property requires society to approve of it being taken out of common hands. In tracing the origins of 'property rights' as understood in Western history, we note the influence of seventeenth-century philosopher John Locke's chapter 'On property' in his *Second treatise on civil government* (1690) and the enclosures movement in England as the origins of such thinking. Locke argued that inalienable property rights derive, not from the government or monarch, but from the labour an individual invests in the land:

> whatsoever then he removes out of the State that Nature hath provided, and left it in, he hath mixed his Labour with it and joyned to it something that is his own and thereby makes it his property.
>
> (Locke, 1690, quoted in Coates, 1998, p124)

Locke maintained that incorporation into an economy or commodity exchange is a necessary precondition for imparting value to anything, including land. By inference, this suggests that land is destined to remain worthless until it acquires the status of a commodity in a market or capitalist economy. Property is, in other words, social. As Patel states, 'there's nothing natural about the way some people are allowed to exclude others from land, for instance' (2009, p102). During the enclosure movement in England, many were aggrieved at this change of social agreement around property. As historian Peter Lindebaugh (2010, p12) explains, 'Enclosure indicates private property and capital: it seems to promise both individual ownership and social productivity, but in fact the concept of enclosure is inseparable from terror and the destruction of independence and community.' This destruction is demonstrated in the following verse found on a notice tacked up as a handbill in Plaistow in 1821 (quoted in Lindebaugh, 2010, p21):

The law locks up the man or woman
Who steals the goose from off the common
But leaves the greater villain loose
Who steals the common from the goose

Thus, what is considered property and how one exercises one's right over that property in relation to others are both socially constructed. For these reasons, given that the institutions of behaviour that determine our collective agreement regarding matters of ownership and distribution of resources *are* social, they can be redefined and renegotiated by people through collective action. The question of concern here is whether Putnam's (2000, p288) 'institutional mechanisms' and Seyfang's (2009) 'socio-technological regimes' are aspects that collective citizen agency can redefine. Equally, that is what is so disturbing about new forms of commodification involving culture and knowledge, as demonstrated by the 'biopiracy' of the intellectual property in seeds. As Patel (2009, p120) observes, 'At the stroke of a pen, the genetic information in seeds that had been bred by generations of peasants became a new El Dorado for transnational seed companies, intellectual property ripe for the taking.'

If property is socially constructed, and governments and transnational seed companies can create and restrict ownership to genetic information or land previously owned by many in common, surely collective citizen agency can also redefine matters of ownership and the distribution of resources into more sustainable systems answerable to need, rather than profit, as their primary motive. Of course this is possible, but – as Maniates (2002), Seyfang (2009) and Spaargaren (2003) have stated – such a change can only occur through collective citizen action, and not through individual consumer behaviour.

The examples of new forms of collaborative and 'collective' ownership that this chapter will discuss offer more than an individual response to over-consumption in that they challenge the status quo of the market system and begin to explore the recreation of a system for exchange based on a new set of social values. In achieving this, one exchange at a time, I speculate that the intangible benefit they offer, in gathering momentum towards finding effective solutions to some of our most pressing social and environmental issues, is of significant value. It empowers individuals to feel they can make a difference, build trust and forge bonds, friendships and associations with others who are also concerned and who are also mobilizing their concern into collective action. Thus, in different ways, these examples help us to rethink the social infrastructure of service systems and, in so doing, they have the potential to contribute to fostering local resilience.

Fostering trust, local resilience and community

In the twenty-first century, there has been plenty of rhetoric regarding the reasons to foster trust and resilience among communities, not least of which is economic. Putnam makes it clear that, when all of us can relax our guard a little, what economists term 'transaction costs' – the costs of the everyday business of life, as well as the costs of commercial transactions – are reduced. This is no doubt why, as economists have recently discovered, trusting communities, other things being equal, have a measurable economic advantage. A society that relies on generalized reciprocity is more efficient than a distrustful society, and 'students of public health find that life expectancy itself is enhanced in more trustful communities' (Putnam, 2000, p135). These findings are reinforced by the work of Howard and Gilbert (2008).

The decline in social capital and social networks that foster resilience in communities has not been substituted by the self-sufficient stability provided by material acquisition, as the industrial capitalists anticipated. Thus, practices of collaborative consumption distinguish themselves from the mainstream market system in that they do not attempt to substitute lost social capital with exclusively owned material value. As discussed with reference to Max Neef's work and Australian indigenous people's practices of satisfying needs, some collaborative consumption initiatives demonstrate the increasing value invested in social capital as an alternative (and direct challenge) to the need for exclusive material ownership as the primary means to needs satisfaction. In a new strategy of assigning value, distinctions that celebrate social capital include:

> measures which support localization and progress toward more self-reliant communities, active measures in reducing ecological footprints and reducing inequity of current consumption patterns, measures which foster community building, nurturing inclusive, cohesive communities which enable collective action and collaboration about things which affect people's lives and building new infrastructures of provision through active ecological citizenship.
>
> (Seyfang, 2009, pp61–2)

These conceptual and value distinctions of framing in which collaborative consumption initiatives operate will be considered in the examples that follow.

Examples exploring a system for exchange based on a new set of social values

In considering examples of initiatives that offer alternatives, Seyfang (2009, p70) analyses grass-roots innovations: niche-based approaches that explore problem framings (e.g. mobility, food energy services) and search for solutions – in contrast to technology demonstration projects that begin with 'technical solutions' to tightly framed problems. This approach is consistent with a similar shift occurring in design, towards a growing awareness that innovation in systems is required, rather than design's more traditional focus on innovation in products. Innovation in service provision differs from traditional improvements to single products or business practices; innovation is needed at the scale of 'socio-technological regimes' (Berkhout, 2002, in Seyfang, 2009, p67). Simultaneously with the realization of this need, collaborative consumption practices have seen an unbounded marketplace for efficient peer-to-peer exchange emerge between producer and consumer, seller and buyer, lender and borrower, and neighbour and neighbour. According to strategist Rachel Botsman and entrepreneur Roo Rogers (2010, pxiv) 'Online exchanges mimic the close ties once formed through face to face exchanges in villages or communities, but on a much larger and unconfined scale. In other words, technology is investing in old forms of trust'.

This image of 'technology investing in old forms of trust' prompts a transformation in considering online exchange as one in which people are held responsible and accountable, as one would expect from a face-to-face exchange. For many, this challenges the relative anonymity and absent accountability with which online transactions are associated. Whether (new) online exchanges adequately emulate the old forms of trust in practice depends upon the service and the 'behaviour' designed into the online negotiation of exchange, and this will be examined in the examples that follow. Notwithstanding this qualification, Brian Chesky, the founder of AirBnB and a graduate of Rhode Island School of Design, predicts 'the status quo is being replaced by a movement. Peer to peer is going to become the default way people exchange things, whether it is space, stuff, skills or services' (Botsman and Rogers, 2010, pxiv).

Botsman and Rogers (2010) outline four underlying principles shared by collaborative consumption initiatives, which are essential for their success: (1) early critical mass; (2) the power of excess capacity (idling capacity); (3) belief in the commons; and (4) trust between strangers. In the next section, I will examine six examples of innovative service provision initiatives that practise collaboration in consumption. These examples are: AirBnB, an international accommodation-sharing exchange; GoGet car share; Zopa and Kiva, both of which are financial lending services; Rentoid, which operates as the rental equivalent of eBay; and FoodConnect, an enterprise in Australia (comparable with international examples) that connects urban households to farmers to enable direct and local food distribution.

In regard to the first of their four principles, Botsman and Rogers state that critical mass is vital for generating both social proof and sufficient choice for consumers to be satisfied. They account for their second principle, the power of excess, by noting that, in the United States, 80 per cent of the items people own are used less than once a month, and so collaborative consumption mobilizes this idling capacity into use. Thus, the first two principles align with an approach that seeks to rationalize efficiency in a manner consistent with the dynamics of the mainstream market system, driven by profit. However, Patel (2009, p171) warns us that the 'increased mismanagement of the planet's resources is almost inevitable when profit driven markets set the terms of value'. With this caution in mind, discussion of the six following examples will be thematic, relating them to each of Botsman and Rogers' principles (2, 3 and 4) in turn. This examination will be followed by a discussion that speculates upon whether participation in these initiatives makes an overall net contribution to fostering resilience.

Collaborative consumption principle 2: harnessing the power of excess capacity

For the purposes of this chapter and this book's overall interest in the reduction of waste, harnessing the 'power of excess capacity' is a trend that offers multiple benefits to the sustainability agenda. It simultaneously offers more efficient use of what is produced, and, as a consequence, it is possible that this could reduce demand for 'products' by satisfying everyone's needs with less 'stuff'. This greater efficiency offers the potential to ensure that everyone still has the use of what they need, while we would not need to produce as much overall to satisfy the net need. Whether the new collaborative consumption would reduce production owing to greater efficiency depends on the way the initiative is set up, and so we will need to examine each example in turn with respect to (a) the use of idling capacity and (b) the overall reduction in consumption and the consequent reduction in production this (should) cause.

AirBnB

Through an online interface and a set of guidelines for expectations and behaviour, AirBnB make it possible for people to arrange to stay with complete strangers. This offers the guest an alternative experience to the anonymity of a hotel, while offering the host opportunities to earn an income from their spare room and meet new people visiting their town. The enterprise began in August 2008, when three colleagues offered to host conference delegates they had never met in a few spare rooms they had between them. Since then, AirBnB has grown, and more than 10,000 trips have been completed to date using the service. With respect to use of idling capacity, this initiative works well, by opening up and offering private spare rooms for use to public guests, as this rate of use would be more frequent than that limited by hosting only guests with whom the host is already familiar. However, although this does rate well in terms of increased efficiency, it does not always follow that this will lead to lower consumption or less overall travel. On the contrary, efficiency gains can be presented as the justification for being able to use more, and thus there may be no net reduction in current consumption levels. The advertising on the AirBnB website suggests that the savings you make by using AirBnB allow you to travel more, and so the onus of responsibility for reduced consumption (as the possible outcome of more efficient use of space) seems to rest with the traveller and not with the initiative itself.

GoGet

GoGet is a carshare business operating in Australia. Similar to Zipcar in the US and the UK, it offers membership of an organization that owns hundreds of cars, so that members can use those cars only when they need to and thus spread the environmental, maintenance and running costs of having a car across a greater number of 'owners'. This also scores well in using idling capacity through prompting more efficient use of fewer cars. Rather than redesign the car, GoGet presents an innovation in systems thinking, through considering the problem framing of mobility and then redesigning the system in response to that problem. GoGet reports that, for every GoGet car, there are seven fewer cars on the road (www.goget.com.au). Thus, this redesign of the system appears to be successful in achieving part (b) of consumption reduction with respect to vehicles.

Zopa

The next two initiatives, Zopa and Kiva, are examples of new systems of financial exchange enabling online lending. Founded in 2005, Zopa claims to be the world's first lending and borrowing marketplace. Its website proclaims that 'By demonstrating that peer-to-peer lending works on a large scale, Zopa has changed the financial sector for good' (http://ukzopa.com). Social lending works within a network of lenders and borrowers, 'when people with spare cash they might otherwise put in their savings account or in the stock market lend it to people looking to borrow' (Botsman and Rogers, 2010, p162). Zopa allows individuals to earn an increased monetary benefit from their savings (a use of idling capacity), rather than offering their savings to a bank to lend out for them; this shift in the redistribution of agency is of prime importance for the initiative.

Thus, the innovation for Zopa is in allowing everyday lenders to profit from lending, in contrast to the dominant system whereby only banks and financial institutions profit from lending. This also 'democratizes' the process, so that borrowers have more options in choosing from whom they borrow. Whether this contributes to less over-consumption is questionable (and beyond the scope of this chapter to determine); however, it is likely that it does not contribute to less overall consumption, as lenders are presumably using the money to fulfil consumer desires.

Kiva

By comparison, Kiva's website describes it as 'a non-profit organization with a mission to connect people through lending to alleviate poverty. Leveraging the Internet and a worldwide network of microfinance institutions, Kiva lets individuals lend as little as $25 to help create opportunity around the world' (www.kiva.org). Kiva's website also defines and discusses 'microfinance':

> Microfinance is a general term to describe financial services to low-income individuals or to those who do not have access to typical banking services. Microfinance is also the idea that low-income individuals are capable of lifting themselves out of poverty if given access to financial services. While some studies indicate that microfinance can play a role in the battle against poverty, it is also recognized that is not always the appropriate method, and that it should never be seen as the only tool for ending poverty.
>
> (www.kiva.org)

This initiative also ranks highly in mobilizing idling capacity. By allowing individuals to lend as little as US$25 each, many who can spare only that much are still enabled to offer support to low-income individuals, and this harnesses the idling capacity of people with extra cash to share for the benefit of those for whom a small loan can help them start a business enterprise that will hopefully provide them longer-term financial independence. As with Zopa, whether this works towards less over-consumption is questionable (and beyond the scope of this chapter to determine); however, it is likely that it does not create further excessive consumption, as Kiva's borrowers are going to use the money to enable economic self-sufficiency, not to purchase luxury goods.

Rentoid

Rentoid is an Australian rental website that operates in much the same way as eBay, except that items advertised on it are available for rent rather than purchase. Similar services exist internationally, such as Zilok in the US, UK and France. Rentoid's website explains: 'We don't need everything we own and we don't own everything we need' (www.rentoid.com). Rather than increasing resources being put into manufacturing more goods, it offers a portal to coordinate the sharing use of those items already produced and using what already exists. As the founder of Rentoid, Steve Sammartino asks, 'now that we can digitally connect to the Internet, how many ladders does Australia really need? Do we really need two million or can we get by with one million?' (Tufvesson, 2008, p10). This initiative scores highly in using idling capacity and it may also reduce overall consumption and production, as the network of exchange allows more efficient use of what has been produced. Furthermore, similarly to GoGet, this online rental network allows the redistribution of the environmental, maintenance and upfront production costs of the item, spreading them across a greater number of 'users' of the item.

FoodConnect

FoodConnect started in Brisbane (capital city of the Australian state of Queensland) and is also now in Sydney. It is a socially and environmentally progressive organisation dedicated to connecting consumers with local farmers through the mechanism of a fairer and fresher approach to food production and delivery. In this manner it furthers the long-standing international tradition of Community Supported Agriculture (CSA). Food connect Brisbane explain 'FoodConnect Brisbane is an award winning social business that works in collaboration with local farmers around South East Queensland to deliver the best food in the world efficiently, affordably and equitably. We are passionate about changing the way food is grown and distributed in this and any country where exploitation of farmers and customers is rampant.' (http://brisbane.foodconnect.com.au/) The innovation in this initiative is not predominantly in its use of idling capacity, nor in its reduction in overall consumption. However, given that the food is distributed directly from farms to homes, the reduced delay from farm to plate elongates the window of opportunity for its consumption in the home, which reduces the volume of food thrown away owing to spoiling.

Collaborative consumption principle 3: invigorating belief in the commons

In the following discussion, I will examine to what extent these initiatives open and redistribute access more equitably among people and consider whether they go as far as ownership held in common. AirBnB describes itself as a 'community marketplace for unique spaces' (www.airbnb.com). Returning to Patel's (2009, p22) observation that, 'What characterizes today's markets is exchange driven not by needs but by profit', it is interesting to ponder what would be considered the primary driver of the AirBnB market? Is it the efficient use of idling capacity (through putting spare rooms to use)? Or the opportunity for hosts to meet new people and make money? Is it for travellers to have somewhere cheaper to stay and enjoy a connection with a personal host (in comparison with the anonymity of a hotel)? There are likely numerous drivers, but it is worth noting that, in Patel's terms, the monetary exchange for an overnight stay operates within the same mainstream system of fee for service, which excludes those who cannot afford the hospitality. Chesky, AirBnB's founder, reports that he was surprised by his grandfather's response when he explained the initiative to him: 'It seemed totally normal to him'; he then realized his grandparents had grown up staying on farms and in little houses during their travels, and AirBnB is, he claims, not very different from that experience. 'We are not the modern invention, hotels are', claims Chesky (Botsman and Rogers, 2010, pxiii).

However, in the AirBnB model, those who cannot afford the hospitality are excluded, and such forms of exclusion are not consistent with the system of Chesky's grandparents, nor with customary hospitality spontaneously offered. Chesky is quoted as saying that, 'what sets the company apart is the access to space that would otherwise be off limits, and . . . he would be honoured to someday stay in the Lincoln Bedroom through the site' (www.airbnb.com). This statement highlights the exclusivity and novelty of social stimulation made possible for those who can afford the cost of access. Thus, the initiative is not successful in redistributing the idling capacity equitably, nor in reinvigorating true belief in the commons, as the system privileges those who can pay for access. This will also be discussed further with respect to principle 4: its capacity to develop trust between strangers.

Similarly to AirBnB, the sharing of a car through a business model such as GoGet is an adaptation of what may have been a friendly loan offered between associates only a few decades ago. The business model certainly promotes membership on the basis that one is buying access to hundreds of cars, owned 'in common'. Access is also offered to anyone who can afford it, and rates are kept low and competitive, particularly because a car can be loaned for an hour at a time, whereas conventional car hire has a minimum daily rate. GoGet scores highly in reinvigorating belief in the commons and providing (more) equitable access than private ownership for many people who cannot afford a car.

With respect to invigorating the commons, Richard Duvall, the initiator of Zopa, was intrigued by the growth of online social ventures and inspired by comments from the founder of eBay, Pierre Omidyar, that, 'eBay wasn't a hobby. And it wasn't a business. It was – and is – a community: an organic, evolving, self-organizing web of individual relationships, formed around shared interests' (Omidyar, 2002). Duvall wondered, 'How could the same concept apply to personal banking?' (Botsman and Rogers, 2010, p164). Thus, the initiator of Zopa sought to create a 'commons' of sorts within the finance industry. However, when we recall Patel's (2009, p22) statement – 'What characterizes today's markets is exchange driven not by needs but by profit' – one could debate whether need or profit drives the lending of money. In mainstream markets, it is certainly profit driven, and Zopa is set up to benefit lenders as well as borrowers, but there is also a strong drive to sidestep the banks, and this provides the need for the exchange. Other examples of lending exist that also seek to sidestep banks, but these are highlighted as assisting people who do not have access to banks in the first place, rather than those who can access mainstream banks but are dissatisfied with their terms and service. Thus, Zopa does create a 'commons' in terms of access to the interface of the online lending, but it does not create a 'commons' of available funds for use – as the use of funds is still subject to the framework of a market driven by profit.

As Kiva is a not-for-profit organization that targets low-income individuals as the recipients of its service, it differs from Zopa, which, by comparison, does not mediate or determine who will benefit from its online lending service. Also founded in 2005, grass-roots innovations such as Kiva are driven by motives of social need and ideology, as evidenced by statements from its website:

> We envision a world where all people – even in the most remote areas of the globe – hold the power to create opportunity for themselves and others. We believe providing safe, affordable access to capital to those in need helps people create better lives for themselves and their families.
>
> (www.kiva.org)

Seyfang (2009, p73) observes that, 'The social economy provides flexible, localized services in situations where the market economy cannot'. Kiva constitutes an example of what Patel identifies as a system driven by need, compared with those driven by profit. If we consider Kiva as an example of new economics, it 'proposes a socio-economic system geared towards quality of life, rather than economic growth per se, and favours localized, self-reliant economies as the basis of sustainable communities' (Robertson, 1999, in Seyfang, 2009, p74; Jackson, 2004). Although the localized economies that benefit from Kiva's lending are not self-reliant, the aim of its lending programme is to encourage this, and the repayment rate of 98.65 per cent indicates its initiative is a successful, functioning system providing enabling solutions. The lending that occurs through Kiva is consistent with the aims of microfinance in pooling small amounts of 'spare' cash for a collected 'common' purpose. Furthermore, Kiva's principles ensure this is redistributed equitably to assist low-income individuals, and so it is a successful model of the third principle.

Rentoid is free to join, and all transactions are subject to a small (5 per cent) commission of the rental fee. Once the transaction has been approved, the two parties contact each other to arrange pick-up or delivery of the item. Thus, the renter makes money from something they already own, while the rentee saves money, as they do not have to purchase the needed item new. Since its inception in July 2007, Rentoid reports that it has accumulated AU\$100 million (US\$103,500,000) worth of stuff for rent and has more than 5000 members (www.rentoid.com). Although Rentoid still relies on a monetary transaction that, if subject to Patel's reading, might constitute alignment with a profit-driven market rather than a needs-driven market, the lister of an item names the price, and many items are available for very reasonable rates, as the site grows in reputation and momentum, generating a 'feel good factor' in sharing what one has with others and potentially reducing their need to purchase things, thus potentially decreasing the amount of resources being put into manufacturing. As Seyfang (2009, p76) highlights, 'grassroots initiatives need not consciously practice "strong" sustainability for them to have an impact concordant with those objectives. Groups doing "simple" activities like furniture recycling, community composting, or running a volunteering project, may nevertheless develop significant sustainability practices.' Rentoid scores well in opening access to more people and, like GoGet, provides more equitable access than private ownership for many who cannot afford to buy the item they need to use.

Subscribers to Foodconnect pay for a weekly box ordered from a selection of local and organic fruit, vegetables, dairy and bakery items, which have been sourced from local farmers and artisans. Within the rationale of being local is support for attuning subscribers to seasonal produce, reducing the financial and environmental costs associated with transporting food across the country and a strong aim to support the sustenance of local agriculture through offering farmers alternative markets to the duopoly that exists in Australian food-distribution markets. Thus, Foodconnect opens a more 'common' marketplace for food distribution than was previously available. This is true for many of the examples in this chapter, as many of them open a more 'common' marketplace for distribution than was previously available. The important distinction, however, is whether that 'common' enjoys equitable access. Although a detailed discussion of what constitutes 'equitable' access is beyond the scope of this chapter, it is important to remain mindful of Patel's distinction between markets based on need and markets that duplicate the profit-driven model.

Collaborative consumption principle 4: developing trust between strangers

With respect to Botsman and Rogers' claim that 'technology is investing in old forms of trust', and the implication that online systems of exchange can assist in developing trust between strangers, this section of the chapter will consider more closely how the six examples identified attempt to develop trust between strangers. As outlined in the first section of the chapter, Putnam (2000, p142) explains that trust can be thick or thin, and that thin trust, which assists with forming bridging social capital, is on the decline. Online exchange systems can operate as an intermediary that connects people and mediates the formation of provisional trust and systems of accountability, as we will see in the following examples. Yet whether that consequently contributes to developing greater trust between strangers is something upon which this chapter can only speculate.

AirBnB's founder, Chesky, believes that a 'trusted intermediary' and secure payment system have a lot to do with its successful record of good behaviour (Botsman and Rogers, 2010, pxiii). This insight into how the trust is mediated is interesting to note, because, while the online interface substitutes for one aspect of social capital, insofar as it provides access to an extended network of others with whom one can exchange and interact, there is still a necessity for provisional trust. The scheme has a set of guidelines for both hosts and guests and also outlines six golden rules of participation. Travellers are asked to 'Communicate, be neighbourly (keep noise down), extra guests (don't invite others without checking), respect the space, notify (so they can address any issue), [and] write a review of the accommodation after the stay so that a user rating is generated for other future travellers to benefit from' (www.airbnb.com). Hosts are directed to 'be transparent, update your calendar, respond in timely manner, check in (be there, be cheerful), uphold reservations, [and] be accessible to address concerns with host first' (www.airbnb.com). These guidelines institute standards of behaviour to which users of the service must conform. They operate in a similar manner to the eight 'design principles' of stable, local, common pool resource management defined by Nobel prizewinner Elinor Ostrom (1990, 2008).

Although it is true that AirBnB is a not a modern invention, rather hotels are, the modern interpretation of Chesky's grandparents' experiences, recreated in the AirBnB experience, involves an exchange of money and a set of 'rules' by which one agrees to abide. Given the international reach of AirBnB and thus the diversity of cultural norms found among its hosts and guests, a set of guiding 'rules of engagement' is understand-ably needed to provide a foundation of agreement within which strangers can connect. Ostrom's work regarding 'commonly' owned resources that are shared supports this model (1990, 2008). The crucial distinction between Ostrom's work and AirBnB, however, is that the AirBnB spaces are not owned in 'common'. Nonetheless, the guide-lines operate in a similar manner by defining common agreement on acceptable practice. Yet, in the case of AirBnB, the 'fee for service' hospitality is an adapted interpretation of the accepted practice of customary hosting, which in many cultures is offered without fee. AirBnB relies on travellers to write 'reviews' of their experiences, which operate as the recommendation (when positive) from which the hosts stand to gain financially. Botsman and Rogers (2010, pxiii) make clear the reason for this: 'The founders [of AirBnB] believe that some form of payment "puts both parties on their best behaviour and makes the whole process more reliable"'. It is interesting that the exchange of a monetary form of value is considered necessary in order for people to treat each other fairly and for the system to be reliable. The implications of this for current levels of social trust are considerable.

Furthermore, with respect to the six 'golden rules' and their role as a form of mediated social trust, it is interesting to note Putnam's (2000, p146) observation that,

> in the US after 1970 the legal profession grew three times faster than the professions as a whole. Whilst the explanation of this explosive increase in our society's investment in formal mechanisms of social control and dispute resolution is not entirely clear, it seems that 'preventative lawyering' or the trend to 'get it in writing', is a major contributor to this explosion.

Putnam (2000, pp146–7) continues,

> Beginning around 1970, informal understandings no longer seemed adequate or prudent. For better or worse, we rely increasingly – we are forced to rely increasingly – on formal institutions, and above all on the law, to accomplish what we used to accomplish through informal networks reinforced by generalised reciprocity – that is, through social capital.

Perhaps the opportunity to get to know new people and places through the public hosting offered by AirBnB will provide opportunities for social capital to be built and for greater social trust to be established through consistent experiences of generalized reciprocity. The measurement of AirBnB's impact in this area could provide interesting insight.

As noted with respect to principle 3 for GoGet car share, the sharing of a car through a business model is an adaptation of what may have been a friendly loan offered between associates only a few decades ago. However, people have become so accustomed to the convenience of their car, and so reliant on it to perform their daily tasks, that loaning it to friends appears to occur less frequently, hence the success of an online system that formalizes and enables such sharing, coupled with the depersonalized trust invested in the sharing 'system' that owns the cars.

Zopa markets itself as 'Sidestepping the Banks for a better deal'. As discussed, the basic premise of social lending has been around for centuries and relied upon relationships of trust between known associates or family members and the customs associated with a loan. Botsman and Rogers (2010, p163) describe customary loans: 'For a loan to happen, three people were required – a borrower, a lender, and a witness – and a handshake'. As Putnam's observations already attest, this kind of lending worked well when we lived in communities where everyone knew everyone else, and reputations were forged face to face. But, as global trade increased,

> a need arose for a central trusted conduit between large-scale suppliers of funds and borrowers, and the model of social lending disappeared. In its place, we saw the rise of financial middlemen – the asset managers, mortgage brokers, pension and mutual funds advisors, and the big banks themselves – who for the most part introduced faceless transactions and overheads, while removing the community loyalty that was the glue in person-to-person lending.
>
> (Botsman and Rogers 2010, p163)

By contrast with the centralized approach, Zopa is moving towards a reinstatement of trust between people in redistributing the agency of lending into the hands of many. However, like other initiatives discussed, this is a provisional and depersonalized form of trust, mediated by the online environment, and is only as 'thick' as the accountability that the online system demands.

Kiva's loan repayment rate of 98.65 per cent is what makes the system sustainable for lenders. Thus, one could speculate it may contribute to developing social trust, at a generalized level, though it is a depersonalized trust, as lenders trust the Kiva 'system', rather than the individual borrowers. Zopa, by comparison, allows the lender to choose to whom they wish to lend. Thus, although an aspect of depersonalized 'trust' needs to be invested in the Zopa model, the risk exposure is spread across the choice to engage with the Zopa 'system' as well as considering the risk associated with the profile of the individual to whom one chooses to lend. Kiva, in contrast, relies on the development of trust in its system and the 'system's' choice of to whom a loan is offered.

For Rentoid, as with GoGet, AirBnB, Zopa and Kiva, it is the website that provides the infrastructure so that people can connect. Foodconnect by contrast has a secondary level of trust developing among subscribers and participants. Their distribution system relies upon 'city cousins', who volunteer to be the local drop-off and pick-up point for subscribers in their neighbourhood. Subscribers' interaction with their city cousin may be limited or more significant, depending on individual circumstances. Yet the face-to-face, physical redistribution with which CSA is involved develops a momentum of its own with respect to social trust and social capital. Foodconnect's website also operates as a noticeboard, providing information about events, advocacy and policy developments for people who are interested in following or contributing to change in food-distribution systems. In this respect, Foodconnect contributes significantly to mobilizing support and generating trust among strangers, forged through common interest and purpose, and not exclusively through economic exchange.

Collaboration in consumption: a catalyst for fostering local resilience?

Harnessing the idling capacity of local resources can contribute to enhancing local resilience and a net reduction in waste. However, as noted in analysis of the second principle of collaborative consumption (harnessing idling capacity), achieving a net reduction needs to be a distinct objective and does not follow directly from harnessing idling capacity. It may rely upon developing local networks of reciprocity and greater knowledge of available resources (both material and intangible). As such development occurs over years and decades and through engaging intergenerational participation, one-off or early participation that is not followed through will do little to foster local resilience. The online mediation of collaborative consumption practices offers a beginning, but would need to be buttressed by, and developed simultaneously with, other real and face-to-face networks.

With respect to fostering local resilience, collaborative consumption practices (as outlined by Botsman and Rogers) do open up privately owned goods for public use, thus beginning a revival of belief in the commons. However, it is important to remember that, if this opportunity is to be harnessed (as Max Neef prompts) to rethink the market system, it will require also considering, as Patel does, that the system could be driven by need not profit, and thus the notion of 'exclusive ownership' needs to be challenged further. Sammartino, the founder of Rentoid, suggests, 'It is about having access to things rather than ownership of them' (Tufvesson, 2008, p10). This statement supports both the indigenous-Australians' perspective outlined previously, that exclusive ownership is not essential to satisfying one's needs, and Max Neef's approach, which posits a range of alternative methods of meeting needs that do not rely on private ownership of material goods, and 'a possibility that the culturally and historically specific consumerist economy is neither an inherent outcome of human-needs satisfaction, nor an inevitable one' (Max Neef, 1992, p203, in Seyfang, 2004, p50).

In many cases of collaborative consumption, items are shared, yet the 'ownership' of the items still rests fundamentally with an individual, and only those who can afford access to the market can benefit from the new 'lending' opportunities. Thus, the belief in the commons may be a critical underlying principle of collaborative consumption, but there is further room for a more radical rethinking of the system if the benefit of the commons is really to be offered up for redistribution. Furthermore, if fostering local resilience is to be encouraged, then alternatives to the profit-driven market are essential to give local enterprises reasons to invest in local networks of relationships and reliance. This would stand in contrast with the economies of scale (and greater monetary profit) associated with expanding scale, which can occur at the expense of investing in local relatedness. Reinvigorating belief in the commons helps focus attention on the local, as clarification of what is tangibly held in common is more easily discussed and negotiated at the local scale in the first instance (Edmonds, 2010).

This brings us to consider how the fourth principle of collaborative consumption, 'trust between strangers', might contribute to fostering local resilience. Greater trust might allow for a more radical rethinking of the distribution system. In the examples discussed, the trust between strangers is mediated by the online environment – the Internet, which some have described as 'the most robust commons in history' (Botsman and Rogers, 2010, p89). Ostrom's research has 'shown that "commoners" can self govern shared resources if they are empowered with the right tools to coordinate projects or specific needs, and the right to monitor each other' (Botsman and Rogers, 2010, p91). Botsman and Rogers (2010, p91) claim that, 'peer to peer platforms enable decentralised and transparent communities to form and build "trust between strangers"'. As my analysis demonstrates, this is true with respect to the thin and provisional trust through which online exchanges are taking place. Yet, as Maniates (2002), Seyfang (2009) and Spaargaren (2003) have stated, the kind of change that is necessary can only occur through collective citizen action, and not through individual consumer behaviour. There is a need for further study to measure the extent to which collaborative practices of consumption are successful in developing extended social trust, which assists networks of relatedness for purposes beyond the single online exchanges that collaborative consumption promotes. Without development of this kind of trust, collaborative consumption may bring us no closer to the collective action necessary to ensure more sustainable and equitable distribution of resources.

In contrast to single online exchanges, Foodconnect (as with other CSA initiatives) seeks to mobilize communities by enabling them to create new 'systems of provision'. These grass-roots innovations offer the potential to generate transformations in production–consumption systems in a way that individuals alone cannot (Maniates, 2002, in Seyfang, 2009, p77). Thus, the social trust that is developed through participation also contributes a greater outcome of collective impact. By joining small, everyday decisions about food, for whatever reason (taste, health concerns, food miles, supporting local growers), communities of citizens participate in that (radical) creative process (Dobson, 2003, in Seyfang, 2004, p77). As such, they represent collective efforts to transform, not simply the market choices available, but sometimes the entire market system itself. They help overcome the principal problem of an individualized approach to greening the market, namely that, when acting individually, consumers are powerless to change the rules of the game and are stuck within current sociotechnological regimes (Seyfang, 2005, 2006a, 2006b, in 2009, p77). There is an additional causal relationship to consider: namely the influence – through education, outreach, literature, farm visits, websites – that local organic food networks have on promoting ecological citizenship and developing communities informed about food, thus, both nurturing the ethics of ecological citizenship and then providing a means for their further expression (Seyfang, 2009, p110).

In the 1995 report, *Yearning for balance*, 75 per cent or more of Americans felt that society had lost touch with what really mattered (Harvard Group, 1995, in Wilkinson and Pickett, 2010, p241). Patel, by contrast, presents examples of 'participatory budget' processes, where citizens gather in forums to decide how funds will be spent in their neighbourhoods – what the priorities are, and which groups will receive government money first. Similar processes in Kerala, India, demonstrate that civic participation is up, but so are levels of satisfaction with government services and responsiveness. Patel (2009, p146) explains that, 'This is what happens when people stop being consumers in the market and become the authors of their lives, political subjects who both preside over resources and develop democratic ways of sharing them'. Thus, participatory government builds better communities (Patel, 2009, p151) and offers ways for groups of people to determine the value of things without sticking prices on them. If collaborative consumption practices are going to contribute to fostering local resilience, they must extend social trust, which assists networks of relatedness for purposes beyond single online exchanges, and promote the development of collective actions that transform the production–consumption system.

Concluding remarks on provisional trust and modern communing

We know that more egalitarian countries live well, with high living standards and much better social environments. We know also that economic growth is not the yardstick by which everything else must be judged. Indeed, we know that it no longer contributes to the real quality of our lives and that consumerism is a danger to the planet (Wilkinson and Pickett, 2010, p262). The initiatives and examples discussed in this chapter begin to explore the possibilities for rethinking the market of exchange in ways that allow alternative forms of value to be expressed. These initiatives are the forerunner of a greater shift, which must ensure greater equality and the development of common-to-all values as the foundation of exchange that will challenge the profit-driven exchanges that have caused the contemporary inequality. This is not to say markets cannot be profitable or create abundance for groups of people; to the contrary, such 'profit' might be measured by the value added to well-being and the growth of social capital and social trust, rather than the narrow sense of 'profit' as an exclusively monetary attribute. Patel's examples of participatory budgeting and governance attest to this possibility. Wilkinson and Pickett (2010, p263) predict that, 'Modern societies will depend increasingly on being creative, adaptable, inventive, well informed and flexible communities, able to respond generously to each other and to needs wherever they arise'. It seems that the practices of collaborative consumption are beginning to explore such territory. It is important, too, that they continue to do so in a manner sensitive to the challenge of identifying how niche social innovations can grow and spread into mainstream society, and 'articulate a theory of change within an approach that might otherwise emphasise the constraints of social infrastructure too heavily' (Smith, 2007). As discussed, without social trust and amidst the degradation of 'thin' trust that Putnam describes, initiatives that foster collaborative and collective action are difficult to sustain, and thus the initiatives discussed contribute to fostering this recovery through connecting people in exchange operating in alternative ways. However, if this movement is to contribute to the greater development of redistributing markets based on need and not profit, further innovation will be necessary. Patel (2009, p162) is optimistic that we can make the necessary changes:

> Everything we know about the kinds of animals humans are can help us in coming up with solutions. We know that while we can be selfish, we can also value fairness; we're capable of co-operation and altruism and can demand justice and democracy.

References

Berkhout, F. (2002) 'Technological regimes, path dependency and the environment', *Global Environmental Change*, vol 12, no 1, pp1–4

Botsman, R. and Rogers, R. (2010) *What's Mine is Yours: The Rise of Collaborative Consumption*, Harper Collins, New York

Boyle, D. (1993) *What is New Economics?*, New Economics Foundation, London

Coates, P. (1998) *Nature: Western Attitudes Since Ancient Times*, Blackwell, London

Dobson, A. (2003) *Citizenship and the Environment*, Oxford University Press, Oxford

Edmonds, A. (2007) 'Metamorphosis of relatedness: the place of Aboriginal agency, autonomy and authority in the Roper region of Northern Australia', PhD thesis, Australian National University, Canberra, Australia

Edmonds, A. (2010) 'Resilience and engagement: some thoughts on the magnetic impact of small change', *Transforming Cultures eJournal*, vol 5, no 1

Hallowell, A. I. (1955) *Culture and Experience*, University of Pennsylvania Press, Philadelphia, PA

Harvard Group (1995) *Yearning for Balance: Views of Americans on Consumption, Materialism and the Environment*, Merck Family Fund, Takoma Park, MD

Howard, M. M. and Gilbert, L. (2008) 'A cross national comparison of the internal effects of participation in voluntary organisations', *Political Studies*, vol 56, pp12–32

Hunter, B. H. (2004) *Taming the Social Capital Hydra? Indigenous Poverty, Social Capital Theory and Measurement*, CAEPR ANU, Canberra, Australia

Jackson, T. (2004) *Chasing Progress: Beyond Measuring Economic Growth*, New Economics Foundation, London

Levett, R., with Christie, I., Jacobs, M. and Therivel, R. (2003) *A Better Choice: Quality of Life, Consumption and Economic Growth*, Fabian Society, London

Lindebaugh, P. (2010) 'Enclosures from the bottom up', *Radical History Review*, iss 108, pp11–27

Maniates, M. (2002) 'Individualization: plant a tree, buy a bike, save the world?', in T. Princen, M. Maniates and K. Konca (eds) *Confronting Consumption*, MIT Press, London

Martin, D. (1995) *Money, Business and Culture: Issues for Aboriginal Economic Policy*, Discussion Paper 101, CAEPR ANU, Canberra, Australia

Max Neef, M. (1992) 'Development and human needs', in P. Elkins and M. Max Neef (eds) *Real Life Economics: Understanding Wealth Creation*, Routledge, London

Omidyar, P. (2002) 'From self to society: citizenship to community for a world of change', keynote address at Tuff's University, May 2002, reported in Botsman, R. and Rogers, R. (2010) *What's Mine is Yours: The Rise of Collaborative Consumption*, Harper Collins, New York

Ostrom, E. (1990) *Governing the Commons: The Evolution of Institutions for Collective Action*, Cambridge University Press, Cambridge

Ostrom, E. et al (2008) 'The Struggle to govern the commons', in J. M. Marzluff, E. Shulenberger, W. Endlicher, M. Alberti, G. Bradley, C. Ryan, U. Simon and C. ZumBrunnen (eds) *Urban Ecology: An International Perspective on the Interaction Between Humans and Nature*, Springer, New York

Patel, R. (2009) *The Value of Nothing: How to Reshape Market Society and Redefine Democracy*, Picador, New York

Putnam, R. (2000) *Bowling Alone: The Collapse and Revival of American Community*, Touchstone, New York

Rigsby, B. (1998) 'A survey of property theory and tenure types', in N. Peterson and B. Rigsby (eds) *Customary Marine Tenure in Australia*, Oceania monograph 48, University of Sydney, Sydney, Australia

Robertson, J. (1999) *The New Economics of Sustainable Development: A Briefing for Policy Makers*, Kogan Page, London

Ropke, I. (1999) 'The Dynamics of willingness to consume', *Ecological Economics*, vol 28, pp399–420

Sanne, C. (2002) 'Willing consumers – or locked in? Policies for a sustainable consumption', *Ecological Economics*, vol 42, pp273–87

Seyfang, G. (2004) 'Consuming values and contested cultures: a critical analysis of the UK strategy for sustainable consumption and production', *Review of Social Economy*, vol 62, no 3, pp323–38

Seyfang, G. (2005) 'Shopping for sustainability: can sustainable consumption promote ecological citizenship?', *Environmental Politics*, vol 14, no 2, pp290–306

Seyfang, G. (2006a) 'Ecological citizenship and sustainable consumption: examining local food networks', *Journal of Rural Studies*, vol 22, no 4, pp383–95

Seyfang, G. (2006b) 'New institutions for sustainable consumption: an evaluation of community currencies', *Regional Studies*, vol 40, no 7, pp781–91

Seyfang, G. (2009) *The New Economics of Sustainable Consumption: Seeds of Change*, Palgrave Macmillan, Basingstoke

Smith, A. (2007) 'Translating sustainabilities between green niches and socio-technical regimes', *Technology Analysis and Strategic Management*, vol 19, no 4, pp427–50

Spaargaren, G. (2003) 'Sustainable consumption: a theoretical and environmental policy perspective', *Society and Natural Resources*, vol 16, pp687–701

Tufvesson, A. (2008) 'Rental revolution', *G magazine*, iss 12, pp10–11

Wilkinson, R. and Pickett, K. (2009) *Spirit Level: Why More Equal Societies Almost Always Do Better*, Allen Lane/Penguin, London

Wilkinson, R. G. and Pickett, K. (2010) *The Spirit Level: Why Equality Is Better for Everyone*, Penguin, London

Part II

Zero waste, enabling technologies and consumption

Policies

Chapter 6

Getting closer to zero waste in the new mobile communications paradigm

A social and cultural perspective

Robert Crocker

Summary

Smart-phones and networked tablets are the latest iterations in an expanding mobile sociality, where access to visual media, information and services has become increasingly important. Promising constant access to a growing range of Internet-based services, these new artefacts are changing the way people communicate, do business and learn about each other and the world. Most commonly sold as fashionable, subsidized 'gifts' attached to short-term service contracts, these devices are used for an average of only 18 months, with the majority of used devices currently stockpiled, and with only around 10 per cent currently surrendered for reuse or recycling in most national markets. By altering current marketing strategies, it should be possible to extend the useful lives of these devices and also ensure a greater degree of user participation in current recycling schemes, in this way substantially reducing the volume of waste created by present early-replacement practices. By better exploiting the software applications that run on these devices, it should also be possible to engage more smart-phone users directly in waste-reduction practices, in this way ensuring that the devices are used for longer and disposed of more responsibly.

Introduction

The mobile phone's dramatic rise to global prominence in the last two decades signals a new, mobile sociality, characterized by 'flows' of information, goods and people and stimulated by continuous communication and dynamic, adaptive social change (Castells, 2000; Ling, 2004; Ling and Pedersen, 2005; Goggin, 2006; Urry, 2007). There are now over 5 billion mobile-phone subscriptions worldwide, with a growing number of advanced economies achieving an extraordinary degree of saturation. In Italy and Germany, for example, many citizens have more than one handset, making the total number in use now equalling 110–140 per cent of their populations (Wikipedia, 2011).

Smart-phones and networked tablets such as the iPad, both direct descendants of the original mobile phone, are the latest dramatic iterations in this techno-social revolution, provoking an unprecedented growth in consumption worldwide, and along the way fulfilling many of the once rather utopian promises made for the Internet and computers. In 2009, around 1.6 billion mobile phones were sold to end-users, with smart-phones already accounting for over 15 per cent of this market. By the second quarter of 2010, smart-phones amounted to a third of all mobile-phone sales in the USA, up 70 per cent from mid 2009. It is predicted that smart-phones will account for 20 per cent of all new phones sold globally this year (2011). Smart-phone sales are expected to reach the 500 million unit mark worldwide by the end of 2011, and one investment consultancy predicts that smart-phones and associated devices such as the iPad will soon overtake in volume PC and laptop sales worldwide (Morgan Stanley, 2010).

The figures from a waste perspective are similarly dramatic: the growth of e-waste globally is around 3–5 per cent each year, with mobile phones steadily increasing their share within this sector (Widmer et al, 2005; Geyer and Doctori Blass, 2010). In Australia, we currently 'hoard' over 80 per cent of our 'replaced' mobile phones, while 'updating' to new ones on average every eighteen months (Zero Waste SA, 2011). Typically, as in the USA and most of Europe, less than 10 per cent of those phones so 'replaced' are handed in to the industry-based voluntary collection programme, with around 3 per cent thrown away with the household rubbish. According to industry sources, there are now at least 16 million old phones 'stockpiled' in Australian homes unused, with 30 per cent of householders having two or more old mobile phones at home, and around 70 per cent having at least one (MobileMuster, 2011), figures not dissimilar to those in the USA and Europe (Silveira and Chang, 2010; Ongondo and Williams, 2011). The volumes represented by these figures are set to increase, with mobile companies such as Apple launching new, key products twice yearly, which will probably stimulate an even more frequent discard and replacement rate. To the mobile-phone mountain, waste authorities will soon have to add an iPad or networked-tablet mountain, which will contain a similar array of toxic metals and chemical residues to deal with (BAN, 2004; Stevels et al below, Chapter 7).

That a revolution in consumption is taking place around these related 'smart' devices is confirmed by the extraordinary popularity of software applications or 'apps' running on Apple's platform, Nokia's Symbian system and now Google's rival Android platform. Apple, as I write, is celebrating the fact that the number of apps available to owners of the iPhone has reached 350,000, an extraordinary figure achieved in less than three years (Apple, 2011a). It is predicted by some market watchers that, in 2012, consumers will spend nearly US$16 billion on apps, with the most profitable genres being those that respond contextually to the new mobile communication paradigm, rather than simply linking us 'on the run' to Internet-based information. So, what do most people seem to want from their apps? Gartner, the consulting group, singles out location-based services, social networking, mobile searching, e-commerce and other payment systems, and mobile-messaging services as the most profitable apps to watch (Gartner, 2011). To this, we could probably add games and entertainment, already two hugely profitable sectors.

Enabling access

There are a number of social changes apparent in this mobile communication revolution, all of which have important consequences for sustainability and zero waste (Campbell and Park, 2008). First, as Ezio Manzini has suggested, we are now moving from a society that considers well-being in terms of accumulating products and the services they might provide, to a society in which well-being is increasingly perceived in terms of access to services, media and information available online (Manzini, 2002). In what Manzini presciently called 'access-based well-being', our quality of life is increasingly conceived of in terms of 'the quantity and quality of services and experiences which it is possible to have access to', and this, he adds, will give rise to 'a new idea of freedom intended as freedom of access' (Manzini, 2002, p141). This puts mobile phones at the centre of any discussion of social and economic sustainability, or should do so (Southerton et al, 2004; Moss et al, 2006; Crang et al, 2007). Certainly, those interested in sustainable design need to broaden their discussion of mobile phones beyond the supply-side problem of e-waste and resource management, to consider in more depth what this extraordinary growth in smart-phones and their apps means in social and behavioural terms. For example, despite the phone's extraordinary global dominance, few writers on sustainable design have yet considered the content provided on smart-phones as a possible tool for behaviour change or 'situational' sustainability (Huang et al, 2009).

As Castells and Urry have shown, mobility – of people, information, media and objects – is a key feature of an emerging global social paradigm (Castells, 2000; Urry, 2002, 2007). In this paradigm, the 'virtual' does not replace the 'real', as was once imagined, but supplements it, enabling new ways of communicating and experiencing what we need or want, or think we do (Nicholson, 2005; Molnar, 2010). The mobile phone's dramatic rise to prominence is both reflecting this ongoing social transformation and shaping it, sometimes in new and surprising directions. As Horst and Miller (2006) show in their study of mobile-phone use in Trinidad, although it is predictable that a technological innovation may be used first to fulfil 'pent-up' desires, such as just the plain advantage of mobile phoning 'on the run', what is less predictable is the way the new device will be used by a particular group, in a particular place, for a particular purpose that derives from a quite specific local context: for example, to buy, sell and swap music (in Trinidad); to engage in voluminous mobile phoning and texting (in Jamaica); or to engage in large volumes of romantic texting (in the Philippines) (Katz and Aakhus, 2002; Katz, 2008; Miller, 2010).

This should be of special interest to designers wanting to respond to the enabling benefits of the mobile phone as a means for achieving greater social sustainability, especially for those groups previously excluded from access to essential services or information, or subject to exploitative relationships (Donner, 2008). In Africa, for example, mobile phones are now providing the essential missing infrastructure of Internet and phone communication, creating exciting opportunities for many poor people to engage in small-scale, mobile e-commerce and e-banking (Harvey and Sturges, 2010). This has been reviving the fortunes of large groups who have been left behind by globalization (Bhavnani et al, 2008). In these countries, where both landlines and computers are too difficult or expensive to use, mobile phones provide a much cheaper infrastructure to enable access to services and opportunities, and often in surprisingly novel ways (James and Versteeg, 2007).

Remaining connected: self, others and relationship

Our desire to own a mobile phone appears to be most closely bound in with a desire to remain connected with friends, business associates or others sharing similar interests, even when the financial costs seem relatively high (Campbell, 2008). This sometimes serious and sometimes playful desire for continuing association, for relationship, has been repeatedly shown to cut across what were once seemingly distinct and separable social or functional domains, of work and life, private and public, local and global (Woolgar, 2005).

The desire to remain connected is also bound up with how we present ourselves, with the smart-phone and iPad now 'must-haves' and important fashion accessories (Campbell, 2008). This is especially true for young people engaged in updating their friends on what they are doing, how they are feeling and who they are with (Ito, 2005; Walsh and White, 2006; Turkle, 2008). The smart-phone and e-tablet can present ourselves (or sometimes heavily edited version of ourselves) to each other, and to the real world around us, in a dynamic relational way. Creatively personalized through accessing our individual collection of files, perhaps of selected photos, images, music, favourite sites, blogs, messages and lists of contacts, as well as favourite apps, this unique and dynamic collage becomes a mirror to the changing self and its desires (Vincent, 2009). For many young people, losing a phone, or even a list of contacts or photos on it, can be a personal as well as a social disaster (Vincent, 2009).

Genuinely innovative social behaviour can also develop, as users come to appreciate the new freedoms and the new dangers bound up with a new technology (Campbell and Park, 2008). One interesting example of this is the phenomenon of 'flash mobs', where, once contacted, a 'mob', defined only by being on someone's list of contacts, will come together for a party, for fun, for some spectacular prank or sometimes, more seriously, for political protest (Rheingold, 2008; Molnar, 2010). The mobile phone's role in the current political upheavals in the Middle East represents an interesting new example of this kind of dynamic mobile sociality. It seems no accident that one of the leading organizers of the recent demonstrations in Egypt was an Egyptian-born Google executive (see also Ibahrine, 2008).

As the sociologist Georg Simmel famously put it, 'the pleasure of the individual is always contingent upon the joy of others' (Simmel, 1949, p255). 'Staying in touch' is a strategy of active social engagement in an overcrowded world, enabling an instant involvement in the unfolding drama of someone else's life (Crang et al, 2007). Many formerly intimate details, pictures, stories or events, are now 'posted' online, accessible through any smart-phone (Katz, 2008, p119ff.). In a society where almost every social contact involves a transaction of some sort, whether it is buying a coffee or driving to an appointment, the financial penalties of paying for a mobile phone might be, in fact, relatively light: there is only one contract and monthly charge for access to a growing range of bundled services, many of them free, and connecting individuals or groups together in new and dynamic ways. As this suggests, having a mobile allows one to stay connected with family and friends relatively cheaply, at a time when almost all socializing has been commoditized and is becoming more costly (Moss et al, 2006).

Mobile obsolescence: from durable to consumable product

If we think of the car's dominant cultural position, as a symbolic extension or expression of the self, an essential means of transport in most modern cities, and also as a rather deceptive expression of freedom (Urry, 2004), the mobile phone falls into a similarly powerful cultural category, again associated with mobility. Like the car and the computer, the mobile phone is a complex, seemingly democratic global product, made up of individual components that have travelled thousands of kilometres before being assembled and shipped to the retailer. Unlike the car, however, the mobile phone, like the computer, becomes technologically redundant quickly, even if this obsolescence is to a great extent perceptual.

This perceived obsolescence, given credence by rapid technological innovation, is assiduously cultivated by manufacturers, service providers and retailers in their marketing plans, and with great effect (Apple, 2011b; Nokia, 2011; Optus, 2011; Telstra, 2011; Verizon, 2011). The aim of the game seems to be to get users to 'trade up' their mobile phone as soon as they can, or as soon as their (typically) eighteen-month or two-year contract with the provider or 'plan' expires (Slade, 2006, pp261–72). This, along with falling hardware and chip prices, is a much more forceful and effective means of 'engineering' obsolescence than the threat of technological redundancy alone, and is already a well-established paradigm in computer and laptop marketing, where similarly dramatic reductions in lifespans have been occurring (Park, 2010). This results in an average working lifespan for most phones of only eighteen months in Australia, only seventeen months in the USA, and twelve months in Japan, and literally millions of perfectly good phones being stockpiled at home, or thrown away, often shortly after this artificially created 'end-of-life' (Miyata et al, 2008; Zero Waste, 2011).

Why is the average lifespan of the mobile phone falling? It is hard to pin down Moore's Law or technological obsolescence as the real culprit. At present, the majority of mobile phones in Australia, as in Europe and the USA, are sold as 'free' or subsidized 'gifts' to the user subscribing to complex service plans, which lock in consumers for up to two years, or as subsidized 'bargains' used to attract users into various 'pay-as-you-go' card or pin-based service plans (Optus, 2011; Telstra, 2011; Verizon 2011; Vodafone, 2011). Consequently, the full cost of the mobile phone is paid for by very few consumers up front, and this is concealed in the plan itself as a notional penalty if the user tries to opt out of the plan before its term. This effectively conceals any 'residual value', as, at the end of the term of the plan, the user is led to believe that, having paid for the phone, there is no residual value at all in the handset, as the provider does not offer a price for the returned phone. In truth, if the phone is working, there is a residual value, which other companies engaged in 'refurbishing' phones recognize and are willing to pay for (Geyer and Doctori Blass, 2010). Retailers and providers do not at present become involved in this trade in refurbished handsets, partly because of a fear this might result in a cannibalization of their own profitable market (Geyer and Doctori Blass, 2010).

The marketing strategies of service providers and retailers typically emphasize the better value of their plan in comparison with those of their rivals, emphasizing the number of 'free calls', 'free texts', 'free data' included in each particular plan offered (Optus, 2011; Vodafone, 2011). This is inherently confusing, as there are so many variables, and many of the higher charges made by the providers are never made clear 'up front' to the user. The handset is attached to this initial marketing campaign as a branded product, whose superior functionality and 'cool' appearance, it is hoped, will influence the buyer to purchase her next service contract (Vodafone, 2011). But, in the often confusing marketing highlighting these alleged financial advantages and perhaps some functional advantages of a particular phone, no reference is made to the environmental consequences associated with the making, use or disposal of the phone, for at present only the manufacturers have any meaningful responsibilities in this field (Lauridsen and Jorgensen, 2010). The handset itself is thus seen by the user mainly as an aesthetic and functional interface to the services the provider can offer, and, from this perspective, its lifespan seems synchronized to the contract, even if most manufacturers would agree that their handsets, properly used, will last up to eight years. Although technological redundancy is often pretended as the reason for the current turnover of phones, this seems unlikely, as most handsets, once sold, will work well with available services for at least four or five years before showing signs of being eclipsed by innovation, as with most computer games consoles (Slade, 2006; Park, 2010).

At the end of the user's plan, perhaps lasting up to two years, the service provider will offer its user a new, apparently more technically sophisticated or cooler handset to secure continuing loyalty (Optus, 2011; Telstra, 2011; Verizon, 2011; Vodafone, 2011). In this marketing strategy, the old phone seems to become obsolete in comparison with the new, 'box-fresh' phone, as it has been paid for by the user within the previous contract or plan, and there is no offer from the provider to buy it back at any market price, but only to 'recycle' it for free if it is handed back. Once the contract is complete, from the provider's point of view there is no residual value in the phone, as its value 'disappears' as the monthly payments add up and the phone is paid off at the term of the contract. To the provider, who has no particular financial interest in 'extended producer responsibility' (Yu et al, 2008; Subramanian et al, 2009) and, in Australia, as in the USA, no regulated responsibility in regard to any return of the phone for recycling or refurbishment, the 'returned' phone has no particular value, and so it is effectively 'written off' and seen as a 'user responsibility' issue (Silveira and Chang, 2010). As waste-management scholars Silveira and Chang remind us, the schemes they examined could be interpreted simply as a way of promoting the environmental consciousness of the companies or charities involved (Silveira and Chang, 2010, pp2283–6). Only Apple offers a 10 per cent discount off the purchase price of a new iPhone, in this way recognizing the residual value of the old phone and encouraging customer loyalty (Apple, 2011c).

Even though providers will let users keep their own older phone, and many producers now offer 'take-back' schemes through prepaid postage packs, a fear of the cost of possible repairs, along with the offer of another new, 'free', more advanced phone, seems to sway most users towards premature disposal (Davis and Herat, 2008; Huang et al, 2009; Park, 2010). If the user decides that another service provider offers a better deal, a better handset or a better degree of customer service, then the handset will normally be disposed of, as the new plan from a rival provider typically comes with a new handset (Slade, 2006). In Silveira and Chang's US-based study, most retail employees they surveyed were not aware of the details of any take-back or recycling scheme, even when it was in store, and did not record how many phones were handed in. They conclude that, under these circumstances, it is very likely that these voluntary schemes themselves could not cope with an increase in scale beyond the present and unsatisfactory 10 per cent rate of return (Silveira and Change, 2010).

Despite their formally green credentials, in such a competitive environment, apparently demanding such a high turnover of new phones, manufacturers must effectively devalue the products they have recently sold through comparison with their heavily advertised 'improved' versions. This accelerates the cycle of purchase and disposal of what are still relatively new phones, to fit in with the cycle of plans promoted by the service providers. The providers' business model requires a constant stream of new sign-ups, evenly spread across the year, and so a more frequent cycle of product announcements from the manufacturers at each cost point in their range provides a distinct commercial advantage. The promotional year, as in the world of fashion, has been reduced to a six-month or even shorter cycle of new product announcements, which often contain relatively minor or incremental aesthetic or technical improvements, but these are sufficient to go to air with, to convince many users that they are 'missing out' if they do not get the next 'best' thing (Park, 2010). So, for instance, the new iPad 2, launched a few weeks ago as I write ('thinner, lighter, faster, and takes pictures'), managed to dominate the news media for days, particularly because it coincided in Australia with the dominant media company News Corp's attempt to launch its new online newspaper, *The Daily*, which is designed to run on an iPad and similar devices (Advertiser, 2011). As with most new smart-phones, this sets out to create the impression that, like the iPhone 3 in comparison with the new iPhone 4, the original iPad is now 'not as good as' the new iPad 2, being 'fatter, slower and less attractive' (Apple, 2011b).

Premature 'end-of-life', hoarding and making waste

Typically, four options confront most users on replacing their handset (or iPad): first, place the 'old' phone in a bottom drawer, as a spare or 'just in case' it might be needed later, an option possibly revealing a continuing attachment to the device as a sort of 'marker' of material or technological progress (Horst and Miller, 2006; Miller, 2010); second, give it to a friend, relative or someone known who might need a working but not new phone, an option taken by a large number also. Together, these two options account for around 80 per cent of users in Australia, as in the USA and UK, with the majority either hoarded or 'stockpiled' (Davis and Herat, 2008; Zero Waste, 2011). A third option is to hand it in at a 'take-back' centre or mail it to the manufacturer, if it has a take-back scheme. This is clearly not as popular as it should be, with only about 10 per cent of users taking this pathway, as there is little real incentive to do so (Huang et al, 2009; MobileMuster, 2011). Worse, in the case of Australia's MobileMuster campaign, the number of hand-ins relative to the number of new phones has slightly fallen over the last two years, at a time of booming mobile sales (2011). This needs some evidence-based analysis and explanation.

Most studies from Australia, Britain and the USA conclude that a similarly large majority of users hoard or stockpile their old phones (Slade, 2006; Huang and Truong, 2008; MobileMuster, 2011; Zero Waste 2011), with the young, and especially young men, the worst offenders. In one study of university students in the UK, alarming numbers of hoarded phones were found, with some male students having up to five or more old handsets in their possession. Given that many of the students surveyed replaced or bought a new phone every year, and that most phones disposed of in this way were still in working order, hoarding is clearly a serious problem confronting waste authorities and government agencies, and a major obstacle to achieving even the most modest goals of waste reduction (Ongondo and Williams, 2011). As Geyer and Doctori Blass show, not just in Australia but globally, only about 10 per cent of the number of new phones sold are in fact 'recycled', with many of those disposed of in the UK and USA sent on to refurbishers for what has become a profitable but largely invisible reuse market (Geyer and Doctori Blass, 2010). An alarming number (at least 3 per cent in Australia, but many more in other developed countries) are still being thrown into the household rubbish at their notional 'end of life' (Ongondo and Williams, 2011; Zero Waste 2011). Given the toxic contents of these little parcels (Slade, 2006; Moolallem, 2008), this is a deeply worrying trend.

Consumer knowledge

Most users are persuaded to replace their phones every two years or sooner, partly because there are few secure alternatives presented to them, and little incentive to resist a common industry-wide promotional strategy involving premature replacement. Although Slade, among others, suggests that this desire to upgrade is largely fashion-driven (2006, pp261–72), it seems difficult to explain this in detail, and there seem to be real and active barriers to keep using one's 'old' phone, as well as many heavily marketed incentives to 'trade up'. In my view, it is perhaps more significant that most users have no access to accurate, independent information on the environmental consequences of their decision to 'upgrade' or replace their phone after only two years or fewer, unless they actively seek this information out from government agencies such as Zero Waste SA or other independent, non-government environmental organizations. They are also often frightened off this option by the unknown costs and inconvenience involved in repairing damaged phones. This is entirely consistent with what is occurring across the whole computer and peripheral sector too: falling prices and technological enticement to 'upgrade', supported by the unknown cost and inconvenience of repairs.

What environmental information is available to mobile-phone users, on provider or manufacturer websites, is extremely coy about what happens to mobile phones sent to recyclers, and never mentions the profitable refurbishing industry willing to pay for used but working phones, a service directly accessible through the Internet. Instead, on these sites is a bundle of rather depressing national or global data including volumes of waste, types of waste and potential toxic threats from the kinds of waste produced by mobile phones (Apple, 2011a; MobileMuster, 2011; Nokia, 2011; SonyEricsson, 2011; and Stevels et al, below, Chapter 7). This kind of 'waste speak' is skilfully matched with the moral imperative of user responsibility when 'take-back' schemes are presented, an 'individualization' of what is a global problem that in this case is clearly not working (Maniates, 2002). As Cooper reminds us, the failure of this kind of voluntary 'user responsibility' to deliver the changes in behaviour now required is still not being acknowledged by many government agencies, despite the mounting evidence that this indeed is the case (Cooper, 2010; Crocker, chapter 1, this volume).

Although most 'fact sheets' or 'FAQs' provided by many producer and provider websites talk of a moral imperative to hand back your old mobile phone and engage in 'sensible' recycling (MobileMuster, 2011; Zero Waste, 2011), the fact that the environmentally minded user may be 'donating' a usable phone with a residual value to a profit-making enterprise is never really explained. Unless the user makes the effort to read the kind of literature referred to in this book, it is very unlikely that he or she will be able to make an informed decision about keeping or disposing of his/her old phone in the 'sensible' way demanded by waste authorities (Geyer and Doctori Blass, 2010).

The gap in consumer information regarding end-of-life choices for mobile-phone owners is frankly alarming, and should be of considerable concern to governments and regulators the world over. In order to 'individualize' the problem of the phone's 'end of life' and avoid any corporate responsibility for such a currently ineffective system of recycling and refurbishment, providers have banded together in many countries to 'volunteer' to solve a problem largely of their own making (Silveira and Chang, 2010). Using the individualizing imperative of 'user responsibility', they have tried to shift the burden of what to do with the old phone to the user, having artificially shortened the phone's potential life through their marketing strategies. Voluntary schemes such as MobileMuster clearly do not work well if, in Australia, only 9 per cent of users donate their old phones (MobileMuster, 2011). Legislators need urgently to reconsider the impact of this style of marketing on the e-waste stream, particularly because this has become the standard for the majority of phones sold in Australia, Europe and the United States. The bundling of cheap phones and 'pay-as-you-go' schemes is not necessarily a better option, as again, in these schemes, it is even easier to dump a phone and switch to another provider's scheme, and again the full price of the enticing new phone is seldom paid by the user.

Present and future end-of-life alternatives

To ignore the impact of marketing, explaining this rapid and accelerating replacement of 'old' phones as the result of individual choice, fashion or the unavoidable impetus of technological innovation is very misleading. Generational change in mobile technology is certainly very rapid, but users seem to be discarding phones independently of real technological improvements, most probably in response to service contracts that steer them to a heavily marketed, shortened end-of-life replacement option. End-of-life information is not provided to them by the service provider, but comes through the media, or perhaps through ads from campaigns such as MobileMuster. The result of this, as Ogondo and Williams (2011) observed in their UK study of university students, is that most consumers do not know how to recycle or dispose of their mobile phones correctly, do not understand what happens to them if they do 'give them back' and have very little understanding of how the market actually works. The result of their survey is consistent with the results of a study undertaken in Australia (Davis and Herat, 2008). Another survey, conducted by Huang and Truong in the USA, shows that a significant percentage still throw their old phone out with the rubbish, with only some (a little more than 10 per cent) giving theirs away or recycling them, and again with the majority stockpiling their old phones, some keeping up to five (2008, p325).

As these surveys suggest, a substantial 'gap' in consumer information is evident, with most users not really understanding or acting upon the 'recommended' way of disposing of their old phones, and a sizeable majority replacing their phones long before they really need to. In the USA, it seems that the average lifespan of a phone in use is still falling, and is now fewer than eighteen months, while, in Japan, it is an extraordinary twelve months (Huang and Truong, 2008; Miyata et al, 2008). It is quite possible that this is at least partly the result of marketing strategies that 'engineer' a perceptual obsolescence for each phone, turning them, perceptually at least, from durables into consumables, an approach that has a direct impact on the volume of discarded phones and ultimately a big impact on e-waste volumes around the world.

From the above, three results of current marketing practices appear to stand out: the first is that the phone is presented to the consumer as a 'gift' paid for in the plan itself, with the paid-for phone retaining no inherent value at the end of the plan, as none is stated or quoted by the provider. This perceived lack of value means that consumers are effectively encouraged to attach no value to the phone outside the boundaries set by the plan. This lack of a residual value, even for phones nominally worth up to US$800 when new, is an obvious disincentive to consumers to dispose of their phone properly, as what appears to have no value is more easily conceived of as disposable.

The second result is that, on the completion of the plan, the user will shop around for a new plan with a new phone, as common uncertainties about possible repairs and the apparent bargain or 'cheapness' of the phone offered with the new plan will become an incentive to opt for taking up a new phone with a new plan. Repairs to phones can be unpredictable and expensive, and there are many anecdotal reports of consumers being overcharged for repairs or having to wait for scarce parts. As with toasters, iPods and other small electronic devices, it often seems a safer option to spend a bit more and get a new device, rather than run the risk of a repair you have to pay for, on top of the guarantee included in a new plan (Cooper, 2010).

Third, no provider in Australia currently informs users accurately what the phone's early retirement means for its environmental impact, as this might perhaps discourage some users from purchasing a new phone and plan. As no legislation requires them to declare this impact, in a highly competitive market it is currently against their commercial interests to do so and break ranks. Instead, they can give the impression they are doing their 'bit' by referring to the industry-wide take-back scheme, MobileMuster (2011). From the perspective of zero waste, this scheme, although similar to other schemes elsewhere, is just not good enough. It has not substantially reduced the number of phones being hoarded in Australia and has not even increased the number of phones being handed in for recycling or refurbishment for two years, despite industry-wide support and many advertising campaigns.

Although more research is needed on the effects of the marketing plans used in the mobile market on the retention and disposal of handsets, it is apparent from this discussion that consumers would be more likely to keep using their phones for longer, and disposing of them properly, if there was clearer information presented to them and the incentive of some financial return on their old, used phone. Under the plans sold by the larger providers, there is no real incentive either to keep using their old phone in a new plan, to surrender it to MobileMuster or to dispose of it properly. Consumers have to actively seek out information on what to do, and this can be confusing to all but the most persistent. They are also given the impression the phone has no residual value, possibly an issue for contract law in many jurisdictions. If providers were required to insert a 'residual value' clause more clearly into their contracts, so that the handset at the end of two years was worth close to what third parties on the Internet are presently willing to pay for it, users might be more likely to sell their phones for refurbishment and resale, or to keep using them under a new contract or plan. If providers were required to explain to users how they could retain their existing phone under a type of extended warrantee with a new plan, they might have some security in knowing that it would not cost them so much if their handset needed repair.

The preceding discussion suggests that 'paper' strategies such as these could well increase the number of working phones being retained for another year or so in many markets across the world. Even a feasible 20 per cent increase in this number could help reduce the rising waste mountain of mobile phones and cut down on the extraordinary and unacceptable number presently being hoarded. Legislation could be introduced to ensure that users be given the option, when the contract is written and signed, to retain their phone at a lesser charge at the end of the first contract on another or extended contract, with a handset guarantee similar to the first plan, or to surrender the still working phone for an agreed price, if they should opt for a new phone with a new contract.

Second, if users were informed by the provider on buying their phone about these end-of-life options, this, plus some agreed payment for a still working phone, could have a dramatic impact on the present lacklustre performance of schemes such as MobileMuster. At present, this essential information is not forthcoming, and most manufacturer websites speak of materials and waste, but only in general, 'supply-side' terms, with very few hints to the user what the responsible option might be (Apple, 2011a; Nokia, 2011; SonyEricsson, 2011). In the meantime, the long-term effect of this style of marketing is to debase the perceived value of the handset to that of a disposable 'consumable' and not a durable, a trend now well established among computer printers, again with severe environmental consequences.

Although some writers have urged more effective design for disassembly, and other production initiatives that might make it easier and 'cleaner' to reuse or recycle handsets (Chapman, 2010), the user's dilemma around replacement is rarely discussed when the problem of product longevity is raised (Cooper, 2010). Indeed, some designers cling to the fiction that a more attractive, 'emotionally durable' and 'classically' stylish phone will somehow encourage users to keep the same phone for longer (Chapman, 2009, 2010; Walker, 2010). Unfortunately, this is directly contradicted by Apple's heavy investment in design for rapid turnover, where a widely appreciated and awarded design such as Jonathan Ives' original Apple iPhone was effectively rendered obsolete in the user's mind by the marketing of the 'must-have', improved Apple iPhone 3 or 4.

Given that decisions to 'upgrade' are to a great extent engineered by an industry-wide marketing strategy, calling this the result of 'fashion' is rather misleading (Mugge et al, 2005; Slade, 2006; Campbell, 2008). As these devices' main function is to enable access to the services provided, we cannot expect their physical form to generate the kind of 'long-term relationship' envisaged by Chapman (2009) without a considerable change to the life expectancy suggested by the associated plan. For this reason, it is unlikely that even a better interface might result in some sort of improved retention of phones (Huang and Truong, 2008). At present, there is considerable evidence to suggest that mobile phones, like laptops, are moving from the status of durable goods to the status of 'consumables', at least in the minds of most consumers (Park, 2010).

Towards mobile-based behaviour change

I would like to finish this chapter by considering one further possible intervention in the story of the smart-phone as a social, enabling device. As Manzini's discussion suggests, smart-phones (and e-tablets such as the iPad) need to be seen primarily as 'enabling devices' (Manzini, 2002) for accessing an increasing range of specific services. Even their value as fashion accessories (Fortunati, 2005) derives ultimately from the promise of what they can do for their users and the access to services they provide. For this reason, designers interested in sustainability need to consider the total 'package' or 'system' being offered through the phone to the user in full, and the kind of use the device in question can be put to, to aid or further the goal of zero waste and sustainability (Hughes, 2004; Huang et al, 2009).

A number of studies have already discussed the liberating potential of the simple mobile phone among poorer developing populations, where they rapidly become an accessible means of selling produce or linking into markets that were once denied them (Bhavani et al, 2008; Donner, 2008). For the users of smart-phones and tablets, green apps are already an important market segment within the booming trade in apps across all platforms, including Apple's leading devices. Searching on the web reveals many reviews of the 'top ten' or 'top seven' green apps, many of them exploiting the connectivity and locational abilities of the device to offer really useful information to the user 'on the fly' (Heimbuch, 2009). Among these are apps that allow one to locate local organic-food supplies, restaurants and other businesses making or doing things within a local economy, while other apps offer extensive advice on changing or 'greening' lifestyles, and others again exploit the phone's considerable power as a calculator to measure energy use in the home or workplace, and map footprints or 'rucksacks' for the user's lifestyle, travel, leisure or other activities.

On my iPhone are a number of tabs indicating services such as weather, maps, iTunes, app store, stocks and YouTube. These are essentially commercial gateways that enable access to a range of mostly simple online services, some 'free' and some available by subscription. It should be quite possible to install a similar 'green' or sustainability gateway that would link the user, not only to useful and accurate information about their own iPhone and its life cycle, battery, energy use and end-of-life options, but also to a bundle of other green apps. In this way, the phone itself could help 'edit' the user's behaviour, as well as change the kind of end-of-life scenario that no one in the industry at the moment should be especially proud of.

Conclusion

The dominant presence of the mobile phone, and now the smart-phone and e-tablet, indicates a new mobile sociality where considerable personal and social resources are invested in the interactive 'system' represented by the mobile phone. As a system rather lightly regulated across the world, government agencies, including Australia's own state-based Zero Waste SA, have expressed a growing concern with the problems presented by e-waste from such mobile devices (Zero Waste, 2011; Stevels et al, below, Chapter 7). Despite the intervention of many government agencies, at present most mobile phones and e-tablets are sold to consumers without any coherent explanation of their internal material toxicity, potential lifespan or end-of-life choices, except in the rather distant terms of formal regulatory statements attached to the phone's warrantee, and sometimes optimistic website statements by manufacturers to demonstrate some slight improve-ments in their environmental-management performance. If interested, consumers have to pursue this information themselves, often against a rising tide of 'green-wash' that now characterizes many of the industries associated with e-waste. From the discussion above, it is clear that a conflict of interest embedded in the way mobile phones and e-tablets are marketed may be a fundamental barrier to behaviour change. The way these devices are sold, attached for 'free' or for very little money to two-year (or fewer) service 'plans', makes the provision of accurate information about end-of-life options and the possibility of staying with an existing phone at the end of a plan an unattractive option, as it is not in the interest of either providers or manufacturers to encourage users to keep their old handsets.

As I have tried to show, the standard timed contract attached to a handset is probably responsible for steering consumers towards a perceptual obsolescence. Given the fact that it is often easier and 'safer' to replace an 'old' phone when one signs up to a new contract, this pathway seems to be artificially inflating the turnover of new phones, to the direct advantage of providers and manufacturers, but at the expense of the community and environment in which this global market operates. Government agencies such as Zero Waste SA become entangled in this problem, because so many phones are now experiencing a premature 'early retirement', and, even if they are stockpiled for some years in our homes, these will eventually join the waste stream, quite possibly going directly into landfill. As many government and intergovernment reports have shown (Stevels et al, below, Chapter 7), this is creating a toxic time-bomb for the future.

As we have seen from the few international surveys on this issue, most consumers are very ill informed about the environmental issues associated with their phones, smart-phones or e-tablets. Most do not know where their phones come from or how or where they are made, and, while some may have been made aware of the toxic materials used in all handsets through government, industry or media efforts, few are particularly well informed either about the potential lifespan or the likely 'end-of-life' scenario facing their devices, a situation made worse by the general paucity of environmental information included with the sale of most phones and e-tablets.

While more comprehensive research on this topic is needed, one option, suggested here, is that, by legislation, or by voluntary industry agreement, all phones could be sold with some residual value at their end of life, and providers could be encouraged to have some more direct and publicly visible link to recyclers and refurbishers, so that the transaction with refurbishers, if there is to be one, can become an added enticement or incentive to the user to dispose of the phone responsibly, or even to keep it, if the new contract could include some repair or maintenance guarantee. This could greatly reduce the number of phones stockpiled and reduce the risk of inappropriate disposal. Similarly, clearer information supplied with or on phones as resident apps, about their environmental impacts and the 'situational sustainability' mobile phones enable (Huang et al, 2009), including information about their real lifespan, would be a great advance on the present situation, improving both the longevity of phones currently in use and also a wide range of lifestyle choices for the users. On smart-phones and iPads, a resident app could become a gateway to other green apps, to provide a pathway for the user to develop a deeper understanding of the goal of sustainability.

The possibility of using the mobile phone for environmental education should be an opportunity that interests many stakeholders in government and industry, including designers working in this industry. It is already providing locational, e-banking, email and other services once restricted to stationary computers linked to the Internet. Why not consider in detail its environmental potential? Why, for example, should access to the sharemarket on our iPhones currently be so much more important than access to more fundamental environmental information?

References

Advertiser (2011) 'Rupert Murdoch unveils *The Daily*', www.news.com.au/.../tablets/...the-daily .../story-fn6vigfp-1225999145465, accessed 3 February 2011

Apple (2011a) www.apple.com/au/environment/reports, accessed 10 March 2011

Apple (2011b) www.apple.com/ipad, accessed 21 February 2011

Apple (2011c) www.apple.com/iphone/apps-for-iphone, accessed 21 February 2011

BAN (2004) 'Mobile toxic waste: recent findings on the toxicity of end-of-life cell phones', A report by Basel Action Network, April 2004, www.ban.org/Library/mobilephonetoxicityrep.pdf, accessed on 11 April 2011

Bhavnani, A., Won-Wai Chiu, R., Janakiram S. and Silarszky, P. (2008) *The Role of Mobile Phones in Sustainable Rural Poverty Reduction*, ICT Policy Division, mobiles4dev.cto.int/system/files/mobile%2520impact%2520on%2520rural%2520areas.pdf, accessed 21 February 2011

Campbell, S. (2008) 'Mobile technology and the body: apparatgeist, fashion and function', in J. E. Katz (ed) *Handbook of Mobile Communication Studies*, MIT Press, Cambridge, MA

Campbell, S. M. and Park, Y. J. (2008) 'The social implications of mobile telephony: the rise of personal communication society', *Sociology Compass*, vol 2, no 2, pp371–87

Castells, M. (2000) *The Rise of the Networked Society* (2nd ed), Blackwell, Oxford

Chapman, J. (2009) 'Design for (emotional) durability', *Design Issues*, vol 25, no 4, pp29–35

Chapman, J. (2010) 'Subject/object relationships and emotionally durable design', in T. Cooper (ed) *Longer Lasting Products: Alternatives to the Throwaway Society*, Gower, Farnham

Cooper, T. (2010) 'Policies for longevity', in T. Cooper (ed) *Longer Lasting Products: Alternatives to the Throwaway Society*, Gower, Farnham

Crang, M., Crosbie, T. and Graham, S. (2007) 'Technology, time-space, and the remediation of neighbourhood life', *Environment and Planning A*, vol 39, pp2405–22

Davis, J. and Herat, S. (2008) 'Electronic waste: the local government perspective in Queensland, Australia', *Resources, Conservation and Recycling*, vol 52, pp1031–9

Donner, J. (2008) 'Research approaches to mobile phone use in the developing world: a review of the literature', *The Information Society*, vol 24, pp140–59

Fortunati, L. (2005) 'Mobile telephone and the presentation of self', in R. Ling and P. Pedersen (eds) *Mobile Communications: Re-negotiating the Social Sphere*, Springer, London, chapter 13, pp203–18

Gartner (2011) 'Gartner identifies 10 consumer mobile applications to watch in 2012', *Gartner Newsroom*, www.gartner.com/it/page.jsp?id=1544815, accessed 20 February 2011

Geyer, R. and Doctori Blass, V. (2010) 'The economics of cell phone reuse and recycling', *International Journal of Advanced Manufacturing Technology*, vol 47, pp515–25

Goggin, G. (2006) *Cell Phone Culture: Mobile Technology in Everyday Life*, Routledge, London

Harvey, J. and Sturges, P. (2010) 'The cell phone as appropriate information technology: evidence from The Gambia', *Information Development*, vol 26, pp148–59

Heimbuch, J. (2009) 'More than a hundred green apps for green shopping, eating, travel and fun', *Treehugger*, www.treehugger.com/files/2009/10/more-than-100-iphone-apps-for-green-shopping-eating-travel-and-fun.php, accessed 22 February 2011

Horst, H. A. and Miller, D. (2006) *The Cell Phone: An Anthropology of Communication*, Berg, Oxford

Huang, M. and Truong, K. N. (2008) 'Breaking the disposable technology paradigm: opportunities for sustainable interaction design for mobile phones', *CHI Proceedings*, Florence, Italy, 5 April

Huang, E. M., Yatani, K., Truong, K. N., Kientz, J. A. and Shwetak, N. P. (2009) 'Understanding mobile phone situated sustainability: the influence of local constraints and practices on transferability', *Pervasive Computing*, January–March, pp46–53

Hughes, T. P. (2004) *Human-Built World: How to Think About Technology and Culture*, Chicago University Press, Chicago, IL

Ibahrine, M. (2008) 'Mobile communication and sociopolitical change in the Arab world', in J. E. Katz (ed) *Handbook of Mobile Communication Studies*, MIT Press, Cambridge, MA

Ito, M. (2005) 'Mobile phones, Japanese youth, and the re-placement of social contact', in R. Ling and P. Pedersen (eds) *Mobile Communications: Re-negotiating the Social Sphere*, London, Springer, chap 9, pp131–48

James, J. and Versteeg, M. (2007) 'Mobile phones in Africa: how much do we know?', *Social Indicators Research*, vol 84, no 1, pp117–26

Katz, J. E. (ed) (2008) *Handbook of Mobile Communication Studies*, MIT Press, Cambridge, MA

Katz, J. E. and Aakhus, A. (eds) (2002) *Perpetual Contact: Mobile Communication, Private Talk, Public Performance*, Cambridge University Press, Cambridge

Lauridsen, E. H. and Jorgensen, U. (2010) 'Sustainable transition of electronic products through waste policy', *Research Policy*, vol 39, pp486–94

Ling, R. (2004) *The Mobile Connection: The Cell Phone's Impact on Society*, Morgan Kaufmann, San Francisco, CA

Ling, R. and Pedersen, P. (eds) (2005) *Mobile Communications: Renegotiating the Social Sphere* (e-book), Springer, London

Maniates, M. (2002) 'Individualization: plant a tree, buy a bike, save the world?', in T. Princen, M. Maniates and K. Conca (eds) *Confronting Consumption*, MIT Press, Cambridge, MA

Manzini, E. (2002) 'Context-based well-being and the concept of the regenerative solution: a conceptual framework for scenario building and sustainable solutions development', *The Journal of Sustainable Product Design*, vol 2, pp141–8

Miyata, K., Boase, J. and Wellman, B. (2008) 'The social effects of Keitai and personal computer email in Japan', in J. E. Katz (ed) *Handbook of Mobile Communication Studies*, MIT Press, Cambridge, MA

Miller, D. (2010) *Stuff*, Polity Press, Cambridge

MobileMuster (2011) 'Quick facts', www.mobilemuster.com.au/quick_facts, accessed 20 February 2011

Molnar, V. (2010) 'Reframing public space through digital mobilization: flash mobs and the futility (?) of contemporary urban youth culture', Harvard Research Paper, isites.harvard.edu/fs/docs/icb.topic497840.files/Molnar_Reframing-Public-Space.pdf, accessed 20 February 2011

Mooallem, J. (2008) 'The afterlife of cell phones', *New York Times Magazine*, January 13, query.nytimes.com/gst/fullpage.html?res=980DE1DD1F3CF930A25752C0A96E9C8B63, accessed 20 February 2011

Morgan Stanley (2010) 'Internet trends', presentation available at www.slideshare.net/CMSummit/ms-internet-trends060710final, accessed 20 February 2011

Moss, M. L., Kaufman, S. M. and Townsend, A. M. (2006) *Technology in Society*, vol 28, pp235–44

Mugge, R., Schoormans, J. P. L. and Schifferstein, H. N. J. (2005) 'Design strategies to postpone consumers' product replacement: the value of a strong person–product relationship', *The Design Journal*, vol 8, no 2, pp38–48

Nicholson, J. (2005) 'Flash! Mobs in the age of mobile connectivity', *Fibre Culture Journal*, vol 6, http://journal.fibreculture.org/issue6/issue6_nicholson.html, accessed 11 April 2011

Nokia (2011) www.nokia.com/environment/recycling/3-steps-to-recycling-your-phone, accessed 10 March 2011

Ongondo, F. O. and Williams, I. D. (2011) 'Greening academia: use and disposal of mobile phones amongst university students', *Waste Management*, in press

Optus (2011) www.optus.com.au/home/mobile-phones, accessed 20 February 2011

Park, M. (2010) 'Defying obsolescence', in T. Cooper (ed) *Longer Lasting Products: Alternatives to the Throwaway Society*, Gower, Farnham

Rheingold, H. (2008) 'Mobile media and political collective action', in J. E. Katz (ed) *Handbook of Mobile Communication Studies*, MIT Press, Cambridge, MA

Silveira, G. T. R. and Chang, S.-Y. (2010) 'Cell phone recycling experiences in the United States and potential recycling options in Brazil', *Waste Management*, vol 30, pp2278–91

Simmel, G. (1949) (trans E. Hughes) 'The sociology of sociability', *The American Journal of Sociology*, vol 55, no 3, pp254–61

Slade, G. (2006) *Made to Break: Technology and Obsolescence in America*, Harvard UP, Cambridge, MA

SonyEricsson (2011) www.sonyericsson.com/cws/company-press-and-jobs/sustainability?cc=au &lc=en, accessed 10 March 2011

Southerton, D., Chappells, H. and Van Vliet, B. (eds) (2004) *Sustainable Consumption: The Implications of Changing Infrastructures of Provision*, Edward Elgar, Cheltenham

Subramanian, R., Gupta, S. and Talbot, B. (2009) 'Product design and supply chain coordination under extended producer responsibility', *Production and Operations Management*, vol 18, no 3, pp257–77

Telstra (2011) www.telstra.com.au/mobile/index.html, accessed 20 February 2011

Turkle, S. (2008) 'Always-on/always-on-you: the tethered self', in J. E. Katz (ed) *Handbook of Mobile Communication Studies*, MIT Press, Cambridge, MA, chapter 10, pp121–37

Urry, J. (2002) 'Globalising the tourist gaze', Cityscapes Conference, Graz, from www.aughty.org/pdf/glob_tourist_gaze.pdf, accessed 20 February 2011

Urry, J. (2004) 'The system of automobility', *Theory, Culture and Society*, vol 21, pp25–39

Urry, J. (2007) *Mobilities*, Polity Press, Cambridge

Verizon (2011) www.verizonwireless.com/b2c/index.html, accessed 21 February 2011

Vincent, J. (2009) 'Emotion and the mobile phone', GBC 2009 proceedings, miha2.ef.uni-lj.si/cost298/gbc2009-proceedings/papers/P103.pdf, accessed 21 February 2011

Vodafone (2011) shop.vodafone.com.au/plans, accessed 21 February 2011

Walker, S. (2010) 'The chimera reified: design, meaning and the post-consumerist object', *The Design Journal*, vol 13, no 1, pp9–30

Walsh, S. and White, K. (2006) 'Ring, ring, why did I make that call? Mobile phone beliefs and behaviour among Australian university students', Youth Studies Australia, vol 25, no 3, pp49–57

Widmer, R., Oswald-Krapf, H., Sinha-Khetriwal, D., Schnellmann, M. and Boni, H. (2005) 'Global perspectives on e-waste', *Environmental Impact Assessment Review*, vol 25, pp436–58

Wikipedia (2011) 'List of countries by mobile phones in use' (modified April 10, 2011), en.wikipedia.org/wiki/List_of_countries_by_number_of_mobile_phones_in_use, accessed 12 April 2011

Woolgar, S. (2005) 'Mobile back to front: uncertainty and danger in the theory–technology relation', in R. Ling and P. Pedersen (eds) *Mobile Communications: Renegotiating the Social Sphere* (e-book), Springer, London

Yu, J., Hills, P. and Welford, R. (2008) 'Extended producer responsibility and eco-design challenges: perspectives from China', *Corporate Social Responsibility and Environmental Management*, vol 15, pp111–24

Zero Waste SA (2011) 'Know e-waste fact sheet', www.zerowastesa.gov.au, accessed 20 March 2011

Chapter 7

Waste from electronics (e-waste) governance and systems organization

Ab Stevels, Jaco Huisman and Feng Wang

Summary

This chapter argues that the performance of take-back and treatment of e-waste systems can be improved substantially. This improvement can be achieved by more fully taking into account the enormous variety in material composition and the potential toxicity of electrical and electronic products – from a technical, organizational and regulatory perspective.

As there is no 'one-size-fits-all' solution in this field, combining smart, tailor-made solutions with economies of scale will result in the best environmental gain/cost ratio. Several examples presented here show how science and engineering have supported, or will support, this approach.

Introduction

The take-back and subsequent treatment of discarded electrical and electronic products (e-waste) has been under discussion for some twenty years. In several regions of the world, this has resulted in legislation to make it happen. In Europe, take-back and treatment systems started to operate in several countries at the end of the last century, with all member states of the European Union (EU) following these after 2005, when the EU Waste Electrical and Electronic Equipment (WEEE) Directive was established. Japan was the first country in Asia to introduce such a system, with South Korea and Taiwan soon following. Hong Kong, Singapore, Australia and Thailand are still at the consideration stage. China introduced its e-waste recycling law in 2009; the basics are therefore in place, but implementation and implementation rules are still in process. In the Americas, several states in the USA and several Canadian provinces have introduced legislation concerning e-waste; and, in other states and countries (for instance, Brazil and Mexico), legislation is under consideration.

Take-back and subsequent treatment have been primarily a political issue, with a strong emphasis on related environmental concerns. At the beginning of this process, a scientific perspective was missing. In the financial domain, a lot of attention was paid to the questions 'who has to pay what' and 'on what basis should this be paid (market share, return share etc.)', rather than addressing the reduction of the overall costs of the system.

This situation has led to rule-making that is delivering insufficient environmental gains for the money spent. In Europe, environmental effectiveness is the primary issue (Huisman et al, 2008a), whereas, in Japan, cost is a primary concern (Yoshida and Yoshida, 2009).

Scientific research on take-back and treatment started just before the turn of the century, but the results were not understood or used by those developing the initial legislation or overseeing its implementation, and so this research had a limited impact on the first round of implementations. Meanwhile, research into take-back and treatment has continued. This gives countries that are still developing their approaches to implementation (such as China, Australia, South Africa and Brazil) the opportunity to benefit from the most recent research. Moreover, present knowledge can assist in overhauling systems already in place, such as the present revision of the WEEE Directive of the EU. We have briefly analysed below how the basic ideas behind this EU directive have to be changed in light of current experience and scientific knowledge. The three main ideas embodied in the directive are:

- Individual Producer Responsibility (IPR). On this topic, it is important to emphasize that some tasks resulting from WEEE can be carried out better collectively, both from an environmental and a cost perspective. Moreover, attributing responsibilities that cannot be properly 'managed' results either in inadequate performance or higher cost (or both). A possible solution for these issues is to keep IPR in place, but to allow selected items to be implemented in a collective form.
- Appropriate treatment of WEEE will realize the directive's envisaged environmental goals. However, in practice, a combination of high collection rates, appropriate treatment and adequate upgrading of secondary material streams is needed to fully realize the environmental ambitions of WEEE. This should be reflected in a stronger differentiation between the various targets of the directive, which should be derived from environmental considerations.
- Design for Recycling (DfR) will result in better environmental performance and will lower or bring back to zero the costs of implementation for the producers. In practice, however, advanced technology, the availability of industrial infrastructures and outlets for secondary materials, and the appropriate organization of take-back systems can all contribute much more than just DfR alone. Even under optimal conditions, many kinds of discarded electronic product result in a financial deficit at the end of their useful life. Such costs pose a financial dilemma: if IPR is strictly applied, this stimulates low environmental performance; however, collective fees do not stimulate efficiency.

Moreover, there are three chief practicalities that call for adaptation in any revision of the WEEE Directive:

- The environmental gains and costs of WEEE differ greatly, depending on the material composition of the products, such as precious metal-, metal-, plastic- and glass-dominated products. This calls for a differentiation of requirements according to composition rather than on application, as currently is the case.
- For some electronic products, such as cooling/freezing systems, lamps and TV monitors with LCD screens, controlling potential toxicity is the dominating environmental issue, whereas for others, such as computers, telecom products and washing machines, recycling is the top priority. A third group, such as TV monitors with cathode ray tube (CRT) screens and several smaller items, should have 'mixed' treatment goals. In the current WEEE Directive, recycling issues dominate, with

the EU's additional Directive on Restriction of Hazardous Substances (RoHS) thought to cover toxicity issues in combination with the so-called Annex II provisions of the WEEE Directive. However, RoHS defined exemptions are not adequately covered.

• Between the EU's member states, there are big differences, both in regards to the administrative procedures used and their reporting duties, but also in what is allowed in practice to reconcile the WEEE Directive's basic ideas with reality. This concerns technical issues such as the organization of recycling systems as well as financing issues, such as whether fees can or cannot be charged.

This chapter will first address the contents of a number of publications from Delft University on the take-back and treatment of e-waste, which reflect current scientific insights on the subject. On the basis of this, a selection of issues addressed in these publications will be presented here that are, in our opinion, most relevant to eco-efficient take-back and treatment systems today.

It should be emphasized here that the focus of this chapter will be a prioritized selection of the most significant issues addressed in these publications, and by no means a comprehensive one. Moreover, organizational matters such as paperwork (registration, proof of compliance) and financial issues (who pays what on what basis, and organizing competition among transport, recycling systems) have not been considered here. Although these are essential to operate take-back and treatment systems in an eco-efficient way, these are felt to be outside the scope of this chapter.

Key publications of Delft and Tsinghua research on the take-back and treatment of e-waste

Research work in this field started at Delft University's Design for Sustainability Lab in 1996. Key publications from this work include:

1   Jaco Huisman, *The QWERTY/EE Concept, Quantifying Recyclability and Eco-efficiency for End-of-Life Treatment of Consumer Electronic Products* (2003): This work allows the mapping of take-back systems and the individual products within these systems from both an environmental and an economic perspective. Moreover, environmental–economic diagrams are introduced in which the effect of 'actions' such as a change in treatment technology, product design, system organization and even legislation can be visualized (and prioritized).

2   Ab Stevels, *Adventures in EcoDesign of Electronic Products* (2007): In Chapters 7–9 of this book, the take-back and treatment aspects of WEEE are addressed. Chapter 7 discusses the historical development and technical aspects of the problem, Chapter 8 focuses on system organization, and chapter 9 addresses legislation.

3   Jaco Huisman, R. Kuehr et al, *Review of Directive 2002/96 on Waste Electrical and Electronic Equipment (WEEE)* (2008): This is an environmental-, economic- and social-impact assessment of WEEE, based on an extensive data collection in the twenty-seven EU member states. Particularly, the scope, collection, recycling, reuse and toxic control of WEEE (Annex II) are considered. On the basis of this analysis, proposals are made to further improve WEEE and its revision.

The documents cited above form the basis for the recommendations presented in this chapter regarding eco-efficient take-back and treatment systems.

General considerations

The goal of take-back and treatment systems

It must be recognized that the goal of take-back and treatment systems for discarded WEEE items is twofold: optimizing material recycling and controlling (potentially) toxic substances. These goals can be partly conflicting; priorities in the collection, recycling and treatment of secondary streams should be adapted according to their material composition. For instance, for products containing high amounts of precious metals, recycling should be focused on recovering these to the very last part per million. This is the case for mobile phones and DVD players in particular, an issue discussed in more depth below.

On the other hand, products containing high amounts of hazardous materials, such as the chlorofluorocarbons (CFCs) in fridges, mercury in lamps and bulbs, and LCD backlights, should get specific targets for the collection and control of such toxics. In this respect, it must be realized that the hazardous effect of chlorinated fluorocarbons (which are the cooling fluids used in fridges) is approximately 10,000 times worse than the same amount of carbon dioxide. For lead, this ratio is 2000:1, for mercury 2500:1, and for chromium 1000:1.

Contrary to what is often thought, there is no specific cost that can be attributed to 'recycling' or to the 'toxic control' of e-waste. The results obtained depend largely on the amount of money spent to achieve the stated goals. A certain minimum amount is required anyway: this is the cost of collecting goods and transporting them to the processors. The cost to be spent on the treatment of this waste is dependent on the targets that are to be reached. On the other hand, it is also useful to have criteria available to set meaningful targets to develop these systems further, and to balance the requirements of dealing with different product categories. Using such criteria can also be helpful in disseminating best-practice procedures and fostering competition among recyclers.

In the three studies briefly described above, the criteria proposed are based on 'eco-efficiency', which is defined as the ratio between environmental gain and cost. This has been worked out in detail for material recycling in Europe. Numerous ideas have been developed on this basis (Huisman, 2003), and eco-efficiency has also been used to rank proposals for the WEEE Review (Huisman et al, 2008b).

The environmental aspects of products to be treated

When products are treated, it must be recognized that the environmental value of materials to be recycled varies greatly. Precious metals have a special position in this respect. Although in terms of weight such metals only occur in tiny amounts in most products (0–50mg), these can dominate the complete treatment strategy. This is demonstrated in Table 7.1, where it is shown that recovering 1mg of gold has the same environmental effect as recovering 1–20g of common metals and plastics (these ratios have been calculated on the basis of the 'eco-indicator 99' system).

Table 7.1 Environmental equivalency of recovering
materials (baseline is 1mg of gold)

Material	Environmental equivalent for 1mg gold
Plastic	20g
Iron	8g
Aluminium	2g
Copper	1.3g
Palladium	0.3mg
Nickel	0.25g
Platinum	0.2mg
Silver	0.08g
Indium	0.05g

Source: supplied by the authors

From Table 7.1, it is apparent that, for relevant products, such as mobile phones and DVD players, and generally for products with miniaturized electronics, treatment should be precious-metal driven: recovering every milligram is the number one priority, rather than recycling as much as possible on a weight basis as the European WEEE directive presently requires.

This has far-reaching consequences for treatment and upgrading. When discarded, products are treated through shredding and separation, and 100 per cent of precious metals should be concentrated in one fraction (the copper fraction). Leakage into the mixed-plastic fraction should be avoided by choosing appropriate settings, or more radically by taking all mixed plastics into the copper fraction. Also, the upgrading of such fractions needs special attention. It has been claimed by Hagelüken and Meskers (2008) that the efficiency of precious-metal recuperation can be more than 90 per cent in specialized smelters, whereas, in standard copper smelters, this is reduced to only 65–70 per cent. In the informal recycling sector, where, typically, precious metals are leached with the help of acids, the efficiency rate is only 25 per cent. As in Europe, investment in a dedicated smelter in China is always worthwhile, from both an environmental and an economic perspective. A social issue here is that those people in the informal recycling sector (in China for instance), who get paid more for disassembling precious-metal-containing subassemblies, should not be exposed to health risks or produce additional hazardous waste in the process they are involved in.

Such special rules should particularly apply to products in which the use of hazardous materials is exempted under the EU's RoHS. In present practice, this issue is pretty much neglected, with little attention paid to how to maximize recycling for these items.

Economic aspects of treatment of products

Like the environmental value of the various materials in electronics, products vary greatly as well. This is shown in Table 7.2 below. This table is based on London Metal Exchange values for October 2009.

Table 7.2 shows similar proportions to the environmental one. This is not surprising, because the amount of energy used to transform minerals (raw materials) into pure ores

Table 7.2 Relative economic value of materials in
electronic products
(baseline is in 1mg of gold)

Material	Price equivalent for 1mg gold
Iron	43g
ABS plastic	13g
Aluminium	10g
Copper	4g
Nickel	1.3g
Silver	0.06g
Indium	0.03g
Palladium	2.5mg
Platinum	0.6mg

Source: supplied by the authors

is proportionately higher, the rarer the metal concerned. On top of this, short-term market fluctuations impact these ratios: in October 2009, the gold price was relatively high owing to instability in the financial market, whereas the price of metals such as iron, aluminium and copper was relatively low owing to the global recession.

Yields of secondary materials can abate collection and treatment costs. Only in a few cases are yields so high that cost turns into an overall yield. This is the case with products that contain a relatively high amount of precious metals, such as mobile phones and DVD players. Products containing a lot of metals have a moderate net cost of treatment. Glass-dominated products have generally a higher cost, and plastics-dominated products have the greatest cost.

Taking this into account, it is obvious that it is best to organize the different types of discarded good according to their material composition. When formulating requirements on collection, recycling and toxic control for each category, the principle of maximizing the environmental gain/cost ratio should be applied, and a balance should be sought between the different categories. So far, the EU has used categories based on application area rather than material composition and cost, and it is likely this organization of the process will be retained in the current revision of the WEEE process. As other countries are still uncommitted in this respect, there is an opportunity for systems to be developed in these places, including in Australia, to be more eco-efficient and to reduce paperwork by following this approach.

Scope

In view of the above, we would recommend that the following products to be treated should be included, irrespective of whether they originate from consumer or industrial applications:

- fridges/ freezers
- washing machines
- CRT- and LCD-based TVs and monitors

- computers
- mobile phones and related items.

Through this product list, 79 per cent of all e-waste on a weight basis is being addressed, and 88 per cent of environmental gain (and of hazard control) is also being addressed, while cost is being kept to a minimum (Stevels, 2007; Huisman et al, 2008b).

The EU has no product list but wants categories of products to be included and wants to make a distinction between commercial e-waste (B2C) and business e-waste (B2B) as well. This leads, in practice, to a lot of discussion about what is 'in' and what is 'out', what is considered to be B2C or B2B, and what to do in cases of mixed B2C/B2B streams. On top of this, the category approach means that a lot of smaller electronic items have to be addressed, for which there is little environmental gain, often at a larger, often administrative, cost.

Flexibility in targets

Setting up and operating a take-back and treatment system is a complex business in which there is a lot to be learned along the way. External developments, such as an increase in understanding from environmental science, advances in treatment technology, developments in the upgrading industry, and last but not least changes in material price, can all have a big impact on the system.

Based on European experience with the implementation of recycling laws over the last ten years, take-back regulation should be split into two parts:

- A basic law setting the guiding principles and responsibilities, where the tasks of the different stakeholders can be described, and where rules can be set for a longer period of time.
- Implementation rules, which are a more flexible set of rules that can be adapted regularly.

These implementation rules might consider:

- scope
- collection amounts
- recycling rates, and
- treatment of secondary streams resulting from primary treatment.

Neither the EU nor Japan has implementation rules. This means that changes have to be made by going through the process of legislation. With its basic law now in place, China is very well positioned to set up an implementation rule system.

System operation

Collection

Appropriate collection of e-waste is crucial to the environmental success of any take-back and treatment system; only if a substantial part of the discarded product is taken

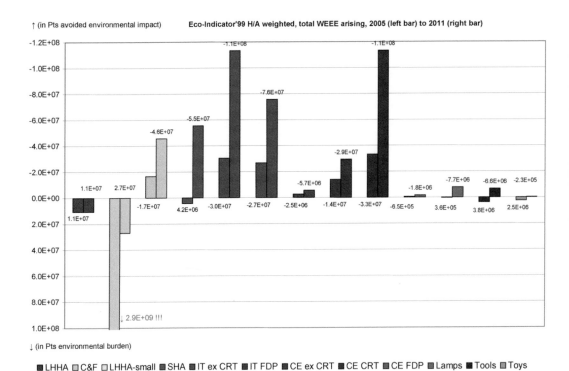

Figure 7.1 Environmental effect of increasing collection of e-waste in the European Union by a factor of 2.

Source: Huisman et al, 2008b

back and treated according to the environmental standards set by regulation can real success be claimed.

In Europe in 2008, some 13 per cent of the WEEE was still being sent to landfill, and 54 per cent was submitted to substandard treatment (see Huisman et al, 2008b); the balance, of 33 per cent, was treated properly. In Huisman et al (2008a), the properly treated percentage of e-waste in Europe in 2005 was estimated to be 25–30 per cent. Volumes of e-waste for substandard treatment are thought to originate chiefly through leaks in the official collection system: for instance, by 'backdoor' trade at shops or informal trading at municipal scrap yards. The final destinations of these streams are often Third World countries. This is not necessarily a problem, so long as it leads to the reuse of the discarded products. But whether this really happens is very doubtful: informal recycling practices with goods originating from Europe have been identified in several non- EU countries.

A similar situation exists in Japan: Yoshida and Yoshida (2009) report that, of home appliances in the waste stream, some 50 per cent end up in the official treatment system; 30 per cent are technically sold for 'reuse' (with 85 per cent being 'reused' overseas); whereas the balance seems to go to other forms of material recovery.

It is concluded that 'stopping the leaks' in the official systems is a number one priority both in Europe and Japan. How this would work out, and how this would look in environmental terms, is shown in Figure 7.1, where the environmental impact of increased collection (by a factor 2) is shown for all product categories.

Figure 7.1 shows that increasing collection would have a dramatic environmental impact, particularly in the category including fridges and freezers (second from left); this is owing to the toxic control of CFCs included in these products. Dramatic gains, both in absolute and relative terms, however, are visible in all categories: for example, in small household appliances, IT products, flat-panel displays and consumer electronics containing CRTs (fourth, fifth, sixth and ninth from left). For lamps (eleventh from left), the gain in relative terms is very high, but in absolute terms pretty modest, because of the mercury control involved.

In China, informal reuse and recycling activities are currently dominating the take-back scene. A lot of material is being bought directly from consumers by peddlers and traders going from door to door (Huisman et al, 2008b). Official systems will have to compete with such forms of collection by giving financial incentives directly to consumers. A demonstration that this could work can be seen in the observation that the economic stimulus package, through which consumers received a discount when an old product was brought back after a new one was bought, was very successful.

Treatment

Generally, it can be stated that the cost of treating discarded electronic products has been stable over the last ten years, or has even fallen. This is owing to (on average) increasing economies of scale at recyclers, better organization of de-production lines and increased investment in advanced equipment. This has led to a situation where the legal requirements for recycling (the recycling targets) could be met (or exceeded) in most cases. Mostly, these requirements are based on weight rather than on the environmental importance of the various material fractions. It can be argued therefore (Huisman, 2003) that some of these targets are not ambitious enough, in the sense that the importance of precious metals and the importance of high-level reapplication are not sufficiently addressed (as noted above).

The treatment of e-waste in the developed world is currently about seeking a careful balance between disassembly (involving high labour costs) and mechanical treatment (shredding/mechanical separation), involving a high investment cost. The material value of most products (see Table 7.1) is such that, in these regions of the world, many products with a weight below some 5kg are not worthwhile disassembling, unless toxicity issues make it mandatory to do so.

In the Third World, particularly in countries such as China and India, there is a third opportunity created by low labour costs: deep disassembly. This means that disassembly takes places into many more fractions (and in more products with lower weights). In this way, purer fractions are obtained (involving lower upgrading costs and better yields), although the obligation of investment in equipment for mechanical treatment is limited.

With respect to 'informal recycling', as practised in such countries, deep disassembly has substantial advantages too, and these are summarized in Table 7.3.

Table 7.3 Positioning deep disassembly between high-tech recycling and informal recycling

Opportunity for:	Informal recycling	Deep disassembly recycling	Hi-tech (shredding) recycling
Components reuse	limited	yes	no
High materials yield	no	yes	moderate/high
Efficient upgrading of secondary fractions	no	yes	moderate
Low cost	yes	moderate	?
Good eco-efficiency	no	yes	reasonable
Low amount of toxic waste	no	yes	moderate
Health and safety	no	yes	yes
Local community	yes	yes	limited
National resources	modest	high	moderate/high

Source: supplied by the authors

From Table 7.3, it can be seen that deep disassembly offers substantial advantages from the environmental perspective (upper three rows). From the cost perspective, the advantages are limited at present (Wang et al, 2008), but improvements are expected to take place in this area owing to the fact that deep disassembly has so far only been carried out at a pilot scale (Wang et al, 2008). Full industrialization will bring economies of scale and therefore further cost reduction. The lowest five rows of the table show that, already, deep disassembly is good for eco-efficiency, helps to reduce waste and contributes to more general sustainability goals such as health and safety, local communities and national resource policies.

Upgrading and the reapplication of materials

From both an environmental and an economic perspective, it is desirable that secondary streams resulting from the treatment of e-waste are upgraded to their purest form. However, the purer the end product, the higher the cost of upgrading will be, and the more losses in the form of waste will result. Such realities of economics and physics are clearly demonstrated in ore processing and in the separation of chemical mixtures, and similar processes, but these are not always realized in the environmental world. Simply going for the highest level of purity or even 'upcycling' are ideals thought to be preferable, but, in practice, however, compromises have to be accepted. So, for example:

- Having the glass of CRTs in a form that can be reused for glass production results in losses of some 30 per cent of its theoretical environmental value (waste). This is still better than using the secondary glass as, for instance, road-fill material.
- Mixed-plastic fractions sometimes are so much a mix of types and colours that the best (eco-efficient) solution is incineration.

Apart from being prepared to accept compromises between yield and quality, sometimes it is also necessary to be prepared to 'sacrifice' some material involved for a 'lead material' to ensure greater value in the upgrading process. So, for instance, in mobile phones, most other materials have to be 'sacrificed' for the recuperation of the precious metals. Huisman (2003) even argued that it is best to process the complete phones in specialized precious-metal smelters, even though the consequence would be that the plastics of the phones are incinerated (only), and the recuperation of the other metals in this process is not optimized.

A study of an integrated lead–zinc smelter (Huisman, 2004) showed that introducing CRT screens in their totality into this process is very advantageous from an environmental perspective. The lead oxide in the glass is transformed into pure lead; the silica and other components of it act only as a flux agent and finally end up in slag. This is better for the environment than upgrading the glass and recycling it into new glass. The only disadvantage is the limited capacity of such mixed smelters in the world!

Technology and design

Economy of scale

Practical experience, as well as semi-empirical calculation (Stevels, 2007), demonstrates that the take-back and treatment of e-waste need economies of scale to ensure the best eco-efficiency of their operation. This is caused by a multitude of factors, ranging from collection (volume of stream), treatment (investment in sophisticated equipment) and upgrading (technology, value of secondary streams in the market) to the presence of sufficient competition between transportation companies, recyclers and system organizers.

It is estimated that some 50,000t per year of WEEE are needed to create sufficient economies of scale in all operations. As take-back and recycling in the EU are organized on the level of member states, the '50,000t rule' indicates that all states with fewer than 10–15 million inhabitants are necessarily eco-inefficient in their WEEE implementations, simply because of their lower populations. This results either in a lower environmental performance than might be otherwise possible (although the EU requirements can still be fulfilled) or in too high prices. However, even in member states with a bigger population, a 'regionalization' of the e-waste issue can occur, including fragmentation due to the presence of too many systems or too many recyclers, or an absence of real market forces, which can lead to a similar sub-optimization. Allowing for the cross-boundary transportation of e-waste in these circumstances would lead to better environmental performance, the development of treatment specialists for certain products or secondary fractions, better investment decisions and lower prices.

Most likely, Japan is eco-inefficient too, chiefly owing to the high cost of take-back and treatment. The presence of two systems only, each having numerous recycling factories, seems to be the chief reason for this. It has been demonstrated that achieving the appropriate economy of scale has a bigger effect on eco-efficiency than having the latest treatment technology, or than introducing products to the market with the best 'design for recycling' (Huisman, 2003; see Stevels, 2007).

This perspective needs to be taken into account when introducing e-waste systems for instance in China, where less-developed provinces will collect insufficient waste to achieve an economy of scale for themselves, or in federated nations, where responsibility for waste is entrusted to individual states (for example, in Australia, Canada and the USA).

Measuring the performance of take-back and treatment systems

The performance of take-back and treatment is related to the goals and targets that have been set for such systems. Therefore, the eco-efficiency criteria discussed above offer a useful yardstick to measure performance. In general, this would be:

$$P_{R \text{ or } TC} = \frac{\Sigma \, (\text{net}) \, \text{environmental gain}}{\text{costs}}$$

where P represents performance of recycling (R) or of toxic control (TC).

The expression '(net)' represents environmental respectively 'toxic' loads involved in collection and transport, as well as losses through fractions resulting from the treatment that still have to be put to landfill (or incineration). 'Gain' means that a comparison is made between two situations: that is, the one with the treatment and the one without. 'Environmental' means, in case of recycling, the environmental value of each material that is recycled. This value is dependent on the environmental load of producing the material that the recycled material is replacing. Generally, these kinds of environmental data are known (Huisman, 2003; Stevels, 2007). In particular, Huisman's study (2003) showed examples of performance calculations as outlined above. This study also showed that the present performance indicator in the European WEEE, the weight-based recycling percentage, is a poor reflection of true environmental performance. In our opinion, increasing the collected amounts of discarded goods has priority over replacing the weight-based percentages, at least until the next WEEE revision can be used to study the performance-measurement issue further, so that a mature and undisputed P_R can be introduced at that moment in time.

This also holds for toxic control performance; here, the principal difficulty is that currently there are no indicators available for 'environmental gain' in this domain. Although some indicators have been proposed, such as the Toxic Potential Indicator (TPI) (Nissen et al, 1997), much more work will be needed to get P_{TC} systems that are workable in practice.

The role of design for recycling

One of the important principles on which early considerations of take-back and treatment were based was the principle of IPR. The idea was that, if individual producers could be held responsible for the costs of recycling, they would start to redesign their products so that the costs of recycling would be reduced to zero. If done smartly, this could even lead to a competitive advantage. However, it has been demonstrated since that the majority of electronic products have a structured recycling cost deficit (see Huisman et al, 2008b), which can be reduced only somewhat by DfR. Moreover, other items, such as achieving economy of scale and having appropriate treatment technologies available, have been shown in practice to be much more important for achieving cost reduction.

In spite of this, the WEEE Directive in its current form is still showing the influence of these discussions and of the 1990s; it is still a mix of a 'design directive' and a real waste directive. It is hoped that, after the revision process, it will be turned into a full waste directive, allowing both individual and collective solutions, but giving priority to those that serve the goal of getting 'the most of environmental gain at the lowest cost'.

Nevertheless, there are strong arguments for eco-design in all this as well. For a given functionality, design for material reduction is to be preferred over DfR – even if the material reduction leads to a lower recyclability of the product. The reason for this is that the efficiency of recycling is mostly (far) below 100 per cent (collection rate, treatment efficiency and the reapplication level of secondary material flows).

Nevertheless, DfR can contribute substantially more in the form of 'design for disassembly'. In this way, it is predominantly serving other goals such as simplifying product architecture (lowering assembly cost) and competitor analysis of fixtures (another form of simplification). Examples of such approaches are discussed by Stevels and Boks (2002).

Conclusion

Owing to the extensive variety in electrical and electronic products and their material composition and weight, and the variety in industrial infrastructures able to treat these products, regulation of the take-back and treatment of these products should be based upon a flexible set of rules. Starting with the goal of maximizing environmental gain at minimum cost, systems can be developed that fulfil the required function. Crucial for the success of such systems are increasing collection, recouping the environmentally most valuable materials to the full, and achieving appropriate economies of scale.

The development of systems to measure the environmental and economic performance of take-back and treatment systems will be essential to support further development. In regions of the world where systems are already in place, there will be ample room for improvement if principles dating from before the turn of the century are replaced by insights that science and engineering have developed into this subject over the last fifteen years. These more recent insights offer particular advantages to countries presently entering the organization and regulation of appropriate systems for the take-back and treatment of e-waste.

References

Hagelüken, C. and Meskers, C. (2008) 'Mining our computers: opportunities and challenges to recover scarce and valuable metals from end-of-life electronic devices', *Proceedings of Electronics Goes Green 2008*, Berlin, Germany

Huisman, J. (2003) 'The QWERTY/EE concept, quantifying recyclability and eco-efficiency for end-of-life treatment of consumer electronic products', PhD thesis, Delft University of Technology, Delft, the Netherlands

Huisman, J. (2004) 'QWERTY and eco-efficiency analysis on treatment of CRT containing appliances at metallo-chimique NV, the eco-efficiency of treating CRT glass fractions versus stripped appliances in secondary copper-tin-lead smelter', unpublished report written for Metallo-Chimique NV, Beerse, Belgium

Huisman, J., Magalini, F., Kuehr R., and Maurer, C. (2008a) 'Lessons from the WEEE Review research studies', *Proceedings of Electronics Goes Green 2008*, Berlin, Germany

Huisman, J., Magalini, F., Kuehr, R., Maurer, C., Ogilvie, S., Poll, J., Delgado, C., Artim, E., Szlezak, J. and Stevels, A. (2008b) *Review of Directive 2002/96 on Waste Electrical and Electronic Equipment (WEEE)*, available at www.step-initiative.org/. 350 pp

Nissen, N., Griese, F., Middendorf, H., Muller, A., Potter, J. and Reichl, H. (1997) 'Environmental assessments of electronics: a new model to bridge the gap between full life cycle evaluations and product design', *Proceedings of International Symposium on Electronics and Environment*, San Francisco, CA

Stevels, A. (2007) *Adventures in EcoDesign of Electronic Products (1993–2007)*, published privately, now available through Amazon.com

Stevels, A. and Boks, C. (2002) 'The lasting advantages of disassembly analysis: benchmarking applications in the electronics industry', *Proceedings of CARE Conference on 'Green Electronics'*, Vienna, Austria

Wang, F., Huisman, F., Marinelli, T., Zhang Y. and van Ooyen, S. (2008) 'Economic conditions for formal and informal recycling of e-waste in China', *Proceedings of Electronics Goes Green 2008*, Berlin, Germany

Yoshida, F. and Yoshida, H. (2009) 'Japan, the European Union and waste of electrical and electronic equipment: key lessons learned', *Environmental Engineering Science*, vol 1, pp21–8

Chapter 8

Life-cycle thinking, analysis and design

Alexander Walker

Summary

The products and buildings that we design and build can be either future-friendly, or not. City environments become traps if they can only operate on large environmental footprints. In contrast, resource-efficient, non-wasteful cities, operating within closed-loop systems, can support a high quality of life with only a small footprint. The longer that the life cycles of our products and buildings are designed to last, the more critical it is to ensure that we are not creating a negative legacy that will damage our social and physical well-being (WWF International, 2006). In an ideal world, the life-cycle impacts of all materials and processes would be fully defined, to allow designers to clearly and unequivocally see which is better from an environmental perspective (Walker, 2007). Designers, engineers and architects have a history of innovation and are therefore well placed to use life-cycle approaches to creatively lock in positive features and to innovatively lock out negative impacts at the design stage. The focus of this chapter will be to analyse the positive role that designers and corporations can and are playing through the use of cyclic approaches in decision-making, to reduce the negative impacts generated by the services, products and buildings that they create.

Introduction

Consumption of materials and energy across the globe is increasing, while the world's resource base irreversibly diminishes, and waste streams and emissions increase. Considerable attention is therefore now being paid to the materials and products that we use to build our cities, in the form of green materials and products, but this raises many difficult questions. What makes a given material 'green', and how do we equate the relative 'greenness' of different products and materials? In a perfect world, the impacts of all materials and processes would be fully defined, allowing designers unambiguously to determine which material is better to use from an environmental point of view. Armed with this knowledge, designers would have the opportunity to intercede early in the design process, in order to maximize the environmental performance of the products and buildings that they design. Typically, the majority of a product's environmental impacts are determined at the design stage. Engineers, industrial designers, architects, product planners and marketers are therefore in key positions of influence to reduce these impacts. They also have the ability to work across the various functional areas within organizations and disciplines involved in the life cycles of products or services, and understand the intimate interactions between people, products, buildings and spaces.

The challenge of industry's fossil-fuel dependency

Over hundreds of millions of years, the earth formed oil from decaying plant matter, and, in less than 150 years, we have consumed more than one-half of the earth's known oil reserves. The ready availability of this low-cost, transportable form of energy is arguably the basis of the wealth we enjoy in most advanced Western economies. The majority of the remaining oil now lies underground, in less-developed economies or in locations much more technologically challenging to access than the regions previously exploited. We are now confronted with the prospect of world peak oil: the point in time when the quantity of oil extracted begins irreversibly to decline (Deffeyes, 2006).

The world will never completely run out of oil, but the oil will, however, become more difficult and expensive to extract, as was clearly demonstrated in 2010 with the BP Deepwater Horizon disaster. Oil security is threatened by even relatively small interruptions to supply, leading to large increases in oil prices, the effects of which then flow into cost increases in the life cycles of food and other forms of manufactured product. Almost every product that we come into contact with has a very intimate connection with fossil fuels, at every stage in its life cycle. Fossil fuels provide energy for raw-material extraction, cultivation, processing, production and transportation of virtually every food and product that we grow, manufacture and build, with many products even being completely made from oil (Economides et al., 2000).

Energy consumption, however, continues to increase dramatically, primarily as the result of population growth. This effect is becoming particularly pronounced in the developing world, as newly affluent populations strive for access to transport, heating, air conditioning, consumer electronics and much, much more. In China's transition to becoming the 'world's factory' for many of the products that we consume, China's economic growth for the past twenty years has been between 8 per cent and 10 per cent per annum, and China has now become the world's second largest importer of oil, the largest being the United States (Luft, 2010). China's need for energy is projected to increase by 150 per cent by 2020 and has accelerated mainly as a result of its dramatic transition from bicycles and paddy fields to cars and factories. With new vehicle numbers growing at 19 per cent a year, China could surpass the total number of cars in the US by 2030, and is now inheriting many of the developed world's environmental degradation issues.

Fossil fuels are intimately intertwined with our manufacturing systems and, in particular, the food production cycle; therefore, as oil becomes scarce and prices rise, the potential for environmental degradation, food shortages and rising energy costs increases. Access to low-cost fossil fuels has been the catalyst for the dramatic growth in human population numbers, and this may be the single greatest impact that fossil fuels have had on earth. Population growth can be directly linked to the rates at which we have been able to extract and exploit fossil fuels. By 2045, earth's population is projected to reach 9 billion. By then, we will need more than double the amount of food that we currently produce to feed this growing number of inhabitants (Cohen, 1996).

Nowhere are fossil fuels more critical to the needs of humanity than in the food cycle. Every organism needs to derive more energy from the food that it consumes, in comparison with the energy that it expends in acquiring its food. Humans have been able to do this very efficiently since the beginning of the industrial revolution. Within the food cycle, oil is used to power ploughing and harvesting equipment, natural gas feedstock is used to manufacture chemical fertilizers, oil is used to manufacture pesticides and herbicides, and we use oil to transport the resulting food that we eat over ever-greater distances. We use far more energy in order to produce food than we will ever attain from consuming food. For every calorie of food we consume, we can invest up to ten calories in growing and transporting the food. For any other organism, this would spell extinction (Heinberg, 2004).

The key factors that will influence our ability to produce enough food to sustain our growing populations are the interconnected issues of climate change, the availability of usable agricultural land and the accessibility of low-cost energy resources. Compounding these issues are the changing patterns of consumption in developing countries, not only from the new middle classes but also the working class, as levels of affluence increase, and the developing world transitions to the consumption of more energy-intensive food, in the form of protein-rich foods such as meat products.

The business case for life-cycle thinking in manufacturing

Per capita consumption of materials and energy across the globe is increasing. Designers therefore have the opportunity to intervene at an early stage in the design process to maximize the environmental performance of the products and buildings they are responsible for designing. Typically, 70–80 per cent of a product's environmental impact is determined at the design stage (European Commission, Enterprise and Industry, 2010). Engineers, industrial designers, architects, product planners and marketers are therefore in key positions to influence and reduce these impacts, often through straightforward methods. A well-designed product tends to embody a balanced combination of the following qualities: usefulness, ease of use, desirability, producibility, differentiation, profitability and sustainability.

Sustainable design

Sustainable design seeks to use materials, energy and water efficiently, while minimizing waste and negative impacts on the natural environment and on the quality of human life. Sustainable design considers environmental impacts at every stage of a product or building's life cycle and seeks to address key environmental issues at their source, by locking in positive environmental attributes such as durability and water- and energy-efficiency, and locking out negative environmental attributes such as toxic or hazardous substances, waste and obsolescence (Resource Smart Victoria, 2005). Other key characteristics of sustainable design are:

- sustainable design objectives incorporated into organizational business strategy;
- the involvement of all company functions, as well as external entities, in the supply chain;
- design decisions based upon measurable data and assessment tools.

Achieving product sustainability through design is emerging as a significant new area of business strategy. The attributes that make a product sustainable are still unclear, however, because the accountability structures that reward organizations or hold them liable are still evolving. Commercial and regulatory environments are changing, and new demands from stakeholders and investors are moving organizations beyond the traditional corporate norms. Consideration of the environment and the social aspects of design is becoming more than just 'a nice thing to do'. There are now a number of key areas that are changing the commercial landscape for manufacturers and are driving more sustainable approaches to business.

Regulatory compliance

A sustainable design approach is now necessary for many exporting organizations to gain entry into new markets. The European Union has demonstrated that governments can and will tackle sustainability issues through the legal system. In Europe, a series of protocols, directives and regulations have been introduced to drive a more sustainable approach through the life cycles of certain damaging categories of product. Three regulatory systems that have had a particularly strong effect have been: the Waste Electrical and Electronic Equipment (WEEE), the Restriction on Hazardous Substances (ROHS) and the Registration, Evaluation, Authorization and Restriction of Chemicals (REACH) directives. These directives have had a global effect by controlling access to attractive European markets (Day, 2005). The link between effective sustainable design and product-oriented regulatory compliance is now well established, and 'regulatory tracking' is now a key requirement in the design of many products, in order to minimize an export-oriented company's commercial risk. European environmental regulation is now generating opportunities for major sustainable design initiatives in the packaging, IT, consumer electronics, white goods and office furniture industries.

Risk management

Many international companies are embracing sustainability in order to address the commercial risks associated with life-cycle input and output price volatility (access to energy, water, raw materials and waste management), tightening environmental legislation, market demands for 'greener' products and services and the introduction of carbon-abatement taxation schemes. Carbon taxes and emissions trading schemes are being implemented globally, in an attempt to reduce consumption patterns through higher energy pricing and material costs. Companies who are proactive and are early adopters of sustainable design practices will be better placed to be cushioned from the worst effects of these changes (Marsden, 2000). Sustainable design could also lead to reduced energy demands of products, giving them a competitive advantage over their less efficient rivals.

Eco-efficiency

Reducing the volume, weight and embodied energy captured in the materials required for a product can reduce the cost of manufacture and the quantity of waste produced over its life. Using recycled materials in a product can reduce costs, absorb waste generated by other products and help reduce the quantity of waste going to landfill. Lighter product weights, smaller overall dimensions and reductions in the quantities of packaging used, can all help to reduce a product's freight costs and associated impacts (Kobayashi et al, 2005). The requirement for specialized handling and disposal needs can be avoided, if hazardous materials are avoided.

Product recalls

Product recalls in response to safety issues, as a result of the inadvertent or deliberate use of toxic materials, can be highly damaging to a company's reputation and are normally extremely expensive to rectify. In 2007, the US Food and Drug Administration learned that certain brands of pet food being sold in the US contained melamine (US Food and Drug Administration, 2009). The consumption of this material caused kidney failure and death in many of the cats and dogs that had consumed the pet food. Melamine is an industrial chemical that has no approved use as an ingredient in the production of animal or human food. Melamine was also, unfortunately, subsequently discovered in Chinese-produced baby milk formula and powdered milk products, resulting in infant deaths and illness.

Value chain management

Environmentally preferable purchasing initiatives introduced by large retailers such as Wal-Mart, Tesco and Marks and Spencer and government purchasing agencies are redefining which products are authorized to be part of their supply chains. The combined effects of green-product interest, eco-labelling and supply-chain eco-discipline are making certifiably sustainable products the norm for access to their distribution networks, as opposed to them simply filling a green market niche. In 2009, Wal-Mart brought together 1,500 of its main suppliers and associates and announced plans for a worldwide 'Sustainable Product Index' (SPI). The SPI requires suppliers to become involved in a range of eco-initiatives, covering plans for greenhouse-gas emission abatement, waste reduction, responsibly sourcing raw materials and ensuring responsible and ethical manufacturing practices (Wal-Mart, 2009).

In 2006, Marks and Spencer launched the 'Look behind the Label' (LBL) initiative, which marketed the environmental and ethical benefits of its products. The success of LBL led to the introduction of 'Plan A', an even more ambitious set of sustainability targets covering climate change, waste, natural-resource depletion, fair trading and health and well-being. Marks and Spencer announced that Plan A's eco-efficiency goals had saved the company approximately £50 million in the 2009/10 financial year (Marks and Spencer, 2010).

New media campaigns

Non-governmental organizations continue to target companies at various points in their product supply chains, in order to encourage the development of sustainable products, production processes and ethical practices. The Internet and social-networking websites are also being used to pressure companies into action, as was seen with the use of the Facebook 'Boycott BP' campaign (Facebook, 2010) and the online petition 'Boycott BP', posted by the consumer advocacy group Public Citizen, who asked consumers to pledge not to buy any BP products for three months, in response to the BP Deepwater

Horizon oil spill (Public Citizen, 2010). Anti-sweatshop campaigns have also forced unparalleled levels of transparency in global footwear and clothing supply chains.

Improved product performance

Designs that improve energy efficiency and decrease direct energy use are making products more cost effective for consumers to use, as can be seen with the trend towards reduced-power-consumption products in the white-goods and brown-goods industries. In addition, reduced component thermal cycling rates can increase the reliability of electronic products, which are normally degraded over time, as a result of large changes in temperature. Reducing the heating, ventilating and air-conditioning demands in downstream products such as computers and computer peripherals and upstream building structures can also ultimately reduce running costs to the consumer (Kwon et al, 2005).

Strengthened market position

Sustainable design is now readily associated with higher levels of product quality, products that are less likely to cause consumer and environmental harm, and products that consumers can feel less guilty about using. Companies are using a widening set of eco-labels and green marketing approaches to differentiate their products as 'green' and to build trust and lasting connections with customers. Product leasing or product take-back schemes (as part of a formal sales agreement) can also alert a company to a customer's interest in making a repeat purchase. In 2005, General Electric (GE) announced the launch of its 'Ecomagination' programme, and, by 2008 (General Electric, 2010), Ecomagination revenues had risen by 21 per cent above their 2007 sales performance figures. Ecomagination is GE's major sustainability programme, covering its products, services and operations. The Ecomagination Product Review (EPR) process provides full third-party verification of GE's environmental performance claims, relative to baseline measures such as benchmarking against competitors' best products and compliance with European regulatory standards (Layne, 2010).

Enhanced commercial dexterity

There is evidence that sustainability initiatives can result in improved employee morale, productivity and employee involvement and enhance an organization's ability to attract and retain high-calibre staff. The implementation of effective sustainable design practices requires a clear articulation of a company's strategic direction with respect to sustainability, and appropriate training is required at all levels of an organization. The cross-functional nature of sustainable design can also lead to more efficient decision-making and communication, a reduction in late changes in product development or process specifications and an overall reduction in product development lead times (White, 2009).

Opportunities for innovation

Sustainable design is being recognized as the next wave of technological innovation and can present a considerable opportunity for organizations to differentiate their products and gain a competitive advantage through innovation and creativity. Although sustainable design approaches may not directly alter population growth, they can, however, influence the impact of products and influence the ways that these products are consumed, by modifying the way that product offerings are valued by consumers in respect to their wants, needs and behaviours (White, 2009).

Life-cycle thinking, closed-loop processes and life-cycle assessment

Life-cycle thinking recognizes that whole product life cycles must be considered, if the true environmental impacts of a product are to be understood and then minimized. Every product that we come into contact with has a very close connection with fossil fuels. Consider the example of a simple plastic garden chair. The energy used throughout this object's life cycle, from cradle to grave, is almost entirely derived from oil and fossil-fuel energy. First, crude oil might be extracted from under the ground somewhere in the Middle East and then transported to an oil refinery and distilled into the various constituent chemicals that are required to manufacture polypropylene. The chemicals are then shipped to a manufacturing plant, which polymerizes the chemicals to create polypropylene pellets. In addition, iron ore might be mined in Australia and shipped to China, where it is smelted into steel, using vast amounts of Australian coal-derived electrical energy, to allow the manufacture of a steel injection-moulding tool. The polypropylene pellets and injection-moulding tool might then be transported to Italy, where an injection-moulding machine constructed predominantly of steel is then used, with the addition of heat and pressure derived from electricity, to manufacture the chair. The chair might then be freighted by sea to Australia and transported to a distribution centre and then on to a retailer, where a customer will eventually drive their car to purchase the chair. The chair is then hopefully used for many years before being transported to a landfill site at the end of its useful life. Waste is not only generated at the highly visible end-of-life, but also at every stage of the chair's extensive life cycle. The volumes of waste generated during raw-material extraction, processing, product manufacture and distribution can be many times the volume of waste eventually materialized at the chair's demise.

The waste that is generated over a product's life cycle, from manufacture, use and disposal, has a number of environmental, social and economic costs linked to its generation. Waste contaminates the surface of the natural environment and landfill sites generate greenhouse-gas emissions, most notably methane from the anaerobic decomposition of food waste. Product and packaging waste is also commonly moved from developed to developing nations, where laws regulating the processing and disposal of hazardous materials are more relaxed or not enforced (Sonak, 2008). The economic costs associated with waste disposal are also high, most often borne by municipal governments and ultimately by the consumer. A similar trail of materials and energy inputs and waste and emissions outputs can be mapped throughout the material extraction, manufacture, use and disposal phases for almost every product or food item that we consume, but not all life-cycle-stage impact profiles are the same for all categories of product. The plastic chair example described previously would have a very different life-cycle 'profile' from that of an electrical appliance. The bulk of a plastic chair's impacts would be realized during the material extraction, processing and disposal

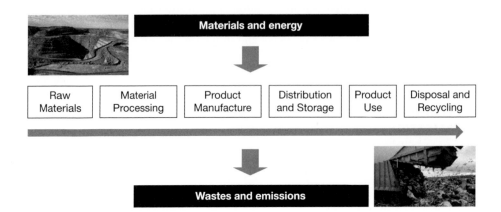

Figure 8.1 Product life cycle.

Source: A. W. Walker

phases, whereas the majority of the appliance's impacts, if it were, say, a toaster, would be realized during its use phase, owing to the energy demands of the product's heating elements. During the use phase of the chair, any impacts would be limited to the use of consumables (such as cleaning products) and would therefore be minimal.

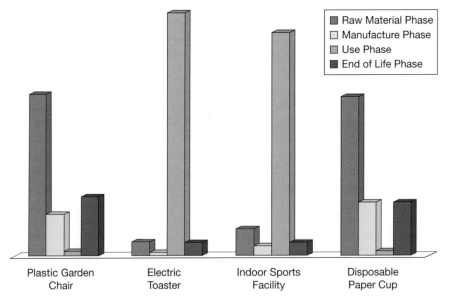

Figure 8.2 Product life-cycle comparisons.

Source: A. W. Walker

Closed-loop processes

In the 1970s, the Swiss architect Walter Stahel first proposed the idea that redesigning products to minimize waste, material resources and energy could potentially be a way of achieving a more sustainable society. He termed this approach 'regenerative design' and 'cradle to cradle', referring to a product's potentially 'closed-loop' cyclic approach. In the more normal 'cradle to grave' end-of-life scenario, products are either incinerated or sent to landfill once they have reached the end of their useful life. As the result of a research project funded by the European Commission, 'The potential for substituting manpower for energy' (Stahel and Reday-Mulvey, 1981), Walter Stahel and Genevieve Reday developed the concept of a 'looped economy' and its potential for employment creation, increased economic competitiveness, increased resource efficiency, increased energy efficiency and waste reduction or prevention. The project recognized that waste is a financial burden on the community and that, if the cost of managing waste were carried by the producer rather than by the consumer, this could lead to manufacturer-initiated waste-prevention strategies, such as waste elimination, remanufacturing of products and the more localized production of products and services. A cyclic system could potentially create an economy based on spiral loops that minimizes material flows, energy flows and environmental deterioration, without restricting economic growth or social and technical progress (Stahel and Börlin, 1987). The key principles of the 'cradle-to-cradle' concept pioneered by Stahel and his colleagues were:

- product design optimized for durability, adaptability, remanufacturing and recycling;
- remanufacturing that preserves the frame of a product after use, replacing only the worn-out parts;
- business models based around 'product leasing' as opposed to 'product selling', where ownership remains with the manufacturer over the entire product life cycle, thereby encouraging product durability and improved quality approaches to product design, manufacture and maintenance;
- extended product liability/stewardship/responsibility, encouraging manufacturers to guarantee low-pollution-use and easy-reuse products.

Cradle to cradle

In 2002, William McDonough, an architect and designer, and Michael Braungart, an ecological chemist, further developed the 'cradle-to-cradle' concept into a system of 'life-cycle development', where waste would be eliminated, or, if unavoidable, products would be designed in such a way that any generated wastes would become nutrients for other manufacturing processes, as is typically found in biological systems, where waste is food (Braungart and McDonough, 2002). Cradle to cradle is a biomimetic approach to the design of products and systems, where waste would either be compostable and act as a biological nutrient (food for the biosphere), or non-compostable and act as a technological nutrient (food for the technosphere). Cradle to cradle as a sustainable design methodology aims to ensure that nutrients are continuously cycled round manufacturing processes as valuable resources, rather than being used once and then disposed of as valueless waste. This approach encourages designs that ensure that a product's output resources, such as materials, water and energy, can be reused as another product's input resources.

Biomimicry

In her 1997 book, *Biomimicry: innovation inspired by nature*, Janine M. Benyus introduced the concept of biomimicry, a design process that uses nature as a model for developing solutions to human-scale problems. Plants, animals and microbes have been patiently perfecting their products for more than 3.8 billion years, turning rock and sea into a life-friendly home (Benyus, 2002). Biomimicry explores new ways of viewing and valuing nature, basing decisions not on what can we extract from nature, but on what can we learn from nature. It is a life-cycle style of designing, as it not only deals with the physical design of an object, but also all aspects of its life cycle, from cradle to grave or, ideally, cradle to cradle.

Life-cycle assessment

If we assume that the earth's population will continue to grow, and we also assume continued economic growth, especially in the developing world, the environmental impacts of our activities will have to be reduced. We will have to develop products and buildings that are radically different from those we currently manufacture and build today. There is no such thing as a sustainable product or building, as all the products and buildings that we design and construct consume energy and materials and generate waste and emissions. The best we can currently hope to achieve are products and buildings that are 'more' sustainable than those we currently make today. Designing more sustainable products begins with the introduction of life-cycle-thinking approaches at the beginning of the design process. It is no longer acceptable to simply focus on the object being designed, when we have responsibility for the whole product system, over the entire life of a product.

Without conclusive knowledge to base life-cycle decisions upon, we are guided by our intuition. Our intuition is normally informed by our acquired knowledge and past experiences, but few designers have detailed knowledge of all upstream and downstream processes involved in a product or building's supply chain. Few designers have smelted steel, polymerized polyethylene or layered and then etched semiconductors used in the products that they are responsible for designing. Environmental design decisions are therefore normally poorly made, as these decisions are based on our intuition. People may ask:

- Are reusable cloth nappies more environmentally friendly than the vast number of disposable nappies used and disposed of during a child's babyhood and infancy?
- Are reusable ceramic cups better for the environment than using waste-generating disposable cups?
- In selecting a sustainable sports surface, is a natural grass playing surface better than an oil-derived artificial grass playing surface?

In the absence of reliable, quantifiable data, we very often intuit the answer that might appear obvious, or the answer we would like to use, to justify our behaviours, or our decisions may simply become paralysed through indecision. If you ask a 'green' question, very often you get a 'grey' answer. The introduction of a more sustainable approach to product development or architecture is often restricted by a lack of easily accessible, reliable, life-cycle data, especially in commercial environments, where many suppliers make environmental claims proclaiming the green virtues of 'singular' aspects of their material, product or service. It is difficult to calculate the impacts of complex production processes operating within complicated ecological systems, especially within dynamic, non-linear design processes, where concepts are constantly evolving and changing as a design develops. In answer to this need for 'sustainable design intelligence', life-cycle assessment (LCA) has been developed, a methodology that considers, where possible, the entire life cycle of a product or service. LCA aims to identify the potential environmental impacts of a product, process or activity in measurable terms, by identifying and quantifying the materials and energy used and the wastes and emissions released to the environment over its life. The adoption of a dogmatic approach to everything we consume may, in some cases, be more environmentally damaging than other alternatives, when the various stages of a product's life cycle are not fully considered.

Green nappies, coffee cups and grass

Green nappies

In 1961, Proctor and Gamble (P&G) launched Pampers disposable nappies, and, by the early 1990s, the disposable nappy had become the symbol of our 'throw-away' society and began to be targeted by non-governmental organizations. In response, P&G commissioned the management consulting company, Arthur D. Little (1990), to conduct an LCA project comparing the respective impacts of disposable and reusable nappies. In this study, Arthur D. Little made the assumption that the number of daily nappy changes would be the same for both reusable and disposable nappies, and that 90 per cent of all reusable nappies are washed at home (10 per cent using a commercial nappy-laundering service). Among other findings, the Arthur D. Little study concluded that laundering a cloth nappy over its lifetime consumes up to six times the water, three times the energy and eight times the emissions to air than are used to manufacture and use a commensurate number of disposable nappies.

Critics felt that this study was flawed in ways that favoured disposable nappies, and, in response to the Arthur D. Little study, Greenpeace commissioned its own research, which gave quite contradictory results. The conflicting results were largely due to the incorporation of different life-cycle inventory data, model assumptions, boundary choices and calculation methods and have prevented a generally accepted conclusion to the nappy debate being reached. The general trends evident in the results of each study were identical, however, in that reusable nappies generate less waste than disposable nappies, but they consume more energy and more water and generate more emissions to air and water.

Green coffee cups

Ceramic, plastic or paper coffee cups? Deciding which is the most environmentally friendly should be obvious, and, as a result, most people intuitively choose ceramic as being the most environmentally benign beverage cup. On further investigation, however, this assumption becomes questionable when ceramic manufacturing processes are taken into account, as ceramics kilns use large amounts of energy, and so do the hot-water systems that are needed to wash soiled ceramic cups, whereas single-use paper and plastic cups – which appear very wasteful – can be manufactured and recycled in large numbers very efficiently.

A life-cycle-energy analysis conducted in 1994 by Martin B. Hocking compared three types of reusable beverage cup (ceramic, glass and reusable plastic) with two types of disposable beverage cup (paper and expanded polystyrene foam). The energy embodied in the manufacture of a reusable ceramic cup was found to be much higher than the energy locked in during the manufacture of a disposable cup (Hocking, 1994). In order for a reusable cup to be more energy efficient than a disposable cup, it must be washed and reused as many times as possible, to fully exploit the energy consumed in its manufacture. In addition, the energy required to freight a reusable cup is normally considerably more than transporting a disposable cup, as reusable cups require bulky protective packaging and tend to be larger and heavier than single-use cups, which in contrast can be tightly stacked and nested with minimal protective packaging.

Hocking concluded that, although a reusable ceramic cup generates much less physical waste than a single-use cup, the ceramic cup would have to be used 1,006 times for it to break even with its polystyrene competitor (Hocking, 1994). This is largely owing to the fact that ceramics kilns are extraordinarily energy intensive, dishwashers required to wash the cup also use energy, and ceramic cups ultimately get chipped, broken and disposed of in landfill sites, as they cannot be recycled. Plastic and paper cups benefit from a reasonably good recycling infrastructure in most developed countries.

In order to reuse a ceramic cup, it also has to be washed. Dishwashers are generally the most energy-efficient way of cleaning dishes, but Hocking's results found extreme sensitivity in respect to the amount of energy that a dishwasher uses, making it very important only to operate a dishwasher with a full load. Dishwashers generally require less energy and use less water than hand-washing, as they are very efficient users of hot water. The efficiency of a dishwasher and that of the energy source that powers it determine how much energy is required for each wash. Hocking based his analysis on Canadian electricity inventory data, and the results could potentially be more detrimental to the case for the reusable cup had the study been repeated using Australian data, owing to Australia's reliance on low-grade coal in the energy supply chain. This sensitivity to washing energy could mean that a reusable cup, if washed by hand or if an inefficient dishwasher powered by an inefficient energy source was used, would never reach break-even with a foam cup, regardless of the number of reuses. As with all LCAs, the data used in Hocking's study are regionally specific, and the LCA will yield different results if conducted using alternative inventory data.

Green grass

Natural grass playing surfaces are the norm throughout most of the world. Natural grass is also a renewable resource, with negative net carbon emissions, but there is also the possibility that the environmental burden produced while maintaining a natural grass playing surface throughout its life may outweigh the environmental load of its oil-based, artificial alternatives. Creating and maintaining natural grass brings with it heavy environmental loads in the form of regular mowing and fertilizer, herbicide and pesticide use (Walker, 2007).

Pesticides are often used on natural grass, not in response to a particular pest, but to prevent any problems arising in the first place. Maintenance staff who come into direct contact with pesticides are at risk of health problems ranging from respiratory and skin irritations to neurological and endocrine-system disorders. In addition, pesticides may find their way into groundwater (Snow, 1996). Grasses do not physically grow as a monoculture in nature, and therefore intruding plants must be managed with the use of herbicides. Natural grass playing fields are in fact a 'biological impossibility' without the significant use of water and chemicals.

Excess usage of fertilizers can throw natural cycles wildly out of balance. When washed into streams and rivers, they stimulate the growth of toxic algae blooms. The algae eventually die and decay, robbing ecosystems of oxygen through the process of eutrophication (Branham et al, 1995). Fertilization also speeds up the growth of grass, which increases the demand for water and the frequency at which the grass then needs to be cut. Grass-cutting machinery also contributes to noise pollution and air pollution, by releasing, for example, hydrocarbons, particulates, nitrogen oxides, carbon monoxide and carbon dioxide (Joyce, 1998).

In this particular study using the available inputs, the indications were that, over the ten-year life of an artificial grass sports playing surface, the manufacture, installation and maintenance of an artificial surface will produce fewer greenhouse-gas (GHG) emissions than a natural grass surface, when all of the heavy environmental burdens in the form of irrigation, fertilizer, pesticide, herbicide use and mowing are taken into account (Walker, 2007). Even though natural grass sequestrates approximately 1t of carbon dioxide each year (Qian and Follett, 2002), the combined effects of the various maintenance activities have an extremely negative impact on natural grass's 'green' credentials (Walker, 2007).

LCA uses

LCA has traditionally been used to measure the relative 'greenness' of a product or service. However, full LCAs are expensive to conduct, require considerable expertise, are time consuming and are therefore difficult to apply iteratively within the design process. This problem has encouraged the development of 'simplified' LCA tools, which allow the evaluation of concepts during the design process. These tools can help to identify ecologically problematic areas within evolving designs, allowing targeted eco-design strategies to be employed to reduce the overall impacts of a particular concept. Ecologically optimized concepts can be compared against each other to identify opportunities for product innovation and to select a final product design direction. At the end of the design process, a 'full-blown' LCA can ultimately be conducted, to accurately define the overall impacts of the final product. LCA enables organizations to:

- identify sources of waste and develop strategies to minimize or eradicate waste within the various stages of a product's life cycle, not only at the product's end-of-life;
- conduct environmental impact comparisons between different products and manufacturing processes;
- identify and redesign design details and manufacturing processes that have high environmental loads;

LCA Procedure: ISO 14044

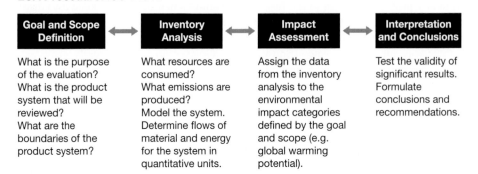

Goal and Scope Definition	Inventory Analysis	Impact Assessment	Interpretation and Conclusions
What is the purpose of the evaluation? What is the product system that will be reviewed? What are the boundaries of the product system?	What resources are consumed? What emissions are produced? Model the system. Determine flows of material and energy for the system in quantitative units.	Assign the data from the inventory analysis to the environmental impact categories defined by the goal and scope (e.g. global warming potential).	Test the validity of significant results. Formulate conclusions and recommendations.

Figure 8.3 Life-cycle assessment procedure.

Source: A. W. Walker

- provide useful 'green' purchasing information to consumers;
- manage business risks such as 'carbon pricing' and 'environmental trading schemes';
- provide comparisons between proprietary products and services and a competitor's products and services;
- position organizations as leaders in sustainability within various markets;
- encourage targeted eco-innovation.

Benefits of LCA

A major benefit of LCA is that the methodology considers all life-cycle stages of a product or service and does not solely focus on the early material selection stages, which have been the traditional hub of the product design process. LCA can be used in comparative studies to help pick a less damaging product concept or help redesign a harmful manufacturing process. It is a quantitative approach to the environmental evaluation of a product or service, removing subjectivity and bias. Its demonstrated use can help position an organization as a leader in sustainability in the eyes of the consumer and encourage an organization to act proactively rather than reactively, as LCA is both comprehensive and authoritative. It can provide customers with information that can influence their purchasing decisions, minimize economic risk, and it can go 'beyond carbon', as a broad range of environmental-impact categories can be evaluated.

Limitations of LCA

The ready availability of reliable data can restrict the effectiveness of an LCA study, as most commonly available information is based on European or US data, and local data may be nonexistent or difficult to gather and access. Using data from another geographic region can lead to inaccurate results. For example, the energy mix in Australia is dominated by coal, which generates high levels of carbon dioxide (CO_2) emissions when burnt. European data on the other hand may include hydroelectric and nuclear power in the energy mix, which would generate lower CO_2 emissions. The full LCA modelling process is detailed and time consuming, and therefore some organizations have developed processes that use 'simplified' LCA tools during the design process and only conduct a 'full' LCA at the end of the development process.

Sports surface selection case study

While designing a building, architects are responsible for specifying a vast range of materials and building components, and each supplier often makes claims for the environmental benefits of their own products or services. Claims extolling the green virtues of one aspect of a system may, however, mask the negative elements of another life-cycle stage. In addition, viewing each building element in isolation ignores the interconnected and interdependent nature of the building's components and life cycles. If an architect is asked to design a 'green sport and recreation centre', how can she decide which sports surface should be used within the facility? The sports surface is arguably the most significant element in a sport and recreation facility, as this is the building component that comes into most direct contact with the user and is therefore subjected to most 'wear and tear', often requiring removal and replacement a number of times during the life of the building.

Specifying and selecting a sports surface involves the simultaneous evaluation of a multitude of performance factors. Assessing the environmental impact is becoming an important component of such surface deliberations. Architects, specifiers and facility operators require objective, consistent and comprehensive data detailing the environmental impacts and waste implications of their selection decisions. This example aims to determine the broader environmental impacts of various constructional styles of indoor playing surfaces, through the application of LCA. The approach involves a process-based analysis, which looks at each individual material and process in the playing surface value chain that is required to manufacture, install, maintain and ultimately dispose of a variety of constructional styles of indoor sports surface (Walker, 2008). Sports surface selection criteria include: purchase cost/life-cycle cost, sport type/use level, athlete safety, playing performance, required approvals systems, aesthetics, surface durability, ease of installation, maintenance and ecological footprint.

Indoor playing surfaces

The quantity and quality of sports facilities encourage community exchanges, sport and recreation and ultimately contribute to the health of the community in which they are situated. Timber indoor sports playing surfaces are the norm throughout most of the developed world and are especially common at the higher competitive levels of indoor sport. Timber is also a renewable resource with negative net carbon emissions (Petersen and Solberg, 2004), but there is also the possibility that the environmental burden developed while using, maintaining and ultimately disposing of a wooden playing surface might outweigh the environmental load of its synthetic alternatives. Installing and maintaining a sports surface brings with it many heavy environmental loads in the form of periodic resurfacing, sealing and disposal (Nebel et al, 2006). The financial cost of installing and maintaining timber playing surfaces is resulting in the increased popularity of synthetic playing surface alternatives. Synthetic surfaces are continuing to gradually replace timber in many parts of the world, as synthetic surfaces avoid many of timber's drawbacks, but could a synthetic surface potentially be more environmentally benign than timber itself?

The life cycle of a flooring surface can be divided into four stages, listed below:

1   Floor production: resource extraction, processing of raw materials, surface manufacture and installation.
2   Floor transport: moving the various constructional elements of the surface to the point of installation. In Australia, most indoor sports surface materials are imported from Europe and North America.
3   Floor use: use and maintenance of the surface, including climatic control.
4   Floor disposal and replacement: removal, disposal or reprocessing of the surface at the end of its useful life.

Definition of goal and scope

The purpose of this study was to assess and evaluate the environmental impacts of alternative constructional styles of indoor sports flooring surfaces with different life expectancies, based on the following commercial construction classifications of flooring:

- hardwood timber sports flooring (twenty-five-year expected life);
- pour-in-place synthetic sports flooring (fifteen-year expected life);
- prefabricated-sheet synthetic sports flooring (fifteen-year expected life);
- prefabricated-tile synthetic sports flooring (ten-year expected life).

If it is assumed that the sports facility will last fifty years, then two timber surfaces, 3.3 pour-in-place surfaces, 3.3 synthetic-sheet surfaces or 5 tile sports surfaces may be needed over the life of the facility. Each life-cycle stage might consist of a number of processes, each of which uses one or more inputs from previous processes and gives outputs to one or more ensuing processes. Each input can be followed upstream to its origin, and each output downstream to its final destination. The representation of connected processes can be generated as a first step and is called the product system, process tree or life-cycle map. Figure 8.4 is an example of the type of information that can be captured for one of the surface types under investigation.

It is widely assumed that, as wood is the result of a living, carbon-sequestrating system, it will be more environmentally benign than various oil-based synthetic alternatives. It would therefore be of considerable interest to the architect and the client for the sport and recreation facility to ascertain whether or not this view can be substantiated through quantitative LCA. The aim of the study will be to present results for CO_2 impacts and water impacts generated from $1m^2$ of playing surface per hour of service provided. The study was limited in the following respects:

- The environmental impact of daily/weekly surface cleaning, subsurface base manufacture and installation and game line-marking processes were omitted, as these processes are repeated for all of the surface types under consideration, regardless of the constructional style.

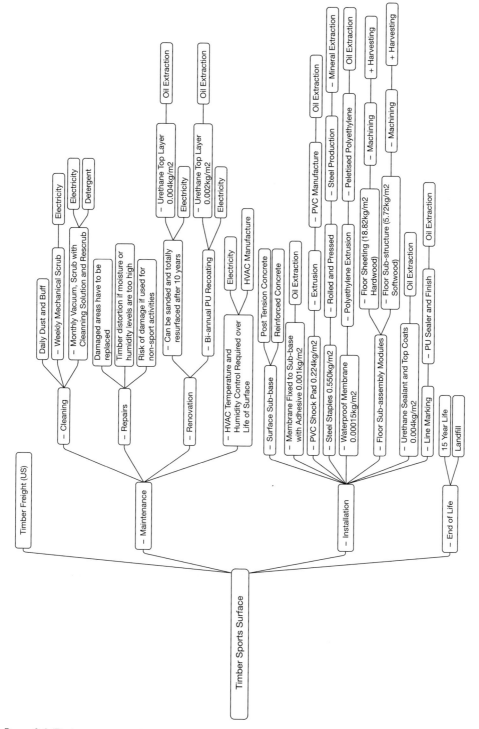

Figure 8.4 Timber sports surface process tree.

Source: A. W. Walker

- In each case, specific manufacturers or manufacturer associations were chosen as the main sources of data.
- Only indoor playing surfaces were considered in the study.
- The scope was limited to CO_2 equivalent and water impacts.
- It was assumed for all calculations that recycling or recovery of the playing surfaces would be limited to landfill or recycling.

Life-cycle inventory analysis

An online, 'streamlined' LCA tool, called Product Ecology Life Cycle Designer, was used to define each flooring surface's bill of materials (BOM), and then data on the environmental load were gathered for each surface life cycle. In this study, the necessary information was gathered from company literature, other LCA studies and the online LCA tool's database. Streamlined online tools such as the one used in this example can be quickly and effectively used by a designer or architect to capture the complex array of inventory data required for an LCA.

Life-cycle impact assessment

GHG emissions are quantified at the component level (Franklin Associates, 2006). This approach requires information regarding the quantity of raw material used in the manufacture of each component and the GHG emission factor associated with the component (IPCC, 2006). In this project, the main focus of the study was global-warming potential and waste potential, and therefore the decision was made to limit the account to CO_2 impacts and water impacts. Once emissions and sequestrations for each component have been calculated, they can be summed for an overall measure of CO_2 and water impacts for each of the flooring systems for each hour of service provided, over the fifty-year anticipated life of the facility.

Life-cycle interpretation and conclusion

LCA results alone will not lead designers and architects to make their final choices, as a surface's performance, cost and durability, the relevant sporting tradition and aesthetic expectations must also be taken into account. In addition, one should always be careful when drawing firm conclusions from a single case study such as this, as the data incorporated into a study will vary greatly from one geographic and climatic location to the next, and different assessment methods and tools may give different and even contradictory answers (Jonsson, 2000).

From this analysis, timber sports surfaces would appear to have larger CO_2 and water footprints, in comparison with the other surfaces investigated. Figures 8.5 and 8.6 show a comparison of all of the sports surfaces included in the analysis and also incorporate a timber sports surface, with the heating, ventilating and air-conditioning equipment (HVAC) energy consumption in the use phase, as internal climatic control is normally recommended when timber sports surfaces are specified. This aspect was included to highlight the potentially 'obscured' role that electrical power consumption can play in the use-phase impacts of timber surfaces. Without due consideration of the energy consumed during the 'use phase' of a flooring system, the specifier's intuition, use of

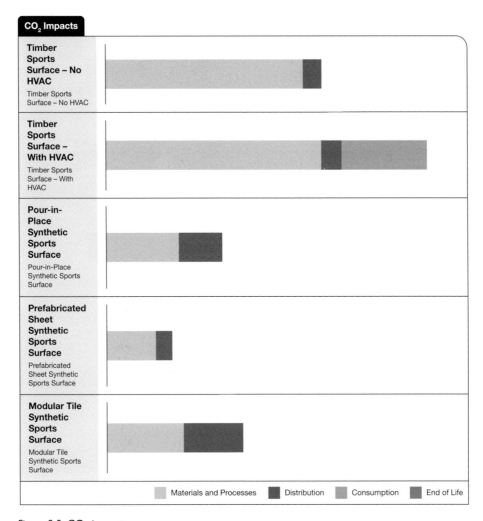

Figure 8.5 CO_2 impacts.

Source: A. W. Walker, using Sustainable Minds Life Cycle Designer, www.productecologyonline.com

questionable 'green' marketing information or acceptance of data that do not take into account the full life-cycle effects of potential design decisions may lead to less sustainable choices. HVAC equipment is recommended for use with timber sports surfaces, as timber is a hydroscopic material. When exposed to varying temperatures and levels of humidity, timber will either release or absorb moisture until it is in equilibrium with the sport facility's surrounding environment. To avoid damage to a timber sports floor, manufacturers recommend that timber sports surfaces should be maintained at a temperature between 13° centigrade and 24° centigrade and humidity levels between 35 and 50 per cent (Maple Flooring Manufacturers Association, 2011). Good airflow must also be maintained, otherwise timber flooring may shrink (low moisture) or cup (high moisture). Synthetic surfaces, on the other hand, require little or no temperature or humidity control, other than what is required for player comfort.

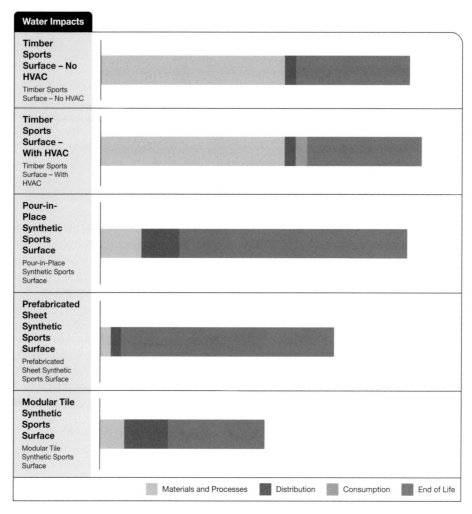

Figure 8.6 Water impacts.

Source: A. W. Walker using Sustainable Minds Life Cycle Designer, www.productecologyonline.com

The extent to which HVAC is required will vary depending on the climatic conditions in the geographic region of the timber surface's installation. The geographic location selected for the installation of all of the surfaces considered in this analysis was Adelaide, South Australia. Only by using comparative life-cycle tools, such as LCA, do the full life-cycle implications of material/component selection decisions become wholly apparent.

Conclusion

With the continued growth of the earth's population, economic expansion and rising rates of consumption and waste generation, the environmental impacts resulting from our activities will have to be reduced. Designing more sustainable products and buildings begins with the introduction of life-cycle thinking approaches at the beginning of the design process. The majority of a product's environmental impacts are 'locked in' at the design stage, and therefore engineers, designers and architects are in key positions to influence and reduce these impacts over a product or building's life. Life-cycle thinking recognizes that whole-product life cycles must be considered, if the true environmental impacts of a product are to be, first, understood and then minimized. Embracing the cyclic approaches that have been developed and perfected by nature, where the waste from one biological process becomes the resource input for another, can help us achieve a more harmonious, future-friendly, resource-efficient tomorrow.

Disclaimer

The content of this chapter is for general information purposes only and does not constitute advice. The authors try to provide content that is true and accurate as of the date of writing; however, we give no assurance or warranty regarding the accuracy, timeliness or applicability of any of the contents. We assume no responsibility for information contained in this chapter and disclaim all liability in respect of such information.

References

Arthur D. Little, Inc. (1990) *Disposable Versus Reusable Diapers: Health, Environmental, and Economic Comparisons*, report to Procter and Gamble, March 16

Benyus, J. M. (2002) *Biomimicry: Innovation Inspired by Nature*, Harper Perennial, New York

Branham, B., Milnert, E. and Rieke, P. (1995) 'Potential groundwater contamination from pesticides and fertilisers used on golf courses', *The USGA Green Section Record*, vol 33, pp33–7

Braungart, M. and McDonough, W. (2002) *Cradle to Cradle: Remaking the Way We Make Things*, North Point Press, New York

Cohen, J. (1996) *How Many People Can the Earth Support?*, W. W. Norton & Company, New York

Day, K. (2005) *Frequently Asked Questions on: Directive 2002/95/EC on the Restriction of the Use of Certain Hazardous Substances in Electrical and Electronic Equipment (RoHS)*, European Commission, Directorate General Environment, www.ec.europa.eu/environment/waste/pdf/faq_weee.pdf, accessed 22 April 2011

Deffeyes, K. (2006) *Beyond Oil: The View From Hubbert's Peak: The Impending World Oil Shortage*, Princeton University Press, Princeton, NJ

Economides, M., Izquierdo, A. and Oligney, R. (2000) *The Color of Oil: The History, the Money and the Politics of the World's Biggest Business*, Round Oak Publishing Company, Katy, TX

European Commission, Enterprise and Industry (2010) *Ecodesign Your Future: How Ecodesign can Help the Environment by Making Products Smarter*, European Commission, Enterprise and Industry, ec.europa.eu/enterprise/policies/sustainable-business/ecodesign/files/brochure_ecodesign_en.pdf, accessed 22 April 2011

Facebook (2010) www.facebook.com/pages/Boycott-BP/119101198107726, accessed 22 April 2011

Franklin Associates (2006) *Life Cycle Inventory of Five Products Produced from Polylactide (PLA) and Petroleum-Based Resins*, Athena Institute International

Hocking, Martin B. (1994) 'Reusable and disposable cups: an energy-based evaluation', *Environmental Management*, vol 18, no 6, pp889–99

General Electric (2010) *Ecomagination*, www.ecomagination.com, accessed 22 April 2011

Heinberg, R. (2004) *Powerdown: Options and Actions for a Post-Carbon World*, New Society Publishers, Gabriola Island, BC, Canada

Intergovernmental Panel on Climate Change (IPCC) (2006) *2006 IPCC Guidelines for National Greenhouse Gas Inventories*, IPCC

Jonsson, A. (2000) 'Tools and methods for environmental assessment of building products – methodological analysis of six selected approaches', *Building and Environment*, vol 35, no 3, pp223–38

Joyce, S. (1998) 'Why the grass isn't always greener', *Environmental Health Perspectives*, vol 106

Kobayashi, Y., Kobayashi, H., Hongu, A. and Sanehira, K. (2005) 'A practical method for quantifying eco-efficiency using eco-design support tools', *Journal of Industrial Ecology*, vol 9, no 4, pp131–44

Kwon, W.-S., Yim, M.-J., Ham, S. J., Lee, S. B. and Paik, K.-W. (2005) 'Thermal cycling reliability and delamination of anisotropic conductive adhesives flip chip on organic substrates with emphasis on the thermal deformation', *Journal of Electronic Packaging*, vol 127, no 2, pp86–90

Layne, R. (2010) 'GE to invest \$10 billion by 2015 under Immelt's "Ecomagination" plan', Bloomberg, www.bloomberg.com/news/2010-06-24/ge-to-invest-10-billion-by-2015-under-immelt-s-ecomagination-plan.html, accessed 28 February 2011

Luft, G. (2010) 'Fueling the dragon: China's race into the oil market', The Institute for the Analysis of Global Security, www.iags.org/china.htm, accessed 22 April 2011

Maple Flooring Manufacturers Association (2011) *Humidity*, Maple Flooring Manufacturers Association, Inc., maplefloor.org/faq/humidity.htm, accessed 15 May 2011

Marks and Spencer (2010) *How We Do Business Report 2010: Plan A, Doing the Right Thing*, Marks & Spencer, plana.marksandspencer.com/media/pdf/planA-2010.pdf, accessed 22 April 2011

Marsden, C. (2000) 'The new corporate citizenship of big business: part of the solution to sustainability?', *Business and Society Review*, vol 105, no 1, pp8–25

Nebel, B., Zimmer, B. and Wegener, G. (2006) 'Life cycle assessment of wood floor coverings – a representative study for the German flooring industry', *International Journal of Life Cycle Assessment*, vol 11, no 3, pp172–82

Petersen, A. K. and Solberg, B. (2004) 'Greenhouse gas emissions and costs over the life cycle of wood and alternative flooring materials', *Climatic Change*, vol 64, no 1–2, pp143–67

Public Citizen (2010) 'BP oil spill', Public Citizen, www.citizen.org/boycott-bp, accessed 22 April 2011

Qian, Y. and Follett, R. F. (2002) 'Turfgrass: assessing soil carbon sequestration in turfgrass systems using long-term soil testing data', *Agron*, vol 94, pp930–5

Resource Smart Victoria (2005) *Design for Environment and Product Innovation*, www.resourcesmart.vic.gov.au/documents/DfE_brochure.pdf, accessed 22 April 2011

Snow, J. (1996) 'Loss of nitrogen and pesticides from turf via leaching and runoff', paper presented at Australian Turfgrass Conference

Sonak, S. (2008) 'Shipping hazardous waste: implications for economically developing countries', *International Environmental Agreements: Politics, Law and Economics*, vol 8, no 2, pp143–59

Stahel, W. R. and Börlin, M. (1987) *Stratégie économique de la durabilité – Eléments d'une valorisation de la durée de vie des produits en tant que contribution à la prévention des déchets*, Société de Banque Suisse, cahier SBS no. 32. Etude réalisée sur mandat de la Société Suisse pour la Protection de l'Environnement; available at www.product-life.org, accessed 11 April 2011

Stahel, W. R. and Reday-Mulvey, G. (1981) *Jobs for Tomorrow: The Potential for Substituting Manpower for Energy*, Vantage Press, New York

US Food and Drug Administration (2009) *Melamine Pet Food Recall – Frequently Asked Questions*, US Department of Health and Human Services, US Food and Drug Administration, www.fda.gov/AnimalVeterinary/SafetyHealth/RecallsWithdrawals/ucm129932.htm, accessed 22 April 2011

Walker A. (2007) 'Grass is not always greener: the application of life cycle assessment to natural and artificial turf sports surfaces', paper presented at the Science Technology and Research into Sport Surfaces conference 2007, UK

Walker A. (2008) 'Going green: the application of life cycle assessment tools to the indoor sports flooring industry', paper presented at the Asia Pacific Congress of Sports Technology, Singapore

Wal-Mart (2009) 'Wal-Mart announces sustainable product index', Wal-Mart Corporation, www.walmartstores.com/pressroom/news/9277.aspx, accessed 22 April 2011

White, P. (2009) 'Building a sustainability strategy into the business', *Corporate Governance: The International Journal of Business in Society*, vol 9, no 4, pp386–94

World Wildlife Fund (WWF) International (2006) *Living Planet Report 2006*, WWF International, Gland, Switzerland

Chapter 9

Green houses

Problem-solving, ontology and the house

Jane Dickson with Victor Buchli

Summary

Through processes of quantifying and visualizing carbon within existing systems of security and risk assessment, the House of Commons Environmental Audit has identified housing as contributing 27 per cent of the United Kingdom's (UK) carbon emissions (Select Committee, 2006). This is further complicated by the fact that this 27 per cent is produced by over 25 million separately owned dwellings and so poses unique challenges to the British government's ability to hit nationally and internationally agreed carbon-reduction targets. Housing has been problematized by linking it to the consumption of energy and identifying it as a site of over-consumption and energy wastage. However, this simultaneously offers the house as a site of transformation whereby the utopian project of sustainability as a response to climate change may be accomplished. Rethinking houses in this way, as a category, reveals the complex and shifting ontological position of the house and how materiality is being regulated and transformed.

> Home is the realisation of ideas.
>
> (Douglas, 1991, p290)

Introduction

In the UK, the materiality of the house, framed in discourses of mitigation and adaptation, is a major topic in current debates about climate change. Processes of making carbon visible and calculable through statistical analysis have implicated the house, as a category, in contributing significantly to the rise of carbon emissions. The house has been linked to the consumption of energy and, further, it has been identified as a site of over-consumption and energy wastage. This creates a link between climate change and security: from personal to resource and food security to national security and the ultimate future security of our children's environmental inheritance and of the very planet (Brundtland, 1987). The alignments between climate change and energy security rewrite the relationships between them (Lovell et al, 2009) and focus government policy on to housing in processes of individualization (Maniates, 2002). Rethinking houses in this way challenges our ideas of the house as a place of safety and security, either architecturally, within the urban environment, e.g. gated and portered residences (Low, 2003), or as ontological security (Hiscock et al, 2001), especially through house ownership (Saunders, 1990; Hollows, 2008). However, it is precisely through its status as agent of security and through its changing physicality that the house has developed a dual identity. In addition to being a potential source of danger, it simultaneously provides a site of transformation and remedy, where carbon can be controlled in the utopian drive towards a zero-carbon society. This challenges any easy definition of the house's contemporary ontological status. This is reminiscent of Derrida's (2007) discussion of the word *pharmakon*, which means both poison and cure. In the project of managing, mitigating and adapting to climate change, the house can now be seen as accommodating multiple ontological identities. Drawing on fieldwork with a sustainability team working at the local-authority level in London, I will discuss how the house as a category becomes a major vehicle for the governance of the reduction of carbon, and how this results in new identifications of, and shifts in, materiality.

What is the problem with houses?

Current governance through housing is managed through processes of problematizing the terms of self-management (Rose and Miller, 2010) and is now being linked to the management of carbon. The house has been identified as a problem through processes of quantifying, visualizing and regulating carbon, or more specifically carbon dioxide as emissions from the combustion of fossil fuels. Two analyses have achieved an almost mythological status within the sustainability agenda in making carbon dioxide visible. One is Girardet's (1992) particularly dramatic calculation of London's ecological footprint (EF) at 120 times the size of the city, which connects the personal scale of everyday life to the planet's security mediated by food and resource management, risk and cost–benefit analysis. Despite reservations about the accuracy of measuring EFs, it has become a valuable policy tool (Moore et al, 2007). Second, the figure most commonly accepted and used to characterize climate change as an energy problem and connect it with housing is the House of Commons environmental audit's (Select Committee, 2006) figure, which identifies housing as contributing 27 per cent of the UK's carbon emissions. This is further complicated by the fact that this 27 per cent is produced by over 25 million separately owned dwellings. This poses unique challenges to the government's ability to reduce carbon when placed against nationally and internationally agreed targets. Both methods of calculation can be and are applied to the house as a discrete unit. They render carbon visible to government through expert knowledge and allow it to be 'thinkable in such a manner as to make it calculable and governable' (Inda, 2005, p5). This leads to specific understandings of housing and implies the need for equally specific actions, or techniques, to be undertaken.

To complement these statistical tools and analyses and in order to act through housing, the government now uses a standard method for calculating home energy, the standard assessment procedure (SAP), which quantifies dwelling emission rates (DER) and is calculated in units of $kgCO_2$ per m^2 per year. A raft of national indicators (NIs) use centrally produced statistical information in order to calculate categories such as household waste (NI 191) and per capita carbon dioxide emissions (NI 186). Local authorities use NI 185 to measure emissions from their own operations, such as transport and buildings, and NI 187 is used to combat fuel poverty. In statistical analyses, calculated carbon becomes linked with energy, the individual and the household. This further identifies houses as consumers of energy and links reduction of energy usage with reduction in carbon.

Success in the project of managing carbon emissions depends to a very great degree on mobilizing the population that lives in these houses. People need to identify their own residences as wasteful and alter both the physicality of the house and their personal carbon-consuming habits. Designs that were built when coal power was cheap and plentiful now lead to the house as a site of carbon wastage. Coal as a fuel was made explicit in house architecture even up until the 1970s, with specifically designed spaces for the provision, storage and consumption of it. Victorian and Edwardian houses were single-skinned (one brick thick), with lime render and mortar to allow moisture to circulate. These houses are uninsulated, with single-glazed, sash windows and huge gaps behind skirting boards and beneath floors. Free-flowing flues were considered the primary ventilation for such houses, built for coal consumption and considered healthful for family and nation (Mosley, 2003). The design of these houses was centred round circulation of fresh air and moisture control. In 1956, the Clean Air Act was introduced to deal with the pollution from domestic houses, and this stimulated the introduction of central heating in the 1960s and 1970s, which led to the reduction of coal provisioning within the house. Energy became less visible, heating became 'on demand', and house design changed accordingly.

Outdated design and materials result in leaks and gaps that allow for the dissipation of excessive amounts of energy, redefining the envelope of the house as wasteful. This is primarily accomplished through calculating thermal transmittance values, or U-values, for different parts of the building envelope. This gives an average calculated value of heat being lost through these different parts, with approximate rates of 10 per cent through windows, 15 per cent through draughts, 25 per cent through roofs, 35 per cent through walls and 15 per cent from floors. Many buildings are now manufactured from concrete, which is portable, flexible, strong and fire-resistant. It has become the most commonly manufactured material in the world, but it is also energy intensive to manufacture, resulting in significant carbon dioxide emissions (van Oss, 2010). Buildings made of concrete may be cooler in summer, but concrete draws out heat in winter and has become identified within carbon calculative systems as wasteful.

In addition to the house, the householder is identified as using or burning too much energy, both by allowing the house to continue its profligate ways and by personal behaviours that lead to over-consumption. This is linked to the idea of taking more than your fair share of the world's resources and, increasingly, of national resources. By identifying housing as a problem within existing systems of environmental and economic risk assessment, an awareness of sustainability as a response to climate change has been developed. Energy assessments have highlighted the dynamic between the permanence and impermanence of the house and its relationship to planetary scales. Sustainability has been coupled with energy consumption, through a reduction based on visualizing and quantifying carbon.

Houses as sites of transformation

Problematized as a site of wastage and over-consumption of carbon, the house exhibits a lack of compliance with the new conditions of being energy efficient. However, this condition simultaneously offers it as a site of problem-solving and transformation. It does so because it already has a long history of being the focus of governance, accomplished through the focusing and collapsing of scales, so that practices, behaviours and new materials become domesticated and normalized. However, it would be a mistake to, as Lévi-Strauss (1983) does, assume too much solidity to houses. Houses are in constant states of change, as Miller (2001) and Clarke (2001) discuss, and this is reflected in the adjective green being turned into a verb. It is precisely this state of constant change and the introduction of new materials and practices that allow the house to become a vehicle for the utopian project of carbon reduction and the move towards zero-carbon living.

Utopia targeted

London's current mayor (2011), Boris Johnson, recently set out a vision for the city in 2015 as 'the greenest big city in the world' (Greater London Authority, 2010b, p1), echoing the Conservative–Liberal Democrat coalition government's commitment to being 'the greenest government ever' (Randerson, 2010, p1). Through processes for the mitigation of climate change and the reduction of carbon emissions, extensive changes to energy supply coupled with economic development are planned to meet and exceed carbon-reduction targets. The UK government, through the Climate Change Act, has committed to an emissions cut of 80 per cent, from 1990 levels, by 2050 (HM Government, 2008). *Delivering London's Energy Future* (Greater London Authority, 2010a) sets a framework for achieving the city's incrementally targeted cuts of 22 per cent by 2015, 38 per cent by 2020 and 60 per cent by 2025; all against 1990 levels. There is a heavy focus on decentralized energy as the means to achieve these, and they are set against an extensive vision of the city working towards a zero-carbon society. Even at this level, the zero-carbon society is still highly aspirational and not yet well defined. This energy future document does not, however, outline a strategy for existing housing, whereas the London borough council with whom I work does have a strategy and counts its housing stock as a resource for achieving the more ambitious targets of a 10 per cent reduction by 2012 and a 40 per cent reduction by 2020, to reach the 80 per cent required by 2050 as advised by Friends of the Earth. These targets are set against 2005 levels, not 1990 levels. Most importantly, all the targets are calculated in terms of reduction of existing emissions, set up against the previous years' levels, not in terms of zero emissions.

As Bulkeley and Betsill (2002) argue, local authorities have a special remit as the linchpins for coordinating scales of government and have been hard at work implementing sustainability since Agenda 21, the document that spelled out local-authority action to mitigate climate change. This has been supported by legislation such as the Sustainable Communities Act 2007, brought in under the Blair Labour government, which aims to promote sustainability as 'the economic, social or environmental well-being of the authority's area' (Department for Communities and Local Government, 2008, p5). Important features of the Sustainable Communities Act include the alignment of sustainability with social issues through linking rising fuel prices to fuel poverty and health, the recommendations for community consultation argued for in section 28 and the fostering of partnerships at all levels to deliver carbon-reduction targets. Linking carbon reduction with already existing programmes allows local authorities to add to the benefits by reducing energy and resource wastage and calculating this into carbon-reduction targets. Action at the local-council level is now seen as of vital importance to the implementation of carbon reduction. By defining sustainability in terms of energy control, and by bundling it with economic advantage, alignments can be set up between users who want to be warm at lower cost, and who may or may not desire to be sustainable, and those council officers who are subject to work and government targets.

Success may depend on two things. One is the council's ability to control its own emissions, and the second is the ability to encourage and enable others to do so. There are 3.2 million housing units in London, with social housing units, owned by local authorities, amounting to 746,000 of that number (Greater London Authority, 2010b). This makes existing housing available to local authorities in London a huge resource to act upon in order to meet their carbon-emission targets. Residential new builds have been legislated to be zero-carbon by 2016 (Department for Communities and Local Government, 2007), and the UK government has also developed the Code for Sustainable Homes (CSH), which is target driven against existing building codes, with code level 6 being defined as zero-carbon. Commercial new builds are to reach this target by 2019 (Greater London Authority, 2010b). Many declare these targets impossible, given the current economy of scale within the building trade (Williams, 2008) or the current economic climate (Barnes, 2007; Williams, 2008). For some housing companies, however, this is not only feasible and desirable: they already have exemplar properties and housing leading the way. Much more fundamental to carbon control is the state of the current housing stock (Royal Commission on Environmental Pollution, 2007). By concentrating on existing houses, attention is focused on consumption rather than production. What this effectively also means is that responsibility for carbon consumption devolves from central government and becomes more focused within communities, households and individuals. As Maniates (2002) suggests, this leaves the individual unable to link scales effectively and powerless to act efficiently. However, in recent years, there has been a proliferation of community groups acting to resolve these scales and forming alliances with local authorities. Groups, such as the Climate Action Network, the SuperHomes network and the Transition Network, as well as individuals, can often be creative and innovative (Bulkeley and Newell, 2010) in their work with local authorities, and local authorities are increasingly looking to partnerships with them to help deliver community action programmes.

The fieldsite

The local authority within London with which I work has three sustainability teams in three core directorates. The first is a single officer based in the Children, Schools and Families (CSF) directorate, whose responsibility is education. The second is a large corporate sustainability team within the Culture and Environment (CE) directorate. They direct the overall sustainability strategy, monitor environmental targets and are responsible for the communication of sustainability issues inside and outside the council. They both work with commercial businesses and run campaigns aimed at the general public. The third team, in which I am primarily based, consists of five officers working in the Housing and Adult Social Care (HASC) directorate; this team concentrates on housing. Like Priemus (2005), this sustainability team regards sustainable housing in the narrow sense, as impact on the environment, calculated in carbon terms. These teams are relatively small compared with overall numbers of council officers, because sustainability has become a widespread core principle across every department within the council, and new projects all have to be justified in terms of their ability to conform to sustainability standards.

What is being transformed materially?

There are a variety of projects researched and tried, but, with the current austerity measures and cuts in funding, the projects that are being preserved and concentrated on are: the provision of cheaper energy; placing physical barriers to encourage council tenants to use less energy; and education and behaviour-change strategies for both social-housing tenants and residents in the wider borough area. Each option has with it greater or lesser involvement and agreement from the people who are targeted by these policies.

First, in accordance with the Greater London Authority targets, great emphasis has been placed on the provision of cheaper, cleaner energy through localized supply such as combined heat and power (CHP) plants. CHP is a system of decentralized generation that produces electricity and captures the by-product of heat and circulates it to near-by houses as district heating. The authority has been buying and supplying bulk energy to its housing estates for decades; however, the provision of CHP plants and the production of cheaper energy place the council now more firmly in the position of producer than of distributor and ensure residents benefit from reduced heating and lighting costs. One such project was initiated by a survey that identified the existing heating network on one estate, including five centralized boilers, as in dire need of repair. The consultation process proposed five scenarios, and each had negative or positive comments attached by the local authority to direct attention to the option that it favoured. The least favoured option, which was refurbishing the five existing boiler houses, along with all the associated pipework and thermostatic controls for all the blocks of flats, attracted negative comments about expense. The favoured option was linking all the estates in the area to a gas-fired CHP plant located at a local hospital and included proposals for a renewal of all associated pipework and the replacement of thermostatic controls in people's homes. For this option, only one boiler would be needed to distribute the power to 1,500 homes, and so this combined the desire for more efficient heating with the reduction of ongoing maintenance and management and had the additional benefit of receiving income from the free electricity generated from the CHP, especially when costed over thirty years. This more efficient use of fuel is estimated to save at least 2,800t of carbon dioxide per annum, a figure the officers equate to insulating 4,000 average semi-detached houses. Directed by the language of the consultation process, the council-favoured option was supported, and the gas-fired CHP project is underway. This energy strategy requires little input from residents in the area, apart from the consultation process (which only a small percentage of residents attended) and allowing access for works to be carried out in the home.

The second strategy the sustainability teams use is to place barriers to consumption now redefined as over-consumption. These interventions are directed at social-housing tenants and form part of regular social-housing refurbishment programmes. They include installing low-flush toilets, aeration taps and shower heads that reduce water and energy consumption. Other measures include installing smaller, more efficient boilers, and these are positioned as saving the tenant money on heating bills and providing warmer living conditions. They also limit hot-water use. Borough-wide insulation programmes are constantly being reassessed, with the intention limited by funding, although a high proportion of properties have now been done. These measures result in a passive reduction that requires little conscious behaviour change from the householder. The aim is to deliver the highest carbon reduction for the greatest value for money. Projects aimed at a reduction in energy consumption tend to be piggy-backed or bundled on to existing home improvement and regeneration programmes, such as 'Warm Front' and the 'Decent Homes Standard', both of which tackle ongoing fuel poverty through improved heating systems and insulation. Carbon-reduction programmes rarely stand alone in this borough, and, if they do, it is because of external funding, and they then become exemplar projects, such as the eco-houses that boast a 70–80 per cent reduction in carbon emissions.

These two strategies alone are unlikely to produce the desired carbon reduction to meet targets, especially when human agency is often regarded as a hindrance to effective carbon reduction. The result is trial projects aimed at changing people's behaviours. These projects, targeting both council tenants and residents in the wider borough area, are often undertaken in partnership with universities and are geared to discover ways to nudge behaviours towards energy conservation. These programmes are difficult, time consuming and expensive and are largely externally funded or run by university-based researchers keen to take advantage of mutual alignments of people and property. They employ social norm theory, which suggests that people simply do not behave in ways that accord with their theorization as rational consumers (Miller, 1998; Ramamurthy, 2003; Power and Mont, 2010). Social norm theory employs descriptive norms: peer perceptions from which, it is suggested, people do not wish to deviate (Schultz et al., 2007). By setting and defining a standard, for example, for recycling or appropriate levels of energy use, people can be encouraged to become 'normal' by comparing themselves with their peers. It is still too early to evaluate the social norm research in this particular council borough. Council officers attempt to manage human agency through two strategies: by educating residents and by making them responsible for their own energy bills. Both strategies encourage and require active participation. Here, there is a set of preconceptions about appropriate behaviours that are set within prescribed limitations aimed at encouraging low consumption of energy. Overheating homes instead of wearing warmer clothes; neglecting to use energy-saving light bulbs; leaving lights and appliances on when not in use; regulating temperatures by opening windows in winter; taking baths instead of showers; and neglecting to draught-proof the home are all behaviours that have come under scrutiny. On balance, it is also recognized that many people simply cannot afford to insulate or draught-proof their homes. As Shove (2003) indicates, people do not think about energy consumption but about comfort, and, for those on low incomes, there is often a stark choice to be made between them.

Educational programmes are then offered to people so that they can learn how to use and monitor their heating fixtures and controls. Despite this, uptake of these programmes is very limited. However, those who do participate often benefit financially, not only, as the council officers believe, because they learn to use their heating controls (in some cases this is true), but because people begin to see energy control in a different way. They cease to have a general awareness and develop a constant awareness of how they regulate their own energy use. Awareness shifts from occasional to daily monitoring of heat against weather patterns and is mediated through conditions of personal comfort. People tend to move away from simple on/off operations limited by time ('I'll put the heat on for an hour'). Often, they do not know what level the control is set at, nor that it is turned up or down once or twice a season. During these programmes, people develop a more nuanced understanding of regulation by altering thermostats and controls to vary the amount of heat on a daily basis. This is intimate involvement of governance in people's daily routines and home behaviours. District heating systems, which have been common in this area since the 1970s, are blamed for these wasteful behaviours, because residents pay a flat fee for all the power they require, regardless of usage. This 'on-demand' usage is seen as encouraging wasteful habits of energy control. However, the issue is not fixed, as the CHP plant discussed earlier will also be a communal heating system.

Much more effective from the council officers' perspective are strategies that make visible and individual each household's energy usage. Officers consider these more effective because, during the process of energy usage being made explicit, rational customers are believed to regulate their own energy supply because they are responsible for paying the full cost. They already possess a financial literacy, and this nudges them to see the links between energy and cost in new ways that develop an energy literacy. Strategies include the introduction of individual household bills, smart meters and pay-as-you-go cards and meters. This again moves away from the flat-fee payment that one informant described as a 'communist system'. By charging them for what they use, tenants are being encouraged to think about their own energy usage, thus making them responsible as self-regulating customers. This idea of making people responsible as individual consumers is mirrored by the UK Local Government Association's 'Small Steps Big Difference' campaign, which is aimed borough wide. This encourages local people to sign up to try to reduce their carbon footprint by taking small steps, such as changing to energy-saving light bulbs and turning off appliances when not in use. The only project within the council to be projected as having a goal of zero-carbon is the zero-waste campaign. This project is punctuated by targets of 50 per cent recycling rates to be achieved by 2020 and the reduction of waste sent to landfill to 35 per cent (against 1995 levels) by the same year. Sustainability teams promote events that feature reused items and encourage reduced purchasing, reselling and composting food waste, with the intention of diverting waste from landfill in order to reduce the impact on an expensive and already overburdened system.

The wider borough homeowner too becomes subject to these educational campaigns, and there are a range of incentives to encourage the greening of privately owned properties, such as advertising campaigns, grants and funds. Local green funds promote the idea of sustainable communities, where residents do the work, volunteering their time to help neighbours. Eco-centres or events such as green summits (which are run by local councils) facilitate the exchange of expert information and research and encourage networking. People participate as willing partners with the council for a variety of reasons, which vary from zeal to spread the word about climate change to the desire to reduce energy bills. House ownership and dwelling now incorporate new, technical kinds of knowledge about window glazing, draught-proofing, recycling and practical statistical information regarding solar panels or wall insulation materials. This new knowledge includes statistical energy calculations and knowledge about materials and equipment. These become embedded in new routines, where the house acts as a site where problems are solved materially. Appliances, walls and roof spaces have to be relearned, recalculated and re-evaluated in terms of carbon input and output and altered accordingly. This is often done with the help of smart meters, which individualize the carbon emissions of each appliance or home-improvement strategy. Householders have developed very sophisticated habits of recycling, and many have become very know-ledgeable about different plastics and single-stream versus multi-stream recycling, or have now specially reorganized their kitchens to accommodate complex domestic waste-management systems (Chappells and Shove, 1999). As Rose argues, this moves to a tipping point where 'the problems of defining and living a good life have been transposed *from an ethical to a psychological register*' (1989, pviii; emphasis in original). It is precisely this change of register that is sought by the council through its various strategies of behaviour change and nudging.

Practice and process

It is the recognition of the house as a site of wastage that makes the conditions of the utopian project possible, by locating that project in the house. This is more than the identification of people with their homes, or linking qualities or characteristics of persons with houses (Carsten and Hugh-Jones, 1995). It is the material interactions and engagements, which Miller speaks of as 'a kind of triad' between people, home and household (2001, p12). It is precisely this which proves to be a process rather than a static state, and, while the home is very highly regulated with rules and meanings, as Rose (1989, 1996) suggests, it is this state of constant change that allows the house to become a vehicle for the utopian project of greening. These material engagements become so domesticated as to be invisible and therefore seem both natural and authorita-tive (see also Douglas, 2002). Douglas describes how routines and scales are materialized and accommodated within the house (1991, p290), grounding the family, producing and reproducing it and creating space over time. Rhythms and cycles are accommodated and materialized in the freezer (Shove and Southerton, 2000) or the store cupboard (Douglas, 1991), which ebbs and flows with seasonal provisions. Large and small scales are materialized in furniture used only at funerals, or closing the curtains nightly, made invisible by close repetition. Power (2005) links domestic temporalities with the cycles of nature found in activities such as gardening and dog-walking, to reveal how diurnal and nocturnal rhythms, seasonal cycles, ageing and decay are entwined and form external agencies that structure and are structured within domestic space. Where scales collapse in the home, it becomes a place where people feel they can exert some measure of control.

When the house is recognized as a process, often multiple processes, it can be seen as neither wholly poison nor cure, but sometimes more, sometimes less. Very few houses in the UK conform to any sort of zero-carbon-emissions standard. Exemplar retrofit projects often achieve an 80 per cent reduction and are considered very successful, but even a Passivhaus can be populated with residents who live high-carbon lives, drive a car or keep a dog (Vale and Vale, 2009). In 2004, the Department for Environment, Food and Rural Affairs (DEFRA) was pessimistic about achieving anywhere near the required targets in the housing sector (DEFRA, 2004). It predicted that the 2010 target of an overall 20 per cent cut in carbon dioxide emissions would fail, and indeed it has. One problem of treating the house as a category is that of homogenization. Looking at the house as a category treats it as a democratizing unit and assumes inclusion. Increas-ingly, one's status as a citizen allows and requires participation in this utopian project. The duty of the new environmental citizen must be to live sustainably in private and public (Dobson, 2009), and, as a consequence, climate denial or refusal to live in an eco-friendly way will become an act of negligence or, worse, malice. However, as Rivlin (2010) argues, not everyone has equal access to the resources needed to become a good green citizen–consumer. More than this, much of the move towards an eco-friendly lifestyle involves a rejection of labour-saving devices (such as clothes dryers and dishwashers), which are energy hungry. For many, the return to human energy is often not welcomed, as it demands time, which is in short supply, or requires different spatial configurations within the home (for example, needing room to dry washing indoors). This can leave people feeling under pressure to change their domestic routines to become eco-friendly and feeling that they have to choose between convenience and a green lifestyle. Much more research needs to be done in this area.

Despite the uncertainty about carbon targets, along with the seemingly 'irrational' behaviours of the residents, and often their unwillingness or inability to participate in energy-reducing and greening projects, national government and local governments, as well as individuals, still consider the house to be a reasonable and appropriate place to regulate carbon. In fact, housing as a vehicle for the reform of carbon is seen in such utopian terms that the Environmental Audit Report (Select Committee, 2006) stated that the correct reduction in house emissions could be used to offset other sectors, specifically aviation. Aviation is widely considered by the government to be vital to the UK economy, and there is, as yet, no viable alternative to the carbon-heavy jet fuel currently in use.

Conclusion

The Western house, which has been the subject of extensive anthropological theory (Carsten and Hugh-Jones, 1995; Buchli, 1999; Low and Lawrence-Zunigais, 2003), has become implicated in further ontological change. A flurry of carbon calculation centred upon it has quantified and identified it as a source of carbon wastage and over-consumption, poisoning the planet. In the UK, national- and local-government policies, aspiring to create communities of eco-active citizens, have focused on the house as a site of intervention. Local governments are promoting processes of behaviour change and are nudging people to change their material culture. As Dobson argues, 'an ecological politics is a quotidian politics', as it rewrites the public/private divide, as feminism and cosmopolitanism did previously (2009, p134). The house is now a site where local government feels it can exert influence on householders and properties in carbon-management schemes, because it is where these scales are linked through already existing systems of governance. The problem house is equally met with optimism that it is the place where it can and should be appropriate to regulate carbon from govern-mental scales to personal ones, and that it can and will be successful enough to offset, or cure, other failing sectors. Nationally agreed and reported targets are implemented and measured at the local level by council authorities. Governance reaches right into people's homes and materializes in regeneration and energy-efficiency programmes. The personal, public and political begin to coincide in new ways. Local authorities are helping to define and encourage appropriate carbon-reduction actions and habits. Houses become places where appropriate consumption must be justified, and the envelope of the house itself must become sustainable as a protector of energy rather than a waster of energy. Often, the wishes of householders and governing bodies align to achieve similar goals, but sometimes they do not. Like Derrida's project of challenging oppositions by complicating the meaning of language through context with the word *pharmakon*, the house has become implicated in narratives of carbon wastage leading to destruction and simultaneously has become a vehicle for producing and materializing sustainability within discourses of mitigation and adaptation. This produces a complex and multiple onto-logical status. How we think about the house has shifted, but its age-old relevance for being the primary means by which we consider and reconsider the relation of the self to the wider world and the maintenance of those relations remains.

References

Barnes, Y. (2007) 'The market for sustainable homes', www.Savills.com/research, accessed 6 January 2011

Brundtland, G. (1987) *Our Common Future: The World Commission on Environment and Development*, Oxford University Press, Oxford

Buchli, V. (1999) *An Archaeology of Socialism*, Berg Publishers, London

Bulkeley, H. and Betsill, M. (2002) *Cities and Climate Change*, Routledge, London

Bulkeley, H. and Newell, P. (2010) *Governing Climate Change*, Routledge, London

Carsten, J. and Hugh-Jones, S. (1995) *About the House: Lévi-Strauss and Beyond*, Cambridge University Press, Cambridge

Chappells, H. and Shove, E. (1999) 'The dustbin: a study of domestic waste, household practices and utility services', *International Planning Studies*, vol 4, no 2, pp267–80

Clarke, A. J. (2001) 'The aesthetics of social aspiration', in D. Miller (ed) *Home Possessions*, Berg, Oxford

Department for Communities and Local Government (2007) *Building a Greener Future: Policy Statement*, Communities and Local Government Publications, Wetherby

Department for Communities and Local Government (2008) *The Sustainable Communities Act 2007, A Guide*, Communities and Local Government Publications, Wetherby

Department for Environment, Food and Rural Affairs (2004) *UK Climate Change Programme Review: Consultation Launch*, Press release 504/04

Derrida, J. (2007) 'The pharmakon', in B. Stocker (ed) *Jacques Derrida: Basic Writings*, Routledge, London

Dobson, A. (2009) 'Citizens, citizenship and governance for sustainability', in W. Adger and J. A. Neil (eds) *Governing Sustainability*, Cambridge University Press, Cambridge

Douglas, M. (1991) 'The idea of a home: a kind of space', *Social Research*, vol 58, pp287–307

Douglas, M. (2002) *Rules and Meanings, Collected Works*, Vol 4, Routledge, London

Girardet, H. (1992) *Gaia Atlas of Cities*, Gaia Books, London

Greater London Authority (2010a) *Delivering London's Energy Future: The Mayor's Draft Climate Change Mitigation and Energy Strategy for Consultation with the London Assembly and Functional Bodies*, Greater London Authority, London

Greater London Authority (2010b) *The London Housing Strategy*, Greater London Authority, London

Hiscock, R., Kearns, A., MacIntyre, S. and Ellaway, A. (2001) 'Ontological security and psycho-social benefits from the home: qualitative evidence on issues of tenure', *Housing, Theory and Society*, vol 18, nos 1 and 2, pp50–66

HM Government (2008) *Climate Change Act*, www.legislation.gov.uk/ukpga/2008/27/contents/enacted, accessed 24 January 2010

Hollows, J. (2008) *Domestic Cultures: Issues in Cultural and Media Studies*, Open University Press, Maidenhead

Inda, J. X. (2005) *Anthropologies of Modernity: Foucault, Governmentality and Life Politics*, Wiley-Blackwell, Oxford

Lévi-Strauss, C. (1983) *The Way of the Masks*, S. Modelski (trans) Blackwell, Oxford

Lovell, H., Bulkeley, H. and Owens, S. (2009) 'Converging agendas? Energy and climate change policies in the UK', *Environment and Planning C: Government and Policy*, vol 27, pp90–109

Low, S. (2003) *Behind the Gates: The New American Dream*, Routledge, London

Low, S. M. and Lawrence-Zunigais, D. (2003) *The Anthropology of Space and Place: Locating Culture*, Wiley-Blackwell, Oxford

Maniates, M. (2002) 'Individualization: plant a tree, buy a bike, save the world?', in T. Princen, M. Manniates and K. Conca (eds) *Confronting Consumption*, MIT Press, London

Miller, D. (1998) *A Theory of Shopping*, Polity Press, Oxford

Miller, D. (2001) 'Behind closed doors', in D. Miller (ed) *Home Possessions*, Berg, Oxford

Moore, S., Nye, M. and Rydin, Y. (2007) 'Using ecological footprints as a policy driver: the case of sustainable construction planning policy in London', *Local Environment*, vol 12, pp1–15

Mosley, S. (2003) 'Fresh air and foul: the role of the open fireplace in ventilating the British home, 1837–1910', *Planning Perspectives*, vol 18, pp1–21

Power, E. R. (2005) 'Human–nature relations in suburban gardens', *Australian Geographer*, vol 36, pp39–53

Power, K. and Mont, O. (2010) 'The role of formal and informal forces in shaping consumption and implications for sustainable society: part II', *Sustainability*, vol 2, pp2573–92

Priemus, H. (2005) 'How to make housing sustainable? The Dutch experience', *Environment and Planning B: Planning and Design*, vol 32, pp5–19

Ramamurthy, P. (2003) 'Material consumers, fabricating subjects: perplexity, global connectivity discourses, and transnational feminist research', *Cultural Anthropology*, vol 18, pp524–50

Randerson, J. (2010) 'Cameron: I want coalition to be the "greenest government" ever', *The Guardian*, 14 May, www.guardian.co.uk/environment/2010/may/14/cameron-wants-greenest-government-ever, accessed 23 September 2010

Rivlin, P. (2010) 'Greening up the citizenry: gender, class and the making of the sustainable self in eco-austerity culture', paper given at the Politics of Consumption, a symposium presented by the Centre for Cultural Studies Research, University of East London,18 May

Rose, N. (1989) *Governing the Soul: The Shaping of the Private Self*, Routledge, London

Rose, N. (1996) *Inventing Ourselves: Psychology, Power, and Personhood*, Cambridge University Press, New York

Rose, N. and Miller, P. (2010) *Governing the Present: Administering Economic, Social and Personal Life*, Polity Press, London

Royal Commission on Environmental Pollution (2007) *The Urban Environment*, The Stationery Office, London

Saunders, P. (1990) *A Nation of Home Owners*, Unwin Hyman, London

Schultz, W., Nolan, J., Cialdini, R., Goldstein, N. and Griskevicius, V. (2007) 'The constructive, destructive, and reconstructive power of social norms', *Psychological Science*, vol 18, no 5, pp429–34

Select Committee (2006) *House of Commons Environmental Audit: First Report*, www.publications.parliament.uk/pa/cm200607/cmselect/cmenvaud/77/7702.htm, accessed 14 December 2010

Shove, E. (2003) *Comfort, Cleanliness and Convenience: The Social Organization of Normality*, Berg, Oxford

Shove, E. and Southerton, D. (2000) 'Defrosting the freezer: from novelty to convenience: a narrative of normalization', *Journal of Material Culture*, vol 5, pp301–19

Vale, R. and Vale, B. (2009) *Time to Eat the Dog? The Real Guide to Sustainable Living*, Thames and Hudson, London van Oss, H. G. (2010) 'Cement' [Advance Release], in *Metals and Minerals: US, Geological Survey Minerals Yearbook 2008*, vol 1, section 16.1–16.38

Williams, J. (2008) *Zero Carbon Homes: Phase 1 – Key Problems*, zerocarbonfutures.org/phase-1-key-results/, accessed 6 January 2011

Chapter 10

Living in harmony with wildlife

Considering the animal's 'point of view' in planning and design

Carla Litchfield, Kurt Lushington, Sue Bigwood and Wendy Foster

Summary

Planet Earth is expected to support an estimated human population of 9 billion people by 2050. One of the questions this brings to mind is whether this large human population will leave room for other species? Already, the health of people, animals (domestic and 'wild') and the environment is inextricably interconnected, and there has been an unprecedented increase in emerging zoonotic diseases, rates of extinction of non-human species and human–animal conflict. As cities and agricultural lands expand, and natural environments shrink, humans and domestic animals are coming into closer and more frequent contact with 'wild' animals, at the same time as numbers of truly wild animals are declining. This chapter explores the 'dark side' of the effect of consumption and technology on the 'built' and 'natural' environment, before promoting connections between disciplines and research areas to foster development of healthy 'green' environments and human pro-conservation behaviours that ensure 'zero waste'. The potential role that conservation psychology and zoos may play in promoting design of sustainable environments for ethical human–wildlife coexistence is discussed. Findings from the Human Zoo Project conducted at Adelaide Zoo (Adelaide, South Australia) illustrate the point that built environments should be assessed from multiple points of view, including those of animals and people visiting or using the site. Only when we take the ecological and behavioural needs of all species in an environment into account can we ensure the welfare of all.

Introduction

2010 – The International Year of Biodiversity . . . The year in which new species continue to be found, but more tigers live in captivity than in the wild . . . The year in which there are 1.8 billion people using the Internet, but 1 billion people still without access to an adequate supply of freshwater.

(WWF, 2010, p6)

As we enter the International Decade of Biodiversity in 2011, it is timely to reflect on the state of our planet. We are in the midst of the world's sixth major extinction event, with vast numbers of species being lost in a geological blink of an eye – frequently before we are even aware of their existence (Dirzo and Raven, 2003). Many of these extinctions are tied to the activities of one species: humans (Pimm and Brooks, 2000). Planet Earth is expected to support an estimated human population of 9 billion people by 2050, or at least 2 billion more than exist today (Kunzig, 2011), with potentially in excess of 150 million of these people displaced by environmental degradation or climate change (Brown, 2008). As human-dominated urban areas continue to 'sprawl', rural land-use patterns change and natural environments shrink and fragment, humans and domestic animals come into closer and more frequent contact with 'wild' or 'free-ranging' animals (Morgan et al, 2004). Humans are also coming into more frequent contact with wildlife, as, globally, tourists seek close encounters with wildlife (Litchfield, 2008), and protected areas become 'tools' for income generation as well as biodiversity conservation (Locke and Dearden, 2005). Disruption of ecosystems through human activities and human intrusion into natural environments has been accompanied by an unprecedented increase in the rates of extinction of non-human species (International Union for Conservation of Nature (IUCN), 2011), emerging zoonotic diseases (Wolfe et al, 2007) and human-animal conflict (Messmer, 2000; Woodroffe et al, 2005).

Estimating the extent of human-induced changes or damage to the environment and biodiversity is difficult. Rockström and colleagues (2009) have attempted to quantify the environmental changes caused by human activities and the biophysical thresholds or earth-system process (planetary) boundaries that must not be crossed to ensure the future of humanity. Of the nine earth-system processes identified, they consider humans to have already crossed the 'safe-operating' boundaries of three of these: climate change, rate of biodiversity loss, and nitrogen and phosphorus cycles. Rockström et al (2009) stress the delicate balance and interconnectedness of the systems across the planet, pointing out that 'significant land-use changes in the Amazon could influence water resources as far away as Tibet' (p474). The Red List of Threatened Species(tm), pro-duced by the IUCN, is used as an indicator of global biodiversity trends, providing data on about 45,000 species of fauna and flora (www.iucnredlist.org). Species facing an 'extremely high risk of extinction in the wild' fall into the 'critically endangered' category (Fearn, 2010, p45). In 2009, the number of species of plant and animal considered to be critically endangered was in excess of 3,200 (Fearn, 2010), with a further 200 species added to this category a year later (IUCN, 2011).

Many of the human-induced threats can be linked back to the size of the human population and its consumption patterns: the amount and type of resources consumed. Under a 'lexicon' or standardized classification system for threats to biodiversity and potential actions to take (Salafsky et al, 2008), most direct threats are limited to human activities (e.g. hunting, logging, off-road vehicle use) that can be countered with appropriate actions (e.g. education and influencing behaviour). At the turn of this century, North America, Europe and Japan made up 15 per cent of the world's population but were responsible for up to 80 per cent of wood-resource consumption, toxic pollu-tion and international travel (Gladwin et al, 1997; Mann, 2000). The emergence of a large, more affluent 'new middle class' or 'new consumers' in developing countries (e.g. India) or 'new economies' (e.g. China), likely to represent 1.2 billion people by 2030, sees increasing adoption of unsustainable 'Western' lifestyles and consumption patterns, such as ownership of private cars and eating large quantities of meat (Lange and Meier, 2009). The extent of our 'over-consumption' or human demands on natural resources is reflected in our ecological footprint and water footprint, as part of the Living Planet Index – another indicator of the health of the world's biodiversity (WWF, 2010). Our ecological footprint or 'human demand on the biosphere' has doubled since the 1960s. During this time, there has also been a 30 per cent decrease in vertebrate species' populations globally, but this figure is twice as high (60 per cent) for the tropical areas of the world, where many of the low-income countries are located (Butchart et al, 2010; WWF, 2010).

Addressing human-consumption patterns is a critical part of conservation, as, without doing so, much of the on-ground conservation work will be in vain, as climate change and pollution create dramatic changes in the landscape. Without a change in the way we as humans think, shop, consume and behave, the continued existence of many species – and ultimately our own species – is tenuous. Our 'disconnect with nature' or con-sumerism 'gone mad' is evident in the global rise of the shopping mall and mega-mall as 'lifestyle destinations', where people 'hang out', communing with designer man-made goods rather than nature (Ahmed et al, 2007). For twenty years, the world's first mega-mall, West Edmonton Mall in Canada – reportedly 'larger than 100 football fields' – was the largest shopping mall in the world (Crawford, 2004, p125), until 2005, when the South China Mall in China, twice the size of Canada's mega-mall, opened its doors (Mitchell, 2008). Across the world in Dubai, the 'City of Gold' in the United Arab Emirates, tourists can escape the searing desert temperatures and go snow skiing at Ski Dubai, and the Versace Hotel opening there in mid 2011 is expected to have its own refrigerated beach for the comfort of its guests (CCP Luxury Industry Management Consultants, 2010). As the number of people making these lifestyle choices increases, our ability to live sustainably continues to decline.

> If everyone in the world lived like an average resident of the United States or the United Arab Emirates, then a biocapacity equivalent to more than 4.5 Earths would be required to keep up with humanity's consumption and CO_2 emissions.
>
> (WWF, 2010, p36)

This chapter investigates some of the anthropogenic changes to our terrestrial environment and related threats to biodiversity, particularly wildlife (with a focus on terrestrial mammals). Areas covered include: issues associated with fragmented habitats; waste disposal; increasing human and semi-wild animal encounters and conflict; and cross-species transmission of diseases. Exploring and understanding the 'dark side' of the effects of consumption and technology on the 'built' (human-dominated) and 'natural' ('wild') environments is necessary to avoid potential pitfalls in future design and management of environments that we share with other species. This chapter aims to facilitate connections between disciplines and research areas to foster the development of healthy 'green' environments and human pro-conservation behaviours that ensure 'zero waste' and prevent the extinction of flora and fauna. As the health of people, animals (domestic and 'wild') and the environment is inextricably interconnected, this chapter explores the potential role that conservation psychology and zoos may play in promoting the design of sustainable environments for ethical human–wildlife coexistence. Findings from the Human Zoo Project conducted at Adelaide Zoo will be discussed to illustrate the point that built environments should be assessed from multiple points of view, including those of animals and people visiting or using the site. Only when we take the ecological and behavioural needs of all species in an environment into account, can we ensure the welfare and survival of all.

Living with wildlife: urban, rural, peri-urban and 'wild' environments

> Several times it was also seen that many people enter the prohibited areas of the park and indulge in nefarious activities. Sometimes they were reported to play cards, booze, roam here and there, burst crackers and throw stones to shoo away the elephants or other wild animals.
>
> (Joshi and Singh, 2008, p69)

In 1950, New York was the only city in the world with more than10 million inhabitants, but, by the year 2000, nineteen cities were home to this many people (almost 10 per cent of the total number of people living in cities globally), with fifteen of these cities located in developing countries (Cohen, 2003). More than 47 per cent of people around the world live in cities (compared with 12 per cent in 1900), and urbanization continues to increase worldwide (Cohen, 2003; Lange and Meier, 2009). Urban sprawl or urbanization into rural areas means that some natural resources will be reduced in size and connectivity as part of urban ecosystems (e.g. trees or forest fragments), and remaining rural or wilderness areas (e.g. forests) subject to even greater human influence, such as decreased native species and increased invasive species (Hansen et al, 2005). Other issues related to our choices of location and consumption include the distance of individuals from the resources they consume (Lenzen and Peters, 2009) and our disconnection from nature (Louv, 2008).

It is too simplistic to view 'human-occupied' landscapes or ecosystems as either urban or rural, as there are 'peri-urban interfaces' representing a 'complex mosaic of rural, urban and natural' ecosystems (Allen, 2003, p136). In developing countries, such peri-urban areas may be villages or rural 'fringe' areas near growing cities (see Figure 10.1), where agricultural lands are acquired and converted to residential housing and commercial shopping areas (Narain, 2009). In Nairobi in Kenya, such interfaces exist within a few kilometres of the city centre, where a fence separates city dwellers from Nairobi National Park, which further south joins the Athi-Kaputiei Plains: an open pastoral savannah where livestock graze alongside migrating wildlife. This ecosystem is changing and fragmenting, as pastoralists begin to settle, grow crops and build fences (Reid et al, 2008). Even within cities, there exists a complex mosaic of urban ecosystems and pockets or fragments of the 'wild' – wetlands, parks, botanic gardens, trees and grasslands along roads, and even backyards (Pickett, 2010).

Biodiversity corridors are one way of providing 'connectivity' or physical links between fragments of natural environments and opportunities for genetic interchange (or breeding) between otherwise isolated populations of animals and plants (Hilty et al, 2006). These corridors exist in connecting wilderness areas, which may be separated by human agricultural areas or settlements, or between urban 'green spaces', and allow movement and migration of animals as well as seed dispersal (Rudd et al, 2002). Poorly planned wildlife corridors, which are the wrong shape and structure for the species of the area and include too many human-use trails, or are too close to human towns and recreation areas (e.g. golf courses), may be unsuccessful in meeting their desired aim and can add to conflict, especially when used by large carnivores such as grizzly bears (Chetkiewicz et al, 2006). Some species, such as bobcats and coyotes, do not always use corridors in California, but also cross through developed areas, showing behavioural

Figure 10.1 Keeping wildlife away from crops or other areas is a growing problem in many parts of the world, as this photo of free-ranging zebras in Uganda shows.

Photo supplied by the authors

adaptations to the presence of humans by being less active during daytime and avoiding developed areas when human activity is at its peak (Tigas et al, 2002). In India, in the foothills of the Himalayas, some wildlife corridors are rendered unusable for elephants and other animals by human activities (Joshi and Singh, 2008). In some corridor areas, there are human settlements, army camps, factories, canals and bridges, temples, grazing cattle, roads and railway lines. Not surprisingly, elephants have come into conflict with people, with numerous people killed by elephants, and elephants killed on roads and by trains (Joshi and Singh, 2008).

In a world populated by humans and their forms of transport, providing safe areas for wildlife to cross roads and railway tracks, or 'wildlife crossings', is vital (Glista et al, 2009). Vehicle-collision fatalities may be high enough to have an impact on the survival of some populations (Roger et al, 2011), or an entire population may even become extinct (Jones, 2000). To prevent road fatalities, exclusion fences are built along highways, or tunnels, culverts or bridges are built as under- or over-passes at major roads (Taylor and Goldingay, 2010). Whether animals choose to use these structures depends on a variety of factors, such as traffic noise levels, location of crossings, dimensions of structure, type of substrate, lighting, airflow and preferences for height or open versus enclosed spaces (Glista et al, 2009). Exclusion fences may reduce road fatalities, but may also create a barrier to movement of some animals, such as moose in Sweden, which may no longer attempt to travel to areas beyond the fence, further fragmenting the population (Olsson and Widen, 2008). Use of physical structures alone will not be effective in the long term, owing to cost, ongoing maintenance and increased need with increasing roads, and so other measures, including changes in human behaviour, such as higher awareness in drivers about wildlife in the area and reducing speed, will be required (Glista et al, 2009).

Living with wildlife: human–wildlife interactions

Jaguars are cultural icons throughout South America, but they are also major predators of cattle. Baboons exhibit social shenanigans that keep ecotourists enthralled, but they also raid crops. Elephants elicit inordinate attention from conservationists, but they are a threat to human life and limb. Pigs, goats and donkeys are valued by animal-rights advocates, but they tear up our parks and reserves (Robinson, 2005, pxiv).

Humans interact with wildlife in a variety of environments (see Figure 10.2), not just in the areas people work and live in. Wildlife also encounters and interacts with humans who travel as tourists specifically to engage in wildlife tourism or as part of other tourism experiences. More than ever before, international tourists are seeking intensely close interactions with large wild animals, whether swimming with orcas in Norway (www.orcasafari.co.uk), cage diving with great white sharks in Australia (www.sharkcagediving.com.au) or tracking mountain gorillas in Uganda (Litchfield, 2008). Viewed as pariahs by some and as the 'golden goose' by others, international tourist revenues have formed the backbone of national economies, have built schools and clinics, and have saved natural habitat (Litchfield, 2008).

A close encounter with wild animals typically requires that the animals become habituated to the close proximity of humans, otherwise they usually flee as humans

Figure 10.2 In the middle of a roundabout on a busy street, people put seed out for pigeons in Sharjah, United Arab Emirates.

Photo supplied by the authors

Figure 10.3 Park rangers sometimes struggle to enforce a 9m buffer distance between tourists seeking the perfect photo opportunity and endangered mountain gorillas in Uganda.

Photo supplied by the authors

approach. This 'escape' behaviour is an anti-predator response, and the distance at which different species, or individuals within a species, flee from an approaching human ('flight initiation distance') varies (Blumstein et al, 2003). If buffer distances are not monitored and enforced, tourists risk inflicting behavioural disturbance and stress on the animals (see Figure 10.3). If tourists do not understand the animals' behavioural repertoire or signs of aggression and stress, then their quest for the perfect photo opportunity or memorable close encounter increases their potential risk of injury. Wild animals can also become dangerous or a problem if people feed them or approach them too closely. Conservation managers intentionally habituate some animals to the presence of humans as part of tourism programmes (e.g. mountain gorillas and chimpanzees in Uganda) (Goldsmith, 2005a). Other animals are simply habituated through ongoing proximity to campsites or recreational areas (e.g. dingoes on Australia's Fraser Island, or monkeys near temples in Indonesia). Species that have a long evolutionary association with humans ('commensal species', such as rats and dogs) may habituate more quickly to the presence of humans (Blumstein et al, 2003).

For urban and landscape planning, it is important to identify species likely to be present in the environment, as some may be viewed as pests, and plans may need to include non-lethal methods of deterring animals (VerCauteren et al, 2005), which themselves may become ineffective once animals habituate to them (see, for example, Shivik, 2006).

Ongoing monitoring of behaviour between humans and wildlife in shared environments is vital for understanding the human–wildlife interface (Fuentes, 2006a), as well as for anticipation of future problems, thus minimizing negative or aggressive encounters, as both humans and non-human animals are 'active agents', influencing each other's behaviour in shared environments (Campbell, 2008). Throughout mainland Asia, wild rhesus macaques (monkeys) have been so successful at adapting to humans and their changing environments that they are sometimes known as 'weed macaques', and are considered as pests by some and holy by others (Maestripieri, 2007). In Europe and North America, some species of bird are the dominant 'urban scavengers', and the presence of humans can exacerbate aggressive interactions between bird species (e.g. gulls and ducks, gulls and crows), individuals within species, and between birds and humans (e.g. gulls diving to 'steal' food from people; Campbell, 2008). Some species, such as grey-headed flying foxes in the Melbourne Royal Botanic Gardens in Australia, may initially be a welcome sight in a city, but, as their numbers grow, they become a pest to be relocated or destroyed (Thomson, 2007). In parts of Africa, where chimpanzees have had aggressive or negative encounters with humans in local communities (inside and outside forests), the response to 'non-threatening' humans (e.g. field researchers) may not be to flee, but rather to 'ignore', 'monitor' or even 'intimidate' people by aggressive mobbing or chasing in some cases, or to make a 'stealthy retreat' (McLennan and Hill, 2010).

A number of threats to wildlife are associated with habituation to humans, such as poaching, behavioural disturbance and stress (Steklis et al, 2004; Muyambi, 2005; Ellenberg et al, 2007; Ahlering et al, 2011), increased incursions into human-inhabited areas, resulting in increased risk of disease transmission (Nkurunungi, 2001; Macfie and Williamson, 2010) and conflicts with local communities due to crop- or bin- or house-raiding (Biryahwaho, 2002). Changes in food availability can be a key factor affecting human–animal interactions associated with human activity. If tourists or other humans feed animals, the animals begin to associate food with humans and places where humans live or visit, and the wild animals may lurk around bins, campsites and tourist spots, such as monkeys in Bali (Fuentes and Gamerl, 2005; Fuentes, 2006b) and dingoes on Fraser Island (Thompson et al, 2003). Rubbish dumps and bins are a source of food, sometimes the main source (Ciucci et al, 1997), particularly in environments where natural sources of food (e.g. prey for carnivores or fruit trees for some primates) are scarce as a result of human activities and changes to the environment (Figure 10.4). Bin-raiding or searching for food has become a major source of human–animal conflict in some areas, which, if the animal is a black bear or polar bear, can be frightening, even if they are not aggressive (Dowsley and Wenzel, 2008) and can lead to fear-based human responses that are detrimental to the animals concerned. This is not the only risk to both animal and human survival, as increased contact can lead to increased disease risk (Karesh, 2010).

Living with wildlife: problems with emerging diseases

Health is not a mirage, as microbiologist Rene Dubos imagined, but an outcome of the constantly changing, complex interactions among the social and ecological conditions in which human societies are embedded (Waltner-Toews, 2011).

Figure 10.4 Rubbish bins are a potential source of food for free-ranging dingoes on Fraser Island in Australia. Dingoes associate people with food, and this has led to human–dingo conflict.

Photo supplied by the authors

The website of the World Health Organization, with its regular updates of information about the latest disease outbreaks, can make even the hardiest of individuals feel uneasy. Over the past thirty or so years, global international tourist arrivals per year have increased by about 500 million (World Tourism Organization, 2000), and more than thirty new diseases have emerged (World Health Organization, 2002). Humans and wildlife are interacting more frequently, whether as humans hunting and butchering animals, humans living with domestic or exotic pets (Pike et al, 2010) or via encroachment.

The changed interactions between humans and wildlife can pose a threat to human health. Animals moving into urban areas may facilitate cross-species transmission of diseases: for example, dingoes infected with *Echinococcus granulosus* (a tapeworm caught after preying on macropods or other mammals), which causes hydatid disease (a debilitating disease of the liver), have been seen in the Queensland city of Townsville and within 6.5km of that state's capital city Brisbane, as well as in other urban areas in Australia (Jenkins and Macpherson, 2003). A related parasite, *Echinococcus multilocularis*, which leads to alveolar echinococcosis in humans, is increasing in prevalence in urban areas in the United States, Europe and China (Deplazes et al, 2004), as wild carnivores, such as foxes, move into larger cities and prey on small rodents. These diseases pale in comparison with some of the newly emerging infectious diseases. International travel and trade assist in the global spread of emerging infectious diseases, with more people visiting unfamiliar, wild places, as the examples of SARS, HIV, avian influenza

Figure 10.5 Close interactions between humans and wildlife may lead to zoonotic disease
transmission, as people feed or photograph animals, such as these monkeys in (a)
Pakistan and (b) Borneo, Malaysia.

Photos supplied by the authors

H5N1 (Schillaci et al, 2005) and H1N1 influenza (Karesh, 2010) show. Over 60 per
cent of the emerging infectious diseases and pandemics are zoonotic, meaning they have
occurred as a result of cross-species transmission of microorganisms from animals to
humans (Pike et al, 2010), and 75 per cent of these originate from wildlife (see Figure
10.5).

Certainly, humans are not the only accidental hosts affected directly by the tide of
emerging infectious disease and decreasing environmental health. The ebola virus
(EBOV) has been described as a significant threat to the survival of western lowland
gorillas and chimpanzees in central Africa (Reed and Cameron, 2011). Some viruses
cause epidemics by adapting to domestic animals and exploiting them as amplificating
hosts (Weaver and Barrett, 2004). For example, in May 2005, avian influenza caused a
major die-off of wild bar-headed geese and other water birds on the Quinghai Lake in
China, and it is suspected that the infection may have stemmed from the domestic poultry
industry (Feare, 2010). Pathogen transmission between animal populations by humans
(via poor hygiene and fomite transmission) has been identified as a major factor in the
global spread of *chytridiomycosis*, a frog disease that is now the worst disease affecting
biodiversity in recorded history. It is thought to have caused the severe decline of up to
200 species of amphibians globally, with many of these now believed to be extinct
(Skerratt et al, 2011).

One of the best ways to mitigate spread of disease lies in maintaining healthy
ecosystems, because these are the key to disease resilience. Although a high level of

biodiversity is where the highest diversity of new pathogens resides, the chance of spill over is greatest when these systems are under pressure. Environmental diseases of contamination and pollution can cause local die-offs and have obscure, chronic and negative impacts on populations. In Esperance, Western Australia, a sudden die-off of wild birds acted as an indicator event for a major investigation into a case of significant lead contamination (Golder Associates Pty Ltd, 2009). Poor environmental health results in lowered immunity and, consequently, increased pathogen prevalence. Although there are a myriad of problems associated with sharing our environments with wildlife, a number of multidisciplinary team initiatives are being implemented to address the problems. For example, the One World – One Health programme monitors and responds to emerging zoonotic disease issues (Karesh, 2010).

Living with wildlife: an impossible dream?

At this point in the chapter, it may appear that living in harmony with wildlife is an 'impossible dream'. Humans do not always understand and manage their own behaviour and relationships well, and many do not have a basic understanding of other species' behaviour, even when they live with them as pets (Boyd et al, 2004). A growing number of conservationists are calling for environments to be set aside as protected areas that are kept free of all human activities (Locke and Deardon, 2005), including tourists and researchers (Goldsmith, 2005b), with field workers and scientists being called upon to develop and abide by more stringent ethical guidelines in order to avoid negative impacts on humans and wildlife alike during the course of field or 'real-world' research (MacKinnon and Riley, 2010). Ultimately, the only way we can live in harmony with wildlife is to change our own behaviour, both as individuals and as local or global communities, and plan environments and ways safely to interact with other species by incorporating knowledge from experts in all aspects of planning and building infrastructure, along with experts in conservation medicine, conservation biology and conservation psychology. The rest of this chapter will focus on the emerging field of conservation psychology and its application in a zoo setting, as a way of encouraging pro-conservation sustainable behaviour.

Conservation psychology: turning the dream of living in harmony with wildlife into reality

> Despite the fact that our technologies give us godlike power to manipulate nature, our genetically inherited brain structures and behavioural propensities are still much the same as those of our stone-age ancestors. Thus, the question of what will happen when men become as gods, might well be rephrased as how will stone-age minds use the might of the gods?
>
> (Small and Jollands, 2005, p348)

As a species, we already have the knowledge and skills to greatly reduce the impact of our activities on the world. As individuals or communities though, there is often a lack of action in applying our knowledge and skills to solving environmental problems. Part of that is related to a lack of knowledge about issues and solutions, but the major problem remains in quickly and effectively translating knowledge and attitudes into pro-conservation behaviours (O'Keefe, 2002). This is where conservation psychology comes into the picture (Saunders, 2003). Conservation psychology is a relatively new field that aims to discover how to change non-sustainable human behaviour in order to protect the natural environment and conserve diminishing natural resources. It draws principles from all areas of psychology and facilitates collaboration with practitioners from other fields, including ecology, biology and social science.

Over many generations, evolution honed our 'automatic' responses (autonomic nervous system) and emotions to help us cope with day-to-day survival. Some of these responses were so vital to survival in the past that they became essentially 'hard-wired' (e.g. tonic immobility or 'fright' response; Bracha et al, 2004). With rapid advances in technology, some of these hard-wired paleolithic responses no longer serve the same 'survival' or adaptive role (Small and Jollands, 2005) and have not had enough time – in evolutionary terms – to adapt to the new environment. These hard-wired physiological responses can play a vital role in creating a better and more sustainable world. On the 'flipside', they can also be used in morally questionable ways, such as in psychological operations during wars, in using the Internet to combat the 'bad guys' (Whitley, 2000) and by advertising and marketing executives to promote sales of products (O'Reilly and Tennant, 2010). Psychological principles of persuasion, attitude and behaviour change have been used effectively in this way for many decades, yet have been largely ignored or underused within biodiversity conservation: 'perhaps because there is sometimes a fine line between persuasion and propaganda, a line most conservationists do not want to cross' (Jacobson, 2009, p63).

Despite their being harmful to our physical or psychological health, our 'supersized' patterns of consumption or addiction (e.g. smoking, gambling) continue. Persuasive advertising can ensure that products known to be harmful continue to be purchased, because they are associated with images or people considered to be 'cool' or 'sexy' or successful. Similarly, corporations sometimes encourage scepticism about research findings that link their products with harmful effects, such as global climate change or health problems (Jacques, 2009). In 2007, the fashion company Diesel increased its sales by draping scantily clad models in iconic landscapes altered by global warming as part of its 'Global Warming Ready' campaign. Global catastrophe was transformed into sexy fashion chic for monetary gain, although the company claimed to be raising awareness about the issue (Dahlen et al, 2010). Using catchy jingles and images of attractive or famous personalities and bombarding people with repetitions of sound or image 'bites' are some of the persuasive techniques advertising employs to influence and change behaviour.

Although some advertising programmes use psychological techniques to encourage specific responses beneficial to their business, without regard to, or understanding of, the long-term consequences for other people or the planet, these same principles of psychology can also be used for 'good'. They can facilitate behaviour change in individuals, by, for example, helping them to overcome an addiction (through the use of behaviour modification therapy or cognitive behavioural therapy). They can also facilitate behaviour change in communities, such as reducing drink driving, speeding or water usage through public-service announcements. To achieve sustainability for our planet, we need behaviour change to occur at both the individual and community level (Oskamp and Schultz, 2006). Psychologists have long known that raising awareness and changing people's attitudes do not always lead to behaviour change. Behaviour change is influenced by many factors, including the person's upbringing or social environment (peers, family and culture) and his/her belief that s/he can make the change (O'Reilly and Tennant, 2010).

Conservation psychology, zoos and pro-conservation environmental design

Zoos have been evolving over the last 100 years, gradually changing from menageries designed to entertain the public to active conservation organizations. Viewed globally, individual zoos are at different stages in this evolution, as is inevitable with major change. There is, however, a growing realization that zoos are one of the few organizations that can operate across the whole spectrum of conservation activities, from *ex situ* breeding of threatened species, research, public education, training and influencing and advocacy, through to *in situ* support of species, populations and their habitats (World Association of Zoos and Aquariums, 2005). Importantly, zoos are unique in that they have a massive audience of visitors whose knowledge, understanding, attitudes, behaviour and involvement can all be positively influenced and harnessed. In Australia alone, in the mid–late 2000s, there was an estimated average of 15.4 million visits to zoos per annum (Aegis Consulting Australia and Applied Economics, 2009). The messages delivered by zoos to their visitors need to be considered carefully to ensure their effectiveness is not reduced by focusing only on the things that are wrong, without providing options for change. Zoos and other conservation agencies have the opportunity to develop effective campaigns directed at changing behaviour, whether reducing consumption of resources (water, energy or meat), fostering volunteering or other 'helping' behaviours, or promoting development and use of more sustainable products or technologies. Zoos also have the opportunity to lead by example in using ecologically sustainable and socially responsible practices (Townsend, 2009) and conducting independent audits of 'in-house' practices, such as recycling (Hae and Ballou, 2009).

Zoos provide an opportunity to showcase environmentally 'green' design features that are also applicable to human facilities, such as green walls and roofs, and can highlight ways in which people (or, conversely, other animals) can become immersed in environments that can resemble either natural or built environments, or can interact with varying levels of contact with wildlife. Observing human and animal behaviour in these environments might offer insights into future planning and design outside zoos, as some zoos are now 'blurring the distinction between people space and animal space' (Coe, 2009). Zoos also offer expertise in developing and managing multi-species exhibits, creating 3D spaces for different species that occupy the same ecosystems but different niches in space (e.g. high-canopy arboreal, low-canopy arboreal, terrestrial and aquatic) or time (e.g. diurnal and nocturnal). This can be viewed as a variation on the multi-use facilities incorporated into urban planning. Zoo designers may need to incorporate 'escape' or 'safe-retreat' areas for less dominant, smaller or more sensitive species or individuals (Pearson et al, 2010). These types of space should also be included in human design as places to escape and recharge. Observing interactions between different species may offer insights into potential problems (e.g. aggressive behaviours, destructive behaviours) or solutions for urban and environmental planning and design. Keeping up to date with the latest developments in zoo design requires searching through the 'grey' literature and online sites (e.g. www.joncoedesign.com and www.zoolex.org), as many projects are not written up for publication in peer-reviewed journals. Zoo designers recognize that 'green space is not always enough' (Coe, 2003, p977) when it comes to animals' physical and psychological well-being in captive environments, as their behavioural needs must also be met.

Human zoo: experiencing a human-built environment from an animal's point of view

In 2007, one of the authors (Carla Litchfield) spent a month in a 1970s-built outdoor zoo enclosure at Adelaide Zoo as part of the 'Human Zoo' project, which aimed to promote community awareness of great-ape conservation, and to get people to think about how different from, or similar to, our 'hairy' cousins we are (see Figure 10.6). This experience led to an 'accidental' finding about thermal discomfort in some captive environments, highlighting the need for humans to experience environments from the animal's point of view. Until a human is literally 'immersed' in an exhibit, s/he cannot really 'feel' what it is like. It will never be possible to truly experience an environment from another species' point of view, as there are many interspecies differences in sensory capabilities (e.g. humans cannot hear the low rumbling vocalizations of elephants or the ultrasonic sounds emitted by bats, or smell every scent like a dog, or see the world as a honey bee does), but we should at least be able to experience the world as our closest relatives, the other great apes, do. Ironically, the importance of physical environments (e.g. temperature) may be overlooked in the planning and design process (Litchfield et al, 2011), with zoo-exhibit designers emphasizing cognitive and psychological well-being (Hosey, 2005). As a case study, the 'Human Zoo' project raises important questions about design principles and shows that, inadvertently, one of the most basic welfare requirements may have been neglected – appropriate thermoregulatory conditions.

To gain a lived experience of zoo-exhibit conditions, four groups of six human participants (including author Carla Litchfield) spent a week in an outdoor enclosure that previously housed non-human primates. An immediate and universal complaint made by the Human Zoo project participants was that they were uncomfortably hot, and this was despite access to a spa pool, hammocks, iced drinking water, as well as shade from a sail and sheltering palm trees. The thermal stress came as a surprise, because apes had been housed in the enclosure for decades, and it had not been evident from prior observation. Upon reflection, we may have misattributed behavioural indicators of thermal stress to psychological rather than physical factors. For example, if an animal was observed to 'hide' in the back areas of an enclosure, this behavioural response might have been attributed to avoidance of, or escape from, the noisy crowd of visitors, when in fact it may simply have been to avoid heat/cold stress by seeking shelter. The Human Zoo project demonstrates the importance of monitoring temperature and shade adequacy, as well as providing shelter and access to other thermoregulatory aids, such as water and cold rocks (Forman et al, 2001) in zoo enclosures.

The effect of thermal stress on humans is well understood. Our building codes, occupational health and safety guidelines, clothing, air conditioning and heating are all aimed at achieving, not just a basically adequate standard, but our optimum comfort. Such principles should also apply to other animal species when we design an environment that includes them. This should not be restricted to captive environments; it should apply

Figure 10.6 The Human Zoo enclosure that one of the authors (Carla Litchfield) spent a month inside to experience an environment from the 'animal's point of view' and promote awareness about human behaviours that endanger wild populations of great apes (e.g. the commercial bushmeat trade).

Photo supplied by the authors

to any spaces that people share with other species. From the scant literature concerning thermal microclimates in zoo enclosures, it is apparent that shade alone may not eliminate thermal distress: climate-controlled structures to reduce all sources of radiant heat may be needed (Langman et al, 2003), and the heat load may be reduced by simple changes such as darkening the colour of gunite surfaces (Langman et al, 1996). Understanding environments in terms of 'thermo-usable' space, rather than size alone, is important, as microhabitats may be unusable in extreme temperatures. A basic understanding of animal behaviour and behavioural needs can allow planners and designers to use appropriate structures, shapes, colours and building materials to create comfortable spaces, thereby maximizing both welfare and well-being and positive interactions between humans and wildlife.

Influencing behaviour in and beyond the zoo: examples from Conservation Ark (Zoos SA)

In 2009, a new discovery centre was opened at Adelaide Zoo: the Westpac Envirodome (www.envirodome.org.au). The Envirodome contains a variety of activities to help people understand their connection with, and impact on, the world around them. The building itself was largely recycled, created by making use of an old ape enclosure, and designed to be an example of a 'green building' based on sustainable design principles. It has a green roof, rainwater-fed toilets, hay-bale walls and passive heating, cooling and lighting.

Water is a vital natural resource that is often taken for granted. To help people understand the balancing act needed to allocate water resources in a modern city, a water sculpture was created within the Envirodome, with water 'raining' intermittently from the ceiling. This sculpture provides zoo visitors with the opportunity to allocate the water from 'rainfall' events to agriculture, household, industry or the environment, or any combination of these areas. The challenge is to keep water moving through the sculpture until the next bout of rain refills the reservoir. The activities in the Envirodome are linked to things people can do in their own life to make a difference, as well as showcasing the building's different design features. Water conservation is emphasized in the toilets: the urinals are waterless, toilets are low water-usage, and water used for washing hands fills the cisterns, and there are also screens that show water savings from using efficient facilities (see Figure 10.7).

Over the last couple of years, Zoos SA has joined two national campaigns initiated by Zoos Victoria to help save great apes: 'They're calling on you' and 'Don't palm us

Figure 10.7 Water-efficient toilet and sink, with screen providing the user with feedback about water savings.

Photo supplied by the authors

off'. The 'They're calling on you' programme identified coltan mining as an activity that threatens gorillas and that could be addressed by targeting mobile-phone recycling, which would reduce the need for new coltan to be mined and provide funds for primate conservation. Barriers to participation were identified, and postage-paid satchels were provided to visitors both to overcome financial barriers and to act as a reminder when they returned home. This particular programme also uses one of zoos' unique features: the ability to connect people with wildlife. At Melbourne Zoo, the programme was linked to an ambassador species, the gorilla, and the connection people develop with the animals and their keepers, harnessed through a call to action made at keeper talks held at the gorilla exhibit. Given that only 4 per cent of satchels taken from a static display were returned, the 28 per cent return rate from keeper talks (Rachel Lowrey, personal communication) shows the benefits of enlisting zoos' unique features to increase pro-conservation actions. The 'They're calling on you' campaign is now encouraging regional participation, with all zoos in Australia being invited to get involved, and ultimately hopes to go global. In any campaign, zoos must decide on one simple message to promote (or behaviour to change) to improve the likelihood of success.

The 'Don't palm us off' campaign was aimed at getting mandatory labelling of products containing palm oil in Australia and New Zealand. The campaign encourages us to swap purchases containing palm oil for ones that do not, until we know that only certified sustainable palm oil is being imported into Australia for the manufacture of snack products and ice creams. As consumers, we have the power to influence retailers; for example, public demand for palm oil-free products has resulted in Woolworths developing its Sustainable Palm Oil Action Plan for palm-oil sourcing and labelling its Homebrand and Select products that contain palm oil appropriately. Every dollar spent is a vote, and many Australians would like to be able to choose *not* to buy products containing palm oil from a sustainable source. Having palm oil listed in a product's ingredients would allow consumers to make informed choices.

The thousands of mobile phones recycled and over 100,000 signatures collected (including over 33,000 Facebook members) for orang-utan-friendly palm oil (Swarna Nantha and Tisdell, 2009) through mandatory labelling in these campaigns show that Australians care about saving great apes. It is vital that we all keep engaging in these simple, pro-conservation behaviours to help save our great-ape relatives and ultimately ourselves.

Responsible interactions with wildlife

One role zoos can play is to promote responsible tourism in habitat countries. People are keen to experience 'close encounters' with wild animals, whether visiting mountain gorillas or swimming with whale sharks or orcas. Wildlife tourism can provide economic incentives to local communities to protect wildlife and habitats, but the potential consequences for local communities should tourism decrease must be considered (Litchfield, 2008), as well as the impacts of travel itself (e.g. contributing to climate change). Zoos are well placed to educate people about responsible tourism behaviours, such as not consuming 'exotic' meats (e.g. bushmeat) or not buying inappropriate souvenirs that may encourage illegal trade or poaching, and following guidelines, such as 'buffer distances' that protect animals from potential disease transmission and behavioural disturbance. One of the authors (CL) has led a number of 'responsible tours' for Zoos SA and Peregrine Travel, as an educational and thought-provoking experience highlighting 'the good, the bad, the ugly' of wildlife tourism, with a portion of costs donated to a conservation project visited. For example, in Uganda, the Jane Goodall Institute Projects were supported (e.g. Ngamba Island Chimpanzee Sanctuary and snare removal programmes in Kibale, Budongo and Kalinzu Forests), and, in Borneo, the Kinabatangan Orang-utan Conservation Project.

Zoos can play a role in more than just tourism though. As part of a long-term study of southern hairy-nosed wombats undertaken by Conservation Ark (Zoos SA) staff, conservation psychology is being used to investigate human–wombat conflict in South Australia. This conflict is arising largely owing to damage caused to property or crops by wombats' extensive burrow systems (Ostendorf et al, 2009). To mitigate this conflict, knowledge about, and attitudes and behaviour towards, wombats will be sampled in participants from local communities and landholders who encounter wombats. These same communities will then be consulted to discover why barriers to non-lethal methods of wombat control exist, and whether they can develop and initiate methods of non-lethal control. Often, the people in conflict with wildlife have solutions that conservationists may never have considered (Treves et al, 2009).

Many zoos and aquaria can also harness their unique ability to connect people with wildlife by providing opportunities for visitors to engage in 'close encounters' with wildlife. This provides an intimate connection with wildlife, but the experiences need to be structured to maximize the impact they have in facilitating pro-conservation knowledge, attitudes and behaviour, while still maintaining the animals' natural behaviours and welfare needs.

Influencing behaviour: evaluating the impact

Zoos have a wonderful opportunity to be a showcase for the natural world, and to share the conservation message with the many people who visit zoos. Conservation-psychology techniques can help zoos achieve their conservation mission, but the message will only be credible if it comes from organizations that 'practise what they preach'. Apart from measuring the success of a programme, evaluation and dissemination of information provide a science-based approach to conservation in the zoo, which increases the credibility of zoos and zoo-based science.

A formal technique that can be used to design programmes that increase the effectiveness of conservation messages is community-based social marketing. McKenzie-Mohr (2000) has combined psychological expertise with social-marketing knowledge to develop the area of community-based social marketing. This approach is used to:

- strategically develop a target behaviour or activity to change;
- identify possible barriers to behaviour change;
- design a strategy based on psychological principles to overcome the barriers;
- pilot the strategy with a small group of people; and
- finally evaluate the impact of the programme once implemented across a community.

Although conservation psychology is only starting to be applied at Conservation Ark (Zoos SA), it is being assessed, with ongoing evaluation allowing changes to be made so that a visit to a zoo results in more pro-conservation behaviours. For example, an evaluation of the 'cheetah encounter' at Monarto Zoo (Adelaide, South Australia) by Tindle (2008) assessed the proximity of cheetahs to, and interaction with, visitors and found the encounter had no negative impacts on the cheetahs. For the human participants, there was improved knowledge about cheetah conservation issues and ways they could help as individuals. Sixty per cent of participants also indicated they would undertake pro-conservation behaviours, although follow-up has not yet been done to determine actual rates of behaviour change. An ongoing evaluation by Monika Szokalski (PhD student) of all the big-cat experiences at Zoos SA is also investigating the effectiveness of all the 'close encounters' offered at Adelaide Zoo and Monarto Zoo in terms of knowledge/attitude/behaviour change in zoo visitor participants and keepers and other staff participants, as well as observing behaviour in the big cats immediately before, during and after the encounters, to ensure these activities do not negatively impact on the animals involved.

Other staff and students are working on projects, such as examining the effectiveness of the 'Don't palm us off' campaign for mandatory labelling of palm oil in Australia and New Zealand (Elissa Pearson, PhD student), and understanding the reasons underlying conflict between people and wombats and the methods used to deal with this conflict (Dr Elisa Sparrow, conservation biologist). In addition, people working in other fields, such as tourism, are also looking at the impact of experiences and messages that people gain from zoo visits (Smith et al, 2011).

Living in harmony with wildlife: impossible dream or sustainable reality?

It is too soon to be able to answer this question. However, the new collaborative efforts made globally to address human and wildlife issues, and the emerging technologies and collaborative fields such as conservation psychology can help make it a sustainable reality. In order to achieve future healthy landscapes, where humans live in harmony with nature and wildlife, humans must change their behaviour in everyday life in two main areas: reduce consumption and waste; and learn how to 'interact' with wildlife in appropriate ways. We must consider all aspects of ethics and welfare when it comes to managing wildlife and developing policy, not only as our moral obligation, but because public attitudes and values are shifting towards humane, non-lethal methods of wildlife control (Fox and Bekoff, 2011) and revision of laws and regulations concerning management of wildlife movements as a result of climate change (Mawdsley et al, 2009), and debates concerning 'personhood' or the moral and legal status of other species are increasing (Gunnarsson, 2008).

When it comes to planning landscapes, infrastructure, buildings and all forms of development that will impact on humans and other species (flora and fauna), as part of an integrated approach to planning across environments, experts in the fields of conservation biology, conservation medicine and conservation psychology should be consulted. By combining One World – One Health principles with an understanding of the biology, behaviour and cognition (e.g. problem-solving abilities) of animals and humans, it will be possible to develop ways of excluding animals more effectively from bins, crops or food, thereby minimizing human–wildlife conflict and transmission of diseases.

By working together and making our passion for conservation contagious, the little changes we make, if well designed, can have big effects, resulting in the rapid change needed to stem the extinctions happening all around us (Gladwell, 2000).

References

Aegis Consulting Australia and Applied Economics (2009) *Report on the Economic and Social Contribution of the Zoological Industry in Australia*, Aegis Consulting Australia, Pyrmont, New South Wales, Australia and Applied Economics, Phoenix, AZ

Ahlering, M. A., Millspaugh, J. J., Woods, R. J., Western, D. and Eggert, L.S. (2011) 'Elevated levels of stress hormones in crop-raiding male elephants', *Animal Conservation*, vol 14, no 2, pp124–30

Ahmed, Z. U., Ghingold, M. and Dahari, Z. (2007) 'Malaysian shopping mall behaviour: an exploratory study', *Asia Pacific Journal of Marketing and Logistics*, vol 19, pp331–48

Allen, A. (2003) 'Environmental planning and management of the peri-urban interface: perspectives on an emerging field', *Environment and Urbanization*, vol 15, pp135–47

Biryahwaho, B. (2002) 'Community perspectives towards management of crop raiding animals: experiences of CARE-DTC with communities living adjacent to Bwindi Impenetrable and Mgahinga Gorilla National Parks, Southwest Uganda', in C. Hill, F. Osborn and A.J. Plumptre (eds) *Human–Wildlife Conflict: Identifying the Problem and Possible Solutions*, Wildlife Conservation Society, New York

Blumstein, D. T., Anthony, L. L., Harcourt, R. and Ross, G. (2003) 'Testing a key assumption of wildlife buffer zones: is flight initiation distance a species-specific trait?', *Biological Conservation*, vol 110, pp97–100

Boyd, C. M., Fotheringham, B., Litchfield, C., McBryde, I., Metzer, J. C., Scanlon, P., Somers, R. and Winefield, A. H. (2004) 'Fear of dogs in a community sample: effects of age, gender and prior experience of canine aggression', *Anthrozoös*, vol 17, pp146–66

Bracha, H. S., Ralston, T. C., Matsukawa, J. M., Williams, A. E. and Bracha, A. S. (2004) 'Does "fight or flight" need updating?', *Psychosomatics*, vol 45, pp448–9

Brown, O. (2008) 'The numbers game', *Forced Migration Review*, vol 31, pp8–9

Butchart, S. H. M., Walpole, M., Collen, B., van Strien, A., Scharlemann, J. P. W., Almond, R. E. A., Baillie, J. E. M., Bomhard, B., Brown, C., Bruno, J., Carpenter, K. E., Carr, G. M., Chanson, J., Chenery, A. M., Csirke, J., Davidson, N. C., Dentener, F., Foster, M., Galli, A., Galloway, J. N., Genovesi, P., Gregory, R. D., Hockings, M., Kapos, V., Lamarque, J.-F., Leverington, F., Loh, J., McGeoch, M. A., McRae, L., Minasyan, A., Hernández Morcillo, M., Oldfield, T. E. E., Pauly, D., Quader, S., Revenga, C., Sauer, J. R., Skolnik, B., Spear, D., Stanwell-Smith, D., Stuart, S. N., Symes, A., Tierney, M., Tyrrell, T. D., Vié, J.-C. and Watson, R. (2010) 'Global biodiversity: indicators of recent declines', *Science*, vol 328, pp1164–8

Campbell, M. (2008) 'An animal geography of avian feeding habits in Peterborough, Ontario', *Area*, vol 40, pp472–80

CCP Luxury Industry Management Consultants (2010) 'Versace Hotel opens in Dubai June 2011', www.cpp-luxury.com/en/versace-hotel-opens-in-dubai-june-2011_1002.html, accessed 27 February 2011

Chetkiewicz, C.-L. B., St. Clair, C. C. and Boyce, M. S. (2006) 'Corridors for conservation: integrating pattern and process', *Annual Review of Ecology, Evolution, and Systematics*, vol 37, pp317–42

Ciucci, P., Boitani, L., Francisci, F. and Andreoli, G. (1997) 'Home range, activity and movements of a wolf pack in central Italy', *Journal of Zoology*, vol 243, pp803–19

Coe, J. C. (2003) 'Steering the ark toward Eden: design for animal well-being', *Journal of the American Veterinary Medical Association*, vol 223, pp977–80

Coe, J. C. (2009) 'Third generation conservation: accommodating wildlife in our daily lives', *Proceedings of the Australasian Regional Association of Zoological Parks and Aquaria (ARAZPA) Conference*, Gold Coast, Australia, 22–6 March

Cohen, J. E. (2003) 'Human population: the next half century', *Science*, vol 302, pp1172–5

Crawford, M. (2004) 'The world in a shopping mall', in M. Miles, T. Hall and I. Borden (eds) *The City Cultures Reader* (2nd edn) Routledge, London

Dahlen, M., Lange, F. and Smith, T. (2010) *Marketing Communications: A Brand Narrative Approach*, John Wiley & Sons, Chichester

Deplazes, P., Hegglin, D., Gloor, S. and Romig, T. (2004) 'Wilderness in the city: the urbanization of Echinococcus multilocularis', *Trends in Parasitology*, vol 20, pp77–84

Dirzo, R. and Raven, P. (2003) 'Global state of biodiversity and loss', *Annual Review of Environment and Resources*, vol 28, pp137–67

Dowsley, M. and Wenzel, G. (2008) '"The time of the most polar bears": a co-management conflict in Nunavut', *Arctic*, vol 61, pp177–89

Ellenberg, U., Setiawan, A. N., Cree, A., Houston, D. M. and Seddon, P. J. (2007) 'Elevated hormonal stress response and reduced reproductive output in yellow-eyed penguins exposed to unregulated tourism', *General and Comparative Endocrinology*, vol 152, pp54–63

Feare, C. J. (2010) 'Role of wild birds in the spread of highly pathogenic Avian Influenza Virus H5N1 and implications for global surveillance', *Avian Diseases*, vol 54(s1), pp201–12

Fearn, E. (2010) 'Some of the world's most endangered animals', in E. Fearn (ed) *State of the Wild 2010–2011: A Global Portrait*, Island Press, Washington, DC

Forman, J. M., Claude, L. N., Albright, A. M. and Lima, M. (2001) 'The design of enriched animal habitats from a biological engineering perspective', *Transactions of the American Society of Agricultural Engineers*, vol 44, pp1363–71

Fox, C. H. and Bekoff, M. (2011) 'Integrating value and ethics into wildlife policy and management – lessons from North America', *Animals*, vol 1, pp126–43

Fuentes, A. (2006a) 'Human–nonhuman primate interconnections and their relevance to anthropology', *Ecological and Environmental Anthropology*, vol 2, pp1–11

Fuentes, A. (2006b) 'Human culture and monkey behaviour: assessing the contexts of potential pathogen transmission between macaques and humans', *American Journal of Primatology*, vol 68, pp880–96

Fuentes, A. and Gamerl, S. (2005) 'Disproportionate participation by age/sex classes in aggressive interactions between long-tailed macaques (*macaca fascicularis*) and human tourists at Padangtegal Monkey Forest, Bali, Indonesia', *American Journal of Primatology*, vol 66, pp197–204

Gladwell, M. (2000) *The Tipping Point*, Abacus, London

Gladwin, T. N., Newburry, W. E. and Reiskin, E. D. (1997) 'Why is the Northern elite mind biased against community, the environment, and a sustainable future?', in M. H. Bazerman, D. M. Messick, A. E. Tenbrunsel and K. A. Wade-Benzoni (eds) *Environment, Ethics, and Behaviour: The Psychology of Environmental Valuation and Degradation*, The New Lexington Press, San Francisco, CA

Glista, D. J., DeVault, T. L. and DeWoody, J. A. (2009) 'A review of mitigation measures for reducing wildlife mortality on roadways', *Landscape and Urban Planning*, vol 91, pp1–7

Golder Associates Pty Ltd (2009) *Esperance Town-Site Human Health and Ecological Risk Assessment*, Department for Environment and Conservation, Perth, Australia

Goldsmith, M. L. (2005a) 'Impacts of habituation for ecotourism on the gorillas of Nkuringo', *Gorilla Journal*, vol 30, pp11–14

Goldsmith, M. L. (2005b) 'Habituating primates for field study: ethical considerations for African great apes', in T. R. Turner (ed) *Biological Anthropology and Ethics*, State University of New York Press, Albany, NY

Gunnarsson, L. (2008) 'The Great Apes and the severely disabled: moral status and thick evaluative concepts', *Ethical Theory and Moral Practice*, vol 11, pp305–26

Hae, E. and Ballou, D. (2009) 'Raising the recycling rate at world-class zoo', *BioCycle*, vol 50, pp31–3

Hansen, A. J., Knight, R. L., Marzluff, J. M., Powell, S., Brown, K., Gude, P. H. and Jones, K. (2005) 'Effects of exurban development on biodiversity: patterns, mechanisms, and research needs', *Ecological Applications*, vol 15, pp1893–905

Hilty, J. A., Lidicker Jr., W. Z. and Merenlender, A. M. (2006) *Corridor Ecology: The Science and Practice of Linking Landscapes for Biodiversity Conservation*, Island Press, Washington, DC

Hosey, G. R. (2005) 'How does the zoo environment affect the behaviour of captive primates?', *Applied Animal Behaviour Science*, vol 90, pp107–29

IUCN (2011) 'IUCN Red List version 2010.4: Table 2: changes in the number of species in the threatened categories (CR, EN, VU) from 1996 to 2010 for the major taxonomic groups on the Red List', www.iucnredlist.org/documents/summarystatistics/2010_4RL_Stats_Table_2 .pdf, accessed 20 February 2011

Jacobson, S. K. (2009) *Communication Skills for Conservation Professionals* (2nd edn), Island Press, Washington, DC

Jacques, P. J. (2009) *Environmental Skepticism: Ecology, Power and Public Life*, Ashgate Publishing, Farnham

Jenkins, D. J. and Macpherson, C. N. L. (2003) 'Transmission ecology of *Echinococcus* in wildlife in Australia and Africa', *Parasitology*, vol 127, supplement S63–S72

Jones, M. E. (2000) 'Road upgrade, road mortality and remedial measures: impacts on a population of eastern quolls and Tasmanian devils', *Wildlife Research*, vol 27, pp289–96

Joshi, R. and Singh, R. (2008) 'Asian elephant (*Elephas maximus*) and riparian wildlife corridors: a case study from Lesser-Himalayan Zone of Uttarakhand', *The Journal of American Science*, vol 4, pp63–75

Karesh, W. B. (2010) 'Emerging diseases and conservation: an update on One World – One Health', in E. Fearn (ed) *State of the Wild 2010–2011: A Global Portrait*, Island Press, Washington, DC

Kunzig, R. (2011) 'Population 7 billion', *National Geographic*, January 2011, ngm.national geographic.com/2011/01/seven-billion/kunzig-text, accessed 11 March 2011

Lange, H. and Meier, L. (2009) 'Who are the new middle classes and why are they given so much public attention', in H. Lange and L. Meier (eds) *The New Middle Classes: Globalizing lifestyles, Consumerism and Environmental Concern*, Springer, Dordrecht, the Netherlands

Langman, V. A., Rowe, M., Forthman, D., Langman, N., Black, J. and Walker, T. (2003) 'Quantifying shade using a standard environment', *Zoo Biology*, vol 22, pp253–60

Langman, V. A., Rowe, M., Forthman, D., Whitton, B., Langman, N., Roberts, T., Huston, K., Boling, C. and Maloney, D. (1996) 'Thermal assessment of zoological exhibits: sea lion enclosure at the Audubon Zoo', *Zoo Biology*, vol 15, pp403–11

Lenzen, M. and Peters, G. M. (2009) 'How city dwellers affect their resource hinterland: a spatial impact study of Australian households', *Journal of Industrial Ecology*, vol 14, pp73–90

Litchfield, C. A. (2008) 'Responsible tourism: a conservation tool or conservation threat?', in T. S. Stoinski, H. D. Steklis and P. T. Mehlman (eds) *Conservation in the 21st Century: Gorillas as a Case Study*, Springer, New York

Litchfield, C., Dorrian, J., Davis, J., Lushington, K. and Dawson, D. (2011) 'Lessons in primate heat tolerance: a commentary based on the "human zoo" experience', *Journal of Applied Animal Welfare Science*, vol 14, pp162–9

Locke, H. and Dearden, P. (2005) 'Rethinking protected area categories and the new paradigm', *Environmental Conservation*, vol 32, pp1–10

Louv, R. (2008) *Last Child in the Woods: Saving our Children from Nature Deficit Disorder*, Algonquin Books of Chapel Hill, New York

Macfie, E. J. and Williamson, E. A. (2010) *Best Practice Guidelines for Great Ape Tourism*, IUCN/SSC Primate Specialist Group (PSG), Gland, Switzerland, data.iucn.org/dbtw-wpd/edocs/SSC-OP-038.pdf, accessed 10 March 2011

McKenzie-Mohr, D. (2000) 'Promoting sustainable behaviour: an introduction to community-based social marketing', *Journal of Social Issue*, vol 56, pp543–54

MacKinnon, K. C. and Riley, E. P. (2010) 'Field primatology of today: current ethical issues', *American Journal of Primatology*, vol 72, pp749–53

McLennan, M. R. and Hill, C. M. (2010) 'Chimpanzee responses to researchers in a disturbed forest–farm mosaic at Bulindi, western Uganda', *American Journal of Primatology*, vol 72, pp907–18

Maestripieri, D. (2007) *Macachiavellian Intelligence: How Rhesus Macaques and Humans Have Conquered the World*, University of Chicago Press, Chicago, IL

Mann, M. (2000) *The Community Tourism Guide: Exciting Holidays for Responsible Travellers*, Earthscan Publications, London

Mawdsley, J. R., O'Malley, R. and Ojima, D. S. (2009) 'A review of climate-change adaptation strategies for wildlife management and biodiversity conservation', *Conservation Biology*, vol 23, pp1080–9

Messmer, T. A. (2000) 'The emergence of human–wildlife conflict management: turning challenges into opportunities', *International Biodeterioration & Biodegradation*, vol 45, pp97–102

Mitchell, S. K. (2008) *Largest Indoor Parks and Malls*, Gareth Stevens Publishing, Pleasantville, NY

Morgan, E. R., Milner-Gulland, E. J., Torgerson, P. R. and Medley, G. F. (2004) 'Ruminating on complexity: macroparasites of wildlife and livestock', *Trends in Ecology and Evolution*, vol 19, pp181–8

Muyambi, F. (2005) 'The impact of tourism on the behaviour of mountain gorillas', *Gorilla Journal*, vol 30, pp14–15

Narain, V. (2009) 'Growing city, shrinking hinterland: land acquisition, transition and conflict in peri-urban Gurgaon, India', *Environment & Urbanization*, vol 21, pp501–12

Nkurunungi, J. B. (2001) 'Habituation of Bwindi mountain gorillas', *Gorilla Journal*, vol 22, pp37–8

Olsson, M. P. O. and Widen, P. (2008) 'Effects of highway fencing and wildlife crossings on moose *Alces alces* movements and space use in southwestern Sweden', *Wildlife Biology*, vol 14, pp111–17

O'Keefe, D. J. (2002) *Persuasion: Theory and Research* (2nd edn), SAGE Publications, Thousand Oaks, CA

O'Reilly, T. and Tennant, M. (2010) *The Age of Persuasion: How Marketing Ate Our Culture*, Counterpoint, Berkeley, CA

Oskamp, S. and Schultz, P. W. (2006) 'Using psychological science to achieve ecological sustainability', in S. I. Donaldson, D. E. Berger and K. Pezdek (eds) *Applied Psychology: New Frontiers and Rewarding Careers*, Lawrence Erlbaum Associates, Mahwah, NJ

Ostendorf, B. F., Taggart, D. A. and Olds, L. (2009) 'Multi-scale distribution patterns of the southern hairy-nosed wombat', *Proceedings of the Surveying & Spatial Sciences Institute Biennial International Conference* (SSC2009), Adelaide, Australia, 28 September–2 October

Pearson, E., Davis, J. and Litchfield, C. (2010) 'A case study of orang-utan and siamang behaviour within a mixed-species zoo exhibit', *Journal of Applied Animal Welfare Science*, vol 13, pp330–46

Pickett, S. T. A. (2010) 'The wild and the city', in E. Fearn (ed) *State of the Wild 2010–2011: A Global Portrait*, Island Press, Washington, DC

Pike, B. L., Saylors, K. E., Fair, J. N., LeBreton, M., Tamoufe, U., Djoko, C. F., Rimoin, A. W. and Wolfe, N. D. (2010) 'The origin and prevention of pandemics', *Clinical Infectious Diseases*, vol 50, pp1636–40

Pimm, S. L. and Brooks, T. M. (2000) 'The sixth extinction: how large, where and when?', in P. H. Raven (ed) *Nature and Human Society: the Quest for a Sustainable World*, National Academy Press, Washington, DC

Reed, P. and Cameron, K. (2011) 'The role in-situ conservation organizations play in disease surveillance programs', *EcoHealth*, vol 7, supplement S11–12

Reid, R. S., Gichohi, H., Said, M. Y., Nkedianye, D., Ogutu, J. O., Kshatriya, M., Kristjanson, P., Kifugo, S. C., Agatsiva, J. L., Adanje, S. A. and Bagine, R. (2008) 'Fragmentation of a peri-urban savanna, Athi-Kaputiei Plains, Kenya', in K. A. Galvin, R. S. Reid, R. H. Behnke, Jr. and N. T. Hobbs (eds) *Fragmentation in Semi-Arid and Arid Landscapes: Consequences for Human and Natural Systems*, Springer, Dordrecht, the Netherlands

Robinson, J. G. (2005) 'Foreword', in R. Woodroffe, S. Thirgood and A. Rabinowitz (eds) *People and Wildlife: Conflict or Coexistence?*, Cambridge University Press, Cambridge

Rockström, J., Steffen, W., Noone, K., Persson, Å., Chapin III, F. S., Lambin, E. F., Lenton, T. M., Scheffer, M., Folke, C., Schellnhuber, H. J., Nykvist, B., de Wit, C. A., Hughes, T., van der Leeuw, S., Rodhe, H., Sörlin, S., Snyder, P. K., Costanza, R., Svedin, U., Falkenmark, M., Karlberg, L., Corell, R. W., Fabry, V. J., Hansen, J., Walker, B., Liverman, D., Richardson, K., Crutzen, P. and Foley, J. A. (2009) 'A safe operating space for humanity', *Nature*, vol 461, pp472–5

Roger, E., Laffan, S. W. and Ramp, D. (2011) 'Road impacts a tipping point for wildlife populations in threatened landscapes', *Population Ecology*, vol 53, pp215–27

Rudd, H., Vala, J. and Schaefer, V. (2002) 'Importance of backyard habitat in a comprehensive biodiversity conservation strategy: a connectivity analysis of urban green spaces', *Restoration Ecology*, vol 10, pp368–75

Salafsky, N., Salzer, D., Stattersfield, A. J., Hilton-Taylor, C., Neugarten, R., Butchart, S. H. M., Collen, B., Cox, N., Master, L. L., O'Connor, S. and Wilkie, D. (2008) 'A standard lexicon for biodiversity conservation: unified classifications of threats and actions', *Conservation Biology*, vol 22, pp897–911

Saunders, C. (2003) 'The emerging field of conservation psychology', *Human Ecology Review*, vol 10, pp137–49

Schillaci, M. A., Jones-Engel, L., Engel, G. A., Paramastri, Y., Iskandar, E., Wilson, B., Allan, J. S., Kyes, R. C., Watanabe, R. and Grant, R. (2005) 'Prevalence of enzootic simian viruses among urban performance monkeys in Indonesia', *Tropical Medicine and International Health*, vol 10, no 12, pp1305–14

Shivik, J. A. (2006) 'Tools for the edge: what's new for conserving carnivores', *BioScience*, vol 56, pp253–9

Skerratt, L., Speare, R. and Berger, L. (2011) 'Mitigating the impact of diseases affecting biodiversity – retrospective on the outbreak investigation for Chytridiomycosis', *EcoHealth*, vol 7, supplement S26

Small, B. and Jollands, N. (2005) 'Technology and ecological economics: Promethean technology, Pandorian potential', *Ecological Economics*, vol 56, pp343–58

Smith, L., Weiler, B. and Ham, S. (2011) 'The rhetoric versus the reality: a critical examination of the zoo proposition', in W. Frost (ed) *Zoos and Tourism: Conservation, Education, Entertainment?*, Channel View Publications, Bristol

Steklis, H. D., Hodgkinson, C., Fawcett, K., Gerald-Steklis, N., Czekala, N., Lilly, A. and Mehlman, P. T. (2004) 'The impact of tourism on mountain gorillas', *Folia Primatologica*, vol 75, supplement 1, pp40–1

Swarna Nantha, H. and Tisdell, C. (2009) 'The orangutan–oil palm conflict: economic constraints and opportunities for conservation', *Biodiversity Conservation*, vol 18, pp487–502

Taylor, B. D. and Goldingay, R. L. (2010) 'Roads and wildlife: impacts, mitigation and implications for wildlife management in Australia', *Wildlife Research*, vol 37, pp320–31

Thompson, J., Shirreffs, L. and McPhail, I. (2003) 'Dingoes on Fraser Island – tourism dream or management nightmare', *Human Dimensions of Wildlife*, vol 8, pp37–47

Thomson, M. S. (2007) 'Placing the wild in the city: "thinking with" Melbourne's bats', *Society and Animals*, vol 15, pp79–95

Tigas, L. A., Van Vuren, D. H. and Sauvajot, R. M. (2002) 'Behavioural responses of bobcats and coyotes to habitat fragmentation and corridors in an urban environment', *Biological Conservation*, vol 108, pp299–306

Tindle, H. (2008) 'Investigating conservation attitudes and behaviour: the impact of human–cheetah interactions within a zoo setting', Honours thesis, School of Psychology, Social Work and Social Policy, University of South Australia, Adelaide, Australia

Townsend, S. (2009) 'Incorporating sustainable practices for zoos and aquariums: a triple bottom line approach', *International Zoo Yearbook*, vol 43, pp53–63

Treves, A., Wallace, R. B. and White, S. (2009) 'Participatory planning of interventions to mitigate human–wildlife conflicts', *Conservation Biology*, vol 23, pp1577–87

VerCauteren, K. C., Shivik, J. A. and Lavelle, M. J. (2005) 'Efficacy of an animal-activated frightening device on urban elk and mule deer, *Wildlife Society Bulletin*, vol 33, pp1282–7

Waltner-Toews, D. (2011) 'Public health in the future', paper presented at the1st International One Health Congress, Melbourne, Australia, 14–16 February

Weaver, S. C. and Barrett, A. D. T. (2004) 'Transmission cycles, host range, evolution and emergence of arboviral disease', *Microbiology*, vol 2, pp789–801

Whitley, G. L. (2000) *PSYOP Operations in the 21st Century*, US Army War College Strategy Paper, Carlisle Barracks, PA, ics01.ds.leeds.ac.uk/papers/pmt/exhibits/660/psyop.pdf, accessed 9 March 2011

Wolfe, N. D., Dunavan, C. P. and Diamond, J. (2007) 'Origins of major human infectious diseases', *Nature*, vol 447, pp279–83

Woodroffe, R., Thirgood, S. and Rabinowitz, A. (2005) 'The future of coexistence: resolving human–wildlife conflicts in a changing world', in R. Woodroffe, S. Thirgood and A. Rabinowitz (eds) *People and Wildlife: Conflict or Coexistence?*, Cambridge University Press, Cambridge

World Health Organization (2002) *Understanding the BSE Threat*, World Health Organization, Geneva

World Tourism Organization (2000) *Tourism Market Trends 2000: Long-term Prospects*, World Tourism Organization, Madrid

World Association of Zoos and Aquariums (2005) *Building a Future for Wildlife: The World Zoo and Aquarium Conservation Strategy*, World Association of Zoos and Aquariums, Berne, Switzerland

WWF (2010) *Living Planet Report 2010: Biodiversity, Biocapacity and Development*, World Wide Fund for Nature, Gland, Switzerland, www.footprintnetwork.org/press/LPR2010.pdf, accessed 27 February 2011

Part III

Zero waste in sustainable architecture and design at the household and building scale

Chapter 11

Sustainable building design and systems integration

Combining energy efficiency with material efficiency

Steffen Lehmann

Summary

Among the most significant environmental challenges of our time are global climate change, excessive fossil-fuel dependency and our cities' growing demand for energy and materials – all likely to be major challenges of the twenty-first century and some of the greatest problems facing humanity. Globally, buildings account for around one-third of energy use and are responsible for over half of total greenhouse-gas emissions (Toepfer, 2007; Brugmann, 2009; Friedman, 2009). Studies show that the efficiency-improvement capacity of buildings is significant: researchers have estimated that the current energy consumption of buildings could be cut by 30–35 per cent simply by using energy more efficiently. Another 25 per cent could be gained by transforming the existing building stock through retrofitting (Hegger et al, 2007; Lehmann, 2008, 2009). Such changes would address the environmental challenges and help to secure social and economic development.

But why are our current construction methods wasting so much material? Why are our current buildings so energy hungry? It is worthwhile reflecting on the origins of the dependency of buildings on air conditioning, which evolved with twentieth-century architecture and is related to other developments that affected buildings in the last century, such as the emergence of the curtain glass facade, the lack of flexibility and adaptability of most buildings and their relatively short lifespan. Such reflection shows that many basic passive design principles have been forgotten or pushed aside. We can, however, still find them in heritage buildings from the pre-air-conditioning era, and we see that they are based on heat avoidance, the appropriate use of local materials, the use of natural cross-ventilation and the harnessing of natural energies offered by the location. This chapter sets out to explain design approaches to energy-efficient and material-efficient buildings and then presents three case studies of such buildings in three different climatic zones. It concludes with a series of recommendations for a holistic pathway to low-to-no-carbon climate-adaptive buildings. High-performance buildings are a key feature of energy reduction and waste minimization. A move towards better design and building practices would ensure limitations on emissions of greenhouse gases for decades to come. In fact, buildings are often described as the 'low-hanging fruit' in the challenge of creating a low-carbon future, because the implementation of energy efficiency and material efficiency in the construction sector has been long overdue and has already started to become a worldwide movement. Also, these changes are often fairly inexpensive and easy to achieve (Kearns et al, 2006).

Introduction

The concentration of our energy supply on fossil fuels has had a continuous and drastic effect on the balance of nature, ecosystems and the overall environment, on water and soil, biodiversity and climatic stability. The use of fossil energy sources has led to a rapid rise in the emission of carbon dioxide and other greenhouse gases into the atmosphere. The use of energy by urban development and buildings is of far-reaching importance. Estimates indicate that, 'at present urban agglomerations account for up to seventy per cent of all CO_2 emissions worldwide, and around forty per cent of CO_2 emissions can be attributed to housing construction and estate development' (Scheer, 2002; see also World Energy Council, 2004; Toepfer, 2007; IPCC, 2007, 2008). An increase in energy efficiency and a reduction in energy demand in buildings must, therefore, be a basic condition for any successful climate-change policy (UNEP, 2007; UN-Habitat, 2010).

It is now widely accepted that human activities are contributing to accelerated climate change and that the built environment (including building design) will play a significant role in the mitigation of, and adaptation to, the impact of climate change (Brundtland/UN Commission, 1987). It is also increasingly understood that there is a complex interplay between various design strategies that can be applied to buildings and the opportunities for increasing their energy efficiency. Energy efficiency has become an integral part of building design.

Energy efficiency is the ability to use less energy more effectively to provide the same level of output. To avoid global warming, we need to take energy efficiency as far as we can and make it a priority. This requires a transformation of how we generate, distribute and consume electricity (by introducing smart grids, new electric transportation and local distribution systems), as most electricity is still produced with the technology of the mid twentieth century. Energy efficiency in buildings means employing strategies in their design, construction and operation that minimize the use of energy imported from utility companies. Commonly quoted examples include insulation of external walls and the use of high-performance glazing, solar hot-water heating and low-energy fluorescent, or LED, lighting. Efficient energy use is achieved by using more efficient and effective technology in all processes of an integrated building design approach that takes advantage of the local climate to provide some, or all, of the heating, cooling, ventilation and lighting needs of the occupants (a 'harnessing-nature' approach). Energy efficiency also helps to reduce emissions of greenhouse gases.

Today it is possible to build 'zero-energy buildings' (ZEBs), which are buildings designed and constructed environmentally responsibly and which produce at least as much energy as they consume. On-site generation of renewable energy through solar power, wind power, hydropower or biomass can significantly reduce the environmental impact of the building. With on-site electricity generation, a ZEB can be used autonomously from the electricity grid supply (off-the-grid), as all required energy is harvested on site (MacKay, 2008).

Material efficiency is the ability to use fewer materials, preferably local materials with less embodied energy, so that, as a consequence, the usage of raw materials, construction methods and physical processes are carried out in a manner that consumes, incorporates or wastes less of a given material (compared with previous measures). For instance, making a usable item out of thinner stock than a prior version increases the material efficiency of the manufacturing process.

'Zero-waste' concepts in design and construction consider the entire life cycle of buildings and express the need for closed-loop industrial and societal systems and construction processes. Better material flow management leads to better material efficiency in the use of raw materials and construction systems and fewer waste streams; it helps in preventing a waste of resources, minimizing material input and reducing the use of non-recyclable materials.

The design of material- and energy-efficient buildings is a complex task for architects and engineers. Truly sustainable design can only be achieved if energy efficiency is combined with material efficiency. It requires a sound understanding of the interlinkages between various technical, environmental, social and economic criteria, as explained in the following parts of this article.

Definitions and background

In future, all buildings will have to be energy efficient by default. The next generation of great buildings will be 100 per cent 'green'.

A question to start with is: what is an energy-efficient architecture (or building)? Energy-efficient buildings are an integral part of the overarching aim to achieve sustainable development. Sustainable development has been defined as 'development which meets the needs of the present without compromising the ability of future generations to meet their own needs' (Brundtland/UN Commission, 1987). Therefore, energy-efficient buildings have to be designed in such a way that they contribute towards the larger vision of building energy-efficient and environmentally sustainable cities. This is achieved by increasing the efficiency of resource (energy) use, but not by increasing resource throughput. This implies that energy is conserved wherever possible, and energy supplies, to a large degree, come from renewable and non-polluting (non-fossil-fuels) sources. It recommends the thoughtful integration of rooftop solar power, solar thermal, wind power, biomass, geothermal or hydro, depending on the site's potential and the kinds of resource the site can supply to harvest renewable energy needs on site.

In general, efficient energy use – most of the time simply called 'energy efficiency' – is the goal of efforts to reduce the amount of energy required to provide products, services or a comfortable indoor climate. For instance, insulating a home allows a building to use less cooling and heating energy to achieve and maintain a comfortable indoor temperature, even if it is very hot or cold outside. Research shows that allowing interior spaces to be naturally ventilated means healthier interior environments and better productivity in workplaces. Importantly, energy-efficient buildings do not have to conform to a particular 'building style': they can be existing buildings adapted for reuse. They are buildings that effectively manage natural resources by taking all possible measures to ensure that the need for energy is minimal during their operation (applying passive and active systems to harvest renewable energy sources). In these buildings, cooling, heating, ventilating and lighting systems use methods, technologies and products that conserve non-renewable energy or eliminate energy use. Cutting energy demand requires the use of design solutions, materials and equipment that are more energy efficient.

Sustainable building design, also known as green or energy-efficient building design, is therefore the practice of creating structures and using processes that are environmentally responsible and resource-efficient throughout a building's life cycle, from concept to design, construction, operation, maintenance, renovation and demolition. Although new technologies are constantly being developed, the common objective is for energy-efficient buildings to be designed to reduce the overall impact of the built environment on human health and the natural environment by efficiently using energy, as well as water, materials and other resources, and reducing waste and pollution.

An Organisation for Economic Co-operation and Development (OECD) report defines 'sustainable buildings' as buildings that are designed on the basis of holistic approaches involving the following five principles:

- resource efficiency: reducing energy needs and materials during construction;
- energy efficiency: reducing energy in building operation;
- pollution prevention: minimizing pollution, environmental impact and damage to health;
- harmonization with environment: making the most of the site, reducing embodied energy and resource depletion;
- applying integrated and systemic approaches (OECD, 2003).

This chapter concentrates on energy use in buildings during their operation, because this is the main field of influence for the building's designer (the architect, engineer or planner). Operational-energy reduction is frequently regarded as a low-hanging fruit that can easily be implemented. However, depending on the level of energy services, the operational-energy consumption can be up to 80 per cent of the total energy demand of a building, along with construction, demolition and the embodied energy in the materials (World Business Council for Sustainable Development (WBCSD), 2009).

The world's built heritage plays an important role in the shift towards a low-carbon society: it contains a large amount of embodied energy. It also offers a large resource of knowledge about design principles and how architects used to operate within the constraints and challenges of extreme climatic conditions, such as, for instance, in a tropical or hot and arid climate. Unfortunately, much of this knowledge has been forgotten, and has not been sufficiently discussed and researched.

'Climate-responsive' means that the building's facade and systems can respond to different climatic conditions, to weather-related changes and to shifting day/night conditions. One of its fundamental principles is to design buildings that are 'low tech', where passive strategies are employed before active ones. Traditional buildings are a great educational source, as they frequently achieve 'more with less': high comfort for building occupants, good indoor air quality, combined with surprisingly low energy requirements. Following the first oil crisis in 1973, a series of architectural pioneers of a low-tech approach, such as the European architects Nicholas Grimshaw, Norman Foster, Renzo Piano, Peter Huebner, Jourda and Perraudin and Thomas Herzog, just to name a few (Tzonis, 2006), proposed environmental alternatives for more energy-efficient buildings.

Energy simulations on the computer can be used at the earliest design stage to assess various design options and alternative building forms, and to explore the effectiveness of different energy-conservation and energy-use-reduction measures. Ideally, energy simulation should continue throughout the entire design process to ensure the desired reductions in energy consumption are achieved, to avoid over-heating and to minimize peak energy load. Computer simulation enables the designer to define the ideal building shape, facade envelope, size of openings and type of glazing, effective sun shading and so on, as early as during the conceptual design phase. Energy simulations are important to refine the final building design, and the use of computer-based tools to solve energy design problems has grown rapidly (Clarke, 2001).

Passive and active design principles for material- and energy-efficient, climate-responsive buildings

Holistic strategies and integrated approaches:

The most successful solutions are now the highly effective combination of passive design principles with some well-considered active systems, for buildings that are built to last longer.

Before electrical heating, cooling and illumination became common, architects used a combination of passive design principles to ensure that interiors were well lit and ventilated through passive means, without any use of mechanical equipment. However, since the early 1950s, most architects and engineers have simply employed air-conditioning systems for cooling, as energy from fossil fuels was cheap and plentiful, and air-conditioning systems allowed for deep-plan buildings, internalized shopping-mall complexes and other highly inefficient air-conditioning-dependent building typologies.

The biggest energy consumers in buildings are technical installations for cooling interiors and lighting. The extensive use of glass surfaces in the facades of buildings (especially in hot, tropical or subtropical climates) and materials that easily store the heat in summer frequently lead to solar overheating, which has led to the widespread use of mechanical systems (air-conditioning systems) (Aynsley, 2006). Buildings in the tropics are a particular challenge owing to the high humidity and temperatures. However, the tropics are home to almost two-thirds of the world's population, and so practical and achievable solutions are of particular relevance. With more careful building design, energy-hungry air-conditioning systems could be avoided in almost any climate. Instead of the use of mechanical air-conditioning systems, substantial improvements in comfort can be achieved by the informed choice of materials appropriate to basic passive energy principles and the optimization of natural ventilation (cross-ventilation, night-flush cooling, mixed-mode systems), summer shading and winter solar heat gain. Solar and wind energy can provide heating, cooling and electric power.

On the other hand, buildings from a pre-air-conditioning era frequently display a convincing application of passive design principles, such as their optimized orientation, the use of evaporative cooling, strategic use of thermal mass, trompe walls, ingenious sun-shading devices for the western facade, solar chimneys, courtyards allowing for cross-ventilation of hot air at the highest point in the room, and natural cross-ventilation adjustable to the changing directions of a breeze. Sub-slab labyrinths for fresh-air intake, activating the thermal mass, have recently seen a comeback in many projects.

Such underground air chambers, called thermal labyrinths, are frequently used to ventilate rooms, with air cooled naturally by travelling a long distance underground through channels in the earth. Energy savings from the use of thermal labyrinths can be significant (Daniels, 1995, 2000). In addition, the use of local materials with less embodied energy (combined with a local workforce and locally available technical know-how) has recently led to regional 'styles' in architecture.

Successful buildings of the future will increasingly rely on the critical examination of, and learning from, buildings of the past (Vale and Vale, 1991, 2000; Hyde, 2000). There is so much we can learn from such studies. For example, which passive design principles have delivered the most energy savings? How has adequate active and passive thermal-storage mass been provided? There is a good reason why passive design principles have traditionally been preferred to (and are now once again being chosen over) active systems. 'We need solutions for buildings that can do more with less technology', argues engineer Gerhard Hausladen, adding: 'The optimization of the building layout and detailing of the facade system are essential for an integrated approach to the design of low-energy consuming buildings and cities' (Hausladen et al, 2005, p41). Just optimizing buildings through the application of passive design principles can deliver energy savings of up to 80 per cent (Hausladen et al, 2005).

A building's location and its surroundings play a key role in regulating its indoor temperature, the illumination of space and the capacity to minimize energy use. For example, trees and landscaping can provide shade or block wind, while neighbouring buildings can overshadow a building and thus increase the need for illumination during daytime. This is why the designer needs to understand the site conditions and the effective application of passive design principles fully (Hall and Pfeiffer, 2000; Gauzin-Mueller, 2002; Treberspurg and Linz, 2008).

Focusing on basic, low-tech passive design principles

For buildings to have the minimum adverse impact on the natural and built environment, energy-efficient building design needs to balance a whole range of requirements from various interlinked issues, including (but not limited to):

- design strategies based on a deep understanding of site and context;
- strategies for energy efficiency (operational and embodied);
- strategies for water efficiency;
- material efficiency: focusing on material flows and embodied energy (life cycle);
- overall material and waste streams during construction, operation and demolition;
- integrating passive design principles, such as optimizing the building's shape and orientation, employing natural ventilation, use of daylight, thermal mass, sun shading, solar gains, the use of courtyard typologies etc.;
- reducing overall greenhouse-gas emissions from construction, operation and demolition;
- integrating community well-being and various social dimensions;
- health and quality of indoor environment (the occupants' comfort).

The need to minimize non-renewable-resource consumption and reduce waste poses significant challenges for the building designer, as well as construction companies, and for building operators during the period of building use. It is obvious that some of the earliest design decisions have a significant impact on energy efficiency and opportunities to use passive solar power or natural ventilation, such as decisions on building orientation, placement on site, compactness and geometry, typology, material choices, facade openings etc.

While recognizing that using more electricity from non-fossil fuels (such as solar and wind power) will help to address climate change, the building designer is likely to focus primarily on cutting energy consumption (Keeler and Burke, 2009). Reducing energy consumption with energy-efficient building design strategies is vital because it helps to preserve finite resources, lowers costs for businesses and consumers and can often be accomplished relatively quickly (again, the low-hanging fruit aspect). The WBCSD points out that,

> realistically, the contribution of renewable energy sources is likely to be constrained for several decades, only increasing slowly, although it can be observed that values and attitudes in society towards renewable energy sources have started to change and will continue to change over time.
>
> (WBCSD, 2009, p12)

Buildings using passive design principles are usually naturally ventilated (or use mixed-mode systems, which are a combination of natural ventilation and additional mechanical cooling during summer months) and are well day-lit to minimize the need for active systems of climate control and artificial lighting (Daniels and Hindrichs, 2007). Green roofs help to cut energy consumption by providing insulation to the building and by acting as filtration for the rainwater-capture system, and at the same time increasing the city's biodiversity.

Studying the built heritage plays an important role in the shift towards a low-carbon society. It offers a large resource of knowledge about design principles and how architects have operated for hundreds of years within the challenges of hot, arid or tropical climates. This knowledge has not been sufficiently discussed, taught and researched. In the light of globalization, it is increasingly necessary for the existing authentic built heritage to be a significant contributor to local identity, helping to define the unique character of a location, supporting local people in their aspirations for social outcomes and providing a marker for collective memory. The diversity and rich complexity of tangible and intangible heritage are a constant inspiration that deserves to be better maintained and protected.

Research in pre-air-conditioning built heritage is particularly relevant for the future of the Asia–Pacific region, where we can find rapid urbanization, sometimes combined with too much reliance on outdated models of urban growth and building designs, thus further increasing energy demands. This can include an unusually high dependency on mechanical (air-conditioning) systems, thereby creating large CO_2 emissions and high operating costs in both residential and commercial building stock. In current discussions about sustainability and climate change, we can observe a re-appreciation and evaluation of the built heritage in harmony with its climatic conditions and geographic location. The Asia–Pacific region's humid tropical climate poses a particularly difficult problem. It has temperatures often around 30° C during the daytime and around 25° C at night, and has a high relative humidity of about 90 per cent. This is typical for

Singapore, Hong Kong, Bangkok, Djakarta, Manila and other large tropical cities suffering from the urban heat island (UHI) effect. Such conditions leave little scope for night-flush cooling, and refreshing breezes (airflow) are often lacking for long periods (Aynsley, 2006). Serious climate engineering strategies are needed, and the dehumidification of the air as part of a cooling process is a preferable option. There are some particularly exciting developments in the innovative area of 'solar cooling'. So far, around 400 installations worldwide already use such innovative solar-cooling technology (Kohlenbach, 2010).

The UHI effect has been particularly difficult for large cities located in tropical regions. Hong Kong, for instance, has a very high population density and is always praised for its efficient public transport systems (Owens, 1986; Newman and Kenworthy, 1989). But the city has an extremely high dependency on air conditioning, and the lack of natural air ventilation in the city has emerged as a serious planning issue. Most buildings are not insulated and lack any external sun shading of their facades.

Brooks and Hyde have pointed out how a site's microclimate can be modified through careful site planning, leading to improved thermal comfort of outdoor spaces, increased capacity for natural ventilation and sun control in buildings, and therefore reduced cooling loads (Brooks, 1988; Hyde, 2000). Traditionally, in cities in Asia and the Middle East, there has always existed a large repertoire of climatically adaptive and culturally sensitive urban form, which is found in the traditional use of courtyard typologies and low-rise housing, even in high-density districts, with narrow, shaded laneways. In addition, there are a variety of passive cooling techniques that can be utilized for particular climate types, such as shaded spaces with courtyards and atria for effective cross-ventilation, open circulation with breezeways and verandahs, roof ventilation, solar chimneys and similar techniques.

The main principles of material- and energy-efficient design include:

- optimal orientation, appropriate window size and sun control (effective shading);
- compact building form (building geometry with less facade surface);
- building mass modified to increase natural airflow through site (catching breezes);
- cross-ventilation and day lighting, with effective external sun shading (e.g. a louvre system for sun control, using vertical shading louvres at the eastern and western facades; these have the advantage of retaining the outside view and are more effective than horizontal louvres);
- passive solar heating for winter months;
- evaporative cooling systems;
- strategic selection of materials for use of thermal mass (e.g. choice of lightweight or heavy construction materials, with exposed, 'activated' concrete surface);
- rooftop vegetation, gardens and water surfaces for improved microclimate and reduced heat load;
- night-flush cooling through openings, activating thermal mass (using night purge);
- sub-slab labyrinths, bringing in outside air through underground, cool air channels beneath the slab;
- white (not dark) facade and roof colouring;
- optimal sun shading devices, with wide roof overhangs to shade windows;
- landscaping for westerly facade protection;
- high insulation of external walls and roofs.

These strategies are often combined to make them work together as a system: for instance, by linking high thermal capacity (thermal mass) for heat-sink effects with passive solar heating, or with cross-ventilation for night-flush cooling (summer cooling). The use of lightweight exterior facade construction elements with low thermal capacity can help to avoid the accumulation, storage and re-radiation of heat.

Deep plans, beyond a maximum of 15m in depth, can significantly reduce the effectiveness of day lighting and natural ventilation, leading to greater dependency on air-conditioning systems, thereby negatively impacting on the occupants' health, thermal comfort, productivity and overall working conditions. Therefore, four of the most applicable and widely used passive design strategies are:

1   avoiding large glazing that receives direct sunlight and is without shading (design of high-quality external shading);
2   reducing the surface-to-volume ratio as much as possible through compact building massing;
3   using window sizing strategically in the design of the building (depending on orientation);
4   maximizing day lighting and natural cross-ventilation through slim building plans.

Building envelopes: the overall important role of the facade

> Good building design offers the user maximum comfort for minimum energy. For building services and technology, the motto must be: as much as is necessary; as little as is possible.

The facade system is the interface between interior and exterior. It always plays an especially significant role in room climate and operational costs. The more effectively the building envelope can react to weather changes and user-specific requirements, the less energy is needed; most of the time, the facade system determines the lighting, glare, ventilation, shading, solar control, insulation, thermal storage, noise reduction etc. (Lieb, 2001).

Research shows that the facade system decides about 60 per cent of the building's energy consumption. The building's envelope is, therefore, crucial for energy efficiency, beginning with the orientation of the building, the use of effective sun shading, lighting and ventilation control, insulation and thermal mass. The building's orientation, the compactness of its shape (geometry), the overall selection of its facade materials and colours, the type of glazing (there is a wide range of absorptive solar protection glazing), the use of sun-shading devices and the size of facade openings all have a significant influence on the energy efficiency of the building design. Engineers even estimate that the decisions made in the design of the facade are responsible for around two-thirds of the building's later energy needs for its operation (Daniels and Hindrichs, 2007).

To increase the efficiency of the building envelope (the barrier between conditioned and unconditioned space), energy-efficient buildings use high-performance glazing with insulated window frames. Over the centuries, facade systems have become thinner and thinner, losing their thermal mass. Most glass curtain wall, high-rise buildings waste a lot of energy because they collect heat like a greenhouse in summer and then use air conditioning to cool the interior spaces. Efficient shading devices for the facade can be used as a solution; however, shading systems that allow for daylight and an unobstructed view, but reduce glare and solar heat gain at the same time, are extremely complicated owing to their contradictory parameters. Using glass for more than 35 per cent of the facade surface means some careful thermal modelling is recommended, as overheating in summer becomes highly likely.

Unless inescapable environmental characteristics, such as high levels of pollution or noise, prevent it, buildings should be ventilated naturally. Double-envelope facades can be a solution for taller buildings (e.g. for office towers) to provide some natural ventilation despite the high wind speeds one might encounter in upper floors. Effective heat protection in summer is crucial, and sun blinds or louvre systems can easily be incorporated in the cavity of double-envelope facades to avoid undesirable heat gain (Lieb, 2001).

Large solar roofs are increasingly being constructed, even in countries with limited sunshine. Active solar walls can generate the entire electrical energy required to operate the building, and light shelves incorporated into the facade can reflect daylight deeper into the inner areas of a building, thus reducing the need for artificial illumination.

The large glass surfaces of modern buildings facing the sun almost always create climatic problems owing to their extreme heat gain. It is increasingly being recognized that performance-based, quantifiable guidance (with exact performance reporting) for designers is needed. In the last decade or so, architects have increasingly raised the issue of traditional 'rules-of-thumb' for passive design principles, which do not sufficiently quantify the effects. More guidance for building designers through exact quantification of the effect of the various available strategies would be helpful.

Embodied energy and operating energy

Calculating the overall energy use of a building (or any other product) is known as life-cycle assessment (LCA); it takes into account: how long the building lasts; how much is the ongoing energy use in the building; and the building's embodied energy, which is the energy used during its construction.

In general, the two different types of energy that are most relevant to a building's ecological footprint and life cycle are the embodied energy in building materials and the operating energy used in the operational use of the building (e.g. an office building's energy demands). Both energy types together define the entire energy life cycle of a building (and, therefore, whole-life carbon emissions) (Lenzen et al, 2008). However, operating costs are frequently seen as more relevant than construction costs, given that most buildings have a lifespan of thirty to thirty-five years or longer, and, over this time period, operating costs can amount to much more than the original costs of construction. This means that investors are looking, not only at initial capital investment costs, but also at long-term operating and maintenance costs. This has driven an increased interest in energy-efficient, green architecture.

The energy payback time is the amount of time an energy system must operate to generate the same amount of energy that was required to manufacture, transport and install the system. Payback times for such systems, for instance for solar PV systems, have significantly dropped in recent years.

'Embodied energy' is the total energy required directly and indirectly to produce (manufacture and/or construct) a product, material or building component and to transport and maintain that product/material so that it is ready for use at a point in time. It is the sum total of the energy necessary for the entire life cycle of a product. For instance, primary energy input (PEI), also known as grey or embodied energy, is the energy required for manufacturing and using a product, measured in megajoules (MJ). It includes all the energy quantities necessary for production, transport, intermediate states and storage, and is an indicator of the environmental impact of the product (Wackernagel and Rees, 1996). Reducing energy embodied in construction materials is an important strategy for mitigating our fossil-fuel dependency.

Embodied-energy reduction means that the overall quantity of energy required by all activities associated with the construction, operation and maintenance of the building (direct and indirect) are kept to a minimum. However, to keep the embodied energy low requires that the designer specifies materials and construction systems that reduce the need for transport during construction, refurbishment and demolition (the sum of all material flows) and tightly controls all processes involved to avoid the creation of waste, pollution and noise. Furthermore, the building designer should always aim for an integration of existing structures and to demolish and rebuild only when it is not economical or practical to adapt, reuse or extend an existing structure. Issues such as adaptive reuse of buildings, lightweight construction systems (with minimized embodied energy), systems for waste prevention, recycling of construction materials, reuse of entire building components and prefabricated modular elements and 'design for disassembly and digital prefab for material recovery' have recently emerged as important fields in energy-efficient building design. This includes the greater influence of supply-chain criteria and the fact that building materials have to be easier to recycle (Lehmann, 2010a).

Sam Hui (2002) discussed the complexity around the aim of reducing embodied energy of buildings without compromising longevity or efficiency. He lists the following strategies:

- reuse existing buildings and structures wherever possible (provided their energy costs in use can be reduced to an acceptable level);
- design buildings for long life, with ease of maintenance and adaptability to changing needs;
- construct buildings and infrastructure out of local and low-energy materials where possible;
- reduce the proportion of high-rise, detached or single-storey developments;
- design layouts that minimize the extent of roadway and utility pipework per dwelling;
- create a holistic strategy to deal with embodied energy.

However, to define the value of embodied energy for a building through a whole life cycle involves many factors: it includes all energy input required to quarry, transport and manufacture building materials, plus the energy used in the construction process. This can easily amount to a quarter of the 'lifetime' energy requirement of a building (Wackernagel and Rees, 1996).

Therefore, it is not just about making everything more energy efficient; it is also about changing the behaviours and attitudes of the property industry, the architects and the construction sector. In this regard, in 1974 (after the first oil crisis), Len Brookes noted on the 'efficiency dilemma': 'If our machines use less energy, will we just use them more?' (Brookes, 1993). Indeed, there is not much gain if energy consumption overall is higher than it would have been if no effort to increase efficiency had been made. When such an increase in consumption cancels out any energy savings, it is called a 'rebound effect'.

The energy used by a building's operation and maintenance ('operational energy') is extremely important. No matter how sustainable a building may have been in its design and construction, it can only remain so if it is operated responsibly and is maintained properly, using as little energy as possible. Operational energy can often be four or five times more than embodied energy over a thirty-five-year life cycle. A frequently quoted rule of thumb is the assumption that the ratio of energy consumption of a building should be in the order of 75 per cent operational and 25 per cent embodied energy. It is, therefore, beneficial to design buildings to take advantage of available natural resources, harnessing and maximizing the benefits from day lighting, solar-energy gains, cooling breezes for natural cross-ventilation, material capacities and all renewable energy sources available from the building's location. Operation of buildings creates exergy (exergy includes waste heat, waste energy, wastewater and all resources that are so far not used). In future, architects and engineers will need to take these unused resources into account through improved inter-coordination of building systems and services.

The most cost-effective steps towards a reduction in a building's energy consumption usually occur during the early design process: reductions of up to 50 per cent of energy use compared with conventional buildings are often possible if best-practice energy efficiency in design strategies is applied.

One of the main causes of overheating in office interiors is the large amount of equipment in use: the internal equipment loads from printers, copy machines, computers, lighting etc. have grown over the last decades, adding significantly to the need to cool down air temperatures to ensure thermal comfort for occupants. It is obvious that change is necessary.

Building materials and construction systems: reducing material consumption, optimizing material flows, enabling recycling

Choosing white, non-heat-storing materials to cut the solar heat build-up and using green roofs can significantly help mitigate the urban heat island effect.

Construction systems have the longest lifespan of all building parts, and decisions about materials for the primary structure are of utmost importance (i.e. whether it is a concrete structure, or steel, brick, timber and so on). The reuse of entire building components will become increasingly important for the construction sector. This is called 'design for disassembly'. Modular prefabrication can play an important role in reducing embodied energy and in zeroing out material waste from construction. Timber offers particular opportunities for prefabricated multi-storey construction systems that store carbon (Kaufmann, 2009).

Material efficiency expresses the degree to which usage of raw materials, construction projects or physical processes are used or carried out in a manner that consumes or wastes less of a given material compared with previous measures. For instance, making a steel beam out of thinner stock than a prior version, without compromising on structural strength, increases the material efficiency of the manufacturing process. Better material flow management can increase material efficiency and prevent waste. Wasting construction materials is a sign of inefficiency and causes great loss of value and resources (McDonough and Braungart, 2002). It is likely that we will see shortages of certain metals and rare earths by 2020. This may involve redesigning both product and process using the following formula:

building material efficiency (BME) = product output (PO)/material input (MI)

Zero-waste strategies consider the entire life cycle of buildings, products, processes and systems. The concept expresses the need for a closed-loop construction system employing the advantages of modular prefabrication, suggesting that the entire concept of waste in the construction process should be eliminated.

Building designs executed to a high material efficiency and economy of means can express their own particular aesthetic and beauty. In fact, we can find highly innovative and aesthetically pleasing minimalist constructions designed during times of material shortage and constraints throughout architectural history. Timber is the only material that is able to store carbon, and it is relatively easy to reuse and recycle. On the other hand, the production of aluminium requires a very high proportion of energy and is therefore responsible for the generation of a large amount of CO_2. For some time, there was a trend in Europe towards super-thick insulation layers, but, increasingly, architects are moving away from the idea of airtight buildings. Besides energy efficiency, there needs to be an equally strong focus on material efficiency and on ways to reduce material consumption in the construction sector. Material efficiency and reduction of CO_2 emissions from operating buildings are rightly seen as top priorities (McKinsey & Company Global Institute, 2007). Increasingly, the emissions and waste from the manufacturing and transport of building materials are being taken into account in the design process (the entire whole-of-life cycle encompasses the implications of design specification from design, to construction, to operation, to disposal or adaptive reuse). Architectural design needs to take the wider urban and ecological context into account, using more locally sourced materials, with the aim of reducing the material demand and optimizing the material flow in the construction process.

In hot and arid climates, effective sun shading is of prime importance, and buildings overshadowing each other are not seen as a disadvantage. For instance, in Abu Dhabi, UAE, 70 per cent of the energy consumed is used to cool buildings. Planned architectural measures are expected to reduce that figure dramatically in a new urban development called Masdar City. Buildings in this new zero-emission city (still under construction in 2011; expected to be completed around 2018) are built so close together that they provide each other with shade and thus reduce air-conditioning requirements. In addition, all buildings are built on concrete pedestals with sub-slab labyrinths, which help to maintain cool temperatures by allowing outside air to be brought in to circulate in underground air channels beneath the building slab. The naturally circulated air cools down in these sub-slab labyrinths before the cooler air is allowed to enter the interior spaces from beneath – all without mechanical systems.

Thermal storage in a building may be decisive for the reduction of cooling loads and depends to a large degree on the storage factor of the external walls and roof system (heat storage capacity). According to Daniels and Hindrichs, in hot–arid and variable–warm regions with great temperature swings between night and day (where night-time cooling is more effective), 'the best way to reduce energy consumption and the investment cost in ventilation and air-conditioning systems is to design a building with not only high storage capacity but also efficient night cooling to improve the storage behavior' (Daniels and Hindrichs, 2007, p164).

Building services and systems: enabling technologies

In future, green buildings will interact with each other, and the wider urban power infrastructure will form zero-emission clusters of buildings that share urban energy technologies, such as a community smart grid and a CHP plant. Buildings and districts interconnected via a smart grid will enjoy a large energy-savings potential.

Compared with the primary structure, building services have a relatively short lifespan; these systems are usually out of date after one or two decades and require exchange (retrofitting), and the disposal of old building components like these could become an unexpected future burden.

Sustainable, energy-efficient building concepts involve providing the cooling, heating and ventilation of the interior spaces using natural resources. In addition, electrical energy can be provided through solar and wind power. There is a strong move towards integrated approaches using smaller technical units and decentralized building systems, where energy is generated on-site and closer to the place of consumption. Flexibility in planning leads to a longer life for buildings. As technical systems and services have a short life cycle, applying technical aids sparingly and making the most of all passive means provided by the building fabric and its natural conditions are essential. Buildings that generate more energy than they consume and that collect and purify their own water are totally achievable (Markvart, 2000).

The era of fully air-conditioned office buildings has passed. The ventilation concepts in a building's design significantly influence its operating costs, maintenance and comfort levels (air velocity). Today, mixed-use systems with a high amount of natural ventilation, or atriums used for better airflow, have become the standard repertoire in the planning of office buildings. Avoiding deep rooms (not more than 6m deep) allows for better natural ventilation and effective day lighting. To avoid overheating in summer, any large window area on the west side should be protected with exterior shading devices. Office buildings are now designed with the optimum combination of thermal storage mass and free night-flush ventilation (these office rooms usually no longer have suspended ceilings to activate the thermal mass of the concrete slab), which makes mechanical cooling unnecessary for most of the year. As a consequence, operating costs are lower, and services take up less space in the building (smaller ducts, units and plant rooms) (Daniels, 2000; Szokolay, 2004).

The excessive use of air-conditioning technology and other quick techno-fix solutions has led to high expectations of indoor living standards and the complacency of architects who solve ventilation and cooling problems by simply putting in the air-conditioning unit (a frequently heard argument). The ubiquitous use of air-conditioning systems across the world consumes a vast amount of energy and has made twentieth-century building types, often with deep plans and closed glass facades, fully dependent on this technology. The question of how much the indoor climate should follow the outdoor climate requires a new discussion and reassessment. Although the fully air-conditioned building raises a series of health questions, most building codes still require that indoor temperatures in offices do not exceed 25° C at any time, even with a 40° C outdoor temperature. Such high requirements are, of course, impossible to achieve without mechanical ventilation.

Global warming means it is time to update this part of the building code and to question the correctness of such high comfort expectations. In addition, the following questions are raised:

- How can energy saving be achieved in the context of expected comfort levels (e.g. legislation requiring a maximum 25° C indoor temperature at any time)?
- How can we allow as much natural daylight as possible into office spaces while also reducing solar heat gain (e.g. glazing qualities on the market)?
- How can we sustainably cool buildings with large glazing areas in hot or tropical climates?

Clearly, more research is needed to answer these questions.

Retrofitting strategies for adaptive reuse: adaptation as long-term strategy

As already mentioned, the built heritage plays an essential role in the shift towards a low-carbon society. We need to look at materials and embodied energy over time. The existing building stock contains a large amount of embodied energy, which should not be lost through demolition. Reusing and refurbishing existing buildings have many advantages over constructing new buildings. Comparative studies in energy consumption and ecological footprint have revealed that the most sustainable buildings are the ones that already exist (based on their primary embodied energy and material flow, measured at year 20 in the building's life cycle) (Lehmann, 2006). Adaptive reuse is more than just retrofitting. The adaptive reuse of existing buildings can give old structures a new role to play and a valuable life extension (Urban Task Force, 1999; Grimshaw, 2009).

Embedding principles of energy efficiency in new buildings is usually much easier than retrofitting existing buildings with environmental upgrades. However, older buildings predominate in our cities, and only a small number of new buildings are added every year to the existing building stock. A Commonwealth Scientific and Industrial Research Organisation (CSIRO) study into embodied energy conducted in 2008 suggested that reuse of building materials in Australia would save about 95 per cent of embodied energy that would otherwise be wasted, and that the retrofitting of existing buildings should be the main focus of future construction (CSIRO and Ambrose, 2008). The study determined that 'the energy embodied in existing building stock in Australia is equivalent to ten years of the total energy consumption of the entire nation'.

Figure 11.1 An energy-efficient office building entirely lit by LED: this office building for Unilever at HafenCity in Hamburg, Germany, is the world's first office building that is exclusively illuminated by LED lighting. LED lighting lasts longer and can achieve a payback on investment in as little as three years. Major savings are achieved from a significantly reduced need to cool the interior spaces in summer. LED lighting produces almost no heat.

Image courtesy of Behnisch Architects, 2010

Retrofitting office and residential buildings will be the next big task for architects. Recent studies show that green buildings earn higher rents and are more sought after by corporate tenants worldwide, thus delivering faster payback to investors and building owners. In a recent study, Eichholtz et al (2009) found that certified green office buildings in the US commanded a premium in rental rates and sales prices over conventional, not-energy-optimized office buildings. In addition, occupancy rates are higher and less volatile than rates in commercial office buildings without green certification (there are now various certification systems in use in different countries, such as BREEAM, CASBEE, DGNB, LEED, GreenStar, Green Mark, just to name a few). Green buildings are not only more attractive to their tenants; they also translate into an improved reputation for the occupying companies, along with economic profitability and improved employee well-being and productivity: 'A green corporate headquarters and the use of green space in general, may signal to stakeholders and customers that a firm has a long-run commitment to a corporate social responsibility policy' (Eichholtz et al, 2009). It is likely that, in future, commercial buildings and office towers that do not meet tenants' green criteria will face higher vacancies, lower rent and value deterioration, while buildings with the appropriate standards will be able to earn more rent and be patronized by high-profile tenants (Kats et al, 2003; Stern, 2007). This makes upgrading existing office buildings and turning them into 'deep green buildings' a profitable investment that reaches its payback point faster (Shiel and Lehmann, 2008).

The reuse of mature, disused buildings means rejuvenating existing structures to suit a new purpose and thereby to extend their life cycle. Adaptive reuse offers many environmental benefits compared with new developments. A good example of the value of existing buildings in terms of sustainability is the recently upgraded building, 39, Hunter Street, in Sydney (built in 1916), which achieved a six-star GreenStar rating. Adaptive reuse is an opportunity to reduce the overall amount of energy and materials consumed; to reduce the operational energy of an existing building by improving its environmental performance; to reduce the amount of waste generated; and to maintain the place's identity in the form of its built heritage (by rejuvenating the previously underutilized or deteriorated building stock). Some architects have now specialized in 'reuse design', designing buildings that use only recycled and reclaimed materials from all kinds of source.

Heating and cooling account for the majority of household energy consumption, but to upgrade old buildings in order to meet modern standards of thermal insulation can be a real challenge. The windows of the old building stock are usually not properly sealed, the walls and roofs are not insulated, and sun shading is missing. However, attaching insulation panels to the external walls (insulation is usually made of polystyrene and other energy-intensive materials) is expensive and unsightly and in many cases doesn't last for more than ten or fifteen years. Another problem is that well-insulated buildings don't breathe and become too air tight: no outside air gets in, and as a result CO_2 can build up quickly inside. The indoor air quality is frequently unhealthy, and mould can build up. To avoid such consequences, occupants need to open doors and windows frequently, after cooking or showering, which again reduces the energy efficiency of the building. In the fight to protect the environment, it may be time to pause and ask: what is really helping, and what isn't?

Clearly, we need a better package of solutions for effectively upgrading older building stock. Designing buildings to incorporate, in the design phase, the later adaptive reuse possibilities raises important questions of longevity, durability, adaptability and end-of-life (disposal/reuse) concepts, e.g. to design plans and floor-to-floor heights suitable for reuse, considering the longevity of materials. Decisions to demolish are often made too quickly and without fully understanding the advantages of keeping good-quality existing structures. The demolition of buildings, if these are not heritage listed, is still too often perceived to be cheaper, easier or more profitable compared with maintaining them for adaptive reuse. Sometimes, legislation encourages demolition and new building. However, not only is there a loss in the sense of material and embodied energy and in the burden of disposal, but there is also a cultural loss of urban fabric.

To increase a building's performance, engineers, industry and architects are continually setting new standards worldwide for energy efficiency using intelligent, integrated technologies that deliver an optimized balance between building performance, comfort levels for occupants and sustainable practices. Considering the entire life cycle of buildings to achieve minimal operational costs and maximum productivity of occupants, the seamless communication between heating, cooling, control of lights and

Figure 11.2 An example of adaptive reuse in Berlin, Germany: the Sasha Waltz Dance Theatre is a renovated and extended factory building in Berlin Friedrichshain overlooking the river Spree. This nineteenth-century industrial building had been disused and empty for decades until a new user and a feasible adaptive reuse concept were finally found. The adaptability of the industrial brick building proved to be excellent for upcycling and for the building's new purpose. This project used an integrated whole-system design approach that combined passive and active measures to reduce energy consumption.

Image courtesy of Spangenberg Architects, 2009

blinds, as well as low-voltage energy distribution, has become an important framework for retrofitting existing buildings (i.e., according to a recent study by Siemens, building automation and energy-management solutions alone can enhance the energy efficiency and productivity of most conventional office buildings' technical infrastructure, with possible energy savings of up to 40 per cent). Intelligent and integrated building and room automation can have a further positive impact on efficiency without sacrificing comfort. Here, further energy savings can be realized simply by using available building automation systems and efficiency monitoring (Siemens, 2010).

Active design principles: on-site energy generation, natural and mechanical cooling

While green, energy-efficient buildings have emerged as a worldwide trend in recent years, including in Asia and the Middle East, they are still evolving as a cultural and technical phenomenon that requires more evidence-based knowledge to formulate reliable best-practice principles. For instance, buildings with double-skin facades have become very popular, but it will need more research into these systems before best-practice guidance can be given to designers. This also applies to on-site energy generation with building-integrated solar photovoltaic (PV) panels, or micro wind turbines, or geothermal energy use (using the energy of the soil, tapping into the warmth or cold of the earth). These are ways of achieving energy autonomy, essentially making an energy generator out of every citizen, instead of them being only energy consumers (Scheer, 2002).

Is it feasible, for example, for a group of buildings to be complemented by a small wind farm or a series of wind generators located on an adjacent site, the wind generators and PV roofs utilizing the inexhaustible energy sources offered by the sun and the wind? The cost-effectiveness of such systems is constantly improving (Droege, 2008; Green Building Council of Australia, 2008). In fact, the costs for solar PV panels have continuously dropped over the last two decades, triggered by advances in research and government programmes in Germany, Japan and China. But further research is needed.

In the context of large-scale energy transition towards more renewable energy sources, harnessing solar power within a city's districts offers particularly interesting opportunities. One of the advantages of solar power is the possibility of harnessing energy on site, with many small units in the form of building-integrated PV panels that are part of the facade or roof design (making roofs and facades solar active, and PVs a part of the urban aesthetic). Solar power is well suited for urban use and one of the few sustainable energy solutions that can easily be integrated into building design, generating energy close to the point of consumption. The main problem is that efficiency of panels has to be doubled; otherwise, there will not be enough space in the city for all the solar panels needed. Again, research is required.

Three case studies in three different climatic zones

In this section, I present three case studies that illustrate the application of the various strategies for energy efficiency: one is located in the temperate and cool climate of Europe (in Germany); one in a hot, tropical climate in Asia (in Singapore); and one in a desert climate in South America (in Chile).

All three cases are energy-efficient, high-performance buildings, which provide a compelling case that improving the energy efficiency of buildings can significantly help governments and municipalities to achieve their greenhouse-gas reduction targets. In addition, such demonstration projects serve as good examples, helping to raise standards and set new benchmarks in the construction sector. The three selected case studies are more than just technologically sophisticated structures built to a high architectural standard; they are also liveable workplaces that offer a more fulfilling relationship with the natural world.

Case study 1

Temperate, cool climate in Europe: Training Academy in Herne, Germany, 1999–2005. Architects: Jourda & Perraudin Architects (Lyon, France); stage 2 with Hegger HSS Architects (Kassel, Germany).

The various energy-efficient design strategies employed in this building include the following:

- This building complex is part of a new generation of buildings that produce more energy than they require for their operation ('energy plus buildings'). Total energy requirement is only 32 kWh/m^2 per annum (p.a.).
- The complex contains the various building parts, such as houses, inside a large overall envelope, creating a protected public atrium space with an in-between microclimate.
- The huge interior atrium space is neither heated nor air-conditioned; it is an intermediate zone as climatic envelope, creating its own protected microclimate, like a traditional glasshouse.
- As a consequence of the large glass envelope, the interior buildings do not have to be completely watertight.
- The structure of the large glass envelope (incorporating the academy, town hall and hotel) is used for collecting passive and active solar energy; its roof and facade are clad with 3,500 PV cells.
- The building incorporates 10,000m^2 of PV modules (on the roof and in the facade), providing a 1MW peak solar-power generation station.
- The timber structure is 100 per cent recyclable.
- To avoid overheating in summer, certain elements of the facade can be opened to ventilate the glasshouse.
- In order to reduce energy consumption in winter and to cool naturally in summer, an air-handling unit with a heat-exchange system has been installed, with the result that 23 per cent of energy is saved in comparison with other buildings of the same insulation level, and CO_2 emissions are reduced to 18 per cent of similarly mechanically air-conditioned buildings.

Case study 2

Hot, tropical climate in Asia: the Zero Energy Building (ZEB, a retrofit/adaptive reuse building of a former school building, the first ZEB in Southeast Asia), at Braddell Road, Singapore, 2008–9. Architects: BCA, Singapore.

Figure 11.3 Energy-efficient civic building: the Training Academy in Herne, Germany.

Photos courtesy of M. Hegger, 2007

Figure 11.4 Energy-efficient retrofit and adaptive reuse: the Zero Energy Building in Singapore.
Images courtesy of BCA, 2009

This project used an integrated whole-system design approach, combining passive and active measures to reduce energy consumption. The active and passive energy-efficiency design strategies employed in this retrofit building include:

- a solar-assisted stack ventilation system: a solar chimney and ducts pull out hot air, while letting cool airflow in for natural ventilation;
- floor diffusers, supplying cool air that, once warm, rises to vents in the ceiling;
- more energy-efficient air-conditioning, detecting carbon dioxide levels and lowering fan speed when fewer people are around;
- efficient lighting, using eco-friendly fluorescent lamps, which cut power usage by 26 per cent;
- dimmers and motion sensors, controlling artificial lighting in the building based on the day and number of people present;
- passive daylight solutions: sunlight is directed via light pipes to illuminate the interior of the building;
- greenery system: the roof is partially a roof garden, and there are wall plants on the facade, which help cut heat transmission into the building;
- plants are used to protect against extreme heat and to create a better-balanced microclimate;
- shading devices, working hand in hand with the greenery system to cut heat transmission;
- high-performance glazing: treated glass, reducing glare and heat entering into the building;
- PV technology: solar panels fitted on the roof, building sides, staircase facade and carpark shelter help to harvest the sun's rays, generating about 200,000kWh p.a., which is sufficient to power thirty four-room apartments over that time frame.

The ZEB retrofitting project is a staged model that can be replicated for other buildings, consisting of: Stage 1 – improving the thermal performance of the envelope. Stage 2 – installing high-efficiency equipment and appliances. Stage 3 – introducing on-site generation of renewable energy.

Case study 3

Desert climate in Chile: European Southern Observatory Hotel in the Atacama Desert, 1998–2002. Architects: Auer & Weber Architects, Munich, Germany.

The passive, low-tech, energy-efficiency design strategies employed in this building include the following:

- Built in extreme dry and arid conditions, 2700m above sea level, the material selection (use of thick concrete prefab panels as facade panels) helps to combat the high temperature differences found in the desert region. The thermally sluggish behaviour of these facade panels and the building structure of concrete have a positive balancing effect on the temperature of the interior spaces.
- The chosen wall system buffers the temperature differences between day and night, creating a balanced inner temperature.
- Concrete has been made by using recycled aggregates and is produced on site.

Figures 11.5 Energy-efficient hotel complex: the European Southern Observatory Hotel in the Atacama Desert, Chile.

Photos courtesy of Auer & Weber, 2005

- In hot, arid regions with great temperature swings between night and day (where night-time cooling is more effective), the best way to reduce energy consumption and to protect the investment cost in ventilation and air-conditioning systems is to design a building with not only high storage capacity but also efficient night cooling to improve storage behaviour.
- Heating is only necessary in individual rooms, with mobile radiators, when the nights are extremely cold.
- To avoid overheating in summer, certain elements of the facade can be opened to naturally cross-ventilate the rooms.
- The roof is partially covered with earth. The building is cut into the slopes, which helps to reduce heat transmission into the building.

Some further strategies for material- and energy-efficient, sustainable buildings

In addition to the strategies discussed in previous sections, the following three strategies are an important part of achieving energy efficiency in buildings.

Using local materials with less embodied energy, avoiding transportation

Buildings that use regional and local materials with less embodied energy and that apply prefabricated modular systems can lead to truly sustainable outcomes. The designer has to, therefore, explore questions about the kinds of material that are locally available and the types of material that appear in the regional, vernacular architecture. This sort of thinking uses opportunities for shorter supply chains, where all designs focus on local materials and technological know-how, such as the type of regional timber in common use.

Prefabrication has come and gone several times in modern architecture, but this time, with closer collaboration with manufacturers of construction systems and building components in the design phase, the focus can be on sustainable prefabrication to reduce material consumption.

We need to support innovation and be aware of sustainable production and consumption, the embodied energy of materials and the flow of energy in closing life cycles. We need to emphasize green manufacturing and an economy of means, such as process-integrated technologies that lead to waste reduction. It is more environmentally friendly to use lightweight structures, enclosures and local materials with less embodied energy, requiring minimal transport. Therefore, we need improved material and system specifications, supported by research into new materials and technological innovation, and reduced material diversity in multicomponent products to help facilitate design for disassembly, value retention and the possibility of reusing entire building components. Success in this area will increase the long-term durability of buildings, reduce waste and minimize material requirements (Head, 2008).

Hegger explored indicators for sustainable material-efficient construction. He points out that selecting materials, products and processes that minimize material consumption and reduce environmental impact involves the following design thinking (Hegger et al, 2006):

- planning a building layout that saves materials and allows flexible utilization;
- optimizing the materials used in regard to their global and regional environmental impact caused by extraction, production and provision;
- selecting materials and products with a preference for local availability to avoid the need for transport;
- saving resources through a preference for renewable and recyclable materials and those with long-term availability;
- recommending materials that can be recycled with minimal loss of properties and composite products that can be reverse-engineered locally.

Making the building's design specific to its site, climate and context

Energy efficiency is not enough on its own. First of all, a building's design should be based on its climatic site conditions, with appropriate responses to location and site context. The designer needs to explore the unique site constraints, climatic conditions and opportunities.

Every site or place has its own unique, individual conditions in regard to orientation, solar radiation, rain, humidity, breezes and prevailing wind direction, topography, shading, lighting, noise, air pollution and so on. Climatic conditions, which should be seen as the fundamental influence for form generation in the design of any project, as well as understanding the site and its context, are essential parameters at the beginning of every design project. Optimizing orientation and compactness to help reduce the building's heat gain or loss is necessary for creating a building with a minimized environmental footprint. Enhancing the opportunities offered by topography and natural setting leads to a building well adapted to the local climate and its ecosystem, and therefore more likely to be energy efficient. We can use the building's envelope to filter temperature, humidity, light, wind and noise.

Owing to the different characteristics of every location, each district or neighbourhood will have its own methods and tailored strategies to reach sustainability and to capture the spirit of the place. Each site or district is different, and to re-engineer existing districts we will need to understand how to take full advantage of each location's potential, and how to fine-tune the design concepts to take advantage of local circumstances. As an aim, all building developments must be in harmony with the specific characteristics, various site factors and the advantages of each location, and be appropriate to their social contexts (cultural, historical, social, geographical, economic, environmental and political). In the future, all buildings should have climate-adapted envelope technologies, with facades that are fully climate-responsive through operable openings. Prevailing winds are usually very directional, which means the predictable constant wind direction and associated thermal effect can easily be used to advantage (Beatley and Manning, 1997; Hotten, 2004).

Maximizing the use of passive design principles

The city that applies deep-green building design strategies and offers solar access for all new buildings is an energy-efficient city. Most of the passive design gains even come for free. Arthur Rosenfeld has extensively researched the benefits of white or reflective roofs, using the simple but effective albedo effect. He found that simply by using white roofs on buildings, combined with good insulation of roofs, buildings can be kept around 3°C cooler in summer, and this leads to 20–25 per cent energy savings (Rosenfeld, personal communication, 19 January 2011). He calculated that making 100m^2 of grey roofing white will offset the emission of 10t of CO_2. More research is needed into how the architect can best apply sustainable design and passive design principles in all their forms and for all buildings (Scott, 2006).

Low-energy, zero-emission designs that apply passive design principles need to be the standard for all buildings. The aim must be to reduce the building's CO_2 emissions and energy use dramatically by introducing compact solar architecture and retrofitting the entire existing building stock. New design typologies will need to be developed at low cost, and we need to produce functionally neutral buildings that last longer. We need to apply facade technology with responsive building skins for bio-climatic architecture, to take advantage of cooling breezes and natural cross-ventilation, maximizing cross-ventilation, day lighting and opportunities for night-flush cooling. Solar architecture optimizes solar gain in winter and sun-shading technology for summer, catching the low winter sun and avoiding too much heat gain in summer. At the same time, when designing buildings, we need to focus on the low consumption of resources and materials, including the future reuse of building elements and design for disassembly.

Barriers to the design and construction of more material- and energy-efficient buildings

To reduce the current energy demand of conventional buildings, a series of barriers and obstacles need to be overcome. According to Sullivan, these barriers include (but are not limited to):

- complacency and inaction between building professionals, architects, developers, investors and building users, and the general lack of a material/energy-aware culture. Changing the habits and behaviour of building users is very difficult;
- inadequate action from various stakeholders resulting in only incremental improvements in efficiency;
- impact of consumer preferences and behaviours (e.g. indoor comfort levels), as well as a lack of knowledge or insufficient awareness about the availability of energy- and material-efficient technologies and advanced design solutions;
- outdated public policies and building codes, combined with a lack of incentives (financial mechanisms) for energy-efficient investments;
- training and education that rise to the challenge of holistic design approaches for more efficient building design;
- complexity and fragmentation in the building value chain, which inhibit a holistic approach to building design, combined with a lack of transparency about energy use, material consumption and its real cost;
- misperceptions: energy-efficient buildings are still perceived in the marketplace to be much more expensive to build than conventional buildings, despite evidence to the contrary (Sullivan, 2009).

However, architecture and urban development must now address the new, complex challenges that have arisen with our throw-away consumer society; architecture will need to deliver more, beyond the classical practicality and beauty, stipulated since Vitruvius. The entire process of building design, construction and product manufacturing must be based on sustainable material flows and opportunities for resource recovery, and R&D in the field of material efficiency and recyclability is increasingly important.

When modelling the impacts of building users' behaviour and their preferences in the use of ventilation, cooling and illumination, researchers found widespread ignorance about inefficiencies and high energy consumption (Lehmann, 2010b). Most building owners and users do not care enough about energy consumption and share the misperception that energy saving is too hard or will reduce comfort levels. This is not correct; however, overcoming these psychological barriers is often very difficult. Furthermore, a recent study indicates that, by just increasing the price of energy, or by introducing carbon trading, the implementation of energy-efficient buildings will only slightly increase (WBCSD, 2009). Other additional steps are required, such as:

- the transformation of the whole building sector;
- business leadership;
- technological innovation;
- awareness campaigns;
- consistently strong regulatory change;
- financial incentives for building developers, owners and users.

What is the real cost of energy-efficient building design? There is plenty of economic evidence that the frequently heard argument 'energy-efficient buildings are more expensive' is not necessarily correct, given the potentially massive operational-energy savings. Implementing passive design principles is free; they do not add any active or mechanical systems such as solar panels or co-generation plants. Active systems can also have a short time frame for discounted paybacks, as short as five to seven years, depending on the selected systems, technology and scale (Dunster and Simmons, 2008).

When designing a building, hundreds of decisions and choices have to be made. For each design decision or choice, there are possibly hundreds of available options, and each option has an associated (and different) cost. In this regard, Edward Mazria noted, on the economic benefits of designing and constructing energy-efficient buildings:

> During any design process, all the time decisions and choices are made about design – the location of a building on a site, building size, shape, colour and orientation, size and location of fenestrations, shading devices, and natural ventilation, heating, cooling and day-lighting strategies to name just a few. Design decisions are usually associated with no-cost, low-cost or cost saving options. Decisions and choices are also made about structure – steel, concrete, wood or metal frame, heavy timber, concrete block, brick, stone, pre-cast concrete or structural insulated panels – and about systems and materials – radiant or forced air heating, exposed or concealed ductwork, lighting systems and fixture types; steel, aluminium, metal clad or wood frame windows with a paint or powder-coat finish, painted gypsum board or thin-

coat plaster finish on metal or wood studs; vinyl, rubber or wood wall base; tile, carpet, sheet vinyl or polished concrete floors with integral or applied colour; etc., etc., etc. Building design is a complex process of trade-offs to meet a specific project budget. The point is, the only design decisions, choices or trade-off's that save owners or tenants money every month and reduce energy consumption and greenhouse gas emissions, are ones that ensure a building design meets the highest energy efficient standards.

(Mazria, 2010)

There are costs and risks in any programme of action, but they are far less than the long-range risks and costs of comfortable inaction.

Looking ahead: recommendations for a holistic pathway to more energy- and material-efficient, climate-adaptive buildings

This chapter advocates that the best solution for creating energy-efficient buildings is a holistic design approach, underpinned by effective legislation: the combination of passive and active design strategies together, adapted to the local climatic conditions. To address global warming, we need to improve building energy efficiency in the construction sector of both developed and developing countries dramatically, with building codes strongly enforcing energy-efficiency requirements. Energy efficiency, water recycling and building materials (material efficiency) are receiving increased attention and have become major contributors to sustainable development. The future trend is for a strong focus on material efficiency and on ways to reduce material consumption and waste creation in the construction sector.

With dwindling raw materials and the depletion of resources, energy and material resources continue to be consumed and wasted at an accelerated rate. Our current energy generation method and distribution network have not changed much since the industrial revolution, and the way we extract virgin materials to consume them ('cradle to grave') has also not changed much either. The construction industry has a huge responsibility to act, as it is one of the most wasteful sectors. Concrete, for example, is responsible for a significant amount of global CO_2 emissions. And, for a while now, researchers have predicted that several construction materials will be exhausted by the end of the century.

The role of buildings in the mitigation of the UHI effect is increasingly being understood. The UHI effect is found in metropolitan areas that are significantly warmer than their surrounding areas; it is a warmer urban microclimate, in a confined local area. The UHI is the product of human activity: a dome of elevated temperatures over an urban area (such as a street, sidewalk, parking lot or group of buildings), which traps heat caused by waste heat from energy-using processes in a city (for instance, the air-conditioning units in Hong Kong's city centre). UHI is caused primarily by urban development, which alters the original land surfaces and their potential for absorbing heat. Green roofs and reflective materials have been found to reduce the UHI effect (Ichinose et al, 2008).

The issue of effective policy and legislation

To develop a holistic pathway to climate-adaptive buildings requires a clear vision of what constitutes a climate-adaptable building, complete with appropriate overall regional variations. These adaptive measures need to be embedded within assessment tools and progressively introduced as experience of the building regulatory framework grows. Policies and building codes will need to be updated appropriately. Examples of such measures might include:

* designing extended-life buildings that have the ability to accept change of usage ('long life – loose fit'). Among other aspects, this impacts on depth of plan, massing of buildings and floor-to-floor heights;
* using thermal-mass (heat-storing) materials and insulation in the design of buildings more strategically to avoid overheating in summer and the rapid loss of heat in winter;
* operating buildings completely passively (without any energy-consuming, mechanical systems operating) for large portions of the year;
* installing district cooling systems that utilize the waste heat through co- and tri-generation systems;
* reducing the volume of materials needed by buildings, particularly the frequently replaced components (services and interior fit-out). UHI reduction measures would allow lower-energy-consuming building systems (this could include electric vehicles, transport modal switching, extensive urban vegetation to mitigate UHI and associated urban rainwater retention).

However, the effective formulation of such policies and legislation has emerged as a very difficult task for governments worldwide. We only rarely question environmental policies, but some have missed their targets. Formulating the right policies and legislation to transform industry is indeed not easy. Sometimes, well-meant legislation has gone wrong; environmental policies have backfired and created an unintended new set of issues. For instance, biofuels were meant to protect the environment, but have in some regions led to the further destruction of rainforests. Banning the incandescent light bulb was seen as a milestone on the path to carbon-neutral living in Europe, but China has been cranking up its mercury production to satisfy demand for the alternative energy-saving bulbs; the new bulbs are classified as special waste in Europe, and the poisonous substances they contain are leading to special landfill dumping. Extreme water saving in some cities has had the harmful effect that there is a lack of wastewater flowing through the sewage systems, and the system is now not getting flushed out enough. Overdoing it with insulation can lead to airtight buildings and create harmful, unhealthy indoor air environments. The European Union plans to ban the stand-by function on electronic appliances to reduce energy consumption, but this might lead to more e-waste (banning the stand-by function will reduce product lifespans).

Concluding remarks and further areas of research

It is important to recognize that building energy and material flows are part of a complex wider system that, in addition to direct energy consumption, includes implications for transport, water use and urban planning (e.g. settlement pattern), and has major social

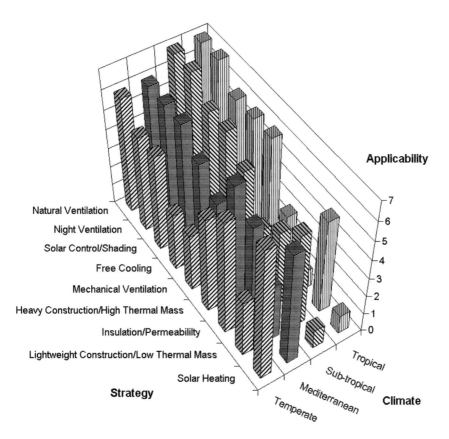

Figure 11.6 Diagram showing the applicability of different energy-efficient building design principles depending on the climatic zone, context and project scale. The building designer needs to identify the most suitable design strategies.

Image courtesy of J. Shiel, from Shiel and Lehmann (2008)

consequences as well as climate-change impacts. This also concerns the supply side, such as energy sources and mix. However, the focus of this chapter is on the energy use of buildings as influenced and defined by the building designer and does not cover the many other aspects of sustainable building. These are necessarily beyond the scope of this chapter.

According to the WBCSD, buildings today account for 40 per cent of the world's energy use (WBCSD, 2009). The resulting carbon emissions are substantially more than those in the transportation sector. New buildings that use more energy than necessary are being built every day, and most of today's inefficient buildings will remain standing in 2030 and beyond. Energy-efficient building design presents a unique challenge and opportunity in the field of architecture and sustainable development. We must start now to transform the building sector decisively and reduce energy demand in all new and existing buildings in order to reduce the planet's carbon footprint and to stabilize CO_2 levels (Harris, 2007; Girardet, 2008).

Understanding site, place, climate and context is a prerequisite for any successful building design. Construction projects typically consume large amounts of energy (embodied and operational), materials and water, and frequently produce a massive amount of waste and have low reuse or recycling rates. On the other hand, energy-efficient buildings offer many advantages compared with conventional buildings, as I have already pointed out. For instance, they last longer, cost less to operate and maintain, and are likely to provide greater occupant satisfaction and productivity. Energy-efficient buildings are not more complicated or expensive than conventional buildings: if every component is carefully considered and is part of an integrated approach, energy-efficient buildings can reach a payback for their slightly higher investment costs within a few years. There is evidence that a short time frame for discounted paybacks of as short as five to eight years is possible for most buildings, owing to significant energy savings during building operation.

Increasing energy consumption by wealthy citizens is a significant contributor to GHG emissions, and more research is needed into strategies to limit their GHG emissions in the most energy-intensive products and services (Shiel and Lehmann, 2008). People in developed countries consume much more energy in their homes and offices than in developing countries, based on larger house sizes (frequently over $40m^2$ per person, e.g. in the US or in Australia), higher expected levels of comfort and more household appliances. However, developing countries' consumption levels have been rising fast, as people become wealthier and their energy-consumption behaviour changes. Allowing improvements in living standards in developing countries while limiting the growth of energy and material consumption will be a significant challenge for the entire globe. It will only be possible if we continue to develop advanced technologies that enable energy-efficient behaviours and create incentives to invest in energy efficiency.

This chapter has argued that truly sustainable design can only be achieved if energy efficiency is combined with material efficiency. The design of material- and energy-efficient buildings is principle-based and leads to minimizing material and energy loads, demand and overall consumption. For instance, the use of measures such as insulation of walls and roofs, sun-protecting glazing, effective sun shading, greening of roofs, LED lighting and maximizing day lighting for workplaces can all be employed to reduce the need for cooling (thus allowing for smaller, less expensive HVAC cooling systems run on mixed-mode). In consequence, the benefits from energy-efficient design of buildings are manifold, economically, environmentally and socially.

Every new building development, ideally, should be energy-efficient, something legislation (and building codes) is increasingly demanding from all new buildings (the European Union has legislated in 2009 that every new building in its member states must be zero-net energy by 2020). The targets of GHG-emission reductions have also been reinforced in the ratified Cancun Agreement at the UN Climate Change Summit in Mexico in December 2010. To achieve energy efficiency and to transform the building sector require a mix of measures tailored to specific geographies, climates and building subsectors. Clearly, strong and bold measures are needed to cut emissions and to stabilize the climate (UNEP, 2007; UN-Habitat, 2010).

Overall, energy efficiency in buildings can be achieved relatively easily and quickly. The biggest culprit for energy efficiency in all building types is the shopping centre. Despite their huge energy consumption through 24-hour mechanical air conditioning and their excessive need for artificial illumination, there are often no immediate incentives to become more energy efficient for their operators, as shopping centres often buy their energy through fixed bulk contracts that are agreed on for long contract periods.

The first step is always to implement energy-efficiency measures in all building design. In the US, Asia and the Middle East, it is still common for fully air-conditioned office buildings to consume electricity in the range of 300–400kWh per m^2 per year. With the available technology, it would easily be possible to reduce this consumption by over 80 per cent, despite the hot, humid climate in these regions.

As I have suggested in this chapter, architects need to refocus more on simple methods to reduce energy consumption and carbon emissions, such as applying a more compact shape and an optimized orientation to buildings, using passive design principles (using technology sparingly), as well as better selecting construction systems and materials. Smart buildings, with sophisticated building energy-management system (BEMS) and smart metering, support grid stability and allow energy generators to consider other options before adding new generation facilities:

- Smart buildings optimize their own energy flow by balancing consumption, storage capacity and decentralized energy generation.
- Smart-building clusters are an interactive part of the grid, providing significant generation capacity and demand-management potential.

In the future, buildings will produce a surplus of electricity that will feed back into the urban power grid. The seamless interaction of clusters of smart buildings with the electrical power grid, through the use of information technology, will enable such buildings to optimize their own energy flow by balancing consumption, storage capacity and decentralized energy generation. Buildings and districts interconnected via a smart grid will enjoy large energy-savings potential. The amount of energy that can be saved through the intelligent networking of power utilities and consumers, enabled through smart metering, varies from case to case. However, experts generally agree that savings of 25 per cent are realistic, depending on the building type. Shopping malls, for instance, open ten to twelve hours a day, but air-conditioned twenty-four hours, seven days a week, have a large savings potential of over 50 per cent. Office buildings, usually unused over the weekend, easily have an energy-savings potential of between 20 and 30 per cent (Siemens, 2010).

Further research is necessary, especially in the area of in-depth evaluation of the performance of highly efficient building technologies and materials. Research is also required in the following areas: the interaction between embodied energy/carbon and operational energy/carbon, including the role of thermal mass; and behaviour change, e.g. changing energy awareness in society and the wasteful habits of building users. As John Dryden noted, 'We first make our habits, and then our habits make us.'

While there were many wonderful innovations that transformed architecture and the building sector during the twentieth century, there were also some less fortunate developmental paths. This has been widely discussed in the literature as a critique of functionalism and modernity. Some of the classic textbooks range from Rachel Carson's *Silent Spring* (1962), to Reyner Banham's *The Architecture of the Well-tempered Environment* (1969), to Ian McHarg's *Design With Nature* (1969) and to the pivotal publications by authors reconnecting architectural design with climatic conditions (such as Koenigsberger et al, 1974; Drew and Fry, 1976; Breheny, 1992; Yeang, 2006).

The field of sustainable-design theories for energy efficiency and the critique of the lack of climate-responsive architecture have constantly expanded.

Importantly, the message is: less energy and material consumption does not mean less user comfort. The technologies to reduce the energy demand of the average building by 50 per cent, just by applying good design principles, are available. It is a matter of changing the approaches of engineers, architects, planners and designers (von Weizaecker, 2009).

To make material and energy efficiency more effective globally, it will now be necessary to up-scale: moving from zero-energy buildings to zero-energy precincts and neighbourhoods.

While we explore how renewable-energy sources can provide sufficient power for an ever-increasing world population to maintain today's lifestyles, we also have to ask how our lifestyles should adapt to the needs of a future low-carbon society, e.g. through behavioural change in the use of energy, water, materials and the automobile. This question has frequently been raised by Glenn Murcutt, an Australian architect experienced in designing houses for extreme climatic conditions, who says: 'Life is not about maximising everything; it's about giving something meaningful back'. He calls it: 'To achieve more with less and to touch the earth lightly' (Murcutt, 2008, quoted in Gusheh and Lassan, 2008, p12).

Acknowledgements

This chapter draws on the work that the author has undertaken as UNESCO Chair in Sustainable Urban Development for Asia and the Pacific, and on the research carried out at the Zero Waste SA Research Centre for Sustainable Design and Behaviour (sd+b). He would like to thank the colleagues who provided image materials and the reviewers for their helpful comments on earlier drafts of this chapter.

References

Aynsley, R. (2006) *Guidelines for Sustainable Housing in the Humid Tropics: Parts 1, 2 and 3*, James Cook University, Townsville, Australia, www.new.townsville.qld.gov.au/resources/3400.pdf, accessed 20 October 2010

Banham, R. (1969) *The Architecture of the Well-tempered Environment*, University of Chicago Press/Architectural Press, Chicago, IL

Beatley, T. and Manning, K. (1997) *The Ecology of Place: Planning for Environment, Economy, and Community*, Island Press, Washington, DC

Breheny, M. J. (1992) *Sustainable Development and Urban Form*, Pion, London

Brookes, L. (1993) 'The greenhouse effect: the fallacies in the energy efficiency solution', *Energy Policy*, vol 18, no 2, pp199–201

Brooks, R. G. (1988) *Site Planning: Environment, Process and Development*, Prentice Hall, New Jersey, NY

Brugmann, J. (2009) *Welcome to the Urban Revolution: How Cities are Changing the World*, ICLEI, Bloomsbury Press, London

Brundtland, G. H./UN World Commission on Environment and Development (1987) *The Brundtland Report: Our Common Future*, Oxford University Press, Oxford/New York

Carson, R. (1962) *Silent Spring*, Houghton Mifflin Publisher, Boston, MA

Clarke, J. (2001) *Energy Simulation in Building Design* (2nd edn), Butterworth-Heinemann /Elsevier, Oxford

Commonwealth Scientific and Industrial Research Organisation (CSIRO) and Ambrose, M. (2008) 'Energy efficient housing and subdivision design', in P.W. Newton (ed) *Transitions: Pathways Towards Sustainable Development in Australia*, CSIRO Publishing, Melbourne, Australia

Daniels, K. (1995) *Technologie des oekologischen Bauens*, Birkhaeuser, Basel/Berlin, Germany

Daniels, K. (2000) *Low-Tech, Light-Tech, High-Tech: Building in the Information Age*, Birkhaeuser, Basel/Berlin, Germany

Daniels, K. and Hindrichs, D. (2007) *Plus Minus 20/40 Latitude: Sustainable Building Design in Tropical and Subtropical Regions*, Axel Menges Publishing, Stuttgart, Germany

Drew, J. and Fry, M. (1964) *Tropical Architecture in the Dry and Humid Zones*, Reinhold, New York

Droege, P. (2008) 'Urban energy transition: an introduction', in P. Droege (ed) *Urban Energy Transition: From Fossil Fuels to Renewable Power*, Elsevier, Amsterdam, the Netherlands

Dunster, B. and Simmons, C. (2008) *The ZEDbook: Solutions for a Shrinking World*, Taylor & Francis, Oxford

Eichholtz, P., Kok, N. and Quigly, J. (2009) *Doing Well by Doing Good? Green Office Buildings*, University of California Energy Institute, Los Angeles, CA

Friedman, T. L. (2009) *Hot, Flat, and Crowded: Why We Need a Green Revolution – And How it Can Renew America*, Picador, New York

Gauzin-Mueller, D. (2002) *Sustainable Architecture and Urbanism: Concepts, Technologies, Examples*, Birkhaeuser, Basel/Berlin, Germany

Girardet, H. (2008) *Cities, People, Planet: Urban Development and Climate Change* (2nd edn), John Wiley & Sons, London

Green Building Council of Australia (GBCA) (2008) *Valuing Green*, GBCA, Sydney, Australia, www.gbca.com.au, accessed 02 March 2010

Grimshaw, A. W. (ed) (2009) *Blue, Issue 1: Water, Energy and Waste*, Grimshaw Architects, London

Gusheh, H. and Lassan, S. (2008) *Glenn Murcutt: Thinking Drawing, Working Drawing*, TOTO, Japan

Hall, P. and Pfeiffer, U. (2000) *Urban Future 21: A Global Agenda for 21st Century Cities*, BM Verkehr, Bau, Wohnungswesen, Berlin, Germany; Taylor & Francis/Spon, London

Harris, G. (2007) *Seeking Sustainability in an Age of Complexity*, Cambridge University Press, Cambridge

Hausladen, G., de Saldanha, M., Liedl, P. and SAGEr, C. (2005) *ClimaDesign: Lösungen für Gebäude*, Callwey Publisher, Stuttgart/ Birkhaeuser, Basel/Berlin, Germany

Head, P. (2008) 'Entering the ecological age: the engineer's role', The Brunel Lecture 2008, London, www.arup.com/Publications/Entering_the_Ecological_Age.aspx, accessed 02 March 2010

Hegger, M., Auch-Schwelk, V., Fuchs, M. and Rosenkranz, T. (2006) *Construction Materials Manual*, Birkhäuser Verlag, Basel/Berlin (Edition Detail, English version), Germany

Hegger, M., Fuchs, M., Stark, T. and Zeumer, M. (2007) *Energy Manual – Energie Atlas. Sustainable Architecture*, Birkhäuser Verlag, Basel/Berlin (Edition Detail, English version), Germany

Hotten, R. (2004) *Sustainable Architecture: Twelve Things You Can Do To Build Effective Low Cost Houses and Cities*, Seadog Press, Monterey, CA

Hui, S. C.M. and BEER (2002) 'Sustainable architecture and building design', www.arch. hku.hk/research/BEER/sustain.htm, accessed 02 March 2010

Hyde, R. (2000) *Climate-Responsive Design: A Study of Buildings in Moderate and Hot Humid Climates*, E. & F.N. Spon, London

Ichinose, T., Matsumoto, F. and Kataoka, K. (2008) 'Counteracting urban heat islands in Japan', in P. Droege (ed) *Urban Energy Transition*, Elsevier, Amsterdam, the Netherlands

Intergovernmental Panel on Climate Change (IPCC) (2007) 'Technical summary', in B. Metz, O. R. Davidson, P. R. Bosch, R. Dave and L. A. Meyer (eds) *Climate Change 2007: Mitigation*, Contribution of Working Group III to the Fourth Assessment Report of the IPCC, Cambridge University Press, Cambridge

Intergovernmental Panel on Climate Change (IPCC) (2008) *Climate Change: Synthesis Report – Summary for Policymakers*, IPCC, Geneva, www.ipcc.ch, accessed 02 March 2010

Kats, G., Alevantis, L., Berman, A., Mills, E. and Perlman, J. (2003) *The Cost and Financial Benefits of Green Buildings*, Report by Capital E to California's Sustainable Building Task Force, Los Angeles/Sacramento, CA, October 2003, www.azdeq.gov/ceh/download/natreview.pdf, accessed 02 March 2010

Kaufmann, H. (2009) *Wood Works. Oeko-rationale Baukunst – Architecture Durable*, Springer-Verlag, Berlin

Kearns, A., Barnett, G. and Nolan, A. (2006) *An Ecological Design Strategy for the Planning and Development of Healthy Urban Habitat*, BDP Environmental Design Guide, Australian Institute of Architects, Sydney, Australia

Keeler, M. and Burke, B. (2009) *Fundamentals of Integrated Design for Sustainable Buildings*, John Wiley & Sons, Oxford

Koenigsberger, O. H., Ingersoll, T. G., Mayhew, A. and Szokolay, S. V. (1974) *Manual of Tropical Housing and Building: Part I. Climatic Design*, Longman, London

Kohlenbach, P. (2010) 'Solar cooling: chilling out in the sun', paper presented at 3rd International Conference on Solar Air-Conditioning, Palermo, Italy, 30 September–3 October, www.solarthermalworld.org, accessed 01 November 2010

Lehmann, S. (2006) 'Towards a sustainable city centre: integrating ecologically sustainable development (ESD) principles into urban renewal', *Journal of Green Building*, vol 1, no 3, pp85–104

Lehmann, S. (2008) 'Cities in transition: new models for urban growth and neighbourhoods', in P. Droege (ed) *Urban Energy Transition: From Fossil Fuels to Renewable Power*, Elsevier, Oxford

Lehmann, S. (2009) 'Interdisciplinary models for collaboration between artists and architects: empowering community, inspiring urban renewal', *UNESCO Observatory*, vol 1, no 4, www.abp.unimelb.edu.au/unesco/ejournal/pdf/lehmann.pdf

Lehmann, S. (2010a) *The Principles of Green Urbanism: Transforming the City for Sustainability*, Earthscan, London

Lehmann, S. (2010b) 'Consumption, zero waste and behaviour change', unpublished report, Research Centre for Sustainable Design and Behaviour (sd+b), University of South Australia, Adelaide, Australia

Lenzen, M., Wood, R. and Foran, B. (2008) 'Direct versus embodied energy: the need for urban lifestyle transitions', in P. Droege (ed) *Urban Energy Transition: From Fossil Fuels to Renewable Power*, Elsevier Publisher, Amsterdam, the Netherlands

Lieb, R. D. (2001) *Double-Skin Facades*, Birkhäuser, Boston, MA

McDonough, W. and Braungart, M. (2002) *Cradle to Cradle: Remaking the Way we Make Things*, North Point Press, New York

McHarg, I. (1969) *Design with Nature*, Natural History Press/Falcon Press, Philadelphia, PA

MacKay, D. (2008) *Sustainable Energy – Without the Hot Air*, UIT, Cambridge, www.withouthotair.com, accessed 10 December 2010

McKinsey & Company Global Institute (2007) *Pathways to a Low-Carbon Economy*, McKinsey & Company, Washington, DC, www.lowcarboneconomy.com, accessed 10 December 2010

Markvart, T. (ed) (2000) *Solar Electricity* (2nd edn), John Wiley & Sons, Oxford

Mazria, E. (2010) 'What additional costs?', Architecture 2030 blog, 10 December 2010, www.architecture2030.org, accessed 10 December 2010

Newman, P. and Kenworthy, J. (1989) *Cities and Automobile Dependence: An International Sourcebook*, Gower Press, Aldershot, Australia

Organisation for Economic Co-operation and Development (OECD) (2003) *Environmentally Sustainable Buildings: Challenges and Policies*, OECD, Paris: e-book, available online at: www.oecd.org, accessed 20 October 2010

Owens, S. (1986) *Energy, Planning and Urban Form*, Pion Press, London

Scheer, H. (2002 (original in German, 1999)) *The Solar Economy: Renewable Energy for a Sustainable Global Future*, Earthscan Publications, London

Scott, A. (2006) 'Design strategies for green practice', *Journal of Green Building*, vol 1, no 4, pp11–27

Shiel, J. and Lehmann, S. (2008) 'Strategies for practical greenhouse gas reductions in the existing building stock', in N. Gu, L. F. Gul, M. J. Oswald and A. Williams (eds) *The Proceedings of ANZAScA 2008*, Print National, Newcastle, Australia

Siemens (2010) *Urban Centres and Their Challenges*, part of the 'Megacities Study', www.siemens.com/sustainability/en/stakeholders/megacities.htm, accessed 20 October 2010

Stern, N. (2007) *The Stern Review: The Economics of Climate Change*, Cambridge University Press, Cambridge, www.sternreview.org.uk, accessed 20 October 2010

Sullivan, M. J. (2009) 'Behavioral assumptions underlying energy efficiency programs for businesses', California Institute for Energy and Environment (CIEE), http://uc-ciee.org/downloads/ba_ee_prog_bus_wpsumm.pdf, accessed 20 October 2010

Szokolay, S. V. (2004) *Introduction to Architectural Science, the Basis of Sustainable Design*, Architectural Press/Elsevier Science, Oxford

Toepfer, K. (2007) 'Architecture–urban planning–environment', in T. Herzog (ed) *The European Charter for Solar Energy in Architecture and Urban Planning*, Prestel, Munich, Germany

Treberspurg, M. and Linz, S. (eds) (2008) *SolarCity Linz-Pichling. Nachhaltige Stadtentwicklung / Sustainable Urban Development*, Springer-Verlag, Berlin, Germany

Tzonis, A. (2006) 'Rethinking design methodology for sustainable social quality', in J.-H. Ban and B.-L. Ong (eds) *Tropical Sustainable Architecture*, Princeton Architectural Press, New York

United Nations Environmental Programme (UNEP) (2007) *Assessment of Policy Instruments for Reducing Greenhouse Gas Emissions from Buildings*, UNEP Sustainable Building and Construction Initiative, Nairobi, Kenya, www.unep.org, accessed 01 November 2010

UN–Habitat (2010) *Fifth World Urban Forum: State of the World's Cities Report 2010/11*, UN, Nairobi, Kenya

Urban Task Force (1999) *Towards an Urban Renaissance*, E&FN Spon Press, London

Vale, R. and Vale, B. (1991) *Green Architecture: Design for an Energy-Conscious Future*, Thames & Hudson, London

Vale, R. and Vale, B. (2000) *The Autonomous House*, Thames & Hudson, London

von Weizaecker, E. U. (2009) 'Interview: why increased efficiency will lead to a more advanced civilization', *Pictures of the Future*, Spring, available at www.siemens.com/innovation/apps/pof_microsite/_pof-spring-2009/_html_en/interview-ernst-ulrich-von-weizsaecker.html, accessed 11 April 2011

Wackernagel, M. and Rees, W. (1996) *Our Ecological Footprint*, New Society Press, Philadelphia, PA

World Business Council for Sustainable Development (WBCSD) (2009) *Energy Efficiency in Buildings (EEB) Report: Transforming the Market*, WBCSD, Washington/Geneva, www.wbcsd.org; www.wbcsd.org/web/eeb.htm, accessed 02 March 2010

World Energy Council (WEC) (2004) *Energy Efficiency: A Worldwide Review*, WEC, London
Yeang, K. (2006) 'Green design in the hot humid tropical zone', in J.-H. Bay and B.-L. Ong (eds) *Tropical Sustainable Architecture: Social and Environmental Dimensions*, Elsevier, Burlington, MA

Chapter 12

Breathing life into the corpse

Upcycling through adaptive reuse

Stephen Ward

Summary

Among the buildings that make up our built environment, there are a significant number that are underutilized or used inefficiently – or at worst have become unusable and fallen into disuse. These are wasted resources, sometimes simply abandoned, but often removed and replaced with new development. In the process, further resources are consumed, and more waste is generated. The alternative is to breathe life into these structures by providing them with a new use. This 'adaptive reuse' not only extends a building's life, but also provides the potential to improve its environmental performance and usefulness – thereby increasing its value.

Three projects are identified in this chapter that were developed from existing built sites, including the redevelopment of an underground water reservoir into an urban park, the conversion of a diesel-engine workshop into a school of architecture, and the reconfiguring of a powerhouse into artists' studios and a public gallery. The projects serve to illustrate the link between adaptive reuse and sustainability, and to demonstrate that it is a process that not only avoids creating new waste, but also offers significant additional benefits to society and the environment.

Introduction: the life of buildings

Unlike the human body, when a building reaches the end of its useful life, there is the possibility that it can be rejuvenated to suit a new purpose. At a practical level, the option of modification – or adaptive reuse – offers many environmental benefits. Compared with new development, adaptive reuse provides an opportunity to reduce the overall amount of energy and materials consumed, to cut the amount of waste generated in construction, and also to decrease the operational energy used in an existing building by improving its environmental performance. Successful adaptive reuse means more than just the recycling of a building – by improving its value, use and performance it is effectively being 'upcycled'.

One of the issues to be considered in the sustainability of our built environments is life expectancy. Some buildings will last for hundreds of years with little refurbishment, whereas others, and especially those designed for obsolescence, might experience various major refurbishments or be demolished within a human lifetime. A building's longevity is dependent on many factors, including the components from which it is assembled, its 'build quality', flexibility to accommodate changes in use, its location and the maintenance undertaken. Building replacement is also affected by external factors: for example, rapid development in technologies may make a particular type of building obsolete, or economic, social and political factors may result in macro change to a larger built environment. These factors can be difficult to predict, and therefore, as with people, the life expectancy of a specific building is difficult to determine at its conception.

As with other consumables, the useful life of a building is not only dependent on its design and physical attributes; it is also affected by the 'value' we assign it, and the resultant care we take to retain it. The buildings, streetscapes and cities that we keep are the ones that are significant to us, either individually or collectively. The decision to change or replace where we live or work will be based on numerous factors, including the emotional or other forms of investment in the place. If we value our environment, it is more likely to be well maintained and 'improved'. If we have a close association with a place, we are less likely to destroy it.

This chapter demonstrates how previously underused and utilitarian building stock can become prized by the community and reinvigorated through the introduction of a new use. In the process, its cultural significance is unveiled, its life is extended, and it helps to encourage society to value and revive a broader range of 'end-of-life' objects that might otherwise be considered waste.

Measuring the impact of construction

The need to consider alternatives to new building projects responds to widespread recognition that the construction industry has a significant impact on economies and the environment. Engineer Robin Spence and architect Helen Mulligan note that gross construction output constitutes 8–12 per cent of GDP in many national economies, and that many of the materials whose production causes loss or deterioration of land and water resources end up in construction (Spence and Mulligan, 1995, p282).

Of all resources used, international studies indicate the construction industry depletes 40 per cent of global raw stone, gravel and sand, and 25 per cent of timber, and consumes 40 per cent of total energy and 16 per cent of water annually (Dixit et al, 2010, p1238). It also generates a large amount of waste, with construction and demolition waste comprising about 40 per cent of waste to landfill globally (Walker-Morison et al, 2007, p1). Construction also impacts on greenhouse-gas emissions, with an estimated 8–20 per cent of emissions in different countries due to the production of construction and building materials, and a further 2.5 per cent globally due to the chemical reactions taking place in cement and lime production (Spence and Mulligan, 1995, p285).

There are a range of environmental indicators that can be used to measure the impacts of material use in construction, but, unfortunately, there is no general agreement on an appropriate range of these indicators, nor are specific benchmarks or standards in environmental assessment applied to building materials. In addition, some indicators are quantifiable, whereas the impact on other indicators is more difficult to assess.

One quantifiable measure is energy. The use of energy in our buildings is directly related to resource depletion and the generation of pollution and waste. It is common practice to measure the energy consumed by buildings as the amount 'embodied' in their materials and construction, and the 'operational' energy consumed in their use. There is widespread debate about the relative importance and impact of these two types of energy.

Until recently, studies have concentrated on operational energy, owing to the high proportion attributed to it in the total life-cycle energy of buildings. Architectural engineer Doug Harris, for example, indicates that the embodied energy of a building may constitute only 15 per cent of its lifetime energy consumption, but notes that 'wide variations remain in the published figures, partly due to local differences in energy efficiency and transport requirements' (Harris, 1999, p754). Operational energy is also considered easier to measure than embodied energy – it can be relatively accurately modelled in the design process or measured during occupation of the building.

Manish Kumar Dixit and his colleagues have identified research from different countries that reveals significant variation in embodied-energy figures, with commercial buildings showing greater variability ($3.4–19.0GJ/m^2$) than residential units ($3.6–8.76GJ/m^2$). Their analysis of the available literature confirms that quantifying embodied energy is difficult, and that a range of methodologies exists. These calculations vary for a number of reasons, including: different system boundaries; the various methods of analysis; location of the study; the age, source and completeness of data; and the variability of technologies used in the manufacture of the material (Dixit et al, 2010, pp1241–3).

Recent analysis of embodied energy does indicate that previous studies may have underestimated its significance. For example, a recent analysis by Robert Crawford et al (2010) of construction assemblies calculated embodied energies that were consistently higher than an earlier analysis by Lawson in 1996. In some cases, these differences were remarkable, at up to twelve times the original calculation (Crawford et al, 2010, p295). These new data indicate that embodied energy is emerging as a crucial factor in the measurement of the sustainability of building projects.

Embodied energy has become an important consideration for another reason. Within a framework of legislative requirements and incentives designed to reduce energy use, it is possible to reduce the operational energy of buildings through more efficient equipment and appliances, improved environmental modelling and advances in material technologies. These measures can make a significant impact on the efficiency of the building when it is first constructed, but can also continue to impact through its life, as services are replaced, and its performance is improved through modification. Embodied energy, on the other hand, only increases over time, as elements are maintained or replaced.

Irrespective of the relative impact of embodied or operational energy, it is the 'net energy' of the building that provides an overall indication of its environmental impact. The net energy of the building is determined by its combined embodied- and operational-energy inputs – but also by its longevity. Net-energy measurement is used in the assessment of life-cycle zero-energy buildings (LC-ZEB); this type of building is characterized by equalizing energy inputs (operational and embodied) and outputs (through energy generation) over its life (Hernandez and Kenny, 2010, p816).

This relationship between the life of the building and the resources and energy used and generated is an important consideration: the longer a building lasts, the less its relative environmental impact. This observation is made at a time when modern construction is often accused of being short lived. For example, in Australia, where cities are comparatively young, commercial and industrial buildings are considered to have a thirty-eight to fifty-eight-year life, with the mean asset life of dwellings between fifty-eight and eighty-eight years (Walker-Morison et al, 2007, p1). Certain types of building, such as speculative office development, can often be refitted within much shorter periods. In most studies, fifty years is considered a typical service life of buildings before they undergo major renovations (Hernandez and Kenny, 2010, p818).

By extending the building's life, together with a deliberate reduction in resource and energy inputs in construction and operation, the opportunity to offset these inputs becomes increasingly possible. This apparently simple concept represents a significant move towards design for zero waste in our built environment.

Defining adaptive reuse

> Tate Modern has nothing to do with the former power station; it is an entirely new museum. We were not interested in the brickwork as a means of tracing history, but much more in finding out to what extent it could enrich a new building.
>
> (Architects of the Tate Modern, Herzog and
> De Meuron; Ursprung, 2002, p149)

Adapting buildings to suit new purposes has taken place since building began, but, as the finite nature of resources becomes ever more apparent, it has become a critical issue. The conservation of our built environment is often placed in the context of retaining, for present and future generations, places that are valued for their ability to inform, to provide experiences and to give inspiration and identity (Stapleton, 2000, p1; Department of the Environment and Heritage (DEH), 2004, p3). This reference to 'present and future generations' is also often used to describe the context of sustainability. In a society that recognizes the principles of 'reduce, reuse and recycle', conservation and adaptive reuse are another way to describe a familiar process that changes a disused or ineffective item into one that can be used for a different purpose. This description can be used at different scales and in different contexts – it can apply equally well to a household container, a building or to larger urban environments and infrastructure.

One general description of building adaption is the work undertaken over and above maintenance to change its capacity, function or performance, or, in other words, any intervention to adjust, reuse or upgrade a building to suit new conditions or requirements (Douglas, 2006, p1). Irrespective of the precise meaning of the term 'adaptive reuse', it indicates that adaptation is a means of extending the useful life of buildings through a combination of improvement and conversion (Bullen, 2007, p22). However, unlike recycling, which implies substantial reprocessing, adaptive reuse can also require little or no physical change to the object and is therefore, by implication, less energy- and material-intensive.

Adaptive reuse needs to be considered amid concern that we are retaining buildings but not making them 'usable' – that we are, in fact, allowing them to decay to a state of ruination. In the United Kingdom, for example, critics of current practices that preserve unused and historic properties describe this as 'the cult of the ruin', where these properties are 'rendered soulless, their past and their purpose evoked only in artists' impressions'. Current conservation practices are contrasted against the more progressive and confident attitudes of the Victorians, who 'studied the past not as relic-worshippers and object fetishists but to stimulate the present' (Jenkins, 2011). This criticism comes at a time when progressively more buildings across the globe are identified as being at risk of damage and decay. This includes not just buildings traditionally recognized as historically significant, such as churches, historic homes and monuments, but particularly industrial buildings – such as the abandoned textile mills of Yorkshire. Although 60 per cent of these mills are estimated to be suitable for commercial or residential reuse, numerous properties are falling into disrepair (English Heritage, 2011).

This neglect of existing buildings comes despite the fact that building adaptation offers the advantage that it can be more economical to convert existing buildings to new uses than to demolish and rebuild. However, whether a building is adapted depends on more than just economic feasibility: the viability of undertaking an adaptive-reuse project is determined by many factors, which individually or combined may preclude adaptation, including:

- the physical and spatial requirements of the new use, including desired internal layout and access to daylight;
- the capacity of the existing structure to accommodate different building loads;
- the physical condition of the building, including its envelope and services;
- the location, including its ability to be accessed; and
- whether the new use is compatible with its site and wider context, or its 'contextual fit'.

The issue of 'contextual fit', as defined by Louise Ellison and Sarah Sayce (2007) in their study of sustainability criteria for commercial buildings, can provide an argument for the retention of existing building stock, or alternatively for its removal. It refers to the appropriateness of both the building and its use within its location and whether it has a positive or negative effect. These effects can range from an increase in the amenity, microclimate or property values of the area, to the deterrence of social and business activity with a resultant depression in land values. Often, these effects can be subtle and difficult to quantify, but they can have a significant and long-term social, environmental and economic impact (Ellison and Sayce, 2007, p301). Adaptive reuse provides an opportunity to introduce a new use – and to potentially replace a less compatible use – into an existing context and therefore act as a catalyst for urban regeneration.

Working with existing buildings imposes limitations that do not necessarily apply to new-build projects. For example, the existing fabric and structure may make it difficult to construct basement carparks, or to meet current building regulations. Adaptive reuse may limit urban densification, whereas new build can intensify the land use more effectively, especially when the cost of land is at a premium. It can be difficult to determine the costs and benefits of adaptive reuse when factored in over the unknown life of the building, particularly when buildings may require extensive and costly refurbishment. It may also be difficult to match the environmental performance of a new building, even with major changes, and ongoing maintenance costs may be unable to meet current sustainability standards.

These practical, environmental and economic limitations need to be considered at the same time as communities and government recognize the contribution that our existing built fabric makes to society. The retention of places with 'cultural significance' has become an important consideration, and this significance impacts, not only on what is retained, but also on how it is retained and what new, 'compatible' uses can be accommodated. Where a building is considered significant, contemporary conservation policies describe compatible uses as those involving changes that require minimal impact to the significant fabric or ones where the changes can be substantially reversible (Australia ICOMOS, 1988). Change to a place is not narrowly defined as changes to its physical material or 'fabric'; it is generally recognized that uses, associations and meanings can also change, and that this can also affect significance (Stapleton, 2000, p3).

Thus, if adaptive reuse is being considered for a building of cultural significance, then historic integrity has the potential to impact on the proposed programme. According to this notion, not only does the new use need to 'fit' the building, but the building also needs to 'fit' the proposed use. If this relationship is incompatible, the project is likely to be compromised by conflicting demands, affecting the viability, use and long-term integrity of the building. At worst, it may result in reuse projects being abandoned, leading to further deterioration of our built assets and acceptance of the aforementioned 'cult of the ruin'.

Adaptive reuse and industrial buildings

Industrial buildings are used in this chapter to illustrate the substantial results that can be achieved through adaptive reuse. The increasing recognition of the value attached to industrial buildings is evidenced by prominent reuse projects such as the Fiat Lingotto Factory in Turin (1989), now a modern complex of concert halls, theatre, shopping arcades and hotel; the Tate Modern in the Bankside Powerstation on the Thames in London (2000); and the Elbe Philharmonic Hall in Hamburg, being constructed above the distinctive Kaispeicher factory building on the Elbe River (due for completion in 2012). While these projects demonstrate the dramatic changes possible, it is also recognized that many industrial buildings are capable of adaptive reuse without major structural refurbishment.

Disused industrial buildings are often associated with decline, attributed 'low value' and considered to be wasted resources. The functions contained within these buildings can be relatively short lived, or subject to change or relocation, resulting from advances in technologies, changing consumer behaviour, the availability of labour and economic impacts. The distinctive issues surrounding these buildings have earned them their own terminology: sometimes they are referred to as 'vips' (vacant industrial premises) or 'brown buildings', which is an adaptation of the use of the term 'brownfield site' used to describe neglected and often contaminated industrial land.

The extent of refurbishment or new work on industrial buildings is occasionally restricted by formal heritage listing, as some carry with them recognized cultural significance or contribute significance to their neighbourhood. Some industrial buildings are associated with historic people and events, or sometimes their association with new industrial methods and building typologies adds to their significance. The social significance of these buildings may also be considerable: in many cases, the surrounding community was established as a result of the industry, and, in some instances, the building or group of buildings accommodated the livelihood of a generation. For many industrial buildings, the functions carried out inside embodied most of their significance.

Researchers in urban regeneration, such as Rick Ball (2002) in the UK, provide interesting information on the reuse potential of vacant industrial buildings over the longer term, by considering both their possible use for other industrial purposes, but also alternative uses. Ball notes that many older buildings occupy prime and central locations compared with later development. Owing to their original function, their occupation of sites such as waterfronts is seen as both desirable and valuable. These are common factors that provided the impetus for the Tate Modern, Lingotto and Elbe Philharmonic Hall developments. Ball's series of studies points to a growing recognition of the potential of industrial buildings – to offer opportunities for reuse (with no or minor change) or for redevelopment for other uses. This is owing, in part, to the flexibility of this building type to accommodate a range of functions, often being characterized by large spans and voluminous spaces. It is also, as Ball explains, largely

> an outcome of the sustainability debate, as ideas of recycling and reuse begin to filter through to all extremities of the built environment . . . The raised political awareness of sustainability and the 'brownfield' debate has clearly spread to the property arena.
>
> (Ball, 2002, p94)

Three adaptive reuse projects

Three projects have been selected to illustrate the opportunities and advantages offered by the adaptive reuse of industrial properties. Although these award-winning projects are sited in Australia (Australian Institute of Architects, 2007, 2008, 2010), the application of the principles and practices illustrates the range of uses and environmental benefits that can be adopted, irrespective of location. Each project represents a different scale, context and background, demonstrating that adaptive reuse can effectively respond to a range of parameters and result in specific and varied outcomes.

The first of these projects, the Paddington Reservoir Gardens, is an urban park located in Sydney. This project transforms abandoned city infrastructure into a public space in a strategy similar to New York's High Line Park. Whereas the High Line is a project built upon the raised freight train tracks constructed in the 1930s, the more modest project in Paddington is located on the site of a subterranean water reservoir. Constructed in two stages in 1866 and 1878, the site served as a reservoir until 1899 when it was decommissioned and then turned into a workshop and garage. A grassed park was added above the garage in the 1930s and used until 1990, when major structural collapse of the roof forced its closure. Architects Tonkin Zulaikha Greer collaborated with Landscape Architects JMD Design and the Sydney City Council to design a valuable community asset from the abandoned site. Part of the site has been transformed into a sunken garden and pond, accessed via a raised boardwalk. In another section, the dramatic brick-vaulted reservoir has been adapted into a multipurpose community space. Previously inaccessible and dangerous, this site has undergone careful stabilization, reconstruction and new construction, to enable it to be better used and valued as a unique urban ruin.

The second case study is the adaptive reuse of a former diesel-engine workshop, originally built in 1951, into a new School of Architecture for the University of Tasmania in Launceston. The existing building, which also served as the exhibition building for the annual Launceston Show, underwent further adaption by Six Degrees Architects and Sustainable Built Environments in close association with the school. The result is an articulation of the previous workshop nature of the building alongside the current

Figure 12.1
Paddington Reservoir (Sydney, Australia) before work to transform it into a public park.

Photographer: Nathanial Hughes

Figure 12.2 Paddington Reservoir Gardens (Sydney, Australia): eastern chamber.

Photographer: Brett Boardman

Figure 12.3 Paddington Reservoir Gardens (Sydney, Australia) after adaptive reuse.

Photographer: Eric Sierens

teaching programme: 'its permanent state of incompletion and adaptation reflects its position as a school of architecture and design – not a gallery for "finished" works, but a workshop for investigation and interrogation of the meanings and possibilities of architecture' (Owen, 2007, p80). Remnants of old equipment such as the gantry cranes remain, and the large internal volume of the building is retained to communicate the previous use of the building and precinct. New insertions are long span and light-weight, designed for removal or change later. These additions are differentiated from retained elements through the use of contemporary detail and materiality. The insertion of a new use into this building came with specific environmental considerations for its new expanded occupation. Thermal comfort and acoustic separation issues needed to be addressed, as well as a specific ecologically sustainable development agenda. The result is a building that is inventive and experimental, reflecting the activities undertaken within.

The final project is the Canberra Glassworks, converted from the Kingston Powerhouse, the city's oldest public building, but one that had been decommissioned over sixty years before. Like the Bankside Powerstation in London, the Kingston Powerhouse offered large, dramatic, cathedral-like spaces ready to accommodate a new use. In this case, the inserted uses include a gallery, artists' studios, a cafe and support spaces. Ostensibly unchanged on the outside, except for a glowing, glazed and illuminated marker, the interior has similarly been retained in its existing state, except for necessary intrusions to accommodate new use. A raised walkway and viewing platform both separate the public from the artists as well as provide a place for observation of

Figure 12.4 School of Architecture, University of Tasmania, exterior.

Photographer: Roger Fay

Figure 12.5
School of Architecture, University of
Tasmania, after adaptive reuse.

Photographer: Patrick Rodriguez

Figure 12.6
School of Architecture, University of Tasmania, after adaptive reuse.

Photographer: Patrick Rodriguez

Figure 12.7
Canberra Glassworks (ACT, Australia) boiler room before construction.

Photographer: Jocelyn Jackson

Figure 12.8 Canberra Glassworks (ACT, Australia) boiler room after adaptive reuse.

Photographer: Tyrone Branigan

the activities within. Where possible, existing materials and infrastructure have been reused for a new purpose, with the intention that no building fabric be removed unless necessary. This is a project that manages to make prominent its new and specialized use and, at the same time, to allow an equal appreciation and interpretation of its former life.

The link between adaptive reuse and sustainability

Recognition of the impact of construction activities on the environment is occurring at the same time as property investors and occupiers become increasingly aware of the vulnerability of property to the sustainability agenda. The property investment sector recognizes that policymakers and environmental campaigners have the potential to make a major impact, with unpredictable results (Ellison and Sayce, 2007, p288). This awareness is resulting in both legislated and voluntary change, including higher performance criteria in building codes and the development and rapid uptake of assessment tools such as LEED, BREEAM and GreenStar. The performance of buildings under the triple bottom line is of particular interest to organizations with a high public profile – and it can be argued that these market leaders have a significant influence over other occupiers. As a result, the long-term impact for property could be, among other things, an increased demand for more sustainable buildings (Ellison and Sayce, 2007, p299). By demonstrating the environmental and social sustainability of their projects, developers are able more readily to attract investment and tenants, and in so doing impact positively on the economic feasibility and long-term viability of the development. This is evidenced by the success of commercial developers of adaptive-reuse projects who market themselves as 'more than just a property company, we're a regeneration company' (Urban Splash, 2011).

Figure 12.9 Canberra Glassworks (ACT, Australia) exterior.

Photographer: Lannon Harley

Given this context, can adaptive reuse provide an opportunity for more sustainable practices in construction? If current conservation practices were adopted for all work, then the answer is invariably yes: guidelines for the conservation of our built environment are built on the premise that changes to important, or 'significant', places should not only be minimized, but be minimal. However, change is often required to enable new uses to be accommodated – these changes need to be considered in the light of both conservation and sustainable construction practices.

Material use and waste

One strategy to minimize waste from building construction and deconstruction, and to capture and make use of the embodied energy that their materials contain, is through their recycling or reuse. The effective recycling of construction materials is impacted by a number of considerations, including the cost and energy associated with sorting and cleaning. The disposal of wastewater, the separation of materials without damage, the need to exclude foreign materials impairing performance, and doubts about the performance standards of recycled materials help to explain a slower uptake of recycling compared with other industries.

Many recycling processes also result in new materials of lower value. Sustainable-design advocates William McDonough and Michael Braungart describe this process as 'downcycling', citing aluminium as a valuable but constantly downcycled material. Recycling of aluminium products such as drinking cans, they argue, invariably results in weaker and less useful products, because the various components of the can contain different materials, including aluminium, manganese alloy, coatings and paint. This downcycling can also result in harmful chemicals, such as paints and plastics, being contained in the new product (McDonough and Braungart, 2002, p57).

An alternative to recycling is reuse, which implies a substantially lower level of reprocessing of a product, such as simply cleaning it ready to be used again. However, the reuse of materials and assemblies comes with its own issues: it is difficult to remove components without damage; the sourcing and availability of reused materials are problematic; there are often limitations inherent in the existing properties of components, such as their dimensions; and the quality of the product being reused is often difficult to determine. These issues are less likely to impact where complete assemblies, or indeed whole buildings, are reused. Whole buildings, or parts thereof, are not required to be disassembled in order to be reused; instead, they form an existing framework for redevelopment. The process of adaptive reuse therefore offers advantages over the use of recycled, reprocessed and reassembled demolition waste.

There is also an argument for adaptive reuse based on the types of material used in construction. In adaptive reuse, the components often retained are the substructure, structural elements and external envelope – elements that embody much of the building's construction energy.

For example, up to 85 per cent of total quantities of finished building products (by mass) in Australia are dominated by concrete, brick and steel (Walker-Morison et al, 2007, p1). These materials are of high density and low value and contribute very significantly to pollution emissions and energy used to transport them (Harris, 1999, p754; Spence and Mulligan, 1995, p286). Not only do these materials constitute the largest quantity of materials used, but the temperatures needed to process them require high production energy, a combination that results in these elements containing a major proportion of the embodied energy of the building.

This argument is supported by evidence that the significant contributors to greenhouse impacts during manufacture are often those same elements that are typically retained in refurbishment work. One study by researcher Andrew Walker-Morison and colleagues identifies the elements that contribute most to greenhouse impacts. In domestic construction, these elements comprise perimeter walls, flooring, internal walls, windows and roofing. In non-residential construction, the major greenhouse impacts are from structural steel, flooring, reinforcing steel, perimeter walls and external cladding (Walker-Morison et al, 2007, p5).

The most energy-intensive materials in construction are therefore those that are generally retained in a building that is being adapted for reuse. The primary structure and substructure, as well as the building skin, although sometimes requiring repair, stabilization, cleaning and modification to improve performance, are generally retained in whole or in part. It therefore follows that, in adaptive reuse, a much lower total embodied energy is required in the construction process – even when substantial refurbishment is required. This, together with the recognition of embodied energy as a major contributor to a building's 'net energy', provides a strong case to extend the life of buildings to ameliorate the embodied component.

The three case studies all demonstrate how the reuse of materials can have significant benefits. At the Canberra Glassworks, the budget required the retention of as much as possible, even to the point where the project architect describes how the original cobwebs can still be seen (Craswell, 2008). At the larger scale, this includes the existing building, but also includes a detritus of found objects: existing timber planks have been reworked as seating for visitors, and coal hoppers have been suspended to form a distinctive ceiling in the theatrical glassmaking exhibition space. The University of Tasmania's School of Architecture retains the existing envelope and structure, with facilities accommodated in a three-storey section running the building's length. The lightweight construction of the new insertion is supported by the existing concrete columns, avoiding the need to introduce new structure or reinforce the old. Likewise, Paddington Gardens retains and stabilizes its original bricked vaults, cast iron and timber. Graffiti, a marker of the reservoir's time as a derelict site, are also preserved. This represents an attempt to avoid the erasing or obscuring of the layers of the past, and to recognize that the passage of time on a building is like a manuscript on which the original writing has been effaced to make room for other writing – otherwise known as a 'palimpsest' (Ward, 2004, p111). Retaining these layers from the past, no matter how 'ugly', helps to communicate the full life of the building, and, in so doing, add to its value to society.

At a more tangible level, studies show that, of construction and demolition waste going to landfill, 81 per cent comprises building rubble (Chiveralls, 2011, p1). The reuse of buildings and their component parts has a direct relationship to the energy and resources consumed in the construction process, but also in the waste generated. Adaptable reuse not only reduces consumption, but also diverts a significant volume of material from entering the waste stream: material that is unlikely to be used again.

Better performance

Although embodied energy is increasingly recognized as a major contributor to environmental impact, it is estimated that greenhouse-gas emissions embodied in base building fabric materials account for only 10–15 per cent of total building greenhouse-gas emissions (Walker-Morison et al, 2007, p6). The remainder is largely attributed to operational energy and therefore dominates the impact of the built environment. Building performance therefore has a direct relationship to energy use and greenhouse-gas emissions. Although the performance of newly built projects is governed by legislative requirements, older buildings often perform poorly in comparison. The option then is to build new, better-performing buildings, or to retrofit existing building stock to improve its energy efficiency.

However, performance is not dependent on the building alone, but also on the services and occupants within that building. In writing about sustainable refurbishment, Nick Baker (2009), for example, argues that each subsystem has a variance in performance of approximately 2.5 (for example, poor-quality management by the occupants can result in 2.5 times more energy use in the same building with the same services). This results in a possible twenty-fold variation between the best performers and the worst performers – an assertion supported by an assessment of ninety-two office buildings in the UK. This significant variation means that, by building new and more efficient buildings, we cannot guarantee a reduction in energy use, especially in non-domestic buildings where overall energy consumption is dominated by processes and activities in the building (Baker, 2009, p5).

The case studies illustrate how adaptive reuse can result in an improvement in building performance through innovation. Changing the use of the building provides an opportunity to 'retune' it, to make use of existing elements and services where appropriate, and also to supplement them with more efficient ones. The approach at the University of Tasmania, for example, was to compress new functions as much as possible to assist in reducing servicing requirements. This also provides opportunities for future expansion and flexibility in the resulting open-plan spaces. The strategy is based on the premise that occupants will accept broader thermal-comfort conditions in certain areas (Fay and Owen, 2008, p4). It could also be argued that occupants are more likely to accept deficiencies as part of the intrinsic nature of an existing building rather than accept poor performance in a new one. Heritage and cost restraints at the University of Tasmania limited the ability to make major alterations to the building envelope to improve thermal efficiency. Strategies developed to counter these restraints included introduction of a thermal labyrinth for pre-cooling of supply air, and radiant heating as an alternative to the conditioning of the large volumes. These moves have resulted in energy use meeting targets of $430MJ/m^2$ per annum, based on actual consumption (Fay and Owen, 2008, p2), representing a 25 per cent improvement compared with external benchmarks.

Despite the restrictions imposed by existing buildings, reuse projects provide opportunities for the introduction of new technologies. In fact, these restrictions may act as an incentive for new and more sustainable technologies to be adopted – to counter any inherited spatial restrictions or limited access to services. Examples of innovation of this type include the reclaiming of heat from glass furnaces for use in the hydronic heating system at the Canberra Glassworks, and the use of existing condensing pits for rainwater storage.

Social impacts

A narrow approach to sustainable development will often have a practical focus that concentrates on the environmental and quantifiable impacts specific to the project. These include how much waste is generated, how much energy and resources are used, what pollution is released, and the health of people and ecological systems on the site. A broader and more holistic approach considers the impact of the development on larger systems (such as transport and waste disposal), but also considers the impact of the development on the community and wider society. For example, compact cities and urban containment are recognized as one means to reduce energy consumption and pollution at a larger scale. The other positive impact of urban densification is in social impacts – it encourages improved public transport and enhanced access to facilities, while reducing social segregation (Bromley et al, 2005, p2409).

Adaptive reuse allows for existing sites to be revitalized, rather than new development at the fringes of the city being sought. Existing buildings located in central, accessible locations provide opportunities to build upon, and encourage the use of, existing transportation and infrastructure. At the University of Tasmania, the relocation from the existing School of Architecture accommodation has provided the potential for reduced car dependency for students and staff.

Reuse can also contribute to social sustainability through the introduction of new uses, including mixed uses, and by providing opportunities for better spaces not able to be provided by new-build projects. For example, the subterranean volume in the Paddington Reservoir Gardens would have been less feasible in new construction owing to the limitations of cost. By optimizing land use and creating a valuable community resource from previously unproductive property, occupation can be increased to the benefit of the community. The gardens, for example, were previously closed to the public owing to their dangerous condition.

Adaptive-reuse projects can also contribute to the development (and retention) of skills and knowledge at the local level. Often, when buildings are conserved, careful repair and reconstruction are required. This work usually uses traditional skills and locally sourced materials, and can be labour rather than material intensive. On the other hand, new-build projects have a comparatively higher materials component. Adaptive-reuse projects can therefore provide direct employment and social benefit – particularly to the local worker. The time required for the repair and stabilization of structural elements, for example, will advantage the worker on site more than the more rapid erection of a new element, whose base materials and manufacture may be sourced from elsewhere. The sourcing of local materials provides additional benefit to the local supply industry and also has a positive impact on the embodied energy used in transporting materials to site. This is exemplified in the Paddington Reservoir Gardens, where existing brickwork has been carefully stabilized, and hardwood columns have been reconstructed to form the base for the new landscaped park above.

It cannot be assumed, however, that adaptive-reuse projects naturally lead to improved social sustainability. The selection of new uses can sometimes have a negative impact. For example, the 'gentrification' of some sites, although successful in the physical regeneration of previously underused areas, can exclude people or segments of society who may have previously lived or worked there. Additionally, adaptive reuse may not provide the optimum solution for densification of a site – for example, an existing building may not be able to be extended to the same height or footprint as new development. Adaptive-reuse projects do, however, offer an advantage when it comes to 'contextual fit', because they already exist and contribute to the site and district. This is supported by a survey of building owners and managers of commercial buildings that found that 82 per cent of respondents felt that retaining older buildings rather than building more new ones would create more interesting communities (Bullen, 2007, pp25–7).

Adaptive-reuse projects can positively impact on surroundings and the reputational capital of stakeholders. They provide the potential for remediation of contaminated sites, with resultant long-term health impacts, such as the work required to the Paddington Reservoir Gardens to remove the contamination resulting from its former life as a petrol station. The re-introduction of civic space by the Sydney City Council, which was publically supported by the community, and the improved environment for staff and students at the University of Tasmania, have a positive impact on direct users and also enhance the image of the providers of these environments. Projects such as the Canberra Glassworks are able to become significant locally, nationally and internationally. Not only do they retain and interpret cultural significance, they also provide an opportunity to showcase new functions in a unique setting and thereby perform a new role as an important cultural facility.

Conclusion: the upcycling of waste buildings

The case studies illustrate that adaptive reuse can provide valuable community resources from unproductive property and, at the same time, revitalize existing neighbourhoods. By breathing life into 'waste' buildings, these projects demonstrate that value can be added – whether measured in economic terms or in how they are perceived by their users and society. The adaptive-reuse process supports the principles of upcycling, where waste is transformed. It is a process that also supports the principles of sustainable development.

Adaptive reuse can reduce the impact on the environment through minimizing landfill; reducing the depletion of non-renewable resources, energy use and emissions; and extending the useful life of the building, resulting in reclaiming embodied energy over a longer time frame. Not only can it bring a building back to life in the immediate term: by contributing to its significance, adaptive reuse has the potential to ensure its survival for a long period.

On the basis of sustainable outcomes alone, there is a strong argument that adaptive reuse should be prioritized over other forms of development. The adaptive-reuse process recognizes that changes may be inevitable to ensure a building's survival, whereas the preservation of buildings in their current state has the potential to turn them into unusable monuments susceptible to further decay. It therefore follows that, if buildings are retained without a new use, then we will need to seek other – and less sustainable – forms of development to compensate.

The design of new construction should also recognize and respond to the potential benefits of adaptive reuse. By designing buildings with a view to later adaptation, functional obsolescence can be avoided, and the transfer to another use made possible, even if that future use is undefined. Numerous old buildings that have been transformed through many cycles of use are testament to the quality and robustness of their original design, which has enabled change to be accommodated.

Importantly, the adaptive-reuse process recognizes the value of our building stock as economic, social and cultural capital that should not be wasted. It is a process that retains those things that have been invested in a building's creation through knowledge, effort and materials. This capital includes physical resources, embodied and operational energy, design effort, artisan skill and labour. Building adaptation means recognizing this capital and reusing what we have available now, instead of letting it go to waste.

Acknowledgements

The author would like to thank Tonkin Zulaikha Greer Architects (Sydney), Tanner Architects (Canberra) and Six Degrees Architects (Melbourne) for their generous contribution to this paper, and to the photographers who kindly provided the permission to publish their images.

References

Australia ICOMOS (1988) *The Australia ICOMOS Charter for the Conservation of Places of Cultural Significance (the Burra Charter)*, Australia ICOMOS, Sydney, Australia

Australian Institute of Architects (2007) 'UTAS School of Architecture', www.architecture.com.au/awards_search?option=showaward&entryno=2007070715, accessed 14 March 2011

Australian Institute of Architects (2008) 'Canberra Glassworks', www.architecture.com.au/awards_search?option=showaward&entryno=2008018858, accessed 14 March 2011

Australian Institute of Architects (2010) 'Paddington Reservoir Gardens', www.architecture.com.au/awards_search?option=showaward&entryno=2010029346, accessed 14 March 2011

Baker, N. V. (2009) *The Handbook of Sustainable Refurbishment: Non-Domestic Buildings*, Earthscan, London

Ball, R. M. (2002) 'Reuse potential and vacant industrial premises: revisiting the regeneration issue in Stoke-on-Trent', *Journal of Property Research*, vol 19, no 2, pp93–110

Bromley, R. D. F., Tallon, A. R. and Thomas, C. (2005) 'City centre regeneration through residential development: contributing to sustainability', *Urban Studies*, vol 42, no 13, pp2407–29

Bullen, P. A. (2007) 'Adaptive reuse and sustainability of commercial buildings', *Facilities*, vol 25, no 1/2, pp20–31

Chiveralls, K. (2011) 'Cleaning up the construction industry', 31 March 2011, www.theconversation.edu.au/cleaning-up-the-construction-industry-31, accessed 3 April 2011

Craswell, P. (2008) 'The power of glass', *Indesign*, vol 32, February, pp196–201

Crawford, R. H., Czerniakowski, I. and Fuller, R. J. (2010) 'A comprehensive framework for assessing the life-cycle energy of building construction assemblies', *Architectural Science Review*, vol 53, pp288–96

Department of the Environment and Heritage (DEH) (2004) *Adaptive Reuse: Preserving Our Past, Building Our Future*, Department of the Environment and Heritage, Australian Government, Canberra, Australia

Dixit, M. K., Fernandez-Solis, J., Lavy, S. and Culp, C. H. (2010) 'Identification of parameters for embodied energy measurement: a literature review', *Energy and Buildings*, vol 42, pp1238–47

Douglas, J. (2006) *Building Adaptation*, Elsevier and RIBA Publishing, Oxford

Ellison, L. and Sayce, S. (2007) 'Assessing sustainability in the existing commercial property stock: establishing sustainability criteria relevant for the commercial property investment sector', *Property Management*, vol 25, no 3, pp287–304

English Heritage (2011) 'Industrial heritage at risk – English Heritage investigates our industrial past', *English Heritage*, 24 March 2011, www.english-heritage.org.uk/about/news/industrial-heritage-at-risk-2011/, accessed 18 April 2011

Fay, R. and Owen, C. (2008) 'Conversion of a heritage listed industrial building', UTas School of Architecture and Design, *BEDP Environment Design Guide*, Royal Australian Institute of Architects, Melbourne, Australia

Harris, D. J. (1999) 'A quantitative approach to the assessment of the environmental impact of building materials', *Building and Environment*, vol 34, pp751–8

Hernandez, P. and Kenny, P. (2010) 'From net energy to zero energy buildings: defining life cycle zero energy buildings (LC-ZEB)', *Energy and Buildings*, vol 42, pp815–21

Jenkins, S. (2011) 'This cult of the ruin renders England's landscape soulless. Better to rebuild', *The Guardian*, 14 April 2011, www.guardian.co.uk/commentisfree/2011/apr/14/cult-ruin-england-castles-abbeys, accessed 18 April 2011

McDonough, W. and Braungart, M. (2002) *Cradle to Cradle: Remaking the Way we Make Things*, North Point Press, New York

Owen, C. (2007) 'UTAS architecture', *Architecture Australia*, July/August, vol 96, no 4, pp76–85

Spence, R. and Mulligan, H. (1995) 'Sustainable development and the construction industry', *Habitat International*, vol 19, no 3, pp279–92

Stapleton, I. (2000) Conference Introduction to *Adaptive Reuse: Continuity and Creativity*, National Trust of Australia, NSW, 9–10 November

Urban Splash (2011) www.urbansplash.co.uk/about-us/our-story/our-mission, accessed 18 April 2011

Ursprung, P. (2002) *Herzog and De Meuron: Natural History*, Canadian Centre for Architecture, Montreal and Lars Muller Publishers, Baden, Switzerland

Walker-Morison, A., Grant, T. and McAlister, S. (2007) 'The environmental impact of building materials', *BEDP Environment Design Guide*, Royal Australian Institute of Architects, Melbourne, Australia

Ward, S. (2004) 'Mulloway Studio', *Artichoke*, vol 6, no 2, pp108–11

Chapter 13

Density, design and sustainable residential development

Alpana Sivam and Sadasivam Karuppannan

Summary

There is a strong belief among many urban-development stakeholders that high density is the way to create sustainable development. In spite of this, people are generally in favour of low-density housing, with the implicit assumption that it has the capacity to improve the living environment. It is often assumed that high densities are inherently unpleasant, and that low densities are inherently good. However, it is quite likely that living conditions in high housing densities are better than in low-density areas, owing to design configuration. Density is important, but it cannot create social, economic and environmentally sustainable residential development alone.

New design paradigms such as New Urbanism and 'smart growth' emerged during the 1980s and addressed the issue of sustainable development. Most stakeholders, however, still consider that density is responsible for creating sustainable development, which is partially true, but not entirely the case. The aim of this chapter is to examine the interrelationships between density, design and their roles in creating sustainable residential development. The method adopted in this study is exploratory in character. The study concludes that, to create sustainable residential development, density and design must fit together like hand and glove.

Introduction

It is often assumed that higher-density developments are more sustainable. The principles of high-density development have dominated recent planning theory, particularly in developed countries. These theories are commonly applied to address the adverse environmental, social and economic effects of urban growth and its concomitant urban sprawl and automobile dominance. Many planning theories have emerged, including New Urbanism, smart growth, urban consolidation, neo-traditional development and transit-oriented development (TOD) to support higher-density housing, particularly in the United States, the United Kingdom, Australia and New Zealand.

Despite these design concepts, people are generally in favour of low-density housing because of the implicit assumption that it has positive effects on the living environment. It is commonly thought that high densities are inherently unpleasant and that low densities are fundamentally good (Forsyth, 2003). From their study of British Columbia's development densities, Alexander and Tomalty (2002) suggest that, even though the ideas of 'smart growth' were supported by many, high density proved to be a very controversial issue. Alexander and Tomalty argue that achieving high density is controversial because, on the one hand, it is supported by environmentalists, transit operators and user groups, and open-space advocates and, on the other hand, it is opposed by developers and owners. The latter group thinks that it will bring undesirable change, including congestion and increased crime, as well as reducing the amount of open space in the neighbourhood. It is quite likely, however, that living conditions in high-density residential developments are better than in low-density areas. Although many people think density is responsible for the creation of good and bad residential environments, they are wrong. Despite their high densities, in many cities' older areas, the living environment is often quite good, for example, Chandani chowk in Old Delhi.

A study of the compact city in the United States led Gordon and Richardson (1997, p96) to conclude that 'low-density settlement is the overwhelming choice for residential living'. Their study demonstrated that a compact city was not a worthwhile planning goal, because the ambition of compact-city principles, in terms of transportation usage, economic stimulation and environmental benefits, had not yet been justified by implementation. These arguments lead to discussion that density alone is not the answer to sustainable residential development, and the link between density and aspects of sustainability remains a challenge for planning theory and practice (Choguill, 2008).

Density creates compact development, but whether residential living is good, bad or sustainable will be owing to a combination of density and design. Design plays an equally important role. Design can influence urban development through the layout of services, distribution of activities and land use, as well as other practices that are inherent in the design process. The economy of planning housing developments depends to a large degree on judicious choices of these variables. High densities reduce the total cost of a dwelling unit. Apart from the effects of density, design parameters such as plot coverage, height, proportion of area under roads, orientation of layout and buildings, and open spaces also influence the cost and environment of residential development. Density itself cannot create a good or bad environment, because density is only a measurement, it is not an independent factor that could create a good or bad urban fabric or built environment (Alexander, 1993; Forsyth, 2003). In spite of new design paradigms, higher densities are still seen as significant elements in achieving sustainable development (Jenks et al, 1996; Williams et al, 2000).

The aim of this chapter is to examine the interrelationships between density, design and sustainable residential development, rather than testing and confirming a hypothesis. The method adopted to undertake this research is exploratory in order to identify the parameters of density and design and their relationship to sustainable residential development. The chapter is descriptive so that the reader will understand the relationship between density, design and sustainability in the context of residential development.

First, the chapter provides an overview of density, design and sustainable development. Then it explains the relationship between density, design and sustainable development and how this helps to create sustainable residential development. Design elements required to create social, economic and environmentally sustainable development are presented, and the chapter concludes with an overview of the roles of density and design and their importance in creating sustainable residential development.

Density and design

The concept of urban density is not new and has been in vogue ever since the garden city movement in England and the early modernists' movement in Germany (Pont and Haupt, 2007). Density has different implications to professionals in different disciplines, such as planners, economists, community organizations, psychologists and ecologists. For example, a psychologist or a sociologist may concentrate on the effects of perceived density on mental well-being. Density is a term that represents the relationship between a given physical area and the number of people who inhabit or use the area. It is expressed as a ratio of population or the number of dwelling units to an area (Jensen, 1966; Magri, 1994; Burton, 2000; Forsyth, 2003; Montgomery et al, 2003; Cuthbert, 2006; Forsyth et al, 2007). The two types of density are net and gross. Net residential density measures the intensity of development with respect to residential area, whereas gross density measures the intensity of development at neighbourhood level (Jensen, 1966; Magri, 1994; Burton, 2000; Forsyth, 2003; Montgomery et al, 2003; Cuthbert, 2006; Forsyth et al, 2007). Churchman (1999, p390) says that, 'density is an objective, quantitative, and neutral term'. It is neutral in the sense that one cannot know immediately whether a given level of density is positive or negative.

Campoli and MacLean (2007) argue that, for many people, density is associated with unattractiveness, congestion and crowding, even if it can be shown that well-designed higher density can achieve a well-built environment and may save land, energy, infrastructure cost and the overall cost of the housing development. They argue that people have a problem in distinguishing the quantitative from the qualitative character of density. Higher density has many advantages in terms of efficient use of infrastructure, housing affordability, energy efficiency and a vibrant street life that improves social interaction (Forsyth et al, 2007). However, density alone is not sufficient to create a good urban environment, and it requires appropriate design. Montgomery et al (2003, p1) conclude that 'issues relating to urban form and density continue to fuel worldwide debate'.

Design is often viewed as an activity that translates an idea into a blueprint and vision for urban, rural and regional areas or for different land uses. The important part is the translation of the ideas through how well a design has been thought out. Design does not have to be new, different or impressive to be successful, as long as it fulfils a need and is functional. Design not only looks at the aesthetic aspects of the built environment, but is also a problem-solving activity. Indeed, design has a 'functionalist' (or 'form follows function') approach. Lloyd-Jones explains design's functionalist approach:

> The functionalist approach suggests that if we analyse the problems that the design sets out to address in sufficient details and in scientific manner, a spatial solution will emerge from this analysis or 'programme'. It suggests that design is a linear process, which if carried out with sufficient rigour, will lead to a single, optimum solution.
>
> (Lloyd-Jones, 2001, p51)

Both design elements and functions have an impact on the sustainability of the built environment. Design has many elements, such as plot coverage, floor-space index, setbacks, mass, height, orientation and climate consideration, that help to create various built environments with same density (see Figures 13.1a and 13.1b).

Figure 13.1 Impact of design on the built environment.

Source: Lincoln Institute of Land Policy (www.lincolninst.edu)

Even though high-rise buildings are generally associated with high residential density, there is no inherent relationship between the two. For example, the two neighbourhoods depicted in Figures 13.1a and 13.1b have exactly the same density, but they look very different. Although they both have the same density, they are not necessarily perceived to be equally dense. What really matters is how the layout is presented. Indeed, layout pattern plays a very important role in creating urban fabric and a sustainable living environment.

There is a strong relationship between density and design. Density is a measurement, but design is an instrument, which creates the built environment. Hence, both density and design play an important role in creating desirable and sustainable built environments in various contexts.

Sustainable development

Newman and Kenworthy (1989) describe how the concept of sustainable development emerged from a global political process that tried to bring together, simultaneously, several important issues:

1   the need for economic development to remove poverty;
2   the need for environmental protection of air, soil and biodiversity, upon which we all ultimately depend; and
3   the need for social justice and cultural diversity.

In solving these issues, local communities will learn to express their values. Indeed, the concept of sustainable development started with human settlement and, from there, it has gone further to address issues of housing and neighbourhood development. Sustainable residential development means 'housing which contributes to community building, to social justice and to economic viability at a local level' (Morgan and Talbot, 2001, p321). Even though there are many definitions of sustainability, it is generally agreed the economy, environment and social equity are the three prime values of sustainability (Chan and Lee, 2009). Sustainable development has become firmly established in the community development and planning literature (Jepson, 2007). However, when it comes to practising sustainable development, it remains largely outside the main stream (Jepson, 2007; Choguill, 2008).

It is generally assumed that the built form is the physical arrangement of various activities and architectural forms to suit land-use regulations (Greene, 1992). There are various schools of thought: for example, some scholars discuss design of urban fabric in physical and environmental terms (Lynch, 1960; Cullen, 1961; Trancik, 1986; Levy, 1999). Others, however, argue that the creation of urban fabric links psychological, sociological and philosophical aspects (Rapoport, 1982; Alexander et al, 1987). Some consider it as an interplay between the environment and social factors (Lawson, 1980; Barnett, 1982). Despite the desire to create sustainable and lively neighbourhoods, the terminology is too inconsistent or vague. Planners and the public cannot refer to a consistent framework that can communicate ideas about neighbourhood design (Greene, 1992). Indeed, sustainable residential development (as part of the built environment) is a combination of physical form, activities and image.

Density, design and sustainable development

It is a common assumption among planners that a suburban development, and particularly a low-density suburb, is not a desirable form of residential development. This type of development has led to unsustainable development due to the increase in surface water run-off, unnecessary energy and infrastructural costs, increased commuting distance, greenhouse gas emissions, car dependency, people's health problems (such as obesity and cardiovascular diseases) and social exclusion (see Churchman, 1999; Jones, 2007). Some scholars assume that 'sustainable urban development runs counter to the principles of the compact city in one fundamental respect: the primacy of process over form' (Neuman, 2005). Planning scholars generally have faith in high-density development and concentration of function as the answer to creating a sustainable city. There is, however, a belief that dense cities are not liveable. Liveability is not, however, only due to density and urban form, but is in fact the result of a combination of density, design and people's perceptions. For example, cities such as Prague, Barcelona and Amsterdam are lively cities, even if they are dense (Neuman, 2005).

Despite the combined benefits being widely recognized, it is argued that sustainability is not intrinsic to the concept of compact development. Churchman (1999) stated that, even though the arguments contradicting low density are accepted and have been an influential component of planning during the past two decades, more questions have arisen regarding the theories of the methods employed, higher density and the soundness of planning. Studies have demonstrated that the 'relation between compactness and sustainability could be negatively correlated, weakly related or correlated in limited ways' (Neuman, 2005, p12). Even though, theoretically, there is a relationship between high density and sustainability, it is not always true. It may influence how urban form is conceived.

The starting point of any sustainable development is the satisfaction of basic human needs, which constitute shelter, health, opportunities for work, access to facilities and a pleasant environment in which to live. Social and environmental goals are often mutually reinforcing. For example, the provision of a range of different kinds, sizes and tenures of housing in a neighbourhood increases both social choice and environmental sustainability. Improving the local environment, reducing traffic and making walking more pleasant enhance people's health and aesthetic enjoyment. They also have the remedial effect of reducing emissions (Barton et al, 1995). There is a strong relationship between urban form and sustainability. Jabareen (2006) argues that there are four prominent types of sustainable urban form: neo-traditional neighbourhood, urban containment, compact city and eco-city. Urban forms have a direct impact on social, economic and environmental sustainability.

Barton et al (1995) recognize people's 'choice' as essential to attaining sustainable development. According to them, the point of good design is not to force a particular kind of behaviour, but to facilitate behaviour that is environmentally compassionate: to open up options that currently may be squeezed out by dominant market trends or policy conventions. It is generally accepted that a city's vitality is tied to its human scale, diversity and the quality of public space (Leccese and McCormick, 1999). Sustainability is a crucial theme for today, and cities are traditionally seen as unsustainable in their own right, but they are a central element of human life and will endure as long as they can be sustained by the natural resources that surround them. There are many

Figures 13.2 Residential area layout, Sheffield, UK.

Source: Google Maps

Figure 13.3 Residential area layouts in Delhi, India: (a) Dwarka and (b) Rohini.

Source: Google Maps

opportunities to reduce the amount of resources cities use and waste if careful design is implemented, i.e. by providing optimum density and through bold political action initiating sustainable policies. The present task is for people everywhere to learn to live increasingly sustainable lives, regardless of the size and form of settlement.

It is not possible to achieve a sustainable and lively development without an integrated approach of density and design that addresses the current issues of our changing environment and social and economic conditions.

Unfortunately, both users and stakeholders generally relate density to the height of buildings rather than the intensity of the development. Further, they far too often think that density alone is responsible for the creation of good or bad residential environments. In fact, height is not the direct measurement of density; the measurement of density is the layout pattern of the residential area. This relationship is demonstrated in Figure 13.2, a layout from Sheffield in the United Kingdom, where layouts 13.2a and 13.2b both have more or less the same density, even though they have different design configurations, different heights of residential blocks and different residential environments.

Another example is from Delhi (Figures 13.3a and 13.3b), where again density is the same in both residential examples, but the layout patterns and heights of the blocks are different. In Figure 13.3a, the height of the residential buildings is ten storeys, whereas in Figure 13.3b it is only four.

Figures 13.4 and 13.5 are from Adelaide, Australia, and juxtaposed they demonstrate how developments with similar layouts and height can have different densities. Note that both are one-storey developments.

It is very clear from Figures 13.4 and 13.5 that Medindie is quite open, whereas Oakden is quite compact. This variation is due to both density and design parameters. Design parameters are the size of residential blocks, street widths and layout patterns. The examples from Sheffield, Delhi and Adelaide demonstrate that density can be increased to create sustainable residential development using design parameters. These examples show that it is not density alone that creates a lively or sustainable neighbourhood, but rather the combination of density and appropriate design that is responsible. The next section explains the design parameters that are responsible for creating a socially, economically and environmentally sustainable residential area.

Design considerations and sustainable development

This section will unfold the design elements required to achieve socially, economically and environmentally sustainable neighbourhoods.

Design considerations for social sustainability

Social sustainability is defined as the improvement and maintenance of current and future well-being and the reduction of social inequality leading to an improvement in the quality of life (Chan and Lee, 2008a). To achieve a good quality of life, interaction is needed within the community. Urban forms of development affect the microclimate of built-up areas, in terms of temperature, relative humidity, air quality, lighting level and ventilation flow, which affects human comfort (Chan and Lee, 2009). Intensity of interaction is very much linked to design elements and layout pattern. For example, residential areas

Figure 13.4 Residential area layout, Medindie, Adelaide, Australia.

Source: PhotoMaps, courtesy of NearMap

Figure 13.5 Residential area layout, Oakden, Adelaide, Australia.

Source: PhotoMaps, courtesy of NearMap

Table 13.1 Design elements required to make residential development socially, economically and environmentally sustainable

Design principles/consideration	Triple bottom line		
	Social	Economic	Environmental
Permeability	✓	✓	
1 Layout pattern			
2 Pedestrian friendly			
3 Street and road layout			
4 Block layout and size			
Diversity	✓	✓	
1 Mixed use			
2 Preserving local character			
Legibility	✓	✓	
1 Massing and scale of the building			
2 Location of public space			
3 Varieties and location of social infrastructure			
4 Good accessibility			
5 Access to social infrastructure and open space			
Robustness	✓	✓	
1 Maximize the use of place			
2 Types and location of recreational facilities			
3 Facilities for diverse population			
4 Affordable living			
Richness	✓	✓	✓
1 Housing diversity and choice			
2 Use of material			
3 Quality of pedestrian walkways and public transport facilities			
Personalization	✓	✓	
1 Protection of local character			
2 Maximization of community participation			
3 Safety and ownership			
Intensity	✓	✓	✓
1 Optimum density			
2 Plot coverage			
3 Height			
4 Reduced carbon footprint			
Climate consideration	✓	✓	
1 Green design including energy-efficient house plan, consideration of solar path			
2 Solar access to roof and open space			
3 Combination of soft and hard surfaces			
4 Consideration of wind direction			

Source: Chan and Lee, 2009; Montgomery, 1998; Bentley et al, 1985

with a row house design and low density tend to reduce social interaction, whereas a dwelling unit that is U-shaped or of medium density increases interaction. Some may argue that, in the 1940s, row-house development promoted a strong sense of social inclusion. It is true, however, that, in previous decades, social life was valued as a community affair, whereas now much of life is self-centred or individualistic. People do not seem to have time to interact with their neighbours, owing to the pressures of modern city life. In these circumstances, the U-shaped layout increases interaction, because this provides a common entry point for everyone. Common areas for passive and active recreation at residential level increase interaction within the community. Pedestrian-oriented neighbourhoods provide opportunities for people to interact with each other. Design is the key to creating sustainable development by improving or enabling social equity, economic vitality and environmental responsibility (Chan and Lee, 2009). In order to ensure social sustainability is achieved through design and density, several design considerations have to be taken into account when preparing residential/urban development (see Table 13.1).

Subsequently, to make residential development socially sustainable, these design elements need to be incorporated in neighbourhood design. It is also observed that, in low-density suburbs, there is less interaction, whereas in medium- and high-density ones there is more. However, as density does not have a fixed standard and varies from place to place, it needs to be identified in its specific context. Hence, social sustainability is the process that addresses the relationship between society, the built environment (design and density) and quality of life in a neighbourhood setting.

Design considerations for economic sustainability

Design elements also have an impact on economic sustainability. The low cost of infrastructure, low construction cost of residential buildings, maintenance of infrastructure and buildings and permeable design lead to economically viable development. Design that takes care of orientation, ventilation, micro- and macroclimate and materials generally enjoys lower maintenance and ongoing costs (Chan and Lee, 2008b).

Li and Brown (1980) argue that better design, buildings in good physical condition and even the perceived image of a neighbourhood can often lead to higher property prices. Economic improvement or development in this context needs to consider many aspects of design, and the most important element is the layout pattern and spatial distribution of activities and social and physical infrastructure. Design also elevates the use of land by providing high-density housing that is of high quality, which leads to increased total revenue (Fishelson and Pines, 1984). The economic sustainability of any residential development is the outcome of the intensity of gross and net residential densities and various design elements. Some of the key design elements are listed in Table 13.1.

Layout and building design are very important aspects of long-term economical sustainability by making maintenance and running costs of infrastructure more sustainable. Layout and design of the buildings could optimize natural lighting and ventilation. Design and density could help maximize the use of land. In any development, 50 per cent of the costs are generally made up of land costs (Sinha, 1982). Therefore, density and land costs are inversely proportionate. The higher the density, the less that land will cost per unit, and this will make any development more feasible and affordable for all groups of people. To create a liveable environment with high density, however, the various design elements need to be considered. Green features related to construction, such as installation of energy-efficient and water-saving devices and use of recyclable and durable construction materials, are important in reducing buildings' maintenance costs. Access to open space and social facilities for all age groups will increase the use of space and make it more economical. Furthermore, more efficient use of land and space and mixed-use development will improve the economic viability of various projects. Providing accommodation for different income groups can make building projects more economically sustainable, because the cost of services and facilities will be shared and will consequently lead to more revenue for local governments. Resources will be saved for future generations through greater efficiency of public transport and safety for pedestrians. In this way, density and design parameters play an important role in achieving socially and economically sustainable development.

Design considerations for environmentally sustainable development

There is a close relationship between development, density, design and environmental quality, and it is necessary to decide the form of development carefully (Chan and Lee, 2009). Design elements and parameters affect the environment at both the macro and micro level. There are studies that examine transport energy and how the relationship between urban structure and building design reduces embodied- and operational-energy consumption and improves environmental sustainability. Rickwood et al (2008) argue that the existence of a relationship between land use and transport is well recognized, but the actual link is contested. It is very clear from the study conducted by Rickwood et al that building design affects both embodied- and operational-energy consumption. However, the authors claim that 'regardless of built form, design is very important in reducing (or increasing) operational use' (Rickwood et al, 2008, p67). This study also argues that urban form is critical for transport consumption. Therefore, there is a need to identify the best design means of transforming current urban structures to be more energy efficient.

Intensity of density also plays an important role in making development environmentally sustainable. Increased density and mixed-use development means more buildings, shops, homes and local services in close proximity will encourage walking and cycling. It will also enable efficient use of services and resources and offer more convenience to citizens. This increase in density means more people should walk or ride bicycles, and thus medium- and high-density buildings will lead to reduced emissions and pollution. Chan and Lee (2009) argue that design considerations such as quality of life, conservation and preservation, integrated design and provision of welfare facilities should be incorporated to sustain the urban environment. Intensity of density needs to be carefully selected, because high densities lead to traffic congestion, and low density increases the cost of public transport.

Various scholars (Montgomery, 1998; Rowley, 1998; Chan and Lee, 2009) believe that design elements are the key components in creating sustainable development. Some of the design parameters that should be taken into account to create environmentally sustainable residential areas are presented in Table 13.1. Sustainability issues vary from country to country, region to region and place to place. In some places, they require consideration of design elements for social and environmental sustainability, whereas, in other circumstances, design elements are required to address economic sustainability. Consideration of design elements will be context-based and thus not universal in application and will vary depending on the priorities of the location.

New Urbanism theory will prove useful in addressing and resolving environmental issues. The sustainability of towns has been envisaged in the New Urbanism movement as involving eco-friendly technologies, energy efficiency, reduction in the use of cars and fuel, and more local production (Hebbert, 2003; Grant, 2006; Chan and Lee, 2009). It is further enhanced when good design principles are used: for example, the positioning of the streets and internal layouts of dwellings in order to lessen the need for heating and cooling. Due consideration in layout and house design to solar orientation will harness the warmth of the sun in winter and protect from the hot summer sun. This will lead to sustainability, because there will be less requirement for heating and cooling. Well-oriented lots will make it possible for buildings to have potentially greater roof space correctly positioned for solar hot-water systems.

Discussion and conclusions

An analysis of the literature demonstrated that there is a strong relationship between density, design and sustainability. However, density alone is not enough to achieve social, economic and environmental sustainability. The earlier sections have demonstrated that design plays an important role in achieving various types of socially, environmentally and economically sustainable urban development. Both density and design are important in creating sustainable urban development. However, density is only a measurement and not the tool to foster the built environment. Our discussion revealed that there are some design parameters, such as pedestrian-friendly, mixed-use, an ability to fulfil people's needs and accessibility, which are vital in achieving sustainable development. Some design parameters are common to sustainable residential development (as seen in Table 13.1). However, there are some design parameters that are specific to individual sustainability issues: for instance, they address local character, which is only relevant to social sustainability. By using local character, the design of a residential area allows people to feel at home and to feel affection and pride in where they live. On the other hand, the same design parameter cannot be used to address economic and environmental sustainability issues.

The sustainability agenda varies from place to place, region to region and country to country. Some design parameters are believed to be common to achieving social, economic and environmental sustainability, but not all. In reality, these design parameters will vary from place to place, depending upon the priority they have been accorded for each component of sustainability. In India, for example, sustainability issues are primarily economic and environmental in character, and therefore the design parameters that are common to them will be relevant to sustainable residential development. In Australia, by contrast, design parameters common to environmental and social issues will help improve sustainable residential development. As density is not a fixed measurement worldwide, the proposed high, medium or low density will vary from place to place and be influenced by such variables as culture and people's perceptions. Thirty-five dwelling units per hectare, for example, represent a high density in Australia, but a very low density in India.

This study has highlighted the importance of density and design considerations in achieving the social, economic and environmental sustainability of residential developments. It is evident that there is a pressing need to change the way in which we develop our neighbourhoods, and, for this, density and design parameters are needed. Density and design parameters have the potential to address triple bottom line principles. In terms of resolving neighbourhood development issues, various authors have concluded that sustainable outcomes are linked to the diverse character of the urban environment. Furthermore, it has been demonstrated that density and design are vital for sustainable residential development to occur anywhere in the world. There is no one density and design parameter that can solve sustainable development problems. The solution will always be contextual.

The more diverse design variables are (for instance, incorporating social, cultural, economic, environmental, transport, housing, land-use and urban-form issues), the greater the opportunity to manage sustainability. Undoubtedly, there is a close relationship between design, density and sustainability. However, to provide social, economic and environmentally sustainable residential development, the impacts of density and design need to be seen in combination, rather than design and density being treated individually. Unfortunately, density alone is not the answer to sustainable residential development, because this only gives the intensity of the development, not the quality and sustainability of the residential development. Therefore, urban managers and planners need to consider both density and design parameters to provide sustainable residential neighbourhoods, rather than density alone.

This study concludes that sustainable residential development is not simply created by increasing housing density. It is also determined by the urban pattern, a factor that continuously transforms our way of living. Density is certainly a contributing factor, but it is wrong to measure intensity of the development alone and disregard the pattern, because it plays a vital role in creating a living environment. Density is only one simple and mechanistic measure of urban form, and, on its own, it has limited meaning. The qualitative differences between densities are more important than the numerical ones. It is only possible to achieve a sustainable residential development using an integrated approach that considers both density and design parameters.

In conclusion, the assumption of many urban-development stakeholders that high density is the most significant element in the creation of sustainable residential development is erroneous. Both density and design make critical (and interrelated) contributions to the creation of sustainable residential developments. Therefore, to create sustainable neighbourhoods, there is a need to consider both density and design parameters, rather than either of these parameters alone.

This study confirms that there is a strong relationship between density and design, as well as demonstrating how both factors contribute to the nature of the sustainable living environment. Density, for example, acts only as a measurement for development intensity, whereas design constitutes the physical elements that create this environment. Finally, this study demonstrates that there is need for planners and stakeholders to consider design elements, along with density, to provide sustainable development. Other research, such as the work done by Rickwood and his colleagues (2008, p57), claims that, 'the nature and form of the urban environment is a critical determinant of the sustainability of our society'. This study is limited to the form of the residential building and the relationship between land use and transport. There is a need to go beyond this concept and consider the density, form and design of the neighbourhood and city morphology, as well as the form of individual buildings and the distribution of land use.

References

Alexander, C., Neis, H., Anninou, A. and King, I. (1987) *A New Theory of Urban Design*, Oxford University Press, New York

Alexander, D. and Tomalty, R. (2002) 'Smart growth and sustainable development: challenges, solutions and policy directions', *Local Environment*, vol 7, no 4, pp397–409

Alexander, E. R. (1993) 'Density measures: a review and analysis', *Journal of Architectural and Planning Research*, vol 10, no 3, pp181–202

Barnett, J. (1982) *An Introduction to Community Design*, Harper & Row, New York

Barton, H., Davis, G. and Guise, R. (1995) *Sustainable Settlements: A Guide for Planners, Designers and Developers*, University of West of England, Bristol

Bentley, I., Alcock, A., Murrain, P., McGlynn, S. and Smith, G. (1985) *Responsive Environments: A Manual for Designers*, The Architectural Press, London

Burton, E. (2000) 'The compact city: just or just compact? A preliminary analysis', *Urban Studies*, vol 37, no 11, pp1969–2001

Campoli, J. and MacLean, A. S. (2007) *Visualizing Density*, Lincoln Institute of Land Policy, Cambridge, MA

Chan, E. H. W. and Lee, G. K. L. (2008a) 'Critical factors for improving social sustainability of urban renewal projects', *Social Indicators Research*, vol 85, no 2, pp243–6

Chan, E. H. W. and Lee, G. K. L. (2008b) 'Contribution of urban design to economic sustainability of urban renewal projects in Hong Kong', *Sustainable Development*, vol 16, no 6, pp353–64

Chan, E. H. W. and Lee, G. K. L. (2009) 'Design considerations for environmental sustainability in high density development: a case study of Hong Kong', *Environment Development and Sustainability*, vol 11, no 2, pp359–74

Choguill, C. L. (2008) 'Developing sustainable neighbourhoods', *Habitat International*, vol 32, no 1, pp41–8

Churchman, A. (1999) 'Disentangling the concept of density', *Journal of Planning Literature*, vol 13, no 4, pp389–411

Cullen, G. (1961) *The Concise Townscape*, Van Nostrand Reinhold, New York

Cuthbert, A. R. (2006) *The Form of Cities*, John Wiley & Sons, Carlton, Victoria, Australia

Fishelson, G. and Pines, D. (1984) 'Market vs social valuation of redevelopment projects in an urban setting', *Socio-Economic Planning Sciences*, vol 18, no 6, pp419–23

Forsyth, A. (2003) *Measuring Density: Working Definitions for Residential Density and Building Intensity*, Design Centre for American Urban Landscape, University of Minnesota, Minneapolis, MN

Forsyth, A., Oakes, J. M., Schmitz, K. H. and Hearst, M. (2007) 'Does residential density increase walking and other physical activity?', *Urban Studies*, vol 44, no 4, pp679–97

Gordon, P. and Richardson, H. (1997) 'Are compact cities a desirable planning goal?', *Journal of the Americal Planning Association*, vol 63, no 1, pp95–106

Grant, J. (2006) 'The ironies of New Urbanism', *Canadian Journal of Urban Research*, vol 15, no 2

Greene, S. (1992) 'Cityshape: communicating and evaluating community design', *Journal of the American Planning Association*, vol 58, no 2, pp177–89

Hebbert, M. (2003) 'New Urbanism – the movement in context', *Built Environment*, vol 29, no 3, pp193–209

Jabareen, Y. R. (2006) 'Sustainable urban forms: their typologies, models, and concepts', *Journal of Planning Education and Research*, vol 26, no 38, pp38–52

Jenks, M., Burton, E. and William, K. (eds) (1996) *The Compact City: A Sustainable Urban Form?*, E & FN Spon, London

Jensen, R. (1966) *High Density Living*, Leonard Hill, London

Jepson, E. J. (2007) 'Sustainability and the Childe thesis – what are the effects of local characteristics and conditions on sustainable development policy?', *Cities*, vol 24, no 6, pp434–47

Jones, P. (2007) 'Practical evaluation tools for urban sustainability', *Indoor and Built Environment*, vol 16, no 3, pp201–3

Lawson, B. (1980) *How Designers Think: The Design Process Demystified*, Butterworth Architecture, London

Leccese, M. and McCormick, K. (1999) *Charter of the New Urbanism*, McGraw-Hill, New York

Levy, A. (1999) 'Urban morphology and the problem of the modern urban fabric: some questions for research', *Urban Morphology*, vol 3, no 2, pp79–85

Li, M. M. and Brown, H. J. (1980) 'Micro-neighborhood externalities and hedonic housing prices', *Land Economics*, vol 56, no 2, pp125–41

Lloyd-Jones, T. (2001) 'The design process', in M. Roberts and C. Greed (eds) *Approaching Urban Design: The Design Process*, Longman Scientific and Technical, Essex

Lynch, K. (1960) *The Image of the City*, MIT Press, Cambridge, MA

Magri, S. (1994) 'Urban density definitions', *Urban Futures*, September, pp49–53

Montgomery, A., Saunders, A. and Chortis, J. (2003) 'Density considerations in managing residential land provision in Perth, Western Australia', paper presented at the State of Australian Cities Conference, Perth, Australia, 3–5 December

Montgomery, J. (1998) 'Making a city: urbanity, vitality and urban design', *Journal of Urban Design*, vol 3, no 1, pp93–116

Morgan, J. and Talbot, R. (2001) 'Sustainable social housing for no extra cost?', in K. Williams, E. Burton and M. Jenks (eds) *Achieving Sustainable Urban Form*, Spon Press, London and New York

Neuman, M. (2005) 'The compact city fallacy', *Journal of Planning Education and Research*, vol. 25, no 1, pp11–26

Newman, P. and Kenworthy, J. (1989) *Cities and Automobile Dependence: An International Sourcebook*, Gower Publishing, Aldershot

Pont, M. B. and Haupt, P. (2007) 'The relation between urban form and density', *Viewpoints*, vol 11, no 1, pp1–3

Rapoport, A. (1982) *The Meaning of the Built Environment*, SAGE, Beverly Hills, CA

Rickwood, P., Glazebrook, G. and Searle, G. (2008) 'Urban structure and energy: a review', *Urban Policy and Research*, vol 26, no1, pp57–81

Rowley, A. (1998) 'Private-property decision makers and the quality of urban design', *Journal of Urban Design*, vol 3, no 2, pp151–73

Sinha, A. (1982) 'Density design and cost study at residential level', Masters thesis, School of Planning, CEPT, Ahmedabad, India

Trancik, R. (1986) *Finding Lost Space: Theories of Urban Design*, John Wiley & Sons, New York

Williams, K., Burton, E. and Jenks, M. (2000) 'Built form and design solutions: Introduction', in K. Williams, E. Burton and M. Jenks (eds) *Achieving Sustainable Urban Form*, Spon Press, New York and London

Chapter 14

Construction management and a state of zero waste

Nicholas Chileshe, Jian Zuo, Stephen Pullen and George Zillante

Summary

Elimination of waste through the efficient use of project resources is fundamental for a state of zero waste. Despite the growing global recognition of the environmental impacts associated with the generation and management of waste across industries, the construction industry, and, in particular, the construction and demolition (C&D) sector, continues to generate a large amount of waste. Furthermore, the majority of the efforts designed to find solutions to total waste elimination have largely focused on the macro and micro levels.

This chapter aims to improve understanding of the application of zero-waste principles to the meso level of C&D. The links between construction management principles and waste minimization are explored. We suggest some drivers for achieving zero waste, such as building procurement teams, empowered work teams, lean designing, education and training, awareness of waste-management systems, senior management commitment, technological innovation, changes to organizational culture and individual behaviour change. We recommend implementing a series of generic, meso-level strategies to help achieve a state of zero waste.

Introduction

The construction industry plays a critical role in a national economy. According to the Australian Bureau of Statistics (ABS) (2010), the construction industry in Australia comprises about 585,000 enterprises and employs about 900,000 people. In total, the industry accounts for approximately 7 per cent of Australia's gross domestic product (GDP). In the state of South Australia, the industry contributes about 6 per cent to the state's GDP and employs more than 60,000 people, thereby making it the seventh largest employer in South Australia. Similarly, the construction industry contributes 6 per cent of the United Kingdom's GDP, where it employs more than 2.3 million people (Worrall et al, 2010). The profitability of the industry can be linked to the effective usage of project resources and, to some extent, the adoption of strategies such as waste management that improve cost-effectiveness through the elimination of waste. In China, the world's biggest developing country, construction activities generate 300 million tonnes of waste annually: 40 per cent of the total amount of that country's waste (Chen et al, 2010; Wang et al, 2010).

Despite the growing recognition of the environmental impacts associated with the generation and management of waste across the construction project life cycle and in particular at the meso level, the implementation of appropriate waste-management strategies aimed at total waste management elimination has had limited effect. This has had a significant impact on the inputs of the construction industry.

There are benefits to be gained from effective waste management, such as the reuse and recycling of waste materials for the construction of new buildings and for the retrofitting of existing buildings: for example, the reduced need for new materials and products. According to Troy et al (2003) and Yan et al (2010), the outcomes of effective waste management reduce the embodied energy used for the manufacture and transportation of materials, which is a very significant part of buildings' life-cycle energy consumption.

Although some studies have identified the need to address the issue of waste management throughout the project life cycle, there is evidence to suggest that the attitude of a large proportion of industry practitioners towards construction and demolition waste is that waste management should only focus on the construction stage. A study by Osmani et al (2007) revealed that waste management is not a priority in the design process, as architects seemed to take the view that waste is mainly produced during site operations and rarely generated during the design stages. However, other studies, such as Poon (2007), dispute this and argue that waste reduction can be achieved through changes in design concepts. A study by Fapohunda et al (2006a) pointed out that resources wastage accounted for 30 per cent of the building cost and implied that construction resource wastefulness (CRW) affects the achievement of clients', contractors', participants' and other stakeholders' objectives. Given the pressing problem of resource use, there is growing evidence of the need to address waste-management issues at state, national and international levels. In Australia, for example, Zero Waste SA developed South Australia's first state-wide waste strategy. In the UK, 'Accelerating Change' was launched in 2002 and has set an improved agenda for all stakeholders in the C&D industry (SFfC, 2005–6a, 2005–6b), which led to the establishment of new approaches such as the Construction Lean Improvement Programme (CLIP), and Lean Construction (LC), both of which are based on the principle of eliminating waste (BRE, 2006).

Before describing the relationship between construction management and a state of zero waste, it is necessary to outline the reasons for pursuing the reduction and elimination of waste in the construction process. The main reasons are cost reduction and environmental sustainability. Containment of costs by avoiding the unnecessary usage of materials (e.g. avoidable cut-offs) has always been a cornerstone of construction project management. According to Yuan et al (2011), significant amounts of construction and demolition waste are also caused by other construction activities, such as cutting corners of construction formwork, poor plastering, deformation during transportation and delivering. In recent years, the traditional cost-management imperative has been equalled, if not surpassed, by the quest for sustainable practices in the design, operation and disposal of buildings and parts of the built environment.

Definitions and background

Before considering the key conceptual and empirical issues affecting the elimination of waste, it is necessary to define the terms 'construction and demolition waste', 'zero waste' and 'construction management'.

Construction and (C&D) waste

Shen et al (2004, p473) define construction waste as, 'building debris, rubble, earth, concrete, steel, timber, and mixed site clearance materials, arising from various construction activities including land excavation or formation, civil and building construction, site clearance, demolition activities, roadwork, and building renovation'. Within the context of the construction-project life cycle, construction waste is defined as the amount that does not add value to the process and would normally end up in landfill. Other C&D waste is generated during the occupancy and operation of buildings, and in the last phase of a project's life cycle, namely demolition. In general terms, the interpretation of waste during the construction and facility management is that of wasted efforts and duplication (of work). Other definitions are provided by Fapohunda (2009), who states that waste resources are non-valued added resources that could either be physical or latent. Simply put, 'wastes' are construction resources that add no value to the overall outcome of an operation and arise through inefficient use of resources such as materials, manpower and machinery.

The BRE Digest 247 (1981 cited in Cooke and Williams, 2004) divides waste into four distinct categories. These four categories are:

1   design waste
2   take off, specification
3   delivery waste and
4   site waste.

The first two categories suggest that waste could be minimized through designs that resulted in waste-cutting on site. Waste building materials represent an unnecessary use of energy in their manufacture and supply. This energy is known as embodied energy and often originates from fossil-fuel consumption. Hence, waste materials also create unnecessary generation of greenhouse-gas emissions and contribute to climate change. Similarly, most construction materials also require water in their production (embodied water), so that waste materials signify wasted water that might be in short supply in some locations. Waste building materials use resources poorly that might be in limited supply. They require disposal in landfill, which is both inconvenient and expensive, owing to the decreasing availability of dump sites. These disadvantages will be explored further.

Zero waste

The term 'zero waste' refers to a philosophy that encourages the redesign of a product's life cycle so that all resources are reused (Wikipedia, 2011). The definition provided by Zero Waste SA (2005) is: ' "zero waste" is a new way of thinking about an age-old problem. It is part of a worldwide movement that recognises the need for change in the way that society manages its waste.' Murray (2002) offers a different perspective and suggests that the term zero waste has its origins in the highly successful Japanese business concept of total quality management (TQM). In the context of buildings, Lehmann (2010) states that 'zero waste' means that buildings are fully demountable and fully recyclable at the end of their life cycle, so that the site can return to being a greenfield site after use.

Given these three definitions, it can be concluded that zero waste as a philosophy would vary according to different organizations' way of thinking. Within the context of construction, note reference to the age-old problem of waste management and the construction industry's tendency to be adverse to change.

Construction management

Traditionally, according to Griffith and Watson (2004), Wideman (1986) and Newcombe et al (1993), construction management as a discipline can be viewed as the act of carrying out construction processes from inception to completion. This process involves a wide range of functions including:

- planning
- motivating
- communication
- coordinating
- controlling
- organizing
- and forecasting a viable operational system for project execution.

One of the functions of construction management is to maximize resource efficiency through procurement of labour, materials and equipment. Furthermore, these construction-management functions are underpinned by the generally accepted seven principles of management:

1   forecasting and planning;
2   organization;
3   commanding or directing;
4   controlling;
5   coordination;
6   motivation;
7   and communication, which encompasses them all.

According to Cooke and Williams (2004), these principles of management were established by classical theorists such as Henri Fayol. The responsibility for these functions varies according to different organizations, although the accepted norm is that the functions are performed by 'construction site managers' or 'construction managers', who are responsible for the smooth running of the project on behalf of the client and the organization. However, an inclusive and internationally accepted definition of construction management (CM) has since emerged. According to Bale (2010, p6), this definition encompasses six stages, namely the CIOB's footprint; a hierarchy of systems; the construction value stream; specialist services; our value system; and CM as an academic discipline. The specific reference to sustainable construction can be found in the third stage of the definition: 'embracing the entire construction value stream from inception to recycling, and focusing upon a commitment to sustainable construction'. It could thus be inferred that CM is closely aligned to the zero-waste ethos through the inclusion of recycling within its definition. The links between site management (which is part of CM) and minimization of waste are highlighted by Formoso et al (1999, cited in Kulatunga et al, 2006). Formoso's study argued that lack of attention of site management to determining waste is a major barrier to the minimization of waste.

The CM functions of 'planning' and 'organization' are linked with waste minimization through efficient site planning. Cooke and Williams (2004) contend that delivery and site waste can be reduced through good site layout planning at the pre-contract stage. Management of materials on site is also the responsibility of the site manager. As observed by Yuan et al (2011), limited site space might affect the effective implementation of construction and demolition waste management.

Zero construction waste and environmental sustainability

Waste construction materials are created at various stages of the life cycle of buildings. During the construction phase, on-site construction waste arises from broken and defective building components, off-cuts and materials packaging. During the operational life of buildings, refurbishments and upgrades will result in waste materials normally destined for landfill or recycling. At the end of a building's life, substantial quantities of waste materials will result from demolition, some of which might be reused and recycled while others would be taken to landfill.

Given that waste streams vary greatly between different project life-cycle stages, the linkages between the construction industry and the state of zero waste as discussed are categorized into three phases. Within the context of the products or outputs of C&D industry, waste from a building complex could be divided into three phases, as follows:

- Phase 1 – waste generated during construction;
- Phase 2 – waste generated during the occupancy and operations of the buildings;
- Phase 3 – waste generated during demolition.

Figure 14.1 illustrates the stages of a building life cycle. Watson (2003) suggests conceptualizing a building's life in two ways. The temporal life cycle represents a sequence of events that follow each other in time, and the physical life cycle represents a flow of materials. As the focus of this chapter is on material flows, the ensuing discussion is based on the physical life cycle of the building and features a 'closed loop' that aims to achieve zero-waste goals.

Figure 14.1 also highlights the potential for how wastefulness from the flow of materials that are transformed at each of the stages could be transmitted to the others. As articulated by Watson (2003), the materials chosen affect the initiation and production stages, the method of assembly affects the construction stage, and the means of disassembly affects the maintenance and disposition stage. Treloar et al (2003) define the 'demolition stage' (depicted in Figure 14.1) as the final and total disassembly of the building, whereas 'construction' is referred to as the assembly of materials and products to erect the finished building. The following section presents a discussion of how waste – as contextualized in the three phases identified earlier, in the form of embodied water, embodied energy and emissions and materials – occurs.

Figure 14.1 Stages in the building life cycle.
Supplied by the authors

Embodied energy and emissions

The energy used in the operation of buildings constitutes a significant portion of national consumption: for example, approximately one-fifth of Australia's energy consumption comes from buildings (Ceuvas-Cubria and Riwoe, 2006) and just over 40 per cent of the UK's does (Department of Trade and Industry (DTI), 2007). For this reason, there has been a focus on improving buildings' energy efficiency. More recently, attention has been paid to the indirect energy consumed by buildings as a result of the manufacture of building materials and the activity of construction. This is known as embodied energy and can amount to a substantial proportion of the life-cycle energy use of buildings, when both the initial (as built) and recurrent (refurbishment and maintenance) embodied energy is considered (Pullen, 2010a). Studies in Australia on a range of building types have indicated that total embodied energy can vary between one-quarter to over one-third of life-cycle energy consumption, depending on the assumed longevity of the buildings (Ding, 2007; Langston and Langston, 2007). As the manufacture and supply of building materials involve the direct and indirect use of fossil fuels, with an associated production of greenhouse-gas emissions, embodied-energy consumption contributes to climate change (IPCC, 2007). Measures to minimize this effect, including the reduction of the waste building materials, will contribute to lowering the impact of buildings on the environment. To this end, in a scoping study to investigate measures for improving the environmental sustainability of building materials sponsored by the Australian government (DEH, 2006a), various options to reduce greenhouse gas and other impacts were suggested including: 'improving the efficiency of materials use, and reducing waste, through design, construction, and demolition stages' (DEH, 2006a, p18).

Eventually, the consideration of embodied energy (and emissions) could become part of a national building energy standard-setting, assessment and rating framework, as suggested in the Australian government's national strategy on energy efficiency (Department of Energy Efficiency and Climate Change, 2010). In the meantime, the significance of embodied energy has been recognized in voluntary building rating schemes, such as LEED (US), BREEAM (UK) and GreenStar (Australia), whereby the use of low-energy embodied materials, minimization of waste and reuse of existing components are rewarded in construction projects by scoring more 'points'.

Embodied water

As the significance of embodied energy in building materials has become more evident, other resources consumed as a result of the construction of buildings have been considered. In particular, the consumption of water is of interest, bearing in mind the shortages of this commodity in certain locations. The production of building components can use water both directly in the manufacturing process and indirectly in the many goods and services that are required by the main process (Crawford and Treloar, 2005). This has been recognized for some time for other products, and water consumption is one of a number of indicators in life-cycle assessment to determine environmental impacts. Embodied-water analysis can be extended to the scale of national economic sectors (Foran et al, 2005). Water use in Australia for the provision of building materials has been projected to increase by 63 per cent over the next fifty years (DEH, 2006b), and so the elimination of waste building products and reuse of demolition materials should contribute to the minimization of water consumption.

Material resources

Despite the fact that most raw materials for building products and built infrastructure will not be exhausted in the short term (DEH, 2006b), the use of existing building materials by the recycling of demolition materials represents an opportunity to reduce additional environmental impacts, such as land disturbance and pollution (Carpenter, 2011).

The existing built environment represents a vast store of resources that has been inherited and that can be used without some of the environmental disadvantages of new developments. In a very broad sense, the World Bank (2001) comments on these resources as follows:

> the key economic reason for the cultural patrimony case is the vast body of assets, for which sunk costs have already been paid by prior generations, is available. It is a waste to overlook such assets.
>
> (World Bank, 2001, p50)

The concept of the built environment representing resources or capital has been explored by Kohler and Yang (2007). They considered the composition and dynamics of the built environment in Germany in terms of mass, energy and monetary flows in the building sector. Such analyses have the capacity to model and predict demolition and the availability of materials for recycling and reuse. This is part of the 'cradle-to-cradle' or 'cyclical-flow' concept and implies a stewardship approach to the management of building and infrastructure stock. Such an approach requires the analysis of material flows through regional and local economies (Kohler and Chini, 2005; Schiller, 2007; Tanikawa and Hashimoto, 2009).

Key drivers for attaining a state of zero waste

The following key drivers are suggested as critical for the attainment of zero waste and are illustrated in Figure 14.2.

The following section presents a brief discussion of each of the drivers identified.

Effective building procurement teams

The construction industry features fragmented approaches where the activities and participating parties are isolated from each other. As a consequence, a confrontational

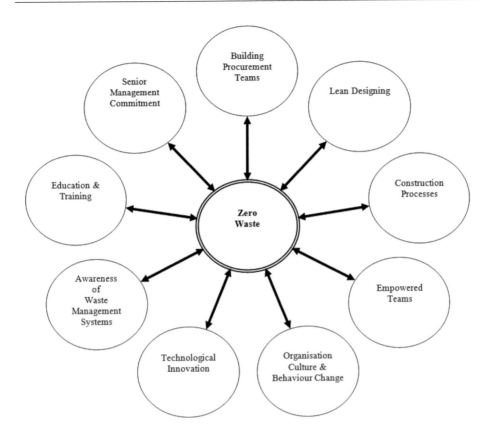

Figure 14.2 Key drivers for attainment of a state of zero waste.

Supplied by the authors

relationship can be formed that affects project outcomes significantly. Within the relevant literature, various approaches for improved teamwork have been suggested. Following the discussion of team working by the UK's Constructing Excellence (2004), the following six elements for effective procurement teams are suggested: (1) team identity; (2) shared vision; (3) communication; (4) collaboration and participation; (5) issues negotiation and resolution; and (6) reflection and self-assessment. Ekanayake and Ofori (2000, cited in Kulatunga et al, 2006) identified procurement as one of the causes of waste. This is manifested through ordering errors, the difficulty of ordering small quantities, and purchased products that do not comply with specifications.

It has been suggested that practices such as supply chain management systems and partnering could act as a platform for enhancing efficient resource use during the production process (Fapohunda, 2009). This would enable the partners to understand and acknowledge the relative importance and benefit of the profit that would accrue by being efficient in the use of resources. The ability to team build is highlighted by Fapohunda (2009) as the second most important ability among the attributes that enhance site managers' performance.

Lean designing

During the design stage, unconscious waste might arise. This wastefulness could be in the form of production information comprising the project objectives, the designer's concepts and, most importantly, the stakeholder's requirements, normally initiated at the feasibility and design stages for implementation at the construction stage. According to Fapohunda et al (2006a, 2006b), during the preparation of construction production information, the design team should always recognize that some wastefulness of resources can occur unconsciously during the construction process owing to design issues. However, despite this awareness of the need for considering wastefulness during the design stage, another study by Fapohunda et al (2007), which aimed at investigating site managers' constraints on construction resource use, established that site managers faced constraints in effectively implementing waste-management strategies as a result of the design team's attitudes towards project change, inefficient communication to effect change and constraints on the implementation of change.

Fapohunda et al (2006a) further identified the following as major sources of CRW in industries: (1) materials, (2) site management, (3) machinery, (4) production information, (5) manpower and (6) the design team. Accordingly, the interwoven waste from these sources requires the integration of each element for effective and efficient building production. Another study by Fapohunda et al (2006b) pointed out that CRW is not only about materials, but also about the inefficient use of labour and machinery. It is evident that labour and plant are used inefficiently during construction processes. Examples of wastefulness were identified in: the design stage (design and specification writing), bill of quantities preparation, cost estimation and resource procurement systems. Adoption of lean construction has the potential to reduce the proportion of non-value-added activities (Harris et al 2006).

Alignment of construction process to waste elimination

Given the definition and conceptualization of the terminologies of 'construction management', it is important to contextualize the process of site management in the waste-elimination process, particularly at the C&D phase. During construction, professionals such as architects are included in the process at feasibility and design stages. It is suggested that architects are included in the process at feasibility and design stages, and other members of the design team need to be aware of and understand the construction method before the final drawings are produced.

As articulated by Fapohunda et al (2008), the architects and design team need to understand the implication of the construction method on their concept of resource usage and how efficient resource use will be achieved. Traditionally, CM or construction site management (CSM) is viewed as the act of carrying out construction processes from inception to completion. Cooke and Williams (2004) suggest establishing procedures for contra-charging subcontractors for any excessive waste created.

Empowered work team

The key to a successful attainment of the state of zero waste is having an empowered work team. Dainty et al (2002) suggest empowerment and related teamwork concepts be evaluated at two interrelated levels: at the individual employee level and at the organizational level, as well as examining teamwork within the project supply chain. Motwani (2001) advocated specific measures of employee empowerment to include the extent of employee interaction with customers and the extent to which employee suggestion systems are used. The importance of employee empowerment or involvement is further highlighted by Brah et al (2002), who posit that empowerment improves worker satisfaction and quality of work life, which improves workers' productivity. In order to understand the concept of empowerment, one has to know what empowerment actually means. Conger and Kanungo (1988) define empowerment as a:

> process of enhancing feelings of self-efficacy among an organisation's members through the identification of conditions that foster powerlessness and through their removal by both formal organizational practices and informal techniques of providing efficacy information.

However, in order to address the issues of empowerment in general, Cassell et al (2001) suggest that larger customers may demand that small to medium enterprises meet certain human resource criteria standards.

Organizational culture and behaviour change

One of the questions posed within this chapter is whether less bureaucracy and a more trusting organizational culture could contribute to the attainment of a state of 'zero waste'. Morgan (1993) states that culture explains that different groups of people have different ways of life. Morgan further argues that it is a metaphor that has considerable relevance for our understanding of organizations. Given that the meso level comprises a variety of team members, including building owners, construction companies, design consultancies and other stakeholders, there is a need to understand how the behaviour of these individuals and teams can affect waste-management practices.

Research has also demonstrated the links between culture and the behaviour of teams (Faniran and Caban, 1998; Teo et al, 2000; Lingard et al, 2001; Teo and Loosemore, 2001). For example, Teo et al (2000, p512) argue that 'the labour intensive nature of construction activity suggests that behavioural impediments are likely to influence waste levels significantly'. This argument is supported by Lingard et al (2001, p809), who state that 'the extent to which reduction, reuse and recycling of waste can be achieved depends, to a large extent, on motivational influences on the behaviour of construction workers'. As highlighted by recent studies such as Zuo (2008) and Zillante (2007), a cultural shift is desirable for achieving better project outcomes and equally important for the continuous development and improvement of organizations. Teo and Loosemore's (2001) theory of 'waste behaviour in the construction industry' perceived waste management as a low priority, and noted an absence of appropriate resources and incentives to support it, and stressed that these deficiencies make the operatives on construction sites considerably more likely to view resource waste as inevitable.

This premise is supported by studies undertaken by Fapohunda et al (2008), which found construction participants believe that resource wastefulness is, to some extent, a normal occurrence that has to be 'budgeted' for during resources estimation. The organizational culture shift that is required for achieving zero waste among the building

Table 14.1 The cultural shift required for zero waste

From	Towards
Bureaucratic systems	Culture-driven systems
Blame culture	'No blame' culture
Rigid organization	Less bureaucratic
Top-down management	Employee empowerment

Supplied by the authors

procurement teams is summarized in Table 14.1. This organizational culture needs to be translated into the project level so that all project participants share a common understanding of, and approach to, waste management. Furthermore, adoption of concepts such as TQM can contribute to an improved organizational culture (Chileshe, 2004).

Given the above requirements, the burning question is why the C&D sector continues to generate the largest amount of waste across the three streams? The answer might be found in a report by Mathews (1992), who sought to identify the barriers to value and competitive advantage in the UK property industry. The conclusion drawn was that the inefficient and uncompetitive nature of the UK development and construction industry was the result of two principal factors that affected the structure of the industry by impeding the efficient creation of value and sustainable advantage. The factors were: (1) significant cultural polarization within the industry and (2) weak links between the elements and participants in the industry's value system.

The desired cultural shift or change in construction could be addressed through training and education, as advocated by McCabe (2004). Organizational culture has the potential to encourage an 'open-door policy', both at operational and project site level. Fapohunda et al (2006a) suggest that site personnel should always bridge the communication gap and operate an open-door policy. This will allow operatives to be ready to share knowledge and contribute meaningfully to the smooth running of an organization and project. Other benefits to be derived from having a good organizational culture include the improved self-esteem and belongingness that would encourage construction-site workers to reach their potential (Fapohunda et al 2006a).

Adoption of technological innovation – BIM

Lack of information sharing at the design stage and throughout the project life cycle contributes to waste generation. The Building Standards Institution (BSI) (2010) observes that this is caused in large part by duplicated work in a complex supply chain. It is evident where data used further down the supply chain were re-entered or recreated by other suppliers, largely because the software used by each part was not interoperable. Unfortunately, despite the growing push from building information modelling (BIM) software as a catalyst for changing the way building projects are run, historically the construction industry has always been reluctant to change its working practices (Griffith and Watson, 2004). As observed by McGeorge and Palmer (2002) and Fryer (2004), the construction industry has been criticized for its inability to innovate and slow adoption of new technology and management methods.

A study conducted in the UK identified poor information flows between all parties to the contract as one of the factors influencing waste-minimization activities. The uptake and adoption of BIM provide immense opportunities and benefits for sustainability and client communication in the construction industry through information management and exchange. According to Luciani (2008, cited in Olatunji et al, 2010), the revolution started by BIM, though new, has truly radical potential and has started rebranding the structure of construction markets. Perhaps the major contribution to the elimination of total waste through the application of BIM can be found in the following three benefits identified by BSI (2010) as forming the heart of BIM:

1   information, once captured, can be reused and repurposed;
2   information can be reviewed and revised, corrected and controlled; and
3   information can be checked and validated.

The benefits of BIM are not just limited to the design stage. BSI (2010) also identifies other areas within the project life cycle where it could be applied. For example, there is scope for the evaluation of environmental impacts associated with waste management during the occupancy of a building. This could take shape through the analysis of energy consumption and its other impacts on carbon generation. Fapohunda et al (2006a) point out that there is need for proper harmonization of product information before any project commences, to prevent avoidable resource wastage thereafter.

Awareness of waste-management systems

Organizational learning is identified in the literature as one of the factors affecting implementation of any change initiative. Deployment of waste-management plans among construction organizations usually involves some change. Zillante and Zuo (2008) assessed the awareness of small construction firms of waste-management systems and concluded that there is not enough pressure to create behaviour change. As a result, small and medium enterprises (SMEs) are only slowly taking up zero-waste concepts, and their waste-management performance suffers. Fapohunda (2009) suggested that making stakeholders aware of the value of wasted resources is one contribution to total elimination of waste. This study also found that involvement of stakeholders and clients enabled them (stakeholders) to understand the cumulative effects of resources wasted during the construction process. Within the Malaysian context, Begum and Pereira's (2008) study found that the contractor's behaviour (as reflected by its attitude and awareness) was dependent on its registration category (large, medium or small) with the national Construction Industry Development Board (CIDB). Furthermore, Begum and Pereira showed that contractors were relatively less aware of waste reduction compared with recycling. Similarly, in China, a study conducted by Yuan et al (2011) found operatives' weak awareness of construction and demolition waste reduction, and clients' weak awareness of construction and demolition waste management were among the obstacles to efficient waste management in the Chinese construction industry.

Awareness of the benefits accrued from effective implementation of waste-management systems should also be extended to employees at the project (site) level.

Staff awareness could be raised via the organization's materials-management policy and through the allowances built into the estimate (Cooke and Williams, 2004). There is also growing evidence for increased general awareness of the issue of waste management among labour-only subcontractors in the UK construction industry (Saunders and Wynn, 2004).

Training towards waste-elimination processes

The decision to implement waste-management strategies commits an organization to a continuous process of development. This calls for the training of every employee (including senior management) in order to cope with both the current demands and also the requirements created by the development process. Fapohunda (2009) recommends that both the design and the construction teams need adequate training in efficient resources use. Alternatively, some new employees may bring with them the necessary skills in waste elimination. It is acknowledged and anticipated that training in waste elimination might be an area of concern for SMEs. Yuan et al (2011) also identify inadequate training and education for practitioners in the Chinese construction industry as one of the major obstacles to improving their performance of waste management.

One way forward, suggested by Love et al (2002), is that organizations must integrate learning within day-to-day work processes, in such a way that they not only share knowledge and continuously improve, but also operate efficiently in response to their changing environments. Fapohunda et al (2006a) suggested that employees should be trained in the efficient use of construction resources, not only in materials usage, but also in manpower and machinery efficiency and effectiveness. They further recommended that, during training, workers should be aware of different incentive schemes available in the project for the efficient and effective performance of their duties.

Senior-management commitment

In the quest for adopting waste-management practices, one of the critical success factors is committed senior management. Egan (1998, p4) identifies 'committed leadership' as one of the five drivers of change that need to be in place to secure improvement in construction processes. Egan (1998, p13) further described committed leadership as 'being about management believing in and being totally committed to driving forward an agenda for improvement and communicating the required cultural and operational changes throughout the whole of the organization'. It could thus be argued that, in order effectively to implement waste-management practices and strive towards the attainment of a state of zero waste, effective senior-management support for waste-elimination principles or initiatives would be required. Consideration of the development and implementation of business waste-minimization policies should form part of this commitment. The requirements could embrace the ethos of the '3Cs' (commitment, championing and communication). Adoption and implementation of waste-management strategies would need to give full consideration to the 3Cs and require a senior-management decision to commit fully to a waste-elimination programme, actively championing waste-elimination strategies and communicating a strong commitment to other employees.

Strategies towards a state of zero waste at the meso level

There are diverse views with regards to strategy formulation. Mintzberg et al (1998) outline the strategy process according to ten schools: design, planning, positioning, entrepreneurial, cognitive, learning, power, cultural, environmental and configuration. However, it is beyond the scope of this chapter to describe them all. For our purposes, strategy is defined as the means by which waste-minimization objectives will be identified. The focus of this section is to identify and describe a series of generic strategies whose implementation at the meso level could hasten the implementation of a state of zero waste. Currently, a number of waste- and resource-management options exist in practice. Roper (2006) examined current practices and trends in the building material waste-management area in the US from a building life cycle or 'cradle-to-reincarnation' standpoint. Some of the strategies Roper found in practice included zero waste, integrated recycling, international approaches, reuse of materials, resource optimization, waste reduction and deconstruction. Similarly, in Australia, Zero Waste SA (2005) has adopted waste-management-practice options ranging from best to worst practice or from least preferable (dispose) to most preferable (avoidance). Their 'hierarchy of waste and resource management' options are as follows:

- avoidance
- reduction
- reuse
- recycling
- recovery
- treat
- disposal.

The waste hierarchy is a national and international guide for prioritizing waste-management practices, with the objective of achieving the optimal environmental outcome (Zero Waste SA, 2005, p7). Zero Waste SA acknowledges the need for a holistic implementation of this framework. Furthermore, given that its 2005 report focuses on only construction and demolition as one of the three waste streams identified as 'waste' going to landfill, its applicability throughout the building life cycle needs careful consideration. Within the broader context of construction management, Lu and Yuan (2011) proposed a framework for understanding waste management studies in construction. Within the framework, the following four major components are identified:

1 a C&D waste-management hierarchy indicating generic waste-management strategies according to their priorities;
2 a project life cycle indicating the stages at which waste management can be conducted;
3 a material life cycle helping to trace and analyse material waste;
4 a C&D waste-management approach spectrum indicating approaches ranging from 'hard' technologies to 'soft' economic/managerial instruments for addressing C&D issues.

Clearly, the first component within this framework encompasses the national and international guide as adopted by Zero Waste SA (2005).

The following section discusses how some of the strategies identified within the hierarchy of waste management might be incorporated during the building life cycle.

Reduction: avoidance of waste generation

Reduction of waste is associated with modifying the attitudes, behaviour and culture of the stakeholders within the construction process. There is a growing body of research in construction management that has linked the effective use of project resources to behaviour (Faniran and Caban, 1998; Teo et al, 2000; Lingard et al 2001; Teo and Loosemore, 2001; Kulatunga et al, 2006; Zillante, 2007; Zuo, 2008). Given the links between zero waste and TQM (Murray, 2002) noted earlier, it is also suggested that construction organizations adopting TQM principles could contribute to their achievement of zero waste. This would occur because one of the critical success factors for TQM is an 'open organization', which manifests itself through the application of a 'more open, trusting organizational culture'. For example, a study by Chileshe (2004) found that adoption of TQM principles such as 'zero defects' resulted in fewer errors and material waste within the building life cycle. Reduction strategy is also considered the most effective and efficient method for managing C&D wastes (Lu and Yuan, 2011). In order to raise the awareness of stakeholders within the construction process, some best management practices (BMPs) should also be adopted. Education and training in waste-minimization strategies for the construction workforce form one such BMP. Kulatunga et al (2006) also recommend development of better communication channels within organizations, and introducing incentives for better waste-management practices. Adoption and implementation of international environmental standards such as ISO 14001 or EMAS could form part of best management practices.

Reduction as a strategy could also be achieved during the design stage of the construction process through the 'designing and specifying convertible structures and materials'. This approach is based on the premise of designers and manufacturers working collaboratively. Other options are associated with the adoption and implementation of smart and reusable components (Fapohunda, 2009). Accordingly, the most significant best practice for waste reduction is for the designers to specify materials that are reusable by designing and specifying panels that could be used several times without being damaged. Pullen et al (2009) identify prefabrication as one construction method that has the potential to improve affordability and sustainability. The benefits of adopting prefabrication are further supported by Tam et al (2007), who found that up to 84.7 per cent of construction waste can be reduced by adopting prefabrication.

Effective partnering and supply-chain implementation enhance efficient resource use during the construction process. Effective use of the principles and practices of CM have the potential to unlock and improve the self-esteem, self-respect and belongingness of employees and workers in the construction industry. At the project level, Cooke and Williams (2004) suggest establishment of procedures for contra-charging subcontractors for the excessive waste created.

Reuse and recycling

The recycling and reuse of building materials can help to reduce the environmental impacts of using new construction products. One of the confounding aspects of improving the energy efficiency of the building stock by demolition and construction of new buildings is the fact that some of the operational energy gains are taken up by the embodied energy of new materials. Faster rates of urban redevelopment have been shown to increase this phenomenon (Pullen, 2010a). However, this effect can be partially offset by the use of recycled materials, which may be available from on-site demolition or from other demolition sites (Pullen 2010b). According to Treloar et al (2003), this is referred to as open-loop recycling (i.e. between industries or building life stages).

Hence, using stocks of existing materials in the construction of new buildings makes sense from the perspectives of resources, energy and emissions. This may include reusing parts of buildings (e.g. facades and structural frameworks), or the recycling and downgrading of materials (e.g. crushed masonry for road-base). In the area of residential building construction, Treloar et al (2003) recommend the reuse of second-hand materials and the use of materials with recycled content as one of the steps for reducing waste. Etxeberria et al (2007) used recycled coarse aggregates obtained from crushed concrete for concrete production. The results showed that the use of recycled aggregates can achieve concrete product of an acceptable quality. Poon and Chan (2007) studied the properties of concrete paving blocks prepared with recycled concrete aggregates contaminated by materials (tiles, clay bricks, glass, wood) commonly found in C&D waste. Their results show that it is feasible to allow a higher level of contamination in the recycled concrete aggregates for making concrete products. Rao et al (2007) pointed out that recycled aggregate concrete can also be used in lower-end applications of concrete. The identified strategies within the reuse and recycling could further be enhanced through the adoption of the best management practice of on-site segregation of waste.

Crowther (1999, cited in Watson, 2003, p11) proposed 'design for disassembly (DfD) or design for deconstruction' as a viable strategy that entails adoption of the reuse, recycling and recovery options within the hierarchy of waste. The deconstruction of buildings has gained more and more attention in recent years as an important waste-management tool (Couto and Couto, 2009). This strategy involves designing the building or some of its components such that they can be easily taken apart at the end of the design's life and separated for recycling or reuse. This approach to waste minimization can be viable through the use of panelized and prefabricated construction components. Fapohunda et al (2008) argue that adoption of standardized products can significantly reduce resources such as labour, materials or equipment, and conversely reduce waste occurrence. Some earlier applications of DfD can be found in the work of architects such as Renzo Piano and Jean Prouve. Prouve's application of prefabrication is demonstrated through the metal house known as the 'Tropical House'. Another example can be found in the work of Piano, who used the DfD principles in the expo building for IBM. However, despite the growing application of DfD ideas within construction and the built environment, it should be noted that DfD, as a concept, originated within the manufacturing industries. It is important, therefore, to acknowledge and identify any challenges associated with its implementation through a building project life cycle.

BMPs used by some of UK construction organizations in their quest for achieving reuse and recycling strategies include the use on construction sites of bins and skips that are colour-coded for each waste stream. This is to ensure that separation of materials is achieved on site and that salvageable resources are retained for future use or resale. There is also evidence that suggests the emergence of DfD as a discipline. Bogue (2007) suggests that for design for disassembly to be successful, it needs to adopt an interdisciplinary approach to the following three areas: (1) the selection and use of materials; (2) the design of components and the product architecture; and (3) the selection and use of joints, connectors and fasteners. Quite clearly, construction management has a role in the selection and use of materials, as well as the joints, connectors and fasteners, through the subject of specifications.

Disposal

The last strategic option available is one associated with disposal, which is linked to the first but focused on identifying sustainable solutions to the disposal of waste generated during the construction and quantified by the amount of material going to landfill. The strategy of disposal is linked to that of 'recycling'.

Within the OECD countries, Austria and Belgium have the highest recycling rates, at about 60 per cent, followed by the Netherlands and Germany at just over 55 per cent, with other countries, such as Australia, considerably lower at 35 per cent (DEH, 2006b). In Australia in 2007, the C&D sector contributed 38 per cent of the 43.8 million tonnes of waste that were generated nationally (ABS, 2010). Concrete, bricks and asphalt constitute a large part of this, with a range of materials, including plastics, metals, glass and timber, making up the rest. According to a report published by the BDA Group (2007), C&D created 51 per cent of the waste dumped in landfill in South Australia. To minimize the demand for disposal sites for construction materials, reduction of on-site wastage and recycling of demolition materials are required. In a report by Hyder Consulting for the Australian government, a number of factors that act as barriers to increased recovery of resources were identified. These factors are the pricing of resources, cost of disposal, community awareness, policy, availability of infrastructure and gaps in information (Oke et al, 2008).

The fourth programme or objective advocated by SA Zero Waste is that of implementing 'effective policy instruments', and the achievability rating for this was 'high', with a number of strategies proposed for its implementation. These are focused on using fiscal and policy instruments, including legislation, mostly related to disposal of waste soil to landfill. There is ample evidence of acknowledgement of the need for compliance and uptake within the construction industry. This is demonstrated through the amount of legislation that stakeholders have to consider when developing a project waste-minimization plan(s) for construction and demolition work. Relevant laws include: the Building Act (2004); the Building and Construction Industry Training Levy Act (1999); the Environmental Protection Regulations (2005); and the Waste Minimisation Act (2001). The role of regulation in the construction industry was demonstrated by Zillante et al (2010). The study highlighted how the Building Code of Australia (BCA) could facilitate cost savings in building construction by allowing innovative or alternative materials, forms of construction or designs. A study conducted by Lu and Yuan (2011) also established that the effectiveness of disposal legislation contributes to waste disposal. (Landfill charges and locations were also found to influence waste disposal.) Lawson et al (2001) established that new taxes were making disposal of C&D waste to landfill uneconomical in the UK.

In summary, adoption of the following principles and strategies could hasten the implementation of a state of zero waste. What is required is the adoption of eco-efficiency strategies in the construction sector, as recommended by Wallbaum and Buerkin (2003). They categorized these strategies into two levels, namely product components and product structure. At the product-structure level, optimization of product technique through alternative product processes is recommended. It could be argued that usage of prefabrication falls into that category.

Some challenges for further research into 'designing for zero waste' are worth mentioning. Given the emphasis of C&D research on the production stage of the building life cycle, the potential for waste-minimization strategies at the initiation or design stage should be pursued further. As articulated by Lu and Yuan (2011), discussion of C&D waste management would benefit from connecting with other disciplines. For example, the discipline of economics could pursue the agenda of economic cost–benefits associated with the current disposal options. Lack of awareness and attitudes of the construction workforce were identified as some of the major barriers to waste minimization. Given this, the disciplines of sociology and psychology are well placed to investigate and address the behavioural issues affecting C&D management and workers in relation to waste minimization. The study of organizational behaviour (OB) also provides a context for deepening our understanding of how construction organizations view waste-minimization interventions. Bennett (1997, cited in Chileshe, 2004) defines the subject of OB as the study of how organizations function and how people relate to them through their conduct, perceptions and intentions, either individually or in groups. Drawing on that definition, it is apparent that waste-minimization strategies could be linked to an analysis of OB. Delivery waste offers the opportunity for areas such as supply-chain management and logistics to help in ensuring that resources optimization is effectively achieved, whereas civil engineering could assess the viability and strength of recovered materials. From these examples, it is evident that, when designing for zero waste, we should embrace the possibilities for interdisciplinary research.

Conclusions

The reasons for seeking a state of zero waste are clear in terms of reducing costs and environmental load and achieving a closed-loop material flow by means of resource recovery. The design and specification of buildings need to be precise and integrated with the construction process to encourage waste minimization. Greater off-site manufacturing of building components will assist this process. To encourage the reuse of buildings at the end of their life, the design and construction process should be undertaken with ease of disassembly as an objective. These considerations indicate that pursuing and achieving a state of zero waste lie squarely among the responsibilities of construction management.

This chapter sought to provide some answers to the fundamental questions raised associated with technology, change, empowered work teams, effective deployment of construction methods and identification of appropriate strategies. Reference was made to some of the objectives contained within the SA Zero Waste report (2005), despite its being limited to only the construction and demolition waste stream. This chapter sought to extend the discussion of some of the challenges faced by the construction industry in eliminating waste by noting that the efficient use of project resources could be extended to other stages of the project life cycle, namely the design, operational and occupancy stages. Some suggestions as to how waste-management issues could be addressed at the meso level were proposed. Overall, this chapter identifies a number of issues affecting the implementation of waste strategies at the meso level.

As articulated by Fapohunda et al (2006a, 2006b), there are clear indications that the companies that survive will be those with good waste-minimization strategies and technological or managerial advantages. Effective and efficient use of construction resources and reduction of either conscious or unconscious resource wastefulness should be of major concern to the construction sector. Similarly, Lu and Yuan (2011) observe that adoption of managerial measures and implementation of technical tools contribute to waste reduction. Following the Zero Waste SA objective of 'fostering sustainable behaviour', this chapter acknowledges the need to take into account the behavioural features of site participants in resources wastefulness and provide an incentive framework for achieving efficient use of construction resources. In response to the challenges of waste management in the construction and demolition sector, this chapter recommends and proposes some key drivers of change. These can be categorized in the following four areas: management issues, employee or worker issues, technological issues and cultural and behaviour issues.

Acknowledgments

This chapter provides a background to the successful ARC Linkage Project: Re-considering sustainable building and design: a cultural change approach (LP110100156). The project team comprises A/Prof George Zillante, Dr Lou J. Wilson, Dr Jian Zuo, Dr Stephen Pullen, Ms Jasmine Palmer, Prof Frank Schultmann and Prof Jiayuan Wang. Industry partners include: Zero Waste SA, The Australian Institute of Building Surveyors (AIBS), The Royal Institution of Chartered Surveyors (RICS), The Australian Institute of Building (AIB), The Campbelltown City Council, Hodgkison Architects and Shenzhen Jianyi International Engineering Consultants Ltd.

References

Australian Bureau of Statistics (ABS) (2010) *Australia's Environment: Issues and Trends*, no 4613.0 Australian Bureau of Statistics, Canberra, Australia

Bale, J. (2010) *CIOB's Professionalism: An Inclusive Definition of Construction Management*, The Chartered Institute of Building, UK

BDA Group (2007) *South Australia's Waste Strategy 2005–2010 Benefit Cost Assessment 2005–2010 Benefit Cost Assessment, Volume 1: Summary Report*, Report to Zero Waste South Australia

Begum, R. A. and Pereira, J. J. (2008) 'Awareness, attitude and behavioural status of waste management: a profile of Malaysian contractors', *Asian Journal of Water, Environmental and Pollution*, vol 5, no 3, pp15–22

Bogue, R. (2007) 'Design for disassembly: a critical twenty-first century discipline', *Assembly Automation*, vol 27, no 4, pp285–9

Brah, S. A., Tee, S. S. L., and Rao, B. M. (2002) 'Relationship between TQM and performance of Singapore companies', *International Journal of Quality & Reliability Management*, vol 19, no 4, pp356–79

BRE (2006) *Construction Lean Improvement Programme (CLIP), Building a better World*, BRE, UK

British Standards Institution (2010) *Construction the Business Case*, Building Information Modelling, British Standards Institution, London and BuildingSMART UK, Surrey

Carpenter, T. G. (2011) *Construction in the Landscape: A Handbook for Civil Engineering to Conserve Global Land Resources*, Earthscan, London

Cassell, C., Nadin, S. and Gray, M. (2001) 'The use and effectiveness of benchmarking in SMEs', *Benchmarking: an International Journal*, vol 8, no 3, pp212–22

Ceuvas-Cubria, C. and Riwoe, D. (2006) *Australian Energy: National and State Projections to 2029–30*, Australian Bureau of Agricultural and Resource Economics (ABARE) Research Report 06.26. Canberra, Australia

Chen, M. Z., Lin, J. T., Wu, S. P. and Liu, C. H. (2010) 'Utilization of recycled brick powder as alternative filler in asphalt mixture', *Construction and Building Materials*, vol 25, no 4, pp1532–6

Chileshe, N. (2004) 'The application of TQM within small and medium sized construction related organisations', PhD thesis, Sheffield Hallam University, UK

Conger, J. A. and Kanungo, R. N. (1988) 'The empowerment process: integrating theory and practice', *Academy of Management Review*, vol 13, no 3, pp417–82

Constructing Excellence (2004) *Team Working*, Constructing Excellence, Watford

Cooke, B. and Williams, P. (2004) *Construction Planning, Programming and Control*, Blackwell Publishing, London

Couto, J. P. and Couto, A. (2009) 'Strategies to improve waste management in the Portuguese construction industry', *International Journal of Environmental and Waste Management*, vol 3, no 1/2, pp164–76

Crawford, R. and Treloar, G. (2005) 'An assessment of the embodied energy and embodied water associated with commercial building construction', *Proceedings of the Fourth Australian Conference on Life Cycle Assessment, Sustainability Measures for Decision Support*, Sydney, Australia

Dainty, A. R. J., Bryman, A. and Price, A. D. F. (2002) 'Empowerment within the UK construction sector', *Leadership and Organization Development Journal*, vol 23, no 6, pp333–42

Ding, G. (2007) 'Life cycle energy assessment of Australian schools', *Building Research and Information*, vol 35, no 5, pp487–500

Department of Energy Efficiency and Climate Change (2010) *National Building Energy Standard-setting, Assessment and Rating Framework*, public discussion paper, National Strategy on Energy Efficiency, Commonwealth of Australia, Canberra, Australia

Department of the Environment and Heritage (DEH) (2006a) *Scoping Study to Investigate Measures for Improving the Environmental Sustainability of Building Material*, prepared by the Centre for Design at RMIT, BIS Shrapnel, CSIRO, Deni Greene Consulting and Synec Consulting, Department of the Environment and Heritage, Commonwealth of Australia, Canberra, Australia

Department of the Environment and Heritage (2006b) *Inquiry into Waste Generation and Resource Efficiency*, submission to the Productivity Commission, Commonwealth Government of Australia

Department of Trade and Industry (DTI) (2007) *Meeting the Energy Challenge: A White Paper on Energy*, UK Energy Sector Indicators 2007 supplement, Department of Trade and Industry, HM Government, www.berr.gov.uk/files/file39511.pdf, accessed 3 February 2011

Egan, J. (1998) *Rethinking Construction*, Department of the Environment, Transport and the Regions, HM Government, London

Etxeberria, M., Vázquez, E., Marí, A. and Barra, M. (2007) 'Influence of amount of recycled coarse aggregates and production process on properties of recycled aggregate concrete', *Cement and Concrete Research*, vol 37, no 5, pp735–42

Faniran, O. O. and Caban, G. (1998) 'Minimizing waste on construction project sites', *Journal of Construction and Architectural Management*, vol 5, no 2, pp182–8

Fapohunda, J. (2009) 'Operational framework for optimal utilisation of construction resources during the production process', PhD thesis, Sheffield Hallam University, UK

Fapohunda, J., Stephenson, P., Griffith, A. and Chileshe, N. (2006a) 'The impact of construction resource wastage on building production', in T. C. Haupt and J. J. Smallwood (eds) *CD-ROM Conference Proceedings, The First Built Environment Conference, CIOB AFRICA*, Association of Schools of Construction of Southern Africa, Johannesburg, South Africa

Fapohunda, J., Stephenson, P., Griffith, A. and Chileshe, N. (2006b) 'Budgeting for waste syndrome (BWS) within the construction industry', in A. Baldwin, E. Hui and F. Wong (eds) *CD-ROM Conference Proceedings of the CIB W89 International Conference in Building Education and Research, BEAR 2006, Construction Sustainability and Innovation Conference*, Kowloon, Hong Kong

Fapohunda, J., Stephenson, J., Griffith, A. and Chileshe, N. (2007) 'Investigation of project manager's restraints (PMR) on construction resources utilisation (CRU)', *Proceedings of the Fourth International Conference in the 21st Century 'Accelerating Innovation in Engineering Management and Technology'*, Gold Coast, Australia

Fapohunda, J., Stephenson, P., Griffith, A. and Chileshe, N. (2008) 'Achieving sustainable construction through efficient construction resources management', *Proceedings of the 17th International Conference on Management of Technology* (IAMOT 2008), the British University in Dubai, Dubai, United Arab Emirates

Foran, B., Lenzen, M. and Dey, C. (2005) *Balancing Act: Triple Bottom Line Analysis of the Australian Economy*, The University of Sydney, www.isa.org.usyd.edu.au/publications/documents/balancingact1.pdf, accessed 3 February 2011

Fryer, B. (2004) *The Practice of Construction Management: People and Business Performance* (4th edn), Blackwell, Oxford

Griffith, A. and Watson, P. (2004) *Construction Management: Principles and Practices*, Palgrave Macmillan, Basingstoke

Harris, F., McCaffer, R. and Edum-Fotwe, F. (2006) *Modern Construction Management* (6th edn), Blackwell, Oxford

Intergovernmental Panel on Climate Change (IPCC) (2007) 'Summary for policymakers', in S. Solomon, D. Qin, M. Manning, Z. Chen, M. Marquis, K. B. Averyt, M. Tignor and H. L. Miller (eds) *Climate Change 2007: The Physical Science Basis*, Contribution of Working Group I to the Fourth Assessment Report of the Intergovernmental Panel on Climate Change, Cambridge University Press, Cambridge and New York

Kohler, N. and Chini, A. (2005) 'Resource-productive materials use', *Proceedings of the 2005 World Sustainable Building Conference (SB05)*, Tokyo, Japan

Kohler, N. and Yang, W. (2007) 'Long term management of building stocks', *Building Research and Information*, vol 35, no 4, pp351–62

Kulatunga, U., Amaratunga, D., Haigh, R. and Rameezdeen, R. (2006) 'Attitudes and perceptions of construction workforce on construction waste in Sri Lanka' *Management of Environmental Quality: an International Journal*, vol 17, no 1, pp57–72

Langston, Y. and Langston, C. (2007) 'Building energy and cost performance: an analysis of thirty Melbourne case studies', *The Australasian Journal of Construction Economics and Building*, vol 7, no 1, pp1–18

Lawson, N., Douglas, I., Garvin, S., McGrath, C., Manning, D. and Vetterlein, J. (2001) 'Recycling construction wastes – a UK perspective', *Environmental Management and Health*, vol 12, no 2, pp146–57

Lehmann, S. (2010) *The Principles of Green Urbanism: Transforming the City for Sustainability*, Earthscan, UK

Lingard, H., Gilbert, G. and Graham, P. (2001) 'Improving solid waste reduction and recycling performance using goal setting and feedback', *Construction Management and Economics*, vol 19, no 8, pp809–81

Love, P. E. D., Li, H., Irani, Z. and Holt, G. D. (2002) 'Re-thinking TQM: towards a framework for facilitating learning and change in construction organisations', *The TQM Magazine*, vol 12, no 2, pp107–16

Lu, W. and Yuan, H. (2011) 'A framework for understanding waste management studies in construction', *Waste Management*, vol 31, no 6, pp1252–60

McCabe, S. (2004) 'Using training and education to create culture change in construction: an exploration of the use of "Egan-inspired" initiatives in large contracting firms in the West Midlands', in R. Ellis and M. Bell (eds) *Proceedings of RICS COBRA 2004*, Construction and Building Research, Leeds, UK

McGeorge, D. and Palmer, A. (2002) *Construction Management: New Directions* (2nd edn), Blackwell Science, Oxford

Mathews, G. (1992) 'Barriers to value and competitive advantage in the UK property industry', Lynton plc

Mintzberg, H., Ahlstrand, B. and Lampel, J. (1998) *Strategy Safari: The Complete Guide Through the Wilds of Strategic Management*, Financial Times/Prentice Hall, London

Morgan, G. (1993) *Imaginization: The Art of Creative Management*, SAGE, Newbury Park, CA

Motwani, J. (2001) 'Critical factors and performance measures of TQM', *The TQM Magazine*, vol 13, no 4, pp292–300

Murray, R. (2002) *Zero Waste*, Greenpeace Environmental Trust, London

Newcombe, R., Langford, D. and Fellow, R. (1993) *Construction Management*, Vol 1, CIOB, UK

Oke, M., Allan, P., Goldsworthy, K. and Pickin, J. (2008) *Waste and Recycling in Australia*, Hyder Consulting Final Report for the Department of Environment, Water, Heritage and Arts (now called the Department of Sustainability, Environment, Water, Population and Communities), Commonwealth of Australia, Canberra, Australia

Olatunji, O. A., Sher, W. D. and Gu, N. (2010) 'Modelling outcomes of collaboration in building information modelling through gaming theory lenses', in I. Wallis, L. Bilan, M. Smith and A. S. Kazi (eds) *Sustainable Construction: Industrialised, Integrated, Intelligent*, I3CON handbook

Osmani, M., Glass, J. and Price, A. D. F. (2007) 'Architects' perspectives on construction waste reduction by design', *Waste Management*, vol 28, no 7, pp1147–58

Poon, C. S. (2007) 'Reducing construction waste', *Waste Management*, vol 27, no, 12, pp1715–16

Poon, C. S. and Chan, D. (2007) 'Effects of contaminants on the properties of concrete paving blocks prepared with recycled concrete aggregates', *Construction and Building Materials*, vol 21, no 1, pp164–75

Pullen, S. (2010a) 'An analysis of energy consumption in an Adelaide suburb with different retrofitting and redevelopment scenarios', *Urban Policy and Research*, vol 28, no 2, pp161–80

Pullen, S. (2010b) 'Recycling of materials to reduce embodied energy consumption in the redevelopment of urban areas', *Proceedings of 44th Annual Conference of the Australian and New Zealand Architectural Science Association*, Unitec Institute of Technology, New Zealand

Pullen, S., Zillante, G., Arman, M., Wilson, L., Zuo, J. and Chileshe, N. (2009) 'Ecocents living: affordable and sustainable housing for South Australia', Institute for Sustainable Systems and Technologies, University of South Australia, www.sapo.org.au/pub/pub16024.html

Rao, A., Jha, K. N. and Misra, S. (2007) 'Use of aggregates from recycled construction and demolition wastes in concrete', *Resources, Conservation and Recycling*, vol 50, no 1, pp7–81

Roper, W. E. (2006) 'Strategies for building material reuse and recycle', *International Journal of Environmental Technology and Management*, vol 6, no 3/4, pp313–45

Saunders, J. and Wynn, P. (2004) 'Attitudes towards waste minimisation amongst labour only sub-contractors', *Structural Survey*, vol 22, no 3, pp148–55

Schiller, G. (2007) 'Urban infrastructure: challenges for resource efficiency in the building stock', *Building Research and Information*, vol 35, no 4, pp399–411

Shen, L. Y., Tam, V. W. Y., Tam, C. M. and Drew, D. (2004) 'Mapping approach for examining waste management on construction sites', *Journal of Construction Engineering Management*, vol 130, no 4, pp472–81

Strategic Forum for Construction (SFfC) (2005–6a) Accelerating Change, www.strategicforum.org.uk, accessed 2 February 2011

Strategic Forum for Construction (SFfC) (2005–6b) 'Welcome to Strategic Forum for Construction', www.strategicforum.org.uk/targets.shtml, accessed 2 February 2011

Tam, V. W. Y., Tam, C. M., Zeng, S. X. and Ng, W. C. Y. (2007) 'Towards adoption of prefabrication in construction', *Building and Environment*, vol 42, no 10, pp3642–54

Tanikawa, H. and Hashimoto, S. (2009) 'Urban stock over time: spatial material stock analysis using 4d-GIS', *Building Research and Information*, vol 37, no 5, pp483–502

Teo, M. M. M. and Loosemore, M. (2001) 'A theory of waste of behaviour in the construction industry', *Construction Management and Economics*, vol 19, no 7, pp741–51

Teo, M. M. M., Loosemore, M., Masosszeky, M. and Karim, K. (2000) 'Operatives' attitudes towards waste on a construction project', *Annual Conference – ARCOM 2000*, vol 2, pp509–17

Treloar, G. J., Gupta, H., Love, P. E. D. and Nguyen, B. (2003) 'An analysis of factors influencing waste minimisation and use of recycled materials for the construction of residential buildings', *Management of Environmental Quality: An International Journal*, vol 14, no 1, pp134–45

Troy, P., Holloway, D., Pullen, S. and Bunker, R. (2003) 'Embodied and operational energy consumption in the city', *Urban Policy and Research*, vol 21, no 1, pp9–44

Wallbaum, H. and Buerkin, C. (2003) 'Concepts and instruments for sustainable construction sector', *UNEP Industry and Environment*, September, pp53–7

Wang, J. Y., Yuan, H. P., Kang, X. P. and Lu, W. S. (2010) 'Critical success factors for on-site sorting of construction waste: a China study', *Resources, Conservation and Recycling*, vol 54, no 11, pp931–6

Watson, S. J. (2003) 'The building life cycle: a conceptual aide for environmental design', in H. Simon (ed) *Proceedings of the 37th Australian and New Zealand Architectural Science Association Conference*

Wideman, R. M. (1986) 'The PMBOK report: PMI body of knowledge standard', *Project Management Journal*, vol 17, no 3, pp15–24

Wikipedia (2011) 'Zero waste', http://en.wikipedia.org/wiki/Zero_waste, accessed 2 February 2011

World Bank (2001) *Cultural Heritage and Development: A Framework for Action in the Middle East and North Africa*, Orientations in Development series, The International Bank for Reconstruction and Development

Worrall, L., Harris, K., Stewart, R., Thomas, A. and McDermott, P. (2010) 'Barriers to women in the UK construction industry', *Engineering, Construction and Architectural Management*, vol 17, no 3, pp268–81

Yan, H., Shen, Q. P., Fan, L. C. H., Wang, Y. W. and Zhang, L. (2010) 'Greenhouse gas emissions in building construction: a case study of One Peking in Hong Kong', *Building and Environment*, vol 45, no 4, pp949–55

Yuan, H., Shen, L. and Wang, J. (2011) 'Major obstacles to improving the performance of waste management in China's construction industry', *Facilities*, vol 29, no 5/6, pp224–42

Zero Waste SA (2005) *South Australia's Waste Strategy 2005–2010*

Zillante, G. (2007) 'The future of building surveying in Australia', PhD thesis, Deakin University, Victoria, Australia

Zillante, G., Pullen, S., Wilson, L., Davidson, K., Chileshe, N., Zuo, J. and Arman, M. (2010) 'Integrating affordable housing and sustainable housing: bridging two merit goods in Australia', in I. Wallis, L. Bilan, M. Smith and A. S. Kazi (eds) *Sustainable Construction: Industrialised, Integrated, Intelligent*, I3CON Handbook

Zillante, G. and Zuo, J. (2008) 'Managing waste – what can small construction firms do to improve their performance?', paper presented to the Australasian Universities Building Educators Association (AUBEA) Conference 2008, Unitec, New Zealand

Zuo, J. (2008) 'Project culture in the Australian construction industry: lessons for China', PhD thesis, University of South Australia, Adelaide, Australia

Part IV

Zero waste in cities, urban governance and material flows

Chapter 15

The metabolism of the city

Optimizing urban material flow through principles of zero waste and sustainable consumption

Steffen Lehmann

Summary

Beyond energy efficiency, there are now urgent challenges concerning the supply of resources, materials, food and water. After debating energy efficiency for the last decade, the focus has shifted to include further resources and material efficiency. This chapter reports the best practice of urban planning principles in regard to material flow, material recovery, adaptive reuse of entire building elements and components (including 'design for disassembly' and the prefabrication of modular building components), and other relevant strategies to implement zero waste by avoiding waste creation, reducing wasteful consumption and changing behaviour in the design and construction sectors. In this chapter, I touch on two important issues related to the rapid depletion of the world's natural resources: the wasteful construction sector and the education of architects and building users (both topics for further research). In the C&D sector, prefabricated multi-storey buildings for inner-city living can set new benchmarks for minimizing construction wastage and for modular on-site assembly. Today, the C&D sector is one of the main producers of waste; however, it does not engage enough with waste minimization, waste avoidance, reuse and/or recycling. In the area of education and research, it is still unclear how best to introduce a holistic understanding of these challenges and to teach practical and affordable solutions to architects, urban planners, industrial designers and others. How, therefore, should urban development and construction methods change and evolve to embed sustainability in the way we design, build, operate, maintain and renew and/or recycle cities? One of the findings of this chapter is that embedding zero waste requires strong industry leadership, new policies and effective education curricula, as well as raising awareness through refocusing research and educational agendas to bring about attitudinal change in regard to wasteful consumption.

Introduction

Since the Industrial Revolution, industrial production and urbanization have constantly increased, using massive amounts of materials, water and energy. The mass consumption of resources causes serious problems, such as global warming, material depletion and the generation of enormous waste. In this chapter, I will explore the notion of a sustainable urban metabolism and the concept of 'zero waste'. There is now a growing interest in understanding the complex interactions and feedbacks between urbanization, material consumption and the depletion of resources. The link between increasing urbanization and increased waste generation has been established for some time. The impact of urban form and density on resource consumption, on the other hand, is still not fully understood. The human population of the planet has increased fourfold over the last hundred years, while – in the same time period – material and energy use has increased tenfold (United Nations, 2010). The United Nations forecasts that the world's urban population will increase by 2.7 billion people between 2010 and 2050. But how can the urbanization of our planet continue, given the currently devastating effect it has?

The pace of urbanization is increasing, and cities face new challenges from the effects of human activity on global systems, which in turn impact on urban life. Climate change is among the most significant of these challenges. It is apparent that cities are the main consumers of resources, and, hence, they are the main sources of the GHG emissions associated with climate change. A holistic understanding and integrated approaches to design, planning and urban management are essential for the effective resolution of urban problems. In most countries, cities keep expanding as their populations grow. It is particularly important to include the peri-urban areas and suburbs in any research and analysis, as they represent the areas of interaction between the urban and rural contexts, where fertile agricultural land is gradually lost.

Given our wasteful patterns of urban development and consumption, it is time to rethink development practice and urban form (Satterthwaite, 2009). But, in order to formulate better urban responses, we require a full awareness of the reasons for, and results of, the current global changes, which mainly occur through:

- demographic changes;
- growing social disparities (especially between north and south, rural and urban populations);
- continuing urbanization, with rapidly expanding cities;
- growing demand for resources (materials, energy, water, food);
- loss of biodiversity and habitat; and
- continuing production methods of industry and agriculture that are too material and energy intensive and therefore unsustainable.

Beyond energy efficiency, there are now urgent challenges around the supply of resources, materials, food and water. After debating energy efficiency for the last two decades, the focus has shifted to include resource and material efficiency (Chalmin and Gaillochet, 2009). Waste was once seen as a burden on our industries and communities; however, shifting attitudes and a better understanding of the reasons for the depletion of resources have led to the identification of waste as a valuable resource (Jackson, 1996). We must now find responsible ways to collect, separate, manage and recover waste. In particular, over the last decade, the holistic concept of a 'zero-waste' life cycle has emerged. This is a cultural shift, a new way of thinking about the age-old problem of waste and the economic obsession with endless growth and consumption.

Complex issues, such as health and the environment, or lifestyles and consumption, are emerging on a global scale in a way that requires approaches that transcend the traditional boundaries between disciplines. In this multidisciplinary context, the relationship between efficiency and effectiveness is not always clear: high efficiency is not equal to high effectiveness, while recovery offers another dimension to their relationship. Today, it is increasingly understood that, just as we now discuss energy efficiency, we also need to discuss resource effectiveness and resource recovery. This includes waste minimization strategies and the concept of 'designing waste out of processes and products' (as advocated, for instance, in South Australia's *Draft Waste Strategy 2010–2015*, Zero Waste SA, 2010).

Every municipality or company can take immediate action to identify its own particular solutions. Separating recyclable materials, such as paper, cardboard, timber, metals, plastics and glass bottles, and consolidating all identified waste categories into one collection point, are some basic measures. However, a waste-stream analysis will always have to be conducted at an early stage, which will involve taking an inventory of the entire waste composition, measuring the volumes of different material categories and its origin, contamination level and destination. A database will then need to be created to enable the municipality to track all waste types and to cross-reference by facility type, so that the amount and type of waste each facility, district or precinct generates can be identified, thus pinpointing where reductions can most easily occur.

The increasing problem of waste as population and consumption increase and materials become scarce

How to change behaviour to avoid waste and reduce consumption

For centuries, waste was regarded as 'pollution' that had to be hidden and buried as landfill. Today, the concept of 'zero waste' directly challenges the common assumption that waste is unavoidable and has no value, by focusing on waste as a 'misallocated resource' (Lehmann, 2010) that should be recovered. It also focuses on the avoidance of waste creation in the first place (e.g. reducing construction waste). That Australia is a wasteful nation is illustrated by the fact that over 40 per cent of our daily food is thrown out and wasted (EPA, 2009). Recent research found that family size, socio-economic status and household income are the primary determinants of household waste, while the effect of environmental awareness on waste-generation behaviour is surprisingly small (EPA, 2009; Sharp, 2010).

This, of course, raises much wider social questions of attitude and behaviour, and our wastefulness has further implications for future urban development (von Weizaecker et al, 1997). How will we design, build, operate, maintain and renew/recycle cities in the future? What role will materials play in the 'city of tomorrow'? How can we increase our focus on more effective environmental education for waste avoidance? And how can we engage sustainable urban-development principles and zero-waste thinking? These are some of the topics discussed in this chapter.

Behaviour change has frequently been listed as the number one hurdle to a more energy- and material-efficient, low-carbon future. If we could only plan better cities and design better buildings, which needed less energy, water, materials and other resources, thus generating less waste, and which facilitated behaviour change simply through their design; for instance, making people less dependent on air conditioning and car driving. We all know there are examples where changes in attitudes and behaviour were mobilized, and consumption was successfully reduced. There are different mechanisms that can be applied to change behaviour and to ensure that more sustainable design solutions are used. Some examples of successful behaviour change initiatives follow:

Behaviour change example 1: make people use bikes instead of cars

As master-planner for the city of Taree, Australia, I devised a concept that got people out of their cars and made them use bikes more frequently: every new resident of the city's waterfront development received a free bike when they moved in, to encourage these new residents to use the bike paths.

Behaviour change example 2: make people fit by motivating them to use the staircase instead of the elevator or escalators

The interactive installation at a staircase in Tokyo's subway station plays music as people walk up and down the stairs.

Behaviour change example 3: boost the use of public transport and clean up the city at the same time.

In Curitiba, Brazil, urban planner Jaime Lerner came up with the idea of giving people free bus tickets and locally produced vegetables when they collected waste and litter from the city's streets; they could trade their recycling credits according to the amount of waste they had collected. The project filled the buses, reduced private-car use, cleaned the city and improved the nutrition of citizens all at the same time.

Behaviour change example 4: store private cars further away than stops for free-looping buses and trams

In Vauban's green district, in Germany, cars are parked at the fringe of the district in so-called 'solar garages', which makes people use more public transport (despite owning a car) and creates residential streets with less traffic, where children can play more safely.

Behaviour change example 5: reduce the need for air conditioning and artificial lighting of workplaces

At the new Council House CH2 building in Melbourne, staff members have shown significantly higher productivity and have taken less sick leave, now that they can individually control their offices' ventilation through operable windows and more natural light. A better and healthier alternative both saves energy and makes employees happier.

Behaviour change example 6: reduce consumption of potable water

At Mawson Lakes, a new master-planned district in Adelaide, South Australia, people save drinking water by using greywater for irrigating their gardens, flushing toilets and washing cars. Over 75 per cent of water usage does not require the high quality of potable water.

Behaviour change example 7: avoid waste creation in offices

Research shows that, when large bins are replaced with smaller ones, less paper waste is created, as office workers are less likely to print out their emails unnecessarily. Some companies have gone so far as to install a display system that shows how much electricity and water is being consumed and how much waste created, and compares the energy use to what is being produced from rooftop solar panels. Sometimes, the individual energy use of company departments is monitored, and departments are encouraged to compete to lower their energy use (including public shaming of departments who are the most wasteful and use more electricity than others).

Behaviour change example 8: ban plastic bags

Government legislation banning free plastic bags in supermarkets in South Australia significantly raised the number of shoppers recycling their shopping bags.

Behaviour change example 9: making public space safer

In Cali, Colombia, a recycling programme was started in low-income neighbourhoods that employed former street toughs as garbage collectors and cleaners of parks and streets; they received training as micro entrepreneurs, which created jobs and reduced street violence.

Behaviour change example 10: taking collective action for waste minimization

In Surat, a textile-industry centre in western India, a voluntary action programme was initiated, promoting waste minimization in manuals and demonstration projects, which led to the installation of an effluent water reuse plant and a reduction of pollution by 80 per cent.

All these initiatives are examples of the various benefits, such as waste prevention and reduced consumption, of behaviour change. Behaviour-change mechanisms differ considerably between developed and developing countries, as well as within the group of developing countries.

It is obvious that the growth of the economy cannot continue endlessly (a fact already pointed out by the Club of Rome, 1972). Our increasing affluence allows us to accumulate massive amounts of stuff, and we build increasingly larger dwellings to store it. So, the core question is how best to change behaviour and shift attitudes to reduce consumption (therefore avoiding the creation of waste in the first place). How do we convince society to consume less? Education programmes aimed at all levels of schooling have proven to be effective. Public education aimed at 'zero-waste' participation is surely a key to success. Changing behaviour is easier in smaller towns, but is more difficult in large cities. Nevertheless, the city of Vancouver in Canada, for instance, has started to implement strategies: Metro Vancouver has plans to ban all compostable organics allowed in residential green bins from disposal to landfills and all forms of waste-to-energy except anaerobic digestion by 2015. As well as removing organics from the waste stream, Vancouver examines other opportunities for waste diversion and minimization, including:

- implementing an e-waste product stewardship scheme;
- rolling-out strategies to promote behavioural change and recycling in the community;
- encouraging businesses to recycle and improve their waste practices.

Most experts agree that the carbon tax under discussion in Australia (in 2011) is unlikely to have any significant effect on the use of energy on its own. The experience in Europe shows that simply putting a price on carbon has had little influence on behaviour. Education to raise awareness is essential, but equally important is that the rules and benefits of waste separation and recycling are well explained. This suggests that the real problem is not technology, but acceptance and behaviour change. What is needed is social innovation and incentives, rather than simply focusing on technological innovation. For instance, the connection between waste policies and emission reductions is not always well understood. What then are the main barriers to zero waste?

- short-term thinking of producers and consumers;
- lack of incentives and technical advice;
- lack of consistency in legislation across the states;
- procurement vs sustainability: the attitude that the cheapest offer gets commissioned;
- lack of community willingness to pay.

Zero waste also includes making consumers responsible for their participation in recycling schemes. A recent survey showed that '83 per cent of Australians wanted a national ban on non-biodegradable plastic bags, while 79 per cent wanted electronic waste (e-waste) to be legally barred from landfills' (Zero Waste SA, 2010). Cities will always be a place of waste production, but there are possibilities that would help them achieve zero waste, whether the waste is recycled, reused or composted (using organic waste for biomass). The Masdar City project in the United Arab Emirates is a good example of a zero-waste city, as is the large Japanese city of Yokohama, which reduced its waste by 39 per cent between 2001 and 2007, despite the city growing by 165,000 people during this period. Yokohama's citizens reached their goal by raising public awareness about wasteful consumption and through the active participation of individuals and businesses. In fact, Japanese cities are most frequently cited when it comes to world's best practice in recycling and waste separation. In Australia, the Zero Waste SA initiative by the South Australian government is highly commendable, achieving significant participation levels.

Germany is among the world's leaders in waste-stream management. When it comes to garbage, the Germans are indeed nation of gatherers and sorters. A news report from March 2011 describes the German approach:

In most cities, there are several coloured garbage cans to choose from: a yellow one for packaging, a blue one for paper, two separate ones for different colours of glass, a brown one for plant waste and a black one for the little that is left over. An orange one for electronics waste is now being introduced in several cities. Astonishingly, only 20 per cent of German garbage ends up in the wrong containers.

(Fleischhauer et al, 2011)

Given the complexity of the waste separation required, this is an impressive performance by German households. Once the rubbish is collected, the sorting continues: automated waste separation with infrared sensors discerns six different types of plastic. But does all the garbage really get recycled? Some of the plastic is recycled and transformed into granules before producing flowerpots. A recent study showed, however, that more than

Figures 15.1 Photos of collection terminals.

These automated waste systems (13,000 units) in Stockholm's green district Hammarby-Sjoestad triggered a positive behaviour change, where the amount of household waste generated was reduced by over 15 per cent per household from 2005 to 2010, and recycling rates rose (90 per cent diversion from landfill was achieved; Sweden still uses incineration for district heating). New technological solutions of automated underground waste collection that can be integrated into residential environments have been developed for new sustainable urban developments: underground waste disposal and transportation systems are easy to use and have become a critical part of green districts (the city of Barcelona has also introduced it). There are different refuse chutes, underground block-based recycling rooms and area-based waste collection points, which makes recycling and the segregation of waste at the source easier for residents. Collection points are carefully located next to bike sheds, easily accessible and clearly visible. They use an airborne pipe system with a vacuum pump. This system of source separation is highly efficient, and the overall transportation of waste is reduced. All combustible waste is converted into district heating and electricity, and the heat from treated wastewater is also converted into district heating. Organic waste is digested into bio solids and used as fertilizer (nutrients and energy contained in the food waste is recovered). All buses in Hammarby-Sjoestad run on biogas.

Images courtesy of Envac Systems, 2010

half the yoghurt cups, plastic juice bottles and packaging foils are incinerated in plants that supply district heating or electricity. Plastic burns well owing to the high quantity of oil in plastics. Under German environmental law, this is legal, as only 36 per cent of plastic rubbish has to be recycled. Today, such plastic burning facilities are everywhere in Germany: municipalities across the country built them during the 1990s in response to a ban on storing garbage in landfills. Indeed, now there are far too many of them, and there is a constant shortage of burnable waste. The result is that firms are buying up as much plastic waste as they can get, even importing it – hardly a contribution to environmental sustainability. The introduction of a deposit on disposable cans and plastic bottles in 2003 by the German government was intended to discourage people from buying them. But the opposite has happened. In 2003, the market share of reusable bottles was 64 per cent. The German government is lobbying the European Union (EU) to require all bottles to be labelled more clearly as reusable or disposable. But it's not an easy problem to solve, because most EU countries do not have a system of paying deposits on disposable bottles.

The link between waste and urbanization

Constantly growing amounts of waste – what can be done?

Global population growth is expected to stabilize in 2050 at around 9 billion human beings (UN-Habitat, 2010b). Current population growth is far from being the main driver of recent economic expansion and the increased consumption of materials, water, fossil fuels and resources. Emerging countries catching up with the standard of living of more advanced economies are, in fact, an even more powerful factor. Although sheer numbers of people have an impact, as incomes rise, increased consumption will stress the planet's natural resources more than population growth.

As a consequence of this 'catching up', waste is accumulating in landfills, rivers and the oceans. In recent years, our oceans have devolved into vast garbage dumps. Thousands of tonnes of waste are thrown into the sea each year, endangering humans and wildlife. As the world's oceans are so massive, few people seem to have a problem with dumping waste into them. However, most plastics degrade at a very slow rate, and huge amounts of them are sloshing around in our oceans. Wildlife consumes small pieces, causing many of them to die, as the plastics are full of poisons. Some plastic products take up to 200 years to degrade. Every year, around 250 million tonnes of plastic products are produced, and much of this produce ends up in the oceans. The 'great Pacific garbage patch' is half the size of Europe, and, in the Atlantic, huge amounts of plastic garbage have recently been discovered (SEA, 2010), the highest concentration being found close to Caribbean islands, with over 200,000 plastic pieces per square kilometre. In the North and Baltic seas, although dumping in them has been illegal for over two decades, the amount of waste found in them has not improved. It is estimated that each year 20,000 tonnes of waste finds its way into the North Sea, primarily from ships and the fishing industry (UN, 2010). Experts warn that we have reached a point where it has become dangerous for humans to consume seafood. Large amounts of waste discharged into the sea and the rising temperature of the oceans create a bacterial bloom, which, combined with a drop of the pH level of the water, kills off the plankton, which is an essential part of the oceans' food chain.

Another big problem concerns the throw-away plastic water bottles made of PET, not only because they significantly contribute to waste creation and carbon dioxide emissions from transporting drinking water around the globe, but also because they release chemicals suspected of being harmful to humans into the water. Together with the largest oil spill in human history, the devastating oil spill in the Gulf of Mexico in 2010, it shows how advanced humanity's destruction of entire ecosystems in the oceans has become.

Given these conditions, the international community has been pushing for four decades for massive bureaucratic efforts aimed at clearing the oceans of waste. In 1973, the United Nations sponsored a pact to protect the oceans from dumping, and, in 2001, the European Union established directives that forbade any dumping of maritime waste into the ocean while in port. However, such directives have been ineffective, and many experts agree that laws and international efforts aimed at protecting the oceans have failed across the board.

With the constant increase in the world's economic activity, there has been a large increase in the amount of solid waste produced per head of population. The waste mix (industrial and urban) has become ever more complex, often containing large amounts of toxic chemicals. The first aim of a sustainable future is to avoid the creation of waste and to select materials and products based on their embodied energy, on their life-cycle assessment and supply-chain analysis. This needs to be understood holistically. Transportation of input materials, as well as the transportation of the final product to consumers (or to the construction site), is a common contributor to GHG emissions. The way in which a product uses resources such as water and electricity influences its environmental impact, while its durability determines how soon it must enter the waste stream. Care needs to be taken in the original selection of input materials, and that the type of assembly used influences end-of-life disposal options, such as ease of recyclability or take-back agreements with the manufacturer. With a huge amount of waste still going to landfill, drastic action is required in urban planning to develop intelligent circular metabolisms for retrofitting districts, and waste collection and treatment systems that will eliminate the need for landfills. Even so, recycling is only halfway up the waste hierarchy: the greenhouse gains lying in the upper half (waste avoidance and reduction) are, largely, yet to be tapped. The focus of attention needs now to expand from the downstream of the materials cycle, from a post-consumer stage, to include the upstream, pre-consumer stage and behavioural change (see Figures 15.2a and 15.2b and Figure 15.3). Figure 15.4 illustrates how future buildings and districts will produce energy and even food.

Limits of growth: understanding waste as a resource and part of a closed-cycle urban ecology

In recent years, researchers have increasingly articulated the need for more sustainable living choices and behavioural change. The estimated world waste production is now around 4 billion tonnes of waste per annum, of which only around 20 per cent is currently recovered or recycled (Chalmin and Gaillochet, 2009). Globally, waste management has emerged as one of the biggest challenges, and it is time that we took a fresh look at how we can better manage the material and waste streams of cities and urban development.

NOW: LINEAR METABOLISM

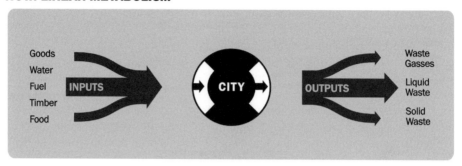

FUTURE: CIRCULAR METABOLISM

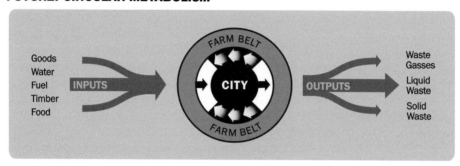

Figure 15.2a The flow of natural resources into cities and the waste produced (recovering waste streams) represents one of the biggest challenges to urban sustainability.

Circular, looping metabolisms are more sustainable than linear ones. This also has economic advantages. Recycling will continue to be an essential part of responsible materials management, and the greater the shift from a 'river' economy (linear throughput of materials: import–use–collect–transport–dispose) towards a 'lake' economy (stock of continuously circulating materials), the greater are both the material gains and greenhouse-gas reductions.

Source: the author, after Girardet, 1999, republished in Rogers and Power, 2000

The issue of our city's ever-growing waste production is of particular significance if we comprehend the city as a living ecosystem with closed-loop management cycles (see Figure 15.2a).

Aiming for zero waste has some serious implications. It is obvious that we must focus, not merely on waste recycling, but also on waste prevention, following the waste-hierarchy diagram (see Figure 15.3). We must give prevention (waste avoidance) more priority; as the saying goes: 'An ounce of prevention is worth a pound of recycling.' Avoidance is the priority, followed by reuse, recycling and 'waste engineering' (up-scaling), to minimize the amount that goes to waste incineration.

A particular concern is the disposal of electrical and electronic equipment, known as 'e-waste'. Of about 16.8 million televisions and computers that reached the end of their useful life in Australia in 2008 and 2009, less than 10 per cent were recycled. Most of the highly toxic e-waste still goes into landfills, threatening ground water and soil quality,

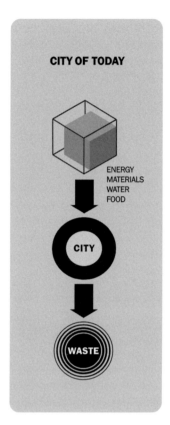
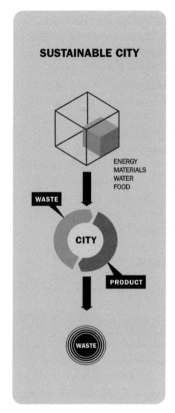

Figure 15.2b The input and output of cities.

This diagram compares the 'conventional' city (high material input, waste-intensive industries) on the left with the more sustainable city (associated with waste minimization, recycling, reuse and resource reclamation) on the right. Increased consumption in emerging cities will stress the planet's natural resources more than population growth.

Source: the author, after Whalley, 2010

and an unknown proportion is shipped overseas (legally and illegally), mainly to China, leading to major environmental problems in the importing countries. About 37 million computers, 17 million televisions and 56 million mobile phones have already been buried in landfills around Australia (data: 2009). This waste contains high levels of mercury and other toxic materials common to electronic goods, such as lead, arsenic and bromide. Several countries are actively pushing for industry-led schemes for collecting and recycling televisions, printers and computers, known as extended producer responsibility (EPR) and product stewardship. In addition, we must expect that the amount of e-waste created in the developing world will dramatically increase over the next decade (Walls, 2006; Easton, 2010).

Discharges are a threat to soil and groundwater, and methane gas discharges (mainly from organic waste in landfill) are a threat in the atmosphere. In the meantime, many

MOST PREFERABLE

LEAST PREFERABLE

Figure 15.3 The waste-hierarchy diagram illustrates how waste avoidance is preferred, above reuse and recycling.

Disposal in landfill represents the lowest level of the waste hierarchy. On the municipality level, a more strategic charging structure (levies) for waste disposal can accelerate sustainable waste management and reward residents who are separating their waste.

Source: diagram by the author, 2008

large cities are producing astronomical amounts of waste daily and are running out of landfill space. Incineration of waste has gone out of fashion, as it has the disadvantage that it releases poisonous substances, such as dioxins and toxic ash, into the environment. Furthermore, burning waste with very high embodied energy is generally not an efficient way of dealing with resources. Environmental groups have successfully prevented the construction of new waste incinerators around the world. Linear systems (e.g. burning waste) have to be replaced with circular systems, which take nature as their model. Much more appropriate is a combination of recycling and composting. Today, recycling 50–60 per cent of all waste has become an achievable standard figure for many cities. The Brazilian city of Curitiba, for example, has managed to recycle over 70 per cent of its waste since 2000; and the city of San Francisco achieved a 77 per cent diversion rate from landfill in 2010.

Organic waste is playing an increasingly important role. The small rural Austrian town of Guessing, for instance, activates the biomass from its agricultural waste and has reached energy autonomy by composting and using the resultant bio-energy to generate its power. The consensus of the literature is that a recommended split for a city where no waste goes to landfill would be:

Recycling and reusing	min. 60%
Composting of organic waste	20–30%
Incineration of residual waste (waste-to-energy) (only what cannot be recycled)	max. 10%

Figure 15.4 Urban farming in the 'Carrot City', designed to use as few resources as possible.

With finite cropland to feed a growing global population, concepts are now being developed that will build vertical farms, where buildings' roofs and facades become sites for urban agriculture and hydroponics. Rotating hydroponic-farming systems give the plants the precise amount of light and nutrients they need, while vertical stacking allows the use of far less water than conventional farming.

Project illustration: 'Carrot City', building design proposal for Dallas with integrated urban farming; courtesy MOV + Data, Lisbon, Portugal, March, 2009

Steel is by far the most recycled material worldwide (it has the longest 'residence time'). However, recent research from Veolia Research Group (Grosse, 2010) shows that recycling in itself is inefficient in solving the problem, as it does not deliver the necessary 'decoupling' of economic development from the depletion of non-renewable raw materials. Grosse and others argue that 'the depletion of the natural resource of raw material is inevitable when its global consumption by the economy grows by more than 1 per cent per annum. The only effect of recycling is that the curve is delayed' (Grosse, 2010, p28). There is evidence that recycling can delay the depletion of virgin raw materials for only a few decades at best. Research shows that recycling rates above 80 per cent are needed for a significant slowdown of the depletion of natural resources. This means that the actual role of recycling in protecting resources is not significant for those non-renewable resources whose consumption tends to grow by above 1 per cent per year.

Even though recycling is an important component of waste reduction, sustainable-development policies cannot rely on it alone. Policies need to aim at reducing the consumption of each non-renewable raw material, so that the annual growth rate remains under 1 per cent. Decoupling economic development from materiality seems to be the only long-term solution. The objective is not to reduce the amount of waste in general, but, rather, to encourage a reduction in the quantities of materials used to make the products that will later become waste.

A closed-cycle urban economy will deliver a series of additional advantages:

- It avoids waste being generated in the first place (and therefore reduces CO_2 emissions).
- It creates closed-loop eco-economies and urban ecosystems with greencollar jobs.
- It helps transform industries towards a better use of resources and non-polluting (non-toxic), cleaner production processes, and extends producer responsibility.
- It delivers economic benefits through more efficient use of resources.
- It supports research into durable, local goods and products that encourage reuse.
- It advocates 'green purchasing' and a product stewardship framework.

Figure 15.2a illustrates the concept of a circular (looping) urban metabolism: the current production–consumption system is typically linear (as in a pipeline) and extends from manufacturing through use to end of life, followed by either recycling or landfill. The idea that this system must be reconfigured in order to promote a series of closed loops, whereby all material and products are reused or recovered, is not new and has been raised many times; however, it has not been adapted by the construction sector.

Figure 15.5a Organics recycling process, Adelaide, South Australia.

This is an important way to return nutrients back to the soil, and there are new process improvements on a massive scale. Metropolitan green organics are collected through council curbside and industrial collections, as well as food organics (food scraps) from hotels, restaurants and supermarkets. Composting and mulching transform the material into a range of high-quality compost, mulch, fertilizer and soil products, to be returned to gardens and parklands.

Photo by the author, Jeffries Plant in Adelaide, South Australia, 2010

Figures 15.5b and c Photos of a renewable energy plant.

This wood-waste-to-energy facility in Ludwigsburg, near Stuttgart (Germany, built 2009–10), is one of Europe's most modern waste-to-energy facilities. In the first stage, the plant provides electricity, district heating and hot water for over 5,000 households and three public pools in the city (output 14.6MW, using an organic-rankine-cycle (ORC) plant). The plant delivers around 5 per cent of the city's heating requirements and 3 per cent of its electricity needs. Much of the waste material (42,000t p.a.) comes as cut-offs and clippings from street greenery, gardens and public spaces. Total investment was €16 million; the plant reduces CO_2 emissions by 18,000t per year.

Photos by the author, 2010

> Waste is nutrients. Waste is precious. We should learn from Nature:
>
> Nature doesn't know 'waste'. In Nature, one species' waste is another species' resource.
>
> (Braungart and McDonough, 2002)

Zero waste and closed-loop thinking in the construction sector

The greatest opportunity to recover resources is probably in the C&D sector, and there is growing interest from architects and planners in zero-waste concepts. One of the main drivers of how we use energy and water is material flow and the embodied energy in materials. Cities are places where all of these concepts come together and can be embedded into practice. Redesigning urban systems with zero waste and material flow in mind will help to transform existing cities and upgrade their recycling infrastructure in low-to-no carbon urban districts. It is time for us to rethink prefabrication and 'design for disassembly', to build resilience into urban systems. This will change the way we design, build and operate city districts in the future. We must remember that zero waste is more complicated than it first seems, and that we still have a long way to go to get from zero emissions to zero waste in the construction sector. For example, facade systems made of composite materials create recycling and resource-recovery problems. No debris should go to landfill. Concrete companies should use sustainable, recycled aggregates. Concrete was previously regarded as difficult to recycle, as closed-loop recycling for concrete structures is expensive. But concrete-related waste is now increasingly used as recycled aggregate (RA) for new concrete structures, and intensive research is being carried out in Japan and China on new concrete-recycling methods. While construction elements in timber and steel are relatively easy to reuse, architects need to focus on the recovery and minimization of off-cuts, which would help create a new market for recovered building by-products made from off-cuts.

Urban planners frequently ask: what is the best scale for the introduction of 'zero waste'? The city district as a unit appears to be a good and effective scale. It means rejoining the urban with the rural community, and therefore neighbourhood and precinct planning must consider both the climate crisis and material scarcity. For instance, planning better cities requires that composting facilities and recycling centres are in close proximity to avoid transporting materials over long distances. Reducing energy embodied in construction materials is an important strategy for mitigating our fossil-fuel dependency. Keeping the existing building stock is very important, as the most sustainable building is likely to be the one that already exists (based on its embodied energy, materials and life-cycle considerations). Retrofitting existing districts is, therefore, essential. 'Today, no other sector of industry uses more materials, produces more waste and contributes less to recycling than the construction sector' (EPA, 2009).

'Design for disassembly' creates the possibility of reusing entire building components in a future project, possibly twenty or thirty years after the original building's construction. It means deliberately enabling 'chains of reuse' in the design, and using lightweight structures with less embodied energy, as well as employing modular prefabrication. Recycling resources that have already entered the human economy uses much less energy than mining and manufacturing virgin materials from scratch.

For example, there is a 95 per cent energy saving when using secondary (recycled) aluminium; 85 per cent for copper; 80 per cent for plastics; 74 per cent for steel; and 64 per cent for paper (Fischer-Kowalski, 1998). Through reuse and recycling, the energy embodied in waste products is retained, thereby slowing down the potential for climate change. If burned in incinerators, this embodied energy would be lost forever. It becomes obvious that all future eco-cities will have to integrate existing structures and buildings for adaptive reuse into their master planning.

Although the worldwide international average for daily waste generation is about 1–1.5kg per capita, countries such as Kuwait and the United Arab Emirates top the list, generating an average of over 3.5kg of waste per person per day (in comparison, the average Australian resident dumps 1.1t of solid waste per year, approximately 3kg per day). According to the 'polluter pays' principle, policies need to penalize those who generate large amounts of waste. Collecting, sorting and treating waste incur huge costs, and so the focus has to be on avoiding and minimizing waste creation in the first place: in the office, in industry, in households, at universities, in restaurant kitchens. Waste-wood-to-energy has frequently become an important component of energy concepts for city districts, as Figure 15.5 shows. Improved waste management and recycling schemes have greatly reduced the volume of waste being 'land-filled'. Waste segregation and recycling also have substantial economic benefits and create new jobs.

Re-using building components and integrating existing buildings (instead of demolition) is a basic principle of any eco-city and eco-building project.

(Lehmann, 2008)

Seeing waste as a resource: solutions in the areas of construction, manufacturing, packaging and composting

Changing manufacturing and packaging processes towards life-cycle-oriented practices

The emerging green economy is a sustainable materials economy based on principles of industrial ecology. New agreements with industry have to be made to reduce waste from packaging dramatically. On the way towards a zero-waste economy, manufacturers will increasingly be made responsible for the entire life cycle of their products, including their recyclability, through an EPR policy. Luckily, many companies are now doing extraordinary things in the area of recycling and are prolonging the life cycle of their products. For instance, the Ohio-based firm Weisenbach Recycled Products, a manufacturer of consumer goods made from recycled materials, holds numerous patents on recycling, awareness and pollution-prevention products. It is both a specialty printing firm and an innovative recycler of waste and scrap, repurposing and 'up-cycling' materials such as plastic caps, glass bottles and circuit boards into over 600 promotional items and retail consumer products. According to the company's president, Dan Weisenbach, there has been a changing perception in the business world, where you are more valued if your company is a 'certified green business':

> Even though conservation has been a core principle in our culture since we started, we believe it is important that we take a step to formalize our commitment to sustainable business. The competitive landscape has shifted and it is important for a company to have a history of environmental leadership and integrity. Choosing to voluntarily document all our efforts in an annual sustainability report is a demonstration of this commitment. We have moved past the bigger is better era. People want to do business with companies they can relate to and who share their values.
>
> (Dan Weisenbach, personal communication, 2010)

For centuries, waste was regarded as pollution that had to be collected, hidden and buried. Today, waste is no longer seen as something to be disposed of, but as a resource to be recycled and reused. It is clear that we need to close the material cycle loop by transforming waste into a material resource. Over the next decades, the earth will be under increasing pressure from population growth, continuing urbanization and shortages of food, water, resources and materials. Waste management, optimizing waste streams and material flows are some of the major challenges for sustainable urban development. There is a growing consensus that waste should be regarded as a 'valuable resource and as nutrition' (Braungart and McDonough, 2002; *Recycling International*, 2008). McDonough and Braungart point out that the practice of dumping waste into landfill is a sign of a 'failure to design recyclable, sustainable products and processes' (2002, quoted after Mallgrave, 2008, p597). All eco-cities have to embed zero-waste concepts as part of their holistic, circular approach to material flows (see Figure 15.2b).

> In closed-loop systems, a high proportion of energy and materials will need to be provided from reused waste, and water from wastewater. We can now move the focus to waste avoidance, behavioural change and waste reduction.
>
> (Walls, 2006)

The manufacturing industry plays an important role in the transition to more sustainable cities. 'Industrial ecology' is a vision of industrial organization that applies the lessons of natural ecosystems to environmental management, where wastes from one process become inputs and opportunities for another (Robins and Kumar, 1999). An 'extended responsibility' means taking a whole life-cycle approach to manufacturing and trade, where producers and retailers adopt an extended sense of responsibility for the social and environmental impacts of their products from 'cradle to grave', by ensuring that: raw materials (virgin materials) are sustainably sourced, there is zero pollution during manufacture, and there are programmes for efficient consumption and recycling after use.

EPR places the responsibility for the future of an item of waste on the initial producer of that product (instead of on the last owner, as in traditional segmentation) (Linacre, 2007; Zero Waste SA, 2009). This leads to the practice whereby an increasing number of manufacturers include in the sale of goods a service for the future recovery and processing of the product at the end of its useful life (a 'take-back' agreement).

Introducing product stewardship: consumption decisions and household practices

There is a clear need for designers to focus more attention on the throughput of material goods consumed in our everyday life, rather than just the end-use energy consumption (Hobson, 2003; Tonkinwise, 2005; Lane et al, 2009). Product stewardship refers to the responsible management of manufactured goods and materials. On the production side, product and industrial designers are critical for stewardship models, such as EPR, that go beyond materials recycling; however, until now, design issues have not figured strongly in product-stewardship schemes, and there is not enough attention to product stewardship of new goods and their disposal at the end of use.

Drawing on social practice theory (Schatzki, 2003; Barr and Gilg, 2006), consumption within the household can be explained as the outcome of the relations between household routines and the surrounding material systems of provision. For product/industrial designers, social practice is a relatively new area of study, and practice-oriented design is only slowly moving beyond the tradition of designers simply focusing on products in isolation and instead acknowledging that 'material artefacts themselves configure the needs and practices of those who use them' (Shove et al, 2007).

Achieving net reduction in material and energy flows implies changes in design and household practices and the introduction of product-stewardship models. Current household practices around the acquisition, use and disposal of common household furnishings and electronic goods depend largely on household type and urban context, including house size and distance to public transport. Research has established that household practices and consumption vary across households and their urban contexts (e.g. suburban dwelling versus inner-city apartment) (Dey et al, 2007; Perkins et al, 2009). Products themselves place constraints on how householders may exercise steward-ship responsibilities, which indicates that household decisions concerning product stewardship, acquisition and divestment are influenced by a range of factors, including the physical spaces of the home, issues of wealth, social status and life stage, cultural values and the habits people establish over time. There is a need for more research into the question of how product stewardship can be extended through new product design in order to explicitly include household consumers' acquisition and better use of products, as well as end-of-life disposal options.

Unfortunately, the manufacturing industry is still lagging behind: one study suggests that almost half of UK companies have no plans for waste minimization and do not keep track of the costs of waste generation, and so generally underestimate the costs of waste management and overestimate the costs of minimization (Jackson, 1996).

Changing behaviour and transforming industries

The scarcity of raw materials, metals and resources

Using fewer materials and better exploiting the value of waste

Energy cost is not limited to heating or cooling energy or lighting energy; it is also related to all the material flows relevant to buildings. For instance, waste from the production of construction materials and components can be much greater than all other waste streams (Jackson, 1996). To make it easier for architects and planners to specify materials according to their impact (including impacts caused by material extraction, or waste creation from the production process), information on materials and components needs to be readily available. In contrast to the Club of Rome's warning in 1972, today, the 'limits to growth' are defined by climate change and the depletion of material resources. We see an increasing challenge due to the scarcity of raw materials, especially metals such as lead, copper and zinc. With natural resources and materials about to run out, we need better resource protection and more effective ways to use them. Several essential metals and resources are already becoming less available. For example, most platinum, zinc, tantalum, lead, copper, cadmium, wolfram and silicon are concentrated in the hands of three countries, under the control of three large companies. This will soon create major challenges for industries in Europe and the US that use many of these metals in their manufacture of products such as televisions or computers. In a resource-constrained future we will see more:

- recycling-friendly designs, with EPR;
- multiple-use (multifunction) devices and expanded product life cycles;
- long-life products and buildings, with optimized material use;
- products using less packaging;
- a variety of ways to avoid the loss of resources during the product's life cycle;
- resource recovery through forward-thinking reuse, remanufacturing and recycling.

Waste that contains precious minerals, rare earth, metals and other nutrients is now understood to be valuable, and organic waste must be returned to the soil. The survival path and rebound effect of materials are understood as extremely critical. Will the landfill sites of today become the 'urban mines' of the future? We can observe the emergence of a new, sustainable industrial society, where new industrial systems are introduced that better reuse and recycle waste, and that are based on a new circular-flow economy (Girardet, 2008; M. Faulstich, personal communication, 2010). In the meantime, the depletion of several natural deposits is drawing closer. In 2008, the Institut der Deutschen Wirtschaft (IDW) estimated the availability and coverage of essential resources and selected metals, as part of a risk assessment for German industry in response to the threat caused by scarcity of raw materials (IDW, 2008). It estimated the years of reserves available for seven metals, as listed:

1	Lead	20 years
2	Zinc	22 years
3	Tantalum	29 years
4	Copper	31 years
5	Cadmium	34 years
6	Wolfram	39 years
7	Nickel	44 years

These metals are becoming scarce and consequently more expensive; for example, iron ore, lithium and copper are already much rarer than oil. This increases the possibility that our landfill sites will become places for urban mining. In addition, it is also important to know what kinds of product we buy. For instance, 40 per cent of the products in our weekly shopping basket contain palm oil, which, if not produced sustainably, can cause deforestation of ecologically precious rainforests. A more conscious use of materials, metals, resources and products is an imperative, and this includes their reuse and recycling (MacKay, 2009).

> Cities are resource-intensive systems. By 2030, we will need to produce 50% more energy and 30% more food on less land, with less water and fewer pesticides, using less material.
>
> (Head, 2008)

The need to change the practice of packaging with a 'product-stewardship' programme

There is a growing need for truly compostable packaging, where everything that arrives at the consumer is useful and does not create waste.

In future, with EPR, the user of packaging will have to pay for the collection of that packaging (Easton, 2010). The rising costs of waste from landfill levies will become its main driver. Essentially, one needs to ask: How much packaging is really necessary? Can the product be packed in another way? There is a need for leadership from a select group of companies (perhaps 5 per cent of all companies) to show how packaging can be reduced, or how products can be taken back from the consumer once the end of the life cycle has been reached, as is done with old tyres. Ikea, Nike and Woolworths have been setting new standards in this area, and BASF only puts new products on the market when there is evidence that the new product has a better life-cycle assessment than the previous one. There have been innovative recycling initiatives for mattresses, bicycles, carpets, paints, construction timber and furniture. We will need more products to be manufactured differently from how they are made now, with zero-waste concepts in mind, and also taking the EPR principle seriously. For instance, in the US, 44 per cent of all GHG emissions result from transporting and packaging products, illustrating the large potential for waste reduction in this area (Easton, 2010).

Case studies of waste management

The following case studies include details of how some cities and regions are trying to overcome the barriers to achieving 'zero waste'. The case studies here look at waste-stream management in the developed world (Australia and Denmark). In the following section, I will discuss two large cities in the developing world (Delhi and Cairo, both rapidly expanding emerging cities).

South Australia's leadership in waste management and resource recovery

Over the last five years, the Australian state of South Australia (SA) has produced a document on zero-waste principles, South Australia's Draft Waste Strategy 2010–2015 (Zero Waste SA, 2010). The strategy offers clear guidelines for SA's waste-recycling and waste-avoidance efforts and has a five-year time frame. The strategy's focus is twofold: 'Firstly, the strategy seeks to maximize the value of our resources; and secondly, it seeks to avoid and reduce waste.' These two objectives are interrelated, and some actions apply to both objectives, proposing new targets for municipal, commercial and industrial, and construction and demolition waste streams. Zero Waste SA is one of the few zero-waste government agencies in the world and is at the forefront of waste avoidance in Australia. Zero Waste SA was established in 2003 and is financed by government levies from landfill. The agency pioneered the ban on checkout-style plastic bags in Australia, in May 2009, and formulated the campaign slogan: 'I recycle correctly and everyone wins'.

In order to increase recycling and reduce consumption, we need to understand the composition of household waste. Only by separation at the source (point of waste creation) can we achieve high recycling rates. Interestingly, recent research at the University of South Australia indicates that the composition of waste varies according to the income level of the people producing the waste. The amount of food waste, for example, tends to be greatest among higher-income earners because, as income increases, there is generally more food waste as consumers purchase greater amounts of fresh food relative to prepared food (Sharp, 2010).

The SA Draft Waste Strategy is not a unique case. All of the European Union member states must compile a waste-prevention programme by the end of 2013, as required by the 2008 revision of their Waste Framework Directive. The EU guidelines are intended to support the formulation of programmes based on the thirty best practices identified by the European Commission.

The waste situation in New South Wales, Australia: a looming crisis?

Australia is the third highest generator of waste per capita in the developed world. In July 2006, only around 50 per cent of waste collected in the state of New South Wales (NSW) was recycled. Of course, it is always cheaper simply to bury waste in landfill than to treat it, but that has dangerous side effects. Electronic waste is still filling up Australian and US landfills (something not allowed in the EU for over ten years), contaminating soil and groundwater with toxic heavy metals. In the meantime, a waste crisis is looming in NSW: the city of Sydney's four landfill sites (Eastern Creek, Belrose, Jacks Gully and Lucas Heights) are reaching capacity and will be full by 2015, according to a recent independent Public Review Landfill Capacity and Demand Report (State Government of New South Wales, 2009). The city's annual 2 million tonnes of waste will have to be moved 250km south, by rail, to Tarago. For a long time, the state government has been inactive and failed to make the move to recycling. It lacks recycling facilities and investment in recycling technology. Recycling needs to be made cheaper than creating landfill, and strong economic incentives are required, as are strategies to get households to reduce their creation of waste substantially. This could be done by reducing bin sizes, raising awareness and by introducing the three-bin system to separate organic/garden waste, recycling and residual waste.

While Sydney's landfill sites are rapidly filling up, and the NSW government has no clear plan to address the crisis, Sydney's waste is forecast to keep growing by at least 1.4 per cent a year (owing to population increase and increasing consumption). Curbside recycling collected in NSW increased from 450,000t in 2000 to 690,000t in 2007. To make things worse, the NSW government raised over US$270 million (€188 million) in waste levies but returned just 15 per cent (US$41.5 million or €28.9 million) of that to local councils for recycling initiatives (State Government of New South Wales, 2009);

most of the collected levy was put towards totally different goals. By contrast, the state government of Victoria gives better support: it raised US$44.7 million (€31 million) in landfill levies and gave it straight back to the agencies responsible for waste management. Despite the smaller levy, Victoria recycled almost 20 per cent more waste than NSW in 2009. The Australian federal government will introduce a National Waste Policy in 2011 (aiming for a 66 per cent landfill reduction by 2014), and hopes are high that this will bring about the urgently required changes.

The situation in the UK is similar. Mal Williams, chief executive of Cylch (a major recycling body in Wales, UK), points out that '90 per cent of household waste is actually reusable without the need for incineration. Waste means inefficiency and lost profit for all' (M. Williams, personal communication, 2010).

Waste management case study from Aalborg, Denmark

Developed countries such as Germany, Japan, Sweden and Denmark are acknowledged worldwide as leaders in waste management. For instance, in some Japanese municipalities, up to twenty-four different categories of waste are separated. There is a great range of opportunities for waste reduction in the wealthier nations.

It is time for us to improve the linkages between material flow, use and recovery and energy and water consumption. To date, little research has been done on measuring the impact of waste-treatment systems themselves and waste-management changes over the longer term. The Danish city of Aalborg has proven that better waste management can reduce GHG emissions and that a municipality can produce significant amounts of energy with sustainable waste-to-energy concepts (see also Figure 15.5b). Two Danish researchers, Poulsen and Hansen, used historical data from the municipality of Aalborg to gain a longer-term overview of how a 'joined-up' approach to waste can impact on a city's carbon dioxide emissions. Their assessment included sewage sludge, food waste, yard waste and other organic waste. In 1970, Aalborg's municipal organic waste-management system showed net GHG emissions by methane from landfill of almost 100 per cent of the total emissions. Between 1970 and 2005, the city changed its waste-treatment strategy to include yard-waste composting, and the city's remaining organic waste was incinerated for CHP production. Of this, waste incineration contributed 80 per cent to net energy production and GHG turnover; wastewater treatment (including sludge digestion) contributed another 10 per cent; and other waste treatment processes (such as composting, transport and land application of treated waste) had minor impacts. 'Generally, incineration with or without energy production, and biogas production with energy extraction, are the two most important processes for the overall energy balance. This is mainly due to the substitution of fossil fuel-based energy,' state Poulsen and Hansen (2009, p861). The researchers calculated that the energy potential tied up in municipal organic waste in Denmark is equivalent to 5 per cent of the country's total energy consumption, including transport. They also predicted that further improvements by 2020 were possible, by reducing energy consumed by wastewater treatment (for aeration), increasing anaerobic digestion, improving incineration-process efficiency and source-separating food waste for anaerobic co-digestion.

This is a pioneering demonstration of how technology can be harnessed to resolve environmental challenges. Aalborg's progress shows how far-reaching waste management can be in attaining energy and GHG reduction goals, and it 'should offer encouragement to other cities embarking on greener waste management strategies for the future' (Poulsen and Hansen, 2009, p862). The potential for emission reduction in waste management is very big. It is estimated that, within the European Union, municipal waste management reduced GHG emissions from 64 to 28 million tonnes of carbon dioxide per year between 1990 and 2007, equivalent to a reduction from 130 to 60kg of carbon dioxide each year per capita. With such innovation in waste treatment, the EU municipal waste sector will achieve 18 per cent of the reduction target set for Europe by the Kyoto agreement before 2012.

A lack of waste-management frameworks in the developing world

Global population growth and increasing consumption

The future will depend on the decisions each of us makes about the way we will consume resources. Is the increase in consumption in the developing world inevitable and unstoppable?

Urbanization has almost reached saturation point in the developed countries. Wealthy nations use the most resources now, but emerging economies are catching up fast. The improved standard of living now being observed in China, India and Brazil, for instance, means that natural resources are being consumed at record levels. Earth's finite resources are more stressed by rising prosperity leading to increasing consumption than by sheer population growth. But the consumption of resources now enjoyed in the wealthiest nations will be impossible to sustain worldwide. The focus has to be on behaviour change and sustainable consumption, as Robert Kunzig notes: 'It's too late to keep the developing world's new middle class of 2030 from being born. But it's not too late to change the ways how they and the rest of us will produce and consume food, energy and materials' (2011, p.24).

Urbanization and demographic transitions are seen as the hallmarks of human progress, and all countries go through them in their own time. Global population today (2011) is around 7 billion people and is predicted to peak at 9 billion by 2045, before levelling out. The UN Population Division predicts that the world will reach 'replacement fertility' by 2030 (UN, 2010). India's population is forecast to grow from 1.2 billion people in 2010 to 1.6 billion people in 2050 (overtaking the population of China by 2030). 'There will be billions more people wanting and deserving to boost themselves out of poverty', as Paul Ehrlich pointed out (1968, p2).

> The increase in world flows of scrap, e-waste, recovered plastics and fibres has turned developed countries into a source of material supply for informal trade in emerging countries.
>
> (UN-Habitat, 2010b)

Informal waste-recycling sectors in the developing world: the cases of Delhi and Cairo

A staggering 95 per cent of global population growth (and most economic growth) over the next forty years will happen in Asia, Africa, Latin America and the Caribbean, according to the United Nations' Population Reference Bureau's 2009 World Population Data Sheet (United Nations' Population Reference Bureau, 2009).

There are ways to improve waste management and change behaviour in developing countries, even if there is no budget or legislation for it. In Curitiba, Brazil, for example, innovative waste-collection approaches were developed, such as the 'Green Exchange Programme', to encourage slum dwellers to clean up their areas and improve public health. The city administration offered free bus tickets and fresh vegetables to people who collected garbage and brought waste to neighbourhood centres. In addition, children in Curitiba were allowed to exchange recyclables for school supplies or toys.

Cities have always been places of economic and social opportunities. Cities always need to find local solutions for waste management appropriate to their own particular circumstances and needs. In Delhi, there is an army of over 120,000 informal waste collectors (the so-called 'kabari') in the streets, collecting paper, aluminium cans, glass and plastic, who sell the waste to mini-scrap dealers as part of a secondary raw-materials market.

It is an informal industry that processes 59 per cent of Delhi's waste and supports the livelihood of countless families. In the Indian capital city, the private sector runs waste management, and the business of collecting and recycling is a serious one for many of the poor, and a relatively lucrative source of income. According to Bharati Chaturved, 1 out of every 100 residents in Delhi engages in waste collection and recycling. Chaturved also estimated that a single piece of plastic increases 700 per cent in value from start to finish in the recycling chain before it is reprocessed. This informal sector of waste collectors saves the city's three municipalities a large amount of money, because they do not need to arrange waste collection, particularly in inaccessible slum areas. In Delhi, more than 95 per cent of homes do not have formal garbage collection (Chaturved, 2010).

For countries such as India or Bangladesh, the introduction of an industrialized clean-up system and associated infrastructure, like those in the developed world, would take jobs from thousands of poor peasants who are willing to work hard and get dirty collecting and recycling the waste of the metropolis in order to feed themselves. An estimated 6 million people in India earn their livelihood through waste recycling. On top of a low standard of living, they now face joblessness, because India's new business-model approach to waste management will replace the pre-existing informal kabari system with a model imported from developed countries. It is an area where India and Bangladesh could probably learn from their neighbour China, as their cities have similar population densities and growth rates (UN-Habitat, 2010b).

Another interesting example of an informal waste-management sector is in the city of Cairo, the capital of Egypt, which has grown to over 15 million people and is one of the most densely populated cities in the world (with 32,000 people per square mile). Low-income households are often located in the most polluted areas of a city. The economy of 'Garbage City' (Manshiyat Naser, the Zabaleen quarter), a slum settlement on the outskirts of Cairo, revolves entirely around the collection and recycling of the city's garbage, mostly through the use of pigs by the city's minority Coptic Christian population. Although the area has streets, shops and apartments, like any other area of the city, it lacks infrastructure and often has no running water, sewage or electricity. The city's garbage is brought in by the garbage collectors, who then sort through the garbage to retrieve any potentially useful or recyclable items. As a passer-by walks down the road,

Figure 15.6 Aerial photo, 'Garbage City', Cairo, Egypt.

Many developing countries have an active informal sector that recycles, reuses and repairs, which achieves recycling rates comparable with those in developed countries, at no cost to the formal waste-management sector, saving the city as much as 20 per cent of its waste-management budget. Cairo, for instance, has grown to over 15 million people and is one of the most densely populated cities in the world. The economy of its 'Garbage City' revolves entirely around the collection and recycling of Cairo's garbage. Although the area has streets, shops and apartments, like any other area of the city, it lacks infrastructure and often has no running water, sewage or electricity.

Photo: courtesy B. Princen, 2009

'he will see large rooms stacked with garbage, with men, women or children crouching and sorting the garbage into what is usable or what is sellable' (Beitiks, 2009, p2).

Families typically specialize in a particular type of garbage that they sort and sell: in one room, children sort out plastic bottles, while in the next room women separate cans from the rest. Anything that can somehow be reused or recycled is saved. Various recycled paper and glass products are made and sold from the city, while metal is sold by the kilogram to be melted down and reused. Carts pulled by horse or donkey are often stacked three metres high with recyclable goods (see Figure 15.6).

The circular economic system in 'Garbage City' is classified as an informal sector, where people do not just collect the trash; they live with it. Most families typically have worked for generations in the same area and type of waste specialization, and they continue to make enough money to support themselves. They collect and recycle the garbage they pick up from apartments and homes in wealthier neighbourhoods. This includes thousands of tonnes of organic waste, which is fed to the pigs. By raising pigs, the Zabaleen people provide a service to those who eat pork in the predominantly Muslim country, while the pigs help to rid neighbourhoods of tonnes of odorous waste that would otherwise accumulate on the streets. Like the famous 'Smokey Mountain' rubbish dump in Manila, Philippines, could this place ever become an official recycling centre?

In most emerging cities, it is still common for solid or liquid wastes to be dumped on some site outside the city, with no provision made to cover the waste or to avoid contamination of local water resources. In India and Egypt, the majority of households do not have a garbage-collection service, and municipal governments are incapable of managing the vast quantity of solid and liquid wastes.

As the cases in Delhi and Cairo illustrate, the increase in world flows of scrap, uncontrolled dumped e-waste, recovered plastics and fibres has turned developed countries into a source of material supply for informal trade in emerging countries. The formalization of this informal economy and the integrated development of a basic waste-management infrastructure remain a major challenge (Lacquian, 2005). Delhi, Cairo, Lagos and other emerging cities have extensive informal 'waste economies', supported by waste pickers, second-hand markets, micro-waste dealers and backyard recyclers. Furedy argues: 'Ironically, such cities where living conditions are very poor, are at the same time models of ecological sustainability in that levels of resource use and waste generation are low and much waste is recycled' (Furedy, 1992).

> A global paradigm shift in urban development and the use of resources is essential. Clearly, a situation where 20% of the world's population consumes 80% of the world's resources cannot go on forever or be allowed to continue.
>
> (Lehmann, 2010)

Composting organic waste and improving urban ecology

Compost is an important source of plant nutrients and is a low-cost alternative to chemical fertilizers. It has become a necessary part of contemporary landscape management and urban farming, as it uses 'reverse supply chain' principles, giving organic components back to the soil, thus improving the quality of agriculture. Paying attention to the nutrient cycle and to phosphorus replacement is part of sustainable urban agriculture. Industrial composting helps to improve soils but requires a proper composting infrastructure. It is important to focus on soil, putting nutrients back into agriculture (for instance, the 'City to Soil' programme in Australia). In Sweden, for instance, the dumping of organic waste to landfill has been illegal since 2005. It is essential to avoid landfill organics such as food waste. All organic waste should be used for composting or anaerobic digestion (see Figure 15.5a).

Food waste is another major concern. Twenty-two per cent of all waste in Australia is food waste. New biodegradable packaging helps to facilitate the processing of food waste. Biodegradable and compostable solutions for food-waste recovery systems, using a kitchen caddy with a biodegradable bag that is collected weekly, has become a common solution. Iain Gulland, director of Zero Waste Scotland, points out that 'over

60 per cent of food waste is avoidable. However, if all unavoidable food waste in Scotland was processed by anaerobic digestion, it could produce enough electricity to run a city the size of Dundee' (I. Gulland, personal communication, 14 September 2010). In South Australia, more than 90,000t per annum of food waste goes to landfill (on average, each household throws out 3kg of food waste per week). This needs to be taken out of the waste stream and diverted into composting or anaerobic-digestion systems (Kahn, 2010).

In this context, urban farming has emerged as a valid urban design strategy, where food is produced and consumed locally within city boundaries, turning disused sites and underused public space into productive urban landscapes and community gardens. Furthermore, such agricultural activities allow for effective composting of organic waste, returning nutrients to the soil and improving biodiversity corridors in the urban environment. Urban farming and similar resource-recovery activities will help to feed the world's predicted population of 9 billion by 2050 (UN, 2009).

Since 2000, the number of hungry people on the planet has been growing rapidly, and agriculture cannot keep up with demand. In China, in the last decade alone, meat consumption has doubled. In India, a 10 per cent rise in food prices means that another 10 million people are pushed into poverty. Declining yields in Africa will lead to further food price increases, and soon food and water (as opposed to oil and territory in the previous century) will emerge as major causes of military conflicts. Climate change and extreme weather events are some of the main reasons for further escalating food prices, according to Lester Brown (Brown, 2006). In this context, composting cycles can support food security, because returning important nutrients to the soil improves harvests.

Conclusions and outlook: challenges for making zero waste a reality

Decoupling material use and waste generation from economic growth

Cities are the main consumers of energy, materials, food and water, and so it is essential that the delivery of urban services (energy, water, transport, waste-stream management and resource recovery) is as efficient as possible. The efficiency and effectiveness of urban services are greatly affected by the urban landform, a city's shape and compactness. The low densities and mono-functional layout of suburbs, for example, are affecting human behaviour, leading to highly inefficient conditions, including an increase in consumption, which contributes to the problem.

Increased material and energy consumption in all nations, coupled with an inadequate and unsustainable waste-management system, has forced governments, industry and individuals to put into practice new measures to achieve responsible, closed-loop solutions in waste management and resource recovery: an industrial green revolution. Achieving 'zero waste' remains difficult and requires continued and combined efforts by industry, government bodies, university researchers, organizations and the people of our communities.

The topic of reducing urban household consumption by optimizing urban form and the need to reduce the material requirements of buildings (in fact, of the entire construction sector) has only recently emerged as an urgent field of research (Dey et al,

2007). Although there is a general acknowledgement that there is a need for improved urban-governance processes and rethinking of urban-development patterns to reduce material consumption and optimize material flows, this is still a relatively new research field, and there is still a lack of reliable data and comparative methodologies. One of the findings of this chapter is that embedding 'zero waste' requires strong industry leadership, new policies and effective education curricula, as well as raising awareness through education and refocusing research agendas to bring about attitudinal change and the reduction of wasteful consumption. Unlimited consumption and growth on a planet with limited resources 'cannot go on forever and is indeed dangerous' (Club of Rome, 1972, p186).

The C&D sector has a particularly urgent need to catch up with other sectors in better managing its waste stream, to increase its focus on reusing entire building components at the end of a building's life cycle. In Australia, for instance, around 40 per cent of all waste to landfill comes from the building sector (EPA, 2009). Increasing the economic value of recycled commodities, such as rare metals in e-waste, paper, glass and plastics, remains an area for future development and investment.

Energy markets will soon compete with material markets for resources. In 2010, the recycling sector in Germany employed over 220,000 people in green jobs. Waste is increasingly being seen in terms of economic sustainability, and this policy issue offers considerable opportunities for the creation of green jobs.

Figure 15.7 Photos of waste management in Germany.

Computer-controlled high-tech plants have conveyor belts where sensors recognize different materials and separate these automatically. Recycling experts agree that 100 per cent recycling and resource recovery is possible technologically; however, behaviour change needs to be mobilized to avoid the creation of waste in the first place. The yellow bin has recently been introduced in German cities (this is bin number four), which is especially for the collection of packaging waste and small e-waste.

A particular challenge in waste management is soil degradation. Composting methods are important to return nutrients from organic materials back to the soil. However, the anticipated global decline in the availability of phosphorous ('peak phosphorous'), which is currently lost as waste from urban areas, is a challenge for food production.

This chapter has touched on some of the complexities around sustainable urban metabolism, waste management and the links between waste streams, urban development and the need for resource recovery. Two of the case studies presented are encouraging models of what could be achieved in the developed world. These cases are of limited value for the developing world, and, for this reason, the informal sector of waste management requires greater research. The importation of waste to developing countries is obviously another interesting but complex issue: on one side, we criticize developed countries for exporting their pollution; on the other side, developed cities provide raw materials for workers in developing countries to mine urban waste. These informal sectors may even hold some lessons for cities in the developed world. Owing to their greater consumption levels, cities in developed countries have much higher material and energy consumption, despite their increased resource efficiency (Lenzen et al, 2008; Rickwood et al, 2008).

It probably makes sense to describe cities in the developed, industrialized world as 'high-consumption cities', to better express the absurdity of low-consumption cities aiming to also become high-consumption cities. The developing world's consumption levels are rising and will continue to increase its hunger for resources. China, for instance, is urbanizing faster than any other country in history, requiring huge amounts of non-renewable materials, energy and water for the production of consumer goods, and increasingly contributing to the depletion of raw-material resources. Asia's 'new consumer', who is part of a newly emerging middle class, with resource-intensive lifestyle habits, materialistic behaviour and mobility needs, is contributing to and accelerating this development. Most of the consumption is going to be in cities. We can define a formula: the environmental impact (I) is a result of the increasing affluence/consumption power (A), a growing urban population (P) and the availability of technology (T). The suggested formula is:

$$I = P \times A \times T$$

It is essential that we continue to reduce wasteful consumption, to avoid the creation of waste in the first place (waste minimization through avoidance), to promote the cyclical reuse of materials in the economy and to maximize the value of our resources to make resource recovery common practice. Waste is a precious resource. The challenges posed by climate change and the depletion of resources are complex – but we have the skills, knowledge and determination to achieve the necessary changes. Changes to human behaviour, to long-held planning habits and to design attitudes will all be necessary. In his latest book, *The Vanishing Face of Gaia: A Final Warning*, James Lovelock outlined the urgency of these changes (Lovelock, 2009; also see Brown, 2006). In 2010, 6.8 billion people on earth consumed resources, energy and materials at an ever-increasing pace and volume. It is therefore essential to use 100 per cent of all old/used resources as new resources and embed the sustainable-city paradigm, while drastically raising the efficiency of the use of resources, energy and materials (see Figure 15.8).

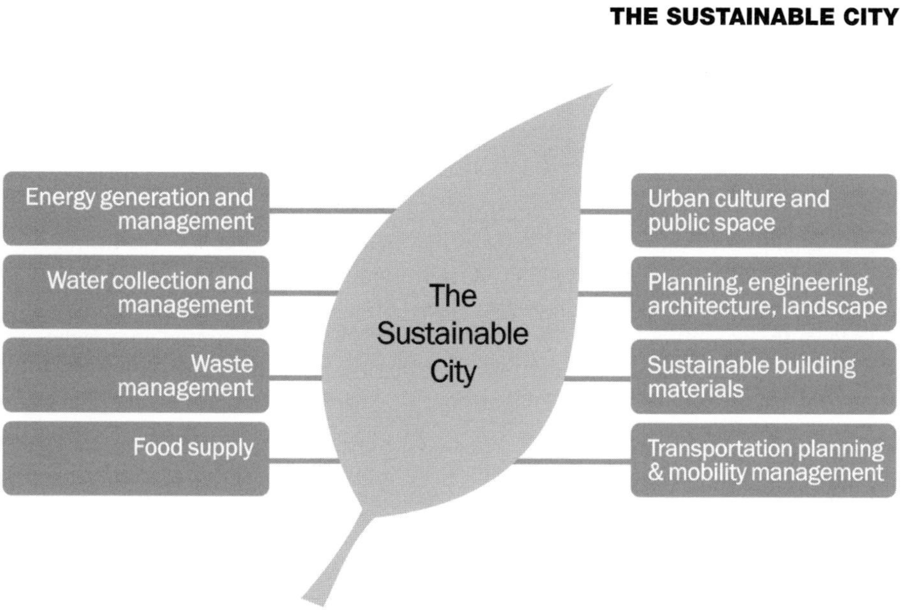

THE SUSTAINABLE CITY

Energy generation and management

Water collection and management

Waste management

Food supply

The Sustainable City

Urban culture and public space

Planning, engineering, architecture, landscape

Sustainable building materials

Transportation planning & mobility management

Figure 15.8 Waste management is an important keystone in the effort to achieve a holistic 'sustainable city', using local and recycled materials.

Diagram by the author, 2008

Challenges and costs can be resolved

Increasing efficiency often leads to increased consumption (which is described as the 'Jevons paradox' and as 'rebound effect'). Changing old consumption habits, wasteful lifestyles or patterns of use is difficult, but educational programmes and tax incentives have been effective in mobilizing behaviour change and motivating a shift in user-behaviour patterns. This includes educating people about how to use technology, buildings, transport systems and recycling facilities. However, behaviour change tends to occur gradually and slowly.

With all the scientific evidence on the causes of global warming now available, there is no reason to delay moves to change our behaviour. Thus, the current key challenge in advancing a sustainable waste-management agenda is the need to bring the general public on the journey to higher recycling rates and waste avoidance, supported by better educational programmes to raise awareness. Unfortunately, governments have often been too slow to respond positively to developments. In addition, we need systems that allow everybody to participate more easily in recycling, including the difficult goods, such as batteries, e-waste and building components. Frequently, the cost of recycling is given as a reason for the slow uptake. Therefore, landfill costs need to rise in proportion to recycling costs. Resource recovery through recycling will not come for free, and so the benefits should always outweigh the costs. Municipalities can influence and accelerate change with strategic levies, such as levies on over-packaging. Recycling costs can be significantly lower if we achieve contamination reduction and better source separation.

Innovative technologies can assist with better automation of materials-recovery facilities and better design for recycling. New modular products and construction systems that can easily be disassembled and recycled ('design for disassembly') will play an increasingly important role, as well as multifunctional devices and extended producer responsibilities.

In the meantime, nothing less than a peaceful green revolution has started, changing the way we design, build, operate, maintain and recycle/renew cities and buildings. Building materials are being more carefully examined, and decisions are made based on the recyclability of these materials. Resource conservation and waste minimization are promoted at all levels, and waste streams are increasingly recognized as 'resource streams' (Furedy, 1992). In fact, the urbanization process has emerged as the incubator and platform for revolutionary change: holistic strategies and integrated approaches for urban development indicate that post-fossil-fuel cities can and must become the most environmentally friendly model for inhabiting our earth. Waste avoidance has to be considered as one of the main drivers for architectural and urban design. Today, the technology and science for zero waste already exist, and recycling experts have recently confirmed that 100 per cent recycling and resource recovery is possible (Rat für Nachhaltige Entwicklung, 2011). In this context, our objective must be to reconcile the scarcity of our natural resources with the huge quantities of waste produced by our cities and industries, waste that we must, unfailingly, recover.

Acknowledgements

This chapter draws on the work the author has undertaken as UNESCO Professor in Sustainable Urban Development for Asia and the Pacific and on the research carried out at the Zero Waste SA Research Centre for Sustainable Design and Behaviour (sd+b). The author wishes to thank the two reviewers for their helpful comments on an earlier draft of this chapter.

References

Barr, S. and Gilg, A. (2006) 'Sustainable lifestyles: framing environmental action in and around the home', *Geoforum*, vol. 37, no 6, pp906–20

Beitiks, M. (2009) 'Incredible "Garbage City" rises outside of Cairo', *Habitat* (Online), 12 November, www.inhabitat.com/incredible-garbage-city-rises-outside-of-Cairo/, accessed 30 October 2010

Braungart, M. and McDonough, W. (2002) *Cradle to Cradle: Remaking the Way We Make Things*, North Point Press, New York

Brown, L. (2006) *Plan B 2.0: Rescuing a Planet Under Stress and a Civilization in Trouble*, W.W. Norton Publishing, New York

Chalmin, P. and Gaillochet, C. (2009) *From Waste to Resource: An Abstract of World Waste Survey, 2009*, Veolia/CyclOpen Research Institute, Paris, France, www.sapiens.revenues.org, accessed 10 September 2010

Chaturved, B. (2010) 'Ragpickers: the bottom rung in the waste trade ladder', *International Plastics Task Force*, January, www.ecologycenter.org/iptf/Ragpickers/indexragpicker.html, accessed 30 October 2010

Club of Rome (Meadows, D.H., Meadows, D.L., Randers, J. and Behrens, W.W., III) (1972) *The Limits to Growth*, Universe Books, New York

Dey, C., Berger, C., Foran, B., Foran, M., Joske, R., Lenzen, M. and Wood, R. A. (2007) 'Household environmental pressure from consumption: an Australian environmental atlas', in G. Birch (ed) *Water, Wind, Art and Debate: How Environmental Concerns Impact on Disciplinary Research*, Sydney University Press, Sydney, Australia

Easton, S. (2010) 'Manufacturers to arrange for recycling of Australia's e-waste', *UPIU*, August, www.upiu.com/articles/manufacturers-to-arrange-recycling-for-australia-s-e-waste, accessed 10 September 2010

Ehrlich, P. (1968) *The Population Bomb*, Ballantine Books/Random House, New York

Environmental Protection Agency (EPA) (2009) *Recover Your Resources: Reduce, Reuse and Recycle Construction and Demolition Materials at Land Revitalization Projects*, EPA, Washington, DC, epa.gov/brownfields/tools/cdbrochure.pdf, accessed 10 October 2010

Fischer-Kowalski, M. (1998) 'Society's metabolism: the intellectual history of material flow analysis, Part I 1860–1970', *Journal of Industrial Ecology*, vol 2, pp61–78

Fleischhauer, J., Kleinhubbert, G. and Neubacher, A. (2011) 'Germany's eco-trap: is environmentalism really working?' *Spiegel.de Online News*, www.spiegel.de, 17 March, accessed 17 March 2011

Furedy, C. (1992) 'Garbage: exploring non-conventional options in Asian cities', *Environment and Urbanization*, vol 4, no 2, pp42–6

Girardet, H. (1999) *Creating Sustainable Cities (Schumacher Briefing #2)*, Green Books, Devon

Girardet, H. (2008) *Cities, People, and Planet: Urban Development and Climate Change* (2nd edn), John Wiley & Sons, Oxford

Grosse, F. (2010) 'Is recycling part of the solution? The role of recycling in an expanding society and a world of finite resources', *SAPIENS*, vol 3, no 1, pp17–30

Head, P. (2008) 'Entering the ecological age: the engineer's role', Brunel International Lecture 2008, London, www.arup.com /Publications/Entering_the_Ecological_Age.aspx, accessed 10 March 2010

Hobson, K. (2003) 'Thinking habits into action: the role of knowledge and process in questioning household consumption practices', *Local Environment*, 8, pp95–112

IDW (2008) *Report: Study 2008*, Institut der Deutschen Wirtschaft (IDW), Köln/Bonn, Germany, www.iwkoeln.de, accessed 1 September 2010

Jackson, T. (1996) *Material Concerns*, Routledge, London

Kahn, R. (2010) Information on food waste, www.ozharvest.org, accessed 10 October 2010

Kunzig, R. (2011) 'Population seven billion', *National Geographic*, January

Lacquian, A. (2005) *Beyond Metropolis: The Planning and Governance of Asia's Mega-urban Regions*, John Hopkins Press, Baltimore, MD

Lane, R., Horne, R. and Bicknell, J. (2009) 'Routes of re-use of second-hand goods in Melbourne households', *Australian Geographer*, 40, pp151–68

Lehmann, S. (2008) 'Sustainability on the urban scale: green urbanism', in P. Droege (ed) *Urban Energy Transition: From Fossil Fuels to Renewable Power*, Elsevier, Amsterdam, the Netherlands

Lehmann, S. (2010) *The Principles of Green Urbanism: Transforming the City for Sustainability*, Earthscan, London

Lenzen, M., Wood, R. and Foran, B. (2008) 'Direct versus embodied energy: the need for urban lifestyle transitions', in P. Droege (ed) *Urban Energy Transition: From Fossil Fuels to Renewable Power*, Elsevier, Amsterdam, the Netherlands

Linacre, S. (2007) *Household Waste: Australian Social Trends*, Australian Bureau of Statistics, Canberra, Australia

Lovelock, J. (2009) *The Vanishing Face of Gaia: A Final Warning*, Penguin Books, London

MacKay, D. J. C. (2009) *Sustainable Energy – Without the Hot Air*, UIT Cambridge Ltd, Cambridge

Mallgrave, H.F. (2008) *Architectural Theory: An Anthology from 1871–2005*, Blackwell, Oxford, p597

Perkins, A., Hamnett, S., Pullen, S., Zito, R. and Trebilcock, D. (2009) 'Transport, housing and urban form: The life-cycle energy consumption and emissions of city centre apartments compared with suburban dwellings', *Urban Policy Research*, vol 27, pp377–96

Poulsen, T. and Hansen, J. A. (2009) 'Wastewater treatment and greenhouse gas emissions', *Waste Management Research*, vol 27, p861

Princen, Bas (2009) www.treehugger.com/files/2009/12/ photographer-capture-life-in-garbage-city.php, accessed 30 October 2010

Rat für Nachhaltige Entwicklung (2011) Report available online at: www.nachhaltigkeitsrat.de/, accessed on 20/4/2011.

Recycling International (2008) September (anonymous), www.environmental-expert.com, accessed 1 March 2010

Rickwood, P., Glazebrook, G. and Searle, G. (2008) 'Urban structure and energy – a review', *Urban Policy Research*, vol 26, pp57–81

Robins, N. and Kumar, R. (1999) 'Production: producing, providing, trading', in D. Satterthwaite (ed) *Sustainable Cities*, Earthscan, London

Rogers, R. and Power, A. (2000) *Cities for a Small Country*, Faber & Faber, London

Satterthwaite, D. (2009) 'The implications of population growth and urbanization for climate change', *Environnement urbain/Urban Environment*, vol 21, pp545–67

Schatzki, T. R. (2003) 'A new social ontology', *Philosophy of the Social Sciences*, vol 33, pp174–202

SEA (2010) *Waste Report 2010*, SEA Organization, Riverside, CA, www.solv.org, accessed 10 August 2010

Sharp, A. (2010) Unpublished seminar on food waste at the University of South Australia, Adelaide

Shove, E., Watson, M., Hand, M. and Ingram, J. (2007) *The Design of Everyday Life*, Berg Publishing, Oxford

State Government of New South Wales (2009) *Public Review Landfill Capacity and Demand Report*, Wright Corporate Strategy Pty Ltd, North Sydney, Australia, www.planning.nsw.gov.au/LinkClick.aspx?fileticket=Xtm8jz6j7WI%3D&tabid=70&language=en-AU, accessed 10 September 2010

Tonkinwise, C. (2005) 'De-materialism and the art of seeing living or: why architecture's self-images lead to McMansions', presentation at the Faculty of Architecture, Design and Planning, University of Sydney, Sydney, Australia

United Nations (2010) *World Urbanization Prospects, the 2010 Revision*, United Nations, Department of Economic and Social Affairs, Population Division, Nairobi, Kenya/New York

United Nations Population Reference Bureau (2009) *World Population Data Sheet*, www.un.org, accessed 20 December 2010

UN–Habitat (2010a) *World Population Growth Forecast, 2010*, United Nations Human Settlements Programme (UN–Habitat), Nairobi, Kenya

United Nations Human Settlements Programme (UN–Habitat) (2010b) *Solid Waste Management in the World's Cities: Water and Sanitation in the World's Cities, 2010*, Earthscan, London, and Nairobi, Kenya

Von Weizaecker, E., Lovins, A. and Lovins, H. (1997) *Factor Four: Doubling Wealth, Halving Resource Use*, Earthscan, London

Walls, M. (2006) *Extended Producer Responsibility and Product Design*, Report to the Organisation for Economic Cooperation and Development (OECD), Resources for the Future (RFF Press), Washington, DC

Whalley, A. (ed) (2010) *Blue: Water, Energy and Waste*, 29, Grimshaw Architects, London

Zero Waste SA (2009) *ZWSA Survey, 2009*, Zero Waste SA, Adelaide, Australia, www.zerowaste.sa.gov.au, accessed 10 December 2010

Zero Waste SA (2010) *South Australia's Draft Waste Strategy 2010–2015. Consultation Draft*, Zero Waste SA, Adelaide, Australia, www.zerowaste.sa.gov.au/upload/about-us/wastestrategy/ DraftWasteStrategyV2.pdf, accessed 10 September 2010

Related websites

Concrete aggregates: regarding recycled aggregates for concrete, see: www.holcimforum.org (accessed 30 October 2010)

Envac Systems, sustainable waste collection systems, based in Sweden; see: www.envac group.com and: www.symbiocity.org (both accessed 1 November 2010)

Gruener Punkt, the German recycling system, introduced 1990: www.gruenerpunkt.de (accessed 1 November 2010)

Kahn, Ronnie: Information on food waste by Kahn on OZHarvest, the not-for-profit NGO, which delivered 6 million meals to people in need between 2004 and 2010; and the 'Love Food – Hate Waste' campaign. Available online: www.ozharvest.org (accessed 10 October 2010). See also: www.lovefoodhatewaste.com (accessed 30 October 2010). Information by John Dee (Australia) on food waste and better shopping methods. Available online: www.dosomething. net and www.foodwise.com.au (accessed 30 October 2010)

SuperUse: Online community of designers using recycled materials and products: www. superuse.org (accessed on 1 November 2010)

World Changing: for more information on new production methods and material innovation, see: www.worldchanging.com and www.transmaterial.net (both accessed 1 March 2010). For more information on new construction methods using timber systems, see also: www. low2no.org (accessed 30 October 2010)

Zero Waste SA Research Centre for Sustainable Design and Behaviour (sd+b), at the University of South Australia, Adelaide, Australia: www.unisa.edu.au/sustainable-design (accessed 1 November 2010)

Chapter 16

Sustainable transport systems and behaviour change

Michael A. P. Taylor and Michelle Philp

Summary

This chapter reviews the implementation of programmes for voluntary travel behaviour change (VTBC), as an important initiative in the search for more sustainable urban transport systems. Significant programmes for VTBC have now been employed in Australia and the UK, among other countries. The basic objective of VTBC is to substantially reduce individuals' use of private vehicles and thus reduce greenhouse-gas emissions from transport. The chapter provides a focus on the current research aimed at developing and applying suitable tools for the evaluation of VTBC projects through the identification of the benefits and impacts of VTBC and the development of survey methodologies for measuring small-scale changes in travel behaviour, as these have emerged as major issues for the proper evaluation of the programmes. The evaluation methodology requires the use of advanced survey techniques and new data-collection technology, with the use of global positioning systems (GPS) by survey respondents being an important innovation. Research results from the evaluation studies are now available. The next research question, then, involves estimating the impacts of future programmes and how the principles of VTBC can be extended to other behaviours impacting sustainability.

Introduction

Since the pre-industrial period, the primary source of the increased atmospheric concentration of carbon dioxide, the most consequential anthropogenic greenhouse gas, is the use of fossil fuels (IPCC, 2007a). Transport represents 14 per cent of greenhouse-gas emissions by source; comparatively, this is the same as the amount of emissions generated by the industrial and agricultural sectors (Stern, 2006). Increasing demand on traffic infrastructure during peak periods results in traffic congestion in all major cities. With increasing car ownership and use, it is logical to expect that congestion will continue to increase, and that the period of congestion will tend to extend over more of the day (Stopher, 2004). Urban congestion can double the fuel consumption and potential emissions of vehicles (Bureau of Transport Economics (BTE), 2000; Bureau of Transport and Regional Economics (BTRE), 2007).

Although technological advances in fuel efficiency could reduce per vehicle emissions in the future, any such improvements will be offset by increased ownership and use of private vehicles (WBCSD, 2001, 2004; Pramberg, 2004; Chapman, 2007; IPCC, 2007b).

The issue of motor-vehicle emissions must be addressed using a multi-pronged approach, focusing on infrastructure and policy, technical improvements and voluntary individual behaviour change (James and John, 1997; Baudains et al, 2001; IPCC, 2007b). Studies have found that, for 40 per cent of trips, there are viable alternatives to the car, and, with minor improvements to alternative travel infrastructure, a further 40 per cent of trips could be completed without a car (Brog and John, 2001; Chapman, 2007). Changes in lifestyle and behaviour patterns can contribute to the reduction of greenhouse-gas emissions and the establishment of sustainable urban transport systems that (Minken, 1999; May and Taylor, 2002; IPCC, 2007b; Taylor, 2007):

- provide access to goods and services in an efficient way for all inhabitants of an urban area;
- protect the environment, cultural heritage and ecosystems for the current generation;
- do not endanger the opportunities for future generations to reach at least the same welfare level as that of the current generation, including the welfare derived from the natural environment and cultural heritage.

It is also important to investigate the possibility of expanding the focus of voluntary lifestyle changes beyond travel to encourage the adaptation of household-wide sustainable behaviours with respect to water, waste and energy consumption.

Voluntary travel behaviour change: the concept

Voluntary behaviour change is defined as change that occurs when individuals make choices for personal reward without a top-down mechanism, regulation of any sort or a feeling of external compulsion (Ampt, 2004; Ker, 2004). This principle can be applied to achieve more sustainable urban transport systems in mitigating and adapting to climate change.

VTBC falls under a general concept known as travel demand management (TDM). TDM was a concept introduced in the 1980s to describe travel interventions made by governments to modify travel decisions, so that desirable social, economic and environmental objectives could be achieved and adverse impacts of travel reduced (James and John, 1997; Ampt, 2001). The focus of TDM has evolved, from programmes encouraging mode change from private motor-vehicle use to more sustainable transport means, to any programme engaged in mitigating the negative impacts of motor vehicles (Ampt, 2001). TDM measures include urban planning to reduce the demand for motor-vehicle travel, and the use of education and information to instigate voluntary behaviour change (IPCC, 2007b).

VTBC schemes aim to shift travel-mode choices to more sustainable options by providing appropriate information, assistance, motivation or incentives to induce people to voluntarily choose to travel in ways that benefit themselves, the community and the environment (Stopher and Bullock, 2003; Chatterjee and Bonsall, 2009). VTBC encompasses a range of programmes including personal travel planning, travel-awareness campaigns, workplace travel plans, school travel plans and car sharing schemes (Chatterjee and Bonsall, 2009). The general consensus is that VTBC programmes lead to reductions in car use while also increasing public-transport use, walking and cycling (Ampt and Rooney, 1998; James, 1998; Ampt, 1999; Rose and Ampt, 2001; Marinelli and Roth, 2002; Stopher and Bullock, 2003; Ker, 2004; Pramberg, 2004; Australian Greenhouse Office (AGO), 2005; Tideman et al, 2006; Bonsall, 2009; Brog et al, 2009; Chatterjee, 2009; Department for Transport, Energy and Infrastructure (DTEI), 2009; Seethaler and Rose, 2009).

In order to motivate, target and develop behaviour change in individuals, VTBC schemes employ psychological principles (Seethaler and Rose, 2003, 2004, 2005; Ampt, 2004). VTBC measures are currently founded on two main social-theory paradigms: community development and social marketing.

Community development is a bottom-up approach to VTBC, using external support to encourage individuals to analyse their current behaviour and the underlying causes for this behaviour, and to develop a plan to change (Ife, 1996; Ampt, 2004).

Social marketing has been traced to Kotler and Zaltman (1971), who used the term to refer to the application of marketing as a solution for social and health problems. Several definitions of social marketing exist, the most fitting with respect to VTBC being: the application of marketing technologies developed in the commercial sector to the analysis, planning, execution and evaluation of programmes designed to influence the voluntary behaviour of target audiences in order to improve their personal welfare and that of society (Andreasen, 1994, 1995). The key features of this definition are the focus on voluntary behaviour change without coercion or enforcement, the concept of exchange in that the individual receives benefits from changing, and the concept that the benefits will accrue to the individual and society, not the marketing body (Ampt, 2003, 2004; Stead et al, 2007a; Powell and Thurston, 2008).

VTBC programmes are undertaken through the application of two general VTBC philosophies: travel blending and individualized marketing.

Travel blending

Travel blending is an approach based around empowering individuals to reduce car use by focusing on their activities and choices (Ampt and Rooney, 1998; Ampt, 1999; Tisato and Robinson, 1999; Stopher, 2004). Travel blending advocates planning in advance to incorporate blending the mode of travel (e.g. car, public transport, walking or cycling) and blending the activities required by the household (e.g. achieving multiple objectives in one trip or at one location) (Ampt, 1999). Travel blending uses a diary-based household interview system in which participants receive a series of four kits containing information booklets and travel diaries, over a nine-week period (Tisato and Robinson, 1999; Rose and Ampt, 2001). The information received from the initial travel diaries is used to provide the household with a summary of its travel patterns and resultant emissions, with suggestions for reducing vehicle use. A subsequent set of travel diaries are recorded four weeks later. Changes in travel patterns from the diaries are relayed back to the household.

Individualized marketing

Individualized marketing is the general term used here to refer to all trademarked schemes that use targeted information for individual travellers to reduce car use and increase use of sustainable-transport modes. Individualized marketing is widely used (Ker, 2004;

Brog et al, 2009) and attempts to shift transport mode by providing information about the transport-related infrastructure and services available to the specific individual (Stopher et al, 2004). This method is based on the assumption that a proportion of the community is uninformed about sustainable-travel options (Taylor, 2007). Information provided generally includes public-transport timetables and route maps, and cycling or walking maps. The technique uses interviews to segment people into three main groups resulting from their responses to a set of simple questions (John, 2001; Ker, 2004). Each household is then provided with a customized implementation plan based on its specific needs as determined during the interview.

VTBC impacts

Generally, the objectives of VTBC schemes are to reduce the amount of car travel or increase the use of more sustainable modes in order to reduce greenhouse-gas emissions; however, there are also a set of beneficial subsidiary effects that have been reported from the implementation of VTBC, as presented in Table 16.1.

Measuring behaviour change

There are two general reasons for measuring behaviour change. First, to provide a method of feedback to participants in VTBC schemes to encourage and support their travel decisions. Second, to evaluate the effectiveness of VTBC interventions regarding the overall effect on reducing car use or the comparative cost and benefits of VTBC versus infrastructure changes, or the comparative effectiveness of intervention types. In undertaking an evaluation, the distinction between these purposes will determine the information and level of detail required. As VTBC has no physical product such as those produced by traditional infrastructure projects, the main focus is in evaluating behavioural outcomes (Morton and Mees, 2005; Chatterjee, 2009). Evaluating behaviour is a significant challenge owing to the many uncontrolled external factors that influence individual decision-making. Evaluation is a controversial area among VTBC practitioners and is widely discussed in the literature (Ampt and Richardson, 1994; Ampt, 2001; Stopher and Bullock, 2003; Taylor and Ampt, 2003; Richardson et al, 2004; Stopher et al, 2004; Morton and Mees, 2005; Stopher et al, 2006; Stopher et al, 2007; Stopher and Greaves, 2007; Stopher and Swann, 2007; Taylor, 2007; Bonsall, 2009; Chatterjee, 2009; Chatterjee and Bonsall, 2009; Cohen, 2009; Stopher et al, 2009). Debate regarding the appropriateness of conclusions drawn in published evaluations demonstrates a need for more robust verification of the impact of VTBC to allow comparison with other TDM options and to determine the most effective way to implement VTBC. The challenge of robust evaluation must be met, not only to improve VTBC implementation, but also to prove its worth as an instrument in developing sustainable urban systems.

Measuring VTBC for participant feedback

The detail and quality of information required to provide participant feedback varies greatly from that required to evaluate the VTBC scheme itself. Rose and Ampt (2001) stated that perfect information is not needed in order for people to change their travel

Table 16.1 Benefits observed from VTBC schemes

Overall benefit	Observed through
Reduction of congestion	• Reduction in distance travelled by car • Reduction in time spent travelling by car • Reduction in car travel at high-demand times or in congested areas • Increase in car sharing
Reduction in air pollution and greenhouse-gas emissions	• Change in mode selection • Reduction in distance travelled • Reduction in stop/start engine losses • Improvement in car maintenance • Reduction in car ownership
Reduction in noise pollution	• Reduction in the distance travelled by car • Reduction in the number of cars
Increased use of environmentally friendly travel modes	• Increases in pedestrian and bicycle activity and public-transport trips
Reduction in land uptake for transport infrastructure	• Less space required to park cars • Reduction in the size of car owned
Increase in revenue from public transport	• Increase in public-transport fare receipts • Increase in public-transport patronage
Improved road safety	• Increase in pedestrian and cycling safety • Decreased frequency of reported accidents
Improved personal safety	• Increased activity and interaction in streets • Reduced reports of local crime
Social benefits to the community	• Increased social interaction and trust at a community level • Increase in recognition of local culture • Decrease in number of 'complaints-without-solutions' to local councils • Increased community-initiated projects
Economic development benefits	• Increase in local shopping • Redevelopment of local facilities to meet community needs • Increase in property prices when local-community efforts increase safety or positive perceptions of the community
Health benefits	• Increase in fitness levels due to more walking and cycling • Increase in health levels due to fewer in-car pollution effects • Decrease in doctors' visits due to social and health rewards • Lower stress levels • Increased levels of satisfaction and self-esteem due to social and health benefits

Source: Taylor and Ampt, 2003

Table 16.2 Objectives for evaluating the effectiveness of VTBC programmes

Objective	Description
Economic efficiency	Impacts related to increased economic efficiency, for example where effective work times are increased owing to less time spent in congested traffic
Liveable streets	Impacts where streets become more liveable owing to increased pedestrian and cyclist traffic, greater social interaction and improved perception of personal security, and less transport infrastructure such as car parks
Environmental protection	Impacts that contribute to reducing emissions
Equity, social inclusion and accessibility	Impacts that improve social interaction, self-esteem and satisfaction
Safety and security	Impacts where there are actual or perceived improvements in personal safety
Economic growth	Impacts that affect local economic development
Finance	Impacts that result in increased revenue for government bodies, such as increased public-transport revenue

Source: Institute for Transport Studies Leeds (ITSL), 2010

behaviour. Participants require suggestions on how to improve their travel behaviour, or support to continue their positive actions. Commonly, travel diaries identifying changes in participant travel behaviour are used to provide quantitative feedback on how participants can improve, or to reward them for their efforts. Travel diaries generally record all trips made, using start and finish time or odometer readings, trip purpose and mode selected. The analysis of the diaries is limited to basic comparisons between the trip time or distance recorded over the life of the VTBC programme, and qualitative review of mode selection to recommend alternatives. The analysis of the diaries is undertaken to act as a guide and support and does not require statistical significance or need to be comparative with other participants. Therefore, the information required to measure behaviour change in this manner is quite basic.

Evaluating VTBC effectiveness

Evaluating a VTBC application requires measuring the impacts of the scheme. Seven objectives, listed in Table 16.2, have been identified for consideration in any VTBC evaluation (ITSL, 2010).

Although there exists a common perception that VTBC will reduce car use wherever it is undertaken, there is an ongoing expectation to provide proof of the impact of VTBC schemes (Cohen, 2009). Conducting a robust evaluation of a VTBC programme is a complicated and resource-intensive procedure. Developing a statistically sound evaluation with a high level of confidence can often overshadow the cost of implementing the scheme itself. The difficulties in evaluating VTBC schemes are discussed in the following sections.

Detecting and measuring change

A baseline understanding of the travel behaviour before VTBC intervention is required in order to determine how travel behaviour has been impacted. VTBC evaluations use before-and-after travel surveys, across the demographic profile of the community and temporally spaced, in order to detect stable changes in travel behaviour. Ideally, these surveys should obtain estimates of the numbers of trips, numbers of activities, total distance travelled by mode, total time spent travelling by mode and the modes of travel used (Stopher et al, 2004, 2009). The reliance on individuals and households to accurately report these factors can decrease the confidence of the evaluation through the introduction of errors. There are two methods to supplement the travel surveys in an attempt to quantitatively verify household travel surveys and reduce self-reporting errors: odometer surveys and GPS surveys.

Odometer surveys record the vehicle kilometres travelled (VKT) by household vehicles. Although odometer surveys do not indicate changes in behaviour such as mode selection or trip chaining, the method reduces error in trip reporting, as missed trips can be inferred from the start/finish odometer readings, and respondents have limited opportunities to falsify information. Stopher and Swann (2007) demonstrate that, for the purpose of tracking household vehicle use over time, odometer surveys involve little burden to respondents, provide targeted, highly accurate data and are representative of the population.

GPS surveys can also be used to supplement household travel surveys. GPS surveys can be undertaken either for cars used in the household or individuals carrying portable GPS devices. Stopher et al (2009) conducted a comparative study of GPS and odometer surveys. The study determined that a GPS panel survey with a sample size of around 200 households was more statistically robust than the comparative odometer survey sampling from over 1000 households. The odometer-survey results were found to be inconclusive in this case and would have ideally required double the sample size to produce statistically significant results. The GPS data also provided a more detailed picture of participants' travel behaviour by capturing details such as the mode of transport, the number of trips made, trip duration and distance travelled. As GPS technology improves with cheaper, smaller and less inhibitive devices, the GPS survey could replace the household travel survey owing to the comprehensive information provided (Stopher et al, 2007).

Control groups – households or individuals unaffected by the VTBC programme – can be used to capture the effect of external influences on travel behaviour over the same period.

The use of before-and-after surveys for the purposes of evaluation can have an impact on the application of the VTBC scheme through a phenomenon known as 'instrument reactivity' (Seethaler and Rose, 2009). Seethaler (2005) found four scenarios are possible regarding instrument reactivity in a VTBC application, where the before surveys affect travel behaviour before the intervention, increase or decrease the uptake response, or have no effect. The study concluded that there exists a residual instrument reactivity, but mitigation measures such as a large interval between the before survey and the VTBC intervention and different branding of materials can be used to reduce this effect.

Variability of travel behaviour

Travel patterns are not static. Travel behaviour can change for many reasons other than VTBC intervention. Changes in household structure, moving house and new jobs are all examples of external influences that affect travel behaviour. Travel behaviour has also been found to be seasonal, changing according to school holidays or to reflect the season (Stopher et al, 2009).

Temporal patterns and rhythms relating to travel behaviour can also be detected at a smaller scale. Axhausen et al (2002) conducted a six-week continuous travel study of 139 German households to undertake detailed observation of the rhythms of daily travel of respondents by comparing the similarity between days, the patterns developed and the interaction between activities, trip duration and frequency. Studies of this type could eventually determine the optimal travel-survey duration in order accurately to represent temporal rhythms and variation.

Travel behaviour also varies geographically in response to factors such as public-transport availability and distance to major business centres (Dodson, 2007). Stopher and Bullock (2003) suggested that the application of VTBC in outer suburbs has a lower impact than in inner metropolitan suburbs. Studies have also shown strong evidence that participants have different characteristics and attitudes to non-participants, with participants forming a minority of the community, representing around three in ten households (Taylor and Ampt, 2003; Taylor, 2007). Socio-demographic characteristics can also affect travel behaviour (O'Fallon and Sullivan, 2004). As such, the evaluation of area-specific VTBC interventions cannot be extrapolated to indicate uptake or impact over the greater metropolitan area.

Statistical confidence

The order of magnitude of the changes generally reported by VTBC programmes is relatively small in statistical terms, requiring a large data set and subsequently large sample sizes in order to report the changes with confidence (Ker, 2004; O'Fallon and Sullivan, 2004; Richardson et al, 2004; Stopher et al, 2004, 2009; Stopher and Swann, 2007).

Generating statistical confidence has proven particularly difficult with small, pilot studies, given their smaller budgets and areas of application. This has given rise to the argument that the comprehensive documented results for existing VTBC applications should provide enough evidence of success, removing the need for evaluation of new applications (Ker, 2004). The predilection for proving the value of VTBC applications often leads to the publication of results drawn from sample sizes too small to derive robust conclusions and no indication of the confidence of the result. This can result in false representation of the success of VTBC applications and may mislead the direction of future applications. Published results need to be methodically and statistically sound, or specify that findings are indicative only.

The method of approach and the parameters selected for analysis in the evaluation surveys can reduce required sample size, but this may increase the complexity of the surveys. Richardson et al (2004) describe several survey design components that affect the sample size required to generate statistically significant results:

- detecting changes in the number of trips undertaken requires a smaller sample size than measuring changes in VKT or travel time;
- repeated cross-sectional surveys (a snapshot of a random selection of the population at a single point in time) require larger sample sizes to detect changes than panel surveys (a longitudinal-style survey gathering data over time using the same population sample);
- daily travel diaries require larger sample sizes to detect changes compared with a weekly travel diary, although the difference can be minimized by using a panel survey and recording the same day of the week for each wave;
- detecting changes in household travel requires smaller sample sizes compared with individual travel data;
- detecting changes in car usage requires smaller sample sizes than public-transport usage.

Seethaler and Rose (2009) provide an indicative example of the sample sizes required for statistical significance with reasonable confidence. The study compared the sample size required to detect a 10 per cent change in VKT for Australian VTBC applications, recorded in weekly travel diaries, using a cross-sectional-survey design compared with a panel-survey design. To estimate the 10 per cent change within a 5 per cent error level, the before-and-after cross-sectional survey required a sample of 758 households, compared with only 242 households with a panel-survey design. Applying the participation rates recorded from other Australian VTBC applications, they concluded that 629 households would need to be recruited to achieve a final sample of 242 households.

The burden on participants resulting from the survey design can also affect the evaluation process. The length of the survey period, the number of waves of a panel survey, and the detail required by the survey can all impact on the response rates and, hence, the data available for evaluation. Motivating and maintaining participation over a period of time have been found to be a substantial challenge (Stopher et al, 2004, 2009).

The design of the evaluation survey has to form a balance between the questions that the evaluator wants to answer and the resources available. A substantial number of evaluations published in the past have not taken this relationship into account and undertook intensive evaluation questions with sample sizes that produce insignificant results. The results from these evaluations are in turn inconsequential, and the resources would be better directed to developing statistically significant relationships.

Evaluating externalities

The indirect benefits, or externalities, of reducing car usage are difficult to quantify, and methods for assessing these changes are not well developed (Tisato and Robinson, 1999; Stopher et al, 2004, 2009). Generally, benefit–cost analysis (BCA) techniques are applied to develop a comparable impact rating based on economic measures, represented as a dollar value. The BCA represents these impacts in monetary terms by valuing the resources consumed at their market value and the impacts on those affected according to their willingness to pay to avoid the negative, and to receive the positive, project outcomes (Winn, 2004).

There have been few comprehensive BCA studies undertaken for VTBC schemes. Ker and James (1999) reported a comprehensive BCA for the application of individualized marketing in Perth, Australia, using conservative values from published sources where project-specific information was unavailable. Other BCA studies that have been undertaken are limited in their consideration of impacts and often focus on a subset of measurable parameters. For example, Tisato and Robinson (1999) and Winn (2004) intentionally neglected health benefits, owing to the difficulty involved in ascertaining their equivalent dollar value.

While there are some major challenges in appraising all the costs and benefits associated with VTBC programmes, the BCAs undertaken suggest that VTBC programmes are highly effective. The benefit–cost ratio (BCR) of other supply-side initiatives to reduce car use is typically 1:2 (Winn, 2004). For VTBC initiatives, Ker and James (1999) reported a BCR of 4:33 under low- and high-impact scenarios; Tisato and Robinson (1999) reported a BCR of 5.7 under an average-impact scenario; and Winn (2004) reported a BCR of 2.9:10. It would be reasonable to assume that the inclusion of the externalities currently not investigated would strengthen the BCA comparison of VTBC against traditional policy or hard-engineering solutions.

Independence of evaluators

The evaluation of VTBC schemes by the same body actioning the scheme can lead to the introduction of bias errors. In order to complete a critical appraisal of a scheme, it is recommended to use independent third-party evaluators to remove this cause of systematic errors (Morton and Mees, 2005; Stopher et al, 2006, 2009; Taylor, 2007). Stopher et al (2009) took this concept one step further, to also remove bias of selection towards intervention participants, by conducting the evaluation surveys in a completely blind manner, where the evaluators surveyed a totally independent sector of the community, with no knowledge of which households had participated.

Evaluating specific VTBC-instrument effectiveness

Evaluating the effectiveness of various VTBC instruments is an important task to help shape future VTBC applications. Direct comparative evaluations between interventions using an individualized-marketing approach, as opposed to a travel-blending approach, cannot be undertaken. This is owing to methodological incompatibility, as individualized-marketing results are measured against the whole target population, whereas travel-blending results are reported with respect to the number of participants (Ker, 2004).

However, it is possible through perception studies to determine which VTBC tools participants feel are most effective in encouraging change. Zhang et al (2009) undertook an extensive perception study of over a thousand participants to evaluate the effectiveness of the four most frequently used tools applied in a large-scale Australian VTBC application. The four tools consisted of a journey plan, a walking and cycling map, an affirmation letter and a local activity guide. Zhang et al (2009) indicated that the cycling and walking map appeared to be the most effective tool, encouraging people to walk more and ultimately achieving the goal of the project to reduce car use to a greater extent than the other tools investigated. In terms of the actual changes in the number of trips made through car driving, public-transport use or travel as passenger, it is interesting to note there was no significant difference found between the treatments.

Summary

Overall, the literature on evaluations conducted for VTBC schemes supports their effectiveness as an instrument in reducing car use. However, as the preceding paragraphs have indicated, there is much refinement and research required to improve this area of VTBC methodology. The challenges of VTBC evaluation for future applications can be summarized as (Stopher et al, 2006, 2009; Taylor, 2007; Chatterjee and Bonsall, 2009):

- determining what questions need to be answered through evaluation;
- conveying the importance of robust evaluation as a tool for improving and advocating future VTBC applications;
- ensuring the independence of evaluators to reduce bias errors;
- measuring changes in the programme participants, the entire targeted populations and in a comparable control group isolated from the intervention over time in order to differentiate between the effects of external factors and the changes related to the intervention;
- collecting comprehensive data, including trip rates, VKT, travel time by transport modes, and choice of travel mode;
- substantiating self-reported travel changes recorded in travel diaries using supplementary GPS or odometer surveys;
- accurately measuring changes over smaller sample sizes;
- minimizing respondent burden to assist in maintaining response rates over time, while providing comprehensive information, which may involve further developing GPS data collection.

Residual behaviour change

While VTBC programmes have been shown directly to affect travel behaviour, it is also necessary to consider effects beyond the active application of the programme. This involves considering what long-term or residual effect VTBC programmes have on participants, the targeted community and, indirectly, on the general population.

Residual behaviour change is reasoned to occur on the same principles that drive participation in VTBC programmes (Ampt, 1999, 2004; Hughes and Di Pietro, 2005; Nye and Burgess, 2008). The personal and environmental gains achieved by changing travel behaviour are typically compatible with the individual's ethics and concept of personal responsibility, providing sufficient motivation for the behaviour change to be sustained (Ampt, 1999, 2004). In Australia, behaviour change has been sustained beyond thirty months (John, 2001; Marinelli and Roth, 2002). German VTBC applications show behaviour change sustained beyond a four-year period (Marinelli and Roth, 2002). Taylor and Ampt (2003) found that behaviour change is sustained and may intensify over the short to medium term.

However, the contemporary nature of VTBC methodologies and the limited duration of evaluations mean there is a lack of historical data from which to infer the lasting effects of VTBC interventions. Longer-term studies are required to determine the duration and extent of behaviour change and whether VTBC is propagated outside the engaged community. These studies could also determine whether maintenance programmes are necessary.

Extending the VTBC concept

The success of VTBC suggests that the principles behind the concept may be successfully applied to other behaviours affecting the sustainability of urban communities. As stated previously, social marketing originally served as a public-health intervention. Marketing campaigns were developed to improve awareness and to prompt voluntary behaviour change towards products and services such as contraceptives, hand soap and immunization (Cairns and Stead, 2009). This practice has been extended further in the public-health sector to facilitate healthy lifestyles. Several examples exist in the United Kingdom of the application of social marketing to encourage voluntary behaviour change with respect to lifestyle choices. Powell and Thurston (2008) described a voluntary-behaviour-change programme with the aim to 'motivate the public to protect its own health and to develop an environment that supports healthy lifestyle choices'. Stead et al (2007a) reviewed the effectiveness of social-marketing interventions in influencing youth versus adult individual behaviour change to prevent smoking, alcohol use and illicit drug use and to increase physical activity. The report found significant short-term positive effects in youth behaviour, with sustained effects more than two years after the intervention. Adult interventions showed mixed results, especially with respect to smoking, yet, however, still proved effective in influencing lifestyle choices. Stead et al (2007b) discussed the use of social marketing to tackle obesity by targeting dietary and exercise behaviour. Powell and Tapp (2009) extended the principles of social marketing to describe a method for confronting problem gambling.

Further case studies are described where social and community-based marketing has been extended to (McKenzie-Mohr, 2000a, 2000b; Abrahamse et al, 2005; Cullbridge, 2010; McKenzie-Mohr, 2010):

- waste minimisation and recycling;
- energy consumption;
- water use;
- biological control;
- sustainable harvests for fishing and agriculture;
- minimizing the use of pesticide, herbicide, fertilizer and other environmental contaminants;
- social problems such as bullying, child abuse, speeding and drink driving;
- green construction and retrofitting.

These examples of voluntary-behaviour-change interventions usually target a limited category of behaviours. In attempting to establish more sustainable lifestyles, there are many behaviours that could be targeted by such schemes. As such, it is valuable to determine if a single intervention can instigate change across multiple behaviours.

The EcoTeam Programme (ETP) targets approximately 100 different household behaviours in order to promote durable, green lifestyle changes in over 20,000 households worldwide (Staats et al, 2004). The six behaviour categories dealt with by the ETP are waste minimization, gas consumption, electricity consumption, water, transport and consumer behaviour. Similar to VTBC interventions, ETP uses information and feedback to generate behaviour change. The ETP operates using groups of six to ten people (from four to six households) who have an existing relationship: for example, neighbours, friends or club members. The group approach increases social pressure to change and sustain green behaviours, and provides long-term community support once the active programme has concluded. Teams meet once a month over the life of the eight-month programme, addressing various behaviour changes over this time. Participants record their individual behaviour changes, measuring energy use, water use, waste reduction and reduction in private-car use. Participants receive feedback during the course of the programme and continue to receive feedback at the conclusion of the intervention on the accumulated effects of the ETP worldwide through quarterly-newsletter updates. The independent evaluation of two ETPs conducted in the United Kingdom (Nye and Burgess, 2008) and the Netherlands (Staats et al, 2004) has found durable changes in participant behaviour. Nye and Burgess (2008) qualitatively reported that the most commonly changed behaviours in the UK ETP were waste minimization and changing consumer behaviour by buying locally grown goods. Staats et al (2004) conducted a three-year longitudinal evaluation for the Netherlands application, finding that improvements in behaviour were maintained or increased two years after the completion of the ETP. The smallest behavioural change measured in the Netherlands case was a 7 per cent reduction in water consumption, whereas the largest change was a 32 per cent reduction in the amount of solid household waste (Staats et al, 2004).

The results of the public-health and ETP applications show that voluntary-behaviour-change principles can be generally applied across different behaviours, resulting in significant and sustainable behaviour change.

Conclusions

The preceding discussion has illustrated that substantial experience and knowledge have been developed by VTBC practitioners. VTBC has been applied in various situations and with different approaches. The consensus stands that VTBC is an effective tool in reducing private-car use and, subsequently, greenhouse-gas emissions, encouraging sustainable cities through the adoption of a sustainable lifestyle. Given this success, practitioners should now turn their focus to consider how to propagate the VTBC concept. It has been shown that the principles of VTBC can also be successfully applied to various lifestyle behaviours, and have the potential to help facilitate the development of sustainable urban communities.

References

Abrahamse, W., Steg, L., Vlek, C. and Rothengatter, T. (2005) 'A review of intervention studies aimed at household energy conservation', *Journal of Environmental Psychology*, vol 25, pp273–91

Ampt, E. (1999) 'From travel blending to living neighbourhoods . . . a vision for the future', *Papers of the 23rd Australasian Transport Research Forum*, www.patrec.org/atrf.aspx, Perth, Western Australia

Ampt, E. (2001) 'The evaluation of travel behaviour change methods – a significant challenge', *Transport Engineering in Australia*, vol 7, no 1/2, pp35–9

Ampt, E. (2003) 'Understanding voluntary travel behaviour change', *Papers of the 26th Australasian Transport Research Forum*, www.patrec.org/atrf.aspx, Wellington, New Zealand

Ampt, E. (2004) 'Understanding voluntary travel behaviour change', *Transport Engineering in Australia*, vol 9, no 2, pp53–66

Ampt, E. and Richardson, A. J. (1994) 'The validity of self-completion surveys for collecting travel behaviour data', *Proceedings of the PTRC European Transport Forum*, Warwick, 12–16 September

Ampt, E. and Rooney, A. (1998) 'Reducing the impacts of the car – a sustainable approach: TravelSmart Adelaide', *Papers of the 22nd Australasian Transport Research Forum*, www.patrec.org/atrf.aspx, Sydney, Australia

Andreasen, A. (1994) 'Social marketing: its definition and domain', *Journal of Public Policy and Marketing*, vol 13, no 1, pp108–14

Andreasen, A. (1995) *Marketing Social Change: Changing Behaviour to Promote Health, Social Development, and the Environment*, Jossey-Bass, San Francisco, CA

Australian Greenhouse Office (AGO) (2005) *Evaluation of Australian TravelSmart projects in the ACT, South Australia, Queensland, Victoria, and Western Australia 2001–2005*, Australian Greenhouse Office, Commonwealth of Australia, Canberra, Australia

Axhausen, K., Zimmerman, A., Schonfelder, S., Rindsfuser, G. and Haupt, T. (2002) 'Observing the rhythms of daily life: a six week travel diary', *Transportation*, vol 29, pp95–124

Baudains, C., Styles, I. and Dingle, P. (2001) 'TravelSmart workplace: walking and the journey to work', *Australia:Walking the 21st Century: A Selection of Conference Papers*, Perth, Western Australia

Bonsall, P. W. (2009) 'Do we know whether travel planning really works?', *Transport Policy*, vol 16, no 6, pp306–14

Brog, W., Erl, E., Ker, I., Ryle, J. and Wall, R. (2009) 'Evaluation of voluntary travel behaviour change: experiences from three continents', *Transport Policy*, vol 16, no 6, pp281–92

Brog, W. and John, G. (2001) 'Personalised marketing – the Perth success story', *Proceedings Marketing Public Transport Conference*, Auckland, New Zealand

Bureau of Transport Economics (BTE) (2000) 'Urban congestion – the implications for greenhouse gas emissions', Bureau of Transport Economics, Canberra, Australia, www.bitre.gov.au/info.aspx? ResourceId=98&NodeId=61, accessed 11 February 2010

Bureau of Transport and Regional Economics (BTRE) (2007) 'Estimating urban traffic and congestion cost trends for Australian cities', Working Paper 71, Bureau of Transport and Regional Economics, Canberra, Australia

Cairns, G. and Stead, M. (2009) 'Obesity and social marketing: works in progress', Symposium on the challenge of translating nutrition research into public health nutrition, Nutrition Society, Dublin, Republic of Ireland, pp11–16.

Chapman, L. (2007) 'Transport and climate change: a review', *Journal of Transport Geography*, vol 15, pp354–67

Chatterjee, K. (2009) 'A comparitive evaluation of large-scale personal travel planning projects in England', *Transport Policy*, vol 16, no 6, pp293–305

Chatterjee, K. and Bonsall, P. W. (2009) 'Special Issue on evaluation of programmes promoting voluntary change in travel behaviour', *Transport Policy*, vol 16, no 6, pp279–80

Cohen, T. (2009) 'Evaluating personal travel planning: if it is prohibitively expensive to get a robust answer then what should we do?', *Transport Policy*, vol 16, no 6, pp344–7

Cullbridge (2010) 'Tools of change: proven methods for promoting health, safety and environmental citizenship', Cullbridge Marketing and Communications, www.toolsofchange.com, accessed 3 March 2010

Department for Transport, Energy and Infrastructure (DTEI) (2009) 'TravelSmart: households in the west', Government of South Australia, Department for Transport, Energy and Infrastructure, www.transport.sa.gov.au/pdfs/environment/travelsmart_sa/Households_in_the_West_Final_Report.pdf, accessed 12 February 2010

Dodson, J. (2007) 'Transport disadvantage and Australian urban planning in historical perspective: the role of urban form and structure in shaping household accessibility', in G. Currie, J. Stanley and J. Stanley (eds) *No Way to Go: Transport and Social Disadvantage in Australian*

Communities, Monash University ePress, Melbourne, Australia, www.publications.epress. monash.edu/toc/nwtg/1/1, accessed 2 March 2010

Hughes, I. and Di Pietro, G. (2005) 'Developing a school travel planning guide', *Papers of the 28th Australasian Transport Research Forum*, www.patrec.org/atrf.aspx, Sydney, Australia

Ife, J. (1996) *Community Development Creating Alternatives – Vision, Analysis and Practice*, Longman, London

Institute for Transport Studies Leeds (ITSL) (2010) *Knowledgebase on Sustainable Land Use and Transport*, ITS Leeds, www.konsult.leeds.ac.uk/public/level0/l0_hom.htm, accessed 16 February 2010

Intergovernmental Panel on Climate Change (IPCC) (2007a) *Climate Change 2007: The Physical Science Basis. Contribution of Working Group I to the Fourth Assessment Report of the Intergovernmental Panel on Climate Change*, Cambridge University, Cambridge

Intergovernmental Panel on Climate Change (IPCC) (2007b) *Climate Change 2007: Mitigation. Contribution of Working Group III to the Fourth Assessment Report of the Intergovernmental Panel on Climate Change*, Cambridge University, Cambridge

James, B. (1998) 'Changing travel behaviour through individualized marketing: application and lessons from South Perth', *Papers of the 22nd Australasian Transport Research Forum*, www.patrec.org/atrf.aspx, Sydney, Australia

James, B. and John, G. (1997) 'Behavioural approaches to travel demand management', *Papers of the 21st Australasian Transport Research Forum*, www.patrec.org/atrf.aspx, Adelaide, Australia

John, G. (2001) 'The effectiveness of the TravelSmart individualized marketing program for increasing walking trips in Perth', *Road and Transport Research*, vol 10, no 1, pp17–25

Ker, I. (2004) 'Household-based voluntary travel behaviour change: aspirations, achievements and assessment', *Transport Engineering in Australia*, vol 9, no 2, pp119–37

Ker, I. and James, B. (1999) 'Evaluating behavioural change in transport – a case study of individualized marketing in South Perth, Western Australia', *Papers of the 23rd Australasian Transport Research Forum*, www.patrec.org/atrf.aspx, Perth, Australia

Kotler, P. and Zaltman, G. (1971) 'Social marketing: an approach to planned social change', *The Journal of Marketing*, vol 35, no 3, pp3–12

McKenzie-Mohr, D. (2000a) 'Fostering sustainable behaviour through community-based social marketing', *American Psychologist*, vol 55, no 5, pp531–7

McKenzie-Mohr, D. (2000b) 'Promoting sustainable behaviour: an introduction to community-based social marketing', *Journal of Social Issues*, vol 56, no 3, pp543–54

McKenzie-Mohr, D. (2010) 'Fostering sustainable behaviour: community-based social marketing', McKenzie-Mohr and Associates, www.cbsm.com, accessed 3 March 2010

Marinelli, P. and Roth, M. (2002) 'TravelSmart suburbs Brisbane – a successful pilot study of a voluntary travel behaviour change technique', *Papers of the 25th Australasian Transport Research Forum*, www.patrec.org/atrf.aspx, Canberra, Australia

May, A. D. and Taylor, M. A. P. (2002) 'KonSULT – developing an international knowledgebase on urban transport policy instruments', *Papers of the 25th Australasian Transport Research Forum*, www.patrec.org/atrf.aspx, Canberra, Australia

Minken, H. (1999) 'A sustainability objective function for local transport policy evaluation', in H. Meersman, E. Van De Voorde and W. Winkelmans (eds) *World Transport Research – Selected Proceedings from the 8th World Conference on Transport Research, Volume 4: Transport Policy*, Elsevier–Pergamon, Oxford

Morton, A. and Mees, P. (2005) 'Too good to be true? An assessment of the Melbourne travel behaviour modification pilot', *Papers of the 28th Australasian Transport Research Forum*, www.patrec.org/atrf.aspx, Sydney, Australia

Nye, M. and Burgess, J. (2008) *Promoting Durable Change in Household Waste and Energy Use Behaviour*, Department for Environment, Food and Rural Affairs and the University of East Anglia, Norwich

O'Fallon, C. and Sullivan, C. (2004) 'Personalised marketing – improving evaluation', *Transport Engineering in Australia*, vol 9, no 2, pp85–101

Powell, J. and Tapp, A. (2009) 'The use of social marketing to influence the development of problem gambling in the UK: implications for public health', *International Journal of Mental Health and Addiction*, vol 7, pp3–11

Powell, K. and Thurston, M. (2008) 'Commissioning training for behaviour change interventions: guidelines for best practice', University of Chester Centre for Public Health Research, www.chesterrep.openrepository.com/cdr/handle/10034/46839, accessed 12 January 2010

Pramberg, P. (2004) 'A national move to change travel behaviour', *Transport Engineering in Australia*, vol 9, no 2, pp49–52

Richardson, A. J., Seethaler, R. and Harbutt, P. (2004) 'Design issues for before and after surveys of travel behaviour change', *Transport Engineering in Australia*, vol 9, no 2, pp103–18

Rose, G. and Ampt, E. (2001) 'Travel blending: an Australian travel awareness initiative', *Transportation Research Part D*, vol 6, pp95–110

Seethaler, R. (2005) 'Evaluating community-based TravelSmart in Melbourne', *Institute of Transport Engineers International Conference Proceedings*, Melbourne, Australia

Seethaler, R. and Rose, G. (2003) 'Application of psychological principles to promote travel behaviour change', *Papers of the 26th Australasian Transport Research Forum*, www.patrec.org/atrf.aspx, Wellington, New Zealand

Seethaler, R. and Rose, G. (2004) 'Application of psychological principles to promote travel behaviour change', *Transport Engineering in Australia*, vol 9, no 2, pp67–84

Seethaler, R. and Rose, G. (2005) 'Using the six principles of persuasion to promote travel behaviour change – preliminary findings of two TravelSmart field experiments', *Papers of the 28th Australasian Transport Research Forum*, www.patrec.org/atrf.aspx, Sydney, Australia

Seethaler, R. and Rose, G. (2009) 'Using odometer readings to assess VKT changes associated with a voluntary behaviour change program', *Transport Policy*, vol 16, no 6, pp325–34

Staats, H., Harland, P. and Wilke, H. (2004) 'Effecting durable change – a team approach to improve environmental behaviour in the household', *Environment and Behaviour*, vol 36, no 3, pp341–67

Stead, M., Gordon, R., Angus, K. and McDermott, L. (2007a) 'A systematic review of social marketing effectiveness', *Health Education*, vol 107, no 2, pp126–91

Stead, M., Hastings, G. and McDermott, L. (2007b) 'The meaning, effectiveness and future of social marketing', *Obesity Reviews*, vol 8, no 1, pp189–93

Stern, N. (2006) *Stern Review – Economics of Climate Change*, HM Treasury, Cambridge University, Cambridge

Stopher, P. R. (2004) 'Reducing road congestion: a reality check', *Transport Policy*, vol 11, pp117–31

Stopher, P. R., Alsnih, R., Bullock, P. and Ampt, E. (2004) 'Evaluating voluntary travel behaviour interventions', *Papers of the 27th Australasian Transport Research Forum*, www.patrec.org/atrf.aspx, Adelaide, Australia

Stopher, P. R. and Bullock, P. (2003) 'Travel behaviour modification: a critical appraisal', *Papers of the 26th Australasian Transport Research Forum*, www.patrec.org/atrf.aspx, Wellington, New Zealand

Stopher, P. R., Clifford, E., Swann, N. and Zhang, Y. (2009) 'Evaluating voluntary travel behaviour change: suggested guidelines and case studies', *Transport Policy*, vol 16, no 6, pp315–24

Stopher, P. R., FitzGerald, C. and Xu, M. (2007) 'Assessing the accuracy of the Sydney Household Travel Survey with GPS', *Transportation*, vol 34, pp723–41

Stopher, P. R. and Greaves, S. (2007) 'Guidelines for samplers: measuring a change in behaviour from before and after surveys', *Transportation*, vol 34, pp1–16

Stopher, P. R. and Swann, N. (2007) 'A 6-wave odometer panel for the evaluation of voluntary travel behaviour change programs', *Papers of the 30th Australasian Transport Research Forum*, www.patrec.org/atrf.aspx, Melbourne, Australia

Stopher, P. R., Wilmot, C., Stecher, C. and Alsnih, R. (2006) 'Household travel surveys: proposed standards and guidelines', in P. R. Stopher and C. Stecher (eds) *Travel Survey Methods: Quality and Future Directions*, Elsevier, Oxford

Taylor, M. A. P. (2007) 'Voluntary travel behaviour change programs in Australia: the carrot rather than the stick in travel demand management', *International Journal of Sustainable Transportation*, vol 1, no 3, pp173–92

Taylor, M. A. P. and Ampt, E. (2003) 'Travelling smarter down under: policies for voluntary travel behaviour change in Australia', *Transport Policy*, vol 10, no 3, pp165–77

Tideman, J., Wotton, B. and Ampt, E. (2006) 'TravelSmart households in the west: new ways to achieve and sustain travel behaviour change', *Papers of the 29th Australasian Transport Research Forum*, www.patrec.org/atrf.aspx, Gold Coast, Australia

Tisato, P. and Robinson, T. (1999) 'A cost benefit analysis of travel blending', *Papers of the 23rd Australasian Transport Research Forum*, www.patrec.org/atrf.aspx, Perth, Australia

Winn, R. (2004) 'Measuring the economic benefits of travel behavioural change programs', *Papers of the 27th Australasian Transport Research Forum*, www.patrec.org/atrf.aspx, Adelaide, Australia

World Business Council for Sustainable Development (WBCSD) (2001) 'Mobility 2001: world mobility at the end of the twentieth century and its sustainability', World Business Council for Sustainable Development, www.wbcsd.org/plugins/DocSearch/details.asp?type=DocDet&ObjectId=MTg1, accessed 4 February 2010

World Business Council for Sustainable Development (WBCSD) (2004) 'Mobility 2030: meeting the challenges to sustainability', World Business Council for Sustainable Development, www.wbcsd.org/plugins/DocSearch/details.asp?type=DocDet&ObjectId=NjA5NA, accessed 4 February 2010

Zhang, Y., Stopher, P. R. and Halling, B. (2009) 'An evaluation of TravelSmart tools for travel behaviour change', *Papers of the 32nd Australasian Transport Research Forum*, www.patrec.org/atrf.aspx, Auckland, New Zealand

Chapter 17

Planning for the sustainable consumption of urban resources

Lou Wilson

Summary

In Australia and other developed countries, urban planning has become aligned with a neoliberal economic agenda to maximize urban growth, with clear implications for sustainable consumption. Planning has found itself caught between pressures on local and state governments to promote urban economic competitiveness, while dealing with national and state policies that contribute to economic, ecological and social crises by encouraging rapid population growth. Hence, urban planning has become structurally inclined to waive community participation and regulations that present impediments to the development and consumption of urban resources. In this model, consultation with stakeholders and communities affected by planning decisions may or may not take into account all of the views expressed and is widely used to legitimate decisions that have already been made. Such processes have significant implications for planning for the sustainable consumption of urban resources. Significant levels of uncertainty are involved in pricing waste abatement and other ecological pressures from a growing population. Optimal solutions require policymakers to have broad knowledge of abatement cost functions, which are difficult to achieve without wide consultation. A case study of the 30-Year Plan for Greater Adelaide suggests that neoliberal planning is significantly in tension with meaningful stakeholder consultation, democratic processes and sustainable consumption of land and housing.

Introduction

Just under two decades ago, the Agenda 21 report of the United Nations Conference on Environment and Development (UNCED, 1992) drew attention to contemporary levels and forms of consumption that, if left unchecked, were likely to prove unsustainable in the twenty-first century. The report drew attention to the wasteful and inefficient overconsumption practices of Western nations, including the United States, the European Union countries, Japan and Australia. Agenda 21 argued for 'sustainable-consumption' policies that would apply not only to the environmental damage that excessive consumption produces but also the effect of the individualizing tendencies of consumerism on community cohesion, social interactions and the availability of public space for positive collective action. These are concepts that are broadly associated with quality of life. Hence, it is unsurprising that sustainable consumption can be defined as:

the use of services and related products which respond to basic needs and bring a better quality of life while minimising the use of natural resources and toxic materials as well as emissions of waste and pollutants over the life cycle of the service or product so as not to jeopardise the needs of future generations.

(Oslo Roundtable on Sustainable Production and Consumption, 1994, definition cited in Prinet, 2011, p10)

A 2003 study led by sustainability theorist and consultant Roger Levett suggests a distinct tension between a philosophy of sustainable consumption and the neoliberal economic agenda pursued by most Western countries, including Australia, since the 1980s. Levett and his co-authors (2003) suggest that neoliberal economics rests on the concept of a utility-maximizing consumer, an ideal agent or household whose rational consumer choices should be as unrestrained as possible to maximize the efficient allocation of resources to the production, distribution and exchange of goods and services.

These ideal consumers in neoliberal economic theory are meant to engage in endless individual acts of balancing costs against benefits to arrive at action that maximizes personal advantage. Under this rubric, the humanity of consumers is neglected in order to build economic models that can explain social and economic behaviour in market economies. It is noteworthy that maximizing personal advantage might involve robbing a bank, using illegal drugs or gratuitous consumption of consumer goods to sate a want. All decisions on consumption, whether socially desirable or not, are considered 'rational' in neoliberal economics. Human motivations (i.e. why we want what we want) are the concern of other disciplines. Neoliberal economists restrict themselves to examining consumer behaviour in specific social or economic environments. That is, neoliberal economists do not examine the biological, psychological and sociological causes of consumption. The focus is only on the external price of consumption to the individual.

In neoliberal theory, the price of consumption is extrinsic or external to the individual, rather than being intrinsic or internal. Cultures, ideology, feelings of pride or honour, familial ties, paternal or maternal care, voluntarism or altruism are not of interest. The Nobel Prize-winning economist Amartya Sen has described other economists who subscribe to the neoliberal economic model as 'rational fools'. Nevertheless, as a range of commentators, including Harvey (2002, 2006, 2010), Saunders (2006), Hamilton (2003) and Levett et al (2003), have noted, neoliberal economic models that favour minimal restrictions on market activity continued to be favoured by governments of all political persuasions. It is not difficult to see why this model has attractions for politicians and policymakers. By ignoring cultural, historical and ideological variables, economists are able to make simple, predictive models of social and economic behaviour that other disciplines cannot. The assumption that economic structures are created out of nothing but the cumulative actions of individuals seeking to maximize personal benefit has an elegant simplicity. If humanity is reduced to the preferences of individuals seeking to get the most satisfaction possible, then a larger model can be constructed that takes these tendencies into account as constants.

In a critique of neoliberal rational-actor models, political theorist Emily Hauptmann (1996) has argued that, by ignoring culture, ideology and, in essence, humanity, neoliberal 'rationality' is antithetical to democratic processes. Elevating 'rational', unrestricted consumption of material goods to the status of a national priority, as governments have done in the USA, Britain and Australia, inevitably requires reducing political responsiveness to social demands for expenditure on schools, health services, parks and other public goods that markets tend to under-provide. Hauptmann (1996) argues that democracy, if it is to be democracy, cannot be reduced to a series of 'rational' choices, because market players are then prioritized above the diverse interests of the mass of the population, that is, the demos.

Similarly, Levett et al's (2003) study of decades of neoliberal policy-making in the UK argues that maximizing individual choice has come at the expense of the declining quality of public goods such as safe communities, clean streets and effective schools. Moreover, the focus of neoliberal economics on the individual consumer, or household, tends to be restricted to the fulfilment of material needs. That is, only material wealth in the form of income, property or other forms of traded goods is maximized by individual consumers or households. There is no room for other types of 'wealth' to be considered, such as 'wealth in time' or 'wealth in space' (Reisch, 2001). This model only explains the allocation decisions of people with formal income. It has no relation to the activities of unpaid workers carrying out 'reproductive work', such as raising children, caring and voluntary work. Unpaid work, care activities and voluntarism are nevertheless necessary to sustain any society. Such activities require environments that make it possible to sustain social reproduction.

In an attempt to refute arguments such as this, the seminal neoliberal economist Milton Friedman (1970) argued that the social responsibility of business is to increase its profits. Friedman was offering a treatise on the virtues of consumption. He did not argue that business should be irresponsible in seeking to maximize profit, but held that the wealth business generated benefited communities. Hence, making money from unregulated consumption was responsible.

In some circumstances, however, the focus of business on profits brings it into tension with the sustainability of communities, broadly defined by Chiu (2003, p245) as the 'maintenance and improvement of well-being of current and future generations'. Urban sociologists John Logan and Harvey Molotch (2007) argue that this tension is between the use value attached to a place by the communities that interact with it as part of their daily lives and the exchange value of making money from the land. Use value in this sense refers to cultural ties, the sense of place that might be attached to iconic heritage buildings and organic ties to community and neighbourhood, which tend to be threatened by unrestrained urban development. Logan and Molotch (2007) refer to a 'growth machine' comprised of those for whom 'the city is their business', an interlocking collection of organizations that include pro-growth developers and investors, but also politicians whose interests align with capitalists seeking a profit from changes to land use.

In Australia, an urban growth machine is fuelled by an expansive immigration policy and pro-fertility entitlements and social policies. The Australian government's permanent immigration programme, comprising the skill and family streams, has averaged 131,000 places per annum over the past decade, with the last three programme years being the highest on record. Temporary migrants have averaged 396,000 persons per year, with the past three years also being the highest intakes on record (Kukoc, 2010). The Australian fertility rate, at 1.81, is one of the highest in the OECD, and is influenced by pro-fertility state and federal government campaigns, including the Australian government's 'baby bonus' payment.

Population growth is causing our cities to expand rapidly and driving up consumption of land and housing. Rapid population growth also places significant pressure on the infrastructure of our cities. Civil engineers Pathak and Shukla (2009, p108) argue that population pressures are causing the 'deterioration of infrastructure facilities, loss of productive agricultural lands and green open spaces, as well as causing air pollution, health hazards and micro-climatic changes'. The deterioration of infrastructure is likely to adversely affect both the social and economic sustainability of settlements, while the loss of agricultural lands and green open spaces has significant social and environmental consequences. The present level of consumption, moreover, is reducing the resources that will be available to future generations to address their needs (Lowe, 2009; Hamilton, 2010). Urban planner Brendan Gleeson (2010) states that our water, energy and even urban climate systems are under severe pressure from antagonized natural systems, as seen in the severe damage from torrential rain and floods that have followed a long drought. Addressing the crisis requires rethinking conventional approaches, institutional systems and the level of resources dedicated to urban resilience.

This crisis has significant implications for urban planning. In Australia and other developed countries, urban planning has become aligned with a neoliberal economic agenda to maximize urban growth and facilitate capital accumulation (Harvey, 2002, 2006, 2009, 2010). Planning has found itself caught between pressures on local and state governments to promote urban economic competitiveness, while dealing with national and state policies that contribute to economic, ecological and social crises by encouraging rapid population growth and the consumption of land and other urban resources (Davidson and Wilson, 2010; Davidson, 2011). Hence, urban planning has become structurally inclined to waive community participation and regulations that present impediments to development (Wilson and Davidson, 2010). In this model, consultation with stakeholders and communities affected by planning decisions may or may not take into account all of the views expressed. The views of marginalized communities and non-economic stakeholders are often neglected. Moreover, consultations are widely used to legitimate decisions that have already been made (Garau, 2008; GRHS, 2009; Wilson and Davidson, 2010, 2011).

Critics of this approach to urban planning have struggled to offer an alternative, despite the inability of the neoliberal model to address mounting social, economic and environmental urban crises. Scholars who argue for alternatives tend to position the current crisis as indicative of 'market failure' to provide public goods. That is, a failure to provide cities characterized by a sustainable level of consumption. Hence, an argument is put for stronger state regulatory interventions to address urban sustainability (Flyvbjerg, 2002; Gleeson et al, 2004; Gleeson, 2010). Environmental economist Cameron Hepburn (2010, p132) suggests that this response lacks an 'appreciation of the fact that both governments and free markets fail a great deal of the time'. Senior environmental economists Simon Dietz and Samuel Fankhauser (2010) note that significant levels of uncertainty are involved in pricing climate-change abatement and the cost of addressing environmental pressure from a growing population. That is, optimal solutions to risks to urban sustainability require state regulators to know each abatement cost function if they are to effectively mitigate and adapt our cities to environmental pressures from a growing population and a changing climate. A comprehensive understanding of these costs and how to address them is difficult to achieve without wide consultation with stakeholders. However, governments are increasingly unwilling to address feedback from consultations that might place restrictions on the market. This is most evident in regard to how the land market is addressed in long-term strategic planning by Australia's state governments.

Long-term urban planning in Australia

In Australia, the everyday regulation of urban environments is generally delegated to local government authorities by state governments that have constitutional mandates over land-use planning. State governments tend to concern themselves with the development of long-term planning strategies that, in recent years, have seemingly embraced the concept of the sustainable consumption of land and urban resources. Sydney, Melbourne, South East Queensland and Adelaide now have long-term plans of up to thirty years that set out expected population and urban growth over coming decades and state government plans to manage the process. The new 30-Year Plan for Greater Adelaide, released in 2010, has marked similarities with Sydney's 2005 City of Cities Plan (Department of State and Regional Development (DSRD), 2005) and the recent update to Melbourne's 2030 plan, Melbourne @ 5 Million (Department of Planning and Community Development (DPCD), 2008) and the South East Queensland Regional Plan 2009–2031 (Department of Infrastructure and Planning (DIP), 2009). In each case, the plans are glossy, coffee-table reports that contain few citations to data that can be checked, at least in the main documents. All contain references to concepts such as healthy cities and the maintenance of community facilities that are associated with sustainable consumption. The newest of these plans, the 30-Year Plan for Greater Adelaide, has a notable emphasis on higher-density, 'transit oriented development' and contains frequent references to 'sustainability', 'social inclusion' and saving the environment.

On the surface there is a commitment in these plans to urban governance that fosters sustainable consumption of land and housing and cooperation between states, local government and grass-roots communities, subject to the characteristics of varying local issues, including environmental concerns. Providing access to green space, a key concern of local communities, is also widely referred to in these plans, as is maintaining urban heritage. There is evidence that maintaining urban-heritage buildings and green environments contributes to the well-being and enjoyment of future generations. The maintenance of heritage buildings provides indications of changes over time and the imprint on the urban fabric left by former generations (Davidson and Wilson, 2009). Such processes are held to help populations to identify who they are and 'what we do and how we lived in the past', as Chan and Lee (2008, p247) argue. Public space is significantly affected by urban-planning regulations and building codes. The quality of a plan might be assessed by how well it addresses the concerns of communities in regard to public life, civic culture and everyday interactions.

However, there is an odd tension between commitments to sustainable consumption and clear intentions stated in the plans to assert greater control over local government authorities, under the rubric of freeing the land market from the constraints of local political pressures and the so-called NIMBY (not-in-my-backyard) syndrome, which is held to get in the way of rational planning. Such plans also indicate a preference for public–private partnerships to foster new urban development. Public–private partnerships require much greater attention by government to the concerns of the development industry in the central decision-making process and to the interests of actors associated with the industry (Wilson and Davidson, 2011). Increasing cooperation of governments with private companies necessitated by public–private partnerships changes the role of the state, with implications for the legitimacy of the planning process. Local governments in Australia have traditionally acted as mediators between market actors and the community. Mediation requires acceptance of the legitimacy of the mediator by competing stakeholders. Planning for land use in Australia has derived its legitimacy from the election of councillors by local communities. Councillors set policy directions in consultation with urban planners and other professionals, who are also tasked with implementing planning decisions. In this sense, councillors are meant to represent the interests of their electors in regard to how land will be used in their communities. Hence, planning for land use is anchored in the democratic legitimacy of elected members acting in concert with planning professionals. The latter bring functional legitimacy to the process by virtue of their qualifications and expertise. State governments also have democratic legitimacy conferred by virtue of election to office. Land-use planning in Australia has always required a degree of coordination with the private sector and between layers of government to improve the built and social environments of communities, in accordance with community consultation, civic culture and everyday interactions (Hutchings and Bunker, 1986). Indeed, the 30-year Plan for Greater Adelaide was largely authored for the South Australian Department of Planning and Local Government (DPLG) by KPMG and Connor Holmes, private consultants associated with the development industry (DPLG, 2010a). While clearly favouring public–private partnerships, the 30-year Plan for Greater Adelaide seems to contain policies that will limit local democracy in order to facilitate urban expansion and the relatively unrestricted consumption of land and housing.

The 30-Year Plan for Greater Adelaide

The central premise of the 30-Year Plan for Greater Adelaide (hereafter referred to as the Plan, unless otherwise indicated) is that Adelaide will grow by 560,000 people from its current population, to 1.8 million by the year 2036 (DPLG, 2010a, p3). How this population increase was estimated is not made clear in the Plan, although it is meant to align with an expansive federal population policy. Demographers discuss population increase or decrease in relation to assumptions made about future levels of fertility, mortality, overseas migration and internal migration, as applied to a base population, to obtain a projected population for the following year. No such discussion appears in the Plan.

Interestingly, the Plan does not refer to Adelaide but rather to a place called 'Greater Adelaide', a term not used in planning documents before the release of the draft Plan in 2009 (DPLG, 2009, p3). Most of the planning for infrastructure and jobs discussed in the Plan refers to the current metropolitan Adelaide area, ranging from the suburbs of Gawler to Willunga (an area of less than 2000km^2, analogous to the 'Adelaide Statistical District' used by the Australian Bureau of Statistics). However, the Plan refers to an area called 'Greater Adelaide', of which the boundaries extend to 9000km^2, covering the area from Port Wakefield in the north to Victor Harbor in the south and Murray Bridge in the west. The Plan suggests that this will be the area subject to urban expansion and will provide a long-term supply of land for consumption by developers in a range of sites over 9000km^2 (DPLG, 2010a, p73).

To put this into perspective, the area of 9000km^2 claimed for 'Greater Adelaide', containing 1.2 million people in 2010, is six times the area of Greater London (1500km^2), a city of 8 million people and more than twice the geographic area of Sydney, an Australian city with four times the population of Adelaide. If 'Greater Adelaide' is considered to be a city, then urban densities in 'Greater Adelaide' are incredibly low, with vast areas of this 'city' being open farmland or vacant land (Wilson and Davidson, 2010). The Plan indicates that more than 14,200ha will be developed for low-density housing on the city's fringes. Three large housing developments are flagged in the Plan for the iconic Barossa Valley wine-growing district to the north of the metropolitan area, and major developments are planned in the semi-rural Mt Barker district of the Adelaide Hills (DPLG, 2010a, p73). Oddly, such peri-urban development is framed in the Plan in terms of containing 'sprawl' and as being in the interest of 'sustainability'. These developments are, of course, within the 9000km^2 claimed as 'Greater Adelaide' and, hence, might be considered urban consolidation, if one accepts the premise that the natural boundaries of Adelaide cover twice the land area of Sydney (DPLG, 2010a, p73). Indeed, much of the Plan seems aimed at appeasing the environmental movement, without challenging the interests of developers who wish to continue to build on the periphery of the city, where land is cheap and construction costs are low.

The 30-Year Plan for Greater Adelaide signifies a strong commitment by the state government to making land available for consumption. This commitment sometimes seems excessive. In a recent case brought before the South Australian Supreme Court by the Gawler Region Community Forum, it was alleged that developers wrote a draft Development Plan Amendment for the state government and started work on a new 2500-home project at Gawler East in Adelaide's north, six months before the public knew the land was going to be rezoned (England, 2011).

This is not to suggest that the South Australian government does not consult on planning matters. In a recent study, politics and policy researcher Rob Manwaring (2010) indicates that the state government has a 'strategic' approach to consultation that suggests the government wants greater public engagement with, and ownership of, the planning agenda, but without the inherent complications of having to commit to address feedback. In essence, this involves an 'announce and defend strategy', whereby a draft plan is drawn up and then presented to key stakeholders and the community, followed by a consultation as a means of selling the plan.

Consultation on the 30-Year Plan for Greater Adelaide

In 2009, copies of a draft 30-Year Plan for Greater Adelaide (subtitled 'Planning for the Adelaide that we all want') and briefings were made available to key stakeholders in Adelaide and regional areas. General community consultation seems to have been confined to eighteen focus groups, conducted by a private consultant who had been contracted by the DPLG. Participants were 'randomly selected' from people living in the Greater Adelaide area, according to a 30-Year Plan Consultation Report available on the DPLG website. No information is provided as to how the random selection of 295 participants from a population of 1.2 million people took place (DPLG, 2010b). Public submissions from interested parties were also called for, many of which were highly critical of the Plan. Over 60 per cent of submissions were from individuals, community groups and commercial organizations, with the rest from local government, professional organizations and state agencies (DPLG, 2010b, p8). The final version of the 30-Year Plan for Greater Adelaide was released in early 2010 and contained some changes to the draft Plan, which are summarized in the 30-Year Plan Consultation Report (DPLG, 2010b). The changes indicate that the plan was recalibrated in minor ways to address the concerns of local government, professional organizations and state agencies. However, a reading of the final Plan and the consultation report suggests that the concerns of some local councils, community groups and individuals in relation to property matters were largely ignored. Indeed, there appears to be only one paragraph that refers to how the concerns of residents and community groups were addressed, in the twenty-one pages of the 30-Year Plan Consultation Report that summarize changes to the Plan. This paragraph states:

> During the consultation process a significant number of submissions were received from the residents and community organisations living in the Mount Barker area. A proportion of these do not support the Plan due to opposition to population growth, concerns on possible future growth in the town and the need for the State Government to commit to infrastructure to support any growth.
>
> (DPLG, 2010b, p29)

Opposition to the population growth and the consumption of land without a commitment from the state to provide infrastructure was evidently deemed to be unreasonable and outside the pale of rational planning by the DPLG. No indication is given as to how these concerns were addressed, and the report simply moves on to discuss, in two sentences, the concerns of the Mt Barker Council, which also appear to have been dismissed, as they are not discussed further. A reading of the 30-Year Plan Consultation Report in relation to the Plan itself also indicates that changes to the Plan concerning the available supply of land for future consumption were minimal and mainly confined to removing parcels of land identified in the original Plan from districts to the south of Adelaide.

In a related matter, the Plan makes provision for the establishment of 'structure plans' for 800m high-density growth zones on either side of major roads, railway lines and tramlines in the existing Adelaide metropolitan area. Local councils will be required to have their development assessment plans comply with the structure plans (DPLG, 2010a, p72). Developments within the zones will be at higher densities than currently exist, and there will be constrained capacity for local residents or communities to appeal a development to local planning authorities. This provision is couched in terms of enhancing urban 'sustainability', with references to saving the environment by encouraging public-transit use. Although there is a significant body of planning literature that supports higher density 'transit-oriented development' (TOD) around transport nodes (usually discussed as railway stations or tram stops associated with mixed-use developments) as a means of reducing sprawl and car usage, there is little to recommend ad hoc ribbon development along congested main roads served by the slow and unreliable bus services that provide public transport on most of Adelaide's main roads. It is revealing that, in the 226 pages of the 30-Year Plan for Greater Adelaide, only five pages discuss public transport and transit corridors, and only in terms of general objectives, whereas many pages are given over to words on the need to find sustainable solutions to rapid population growth by increasing urban densities to save the environment.

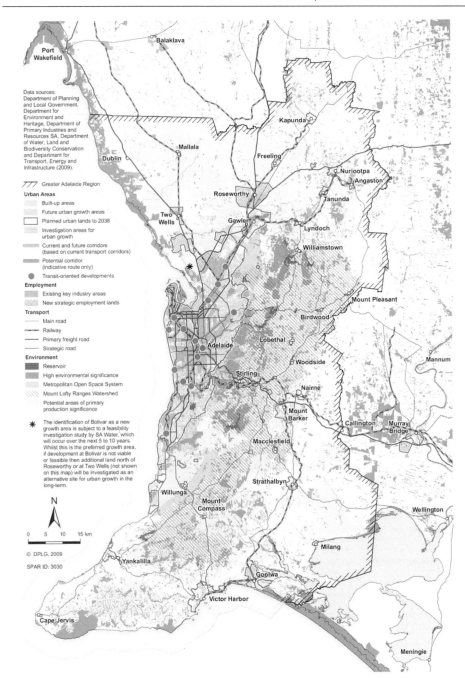

Figure 17.1 Illustration of the 30-Year Plan for Greater Adelaide.

Source: Report DPLG, 2010a

Conclusion

The new 30-Year Plan for Greater Adelaide is illustrative of a neoliberal policy agenda to promote relatively unrestricted land and housing consumption. The Plan, if implemented, will work to exclude the interests of actors other than land developers and state agencies from influence over decision-making in significant areas of the planning process and diminish the capacity of local government and local communities to address their concerns on land-use matters.

Adelaide's Plan offers a claim that the city's boundaries should incorporate a region more than four times the size of the current metropolitan area. This allows the state government simultaneously to argue that it is engaging in urban consolidation, thus (on paper) addressing concerns of environmentalists and planners concerned about sprawl, while providing space for developers to continue to build on the fringe of the city. There are also plans to free up more land in the inner city using similar justifications. In this sense, there is a superficial attempt in the Plan to include the interests of a plurality of individuals, communities and social organizations, but the clear intention is to facilitate relatively unrestricted consumption of land and housing. Opponents of the Plan who are not appeased by these arguments, and whose dissent can safely be ignored, might expect to be positioned as selfishly standing in the way of both good environmental outcomes and economic growth.

The Plan, and others like it, will do little to address the concerns of communities in Adelaide affected by development, particularly those who may find themselves living in higher-density-structure zones or rural towns that are engulfed by greenfields development. The latter might find avenues for consultation and appeal against developments that affect their interests to be increasingly limited under the Plan. In this sense, the Plan also illustrates a clear tension between neoliberal planning and democracy. As Hauptmann (1996) has suggested, a policy that prioritizes the market and the facilitation of consumption necessitates the marginalization of the interests of non-economic actors and the undermining of democracy by ignoring the 'non-rational' demands of the demos.

The lack of concern with the interests of actors other than commercial interests and state agencies that is evident in the Plan and the associated consultation report also has implications for how governments respond to the environmental pressures on our cities associated with climate change and a growing population. As Dietz and Fankhauser (2010) have shown, significant levels of uncertainty are involved in pricing climate-change abatement and the cost of addressing environmental pressure from a growing popula-tion. Arriving at optimal solutions to risks to urban environments requires state regulators to know each abatement cost function, if they are effectively to mitigate and adapt our cities to environmental pressures from a growing population and a changing climate. However, a comprehensive understanding of these costs and how to address them is difficult to achieve without wide consultation with diverse stakeholders. These costs are also unlikely to be addressed unless governments exhibit a willingness meaningfully to address stakeholder concerns other than those of market actors and state agencies.

In the case of the 30-Year Plan for Greater Adelaide, it is evident that consultation was seen as a means of defending the Plan. The consultation process seemed to offer a limited public engagement to minimize the complications of having to commit to address the feedback of non-market stakeholders. Indeed, the concerns of some of the latter stakeholders, notably the Mt Barker council, residents and community groups, appear to have been dismissed as irrational because they raised a concern that significant future population growth in the town was being flagged without a state-government commitment to provide schools, roads, sewers and other infrastructure necessary to sustain the new population. These are the kinds of abatement cost that Dietz and Fankhauser (2010) indicate must be considered by governments to address the risks to sustainable urban futures presented by a growing population and a changing climate.

A policy of ignoring feedback that is in tension with neoliberal planning does not bode well for the capacity of governments to address the challenges our cities face from a growing population, climate change and the relatively unrestricted consumption of land and housing. Neoliberal policies that consider only the concerns of commercial interests and state agencies, while ignoring the demos, are unlikely to offer a plan for the sustainable consumption of land and housing. Moreover, without wide, and meaning-ful, consultation, governments might not be able to price climate-change abatement and the cost of addressing environmental pressures from a growing population.

In summary, the case of the 30-Year Plan for Greater Adelaide suggests that neoliberal planning is significantly in tension with the sustainable consumption of land and housing. This model of planning also has implications for the capacity of governments to address climate change and seems antithetical to democracy. Planning for the sustainable consumption of urban resources might require a rethink of how we plan for our future in Australia.

References

Chan, E. and Lee, G. (2008) 'Critical factors for improving social sustainability of urban renewal projects', *Social Indicators Research*, vol 85, no.2, pp243–57

Chiu, R. (2003) 'Social sustainability, sustainable development and housing development: the experience of Hong Kong', in R. Forrest and J. Lee (eds) *Housing and Social Change: East–West Perspectives*, Routledge, London

Davidson, K. (2011) 'Reporting systems for sustainability: what are they measuring?', *Social Indicators Research*, vol 100, no 2, p351–65

Davidson, K. and Wilson, L. (2009) 'An integrated model for the assessment of urban social sustainability', conference paper, State of Our Cities Conference, University of Western Australia, Perth, November

Davidson, K. and Wilson, L. (2010) 'Towards a new framework for urban sustainability', paper presented to the International Society of Ecological Economics Society Conference, Oldenburg, Germany

Department of Infrastructure and Planning (DIP) (2009) South East Queensland Regional Plan 2009–2031, Department of Infrastructure and Planning, Queensland Government, Brisbane, Australia

Department of Planning and Community Development (DPCD) (2008) *Melbourne 2030, Melbourne @ 5 Million*, Department of Planning and Community Development, Victorian Government, Melbourne, Australia

DPLG (2009) *Planning the Adelaide We All Want: Progressing the 30-Year Plan for Adelaide*, Department of Planning and Local Government, Government of South Australia, Adelaide, Australia

DPLG (2010a) *The 30-Year Plan for Greater Adelaide: A Volume of the South Australian Planning Strategy*, Department of Planning and Local Government, Government of South Australia, Adelaide, Australia

DPLG (2010b) *The 30-Year Plan for Greater Adelaide Consultation Report*, Department of Planning and Local Government, Government of South Australia, Adelaide, Australia

Department of State and Regional Development (DSRD) (2005) *Sydney City of Cities Plan*, Department of State and Regional Development, NSW Government, Sydney, Australia

Dietz, S. and Fankhauser, S. (2010) 'Environmental prices, uncertainty, and learning', *Oxford Review of Economic Policy*, vol 26, no 2, pp270–84

England, C. (2011) 'Land developers "wrote state policy"', *The Advertiser*, March 27, p3

Flyvbjerg, B. (2002) 'Bringing power to planning research', *Journal of Planning Education and Research*, vol 21, pp353–66

Friedman, M. (1970) 'The social responsibility of business is to increase its profits', *The New York Times Magazine*, September 13

Garau, P. (2008) 'Revisiting urban planning in developed countries', regional study prepared for the *Global Report on Human Settlements – Planning Sustainable Cities*, United Nations Human Settlements Programme, UNHABITAT, Earthscan, London, p79

Gleeson, B. J. (2010) *Lifeboat Cities*, UNSW Press, Sydney, Australia

Gleeson, B., Darbas, T. and Lawson, S. (2004) 'Governance, sustainability and recent Australian metropolitan strategies: a socio-theoretic analysis', *Urban Policy and Research*, vol 22, no 4, pp345–66

GRHS (2009) *Global Report on Human Settlements – Planning Sustainable Cities*, United Nations Human Settlements Programme, UNHABITAT, Earthscan, London

Hamilton, C. (2003) *Growth Fetish*, Allen & Unwin, Sydney, Australia

Hamilton, C. (2010) *Requiem for a Species: Why We Resist the Truth About Climate Change*, Allen & Unwin, Sydney, Australia

Harvey, D. (2002) 'The art of rent: globalization, monopoly and commodification of culture', *Socialist Register*, socialistregister.com/recent/2002/harvey2002, accessed 21 June 2010

Harvey, D. (2006) *Limits to Capital*, Verso, London

Harvey, D. (2009) *Cosmopolitanism and the Geographies of Freedom*, Columbia University Press, New York

Harvey, D. (2010) *The Enigma of Capital and the Crises of Capitalism*, Profile Books, London

Hauptmann, E. (1996) *Putting Choice Before Democracy: A Critique of Rational Choice Theory*, State University of New York Press, Albany, NY

Hepburn, C. (2010) 'Environmental policy, government, and the market', *Oxford Review of Economic Policy*, vol 26, no 2, pp117–13

Hutchings, A. and Bunker, R. (eds) (1986) *With Conscious Purpose: A History of Town Planning in South Australia*, Wakefield Press, Kent Town, Australia

Kucok, K. (2010) 'An overview of emerging challenges, government planning and reforms in the context of Australia's temporary and permanent migration programs', paper presented to the 15th Biennial Conference Australian Population Association, 30 November to 3 December

Levett, R. with Christie, I., Jacobs, M. and Therivel, R. (2003) *A Better Choice of Choice: Quality of Life, Consumption and Economic Growth*, Fabian Society, London

Logan, J. and Molotch, H. (2007) *Urban Fortunes: The Political Economy of Place* (20th anniversary edn), University of California Press, Berkeley, CA

Lowe, I. (2009) *A Big Fix*, Black Inc, Melbourne, Australia

Manwaring, R. (2010) 'Unequal voices: "strategic" consultation in South Australia', *The Australian Journal of Public Administration*, vol 69, no 2, pp178–89

Pathak, V. and Shukla, S. P. (2009) 'Urban growth monitoring techniques for sustainable development', in S. N. Chauhan (ed) *Recent Trends in Management, Technology and Environment*, Macmillan Publishers India Limited, Kolkata, India

Prinet, E. (2011) 'Sustainable consumption and production', Background Paper, No. 1, North American Workshop on Sustainable Consumption and Production and Green Building, Ottawa, Canada, 31 January to 1 February 2011

Reisch, L. (2001) 'Time and wealth: the role of time and temporalities for sustainable patterns of consumption', *Time & Society*, vol 10, no 2/3, pp367–85

Saunders, P. (2006) 'Unleashing (labour) market forces: the social policy implications of industrial relations', *University of New South Wales Law Journal*, vol 29, no 1, pp80–90

United Nations Conference on Environment and Development (UNCED) (1992) *Agenda 21 and the United Nations Conference on Environment and Development Proceedings*, Oceana Publications, New York

Wilson, L. and Davidson, K. (2010) 'Adelaide's 30-Year Plan: a "sustainable" urban growth machine?', paper presented to the Asian Conference on the Social Sciences: East Meets West in Pursuit of a Sustainable World, Osaka, Japan, 18–21 June

Wilson, L. and Davidson, K. (2011) 'Regulating land use for profit: the case of Newport Quays', *Journal of Australian Political Economy* (accepted for publication March 2011)

Chapter 18

Development of multifunctional urban land uses using water sensitive urban design

Simon Beecham

Summary

There are often competing demands for the ever-decreasing available land space in our towns and cities. In many cities, this has led to new transport infrastructure going underground. However, most of our landspaces are still monofunctional, including the areas on which we currently park our cars. Not only is this not sustainable, into the future it will not be economically viable. This chapter explores the concept of multifunctional urban land use, with a specific emphasis on water-sensitive urban design (WSUD). Instead of dedicating areas of land to a single land use, such as water conservation, flood control, water-quality treatment or public amenity, the possibility of using the same land to serve all these purposes is explored through comparative case studies. A multifunctional approach to urban land use is presented through which habitat connections, flood storage, water reuse and social amenity are all integrated into the same land corridors. This approach can be economically competitive, as it could potentially release flood-prone fringe areas for development, which in turn could provide the economic driver to achieve higher-level outcomes, such as the enhancement of urban ecology.

Approaches to urban development

In recent years, most storm-water-management regulations have been concerned primarily with reducing peak flows and volumes of run-off into the storm-water system. While this is still very important, little attention has been given to the quality of the water that is reaching the waterways. These waterways support sensitive ecosystems that can be easily impacted by increased storm-water pollution. It is important to ensure that future developments are implemented using an integrated urban water-management approach. This can be achieved through the integration of water-quality controls, flood detention and WSUD (Collins et al, 2008). Equally important is the need to design smarter, more resilient and, most of all, adaptive water systems. Examples of such adaptive water systems include permeable pavements (on which cars can be parked) with underlying storage and vegetated storm-water systems that include below-soil storage systems to enable the vegetation to be sustained during longer inter-event dry periods. Both these systems achieve multifunctionality of land use by providing flood control, storm-water treatment, habitat connectivity and public-space amenity.

In developing countries, both sustainable water management and multifunctional land use are being practised (Beecham, 2011). Malaysia is a particularly interesting country to study, as it is rapidly urbanizing. Rainfall in Malaysia is typically characterized by very intense and short-duration storm events, which makes urban water management very challenging. The regular traffic gridlocks that occur in Kuala Lumpur (the capital city) following rainfall deluges are a result of these issues. However, urban planners and engineers are looking for ways to both control and make better use of water in our ever-expanding cities. This chapter compares innovative storm-water-management methods currently being implemented in both Australia and Malaysia.

Water-sensitive urban design

The term water-sensitive urban design first appeared in various Australian publications exploring concepts and possible structural and non-structural practices in relation to urban-water-resource management during the early 1990s. Comparable design philosophies, such as sustainable urban drainage systems (SUDS), were simultaneously developing in Europe and the United States. SUDS is now generally referred to as SuDS to reflect the wider application of sustainable drainage systems. In the USA and Japan, SuDS is known as low-impact urban design (LIUD), or simply low-impact development (LID). WSUD, LID and SuDS embrace the concept of integrated land and water management and, in particular, integrated urban-water-cycle management. This includes the harvesting and/or treatment of storm-water and wastewater to supplement (normally non-potable) water supplies. More generally, WSUD focuses on the interaction between the urban built form and the natural water cycle.

Various planning frameworks and technical guidelines have been developed across Australia to support the local adoption of WSUD. The most recent of these is South Australia's *Water Sensitive Urban Design Technical Manual for the Greater Adelaide Region* (Department of Planning and Local Government, 2009). The aim of this particular manual is to:

- demonstrate how WSUD can be successfully incorporated into a range of projects, illustrating example measures;
- provide a consistent approach to the planning and design of WSUD measures for urban development across the greater Adelaide region;
- inform and guide urban-management decision-making processes;
- help increase awareness and appreciation of WSUD; and
- encourage the consideration of factors including landscaping, biodiversity and greenhouse-gas emissions early in the design process.

The South Australian government's vision of WSUD in the greater Adelaide region is that it will stabilize and improve the health of the region's coastal waters, inland watercourses and groundwater systems, while maintaining and enhancing human health and reducing the ecological footprint of the region.

Other key objectives of implementing WSUD in the Adelaide region are to:

- move towards a natural flow regime (for example, lower flows to reduce erosion of creeks and improve or maintain ecological value);
- manage risk in relation to drought, flood, climate change and public health;
- protect, enhance, value and conserve water resources;

- encourage leading practice in the use and management of water resources so as to increase water efficiency, reduce reliance on imported water and apply at-source reduction of impacts on water quality, flooding, erosion and sedimentation;
- raise awareness and catalyse change in the design, construction and management of urban development and urban infrastructure; and
- recognize and foster the significant environmental, social and economic benefits that result from sustainable and efficient use of water resources.

These guidelines were developed following a set of principles that underpin the objectives for water management and the implementation of WSUD in the greater Adelaide region, including:

- incorporate water resources as early as possible in the land-use planning process;
- address water-resource issues at the catchment and subcatchment level;
- ensure water-management planning is precautionary and recognizes intergenerational equity, conservation of biodiversity and ecological integrity;
- recognize water as a valuable resource and ensure its protection, conservation and reuse;
- recognize the need for site-specific solutions and implement appropriate non-structural and structural solutions;
- protect ecological and hydrological integrity;
- integrate good science and community values in decision-making; and
- ensure equitable cost sharing.

From these principles, it can be seen that WSUD embraces the concept of integrated land and water management, in particular integrated urban-water-cycle management. Typical WSUD components include rainwater tanks, grassed swales, biofiltration swales, bioretention basins, sand filters, infiltration trenches and basins, vegetated filter strips, permeable pavements, wetlands and ponds (Beecham, 2010b). These components can be combined into very sophisticated systems (Dunphy et al, 2007) that treat storm-water to almost drinking-water standards.

Permeable pavements for storm-water reuse

Pavements are ubiquitous in urban areas. For developers, industrial facilities and local authorities addressing storm-water and associated water-quality regulations, pavements are very much at the forefront of planning issues. Pavements designed for use by vehicular traffic typically consist of a subgrade, one or more overlying courses of compacted pavement material and a surface seal. An integral aspect of conventional pavement design involves preventing entry of water to the pavement via the seal to protect the integrity of the underlying base course, sub-base and subgrade.

Conversely, a permeable pavement has quite different objectives and design requirements from conventional pavements. The permeable pavement is designed to infiltrate storm-water through to the underlying layers. Water passes to the open-graded, single-sized gravel substructure and is drained through to the subgrade. These pavements therefore perform the dual functions of supporting traffic loads and of storm-water drainage. Pollutants within the storm-water also infiltrate, with the majority being trapped within the pavement layers.

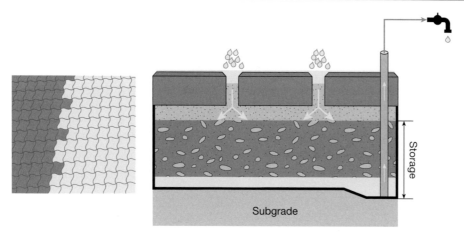

Figure 18.1 The pavement reuse concept (left: plan view; right: cross-section).
Image courtesy of the author

Permeable pavements can be designed to incorporate an underlying storage volume for water harvesting and reuse, flood attenuation and/or enhanced water-quality treatment. Permeable pavements thus present a unique opportunity to harvest and store urban storm-water that would otherwise contribute to overland run-off into the conventional storm-water pipe and channel network. With minimal surface infrastructure, permeable pavements provide a serviceable, hard-standing area that facilitates water harvesting, treatment and reuse (Beecham, 2010b).

There are several options for the design and construction of such a system. After infiltrating through the pavement surface, the storm-water can be stored in a submerged tank, or in proprietary plastic cell systems. It can also be stored in a matrix of base-course aggregate contained within an impermeable membrane. This is shown in Figure 18.1.

Researchers at the University of South Australia recently completed construction of a conceptual prototype facility, shown in Figures 18.2 –18.4, which features a pavement the size of a standard car space (in accordance with AS/NZS 2890.1). Storage is provided within a limestone base-course aggregate material. There is also a window cut into the side to view the depth of the water in the reservoir.

In constructing the permeable pavement, a procedure similar to the construction of a standard pavement was followed. Excavations were undertaken according to plans, ensuring adequate water-storage volume was available. Laboratory tests indicated that voids in the base-course aggregate material were 40 per cent of the overall sub-base volume. This initial testing suggested that the overall storage of this facility is approximately 3,600l. The excavation varied between 650mm and 750mm in depth overall, sloping downward to a sump at one end, where a submersible pump was located.

A 0.75mm polypropylene material was used to line the excavation. To access the stored water, a storm-water pipe was installed prior to filling. The pipe was perforated at sufficient intervals to allow the ingress of water, while preventing the ingress of aggregate stones to the submerged pump reservoir.

Figure 18.2 Pavement excavation.

Image courtesy of the author

Figure 18.3 Laying of the impermeable lining and base-course aggregates.

Image courtesy of the author

Figure 18.4 The completed UniSA prototype facility at the University of South Australia, Adelaide, Australia.

Image courtesy of the author

Following the placement for the storage access pipe, 14t of 20mm dolomite aggregate were placed on top of the liner and compacted using a vibrating plate compactor. Permeable pavers were laid in a similar fashion to conventional concrete block-paving units. The upmost layer of aggregate (the 'laying course') was screeded to a desired level, and pavers were placed according to manufacturers' instructions. The pavement itself was then compacted with a vibrating plate compactor. The installation of appropriately designed edge restraints completed the construction.

The storm-water harvested from this system is extracted using a small solar pump and is used to irrigate plants in an equivalent-sized adjacent rainwater garden. The total installation cost of this system was AU$3100 (€2316). The most significant feature of the permeable paved car space shown in Figure 18.4 is that it is a clear example of multifunctional land use. Effectively, it is a 3600l rainwater tank on which a car can be parked. If located on a residential driveway, all storm-water downpipes from the house could be piped straight into the base of the system, allowing the permeable paving to harvest surface run-off from the property via direct infiltration.

Investigating the use of recycled construction waste materials

Despite a growing global awareness about the benefits of porous and permeable types of paving, they have not been widely adopted in Australia. This limited use is mainly due to concerns over their reduced structural capabilities, their potential to pollute groundwater and their perceived higher costs. For a number of years, the University of South Australia has led a research and development programme that aims to address some of these issues with the development of enhanced porous pavement construction materials (Beecham and Myers, 2007). There are three significant aims in this programme:

1   The development of optimized porous concrete mix designs using recycled building materials as aggregates. Inclusion of recycled fibres and pozzalanics, such as silica fume, is also being investigated. Testing has been undertaken to examine the load-bearing capacity, fatigue life, hydraulic conductivity and pollutant-removal processes inherent in the novel pavement construction materials (Lian and Zhuge, 2010).
2   The development of a numerical model for the simulation of the microstructure behaviour of the materials. The model has been calibrated using laboratory test specimens analysed with the use of scanning electron microscopy (SEM) and three-dimensional X-ray microtomography. This has provided a detailed understanding of the complex relationship between structural strength and porosity. It will further allow the determination of optimal mixes for permeable-pavement design (Lian et al, 2011a).
3   The development of a model to simulate the hydrologic behaviour and treatment processes occurring within the permeable-pavement base-course material (Lian et al, 2011b).

The use of recycled construction materials is also a programme priority. A further objective of this programme is to investigate the options available to develop a new, high-strength permeable-pavement base-course material, particularly one that can carry higher traffic loads. A variety of cement-treated base-course materials were selected for the preliminary investigation. These cement-treated permeable base courses consist of specially formulated mixtures of Portland cement, uniform open-graded coarse aggregate and water. More recently, experimental trials have involved the use of recycled fibres in the mixture.

Determining the amount of cement necessary to achieve the balance between high void space and adequate strength of material is a pivotal concern to ensure that only sufficient cement to coat the aggregate is used. The strength properties that were evaluated consisted of compressive strength (shown in Figure 18.5), flexural strength (shown in Figure 18.6), and resilient modulus. Tests have also been performed to measure the porosity and the coefficient of permeability of the porous-concrete products.

This study demonstrated that concrete compaction methods affect ultimate strength. Samples prepared using a vibration table tended to display much higher structural strengths. Further complexity is introduced through the use of recycled construction waste. These materials often had higher water-absorption ratios, and, to ensure that this did not unduly influence the test results, the experiments were performed when the construction-waste (crushed) aggregates were under both soaked and dry conditions.

Figure 18.5 Compressive-strength testing of porous concrete.

Image courtesy of the author

Figure 18.6 Flexural-strength testing of porous concrete.

Image courtesy of the author

Case study: water-sensitive urban drainage systems in Malaysia

An example of Malaysian best practice in integrated urban water management is the recent adoption of the principles of WSUD into the upgrade design for the Humid Tropics Centre (HTC) in Kuala Lumpur. As shown in Figure 18.7, porous paving, rainwater tanks, green roofs, vegetated swales and bioretention basins are integrated into a space-constrained office complex. This has been designed as an exemplar case study of WSUD for Malaysian conditions (Beecham and Fallahzadeh, 2011).

Malaysian and Australian responses to WSUD can be compared via their respective permeable-pavement designs. The design shown in Figure 181.7 was undertaken in accordance with the *Malaysian Urban Stormwater Management Manual*, known locally as 'MSMA' (Department of Irrigation and Drainage, 2009). The permeable-pavement system shown in Figure 18.7 is 279.5m² in area and was designed for a two-year average recurrence interval (return period) design rainfall event of 15 minutes' duration and an intensity of 181.2mm per hour. This immediately demonstrates the very high rainfall intensities faced by designers in Malaysia. Indeed, this design storm is very close to the 100-year average recurrence interval, 5-minute-duration design storm for Adelaide Australia, which is 186mm per hour. The MSMA design process involves the following steps, with only the summary calculations shown for conciseness:

Step 1: Determine the permissible site discharge (PSD).

PSD = 7l/s

Step 2: Determine the site storage requirement (SSR).

SSR = 7.4m³

Step 3: Determine the required reservoir depth (d).

d = 105.9mm

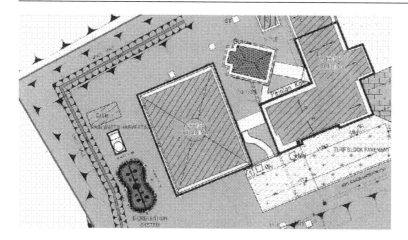

Figure 18.7 WSUD features at the Humid Tropics Centre, Kuala Lumpur, Malaysia.
Drawing courtesy of both HTC and ZHL Engineers, Malaysia

To compare this with Australian design practice, the PERMPAVE software (Beecham et al, 2009) was run for the same two-year average recurrence interval event (15 minutes' duration) for Adelaide, Australia. This design storm has a much lower rainfall intensity, at 35.6mm per hour. PERMPAVE is freely available from the Concrete and Masonry Association of Australia (www.cmaa.com.au). Figures 18.8 and 18.9 show screenshots from the program output.

For the Australian design, the main limiting factor is the maximum infiltration rate through the pavers, rather than the depth of base course required to infiltrate and store the design storm run-off. A base-course depth of 100mm provides 11.2m^3 of storage when the voids ratio is 0.4. This is sufficient to cope with the run-off volume from the two-year event. However, because of the lower rainfall intensity, the peak inflow to the Adelaide system is 3.9l/s, compared with 13.9l/s for the Malaysian design storm event. This means that high infiltrative capacities are required for pavement systems in Malaysia. It also means that partial clogging of permeable systems is likely to have more significant affects on system performance in Malaysia than in Australia. Pezzaniti and his colleagues (2009) showed that partially clogged systems in Adelaide can still continue performing adequately for over ten years, with minimal maintenance. This is unlikely to be the case in Malaysia, but further research would be required to accurately determine the differences.

In Malaysia, permeable pavements are not yet designed for harvesting and reuse of storm-water. However, the average annual rainfall in Malaysia is 2500mm, which results in high volumes of urban run-off. Therefore, permeable pavements with significant underlying storage would provide both effective flood control and high security of supply for storm-water reuse.

Conclusions

This chapter has examined how sustainable water management can be achieved using multifunctional urban landuses. It has presented examples of how using innovative WSUD

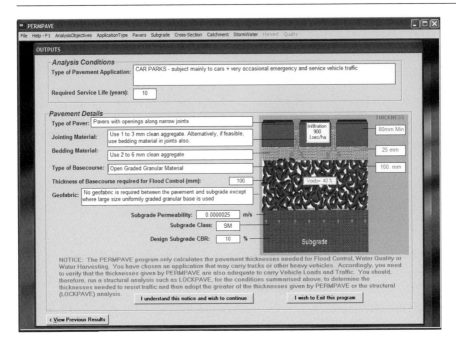

Figure 18.8 PERMPAVE computed inflow hydrograph.

Image courtesy of the author

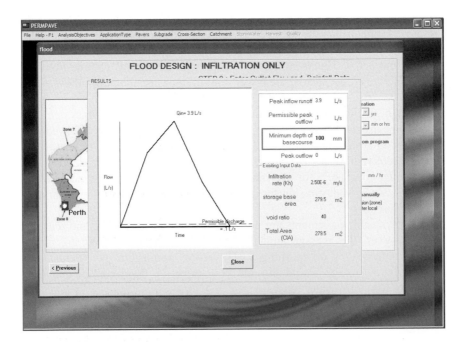

Figure 18.9 PERMPAVE program outputs.

Image courtesy of the author

technologies achieves flood control in Kuala Lumpur, Malaysia, and Adelaide, Australia. The design approaches used in both countries have been compared, and the emerging use of permeable pavements for water harvesting and reuse has been discussed.

This chapter has also clearly identified that more research is needed to inform practice in the areas of water-quality treatment, flood control and water harvesting and reuse. One of the most important considerations in storm-water management is the provision of sufficient water storage. If the development of WSUD in Australia can be criticized, it would have to be for the way in which inadequate attention has been paid to the incorporation of sufficient storage volumes (Beecham, 2010a). Developing countries such as Malaysia can learn from these experiences.

Acknowledgements

The support of the Australian Research Council for funding under grant LP110100222 is gratefully acknowledged, as is the ongoing support provided by ZeroWaste SA, the SA Water Corporation and HydroCon Pty Ltd. The support of Alan Pearson, Professor Brian Shackel of UNSW and the Concrete and Masonry Association of Australia (CMAA) is also acknowledged. Our deep gratitude is also extended to Associate Professor Lariyah Sidek of UNITEN, Putrajaya, and to Zul Mohd Roseli, Director of ZHL Engineers Sdn. Bhd., Malaysia, for their considerable assistance in comparing Malaysian and Australian design techniques for WSUD technologies.

References

Beecham, S. (2010a) 'Planning for multi-functional urban landuse using sustainable water management', keynote paper presented to the 4th International Conference on the Built Environment in Developing Countries, Penang, Malaysia, 2–3 December
Beecham, S. (2010b) 'Water sensitive urban design', in C. B. Daniels (ed) *Adelaide: Water of a City*, Wakefield Press, Adelaide, Australia
Beecham, S. (2011) 'Using water sensitive urban design to achieve multi-functional urban landuse', keynote paper presented to the Stormwater Industry Association of Queensland State Conference, Gold Coast, Australia, 25–27 May
Beecham, S. and Fallahzadeh, R. (2011) 'Innovative approaches to urban water management in developing countries', paper presented to the 5th International Conference on Sustainable Development and Planning, New Forest, UK, 12–14 July
Beecham, S. and Myers, B. (2007) 'Structural and design aspects of porous and permeable block pavements', *Journal of Australian Ceramics Society*, vol 43, no 1, pp74–81
Beecham, S., Pezzaniti, D., Myers, B., Shackel, B. and Pearson, A. (2009) 'Experience in the application of permeable interlocking concrete block paving In Australia', paper presented to the 9th International Conference on Concrete Block Paving, Buenos Aires, Argentina, 18–21 October
Collins, A., Morison, P. and Beecham, S. (2008) 'Deemed to comply stormwater management requirements for Parramatta city council', paper presented to the Stormwater Industry Association New South Wales and Queensland Conference, Gold Coast, Australia, 8–11 July
Department of Irrigation and Drainage (2009) *Malaysian Urban Stormwater Management Manual* (MSMA), Department of Irrigation and Drainage, Kuala Lumpur, Malaysia
Department of Planning and Local Government (2009) *Water Sensitive Urban Design Technical Manual for the Greater Adelaide Region*, Government of South Australia, Adelaide, Australia

Dunphy, A., Beecham, S., Vigneswaran, S., Ngo, H. H., McLaughlan, R. and Collins, A. (2007) 'Development of a confined water sensitive urban design system using engineered soils', *Journal of Water Science and Technology*, vol 55, no 4, pp211–18

Lian C. and Zhuge Y. (2010) 'Optimum mix design of enhanced permeable concrete – an experimental investigation', *Construction and Building Materials*, vol 24, no 12, pp2664–71

Lian, C., Zhuge, Y. and Beecham, S. (2011a), 'Numerical simulation of the mechanical behaviour of porous concrete', *Engineering Computations* (accepted for publication, in press)

Lian, C., Zhuge, Y. and Beecham, S. (2011b), 'Modelling pervious concrete under compression loading – a discrete element approach', *Advanced Materials Research*, 168, pp1590–600

Pezzaniti, D., Beecham, S. and Kandasamy, J. (2009) 'A laboratory and field investigation into the effective life of permeable pavements', *Journal of Water Management*, vol 162, no 3, pp211–20

Conclusion

The culture and politics of zero waste: looking ahead

Robert Crocker and Steffen Lehmann

Consumption, sustainability and zero waste

'Consumption' is a problematic word. Its nineteenth-century economic origins sit somewhat uneasily on top of its earlier pejorative meaning, 'destroying', 'using up', or 'laying waste' something. In contrast, in our now common economic parlance, consumption came to mean, in opposition to 'production', the economic activity of buying and using (up) goods and services or resources (Williams, 1983, pp78–9). This narrower economic definition, linked to the economic ideas of 'demand' and 'supply', has been progressively broadened over the last two decades by social scientists and historians interested in 'consumer culture', that is the activities and behaviours that we engage with when we consume. From this cultural perspective, consumption can be said to shape our attitudes, lifestyles, expectations and beliefs. In fact, consumption can be said to act like a window or frame through which we see the things and services we imagine we need, as well as the value we attribute to them (Sassatelli, 2007).

Through the continual 'advice' we receive daily from the media, consumption becomes a cultural viewpoint that continuously refocuses our attention on the alleged benefits or advantages of using or owning particular goods or services (Lees-Maffei, 2001). The 'manufactured desires' created by the media, presented in a veritable cascade of often misleading, even sometimes manipulating, information, cause the 'bigger picture' of the origins and contexts of our material world to recede into the background of our awareness. The concept of 'sustainability', like that of 'zero waste' and 'resource recovery', on the other hand, reminds us to refocus on what is beyond this narrow 'consumption' frame or window. This represents almost a return to the previous meaning of consumption, to 'use up' or 'destroy' something, possibly something we value. Waste, like the resources and manufactured goods we presently 'use up' and discard at an unprecedented rate, is defined only by the fact that it lies 'outside' or beyond this consumption frame (of use, ownership or economic opportunity): by definition, it is what is unwanted, unvalued, abandoned or not seen anymore as of value in the world of consumption.

Because of the narrow scope presented to us by the frame of our consumer culture, those concerned about its destructive and wasteful effects have, over the last fifty years or so, devised increasingly sophisticated ways of bringing back into view what had been formerly excluded: ecological economics, industrial ecology, life-cycle thinking, resource recovery and sustainable design are all members of this expanding family of interrelated disciplines that seek to broaden our vision of our material world beyond the narrow focus of use or ownership. These have become the basis of scholarly investigations and evaluative tools now used in a growing body of scholarship attempting to break down the confining walls that frame the narrow window of our consumer culture (Papanek, 1995; Wackernagel and Rees, 1996; Rees, 2002; Hertwich, 2006; among others). Sustainability is perhaps the most important recent iteration of this conceptual development, as it brings to the fore a consideration of our environmental and social crisis in terms of legacy. It urges us to consider the results of our various destructive activities and their legacy on this planet for the future of the world, of our children and grandchildren (Brundtland/UN World Commission on Environment and Development, 1987; Ehrenfeld, 2008, pp48ff.).

Zero waste, on the other hand, is a similarly future-focused concept, but one conceived in terms of the increasingly complex composition of our waste stream: it is the ideal future of a system that, at the moment, creates mountains of often toxic or dangerous waste, much of which cannot be broken down organically. As a concept, zero waste demands a commitment to 'design out' all present and future waste from the life cycle of every product, building or system – an extremely ambitious programme, but one that, like sustainability itself, is critical to our survival and future (Phillips et al, 2011; Zero Waste SA, 2011). As Walker points out in his essay on life-cycle thinking (Chapter 8), most waste originates in the first decisions taken by designers at the beginning of a project, and this can be seen also in the work of architects, construction managers, builders and planners. For this reason, zero waste as a concept needs to be incorporated into the 'standard' education of these professionals, so that more effective, efficient use of resources becomes possible, and 'designing out' waste becomes a framework all professionals strive to work within. In this context, waste avoidance, recyclability and material efficiency have to become some of the basic aims for all designers, including planners, architects, engineers and project and production managers. In many of the other essays in this book, discussions based on practical and pragmatic ways of 'designing out' waste can be found: in buildings (Lehmann, Chapter 11, and Ward, Chapter 12), construction sites (Chileshe et al, Chapter 14), residential development (Sivam and Karuppannan, Chapter 13), zoos and wilderness areas (Litchfield et al, Chapter 10) and water-provision systems in urban areas (Beecham, Chapter 18). Other essays in this book broaden the concept of zero waste even further to include, not only the design-based 'locking out' of 'waste' in all material flows, but also our habitual, sociotechnical waste of energy, fuel, water and other resources, whether this is in a single industrial object, such as an iPhone (Crocker, Chapter 6), a housing estate (Dickson, Chapter 9) or a whole city (Lehmann, Chapter 15).

Zero waste as a concept urges us to consider waste, not just as what is 'not owned' or 'not needed' or, by definition, 'out of the picture', but as a part of the material cycle itself, as a potential resource, or as industrial or organic 'food' to be reused, or to be returned without toxic side-effects to the natural cycle, from which all our material flows are extracted (Braungart and McDonough, 2002). Like a magic mirror that suddenly reveals the witch in the fairy tale as she really is, rather than the beautiful princess she has made herself out to be, terms such as sustainability and zero waste, rather than being only 'utopian' or, worse, 'impossible', confront us directly with the true material realities of our present crisis and its growing list of devastating consequences, forcing us to cut through the genial manipulation of marketing, of 'green-wash', of commercially inspired misinformation and the continuing misapplication of material values that our present consumer culture seems to require. Through the skilful deployment of these terms in the kinds of scholarly domain sampled in this book, we are faced, rather abruptly, not only with a vista of our own collective folly and its destructive consequences, but also, more positively, with what steps we can take to transform this rather dire scenario into a more hopeful future.

Sociotechnical systems and behaviour change

As we have suggested, one of the great engines of consumption is technological innovation and the resulting sociotechnical systems and infrastructures that over time this engenders, and many of the essays in this book reflect on the consequences of this in a number of different domains. First, it is worth emphasizing that technological innovation and constant media saturation stimulate us to try out new products, systems and experiences, and these can result in dramatically changing our behaviour (Shove, 2003a). Over time, new products or systems, once widely adopted, become 'normalized' into everyday life and become what economist and sociologist Thorstein Veblen once described as the ordinary and expected 'standards of decency' we aim to attain and then retain (in Dwyer, 2009; and see Schor, 2007). These, in time, become synonymous with what is regarded as 'normal' in everyday life, from flat-screen TVs and houses full of power-hungry appliances, to two fridges, multiple cars in every garage and holidays involving cheap, long-distance jet travel (Smart, 2010; Urry, 2010). A recent report by the German government revealed that the average German citizen consumes 40t of material resources per year (Rat für Nachhaltige Entwicklung, 2011); this amounts to 110kg per person per day. This amount is not only waste generated but contains to a large degree the non-renewable commodities used up for the production of consumer goods.

Technology has always played a central role in locking us into various unsustainable sociotechnical regimes: through innovations that introduce new 'must-haves', we tend to collectively submit to the effects or consequences of these, which often overturn or replace what was there before their arrival. So, plastic cartons are now synonymous for most of us with milk, juice or soft drinks, whereas, only a generation ago, milk was something delivered to the door in a reusable glass bottle, and most other drinks came in reusable glass bottles or steel cans (see Crocker, Chapter 1). Being cheap, 'free' or in some way more convenient, these new objects or systems, once adopted, increase our collective requirements for resources, fuel and energy, and result in more waste and more packaging, and now on a global scale. One result is that there is a vast and growing continent of plastic trash floating in the Pacific Ocean, no doubt a good proportion of it directly traceable to simple changes in behaviour, such as the global adoption of plastic containers for milk and juice (Moore, 2003). This vast waste-mass in the Pacific is one result of a global commercial and logistical infrastructure built up over the last fifty years, delivering a vast, maladapted and extremely wasteful system of provision to us, a huge investment in misdirected skills, money, materials and marketing, but one that has become an important component in our global economy. Much scholarship in zero waste and sustainable design is thus directed at the problem this and other similarly unsustainable systems have created. The problem, as many have noted, is not our technology or science itself, which are quite capable of solving most of our problems, but systems and infrastructures such as these that have, over time, locked us into extremely wasteful and environmentally destructive behaviours that cannot easily be reversed, in the process devastating also the lives of other creatures and their environments (Litchfield et al, Chapter 10). As Strasser's essay on the now 'alien' experience of material life in the not so distant past suggests (2003), an accurate historical understanding of the slow process that has resulted in new sociotechnological systems and accompanying changes in attitudes and behaviour is of vital importance for those interested in reversing or ameliorating their destructive grip on us today.

Most attempts to legislate controls on the serious environmental issues associated with new technological devices and systems, with few exceptions (such as tobacco products), tend to accept the relationship between technological innovation and consumer desire as a fixed and almost sacrosanct phenomenon, and something that – with few exceptions – should not be interfered with, for the sake of 'the market'. And this rather wary reluctance to legislate what happens in marketing and retail is probably cemented in place by the globalized production and distribution of most technological products and systems, and the importance of global trade to our economies: no government on its own, it seems, can easily legislate to control an economically successful technological genie once it has been let out of its bottle. This tends to push responsibilities for the environmental consequences of many technological products and systems downstream to the manufacturer or upstream to the user, leaving out of the picture the promoter, retailer or 'provider', in whose direct interest it might be to increase the circulation of new products to increase sales, regardless of the waste or environmental problems that this increased volume and early obsolescence might entail (just think of the ever-growing amount of e-waste and food waste generated). This legislative neglect of the 'meso' level in the material stream follows the logic of many earlier attempts at 'life-cycle'-based policy-making and legislative remediation. So, while the material flows of products, their origins, use and disposal might be carefully studied to improve policy response and legislative control, the social and retail contexts of purchase and use tend to be left out of this picture and to the social scientists (Smart, 2010; Urry, 2010).

Following Veblen's insight, Elizabeth Shove has emphasized the 'ratchet-like' path-dependency created by our socialization of technological innovations, focusing especially on the domestic example of washing machines and the other 'orchestrated' devices of convenience we surround ourselves with (Shove, 2003b, p399). The attitudes and daily routines that are generated around new domestic or workday systems of convenience (for instance, car ownership), comfort (air conditioning) or cleanliness (washing machines and dryers) tend to 'lock in' behaviours that are normalized over time and cannot easily be modified. Each innovation, like a new star or sun, pulls us into a dependent but ultimately self-destructive orbit, following new routines that evolve into expected 'standards', which over time become extremely hard to break free of.

'Behaviour change' is a term now widely used to suggest possible ways of 'nudging' our attitudes and behaviour into more sustainable routines and expectations. Given the force of habit and routine, and the way that each new innovation tends to eclipse the previous 'standard', this is not an easy task and is much debated and discussed in the literature (see Davison et al, Chapter 4). What is apparent from the essays in the first part of this book is that substituting more sustainable routines and behaviours requires interdisciplinary research that re-examines in some detail the connections between social or sociotechnical routines, resulting consumption patterns, established behaviours and the attitudes they involve, and their often negative social, psychological or material consequences, in quite specific contexts. Each domain of everyday life throws up complexities and specific issues that demand close attention, from the impact that our dominant car-based transport system might have on the creation of more 'walkable' local communities (Crocker, Chapter 1; Taylor and Philp, Chapter 16), to the impact of the 'time squeeze' of paid work on the capacity of many households to engage with more sustainable behaviours (Skinner et al, Chapter 2). Similarly, we can see how the impact of consumer culture's neophilia on young children's attitudes towards value can perhaps be addressed through an educational agenda that encourages valuing what is 'used' or 'old' but still precious to its owners (Nichols, Chapter 3).

Governments have traditionally used social marketing to try and influence and shape behaviour, and it is usually informed by detailed research, ensuring that the expense and time frames involved in such marketing campaigns are not wasted, and that some socialization of desired behaviours can take place, often linked to a strategy of information, 'carrots' and 'sticks'. But the process of change itself also needs to be addressed, and this is examined in some detail in a case study of domestic food waste, which is one of the most persistent and problematic domestic examples of wasteful behaviour (Davison et al, Chapter 4). Certainly, just telling people to save water or power, or avoid using their car, is usually insufficient on its own; rather, it requires considerable background research into the specific routines and attitudes we might be intending to modify, and how this modification might be 'locked in' through a regime, perhaps, of incentives and new barriers or costs. As is repeatedly argued by the different authors in this book, 'individualization', especially where the individual is 'moralized' for behaviour that perhaps he or she cannot afford to change, cannot really work without some measure of socialization taking place, where alternatives are clearly presented, and change is encouraged with some rewards or incentive system, in a supporting social context (Verbeek, 2006). This 'socialization' is especially evident in new collaborative-consumption ventures, where individuals and households are enticed through new ventures to band together to gain access to services or useful appliances, such as tools, cars or holiday houses, that otherwise they might not be able to afford, or might only need occasionally (Edmonds, Chapter 5).

Rather like trying to get people to drive safely in a culture that emphasizes the importance of speed, of getting there on time, and of the individual power and freedom embodied in a car, modifying 'unsustainable' behaviours in most life domains is not a 'one-shot' job, or simply a matter of moralizing the behaviour of the individual (Verbeek, 2006). Providing incentives and removing barriers to more sustainable behaviour, and perhaps increasing the costs associated with the targeted unsustainable behaviour, can only work if the domains in which the behaviour we set out to modify are thoroughly understood and closely examined. Technology is a critical issue in many social domains, partly because it introduces change so rapidly and tends to lock in behaviour that then becomes dependent on the technology concerned. For this reason also, using technology to modify behaviour into avenues that are more sustainable also has great potential, and this is really where many of the chapters in the later parts of this book take their cue. Whether it is using mobile phones to improve awareness of sustainable-behaviour choices and opportunities (Crocker, Chapter 6), using more effective recycling regimes for e-waste based upon recent scientific evidence, rather than not yet quite effective policy regimes (Stevels, Chapter 7), or using recent developments in life-cycle analysis to ensure a better material or product choice in certain domains (Walker, Chapter 8), technology can play a vital role in enabling more sustainable behaviours, or better outcomes in waste reduction.

Redesigning the built environment

The difficulties involved in developing successful programmes for behaviour change in the face of unsustainable sociotechnical regimes signal many of the major themes found in discussions of the built environment and waste reduction in the second half of this book. The importance of life-cycle thinking, first discussed from the 'micro' view of an industrial designer (Walker, Chapter 8), becomes apparent in the discussions around buildings and cities in the third part of the book: building waste, whether from construction, operation, use or demolition, represents an extraordinary 40 per cent of most landfill around the world, while the energy consumption involved in using most modern buildings stands at an unedifying 43 per cent of global GHG emissions (see Lehmann, Chapter 11).

The generation of carbon emissions is mostly associated with people's everyday lives and lifestyles, including life-sustaining necessities (e.g. food, clothing), life-enhancing commodities (e.g. fridges, television sets) and the impact of entertainment (e.g. books, CDs). Treloar et al (2000) have argued that there is a need to consider, not only the life-cycle energy of a building, or of the products inside this building, but also the life-cycle energy attributable to activities undertaken by the actual users of the building, an argument that returns us again to the importance of behaviour change addressed in the first part of this book.

Buildings and cities, shaped since the Second World War primarily through massive tax-payer funded expansions of car-based transport infrastructure and the so-called 'oil economy', have resulted in more and more 'modernized' and suburbanized cities and towns, dependent both on the car and on centralized systems of energy, water and waste provision, each with their own set of complex but largely concealed energy, resource and waste problems (Lehmann, 2010). A small country such as Switzerland, for example, after the war moved into the kind of 'dual' economic development that became typical across Europe and now much of the world: an older, primary economy of small farms, artisans and skilled trades (connected to traditional industries such as clock- and watch-making), and a newer, secondary economy tied to the new industries thrown up by the war, employing mainly semi- or unskilled people, often for wages that were as high as those enjoyed in the first economy (Pfister, 1998). In many Western countries, this apparently more technologically sophisticated and 'advanced' type of economy enjoyed massive government subsidies, as, at that time, it seemed to represent the future. The promise these new industries offered was founded in science and new technologies and resulted in massive expansions of industries associated with the use of fossil fuels and the inventions of the Second World War; thus, the new communication technologies, plastics, chemicals and transport became the backbone of most advanced economies in the second half of the twentieth century (see Meikle, 1995). Unfortunately, we have now seen the consequences of that 'future', and it is not what it was once made out to be: car-based transport is a major contributor to GHG emissions, virgin materials are getting depleted, and oil-based chemicals have now become a major problem in environments all over the world: they crop up as toxins in the food chain, and oil-based plastics are a major component of waste that cannot be easily reused or returned to the soil. 'Peak oil' is imminent, and the future, whatever it might bring, will probably not be based on this finite resource that is increasingly difficult and expensive to extract (Heinberg, 2007). Industry has already started searching for a new generation of biodegradable plastics, but, whatever the ameliorating impact of this change in materials technology, we will have to try and ensure that their use is more responsible and set within a frame that is not so narrow or wasteful.

The legacies of economic 'modernization' and 'development' since the Second World War are embedded in many of the issues discussed in the second half of this book: environmentally inefficient urban and residential developments tied to the car and its infrastructure (Sivam and Karuppannan, Chapter 13; Taylor and Philp, Chapter 16; Wilson, Chapter 17); buildings and suburbs that are often wasteful and environmentally destructive to construct, maintain, use and demolish (Chileshe et al, Chapter 14); low-density 'oil-economy'-based cities such as Los Angeles and Brisbane, where a relatively low density of urban populations is spread over many square miles, and over half the available urban land, much of it agriculturally fertile, is devoted to car use alone (Lehmann, Chapter 15); and, on top of this, an extraordinary devastation of the lives and habitats of other creatures we share this planet with (Litchfield et al, Chapter 10). Engineers and architects are very much on the 'front line' in the required redesign and reshaping of these unsustainable legacies, so that current wasteful practices can be abandoned, and new buildings, or old ones sensitively adaptively, are reused (Ward, Chapter 12), as well as creating new developments and provisioning systems that 'lock in' more sustainable behaviours and 'lock out' the unsustainable traditions of the post-war city.

Looking ahead: 100 per cent resource recovery

For a long time, zero waste has been seen as a relatively utopian or visionary concept. But today, it has emerged as a real option in our ordinary lives and as an essential perspective in our industries. At a fundamental level, zero waste defines an essential requirement for a sustainable future: an end to the 'throwaway', 'drive-through', 'borrow-to-spend' society, towards a society based more on living intelligently with what we already have. To achieve this, recycling alone will not be enough. With clever strategies for waste avoidance, zero waste has now become a real possibility, and certainly a necessity, and has moved from being the seemingly utopian concept of some twenty or thirty years ago, when the chemist Paul Palmer coined the term in 1974 (Palmer, 2005), to a concept that is grounded in reality: the science and technology for achieving zero waste exist. Recycling experts confirm that 100 per cent recycling and resource recovery is possible. For instance, new methods have been developed in Europe to collect all products containing rare and precious metals more efficiently (e.g. cars and e-waste), to ensure the highest recycling rates. Technologically it's already possible, and a number of 'demonstrator' projects around the world have made this clear; however, it is the behaviour change needed for zero waste that, as we have seen, still lags behind. As the essays in this book show, progress towards a zero-waste society is achievable in every domain. The problem is shifting the often-vast resources and investment we currently deploy on unsustainable and wasteful practices into more sustainable ones, many of which have been suggested or described in some detail in this book.

References

Braungart, M. and McDonough, W. (2002) *Cradle to Cradle: Remaking the Way We Make Things*, North Point Press, New York

Brundtland, G. H./UN World Commission on Environment and Development (1987) *The Brundtland Report: Our Common Future*, Oxford University Press, Oxford/New York

Dwyer, R. (2009) 'Making a habit of it: positional consumption, conventional action and the standard of living', *Journal of Consumer Culture*, vol 9, pp328–47

Ehrenfeld, J. R. (2008) *Sustainability by Design: A Subversive Strategy for Transforming our Consumer Culture*, Yale University Press, New Haven, CT

Heinberg, R. (2007) 'Out of time? The end of oil', *Public Policy Research*, vol 14, no 3, pp197–203

Hertwich, E. G. (2006) 'Accounting for sustainable consumption: a review of studies of the environmental impacts of households', in T. Jackson (ed) *The Earthscan Reader in Sustainable Consumption*, Earthscan, London

Lees-Maffei, G. (2001) 'From service to self-service: advice literature as design discourse, 1920–1970,' *Journal of Design History*, vol 14, no 3, pp187–206

Lehmann, S. (2010) *The Principles of Green Urbanism: Transforming the City for Sustainability*, Earthscan, London

Meikle, J. (1995) *American Plastic: A Cultural History*, Rutgers University Press, New Brunswick, NJ

Moore, C. (2003) 'Across the Pacific Ocean, plastics, plastics everywhere', *Natural History*, vol 112, no 9, November, www.mindfully.org/Plastic/Ocean/Moore-Trashed-PacificNov03.htm, accessed 10 March 2011

Palmer, P. (2005) *Getting to Zero Waste: Universal Recycling as a Practical Alternative to Endless Attempts to 'Clean Up' Pollution*, Purple Sky Press, Sabastipol, CA

Papanek, V. (1995) *The Green Imperative: Ecology and Ethics in Design and Architecture*, Thames and Hudson, London

Pfister, C. (1998) 'The 'Syndrome of the 1950s' in Switzerland: cheap energy, mass consumption and the environment', in S. Strasser et al (eds) *Getting and Spending*, Cambridge University Press, Cambridge

Phillips, P. S., Tudor, T., Bird, H., Bates, M. (2011) 'A critical review of a key waste strategy initiative in England: zero waste places projects, 2008–2009', *Resources, Conservation and Recycling*, vol 55, pp335–43

Rat für Nachhaltige Entwicklung (2011) Report, available online, www.nachhaltigkeitsrat.de/, accessed 20 April 2011

Rees, W. E. (2002) 'An ecological economics perspective on sustainability and prospects for ending poverty', *Population and Environment*, vol 24, no 1, pp 15–46

Sassatelli, R. (2007) *Consumer Culture: History, Theory and Politics*, SAGE, London

Schor, J. B. (2007) 'In defense of consumer critique: revisiting the consumption debates of the twentieth century', *Annals of the American Academy of Political and Social Sciences*, vol 611, pp16–30

Shove, E. (2003a) *Comfort, Cleanliness and Convenience: The Social Organization of Normality*, Berg, Oxford

Shove, E. (2003b) 'Converging conventions of comfort, cleanliness and convenience', *Journal of Consumer Policy*, vol 26, no 4, pp395–418

Smart, B. (2010) *Consumer Society: Critical Issues and Environmental Consequences*, SAGE, London

Strasser, S. (2003) 'The alien past: consumer culture in historical perspective', *Journal of Consumer Policy*, vol 26, pp375–93

Treloar, G., Fay, R., Love, P. E. D. and Iyer-Raniga, U. (2000) 'Analysing the life cycle energy of an Australian residential building and its householders', *Building Research and Information*, vol 28, no 3, pp184–95

Urry, J. (2010) 'Consuming the planet to excess', *Theory, Culture and Society*, vol 27, pp197–212

Verbeek, P. P. (2006) 'Materializing morality: design ethics and technological mediation', *Science, Technology and Human Values*, vol 31, pp361–80

Wackernagel, M. and Rees, W. (1996) *Our Ecological Footprint*, New Society Press, Philadelphia, PA

Williams, R. (1983) *Keywords: A Vocabulary of Culture and Society*, Fontana Paperbacks, London

Zero Waste SA (2011) 'Publications', available online, www.zerowaste.sa.gov.au/resource-centre/publications, accessed 20 April 2011

Glossary of terms

Active systems generally refers to mechanical heating, ventilation and airconditioning (HVAC) systems (as opposed to passive systems).

Albedo is the amount of heat (solar radiation) from the sun that Earth or a surface reflects back into space. Snow- and ice-covered surfaces have high albedo, reflecting back most of the warmth they receive, while low-albedo oceans, land and plants absorb most of the heat that falls on them. As polar ice melts, the planet's overall albedo is lowered, and it soaks up more solar heat. White or reflective roofs are a simple and effective way to avoid overheating; retrofitting white roofs to single-storey houses can deliver around 20–25 per cent energy savings.

Anthropogenic means resulting from human activities (e.g. global warming is understood to be anthropogenic, human-induced, resulting from human activities).

Autonomous means that a building or district is operating independently of any inputs except those available in its immediate environment.

Balance of plant means the optimization of a technical plant's equipment to maximize energy and water efficiency, as well as minimizing pollution and waste.

Bio-climatic in architecture means to respond to the climate with minimal reliance on non-renewable energy for achieving comfort. Climate-responsive is a design approach that seeks to achieve year-round comfort using exclusively passive means, thereby significantly reducing energy consumption.

Biodegradable applies to any material that the natural world can absorb, if given time and the proper conditions, including sun, water and air. Active agents in this process include bacteria, fungi, unicellular organisms, insects and rodents.

Biodiversity is the variety and essential interdependence of all life forms within a given ecosystem or community (the different plants, animals and micro-organisms, the genes they contain and the ecosystems they form). It is generally thought that the more species an ecosystem has, the healthier and better it is.

Biomass is a renewable energy source derived from wood or biogas, comprised of living or recently dead biological material (plant or animal matter) that can be converted into bio-energy and fuel.

Brownfield site defines land, or premises, that has previously been used or developed and is currently not fully in use, lying vacant, underused or abandoned. In some cases, it may be partially occupied or used; or it may be vacant, derelict or contaminated. Typical brownfields are docklands, heavy industry plants or military areas that are no longer in use. The opposite of brownfields are greenfields: previously undeveloped open space.

Building-integrated photovoltaic (BIPV) describes photovoltaic systems that are integrated into the building's structure or facade cladding. This normally replaces parts of the building envelope, such as the roof, skylights or facades.

Carbon is a chemical element essential to all forms of life on earth, which bonds with oxygen to form carbon dioxide, a potent greenhouse gas. Carbon dioxide (CO_2) is a colourless, odourless gas produced by animal respiration or the decay of plant or animal remains, and it is a by-product of the burning of fossil fuels. Of the six principal greenhouse gases that contribute to climate change, CO_2 is the one most directly affected by human activity.

Carbon cycle describes the natural process of the worldwide passage of carbon between four 'reservoirs': the oceans, the atmosphere, the ground and the bodies of all plants and animals. When one reservoir gives up too much carbon and overloads another, a delicate balance is upset, with uncertain results.

Carbon footprint is the amount of total CO_2 emissions produced annually by all activities – for instance by a person's daily life, a company, building or city. There is still some dispute over the best way to calculate and measure the carbon footprint of a city, district or building accurately.

Carbon neutral means to reduce the net amount of CO_2 emissions for which a city, building or company is responsible to zero. In practical terms, it is impossible to attain total carbon neutrality; it means a city or organization reduces its carbon emissions as much as it possibly can, and then offsets the remainder (which moves part of the responsibility to the offsetting projects).

Carrying capacity refers to the upper limits of an urban development beyond which the quality of human life, health, welfare, safety or community character and identity might be unsustainably altered. Carrying capacity is the level (upper limit) of land use or human activity that can be permanently accommodated without causing irreversible changes in the quality of air, water, land or plant and animal habitats.

Combined heat-and-power (CHP) is an energy-conversion process that uses a heat engine or powerstation to simultaneously generate electricity and usable heat (frequently waste heat, which would otherwise be lost). Primary energy sources include a variety of fuels (natural gas, biomass and fossil fuels) and renewable energy sources. Also called co-generation, it is the simultaneous production of two forms of useful power from a single fuel source in a single process, e.g. the reuse of waste heat to provide space heating. If the waste heat is also used to produce chilled water for cooling through the use of an absorption chiller, it is called tri-generation.

Compactness (the A/V ratio) is the ratio of the surface area of a building to the enclosed (heated/cooled) volume. Typical A/V ratio values vary from 0.4 for compact, multistorey buildings to 1.1 for inefficient, detached bungalows in suburbs. The A/V ratio is an important factor in the calculation of energy consumption. The more compact the urban form (with smaller facade surfaces and therefore less solar gain in summer or heat loss in winter), the more energy-efficient is the building.

Cost–benefit analysis describes a method of evaluating projects or investments by comparing the present value of expected benefits with costs. It's a useful technique for making transparent the benefits of up-front investments in sustainable design features or technologies by revealing estimated payback times.

Courtyard is an outdoor patio space, open to the sky and enclosed by walls or buildings, commonly found in Mediterranean, Latin American or Asian cultures and used for natural cross-ventilation.

Cradle-to-grave measures the environmental impact of a product from the extraction of its raw materials until the product is disposed of (i.e. goes to landfill). This includes transport to the construction site. Opposite: cradle-to-cradle.

Density and floor space ratio (FSR) is a measure of the built environment in either the number of habitable rooms per hectare, or the number of dwellings per hectare. It determines the spatial property, ensuring that overcrowding or overdevelopment is not an issue. Density describes the average number of people, households (families) or housing units (dwellings per hectare) on one unit of land; for instance, density can be expressed as dwelling units per hectare (or acre). FSR is the primary way of controlling the size of buildings, with the maximum FSR requirements varying in different zones and areas. On the other hand, if the density is too low, sustainability cannot be achieved. FSR, or floor area ratio (FAR), is the total floor area of all buildings or structures on a lot, divided by the total area of the lot (1ha is 10,000m^2; 100ha is 1km^2).

Dump is the correct name for what the garbage industry would like us to call a landfill, because 'dump' has historical connotations of irresponsibility, whereas landfill mendaciously proclaims a thoughtful and responsible process of filling land that was until now empty.

Eco-city enhances the well-being of its citizens and of society through integrated urban planning and management that fully harnesses the benefits of ecological systems and renewable energies – aiming for zero emissions and zero waste. An eco-city or eco-district protects and nurtures these assets for future generations.

Ecological footprint (EF) is a measure of environmental impact, defined as an index of the area of productive land and aquatic ecosystems required to produce the resources used, and to assimilate the wastes produced, by a defined population at a specified material standard of living. See www.ecologicalfootprint.com

Ecosystem describes the species and natural communities of a specific location, interacting with one another and with the physical environment. The terms 'ecology' and 'ecosystem' were coined by the German biologist Ernst Haeckel in 1866.

Embodied energy is the total energy required directly and indirectly to produce (manufacture or construct) a product, including transportation and maintenance of that product/material until it is ready for use at a point in time. It is the sum total of the energy necessary for the entire life cycle of a product. Environmental product declarations (EPDs) give information on the entire life cycle of a product.

Energy efficiency/energy effectiveness is the ability to use less energy to provide the same level of output. Energy efficiency in buildings means employing strategies to minimize the use of energy imported from utility companies. Examples include: insulation, high-performance glazing, fluorescent and LED lighting. Efficient energy use is achieved by using a more efficient/effective technology in processes and helps to control emissions of greenhouse gases. Efficiency is, of course, an engineering concept for maximizing output from a given input.

Energy-efficient building retrofit programme unites many of the world's largest energy service companies, financial institutions and cities in an effort to reduce energy consumption in the existing built environment. This includes municipal, educational, private, commercial and public-housing sectors. By 'retrofitting' (upgrading) existing buildings to incorporate more energy-effective products, technologies and systems, energy consumption can be significantly reduced through improving a building's fabric and installations. Energy effectiveness is the ratio between useful output and the energy needed to achieve it.

Evaporative cooling is a physical process where liquid, typically water, is evaporated into surrounding air and cools an object or liquid in contact with it.

Exergy is the maximum work potential of a material; the quality and unused part of the energy potential (e.g. the use of waste heat or wastewater).

Extended producer responsibility means that the producer or manufacturer bears responsibility for the disposal and recycling of the goods sold. It will be an interesting change for battery manufacturers, packaging companies and other industrial allies, who are opposed to any recycling.

Feed-in tariff (FiT) is a policy that guides the reimbursement of private producers of renewable energy above the usual market price. It is a long-term tariff paid by a utility company for electricity that it must purchase and that is fed back into the grid from a renewable energy source. The price for this electricity is guaranteed by the government.

Fossil fuels are non-renewable (finite) resources, including coal, oil and natural gas, which were generated over millions of years from the organic remains of prehistoric plant and animal matter, and which when burnt release CO_2/greenhouse gases into the atmosphere. Long before these combustible geological deposits run out, they will become uneconomic to extract. Transforming the primary energy into the net energy used by consumers at the end of the energy chain (e.g. as electricity or district heat) leads to losses inherent in the conversion and transmission process. The opposite of fossil fuels are renewable (infinite), clean energy sources.

Geothermal energy, also known as ground-source energy, is a natural resource of heat energy contained within the Earth's crust, emitted in form of hot water or steam. The heat is transferred from the planet's molten core to water and rocks and lies fairly close to the surface, where it can be tapped to produce energy. It can be extracted and used, either indirectly to generate electricity or directly for heating applications. This includes use in heavy and light industry, domestic heating, plant growing and many other applications.

Global radiation is the quantity of solar energy incident on the Earth's surface, related to a horizontal surface. It consists of direct and diffuse, non-aligned radiation, depending on the solar altitude angle (which is dependent on latitude and time of year) and on atmospheric disturbances (clouds, particles). For instance, in Germany, the annual total global radiation is around $1000kWh/m^2$ per annum. In Australia, it is around $2000kWh/m^2$ per annum.

Green roof is a vegetated roof that has the potential to assist in mitigating poor urban air quality and heat-island effects, provide buildings with thermal and acoustic insulation, collect rainwater and increase occupant amenity and biodiversity. Usually, extensive planting is used for green roofs. A 'living roof' is an area of green space that provides a habitat for birds and wildlife and increases biodiversity. See www.greenroofs.org

Green urbanism is a conceptual model for zero-emission and zero-waste urban design that arose in the 1990s, promoting compact, energy-efficient urban development and seeking to transform and re-engineer existing city districts and regenerate the post-industrial city centre. Green urbanism promotes the development of socially and environmentally sustainable city districts.

Greenfield sites are the opposite of brownfields. They are 'virgin lands', sites that are not yet developed for intensive or urban use, such as meadows, parks and forests. Greenfield sites have not experienced any previous development.

Greenhouse gas (GHG) is any gas that, once emitted in the atmosphere, contributes to the warming of the Earth (e.g. CO_2, ozone or methane). The greenhouse effect is the process by which greenhouse gases allow incoming solar radiation to pass through the Earth's atmosphere, but prevent part of the outgoing heat from escaping, thus increasing temperatures.

Grey-water systems are systems that focus on the reuse of water generated from domestic processes such as dish washing, laundry and bathing for either indoor use or in irrigation.

Hannover Principles were propounded by William McDonough and Michael Braungart in 1999 and include statements such as: 'Insist on rights of humanity and nature to co-exist', 'Eliminate the concept of waste' and 'Understand the limitations of design'. The Hannover Principles are a set of statements about designing buildings and objects with forethought about their environmental impact, their effect on the sustainability of growth and their overall impact on society, including the optimization of the full life cycle of products and processes, to approach the state of natural systems, in which there is no waste.

Heat storage capacity is the value that designates the ability of a building component to store thermal energy. It is the product of the specific heat capacity, the material density and the thickness of the specific component. The amount of heat gained by a space from all sources (including from people, incoming and reflected radiation, internal loads from machines, computers, lights etc.) represents the amount of heat that must be removed from the space to maintain the desired indoor conditions; this is called cooling load.

Incineration means the burning of unwanted excesses, requiring additional fuel or gas, and is thus wasteful, not only of the incinerated and lost material but also of resources.

Infill is the act of building on a vacant lot within an otherwise developed neighbourhood. Urban infill development occurs in the established areas of a city.

Integrated design is a multidisciplinary approach that brings together all the stakeholders in the building process at an early stage to maximize building comfort and usability, while minimizing resource use.

Intergovernmental Panel on Climate Change (IPCC) is the United Nations' independent international group of scientists, established in 1988, with headquarters in Switzerland. The IPCC is an official, leading advisory body to the world's governments, issuing periodic assessments on global climate change and its effects. In 2007, the IPCC was awarded the Nobel Peace Prize for its research into climate change (see www.ipcc.ch).

Kyoto Protocol is a codicil to the United Nations Framework Convention on Climate Change. Following the 1992 Earth Summit in Rio de Janeiro, the UN produced the 'United Nations Framework Convention on Climate Change' (UNFCCC). In this groundbreaking treaty, industrialized signatories agreed to reduce their emission levels to below 1990 levels. The Kyoto Protocol – a codicil to the UNFCCC – is an international agreement that was signed in Japan in 1997 and commits most industrialized countries to reducing their emissions by 6–8 per cent below 1990 levels by 2012. It was signed by 175 nations; however, some of the world's largest contributors of CO_2 emissions (for instance, the US and China) have not ratified the Kyoto Protocol and are not bound by these targets. It will expire by 2012 and will be replaced by a new global agreement. See www.kyotoprotocol.com.

Life-cycle assessment (LCA) is a technique for measuring and assessing the environmental aspects and potential impacts associated with a product or process, by compiling an inventory of inputs and outputs and analysing the results of the inventory. This includes all inputs (i.e. raw materials, water, and energy) and outputs (i.e. the end product, waste, emissions) of manufacture, transport, use, maintenance and disposal of the product.

Low-impact materials are building materials that use fewer resources and produce less pollution over their life cycle compared with conventional building materials.

Material efficiency expresses the degree in which usage of raw materials, construction projects or physical processes are used or carried out in a manner that consumes or wastes less of a given material compared with previous measures. For instance, making a steel beam out of thinner stock than a prior version, without compromising on structural strength, increases the material efficiency of the manufacturing process. Better material flow management can increase material efficiency and prevent waste. Wasting construction materials is a sign of inefficiency and causes great loss of value and resources.

Mega-cities are metropolitan areas with a total population exceeding 10 million people. Mega-cities include rapid growth, new forms of spatial density of population, formal and informal economics, as well as crime, poverty and high levels of social fragmentation. Recently, with the urbanization in Asia, the number of mega-cities has significantly increased.

Millennium Development Goals (MDG) were formulated by the United Nations and adopted in 2000. The eight MDGs aim to halve extreme poverty by 2015. The MDGs are much wider than the issue of global warming. See www.un.org/millenniumgoals.

Mitigation and adaptation: mitigation means the first steps taken to fight the effects of climate change by reducing CO_2 emissions. The second response to global warming is adaptation. As the environment changes, governments, businesses and designers have to be prepared to adapt to a set of new challenges and be ready to take opportunities that arise.

Mixed-use (MU) describes a development that combines residential, retail, commercial and/or office uses, clustered together: either layered vertically in a single building, or in a horizontal arrangement in adjacent buildings.

Natural ventilation is caused by natural convection; it is non-mechanical airflow through operable windows, doors, louvres and other openings due to differences in thermal and pressure gradients.

Net-zero buildings (NZBs) are buildings that draw no net energy from the grid on an annual basis. This is achieved through a combination of energy efficiency and on-site (off-grid) generation. All new buildings in the EU will have to be net-zero buildings from 2018 onwards.

One-planet living is a programme developed by UK-based initiative BioRegional. It involves ten guiding principles to healthy living and preserving the Earth's scarce natural resources. These include: zero carbon, zero waste, sustainable transport, use of local and sustainable materials, local and sustainable food, sustainable water, natural habitats and wildlife, culture and heritage, equity and fair trading, and overall health and happiness. Each city dweller has a certain global area and a certain amount of resources at his/her disposal, calculated proportionally. See www.oneplanet living.org.

Orientation means a building's on-site placement in regard to the direction of prevailing winds and solar position, and its resulting sun exposure.

Parts per million (ppm): most scientists agree that the sustainable level of GHG concentration in the Earth's atmosphere is around 280 ppm. Several climate-change agreements focus on limiting the concentration to 350 ppm.

Passive design is an integrated building-design approach that takes advantage of the local climate to provide some or all of the heating, cooling, ventilation and lighting needs of the occupants (and is akin to a 'harnessing nature' approach). For instance, thermal energy is collected and stored by natural means, exploiting the building's orientation, layout and form and the choice of materials in relation to solar radiation, which reduces the building's energy requirements. A typical passive-design strategy is night purging: the flushing out of internal spaces with lower night temperature air levels, thus naturally cooling down built-up heat from daily internal loads and solar gains to avoid overheating. Passive solar design is one of the simplest and best-established forms of adaptation to climates with intense heat or humidity. It includes site orientation, sun shading, cross-ventilation, evaporative cooling and other strategies to reduce operational-energy needs.

Passive (solar) heat gain involves the increase in temperature in a space, object or structure resulting from solar radiation. The amount of heat gain increases with the strength of the sun and is affected by any intervening material that transmits or resists the projected radiation (e.g. sun shading or glazing).

'Passivhaus' Standard (Germany), similar to the Minergie Standard (in Switzerland), is concerned with high insulation and reduced energy consumption, below $15kWh/m^2$ per annum. See www.passiv.de and the Swiss standard: www.minergie.ch.

Photovoltaic (PV) cells are solar panels able to transform the sun's radiation into electricity (converting light into direct current). PV devices capture photons of light from solar isolation and convert them into electrical energy stored as direct current (DC). Conversion is direct, with the generated power fed directly into existing power supplies. The effective energy storage of the gained power is still a challenge.

Post-occupancy evaluation (POE) is the systematic data-gathering and analysis, comparing the actual building performance with stated performance criteria (usually undertaken by facility managers), after the building has been completed and occupied for at least one year. POE seeks to measure and evaluate technical performance, fitness for purpose and user satisfaction.

Prefabrication describes building components (usually modular) fabricated or manufactured prior to delivery and on-site assembly. Prefabrication enables 'design-for-disassembly' for the reuse or recycling of components and materials of a building at the end of its life. This mainly applies to timber, steel and concrete elements with reversible joining details. See www.fabprefab.com.

Primary energy input (PEI), also known as grey or embodied energy, is the energy required for the manufacturing and use of a product, measured in megajoules.

It includes all the energy quantities necessary for production, transport, intermediate states and storage; it is an indicator of the environmental impact of the product.

Rating tools can be used as an assessment of measures for building performance. Examples of these are LEED, BREEAM, CASBE, Green Mark, GreenStar or DGNB, where a building's capabilities are rated according to specific criteria, giving a better understanding of its overall performance.

Recycling means a cyclic process of respecting the ecological integrity of all products and materials, by extending their use or form, so that their useful material cycle does not end in landfill or incineration. Closed-loop recycling means a recycling system in which a particular mass of material is remanufactured into the same product. The 'cradle-to-cradle' approach ensures that materials and products are considered and accounted for throughout their life cycle (instead of 'cradle-to-grave'). Recycling is the way to recapture most resources (through diversion, instead of destroying the resource); it is an umbrella term that includes more specific terms, such as reuse, remanufacture, recapture, reclaim and recover. Unfortunately, most of the so-called recycled materials are actually placed into dumps whenever the cost of low-grade-material recovery exceeds its potential revenue. In the same way, 'non-recyclability' is a notion repeatedly asserted by garbage personnel and regulators, which holds that any unwanted item that presents the slightest difficulty in designing a process for reuse is inherently incapable of being reused by any method.

Renewable energy sources are any sources of energy that can be used without depleting natural reserves. They include: wind, geothermal, water/hydro/wave/tidal, biofuels, biomass, solar and solar water heating. Renewable energy is energy generated from natural resources that are infinite, inexhaustible (unlike fossil fuels), can be naturally replenished and are not derived from burning hydrocarbons. By using regenerating natural resources and converting them into needed energy, we ensure that energy is produced with minimal waste and harm to the Earth. Renewable (alternative) energy technologies include wind turbines, solar panels and hydroelectric dams.

Smart-grid networks are networks supported by digital technology capable of exerting 'smart control' over all aspects of the electric power sector, including: generation, transmission, distribution, customer service and power dispatch at all voltage levels. Smart grids deliver power in an efficient manner and can better integrate power from renewable sources.

Solar cooling systems use the process of absorption (sometimes adsorption), where heat is evaporated, and the condensation of vapours provides a cooling effect (e.g. with chilled water). Solar cooling provides a much more sustainable method of cooling, with a pollution-free process.

Solar energy is solar radiation exploited for hot-water production and electricity generation by flat plate collectors, photovoltaic cells or solar thermal electric plants. Solar radiation is short-wave radiation emitted by the sun, which has a distinctive range of wavelengths (spectrum).

Solar gain (Q) is measured in kilowatt hours per annum. It describes heat that contributes to heating up the interior of a building and to reducing the heating requirement, owing to the incidence of solar energy on transparent and opaque building components. The location of the building, its orientation, the inclination and size of the building components and the amount of radiation absorbed by the facade material all influence this energy input. Solar gains occur in all building components, but they are very much greater with transparent components than any other components. High solar gains (e.g. from the strong western sun) can lead to overheating in a building.

Solar hot water is water that is heated by the use of solar energy using a renewable energy source: the sun. Solar hot water (SHW) systems are now compulsory for all developments in many countries.

Strategy is a carefully devised plan of action to achieve a goal, and the art of developing and carrying out such a plan. Central to strategy is the recognition of a lack of total control. Through strategic action, other parties are inspired, are seduced, challenged or forced to act.

Sustainable is derived from the Latin verb *sustinere* (to support) and describes relations that can be maintained for a very long time, or indefinitely. The idea of 'sustainable urban development' probably originated at the 1992 UNCED Conference and Earth Summit in Rio de Janeiro, and is based on the concept of balanced environmental planning instruments and methods.

Sustainable urban development is development that considers environmental, economic and social impacts and has the ability to maintain activities, without using up excessive amounts of resources and creating a future debt that is not offset by equal levels of future benefits. It is suggested that cities should have a defined commitment to sustainable urban development and aim to reduce poverty and balance the social, economic and environmental needs of present and future generations. Sustainable urban planning is defined as planning that optimizes the use of the built environment, transportation systems, energy, water and land, while aiming to minimize the negative impact of the community on the natural environment.

Thermal mass defines the availability of a material to act as a storage medium for heat; it is measured as a function of a material's specific heat and its density. Materials suitable for thermal mass (for instance, a trompe wall) are heavy materials with the ability to store large amounts of heat energy, such as concrete, masonry, brick or rammed earth walls.

Transit-oriented development (TOD) is a form of development that emphasizes forms of transportation other than by privately owned cars – such as walking, cycling and mass transit – as part of its urban design. Transit-oriented neighbourhood development locates activity centres, composed of office space, housing and retail as multistorey, compact, mixed-use development, around a transit stop. These activity centres offer a variety of housing options, such as apartments, townhouses and duplexes, often above ground-floor commercial premises.

Treaty of Basel is an international treaty signed by most developed countries that prohibits the export of so-called hazardous waste to developing countries.

Typology is the classification system according to general building type, which, in architecture and urban design, could include the range of common identity, plan geometry, spatial pattern and functional programmes.

UNESCO, the United Nations Educational, Scientific and Cultural Organization, currently has 193 member states. See www.unesco.org.

UNFCCC, the United Nations Framework Convention on Climate Change is an international treaty founded on the Kyoto Protocol; the UN Climate Secretariat is based in Bonn, Germany. See www.unfccc.int.

UN-Habitat, the United Nations Human Settlements Programme, is based in Nairobi, Kenya. UN-Habitat promotes socially and environmentally sustainable cities and towns. See www.unhabitat.org.

Urban design involves various disciplines and applies the art of planning to the three-dimensional form of the city, its public-space networks, masses, open spaces and distribution of activities. Good urban design considers the full complexity of the city and its buildings in relation to their context, layers of history and local typology. The resulting urban form encompasses the pattern and density of land use and the nature of transportation within cities and towns.

Urban farming (urban agriculture) is the practice of cultivating, processing and distributing food in or around a town or city. Urban agriculture contributes to food security and safety by increasing the amount of available food to people living in cities and allows fresh vegetables, fruit and meat products to be available to the urban consumer. Urban farming ensures that the city's community consumes natural produce at nearby urban residences and minimizes the need for transportation of these products. 'Local food' is usually food that has travelled less than 200km from producer to consumer.

Urban growth is fuelled by the natural increase of a city, as well as by net in-migration. Urban growth is usually the dominant factor behind an urban centre's growing population.

Urban heat island (UHI) effect is found in metropolitan areas that are significantly warmer than their surrounding areas. It creates an urban microclimate in a confined local area. It is created by human activity: a dome of elevated temperatures over an urban area (such as a street, sidewalk, parking lot or building) that traps heat, caused by waste heat from energy-using processes in a city (for instance, the air-conditioning units in Hong Kong's city centre). The differences in temperature are usually greater at night and in winter months. It is caused primarily by urban development, which alters the original land surfaces and their potential for absorbing heat. It is also caused by waste heat from air-conditioning units, generated by the use of energy. As the population of an area grows, the land alteration becomes greater, thus increasing average temperatures in the region.

Urban sprawl is a low-density pattern of residential urban growth; the spreading of a city and its suburbs to the surrounding urban fringe, pushing the city boundaries outward. Sprawling neighbourhoods are usually dominated by single-family homes away from urban centres. They are highly car-dependent, have low population densities, involve single-use zoning with rigid separation between uses, have low-density land use and lack public-transportation options. Sprawl is often characterized by placeless commercial strip development along main streets and otherwise large expanses of low-density or single-use development, where the major form of transportation is the car. Urban planners try to adapt pedestrian-friendly neighbourhood qualities to these regions, as well as attempting to create higher-density and more compact, mixed-use communities in close proximity to work and retail. Sprawl negatively impacts on land and water quantity and quality and can often be linked to a decline in social capital. For instance, the lack of land-use diversity (typical of suburbs) results in and increases car dependency. A growth boundary is usually necessary to curb sprawl and similar scattered development that leaves large tracts of undeveloped land between developments.

Urbanization is the increase in the proportion of a population living in urban centres (cities and towns), caused by a net movement of people from rural to urban areas, accompanied by manufacturing and commerce replacing agriculture, and associated patterns of land use. Urbanization is driven by economic growth and a concentration of new investment in particular urban areas.

U-value of materials, also known as the overall heat transfer coefficient, is measured in square metre kelvin per watt. U-value is the reciprocal of R-value (the thermal insulation factor of a material). It measures the rate of heat transfer (flow) through a building element (e.g. glazing or a window frame) over a given area, under standardized conditions. It is a specific thermal performance characteristic value that designates the heat flow through the element or material, taking into account the number of panes of glass, the nature of coatings, material thickness, quality of the seals and the filling in any cavities between the glass panes.

Waste describes anything not wanted by its current owner and deemed as 'not of use to anyone'.

Waste minimization is aimed at reducing the production of waste through education, behaviour change and improved production processes, rather than aiming to increase technology to improve treatment of waste. The idea of minimization is not centred on technological advances; it can be viewed as a method of managing existing resources and technology in order to maximize the efficiency of available resource use. Minimizing waste generation has the potential to reduce costs or increase profits by maximizing the use of resources and by reducing the amount of waste to be disposed of; thus the cost of waste management is also decreased. Action for waste avoidance and waste minimization can be taken at many levels. Waste avoidance for individuals includes: buying goods in bulk; reconsidering superfluous purchases; purchasing products in materials/packaging that are readily recycled; use of alternatives, e.g. landscaping that creates mulched gardens in place of lawns; and use of composting and vermiculture practices. Waste minimization in industry includes: introducing changes in product design to reduce materials consumption; using crates instead of pallets to avoid the need for shrink wrap; incorporating eco-design technology into production processes; adopting cleaner production practices that ensure waste avoidance through efficiency measures; and conducting regular audits and monitoring of waste-reduction/resource-recovery practices. Waste minimization for local government includes: encouraging community 'avoidance' activities, e.g. promote competitions rewarding initiative in this area of resource recovery; leading by example, e.g. display mulched gardens throughout the munici-pality; and providing facilities and infrastructure to assist industry, business and the community to undertake resource-recovery practices, e.g. kerbside recycling and resource-exchange registers, and initiating greener procurement programmes.

Waste processing is the range of activities characterized by the treatment and recovery (use) of materials or energy from waste through thermal, chemical or biological means. It also covers hazardous-waste handling. Generally, there are two main groups of processes to be considered: (1) biological processes, such as open composting, enclosed composting, anaerobic digestion and vermiculture; and (2) thermal processes, such as incineration and gasification. Examples of reuse initiatives include: (1) product reuse – retreading tyres, recovery of demolition materials, reuse of plastic bags, second-hand clothing, reconditioning and repair of furniture and appliances; (2) materials reuse – liquid-paper board for seedlings planters, bottles, scrap paper for notes/phone messages, mulching; (3) durable packaging – e.g. milk crates, bread trays, string or calico shopping bags. Some of the positive effects associated with processed waste include: more effective use of resources; employment opportunities in the service and repair industries; support for charity-based stores; better protection of products, as durable packaging is more robust; and changes in attitudes towards disposable products. Waste treatment is the technical umbrella term for any kind of modification applied to waste.

Waste recycling is the breaking down of materials from waste streams into raw materials, which are then reprocessed either into the same material (closed loop) or a new product (open loop), generally including waste separation and material reprocessing. There are various materials that are capable of being recycled, and technology is advancing to allow the recycling of more materials. The benefits of recycling do not lie solely in diversion of waste away from disposal but, even more importantly, in the reduction of the amount of virgin resources that need to be harvested and processed for the manufacture of new products.

Zero-energy buildings/zero-energy districts are buildings or city districts that were constructed environmentally responsibly and produce at least as much energy as they consume.

Zero waste as a concept considers the entire life cycle of products and buildings and expresses the need for closed-loop industrial and societal systems and construction processes. It means that all products, buildings and cities are designed in a way that resources can be recovered. Zero waste means 100 per cent of waste is diverted from landfill, and organic waste is composted and returned to the soil. It also includes the scrutiny and transformation of manufacturing methods for construction materials and their supply chains by asking: are the building materials fully recyclable? As a consequence of embedding zero-waste concepts, better material-flow management leads to optimized material efficiency in the use of raw materials and construction systems, preventing the loss of resources, minimizing material input and reducing the use of non-recyclable materials. Zero waste includes a system to recycle all manner of chemicals in any way possible.

Zero-waste online resources

This list was compiled by Atiq U. Zaman, UniSA sd+b in April 2011.

All website links were active at this date.

Africa

Institute for Zero Waste in Africa: www.izwa.org.za

North America

Calrecycle: www.calrecycle.ca.gov
County of Hawaii: www.hawaiizerowaste.org
Eco-Cycle: www.ecocycle.org/index.cfm
Oakland: www2.oaklandnet.com/Government/o/PWA/o/FE/s/GAR/OAK024364
Zero Waste Alliance: www.zerowaste.org/about.htm
Zero Waste America: www.zerowasteamerica.org/index.html
California Against Waste: www.cawrecycles.org/issues/zero_waste
Zero Waste Network: www.zerowastenetwork.org

Australasia

Zero Waste Singapore: www.zerowastesg.com
Zero Waste Japan: www.greenpeace.or.jp/campaign/toxics/zerowaste/localgov/
    kamikatsu_en_html
Zero Waste Community in Japan: www.no-burn.org/article.php?id=376
Zero Waste India: www.zerowasteindia.org
DISHA: www.dishaearth.org/Municipal%20Waste.html
CSIRO: www.csiro.au/csiro/channel/_ca_dch2t.html
Sustainability Victoria: www.sustainability.vic.gov.au/www/html/1344-towards-
    zero-waste.asp
Towards Zero Waste: www.zerowastewa.com.au
WOW – Wipe Out Waste: www.wow.sa.gov.au/index.php?page=organics
Zero Waste Australia: www.zerowasteaustralia.org/about
Zero Waste Brisbane: www.brisbane.qld.gov.au/environment-waste/towards-
    zero-waste/index.htm

Zero Waste SA Research Centre for Sustainable Design & Behaviour (sd+b):
    www.unisa.edu.au/artarchitecturedesign/ZeroWasteSAResearchCentre/default.asp
Zero Waste SA: www.zerowaste.sa.gov.au
Zero Waste Sydney: www.cityofsydney.nsw.gov.au/zerowaste
Zero Waste New Zealand: www.zerowaste.co.nz

Europe

Zero Waste Europe: www.zerowasteeurope.eu/principles-zw-europe
Zero Waste Scotland: www.zerowastescotland.org.uk
Zero Waste UK: www.zwallianceuk.org
Gruener Punkt: www.gruener-punkt.de/en
Zero Waste Future: www.zerowastefuture.com/zero-waste-world.aspx

International

GAIA: www.no-burn.org/article.php?list=type&type=90
Getting to Zero Waste: www.gettingtozerowaste.com
Global Recycling Network: www.grn.com
My Zero Waste: http://myzerowaste.com
Zer0-M: www.zer0-m.org
Zero waste around the world: www.grrn.org/zerowaste/zw_world.html
Zero waste Institute: www.zerowasteinstitute.org

Zero-waste initiatives within different business organizations

Battery Council International: www.batterycouncil.org
Epson: http://global.epson.com
Fujitsu: www.fujitsu.com/global
General Motors: www.gm.com
HP: www8.hp.com/au/en/home.html
IKEA: www.ikea.com
Interface Inc.: www.interfaceglobal.com
Toyota: www.toyota-global.com
Walmart: walmartstores.com
Xerox: www.xerox.com

Academic journals for zero-waste research

Annual Review of Environment and Resources, Annual Review. USA
    www.annualreviews.org/journal/energy
Bioresource Technology, Elsevier. USA
    http://journals.elsevier.com/09608524/bioresource-technology/
Environmental Science & Technology, American Chemical Society. USA
    http://pubs.acs.org/loi/esthag
Global Environmental Change, Elsevier. UK
    www.elsevier.com/wps/find/journaldescription.cws_home/30425/description
    #description
International Journal of Environment and Waste Management, Elsevier. UK
    www.elsevier.com/wps/find/journaldescription.cws_home/404/description
    #description
Journal of Material Cycles and Waste Management, Springerlink. Germany
    www.springerlink.com/content/110360/
Journal of the Air and Waste Management Association, AWMA. USA
    www.awma.org/public/
Journal of Waste Management, Elsevier. UK
    www.elsevier.com/wps/find/journaldescription.cws_home/404/description
    #description
Waste Management and Research, SAGE. USA
    http://wmr.sagepub.com/
Journal of Urban Planning and Development, ASCE. USA
    http://ascelibrary.org/upo/
International Journal of Environment and Waste Management, Inderscience. UK
    www.inderscience.com/browse/index.php?journalCODE=ijewm
International Journal of Interdisciplinary Environmental Science, Cambridge
    University Press. UK
    http://journals.cambridge.org/action/displayJournal?jid=ENC
International Journal of Landscape Ecology, Planning and Design, Elsevier. UK
    www.elsevier.com/wps/find/journaldescription.cws_home/503347/description
    #description
International Journal of Sustainable Development & World Ecology, Taylor and
    Francis. UK
    www.tandf.co.uk/journals/titles/13504509.asp

International Journal of Sustainable Development and Planning, WIT. UK
   http://journals.witpress.com/jsdp.asp
Journal of Sustainable Development, John Wiley & Sons. USA
   http://onlinelibrary.wiley.com/journal/10.1002/(ISSN)1099-1719
SAPIENS – Surveys and Perspectives Integrating Environment & Society, Veolia
   Research Institute, Paris. France
   www.sapiens.revues.org

Index

Note: page numbers in *italic* type refer to Figures; those in **bold** type refer to Tables.